DECORATIVE
ARTS

DECORATIVE ARTS

JUDITH MILLER

DK Publishing

LONDON, NEW YORK,
MELBOURNE, MUNICH, AND DELHI

A joint production from **DK** and
THE PRICE GUIDE COMPANY

DORLING KINDERSLEY LIMITED
Senior Editor Angela Wilkes
Senior Art Editor Mandy Earey
Editors Anna Fischel, David Tombesi-Walton,
Sylvia Tombesi-Walton, Diana Vowles
Art Editors Ian Spick, Simon Murrell, Victoria Short
Managing Editor Julie Oughton
Managing Art Editors Christine Keilty,
Heather McCarry
Art Director Bryn Walls
Creative Publisher Jonathan Metcalf
Publishing Director Jackie Douglas
Production Linda Dare
DTP Designer Adam Walker
Picture Library Richard Dabb
US Editor Christine Heilman

THE PRICE GUIDE COMPANY LIMITED
Publishing Manager Julie Brooke
Editorial Assistants Jessica Bishop, Sandra Lange,
Carolyn Malarkey, Karen Morden
Digital Image Coordinator Ellen Sinclair
Picture Research Liz Moore

CONTRIBUTORS
Chief Contributor Daniel Dunlavey
Contributors Simon Adams, Theresa Bebbington,
Anna Fischel, Albert Hill, Frankie Leibe, Alycen Mitchell,
Anna Southgate, John Wainwright

First American Edition, 2006
Published in the United States by
DK Publishing, 375 Hudson Street,
New York, NY 10014

06 07 08 09 10   10 9 8 7 6 5 4 3 2 1

A Cataloging-in-Publication record for this book is available
from the Library of Congress.

ISBN-13: 978-0-7566-2349-4
ISBN-10: 0-7566-2349-9

DK books are available at special discounts for bulk purchases for sales promotions,
premiums, fund-raising, or educational use. For details, contact: DK Publishing
Special Markets, 375 Hudson Street, New York, NY 10014 or SpecialSales@dk.com

Color reproduction by Colourscan, Singapore

Printed and bound in China
by Leo Paper Products Ltd.

Discover more at
www.dk.com

FOREWORD

The desire to decorate our homes is centuries old. From prehistoric humans painting the walls of their cave, to an 18th-century aristocrat collecting the new European porcelain, to the late-20th-century desire for individualism and design, the objects with which we surround ourselves make our homes our own.

I have always been fascinated by the influences on the decorative arts and their stylistic changes, as well as the stories of the craftsmen and designers who have influenced the course of style through the decades. This book tells those stories and explains the impact they had around the world.

This tradition of craftsmanship goes back to ancient Greece and Rome; it can be seen in the delicate porcelain figures of Johann Joachim Kändler at Meissen in the 1730s and 1740s, the glass of Émile Gallé at the end of the 19th century, the exquisite Rookwood vases painted by Kataro Shirayamadani, and the furniture of Senior and Carmichael, as shown in the desk on the right, in the early years of the 21st century.

As technology developed, mass production became possible, and many of the decorative arts from the past 200 years reflect this. Factory-made ceramics in the mid-19th century, like the Rococo Revival vase on the left, enabled thousands of newly affluent middle class families to share the decorative possibilities that had, until then, been available only to the wealthy few. The decorative arts became central to all our lives. In the late 20th century, even the humble corkscrew gained a design aesthetic that brought it into the realm of decorative art.

I hope that you find the story of the decorative arts as intriguing as I do and that this book will give you a lifelong interest in the styles and history of this fascinating subject.

Judith Miller.

CONSULTANTS

Paul Atterbury
Freelance writer and lecturer specializing in 19th- and 20th-century art and design, particularly ceramics *Age of Excess*

John Axford
Director, Woolley & Wallis Fine Art Auctioneers, Salisbury, Wiltshire *Ceramics 1700–1900*

Keith Baker
Consultant and valuer *Arts and Crafts, Art Nouveau*

Lynda Cain
Vice President American Furniture & Decorative Arts, Samuel T. Freeman and Co., Philadelphia *Folk Art*

Dudley Browne
Lamp and Glass Division, James D. Julia Inc., Fairfield, Maine *Age of Excess, Arts and Crafts, Art Nouveau*

Max Donnelly
The Fine Art Society, London *The Aesthetic Movement, The Glasgow School, Christopher Dresser*

Dr Graham Dry
Jugendstil and Art Deco specialist, Von Zezschwitz Kunst und Design, Munich *Art Nouveau, Birth of Modernism, Art Deco*

Yves Gastou
Galerie Yves Gastou, Paris *Art Nouveau, Art Deco, Mid-century Modern, Postmodern and Contemporary*

Dr Henrietta Graaf
Furniture historian and lecturer at the Technical University of Munich *Furniture 1700 to the present day*

Jeanette Hayhurst
Jeanette Hayhurst Fine Glass, London *Glass 1700 to the present day*

Mark Hill
20th-century specialist *Mid-century Modern, Postmodern and Contemporary*

Liz Klein
Consultant and collector's agent specializing in 20th-century decorative arts *Mid-century Modern*

Maître Lefèvre
Maison de Ventes Beaussant-Lefèvre, Paris *France 1700–1900*

Nicholas Lowry
President and Poster Specialist, Swann Auction Galleries, New York *Art Nouveau, Art Deco, Mid-century Modern Posters*

David Rago
Expert and Partner, Rago Auction Center, Lambertville, New Jersey *Arts and Crafts, Art Nouveau, Birth of Modernism*

John Sollo
Expert and Partner, Sollo:Rago Modern Auctions, Lambertville, New Jersey *Mid-century Modern*

Hervé de la Verrie
Head of European Ceramics and Glass department, Christie's, Paris *Ceramics 1700–1900*

Patrick van der Vorst
Director and Head of Continental Furniture Department, Sotheby's, London *Furniture 1700–1900*

Professor Jonathan M. Woodham
Director, Centre for Research Development (Arts & Architecture), University of Brighton, Sussex *Postmodern and Contemporary*

Dr Alfred Ziffer
Art historian and lecturer. Curator of the Nymphenburg Porcelain Bäuml Collection Editor of *Keramos* *Ceramics 1700 to the present day*

PRICE BANDS

Some of the pieces in this book are accompanied by a number that gives an indication of value:

① $200–1,000
② $1,000–2,000
③ $2,000–4,500
④ $4,500–9,000
⑤ £9,000–18,000
⑥ $18,000–36,000
⑦ $36,000–90,000
⑧ $90,000–180,000
⑨ $180,000–450,000
⑩ $450,000 upward

IMAGE ON PAGE 1
LOÏE FULLER Raoul Larche was known for his sculptures of dancer Loïe Fuller. As here the gilt-bronze forms often doubled as lamps. *H:12½ in (32 cm).*

IMAGES ON PAGES 2–3
SWEDISH CONSOLE TABLE Supporting a marble top, this table's giltwood frame is carved in deep relief, in Louis XV style, with a lion mask, dragons, flowers, and scrolling foliage. *c.1760. W:39 in (99 cm).*

BOHEMIAN OVERLAY GLASS This lidded goblet made in ruby red over clear overlay glass was wheel-engraved by August Böhm with a forest landscape with a deer on the bowl and grapevines around the lid. *c.1850. H:21 in (53 cm).*

TUDRIC MANTEL CLOCK Designed by Archibald Knox for Liberty & Co's Tudric range, it has a pewter case with stylized leaf decoration, and an enamelled dial with berry motifs and copper Arabic numerals. *c.1905. H:8¼ in (21 cm).*

LORENZL FIGURE This stylized figure is cast in bronze from a model by Josef Lorenzl and patinated with a silver finish. It has an onyx base. *H:15 in (38 cm).*

HEART CHAIR Verner Panton's sculptural chair takes inspiration from the work of Arne Jacobsen. The metal frame and foam construction is fully upholstered in a bright red fabric. *1958. H:40 in (101.5 cm).*

GLASS SCULPTURE This is made from an opaque orange half-globe and a quarter-globe in clear orange glass by Milos Balgavy. *D:9¾ in (25 cm).*

IMAGES ON PAGES 4–5
BALUSTER-SHAPED VASE The scrolling form is encrusted with applied flowers in extravagant English Rococo Revival style. *1850s. H:10¾ in (27 cm).*

VENUS DESK Made by Senior and Carmichael for the Marchioness of Bath, the sycamore canopy of this mechanical cylinder yew desk was inspired by the scallop shell in Botticelli's painting *Birth of Venus. 2005.*

CONTENTS

5 Foreword
6 Consultants
7 Contents

DECORATIVE PAST
4000BCE–1600CE
10 The Ancient World
12 Eastern Influence
14 The Middle Ages
16 The Renaissance

AGE OF ORNAMENT
1680–1760
20 Lavish Opulence
22 Elements of Style
24 FURNITURE
  Régence to Rococo
  From Walnut to Mahogany
28 The Huguenots
30 CERAMICS
  Pottery in Europe
  Tin-Glazed Earthenware
  The Arcanum
  Porcelain
38 GLASS
  Enamelled glass
40 Asian Influence
42 METALWARE
44 CLOCKS
46 TEXTILES

NEOCLASSICISM
1760–1840
50 A New Classicism
52 Elements of Style
54 The Ancient World
56 FURNITURE
  A Classical Style
  Late Neoclassical
  The Empire Style
  Furniture Gallery
64 CERAMICS
  British Pottery
  Tin-Glazed Earthenware
  Neoclassical Porcelain
  Ceramics Gallery
72 GLASS
  Cut and Engraved Glass
  Colored Glass
  Glass Gallery
78 METALWARE
80 CLOCKS
82 OBJETS DE VERTU
  Precious Gifts
  Tea and Snuff
  American Folk Art
88 TEXTILES
  The Silk Trade
  Samplers
92 SCULPTURE

AGE OF EXCESS
1840–1900
96 19th-Century Revivals
98 Elements of Style
100 FURNITURE
  An Age of Revivals
  Battle of the Styles
  Furniture Gallery
106 CERAMICS
  Folk Ceramic Revival
  English Ceramics
  American Ceramics
  Sèvres
  Meissen
116 GLASS
  Surface Techniques
  Cut Glass
  Historical Styles
122 METALWARE
  Silverware
  Victorian Ingenuity
  Metalware Gallery
128 Pattern Books
130 CLOCKS
132 SOUVENIRS
134 TEXTILES
  Eastern Carpets
  Needlework
138 SCULPTURE
  French Bronzes
  American Sculpture

ARTS AND CRAFTS
1880–1920
144 Traditional Values
146 Elements of Style
148 The Aesthetic Movement
150 FURNITURE
    Morris and Co.
    The Stickley Dynasty
    American Workshops
    Furniture Gallery
158 CERAMICS
    Rookwood
    American Art Pottery
    New Glazes
    British Ceramics
    Ceramics Gallery
168 Exotic Influences
170 GLASS AND LAMPS
    Leaded Glass
    Lamps
174 METALWARE
    The New Guilds
    Liberty & Co.
    American Metalware
    Metalware Gallery
182 CLOCKS
184 TEXTILES

ART NOUVEAU
1880–1915
188 Sinuous Contours
190 Elements of Style
192 FURNITURE
    A French Revolution
    The Style Evolves
    German Jugendstil
198 CERAMICS
    Innovative Glazes
    Tradition and Innovation
    American Art Pottery
    Ceramics Gallery
206 GLASS
    Émile Gallé
    Cameo Glass
    Iridescent Glass
    Louis Comfort Tiffany
    Glass Gallery
216 LAMPS
218 METALWARE
    French Luxury
    Northern Europe
    Georg Jensen
    Metalware Gallery
226 CLOCKS
228 TEXTILES
230 SCULPTURE
232 POSTERS
    French Street Art
    Europe and Beyond

BIRTH OF MODERNISM
1860–1920
238 Dynamic Designers
240 Elements of Style
242 Christopher Dresser
244 FURNITURE
    The Glasgow School
    The Wiener Werkstätte
    The Bauhaus
    Le Corbusier
    Frank Lloyd Wright
254 CERAMICS
    European Modernism
    The Birth of Studio Pottery
258 GLASS AND LAMPS
260 METALWARE
262 TEXTILES

ART DECO
1920–1940
266 Stylish Modernity
268 Elements of Style
270 FURNITURE
    A Change in Style
    Simple Design
    Furniture Gallery
276 Exotic Influences
278 CERAMICS
    French Ceramics
    Figurines
    Female Designers
    Ceramics Gallery

286 GLASS
 Lalique
 Daum and French Glass
 Cut and Engraved Glass
 Glass Gallery
294 LIGHTING
296 CHROME AND PLASTIC
298 METALWARE
 European Silversmiths
 American Metalware
 Metalware Gallery
304 CLOCKS
306 TEXTILES
308 SCULPTURE
310 POSTERS

 MID-CENTURY MODERN
 1940–1970
314 A New Optimism
316 Elements of Style
318 FURNITURE
 Scandinavian Trends
 American Studio
 Bent Ply
 Charles and Ray Eames
 Modern Materials
 Plastic Furniture
 Furniture Gallery
332 CERAMICS
 Scandinavian Ceramics
 The Mass Market

 Studio Pottery
 Figures and Forms
 Ceramics Gallery
342 GLASS
 Colored Glass
 Textured Glass
 Timeless Murano
 Modern Italian Glass
 Studio Glass
 Glass Gallery
354 LIGHTING
 Sculptural Lighting
 Rods and Rays
 Lighting Gallery
360 METALWARE
 Fluid lines
 Metalware Gallery
364 PRODUCT DESIGN
366 Pop and Plastics
368 TEXTILES
370 POSTERS

 POSTMODERN AND
 CONTEMPORARY
 1970 ONWARDS
374 Eclectic Diversity
376 Elements of Style
378 FURNITURE
 Seeds of Postmodernism
 Contemporary Furniture
 Wendell Castle
 Furniture Gallery

386 PRODUCT DESIGN
 Alchimia
 Ettore Sotsass
 The Memphis Group
 Revolutions in Design
 New Technology
396 CERAMICS
 Abstract Expressionism
 The Funk Movement
 Vessels of Ideas
 Factory Ceramics
 Ceramics Gallery
406 GLASS
 Colorful Forms
 Clearly Optical
 Figures and Materials
 Glass Gallery
414 LIGHTING
416 METALWARE

418 Useful Addresses
420 Further Reading
421 Glossary
426 Dealer Addresses
430 Index
438 Acknowledgments

DECORATIVE PAST

FROM THE EARLIEST TIMES, HUMANS HAVE FELT THE NEED TO DECORATE THEIR HOMES. FROM CAVE PAINTINGS TO SILVER CANDELABRA, PORCELAIN FIGURES TO EAMES CHAIRS, THE WAY WE DECORATE OUR HOMES REFLECTS THE AGE WE LIVE IN.

THE ANCIENT WORLD

From ancient times until fairly recently, only the wealthy could afford the decorative items needed to furnish a home. Furniture, ceramics, silver- and metalware, glass, tapestries and carpets, and sculpture were out of reach of most people.

The items people have used to beautify their homes have changed with fashion and technology—until Johann Friedrich Böttger at Meissen discovered the formula for hard-paste porcelain in 1709, European potters had to use less refined earthenware. Meanwhile, the popularity of Classical decoration in the 18th century was fueled by the discovery of Herculaneum (1738) and Pompeii (1748). By the early 19th century, Napoleon's campaign in Egypt (1797–98) and the publication in 1802 of Baron Vivant Denon's *Aventures dans la basse et la haute Égypte* (Adventures in Low and High Egypt) inspired the fashion for the Neoclassical and, later, the Empire style.

Nationality also has its bearing on the decorative arts, dictating everything from which woods are used for furniture to the flora and fauna that inspire its decoration. The decorative arts have been with us since cave dwellers drew pictures of hunting on the walls of caves. But the best records of early decoration probably come from the relics of early civilizations that have been found in the Mediterranean countries.

EGYPTIAN CIVILIZATION

With the rise of the first great civilizations in Mesopotamia, advances such as writing and irrigation spread throughout ancient Egypt, Greece, and Rome. As early as 4,000 BCE, Egyptian artists had devised a series of rules governing the proper depiction of the human figure, based on a simple grid system. Combined with "frontalism," whereby heads are always shown in profile and torsos from the front, these guidelines marked the beginnings of a formal approach to art.

During the first years of the New Kingdom, from around 1,500 BCE, Egypt had become a cosmopolitan place. Its citizens were wealthy enough to support a class of craftsmen. The more affluent members of society enjoyed state-of-the-art creature comforts such as headrests and boxes for cosmetics, made from native woods such as acacia, sidder, and fig, or imported cypress and cedar. The wood might be inlaid with ebony, ivory, semiprecious stones, or painted to look like them. Master craftsmen worked with teams of apprentices, acting as project managers and taking final responsibility for the results of these group efforts. Unlike the uniform style of Egyptian funereal art, decorative pieces for the home were varied, lively, and sometimes even experimental.

GREEK POTTERY The krater was used for mixing wine with water at *symposia*, or drinking parties. The red-on-black decoration shows a figure sitting on an X-framed stool, a Classical furniture form still copied today. The Greek key pattern below the figures is a recurrent Classical motif.

EGYPTIAN BRONZE Called a situla, this bucket held holy water for sprinkling at religious ceremonies. It is decorated with images of gods and ancestral rulers.

VILLA OF THE MYSTERIES, POMPEII Pompeii became a Roman colony in 80 BCE, and heralded in the so-called Architectural style, which used trompe-l'oeil effects to blur reality and illusion. A screen of painted pillars on a plinth, apparently supporting a cornice, made the wall surface appear set back in space.

GREEK ORDER

The Greeks, like the Egyptians, valued the look of their homes and possessions. It was the Greeks who first developed a uniform architecture based on "orders." The Doric, Ionic, and Corinthian orders (*see p.54*) dictated the proportions and stylistic features of every part of a building. Decorative artists from almost every historical period since have referred back to them.

Throughout the Greek world, from city-states such as Athens to the Aegean islands and the colonies of southern Italy and Sicily, specialist potters produced a range of decorative homeware. Among the earliest decorative drinking wares was the rhyton, which evolved from the use of ox horns as cups. In time, the horn was replaced with a ceramic replica, molded or carved with an animal's head at the foot and, often, with a decorative frieze around the rim. The urge to replicate natural forms

has driven decorative artists throughout history. The rhyton was complemented by other vessels, especially the amphora, for storing oil or wine. The krater, used by the Greeks to mix wine with water for parties, was often decorated with images of Dionysus, the god of wine and inebriation. In the Roman world earthenware oil lamps were mold-cast with a variety of decorative subjects ranging from the devotional to the erotic.

ROMAN GLASS

Evidence for the use of glass in the ancient world is widespread. The Roman historian Pliny attributed the discovery of glass to a troupe of seafaring merchants who used chunks of the saltpeter their ship was carrying to prop up their cooking pots on the beach. The cooking fire fused the sand and ashes with the saltpeter to form the first man-made glass. While this tale is impossible to verify,

archaeologists have unearthed countless examples of refined glassware from ancient times, even leading to speculation that our current mastery of the art has not yet reached the same standard.

ROMAN GLASS This tiny honey-colored container is an *unguentarium*, or ointment bottle. *1st–3rd century CE. H:3¼ in (8.5 cm).*

EASTERN INFLUENCE

A separate decorative art tradition evolved in the East. The sophistication of surviving artifacts from Neolithic China (4,000–2,000 BCE) is far greater than anything that was produced in the West at the same time.

The ancient Chinese valued jade for its beauty and purity and had been using it for 5,000 years before Confucius said: "When I think of a wise man, his merits appear to be like jade." From the earliest days, Chinese artisans carved jade into exquisite sacrificial vessels, decorative objects, and functional tools and utensils. Even musical instruments such as flutes and chimes were made from blocks of jade. The unparalleled ritual significance of this exalted stone is demonstrated by the existence of jade burial

ALEXANDER VASE This rare Chinese vase from the Yuan Dynasty is painted in underglaze cobalt blue with gourd plants, relating the decoration to the double gourd shape. *Mid-14th century. H:18¾ in (47.5 cm).*

suits, such as that of the prince Liu Sheng, who died in 113 BCE. This extraordinary suit was constructed from almost 2,500 pieces of jade sewn together with gold thread.

The next most significant material in early Chinese decorative art was bronze. During the Shang dynasty (1,700–1,027 BCE), Chinese metalworkers produced a variety of decorated bronze vessels for ceremonies and banquets. These were cast in ceramic relief molds and then carved with complex motifs. The fearsome taotie mask often appears, depicted with horns, fangs, and staring eyes.

CHINESE PORCELAIN

The most outstanding and influential achievement of the Chinese decorative art tradition was porcelain. Fine stoneware was being produced during the Shang dynasty and, by the time of the Eastern Han, around 25 CE, Chinese ceramicists had perfected hard-paste porcelain.

During the Tang dynasty (618–907 CE) there was already a lively export market with the Middle East. This trade route proved especially beneficial, as it was the cobalt pigment that was imported from the Middle East which enabled Chinese ceramicists to create the first blue and white wares during the Yuan dynasty (1280–1368).

THE BYZANTINE TRADITION

After Diocletian divided the Roman Empire in two in 286 CE, the powerful Emperor Constantine founded a new capital, called Nova Roma or Constantinople, on the site of the ancient

HAGIA SOPHIA Embodying the spiritual side of Byzantine art, the temple's many windows allow light to play over the huge dome and columns, polychrome marbles, gold ornaments, exquisite mosaics, and calligraphy.

city of Byzantium in 330 CE. This created a bridge from East to West. Byzantine art soon became a force in its own right, spurred on by the Christian zeal and economic prosperity of the new state. Constantine's son and heir, Constantius, began work on the great Christian temple known as the Hagia Sophia, which was eventually completed by Justinian I in 537 CE. Considered by many to be the eighth wonder of the world, this building is among the supreme achievements of Byzantine art. The interior is decorated with mosaics and pillars of the local marble.

The decorative arts of Byzantium were often intended to educate or serve a moral purpose. Figures are depicted in stiffly formal poses, and colors tend to be bright and bold so that the

THE ALHAMBRA This citadel and palace in Granada, Spain, was built for Moorish kings of the 13th and 14th centuries. Its rich, abstract decoration has influenced designers ever since.

characters and stories represented can be easily recognized and understood. The role of decorative art as an educational medium, capable of bringing about a positive change in the owner or viewer, has since been explored in many historical periods.

ISLAMIC ART

The Muslim conquest of southern Spain from the 8th century exposed Europe to Islamic art for the first time. Portraiture and any depiction of the human form were forbidden in the Koran, in case they led to idolatry— worshiping a mere likeness instead of God and the prophets. As if to compensate, early Islamic artists excelled in abstract and geometric surface decoration. Complex repeating geometric designs, often based on natural

IZNIK DISH The surface is decorated with two saz leaves, carnations, and tulips within a blue ammonite scroll border. *Mid- to late 16th century. D:12 in (30.5 cm).*

forms, are known as arabesques to this day. The religious aspect of Islamic art, and in particular its veneration of the prophet Allah, centers around the beautification of Arabic calligraphy, especially verses from the Koran. Inscriptions in highly stylized, flowing Arabic script abound in Islamic decorative art and serve the same devotional function as, for example, depictions of the crucifixion in Christian art. The many strands of early Islamic decorative art were drawn together in ambitious projects such as the Alhambra fortress in southern Spain, begun in the 13th century.

CERAMIC ADVANCES

One of the most significant Islamic contributions to ceramics was the perfection of luster decoration in the 9th century. This costly and complicated technique makes use of metal oxides to impart a shining metallic surface to pottery.

During the 11th century, Islamic potters developed fritware in imitation of Chinese porcelain. This material was a combination of ground quartz, glass frit, and white clay. Ottoman potters produced a particularly fine type of this ware from the late 15th century. Known as Iznik pottery, it was covered in a white slip that acted as an ideal ground for further polychrome decoration.

ENGLISH FLOOR TILE This medieval square earthenware tile has a slip decoration of a griffin, a mythical winged creature with an eagle's head and lion's body. W:5 in (12.5 cm).

THE MIDDLE AGES

While artisans in East Asia and the Islamic world continued to build directly on their ancient decorative traditions, something very different happened in the West. With the fall of the Roman Empire after Rome was sacked in 476 CE, Western Europe was abruptly cut off from the Classical past. In its place, the first singularly European decorative style developed, known today as Gothic. Originally a distillation of influences ranging from Burgundian, Byzantine, and Islamic to Norman, the Gothic style flourished from the mid-12th century and dominated European decorative art for around 400 years. The roots of the Gothic style are ecclesiastical, and its greatest legacy is the network of extraordinary cathedrals and abbeys that dominate the landscape of northern Europe.

GOTHIC ARCHITECTURE

The pointed arch was one of the most important architectural innovations of the period, allowing the construction of larger and more complex buildings with massive interior spaces. Such was its dominance that the pointed arch, together with associated decorative devices such as trefoils, quatrefoils, and tracery, was used extensively not just in the architecture of the Gothic period but throughout the decorative arts.

Using technical devices such as vaulting and immense flying buttresses, the architects of the Gothic cathedrals were able to fit extremely large windows, flooding the interiors with light. Combined with the predominance of primary colors and gold in the decorative scheme, the effect was striking. The Byzantine roots of Christian art are evident in the Catholic Gothic style. Both share the aim of impressing upon a largely illiterate population the glory of God and, along with it, the supreme power of the Church.

STAINED GLASS

Of all the decorative innovations of the Gothic period, the most awe-inspiring are the great stained glass windows depicting scenes from the Bible and lives of the saints. There is evidence for the manufacture of stained glass dating back to Saxon times, but medieval craftsmen took the art to unscaled heights. Outstanding surviving examples include *Notre Dame de la Belle Verrière* (Our Lady of the Beautiful Window) at Chartres in northern France. The upper sections date from the 12th and 13th centuries and, despite their great age, the colors remain vibrant. The opulence of the church extended beyond the buildings to the sumptuous robes of the clergy and the fine metalware used during mass. These were usually of gold and silver and could even be encrusted with enamels or precious stones. Much of the most exuberant metalware was lost during the

WINCHESTER CATHEDRAL The pointed arches of Gothic architecture, with carved and pierced trefoil (three-leaf) and quatrefoil (four-leaf) ornament, were motifs that inspired decorative arts of the Middle Ages and later revivals.

SILVER SPOON This elaborately engraved and plated spoon has a stylized motif based on plant forms.

LADY OF THE UNICORN The most famous of the *mille-fleurs* (thousand flowers) Tournai tapestries is also the most enigmatic. It depicts an allegory involving a beautifully dressed lady, a unicorn symbolizing chastity, a tame lion, and other animals among the flowers. *Late 15th century.*

Reformation of the 16th century. This attempt to reform the Roman Catholic Church resulted in the start of the Protestant Church.

ART FOR THE HOME

Secular art of this period was expected to be as pious as religious art, although it was often open to interpretation. A series of tapestries known as the Lady and the Unicorn group, made in Flanders during the late 15th century, represents a high point of medieval decorative art and illustrates the thin line between the sacred and the profane.

The six panels—one representing each of the senses and one entitled *À Mon Seul Désir* (My Only Desire)—can be seen either as a young woman's rejection of worldly pleasures or as a narrative depicting the seduction of a unicorn. Throughout

history, designers have defied powerful regimes with similarly sophisticated subtlety and suggestion.

INTERNATIONAL GOTHIC

Depictions of the human figure in tapestries, manuscripts, stained glass, and paintings during the Middle Ages often exaggerated courtly grace. The proportions of the body were skewed as artists elongated the limbs and necks of their subjects. Called the International Gothic style, it reached its height toward the end of the 14th century. In reaction to the attenuated proportions, many artists started to strive for a less stylized depiction. However, knowledge of anatomy was poor and this frustrated attempts to produce realistic portraits. Even so, the rigidity that characterizes so much early Christian art was slowly giving way to naturalism.

OUR LADY OF THE BEAUTIFUL WINDOW In Chartres cathedral in France, the use of strong primary colors made stained glass Biblical stories all the more vivid. The Virgin Mary, with Jesus on her lap, is the largest image in the windows of the nave, surrounded by lives of the saints.

THE RENAISSANCE

The move away from extreme stylization to observing and recording nature gradually gathered pace. In the wealthy city-states of early-15th-century northern Italy, architects, scientists, philosophers, and artists rediscovered the lost learning of the Classical era and applied it to their work. Reviving the ideas of the Greek philosopher Aristotle, the rich and powerful saw the ownership and display of beautiful works of art as a virtue. The Renaissance began, with far-reaching consequences for the decorative arts, as affluent patrons poured money into commissions to display their prosperity and taste. The pioneers of the Renaissance spirit believed that they were reconnecting themselves with their Classical heritage after a hiatus characterized by barbarism.

ITALY REDISCOVERS ITS PAST

The term "Gothic" was first coined by Renaissance thinkers to disparage medieval culture by linking it with the rampaging hordes—Goths—who had laid waste to Western Europe after the fall of the Roman Empire. Evidence of past Roman glories was everywhere in Rome, Florence, and Venice—the centers of this new movement. Regular discoveries further reinforced the belief that Classical art was superior to anything produced since. The Laocoon Group, a particularly fine Rhodian marble statue depicting the death of the Trojan priest Laocoon, was escorted to the Vatican by a rejoicing crowd on its rediscovery in 1506. Most discoveries were of architecture, sculpture, and Roman sarcophagi. They inspired sculptors, furniture-makers, and other decorative artists to

MAIOLICA **ALBARELLO** Italian maiolica—tin-glazed earthenware—was often used to make drug jars. The waisted shape gives a secure hold, while the label, sandwiched by colored decoration, describes the contents. *16th century. H:8½ in (21.5 cm).*

use motifs from the Classical orders such as acanthus leaves and fluted columns in their own work. Swags and friezes, urns and trophies, sphinxes and putti (naked cherubs) all appeared.

Excavations revealed the *grottes* (underground ruins) of Nero's *Domus Aurea* (Golden House) beneath the Aventine Hill in Rome during the late 15th century, and contributed directly to the grottoesque style of the early Renaissance. The walls of Nero's state apartments were decorated with grotesques—arabesques with animal, human, and mythical figures added. Most early designers used elements from the grotesques. Between 1518 and 1519, Raphael revived them in their original completeness as whole schemes to decorate the walls of the Vatican Loggie.

ARCHITECTURE AND CRAFTS

Italian architects used the texts of their ancestors as a foundation for their own work—in 1570, Andrea Palladio published *Quattro Libri dell'Architeturra*

VILLA CORNARO Constructed in 1552–53, Andrea Palladio designed the interior to ideal Classical proportions. The spatial harmony is reflected in the balanced decoration, including grotesques in the domed ceiling.

decoration. One difference was that Venetian glassmakers used soda ash, resulting in a malleable product particularly suited to hot techniques such as blowing and lampwork.

Islamic crafts also informed ceramic art of the period—tin-glazed earthenware from Morocco inspired the creation of Italian maiolica, the name itself born of the misconception that the Moroccan wares came from Majorca.

BERNARD PALISSY DISH The eccentric French potter cast reptiles from nature and applied them, surrounded by leaves, rockwork, and water, to lead-glazed earthenware. *16th century.*

MOVING INTO MANNERISM

From Italy, Classical decorative ideals spread north through France and eventually the rest of Europe. In the 1530s two Italian artists, Rosso Fiorentino and Francesco Primaticcio, were commissioned by the French king François I to decorate his palace at Fontainebleau. Fiorentino and Primaticcio brought with them the full repertoire of Classical motifs, but by then the Renaissance style in Italy had developed into Mannerism, which was characterized by sinuous and contorted forms, often within grotesques. This sophisticated style often distorted Classical ideals—elongating the human figure, for instance. Northern European craftsmen discovered the themes and motifs of the Renaissance and Mannerism simultaneously, and the result was a combination of styles their Italian counterparts would never have considered. The strapwork that the Italian artists introduced to Fontainebleau was particularly influential, and became one of the hallmarks of northern European Renaissance and later styles.

One of the quirks of the courtly Mannerist style was a love of precious, bizarre materials or clever use of them. The ceramics of French potter Bernard Palissy were one example. He took casts from real animals such as frogs, snakes, and lizards and applied them to dishes, using translucent colored glazes that made the reptiles and amphibians look even more realistically scaly or slippery. His wares were widely copied for the grottoesque value that still held great appeal.

VENETIAN EWER Glass has been made on the Venetian island of Murano since the 13th century. This ewer—blown from glass that imitates chalcedony—features an applied handle and spout. *c.1500.*

(Four Books on Architecture), a direct descendant of *De Architectura* (On Architecture) by Vitruvius, despite the one and a half millennia that separate the two texts. Palladio designed villas and churches in a Classical style that later became highly popular in Britain.

Within the home, wealthy newlywed couples in Italy were given a *cassone*, a richly decorated marriage chest that would be the centerpiece of the interior. Otherwise, furniture was usually simple.

Glass firms on the Venetian island of Murano were at the forefront of the European glass trade— the island's industry was strictly regulated and more than 3,000 glass-blowers were working there by the end of the 15th century. Production at this point was heavily influenced by the prized Islamic glass of the East, particularly in terms of gilding and enamel

FRENCH ARMOIRE This cupboard is decorated with pilaster figures and attributed to Hugues Sambin, who worked in Burgundy. French furniture tended to imitate that of Italy after Italian artists decorated Fontainebleau for the French king. *1550–80. H:79 in (200 cm).*

AGE OF
ORNAMENT
1680–1760

LAVISH OPULENCE

AFTER MORE THAN A CENTURY OF DESTRUCTIVE WARFARE, WHICH
HAD BEEN MOTIVATED AS MUCH BY POLITICAL DIFFERENCES AS
RELIGIOUS ONES, RECOGNIZABLY MODERN NATION STATES BEGAN
TO EMERGE ACROSS EUROPE FROM ABOUT 1650.

GERMAN ROCOCO MIRRORS This pair of
wooden mirrors is carved and stuccoed with
typically Rococo asymmetry, *rocaille* (rockwork),
leaves, and flowers. *Early 18th century.*
H:39 in (98 cm).

EMERGING STATES OF EUROPE

Power was increasingly centralized under the
monarch, although in Britain and the Netherlands
parliaments were gaining power, and as a result
national identity began to replace
regional or local affiliation.

During the reign of the
autocratic Louis XIV
(1643–1715), France
aggressively extended its
territory and influence
through a series of wars
with its neighbors,

DUTCH CHAIR Made of walnut
with floral marquetry, the chair is
carved with shells and has a solid
vase-shaped splat, cabriole legs, and
claw-and-ball feet. *18th century.*

notably Spain and the Netherlands. By the start
of the 18th century it had confirmed its status as
the leading power in Europe. England and the
Netherlands—commercial rivals for much of the
period—were briefly united against the French
threat under the Dutch King William of Orange
from 1688 to 1702.

Both countries grew increasingly rich on
international trade and colonial expansion, while
the union of the English and Scottish parliaments
in 1707, a century after the union of their crowns,
gave birth to a strong and stable United Kingdom.

In central Europe, Austria fought off an Ottoman
Turk siege of its capital, Vienna, in 1683, to emerge
as the major power in the region. To its north,
Prussia, under Frederick William I (1713–40) and
his son, Frederick II, "the Great" (1740–86),
became the dominant state in northern Germany.
Both Germany and Italy, however, remained

merely geographical descriptions, as each of them
was a collection of small and disunited kingdoms
and principalities often fought over or controlled
by outside powers.

THE WIDER WORLD

Outside Europe, the first of the three long-lived
Manchu emperors, Kangxi, reigned from 1662 to
1722, presiding over a lengthy period of stability
and increasing wealth. Trade in tea, porcelain,
spices, and silk between China and Europe
flourished, while European merchants, notably
the British, French, and Dutch, established
commercial bases and small colonies
throughout southern and eastern Asia.
Although in relative decline during this
period, both Spain and Portugal continued
to derive great wealth from their colonial
empires in the Americas.

THE ENLIGHTENMENT

Intellectually, the leading movement of the
period was the Enlightenment, a Europe-
wide shift in favor of rational thought and
scientific discovery at the expense of religion
and superstition. New ideas in philosophy,
politics, and economics were accompanied

CHÂTEAU OF VERSAILLES Louis le Vau, architect to Louis XIV,
remodeled Versailles between 1661 and 1670, turning a small
château into a grand and luxurious Baroque palace. It was the
official residence of the French court from 1682 to 1789.

HÔTEL DE SOUBISE, PARIS The four tall windows of the oval salon are reflected in three corresponding mirrors. The white and gold *boiseries* (wood paneling) are decorated with Rococo shells, garlands, and cupids. Above the *boiseries*, under the elaborate cornice, eight paintings by Charles-Joseph Natoire recount the story of Psyche.

by discoveries in astronomy, physics, biology, and botany. One practical result of the Enlightenment was safer navigation at sea and a substantial increase in overseas exploration and trade.

Artistically, the dominant style in Europe and its overseas possessions remained the Baroque. A flamboyant, theatrical style that grew out of the Renaissance, Baroque was used for religious and secular buildings. Its emphasis on order and proportion appealed to monarchs seeking to build capital cities and palaces that glorified their rule. The centers of Rome and Paris were remodeled as Baroque cities. Almost all of St. Petersburg and the great palaces of Louis XIV at Versailles, the Habsburg palace of Schönbrunn in Vienna, and

the Royal Palace of the Prussian kings in Berlin, as well as the London skyline after the Great Fire of 1666, owe much to the Baroque style. Toward the end of the period, a lighter, more playful and colorful style known as Rococo predominated, at first in France and then in Germany and Austria.

The new grand palaces and large town houses that sprang up across Europe required furnishing and decorating in the latest style. The first true porcelain in Europe was produced at the Meissen factory in Saxony, Germany, in 1713; the quality of its output was only matched some 40 years later by the French national porcelain factory first at Vincennes and then, after 1756, at Sèvres. Fine silverware was produced in Paris and London,

furniture in many European cities, and large-scale tapestries by French workshops. Such items, although hand-produced at great cost, were bought in large numbers by monarchs, aristocrats, and wealthy merchants anxious to impress with their style and opulence.

BOHEMIAN GOBLET Now the Czech Republic, Bohemia was a long-established glassmaking center in the 18th century. This goblet depicts a battle scene, and has a baluster-shaped stem. *c.1730. H:7¼ in (18 cm).*

ELEMENTS OF STYLE

As the 17th century drew to a close, the decorative arts were slowly released from the formal strictures of the heavy Baroque style and began to flourish anew. Artisans enjoyed a new freedom to imbue their work with a more personal aesthetic. The Rococo style was brought to fruition in extravagant commissions for the aristocratic Paris society that flourished during the Régence (1715–23). Asian influences and the vast natural resources of the New World contributed to the heady atmosphere of the time and also had a direct effect on its decorative art.

RUSSIAN BEAKER
REPOUSSÉ WORK
The combination of embossing, or hammering, a relief design into metal, and then chasing to add further fine detail to the surface, is known as repoussé decoration. This design featuring scrolls and birds in high relief is typical of repoussé work of the Rococo period.

FRENCH CARTEL CLOCK
S-SCROLLS
Frequently seen adorning the corners and aprons of furniture of this period, the S-scroll is derived from the Classical volute that was first used on the capitals of Ionic columns and is thought to be inspired by rams' horns. Cartouches of multiple scrolls were very popular in Baroque and Rococo decorative arts.

MEISSEN FIGURE GROUP
BRIGHT COLORS
By the turn of the 18th century a wide range of bright enamel colors was available to painters and decorators of ceramics and glass. Also known by the French name *petit feu*, overglaze enamels changed the face of ceramic design, allowing for brighter and more durable colors.

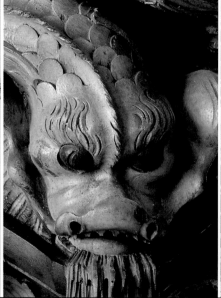

SCEAUX PLATE
SPRIGS OF FLOWERS
Rococo designers respected and imitated natural forms. The extensive palette available led to realistic representations of flowers and foliage. European porcelain manufacture was still in its infancy, and decorators frequently used scattered flower sprays to cover small blemishes and firing faults.

ENGLISH CANDLESTAND
FANTASTICAL BEASTS
A legacy of Classical mythology bearing the influence of the Renaissance grotesque style, fantastical beasts were used frequently in the Baroque and Rococo styles. The naturalistic inclinations of Rococo designers limited them to dragons in the Asian tradition or sea creatures based on mariners' tales.

AUBUSSON TAPESTRY
VIBRANT FABRICS
Great tapestry factories in France and the Low Countries continued to flourish during this period. Tapestries were used extensively to adorn walls and cover furniture. Needlework was a popular art form, and many seats were upholstered with petit-point embroidery, particularly in France.

CHANTILLY COOLER
CHINOISERIE
The increasing fascination with the Orient resulted in a European interpretation of Chinese decoration known as Chinoiserie—an imaginary version of China complete with latticework, fretwork, dragons, Chinese figures, and pagodas. It was used on ceramics and Chinese Chippendale furniture of the period.

LOUIS XV TABLE
EXOTIC TIMBERS
During the 18th century, Europe began to import more and more luxury goods. Along with tea, spices, and fine porcelain, merchants also satisfied a new demand for exotic hardwoods, which were much admired for their rich colors and lent an air of opulence when inlaid into furniture.

SWEDISH BEAKER
ENAMELED GLASS
The European glass market was dominated by Bohemia during this period. Among the many specialties of the region was enamel decoration, ranging from the stark monochrome of *Schwarzlot*, or "black lead" enamel, to pastoral themes picked out in multiple colors and gilt.

GERMAN MIRROR
ASYMMETRY
After the heavy formality of the Baroque period, the Rococo era represented a lighter, more playful style. Asymmetry was an important aspect of this more fluid aesthetic. The more realistic representation of nature that flourished during the period recognized the essential disorder of the natural world.

QUEEN ANNE WALNUT SIDE CHAIR
SHELL MOTIF
The term "Rococo" is derived from the French word *rocaille* (rockwork) and refers to the irregular rock and shell forms on grotto ornament. Shell motifs—especially scallops, or cockleshells—are found frequently on Rococo silver, ceramics, and furniture. In the late 18th century the conch shell gained popularity.

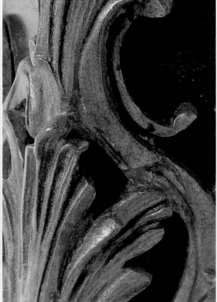

FRENCH RÉGENCE COMMODE
METAL MOUNTS
Cast-bronze and gilt-metal mounts were initially used to protect the vulnerable corners of ornate veneered furniture, but they quickly became decorative elements in their own right. The casting of ormolu mounts was a specialty industry in France, and popular motifs included scrolls, masks, and foliate designs.

GEORGE I SECRETAIRE
JAPANNING
The practice of japanning furniture spread across Europe and the American colonies during this period: shellac varnish was applied to the surface in imitation of Japanese lacquer. A wide range of colors was used, but a white surface provided the most suitable base for further painted decoration, often of Asian scenes.

ITALIAN TABLE
CARVING AND GILDING
Furniture made of softer indigenous woods, rather than more expensive tropical hardwoods, was frequently carved with elaborate scrolls and smothered with gesso and gilding to provide a more lavish decorative effect. The carving was often carried out by specialists trained in the art of sculpture.

FURNITURE

THE DESIRE FOR MORE COMFORTABLE LIVING PROVIDED AN IDEAL CLIMATE FOR A NEW LOOK IN FURNITURE DESIGN AND A MOVE AWAY FROM THE RESTRAINTS OF CLASSICISM AND INTO THE REALMS OF FANTASY.

RÉGENCE TO ROCOCO

The new style had its origins in the refurbishment of the Palais Royal in Paris under Philippe, duc d'Orléans, regent to Louis XV from 1715 to 1723. Architect Gilles-Marie Oppenord introduced a look that was, essentially, curvaceous—a mass of swirling lines incorporating carvings of foliage and flowers in arrangements that were fanciful and deliberately asymmetrical.

A cohesive, unified design was key: chairs were upholstered in elegant silks, satins, and damasks that matched drapery; carved ornament on the furniture echoed motifs in wall paneling and doors; and colors were light and subtle, reflected in elaborately carved gilt-framed mirrors. Much of the design was influenced by women, whose desires to entertain at leisure inspired the creation of the drawing room, or salon. This is evident in the "feminine look" of the period.

LOUIS XV

The fashion for asymmetry was most extravagant during the reign of Louis XV (1715–74). Natural motifs— shells, flowers, and husks—were used in abundance, alongside arabesques, C-scrolls, and S-scrolls, in a bid to create the desired effect. This signaled the arrival of the *genre pittoresque*, later named the Rococo style. A derivation of the phrase *rocaille coquille* (rock and shell), the term refers to the rockwork and grottolike features that became synonymous with the look.

FASHIONABLE FORMS

Furniture tended to be smaller and more elegant than under Louis XIV, making maximum use of the curve motif in pieces such as tables and commodes with serpentine edges, chairs with undulating top

SECRÉTAIRE À ABBATANT This piece has a marble top, ormolu banding with shell and foliate scrolls at the corners, and a tulipwood veneer with floral marquetry. Stamped Joseph. *c.1760. H:45 in (114 cm).*

The ornate marquetry-work **apron** is embellished with carving

TABLE EN CHIFFONIÈRE This tulipwood-veneered table has cabriole legs with ormolu mounts and sabots. The top and undershelf marquetry floral cartouches have banded purplewood borders. *c.1755. H:26¼ in (66.5 cm).*

LOUIS XIV COMMODE The top, sides, drawer-fronts, and apron of this piece are decorated with floral, fruit, and foliage marquetry work and augmented with gilding and gilt-bronze mounts. Attributed to Thomas Hache. *1680–90. W:51¼ in (130.5 cm).*

Gilt-bronze sabots take the form of animal hooves under foliage rails, and the ubiquitous S-shaped cabriole leg. The prestigious marble-topped commode existed in a variety of styles, a favorite being the two-drawer version designed by Charles Cressent. The *fauteuil*—an upholstered, open-sided armchair—exemplified the desire for greater comfort, the frame adapted to accommodate fashionable hooped skirts. Close relations were the fully upholstered *bergère* and the fully upholstered sofa, or settee.

The new salons included tea tables, games tables, and sewing tables. Folded away at the edge of the room, such pieces were opened up as the need arose. Writing tables—primarily housed in the bedroom—were also popular. In addition to the men's *bureau plat*, largely unchanged from Baroque forms, there were now smaller, more elegant writing desks for ladies.

A TASTE FOR THE EXOTIC

Designs were executed in a range of techniques, and exotic woods such as amaranth, purplewood, and kingwood were used to create intricate marquetry inlays that became the height of fashion. Many pieces were finished with ormolu mounts; ostensibly applied to protect vulnerable corners, these were nevertheless exquisite in design.

In France, a process for imitating—more economically—Chinese lacquerwork was developed by Martin Frères and called *vernis Martin*. In Venice, *lacca povera* (poor man's lacquer) had the same effect. The technique involved pasting colored images onto furniture and applying several coats of varnish to achieve a glossy finish. In England, Thomas Chippendale often used Chinese elements in his furniture designs.

A fashion for carved and painted wood was common in regions of Italy and Scandinavia, where native woods such as pine, beech, and lime were soft and, therefore, particularly suited to intricate carving. Where the wood was inferior in quality, pieces were also covered in gesso and gilt.

MASTERS OF THE STYLE

Most of the finest Rococo pieces originated in France—Charles Cressent's two-drawer commode became a seminal design of the period, for example. François Cuvilliés did much to introduce the style to Germany, creating exemplary interiors at the Munich Residenz for the Elector of Bavaria. In Italy the work of Pietro Piffetti epitomized the Rococo style, with intricate marquetry in exotic woods, ivory, and mother-of-pearl.

GILTWOOD *FAUTEUIL* One of a pair made by N. Blanchard in the reign of Louis XV, this chair has a characteristically curvaceous frame carved with floral, fruit, and foliate motifs. These are echoed in the petit-point reupholstery. c.1755. W:28 in (71 cm).

LOUIS XV INTERIOR The Louis XV Blue Room in Paris's Musée Carnavalet is decorated and furnished in the lighter, airier Rococo style, which supplanted the heavier, more ornate Classicism popular during the reign of Louis XIV.

LOUIS XV MIRROR The openwork giltwood frame of this archetypal French Rococo mirror comprises an elaborate concoction of scrolling foliage, trailing and interlaced flowers, and *rocaille*. c.1755. H:46½ in (118 cm).

SWEDISH CONSOLE TABLE Supporting a marble top, this table's gilt-wood frame is carved in deep relief, in Louis XV Rococo style, with a lion mask, dragons, flowers, and scrolling foliage. c.1760. W:39 in (99 cm).

Ormolu drawer-pulls are in keeping with other adornments

LOUIS XV *BUREAU PLAT* Veneered in tulipwood and purplewood, with elaborate satinwood marquetry of stylized shells and foliate scrolls, this piece is further enriched with similar motifs in the elaborate ormolu mounts. c.1745. W:76 in (193 cm).

FROM WALNUT TO MAHOGANY

The high-Rococo style that developed in France spread to much of Europe, but in some regions the flamboyance was simply too much. Instead, designers took their lead from developments in the Low Countries and England, where a more restrained version of the style prevailed.

AN EMPHASIS ON WOOD

At the beginning of the 18th century, walnut was the wood of choice throughout much of Europe. It was a good, hard, indigenous wood, and it was suitable for carving. It grew rich in color over time and had exciting figuring—particularly when selected with burrs or from root timbers. For these reasons, there was a tendency to rely on the wood itself for ornament. Although techniques such as marquetry and lacquerwork existed, these were an exception to the rule and prohibitively expensive to all but the wealthiest of patrons.

From 1725 onward, mahogany began to take the place of walnut, primarily in England, and later across the rest of Europe. Mahogany found favor in the early American colonies, though it was also common to find regional pieces produced in native woods such as maple in New England, cherry in Connecticut, and walnut in the southern states.

The increased use of mahogany coincided with a blight on walnut trees in Europe, which made their wood rare and expensive, and the removal of import taxes in the 1730s, which significantly reduced the cost of importing mahogany from the West Indies. Because mahogany is a harder wood than walnut, it was a better choice for carving and piercing with intricate decoration. Its darker color married well with gold, silver, or bronze ornament, and it was not long before the wood became associated with the more elaborate styles of French Rococo, Palladian, and Chippendale furniture.

STYLE AND ORNAMENT

Although the Rococo style was more restrained than contemporary French and Italian furniture, concessions were made, not least the cabriole leg, less exaggerated *bombé* forms, and broken or arched pediments. Ornament was often

GEORGE II ARMCHAIR The mahogany frame is carved in deep relief with shell motifs and acanthus leaves. The legs terminate in claw-and-ball feet. Made in the style of Giles Grendey. *c.1740. H:39¾ in (101 cm).*

QUEEN ANNE WALNUT SIDE CHAIR This piece (one of six) has a vase-shaped splat, cabriole legs with pad feet, and a drop-in seat with period-authentic upholstery. By John York of Warwickshire. *c.1710. H:45 in (114 cm).*

GEORGE I SECRETAIRE This piece is modeled as a walnut-veneered chest-on-chest, and its upper drawers—the fourth of which is a fold-down writing surface—are flanked by carvings of griffins, flowers, and fruit. *c.1725. H:87½ in (222 cm).*

The broken pediment frames a scrolling Rococo cartouche carving

PALLADIANISM

From the 1720s a style emerged in England that rejected the asymmetrical frivolity of contemporary French design. It was inspired by, and takes its name from, the Italian architect Andrea Palladio, whose own buildings were influenced by the mathematical precision of ancient Classical architecture. The result was a formal style based on symmetry and geometric forms. Such buildings were furnished with massive furniture, often embellished with pediments, pilasters, and fielded panels. Some designers made the occasional concession to the Rococo style by decorating pieces ornately with swirling ribbons and shell motifs, but the overall look remained symmetrical. A leading exponent of the style was William Kent, who designed Holkham Hall in Norfolk.

GEORGE II CONSOLE TABLE The *alabastro fiorito* top of this table rests on a gilt-gesso, carved wooden base with a lambrequin-collared female mask and caryatids. Attributed to William Kent. *c.1730. W:56 in (143 cm).*

The acanthus-scroll stretcher has a double scallop shell at the center

WILLIAM AND MARY HIGHBOY Made in New England in flame birch and maple, this two-part highboy—the lower with a scalloped skirt—has ringed ball feet united by cockbeaded stretchers. *c.1700. H:66 in (167.5 cm).*

The vasiform back splat is typical of American Queen Anne chairs

GEORGE II MAHOGANY CARD TABLE This table has a shaped apron with a carved shell motif and is raised on shell-carved cabriole legs with webbed pad feet. The foldover top hides a baize-lined interior with candle stands. *c.1750. W:33¾ in (86 cm).*

Shell carving at the top of the chair leg

QUEEN ANNE DINING CHAIR With a serpentine-crested top rail terminating in scrolled ears, a vasiform back splat, and shell carvings, this walnut-framed dining chair made in the Delaware Valley is typical of the American Queen Anne style. *c.1760.*

limited to a single shell motif on the knee of a cabriole leg or a claw-and-ball foot. The occasional piece may also have been painted in pastel colors and gilt. Although marquetry was not as fashionable in England, it was still popular in the Low Countries, where designers created realistic floral displays. In England, inlaid detail took the form of elegant feather- or crossbanding.

TYPICAL FURNITURE

The first quarter of the century saw the emergence of the style referred to as Queen Anne. Its most recognizable form was the Queen Anne chair with its rounded back, vase-shaped back splat, and cabriole legs. This design was produced widely in England, the Low Countries, and the American colonies. The chair was most commonly made from solid walnut or oak with a walnut veneer.

Another form particular to these regions, and Germany, during the first half of the 1700s was the bureau cabinet—a two-door cupboard above a chest of drawers. Sometimes the cupboard doors were glazed for displaying ceramics. Some versions also housed a writing surface, a form known as a secretaire cabinet. A close relation, the chest-on-chest, was an architectural piece, often seen with a pediment and fluted pilasters.

Almost exclusive to the early American colonies was the combination of highboy and lowboy,

which rivaled the prestige of the commode in France. Designed en suite for the bedroom, each had a similar form and ornament. With its many drawers, the highboy served as an essential storage piece, while the lowboy functioned both as a dressing table and a writing table.

As in France, the more sociable climate gave rise to the creation of a number of smaller pieces of furniture. These were particularly suited to entertaining and included tea tables, which sometimes took the form of a round tilt-top table on a tripod base, and card tables, which satisfied an increasing fascination with gambling.

A TOUCH OF FLAIR

Despite the prevailing climate of restraint, Thomas Chippendale's designs stand out as having more exuberance. In his publication *The Gentleman and Cabinet-Maker's Director* (1754), he presented designs for a host of furniture forms elaborately decorated in different styles. Alongside drawings for richly ornamented French pieces with scrolling ribbons and foliage, Chippendale also offered Chinese-inspired designs featuring pagoda surmounts, fretwork galleries, and bamboo-effect carving, as well as Gothic-inspired designs incorporating pointed arches and quatrefoils.

QUEEN ANNE DRESSING TABLE The mahogany carcase of this American piece houses four drawers flanked by chamfered and fluted corners. The cabriole legs have claw-and-ball feet. *c.1750. W:34½ in (87.5 cm).*

THE HUGUENOTS

FEARING PROSECUTION AFTER THE 1685 REVOCATION OF THE EDICT OF NANTES, LARGE NUMBERS OF THE FRENCH PROTESTANT COMMUNITY, KNOWN AS THE HUGUENOTS, LEFT THE COUNTRY. THEY TOOK WITH THEM THE SKILLS THEY HAD DEVELOPED IN A RANGE OF ARTISTIC DISCIPLINES AND SPREAD THEM ACROSS EUROPE AND THE WORLD.

The revocation of the Edict of Nantes by Louis XIV sent shock waves through the Huguenot community of France. Prevented from worshiping freely, at the end of the 1600s Huguenots fled the country in droves. A good number of them were craftsmen, and the host countries—primarily the Protestant Low Countries, Prussia, Switzerland, and Britain—gained from their skills. Many Huguenots also benefited from opportunities farther afield: Dutch colonists encouraged travel to the Cape, where several families had success in viticulture; while British colonial interests afforded travel to the early American colonies, where immigrants set up a number of communities.

HOGARTH ENGRAVING Entitled *Industry and Idleness—The Fellow Apprentices at Their Looms*, this engraving shows silk weavers working in Spitalfields, London. It is accompanied by proverbs, including: "The hand of the diligent shall maketh rich." *1747.*

Lamerie silver ewer

SILVER DISH AND EWER Made by Paul de Lamerie for Algernon Coote, Sixth Earl of Mountrath, these items display the Earl's coat of arms, as well as delicate scrolling flowers and foliage, intertwined with human figures, typical of Lamerie's designs. *1742–43. Dish: D:30 in (75.75 cm); Ewer: H:18¼ in (46.5 cm).*

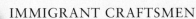

Lamerie silver dish

SILVER SAUCEBOAT Made by Nicholas Sprimont, this sauceboat in the form of an upturned shell features cast and applied Rococo-style decoration to the body. The foot is in the shape of shells and plant forms, which, combined, take on the appearance of a dolphin—a popular motif of the era. *c.1745.*

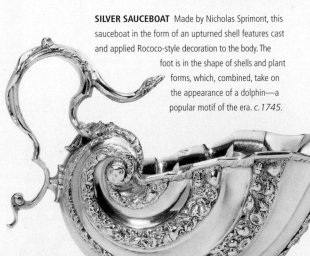

IMMIGRANT CRAFTSMEN

In the previous century, monarchs had used foreign craftsmen to furnish their palaces in the latest fashions. The concept of using talent from abroad was therefore not a new one. The difference now lay in sheer volume. More than 200,000 Huguenots left France, seeking employment abroad. In a climate of social change, they were not working exclusively for the elite but also contributing to the production of domestic wares for middle-class households.

A MAN OF INFLUENCE

Daniel Marot had a considerable impact across all decorative arts. An architect and designer, he made engravings of designs by Jean Bérain before leaving France to work for William of Orange, first in the Netherlands and then in England. He published numerous designs of his own for ornaments, furniture, and textiles, which were copied and reinterpreted by many contemporary craftsmen. Marot excelled at integrating form and ornament in his designs in a style that was primarily Classical.

WEAVERS AND SILVERSMITHS

Most Huguenots who came to England ended up in London. Spitalfields, an area known for producing silk, attracted weavers on a large scale and soon became the center of the silk industry, earning the nickname "weaver town." Among the immigrants was James Leman, who stood out as an accomplished designer as well as a

manufacturer, a rarity at the time. His designs were bold, often abstract, incorporating motifs ranging from stylized flowers to accurate botanical drawings, and from Classical architectural forms to elaborate Chinoiserie.

Around Soho, other Huguenots were making a name for themselves in silverware, among them Paul Crespin and Nicholas Sprimont. They produced pieces in unmistakable Rococo style, often with elaborate scrolling ornament and asymmetrical motifs, and created several outstanding items for Frederick, Prince of Wales, among other wealthy patrons. In 1746 Sprimont set up the Chelsea Porcelain factory, where the influence of his work with silver can be seen on early pieces.

But it is Paul de Lamerie who stands out as the genius of the age, becoming the leading exponent of silverware in the Rococo style. Lamerie emigrated to the Netherlands at the end of the 1600s and followed William of Orange to England when he became king. He trained under one of the most accomplished London goldsmiths of the time, Pierre Platel, creating exquisite, well-proportioned pieces in the Régence style. His work reflected the high style that was fashionable in France, and he excelled at producing pieces that combined form with often-dense relief ornament. At the peak of his career, Lamerie had an impressive list of clients among London's nobility and wealthy middle classes.

SILK BROCADE Made in Spitalfields, London, by Huguenot weavers, this yellow silk fabric is brocaded with naturalistic flowers in polychrome and silver threads. P. A. Ducerceau's publication *Bouquets Propres pour les Étoffes de Tours* provided weavers with a rich sourcebook of floral imagery.

CERAMICS

AT A TIME WHEN MANY WESTERN POTTERS WERE MIMICKING ASIAN WORKS,
AND A SELECT FEW STROVE TO DISCOVER THE SECRET OF PORCELAIN, OTHERS
CONTINUED TO REFINE TRADITIONAL FORMS AND DECORATIONS.

POTTERY IN EUROPE

First developed by potters in ancient China, by
the Middle Ages stoneware was also produced in
Germany; from here it spread throughout Europe.

The fine, robust body of stoneware is created
by firing clay at about 2,500°F (1,400°C). The
high temperature melts the components of the
clay, forming a nonporous body. Some types
of stoneware are translucent when held to the
light, in a way that is similar to porcelain.

THE GERMAN LEAD

Germany was at the forefront of the pottery
industry. Soon each region developed its preferred
style of stoneware, embracing the various styles
and properties the material allowed. For example,
many pieces produced in the town of Sieburg
(now Bad Karlshafen), in the northwest of the
country, had a fine, white body. In the Westerwald,
stoneware featured a gray body and was used to
make items such as a narrow-necked jug called an
Enghalskrug and a globular-shaped tankard known
as a *Kugelbauchkrug*. In Cologne, stoneware was
made with a brown body that became synonymous
with the bellarmine jug, a globular bottle with a
bearded mask or neck.

A large quantity of German stoneware was
imported to Britain in the 17th century, which
inspired British potters to develop their own range.
The London potter John Dwight patented a whitish
stoneware in 1672. In the early 18th century, many
potters in Europe, including the German Johann
Friedrich Böttger (*see p.34*), became admirers of
a fine, red stoneware produced in Yixing, China.
Much copied, this Chinese stoneware had a thin
body, making it suitable for tableware, especially
coffee and tea services.

*The Staffordshire
red ware* body was
inspired by Dutch imitations of
Chinese Yixing stoneware

STAFFORDSHIRE MUG
The red ware body of this
mug displays delicate applied
cream-colored decoration in
the form of flora and fauna,
including a lion and a unicorn.
c.1760. H:4¾ in (12 cm).

RHENISH BELLARMINE Named
after, and bearing an image of,
Cardinal Roberto Bellarmino
above a lion medallion, this style
of brown, salt-glazed stoneware
vessel originated in Cologne.
c.1750. H:8¼ in (21 cm).

ANNABERG JUG A molded
relief of a Madonna and Child
decorates this bulbous stoneware
jug. They sit among a palm frieze in
bright polychrome against a shiny
brown-black glaze ground. *c.1700.
H:8¼ in (21 cm).*

CREUSSEN STEIN Characteristically squat, the tin-mounted, salt-
glazed stoneware body displays hunting scenes flanked by bands
of stylized flora, all in applied relief and painted with blue, black,
yellow, and white enamels. Other favored subject matter included
apostles, electors, and the planets. *c.1680. H:8½ in (21.5 cm).*

EARTHENWARE

Earthenware is produced by firing coarse clay, often containing impurities, at about 1,500°F (800°C). This is a much lower temperature than is required to produce stoneware, and it endows pottery with a fundamental difference: tiny air spaces remain in the body, resulting in earthenware being porous. An earthenware body is usually reddish brown, as found in British clay, or buff, which can be seen in Delft earthenware when it is chipped. In order to make earthenware waterproof, a glaze must be applied. As well as tin glaze, lead glaze, which is shiny and transparent, was often used on earthenware. Metal oxides were sometimes added to give the glaze a color.

DECORATIVE TECHNIQUES

Decorating pottery with an incised pattern—a technique known as sgraffito—had been done for centuries. The technique involves cutting a motif into wet clay. In the 17th and 18th centuries the incised areas were sometimes painted.

Other decorative techniques soon developed. To create a three-dimensional decoration, for example, ornamental elements were formed in a mold and then applied to the body before firing. Slipware was produced—particularly in Staffordshire, Wrotham in Kent, and north Devon, all in Britain—by dipping a red earthenware body into a brown or white slip. The vessel was then decorated by slip-trailing, applying different colored slips in a trail, not unlike the way a cake is decorated.

Wares were sometimes handpainted with overglaze decoration. In this instance, enamel paints were applied to the glazed surface. They fused together once the piece was returned to the kiln. Underglaze decoration involved use of a metal oxide for a design after an initial firing but before applying the glaze.

STAFFORDSHIRE CHARGER In this example of Burslem slipware, the robust, contrasting colored decoration, in the form of a coat of arms within a spiraling border, is probably by Ralph Simpson. c.1680. D:12½ in (32 cm).

Brickwork pattern is slip-trailed by hand

SLIPWARE NIGHTLIGHT Modeled as an English mansion, this nightlight has architectural details that are slip-trailed in lead-glazed brown clay on the red clay shell. c.1760. W:6½ in (16.5 cm).

SALT-GLAZED STONEWARE

A particular type of hard, translucent glaze can be created on stoneware by throwing salt into the kiln while firing the object at a high temperature during the glazing stage. As the salt vaporizes, it leaves behind sodium, which fuses with silicates in the clay, forming a thin, glassy surface. Because of iron impurities within the clay, most salt-glazed stoneware has a brown color, although some are a buff or whitish color. Red lead was sometimes added to create a more glassy appearance. The glaze may be pitted, with a texture similar to orange peel.

This technique was first employed in Germany, where gray clay was used to produce tankards and bottles, but it spread to Britain in the late 1600s. In Staffordshire in around 1720, a fine, white, salt-glazed stoneware was created that was stronger than other bodies used at the time. It was inexpensive to produce, and large quantities were exported to the rest of Europe and North America, particularly as domestic tableware. A variety of decorative shapes were produced, including teapots modeled as camels and houses. The wares were sometimes decorated with molded or incised patterns. Tiny clay chips were occasionally added to the glaze—for example, to create the appearance of fur on a bear.

STONEWARE TEAPOT The English-made, salt-glazed body and cover of this teapot are handpainted with romantic imagery of a courting couple in parkland and with a flutist on the reverse. c.1760. H:7 in (18 cm).

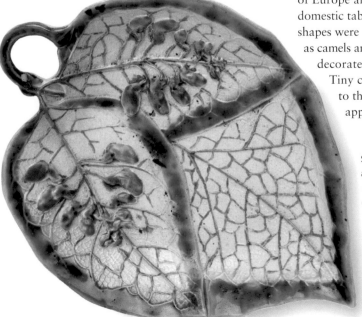

STAFFORDSHIRE DISH Made in the form of a leaf with a curled stalk handle, this salt-glazed stoneware dish is molded with pea flowers in relief, and painted in shades of green, yellow, and pink. c.1760. W:6¾ in (17.5 cm).

STAFFORDSHIRE JUG Molded with the head as a cover, this bear-baiting salt-glazed stoneware vessel is typically finely wrought and thinly potted. It is covered with tiny clay parings simulating fur. c.1760. H:10 in (25.5 cm).

TIN-GLAZED EARTHENWARE

In the 9th century, many years before Germany made its mark on the pottery industry, potters in Mesopotamia (now Iraq) were also inspired by Chinese ceramics. In a bid to replicate its appearance, they covered their earthenware with a tin glaze that provided an opaque white background for painting on decoration. They also developed luster glazes.

These forms of decoration spread through the Islamic countries and eventually reached Spain, parts of which were still under the rule of the Moors, in the 13th or 14th century. Hispano-Moresque lusterware was produced in the regions of Malaga and Valencia in the 14th and 15th century, often in the form of dishes and drug jars known as *albarelli*. These have a cylindrical form with a neck and foot more narrow than the body—a Persian form that spread, along with tin-glazed earthenware, to Italy (*see Maiolica box, right*), France, Germany, the Netherlands, and Britain.

MOUSTIERS PLATE The shape, creamy-gray glaze, and decoration—polychrome groups of caricatured figures among flora and fauna—are typical of Moustiers faience of the early 1700s. *D:9¾ in (25 cm).*

FRENCH FAIENCE

French tin-glazed earthenware is known as faience, after the Italian city of Faenza. Its production began in 1512, with the arrival of Italian potters in Lyon. At first, wares followed the Italian style, but by the mid-1600s they adopted a native Baroque style, in which ocher and blue were the dominant colors used to depict bold mythological figures. Blue-and-white Asian motifs, inspired by Chinese exports, became the norm by the end of the century.

An important pottery center in the 1700s was Rouen, which produced wares with intricate patterns based on lacework, lambrequins, or ironwork. Some French products were left blank or only lightly decorated, in a style known as *faience blanche*. Another style that became popular in the early 18th century was the so-called *grand feu*. This involves painting the decoration on to an unfired glaze with high-temperature enamels—blue, purple, green, yellow, orange-red, and red—before firing. Strasbourg, Lunéville, Marseilles, and Sceaux led the industry.

HANAU EWER Known as an *Enghalskrug*, this German jug has a typically long-necked and footed, bulbous body. It is decorated with Chinoiserie-style flowers, birds, and insects, rendered in Scharffeuer cobalt blue on white. *c.1725. H:12½ in (32 cm).*

ITALIAN SANDER The tin-glazed, fluted drum-shaped body of this sander is decorated with naturalistic landscape imagery in the Chinese style, rendered in green and black, a favorite Italian palette. *c.1750. D:2¾ in (7 cm).*

D'APREY PLAQUE Made in the factory of Jacques Lallemant de Villehaut, Baron d'Aprey, this plaque has a faience body painted with a landscape characteristic of pastoral French Rococo imagery. *c.1750. W:13¼ in (33.5 cm).*

Strasbourg also produced wares using the *petit feu* technique, in which colors are painted onto the glaze after it is fired. The pottery is fired again at a lower temperature, which means brighter colors can be used, including crimson, vermilion, and pink.

GERMAN PRODUCTION

Introduced by Dutch potters in the late 1600s, German Fayence was decorated in a style similar to Delft ware, with blue-and-white Asian themes. Fayence was occasionally painted with manganese and yellow in addition to blue, as well as *petit feu*. *Enghalskrugen* (jugs with a narrow neck) and deep dishes were common forms, as was plain hollow ware. In the 18th century the Chinese themes were replaced by local, native motifs, including figures, landscapes, the double-headed eagle, and coats of arms. Common shapes include the *Walzenkrug* tankard, tureens, plates, dishes, and figures.

MAIOLICA

Throughout the 18th century, Italian potters continued to make their traditional tin-glazed earthenware, which was inspired by Hispano-Moresque wares imported through a port on the island of Majorca. These wares were named *maiolica*, the Tuscan name for Majorca. One of the most important Italian maiolica centers was the city of Faenza, where pottery production was well established by the mid-15th century. Early wares were decorated in green and purple, depicting figures, animals, and heraldic beasts. A palette dominated by blue followed, and by the 16th century pictorial paintings with episodes from Classical literature or Biblical, mythological, or allegorical scenes covered huge expanses of large dishes, plaques, and other objects—a style known as *istoriato*. The style was particularly popular in the town of Urbino. Other important centers include Castelli, Deruta, and Montelupo, all in central Italy.

ITALIAN MAIOLICA PLAQUE Of rectangular form, this plaque has a grayish-cream glazed body decorated with the Madonna and Child in shades of blue, green, yellow, and manganese. *Mid-1700s. W:15 in (38 cm).*

DUTCH POTTERY

Dutch potters soon began to imitate the blue-and-white decoration of the Chinese porcelain imported by the Dutch East India Company in the early 17th century. It was known as *kraak* porcelain—after the Portuguese carracks, or merchant ships, which transported the wares from China. Delft became the preeminent center for this product by the mid-1600s, and it even gave its name to the pottery, which is now known as Delft ware.

Dutch potters also painted Dutch landscapes and Biblical subjects on their pieces, which included hollow ware, tiles, plaques, flower holders, and many more forms. By the end of the 17th century they also used a polychrome palette that imitated the Chinese *famille verte* and *famille rose* palettes, as well as Japanese Imari and Kakiemon porcelain.

Tin-glazed earthenware was first produced in Britain in the 1500s, but most of it was made in the 17th and 18th centuries. This pottery is known as delftware.

In the 17th century, Chinese porcelain was a luxury item in Britain. In order to satisfy the appetite of the middle classes for this type of item, British potters created a Chinese-inspired product that was less refined than its Dutch counterpart, with a softer body. Typical decoration included stylized flowers, oak leaves, and the monarch's portrait on such forms as drug jars, dishes, and salts. The blue-dash charger, with a rim decorated with

DELFT PLATE This plate is decorated in the cobalt-blue and white palette. The design, possibly inspired by a contemporary print, shows cabinet-makers at work within a floral border. *c.1760. D:12½ in (31.75 cm).*

DELFT BASIN Decorated in the Chinese export palette of cobalt blue on white, this basin has a central image of fruit, flowers, and leaves circumscribed by a gently scrolling foliate border. *1720s–40s. D:10¾ in (27.5 cm).*

broad strokes of blue, was popular in the late 1600s. In the 18th century British delftware became more delicate and was made in a larger range of shapes, including wall pockets, punch bowls, and puzzle jugs, often painted with British figures, landscapes, and buildings, as well as Chinese designs.

DELFTWARE FLOWER BRICKS The polychrome Chinoiserie landscape on these flower bricks is rendered in a more open and delicate style than pre-18th-century equivalents. Made in London. *1730–40. H:6 in (15 cm).*

DELFTWARE POSSET POT Made in either London or Bristol (the painting style possibly indicates the latter), this blue-and-white piece features flowering shrubs, birds, and commemorative decoration ("E.I.P."). *1689. D:9¾ in (25 cm).*

THE ARCANUM

AMONG EUROPEAN ARISTOCRATS, PORCELAIN WAS
CONSIDERED MORE DESIRABLE THAN GOLD. THIS LED
TO THE RACE FOR THE ARCANUM—THE SECRET TO
MAKING HARD-PASTE PORCELAIN, WHICH THE CHINESE
AND JAPANESE HAD GUARDED FOR CENTURIES.

MEISSEN MILK JUG Of octagonal form and characteristically
bulging near the foot, this milk jug has a scroll handle and a
domed cover with a cone knop. It is painted with the Quail
pattern in the Kakiemon palette. *c.1730. H:6½ in (16.5 cm).*

JOHANN JOACHIM KÄNDLER

Some of the best Meissen porcelain was produced when
Johann Joachim Kändler was chief modeler (1733–75).
First he created a series of large, naturalistic animals and
birds, some as tall as 3 ft (1 m), for Augustus the Strong's
Japanese Palace. Because these elaborate figures were
expensive to produce, they soon gave way to small figures
and groups, including Commedia dell'Arte actors, exotic
figures, shepherds, aristocrats, street vendors, dogs, and
monkey musicians. Originally modeled in the Baroque
style, the figurines took on the Rococo fashion for light-
heartedness with flowers and scrolls after
Kändler visited Paris in 1747. These
exquisite pieces were the height
of fashion, often displayed on
the dining tables of the rich.

MEISSEN FIGURE GROUP Modeled by Kändler, this group shows a
lady with a pug on her lap attended by a Moorish servant. The modeler's
typically vigorous and exotic style is accentuated by a rich polychrome
and gold palette. *c.1740. H:6 in (15 cm).*

Augustus the Strong, Elector of Saxony and
King of Poland, was a powerful man who had
built up a spectacular—and expensive—collection
of Asian ceramics. He was eager to find the secret
of the Arcanum, so that he could increase his
collection—and his coffers—by making and selling
the first European hard-paste porcelain. To this
end, Augustus had employed Ehrenfried Walther
von Tschirnhaus, a scientist and mathematician.
However, the work was expensive, and the Elector
was short of funds.

AN ALCHEMIST'S BOASTS

At the time, one way to gain patronage for
chemical experimentation was to claim the ability
to make gold from base metals. However, this was
a dangerous strategy: a lack of success meant the
possibility of execution.

One man who made such a bold claim was
Johann Friedrich Böttger, a skilled chemist who
had knowledge of both pharmaceutical and
metallurgical techniques. In 1707, Augustus
imprisoned Böttger in Dresden, the capital of
Saxony, both as punishment for failing to
produce gold and to secure the secret of doing
so if he did succeed. Böttger was also forced to
collaborate with von Tschirnhaus on his formula
for making porcelain.

SUCCESS AT LAST

Von Tschirnhaus was using nearby
deposits of kaolin for his
experiments, but his
porcelain formula lacked
the traces of potash
mica found in its
Chinese counterpart.
Meanwhile, Böttger
began building kilns that
could produce the high
temperatures required.

At first he developed a new
type of red stoneware, known
as *Böttgerporzellan*. This was so
hard that it could be polished on a
lapidary's wheel. Then, after von
Tschirnhaus's death in 1708, Böttger made
refinements to the experiments the two men had
worked on and succeeded in producing Europe's
first hard-paste (or true) porcelain in 1709.

MEISSEN FIGURE Made when Johann
Gottlob Kirchner was chief modeler, this
figure depicts an Asian woman on a
sectioned socle. She is dressed in a long
robe painted with polychrome decoration,
including *Indianische Blumen* (Indian
flowers). *c.1725. H:4½ in (11.75 cm).*

MEISSEN'S MODEL

The Elector set up a manufactory in Meissen,
a town near Dresden, in 1710. The factory
produced luxury items that differed from the Asian
wares, based on the shapes and decoration used for
contemporary silverware. However, demand was
slow, and the fashion for all things Asian became
stronger than ever.

The Meissen factory managed to survive and
became an economic success by 1713. It had
attracted some of Europe's best painters and
modelers, whose work included gold-gilt and
Asian-inspired decoration, including the Kakiemon
palette. Meissen became, and still is, one of Europe's
most respected porcelain manufacturers.

Meanwhile, Böttger was eventually freed in
1713. He died in 1719, the same year that hard-
paste porcelain was first made in Europe outside of
Meissen, at Claudius Innocentius du Paquier's
factory in Vienna.

MEISSEN TEAPOT Made
from early Meissen porcelain
(*Böttgerporzellan*), this teapot
is decorated with gilt-crested oval
reserves showing Chinoiserie scenes
painted in iron red and purple.
c.1725. H:5½ in (14 cm).

AUGUSTUS THE STRONG'S JAPANESE PALACE Drawn, painted, and
engraved by Bernardo Bellotto, a nephew of Canaletto, this view includes
Augustus's Japanese Palace (on the left). Begun in 1714 and enlarged in
1722–33 in the late Baroque style, the palace was originally intended to
house Augustus's Asian porcelain collection. *1748.*

PORCELAIN

With the help of former Meissen employees, the Vienna factory produced hard-paste porcelain in 1719. At first the shapes were symmetrical Baroque forms with scrollwork decoration. Asian-inspired floral motifs were used, as well as battle and hunting scenes and Chinoiserie. From around 1750 Vienna began producing Rococo-style wares, as well as figures modeled by Johann Josef Niedermayer. Other 18th-century German factories producing hard-paste porcelain were Höchst, Frankenthal, Nymphenburg, Fürstenberg, and Ludwigsburg.

The Italian firms of Capodimonte and Doccia also worked with hard-paste porcelain. Both companies produced tea and table services and specialized in figures.

FRENCH SOFT-PASTE PORCELAIN

European firms that could not make hard-paste porcelain or did not have access to kaolin produced soft-paste porcelain. At first the French Saint-Cloud factory decorated its small wares—cutlery handles, snuff boxes, and spice boxes—with underglaze blue borders of *lambrequins*. From about 1730 the body was left white and was sometimes molded with Chinese-inspired cherry blossoms, wading birds, or overlapping leaves.

Chantilly covered its porcelain with an opaque creamy-white glaze that hid imperfections. The decoration on its plates, teapots, jugs, and jardinières was inspired by Chinese *famille verte* and Japanese Kakiemon style. By the mid-1700s it used a scattering of small sprays of European flowers.

The style of the Vincennes factory (est. c.1740) was influenced by Meissen, but with a softer palette and more natural brushstrokes. Early pieces are heavy and decorated with landscapes, sprays of flowers, figures, and scrollwork borders. In 1748 the factory introduced more elegant Rococo-style forms. Vincennes moved in 1756 and became known as Sèvres.

VINCENNES CUP AND SAUCER The soft-paste porcelain bodies of these pieces were painted by Pierre Rosset with medallions and garlands of flowers in polychrome and gold on white and celestial blue. *1754. Saucer: D:3¾ in (9.5 cm).*

SOFT-PASTE IN EUROPE

In Flanders Tournai made porcelain tableware with basketweave and spiral borders decorated in underglaze blue with scenes from Aesop's fables

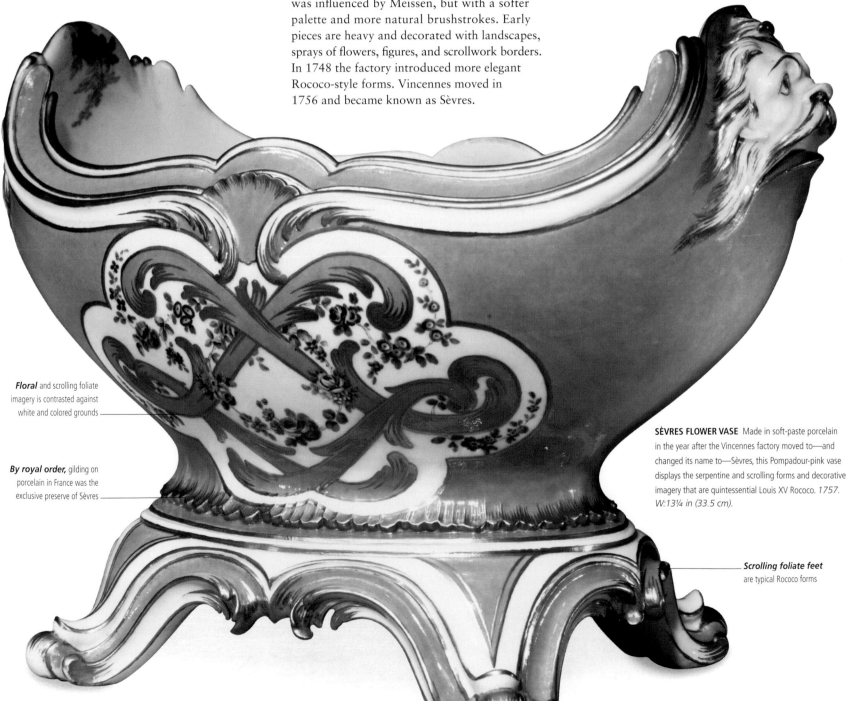

Floral and scrolling foliate imagery is contrasted against white and colored grounds

By royal order, gilding on porcelain in France was the exclusive preserve of Sèvres

SÈVRES FLOWER VASE Made in soft-paste porcelain in the year after the Vincennes factory moved to—and changed its name to—Sèvres, this Pompadour-pink vase displays the serpentine and scrolling forms and decorative imagery that are quintessential Louis XV Rococo. *1757. W:13¼ in (33.5 cm).*

Scrolling foliate feet are typical Rococo forms

DU PAQUIER VASE Made at Claudius Innocentius du Paquier's factory in Vienna, this vase is decorated with a polychrome *Indianische Blumen* (Indian flowers) pattern, inspired by Japanese and Chinese porcelain. *c.1725. H:11 in (27.5 cm).*

Manganese purple, yellow, green, and iron red dominate the polychrome palette

Polychrome painting is contrasted with gilt edging

ANSBACH FIGURE The young boy with a wine glass and jug represents Fall. The figure is from a series entitled The Four Seasons, a popular subject matter in the Rococo era. *c.1760. H:7 in (18 cm).*

OVAL TOURNAI PLATE The soft-paste porcelain body is decorated with a large bouquet and smaller sprigs of flowers within a swagged floral border, in a palette dominated by purple, puce, and blue. *1755–65. L:17¼ in (44 cm).*

and exotic birds. Tournai is also known for figures and groups. The Ansbach factory in Bavaria specialized in figures. The porcelain body was a brilliant white and the painting of good quality.

BRITISH SOFT-PASTE PORCELAIN

Porcelain production in Britain became established around the mid-1700s. Worcester produced a finely potted body with a thin glaze for tea and coffee wares and decorative tableware. These often had molded decoration. Early wares had Chinoiserie motifs and flowers, but by the late 1760s strong background colors and Rococo-style panels of exotic birds and flowers became favored.

Early Chelsea wares copied contemporary Rococo silver forms and were unadorned. By 1749 the decoration was inspired by the Japanese

Kakiemon style, which evolved into the rich colors and gilding used between 1756 and 1769, in imitation of Sèvres. Chelsea produced tureens in the shape of animals and vegetables, Meissen-style figures, and plates with botanical designs.

The Bow factory produced wares for a wider market. Some were decorated in underglaze blue with Chinese-inspired patterns, as well as molded *blanc-de-Chine* cherry blossoms.

Derby began producing porcelain in around 1748. Its *blanc-de-Chine* Chinoiserie figure groups are among the best of its production. The factory was bought by Duesbury & Heath in 1756, and production was soon influenced by Meissen. Derby's Rococo figures have scrolling bases and bocage, a type of tree ornament. Tea services, tureens, dishes, and baskets were painted with birds and flowers.

Lowestoft manufactured wares with underglaze blue decoration that followed Chinese patterns. The Longton Hall factory made domestic wares decorated with delicate multicolored painting, as well as Meissen-inspired figures.

Richard Chaffers's Liverpool factory mostly used a blue-and-white palette for its soft-paste porcelain. Some wares, however, were decorated in the *famille rose* palette. Lund's Bristol used Cornish soapstone to produce soft-paste porcelain. The heavy glaze used often blurred the underglaze blue decoration.

Chinese scenes in well-controlled underglaze blue are typical of Liverpool porcelain

Botanical imagery was a popular subject matter for Chelsea in the 1750s

CHELSEA CUP AND SAUCER Their creamy-white porcelain bodies and Meissen-style polychrome floral decoration date these items to Chelsea's Red Anchor period (1752–56). *Saucer: D:5¼ in (13.5 cm).*

The Kakiemon palette includes cerulean blue, iron red, turquoise, brown, yellow, and gold

WORCESTER VASE Of waisted, beakerlike form, this vase is painted in the Kakiemon palette with Chinoiserie imagery, comprising a ho-ho bird on rockwork, flanked by flowering branches. *c.1755. H:5½ in (14 cm).*

LIVERPOOL COFFEE POT Made at Richard Chaffers's factory, this pot has a baluster-shaped body and dome cover. Both are painted in the Chinese style with a Jumping Boy pattern in underglaze blue. *c.1760. H:7¾ in (19.5 cm).*

LONGTON HALL TUREEN Made in the shape of a melon, this soft-paste porcelain tureen is decorated in shades of yellow, green, and puce. Longton Hall was famous for its vegetable and fruit forms. *c.1755. W:9½ in (24 cm).*

GLASS

IN THE 17TH AND 18TH CENTURIES SODA AND LEAD GLASS WERE
DECORATED WITH ENAMELS, AND WERE CUT, STIPPLED, ENGRAVED,
AND, WITH THE ADDITION OF VARIOUS OXIDES, COLORED.

ENAMELED GLASS

Colored enamels were first used on glass by the
Romans, and then by Islamic glassmakers from
the 13th century onward. Enameling flourished
in Venice in the 15th century, particularly on
cristallo glass, a lightweight, thin, clear glass
developed by Angelo Barovier in around 1450.

Enamels arc made of powdered glass mixed with
a colored oxide and oil. After being painted onto
a surface, they are heated in a furnacc to form a
hard material that is bonded onto the glass. Early
decorative patterns tended to be simple, such as
lines and dots, and were restricted to borders.
Later, more complex patterns, including coats of
arms and mythological figures, were
created. German and Bohemian
glassmakers adopted enameling in
the mid-16th century, and the
technique flourished in central and
northern Europe during the 17th and
18th centuries. Enameling was most
commonly applied to drinking
vessels. These included the *Humpen*,
a cylindrical beaker, and the *Römer*,
a heavy footed and stemmed glass
akin to a wine glass.

Patterns were often applied by
Hausmaler, enamelers who worked at

Landscape scenes are a
typical *Schwarzlot* subject

*The opaque
Milchglas body* is
in imitation of porcelain

MILCHGLAS TANKARD Made in either Germany or Bohemia,
this piece has a pewter-mounted *Milchglas* body. It is colorfully
decorated with medallions depicting a cipher and portraits under
a crown and among foliage. *c. 1740. H:9 in (23 cm).*

SCHWARZLOT GOBLET The funnel bowl is raised on
a cut pedestal stem and embellished with *Schwarzlot*
(black lead) enameling in the form of a hunting scene.
Made in Saxony. *c.1730. H:8¾ in (22.5 cm).*

The naivety of the
painting, especially in the
lion's almost-human face,
is characteristic of the
style and period

SWEDISH BEAKER This cylindrical beaker depicts, in vivid polychrome
enamels, Carolus (Karl) XII of Sweden in military attire, with a lion at his feet.
The reverse is decorated with an equally colorful floral spray and the three
crowns of the Swedish royal coat of arms. *c.1715. H:9¼ in (23.75 cm).*

home. In the mid-17th century Johann Schaper, a *Hausmaler* in Nuremburg, developed the use of transparent brown and black enamels. Known as *Schwarzlot* (black lead), this style remained fashionable until the 1750s and was adopted by the Bohemians, whose leading exponent was Ignaz Preissler. Designs were usually based on natural themes, including flowers, landscapes, and hunting and mythological scenes. Political and commemorative themes are also known.

GILDED GLASS

In the early 18th century *Zwichengoldglas* was developed. Gold or silver leaf was applied to a body, engraved with a design, and then covered with a layer of clear glass. Decorative motifs were similar to those on enameled glass, and gilding was often used in combination with enameling.

COLORED GLASS

In the late 15th century a "milky" opaque white glass, known as *lattimo*, was developed by the Venetians. It resembled the highly coveted porcelain imported from China and became popular during the 17th and 18th centuries.

The technique had spread to Bohemia by the 18th century, where it was known as *Milchglas*. Bohemian glassmakers also produced innovative colored glass, most notably a deep, strong blue glass created by adding cobalt oxide to the glass mix. As with *Milchglas*, this provided a perfect foil for colored enamels.

At the end of the 17th century Johann Kunckel, a director at the Potsdam Glasshouse, developed a deep pink glass, by adding gold chloride to the mix. It was known as *Rubinglas* or *Goldrubinglas* (gold-ruby glass). As it was expensive to produce, it was often finely engraved or cut. Caspar Wistar, a German glassmaker, emigrated to North America in the early 18th century and founded the first American glass factory, Wistaburgh Glassworks, based in New Jersey.

BEAKER WITH COVER On the front of this gray-tinted Bohemian footed beaker are two cooing doves and stylized floral ornaments; the back shows architectural landscapes. *c.1700. H:10¼ in (26 cm).*

ALPINE REGION BOTTLE The semi-opaque brown-glass body is hand-trailed with spirals of opaque white *Milchglas. Mid-1700s. H:4½ in (11.5 cm).*

ENGRAVED GLASS

Although engraved glass was made by the Romans and then the Venetians, it was not until the second half of the 16th century that the techniques spread to the rest of Europe.

Diamond-point engraving, in which the design is lightly scratched onto the surface of the glass with a sharp stylus, could be used on thin *cristallo* glass, as the engraved line was so shallow. Stipple engraving is similar, but uses patterns of dots made by tapping the stylus on the glass. Stipple-engraved pieces are less common, as the process was more time-consuming.

Both types of engraving enjoyed a golden age when they were brought to the Low Countries, then Germany and Bohemia, by Venetians during the 17th century. Notable exponents included Willem Mooleyser and Frans Greenwood. Patterns were more complex than many enameled examples, and included political and mythological figures and portraits, and scrolling fruit and floral motifs. Many were applied to drinking vessels, including the lidded *Pokal* and goblets.

Wheel engraving, in which a spinning wheel is used with abrasive paste to cut a design onto glass, was revived in Europe in about 1600. Germany and Bohemia became centers of production, and the technique was brought to Britain in around 1720. George Ravenscroft's lead crystal glass provided a robust body that was perfect for engraving, ensuring Britain remained an important center of glass production.

ENGRAVED COVERED GOBLET The delicate floral and foliate decoration to the bowl and cover of this glass is by Georg Ernst Kunckel of Thuringia. *1726–30. H:12¼ in (31.25 cm).*

FRENCH GOBLET This glass has a stepped, circular foot and a baluster stem with a heart-shaped knop. The bowl is engraved with stylized heart shapes. *c.1700. H:8½ in (21.5 cm).*

FAÇON DE VENISE

Glass made in the 15th-century Venetian style but not produced in Venice is known by the French term *façon de Venise*. This ornate, delicate glass was made throughout Europe by emigrant Venetian glassmakers, and those they taught, during the 16th and 17th centuries. It was often produced in a gray-toned soda glass and could be elaborately decorated with *filigrana*— thin strands of clear or, more usually, white-colored glass contained in rods, which were shaped into a pattern.

Serpent-stemmed drinking glasses were a popular form, as were tazze and covered goblets. Ornate curls and geometric shapes were also common. Diamond-point engraving can sometimes be found on the bowls of *façon de Venise* glasses made in the Low Countries.

FAÇON DE VENISE GOBLET Made in the southern Low Countries, in the style of 15th-century Venetian glass, this goblet combines clear and colored (blue) glass and features a typically ornate snakelike pattern in the stem. *1690s. H:12¼ in (31 cm).*

ASIAN INFLUENCE

CHINA DEVELOPED THE FIRST HARD-PASTE PORCELAIN IN THE 10TH CENTURY, AND BY THE 1700S VAST QUANTITIES OF CHINESE WARES WERE SHIPPED TO EUROPE, WHERE—ALONG WITH JAPANESE CERAMICS—THEY HAD A HUGE IMPACT ON EUROPEAN POTTERY.

CHINESE WUCAI VASE
This Transitional period vase of baluster shape has a carved and pierced wooden stand and cover. It is painted in the *wucai* palette, with squirrels, grapevines, and rockwork. *c.1650. H:11¾ in (30 cm).*

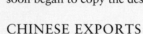

CHINESE PLATE Salvaged in 1985 as part of The Nanking Cargo from a Dutch ship sunk in 1752, this Qing dynasty blue-and-white export plate features a Lattice Fence pattern, with a pagoda, willow, and pine. *c.1750. D:16½ in (42 cm).*

The strong translucent body of Chinese porcelain, as well as its decoration, was greatly admired by wealthy Europeans. The Portuguese first imported large quantities of Chinese porcelain made specifically for the West, decorated in blue and white, during the Wanli reign (1573–1619). These delicate wares were decorated in a thin, watery blue color and often featured birds, animals, plants, and landscapes. Peonies, chrysanthemums, and lotuses were commonly used. European potters soon began to copy the designs on their own work.

CHINESE EXPORTS

During the Transitional period (1620–83), Chinese potters produced new shapes and decoration that catered to European tastes. They used European shapes such as saltcellars, candlesticks, and flasks. They also made technical advances, improving the quality of the porcelain. The cobalt-blue glaze on wares from this period has a purplish tone and more naturalistic brushstrokes. Landscape painting became the favorite form of decoration, but narrative scenes were also popular.

Porcelain made during the Kangxi period (1662–1722) is of a higher quality than earlier wares, except pieces made for the emperor and his court. Flowers and plants among rocks are popular themes on these pieces, as are craggy landscapes, which were replaced by idealized scenes of bending trees and pavilions on islands.

JAPANESE PORCELAIN VASE
Made in Arita, this vase is in the shape of an ancient bronze urn and molded in shallow relief with chrysanthemums, rocks, and waves, in iron red, blue, and green. *c.1680. H:6¾ in (17 cm).*

COLORFUL CHOICE

Along with the popular, inexpensive blue-and-white, the Chinese also used polychromatic palettes. These include the mid-16th-century *wucai* ("five color") palette, in which underglaze blue is used as a wash or outline and overglaze iron red, green, yellow, brown, and black provide the pattern. The *famille verte* ("green family") palette, first used during the Qing dynasty (1644–1911), is similar to the *wucai* palette but uses a prominent brilliant green and a duller blue. The 18th-century *famille rose* ("pink family") palette is dominated by rose pink.

Not all wares were colored: the French term *blanc-de-Chine* refers to the white porcelain exported to Europe from China in the 17th and 18th centuries.

JAPANESE PORCELAIN

Almost all early Japanese porcelain was produced in Arita, on Kyushu, the main western island close to Korea. Korean potters arrived in this area in the late 16th century and discovered kaolin.

The region is known for three distinct styles. The 17th-century painter and potter Sakaida Kakiemon, thought to have discovered enameling in Japan, has given his name to Kakiemon ware. Nigoshide, a milky-white porcelain, was used for bowls, vases, and bottles sparsely painted in iron red, blue, turquoise, black, yellow, and occasionally purple enamels. The colorful Imari palette, developed in the late 1600s, saw tableware and large ornaments adorned with textile-inspired patterns, using a dark underglaze blue and iron red, yellow, gold, green, purple, and sometimes turquoise enameling.

LACQUERING AND JAPANNING

East Asia is the home of lacquering, a technique first used in 4th-century-BCE China but perfected in Japan, which involved applying numerous layers of varnish onto wood, leather, or fabric. The varnish came from the sap of the *Rhus vernicifera* tree, and when dried it formed a hard, protective shell that could be carved. Lacquer is often found on furniture, boxes, and *inro*, a type of container with figurative or naturalistic designs highlighted in gold against a typically black or red background. The great demand for the product in Europe led to the development of japanning. For this type of lacquering, the varnish was made from deposits of *Coccus lacca* (the lac beetle). To create the illusion of depth, sawdust and gum arabic were used to build up areas. Japanning can be found in black, scarlet, or green, often decorated with gilt Chinoiserie.

QUEEN ANNE KNEEHOLE DESK Richly japanned on a blue-green ground, this desk features gold Chinoiserie, including elephants, a pavilion, and a warrior on horseback. *c.1710. W:30¾ in (78 cm).*

DETAIL FROM A GEORGE I SECRETAIRE The door is white japanned all over and decorated with Chinoiserie scenes of dignitaries. The delicately painted figures are rendered in a palette of iron red, yellow, blue, gray, and black. *c.1725.*

METALWARE

MANY NEW SILVER FORMS APPEARED IN THE LATE 1600S. HOWEVER, DUE
TO CHANGES IN FASHION AND THE FACT THAT SILVER WAS OFTEN MELTED
DOWN TO FINANCE WARS, FEW ITEMS FROM BEFORE 1700 HAVE SURVIVED.

ROCOCO CHOCOLATE POT Fashioned in silver
by Charles-Louis Gerard, this waisted pot is raised
on four animal feet and decorated with gadroons,
shell motifs, and armorials. The handle is of ebonized
wood. *1716. H:10½ in (26.5 cm).*

THE NEW LUXURY BEVERAGES

Tea, coffee, and chocolate were first brought to
Europe in the late 17th century and only drunk
by the wealthy few who could afford silverware.
The shape of the earliest teapots was based on
globular Chinese porcelain teapots, but by the
early 1700s the pear-shaped teapot was common
in Britain, Germany, the Low Countries, and North
America. It had a domed, hinged lid, and the
handle and knop on the lid were often made of
wood or ivory, which retained the heat created by
the hot liquid. In Britain, teapots were occasionally
octagonal, imitating the shape of coffee pots.

Early teapots were small (tea was expensive)
and decoration was sparse, usually limited to an
engraved family crest or coat of arms or cut-card
work. By the 1730s teapots were made in a
spherical bullet shape and were more ornately

decorated, with chased or engraved flowers, scrolls,
and strapwork near the lid. North Americans
preferred an inverted pear-shaped pot on a short
stem with a wide foot. A curvaceous body and
spout are more symbolic of the Rococo style,
as are the double-scroll handle and embossed
and chased scroll decoration.

Early 18th-century coffee pots had either a
cylindrical or octagonal body, with a straight
or curved spout and a wooden handle.
Again, decoration was limited to armorials
or cut-card work. By the 1740s pots had
a flatter lid, a scrolled handle, and a beak-
shaped spout. Coffee pots evolved into
a baluster shape, then a pear shape
by 1760. Gadrooned rims and
decorations of shells, flowers,
and scrolls can be found

The carving of the
ebonized wood handle is
naturalistic and dynamic

Fixed finial, typical
on coffee pots

*The spout is
chased* to form a
dog's head, neck,
and collar

Gadrooning, or lobed
decoration, was popular in the
16th, 17th, and 18th century

ROCOCO COFFEE POT Made by William Shaw III, this
pot is of footed baluster form, has an ebonized wood
handle, and is decorated with fruit, flowers, strings of
husks, and scrolling foliage. *c.1760. H:12¼ in (31 cm).*

SILVER TEAPOT The body and cover are
selectively gadrooned and engraved. The
ebonized wood handle is shaped like a
black African. By Henri Louis Le Gaigneur.
c.1740. H:7½ in (19 cm).

on both of these latter forms. The pear shape was originally developed in France, where silversmiths made pots with three feet, a straight handle, and a small pouring lip. The decoration was also more in keeping with the Rococo style.

Chocolate pots were based on the shape of contemporary coffee pots but had a hinged finial where a swizzle stick could be inserted to mix the chocolate. Few were produced after 1750.

DINING SILVER

Complete dinner services, with plates, tureens, and other serving items became fashionable in France in the late 17th century. Early plates and salvers, used as stands for caudle cups—small, two-handled silver cups—were often plain, decorated with only a family crest or coat of arms. However, by the 1730s, the plain rim was superseded by a wavy one with gadrooning; and by the 1740s the Rococo-style gadrooned borders with shells were common.

Entrée dishes were introduced in the late 17th century, sauceboats first appeared around 1715, and soup tureens around 1720. These were often produced with matching decoration as part of a service, and early examples were plain, decorated with a coat of arms. By the 1730s and 1740s, especially in France, the decoration had become more ornate, with scrollwork and shells, and more extravagant pieces were decorated with vegetables, shellfish, and game.

OTHER SILVERWARE

The wave of Huguenot immigration to the Low Countries and Britain in the 1690s strongly influenced the style of silverware (*see p.28*). Soon the base, stem, and sconce of a candlestick

ENGLISH SILVER SALVER Made by William Justus of London, this has a C-scroll rim with shell clasping around a chased border of scrolling foliage and fish-scale panels, all around a central engraved cartouche. *1747. D:11½ in (28.5 cm).*

PAIR OF CANDLESTICKS These silver candlesticks by John Cafe of London are case cast in a late Rococo style. They have selectively lobed baluster stems and spreading bases with scalloped corners. *1751. H:7¾ in (19.5 cm).*

were cast separately in solid silver, then soldered together. The stem had a plain baluster shape with knops, which remained popular until the mid-1700s, and the base was round, square, or angled. By the 1730s the previously plain candlestick was ornately decorated with Rococo-style shells and flower-shaped nozzles; some exceptional examples have cast stems in the shape of female figures holding the socket for the candle.

Many other silver items were made in the Rococo style, including tea canisters (later known as tea caddies), sugar bowls, and cream jugs. A variety of items were made for serving wine during dinner—jugs, wine coolers, and monteiths (for cooling wine glasses)—and for condiments. More unusual silver items can be found in the form of andirons, used to hold logs on the hearth of a fireplace.

METAL MOUNTS

A variety of Chinese porcelain imported into Europe was embellished with ornate metal mounts in the 1500s, but the fashion reached the peak of its popularity in the 1700s, particularly in France. Gilt bronze, silver, and sometimes gold were used to make the mounts, which might be added to protect the piece, to westernize the form by creating handles and bases, or to help adapt the piece into a new form. In the early 18th century, French dealers of luxury items purchased Chinese exports from the Dutch East India Company and instructed metalworkers to decorate them. The porcelain was often modified to fit the mounts.

Chinese celadon glazes are found in grayish-, bluish-, and olive green

Each Buddha is carved in sandstone and turquoise-enameled

Dolphins are a recurring motif

PAIR OF LOUIS XV ANDIRONS Fashioned in gilded bronze in the style of Jacques Caffieri of Paris, these fire dogs feature reclining male and female Chinese figures raised on volutes. *1760s. L:7 in (18 cm).*

The volute acts as a resting place for the figure

FRENCH PERFUME FOUNTAIN The Chinese celadon-glazed vase of this piece has a gilded rim and is flanked by a pair of Buddhas atop gilded-bronze bases of plant forms and dolphins. *c.1760. H:12½ in (32 cm).*

CLOCKS

THE DAZZLING ACHIEVEMENTS OF BAROQUE AND ROCOCO CLOCK-MAKERS, ESPECIALLY THOSE WORKING IN FRANCE, REMAIN WITHOUT PARALLEL IN TERMS OF DECORATIVE IMPACT AND EXUBERANCE.

THE COURT OF THE SUN KING

That the French should rise to such heights in the field of clock decoration during the reign of Louis XIV, the Sun King, is surely no coincidence. The king himself had a particular interest in time, running his days, and those of his sizable retinue, to a strict timetable. Such was his punctiliousness that he kept no fewer than four clock-makers in his entourage. Their most famous charge—the astronomical clock by Passement—keeps time at Versailles to this day.

The patronage of Louis XIV's court could seal the fortune of any fashion and ensure its replication in elite circles across Europe for many years. The French clock-making industry of the 18th century is, however, more remarkable for the intricate decorative schemes devised by its craftsmen than for the quality or accuracy of its movements. Several horologists owe their long-standing reputation to the efforts of the cabinet-makers and metalworkers who enshrined their machinery in such palatial housings.

ELABORATE CASES

Clock cases of the period were usually made from wood, metal, or a combination. Designs varied from architecturally severe bracket clocks to ethereal cartouche-shaped wall clocks. Decorative embellishments were similarly diverse. Boullework was just as prevalent on clock cases as it was on other furniture at this time. Some cases exhibit brass and tortoiseshell inlays in intricate scrolling designs reminiscent of waves, tongues of flame, or foliate tendrils. Wooden and metal surfaces might be painted or enameled with convoluted foliate designs or sprays of flowers in a naturalistic style, similar to those found on porcelain of the period.

Background colors include bright greens and deep reds, chosen to complement the gilt-metal mounts that were so prevalent—whether complex openwork scrolls, which were the very epitome of Rococo design, or the more substantial structural additions of bracket or scroll feet, caryatid pillars, and floral finials.

Many of the most striking metal mounts take the form of cast figures. Stock Rococo representations of women in pastoral dress, taken straight from popular paintings of the day, can be seen alongside figures drawn from antiquity, including putti and allegorical representations of Father Time.

The numerals
are set on a white-enameled dial

CARTEL CLOCK The openwork case of this Parisian-made, gilded-bronze, cartouche-shaped clock features doves and two quintessential Louis XV Rococo motifs: scrolling foliage and putti. c.1750. H:23 in (58.5 cm).

The acanthus leaf mounts are in gilded bronze

BRACKET CLOCK Made by Duhamel of Troyes, this clock has a Louis XV Rococo scrolling form, accentuated by gilded-bronze scrolling-foliage mounts and polychrome-painted flowers. c.1750.

French cartel clock cases are usually cast in gilded bronze, as here, or brass

EXTENSIVE DECORATION

The clock cases with the strongest association with this fertile period are made entirely from metal. Gilded bronze, or ormolu, was especially prized for its luster and decorative versatility. The gossamer-thin openwork designs and extensive pierced decoration favored by some designers were ideally suited to ormolu, and metalworkers were able to manipulate sturdy metals into contortions that would have been impossible in wood. The most unrestrained Rococo clocks lack even a basic form and are delineated by branching leaves, hanging figures, and roaming scrolls around the clock face. This chaos is tempered only by the familiarity of the clock face: most are white-painted or silvered-metal disks, but some are made up of individual numerals picked out in enamel on an engraved metal ground.

REGULATOR CLOCKS

Regulators, first produced in England and France in the mid-17th century, represented a new breed of timepiece. They tended to be less decorative than other longcase clocks, since their function was to keep accurate time: other household clocks and watches would be set by the time shown on the regulator. For ease of reading, regulator dials give greater prominence to the minutes than the hours and often have a subsidiary dial for seconds. Regulator mechanisms, which do not strike, are the most carefully constructed and sophisticated of the period.

EBONY BRACKET CLOCK The caddy top has a carrying handle, and there are embossed pierced panels on the globe finials. The backplate is inscribed "Nicolas Masey A Londres." c.1680. H:15¼ in (38.5 cm).

Each numeral is set within its own white-enameled plaque

BOULLE BRACKET CLOCK This clock's tortoiseshell-veneered case has a domed and galleried surmount, with caryatids and corner consoles. These, like all the mounts, are in gilt brass. Made by Jacques Hory of Paris. c.1690. H:27½ in (70 cm).

PENDULES RELIGIEUSES

The *pendule religieuse*, or "church clock," is a subcategory of the bracket clock that became prevalent in France in the late 17th century, during the reign of Louis XIV. Of relatively sober design, at least compared with many of the more elaborate excesses of high Rococo horology, these clocks take their name from a supposed similarity to church architecture. The basic form of the *pendule religieuse* is the high arch over the top of the clock face, which can be seen as an imitation of the high, round arches of the ancient Romanesque churches scattered throughout France.

These clocks are usually made from the most opulent materials. Cases are frequently cut from ebony and other rare woods, and feature lavish inlaid decoration, often of Boulle type. Inlays of copper, ivory, and even tortoiseshell add to the understated sumptuousness of these timepieces. Foliate scrolls and asymmetric enameled floral decoration both help place the clocks firmly within the Rococo decorative tradition.

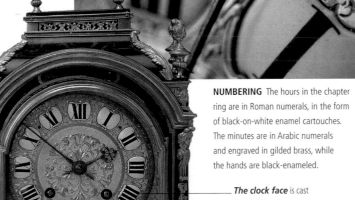

NUMBERING The hours in the chapter ring are in Roman numerals, in the form of black-on-white enamel cartouches. The minutes are in Arabic numerals and engraved in gilded brass, while the hands are black-enameled.

The clock face is cast in gilded bronze

The scrolling foliate and floral decoration beneath the dial is in applied enamel

BOULLEWORK CLOCK The wooden body of this clock by Pierre Margotin is decorated with tortoiseshell veneer and brass Boullework. It also has gilded-bronze mounts, including caryatids, scrolling acanthus leaves, and flaming urns. c.1700. H:19¼ in (49 cm).

SIGNED WORK The mechanism bears the engraved signature of Pierre Margotin, who is known to have worked in Paris for most of the second half of the 17th century.

BOULLE PENDULA CLOCK Made by Voisin of Paris during the Régence, this piece features gilded brass on brown tortoiseshell Boullework, figural mounts, and an equally elaborate socle with masks and scrolling foliage. c.1730. H:49¼ in (125 cm).

TEXTILES

IN EUROPE, THE TRADITION FOR TAPESTRIES CAN BE TRACED AS FAR BACK
AS ANCIENT GREECE AND THE WORLD OF HOMER'S *ODYSSEY*, WHILE SILK
HAD LIKEWISE BEEN WOVEN IN CHINA FOR MILLENNIA.

MULTIFUNCTION TAPESTRIES

Weaving cloth has always had both a useful
and a decorative purpose. In the Middle Ages
in Europe, wall hangings kept out drafts and
blanketed rooms with pictures taken from
mythology, morality tales, or nature. In church,
tapestries depicting religious scenes helped
imprint stories from the Bible on the minds
of an illiterate congregation.

Tapestries are made on a loom by weaving
colored weft threads (which run horizontally)
between undyed warp threads (which run
vertically) to create an image or pattern. Each
area of color is built up separately, following
a paper or canvas design known as a cartoon.
The colored threads are wound onto bobbins.

RISE OF FACTORIES

France and the Low Countries were at the
forefront of tapestry-making. Two factories stood
out: Gobelins and Aubusson. The former was taken
over by Louis XIV's minister of finance, Jean-
Baptiste Colbert, in 1662. Under the artistic
directorship of court painter Charles Le Brun,
Gobelins produced tapestries of unrivaled
technical brilliance, the subtle shading of which

increasingly resembled paintings. Le Brun
created cartoons for *portières* (tapestries
meant for hanging in front of doors) showing
a triumphal cart filled with trophies, with
Louis XIV's fleur-de-lys coat of arms and
his Sun King emblem. The Story of the
King ran to 14 large panels, and there was
also a series of 12 Months, showing a
different royal residence for each one.

Le Brun's Baroque style suited the pomp
and formality of the Sun King's court.
With the advent of the Rococo style, more
frivolous designs were introduced, following
cartoons by François Boucher, who specialized
in erotic mythological scenes. His 1758 series,

AUBUSSON TAPESTRY Woven in wool and silk for an upholstered settee, this
tapestry has picturesque flora and fauna imagery inspired by the fables of 17th-
century French poet Jean de La Fontaine. *Early 1700s. W:52½ in (133 cm).*

FLEMISH TAPESTRY Woven in wool, this tapestry displays the overall green
color cast and flora and fauna imagery—a wooded landscape with a castle
in the distant background—typical of *verdure* work. *Early 1700s. W:69 in
(175 cm).*

AUBUSSON TAPESTRY The scrolling leaf border of this tapestry, woven in wool
and silk, frames an exotic Chinoiserie landscape with birds and a pagoda, in the
style of French designer Jean Pillement. *Early 1700s. W:89¾ in (228 cm).*

AUBUSSON TAPESTRY The *verdure* silk and wool weave of this tapestry depicts woodland scenes with *a manoir* in the background, all within a ribbon-bound floral border. *c.1865. L:114 in (290 cm).*

VERDURE TAPESTRIES

From the Middle Ages until the reign of Louis XIV, most factories in northern Europe produced *verdure* tapestry hangings. Revolving around the theme of natural woodlands tamed by man, these showed formal or wild gardens, game preserves, or game parks, sometimes with castles or mansions in the background. Often they included animals and birds as well, and the color palette focused on greens, browns, and other complementary shades. *Verdure* tapestries were often surrounded by a wide border.

FLEMISH TAPESTRY Woven at the Schaerbeck factory in Brussels, this piece was designed in the *verdure* style by M. Chaudoir. It depicts a wild garden made up of numerous independent vignettes. *Early 1700s. W:104 in (264 cm).*

Loves of the Gods, found favor with English as well as French patrons. Today it can be admired at Osterley Park in Middlesex, England.

After a checkered time during the French Revolution, Gobelins is still in production today, working to designs of artists such as Henri Matisse.

At Aubusson weavers worked at home on low-warp looms rather than at a central location. Unlike Gobelins, this factory catered more to the middle classes, with simpler, coarser tapestries. Motifs were taken from the Bible or mythology, or they depicted *verdures*, or gardens. They also copied designs such as The Hunts of Louis XV

from Gobelins and Beauvais, another royal factory that incorporated Jean Bérain grotesques and scenes from the comedies of playwright Molière.

Like Gobelins, Aubusson continues today, working to cartoons by 20th-century artists such as Raoul Dufy and Graham Sutherland.

EUROPEAN SILKS

The natural fiber that produces silk comes from the cocoons of a moth native to China, so it is no surprise that the material was first used for textiles here. In 1667 Jean-Baptiste Colbert banned foreign imports of silk, an action that single-handedly put the factories of Lyon on the silk-manufacturing and weaving map. Soon the European silk industry had shifted from Italy and Spain to France. The Lyon factory alone employed more than 3,000 weavers.

In fashion-conscious Europe, designs changed every year. One Lyon range, Bizarre, in gold or silver, with swaying flowers and leaves, jagged lines, and asymmetrical architectural motifs, was a forerunner of the Rococo style. The range existed alongside more formal Baroque patterns, which gave way in about 1730 to naturalistic flowers and fruit, at the instigation of the innovative silk designer Jean Revel.

When the Edict of Nantes was revoked in 1685, many Huguenot weavers fled to London and found work at the Spitalfields silk factories (*see p.28*). In the early 1700s they stuck to Bizarre patterns, then adopted the Rococo style, with designs featuring dainty posies of flowers and ribbons.

Ever capricious, the fashion industry lost interest in patterned silks, and the industry went into terminal decline in the 1770s.

FLORAL SILK The floral pattern of this silk, woven in a weight suitable for curtains or wall hangings, was probably inspired by the exotic decoration found on imported Chinese silks and lacquer wares. *Early 1700s. L:41 in (104 cm).*

RÉGENCE SILK A Jacquard-woven silk *lampas* (damask), this displays an all-over pattern of formalized branches, leaves, and blooming flowers in a redcurrant, cream, and green palette. *1710–30. W:49¼ in (125 cm).*

AUBUSSON *PORTIÈRE* Designed to frame a doorway, and woven in wool and silk, this item presents a highly naturalistic woodland imagery in autumnal colors, set against a mountainous backdrop. *Mid-1700s. H:134¼ in (341 cm).*

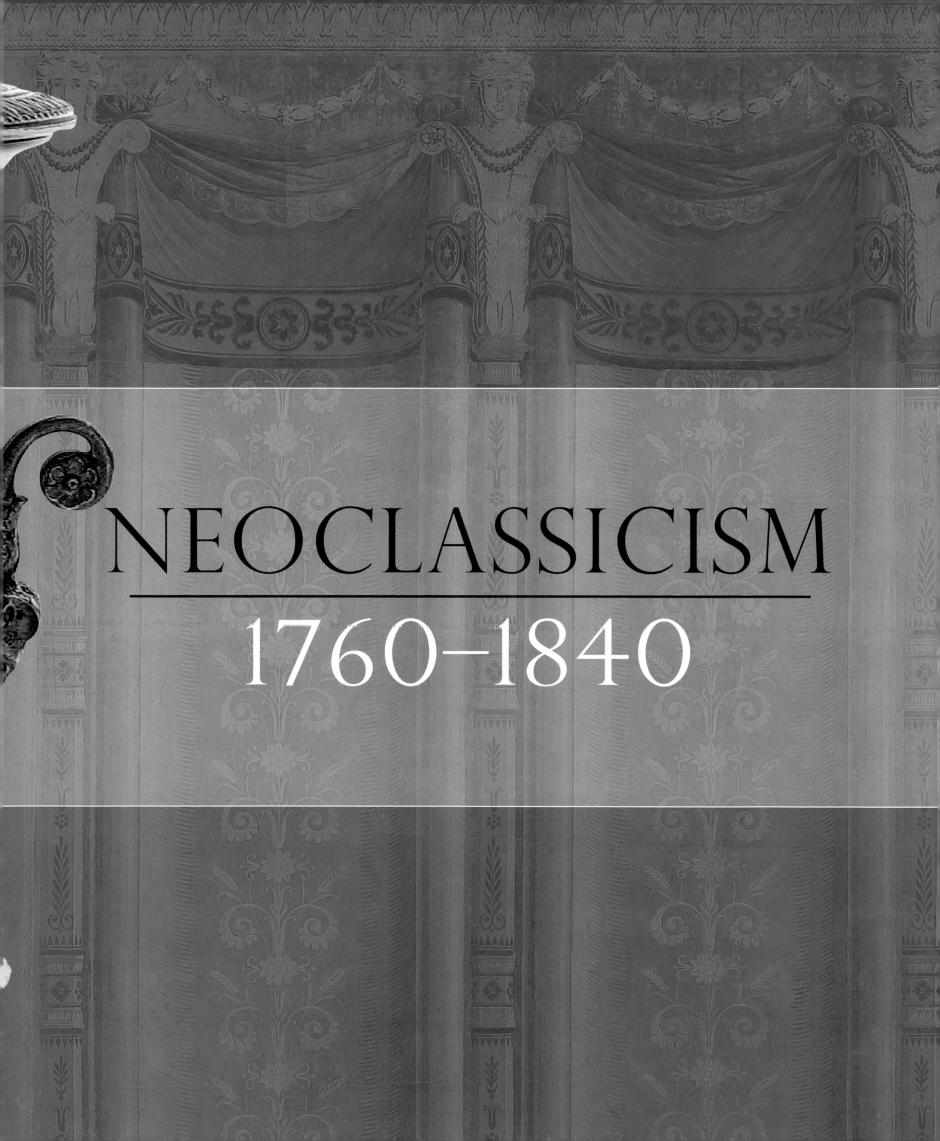

NEOCLASSICISM

1760–1840

A NEW CLASSICISM

IN DIRECT IMITATION OF GREEK AND ROMAN MODELS, NEOCLASSICAL STYLE WAS INSPIRED BY THE EXCAVATIONS OF HERCULANEUM (1738) AND POMPEII (1748), WHERE VILLAS CONTAINING ARTIFACTS WERE UNCOVERED BENEATH THE ASHES OF MOUNT VESUVIUS.

GRAND TOUR

A steady stream of visitors began to visit the ancient sites around Rome in order to learn more about the Classical world. For a gentleman, such sites were part of the Grand Tour he undertook to complete his education. This renewed interest in ancient Greece and Rome led in turn to the development of a revived Classical style.

NEOCLASSICAL STYLE

Neoclassicism was a comprehensive style that encompassed painting, architecture, literature, and music, as well as the decorative arts. In furniture, the elaborate decorations and gilding of Rococo gave way to straight lines and geometric motifs. Chairs were modeled on the curule, sat on by the highest civil officials of ancient Rome, and beds on the triclinium, or reclining couch. Bronze acanthus leaf sprays, fan-shaped floral palmettes, and other Classical motifs were applied as decoration. Silverware became more formal and less ornate,

while rooms were now decorated in pale-colored wallpaper with repeating arabesques.

The Neoclassical style varied from country to country, developing into the grand Empire style in France, the Regency style in Britain, the relaxed Biedermeier style in Germany, and the light Gustavian style in Scandinavia. It also spread to the newly independent United States, where it resulted in the elegant Federal style.

Neoclassicism owed its intellectual birth to the Enlightenment, whose philosophers, notably Voltaire and Diderot, believed in the promotion of public morality through art and the social responsibility of the artist and craftsman: their work should be designed for the collective well-being and education of the community. The noble simplicity and symmetry of antiquity as expressed through Neoclassicism was much better suited to this task than the frivolous decoration of the Rococo. In this respect, Neoclassicism can be seen as the artistic flowering of the Enlightenment.

FEDERAL MAHOGANY CHAIR The molded and rope-carved back encloses an urn and Prince of Wales feathers, draped swags, and leaves, above a serpentine seat on reeded, tapering legs. *1790. H:38½ in (98 cm).*

FOUR REVOLUTIONS

The Neoclassical style can also be seen as the artistic response to the four revolutions of the 18th century. The first of these was the agricultural revolution that began in Britain during the early 1700s and spread across the Continent. The enclosure of common land, better crop and animal breeding techniques, and new farm machinery led to a rise in agricultural production. This reduced food prices and created a wealthy land-based middle class and aristocracy that sought an artistic style suited to their rural status.

During the 1760s an industrial revolution in Britain transformed the country and later most of the Continent. New inventions such as the spinning jenny to spin cotton thread, steam engines to power the new weaving machines, and canals and later railroads to deliver coal and iron and take away finished goods, made it possible to mass-produce cotton and woolen cloth, ceramics, and

PAVLOVSK PALACE, RUSSIA
Catherine the Great had this imperial residence built from 1777 for her son. Its Classical exterior, influenced by the Italian architect Andrea Palladio, is followed through indoors in Italian and Grecian halls.

PARIS VASE One of a pair, the vase is in the resplendent Napoleonic Empire style, painted with a woman in an interior and with caryatid handles. *Early 19th century.*

other household items in specially built factories. Workers left their small cottage industries to work in the factories, leading to fast growth in towns and cities at the expense of the countryside. This revolution created new industrial classes of factory owners and workers that transformed the economics and politics of many European nations, while mass production affected design styles and techniques.

REPUBLIC AND EMPIRE

In the 13 British colonies on the Atlantic coast of North America, discontent with repressive British rule and taxation without representation led to revolt in 1775 and a declaration of independence in 1776. The United States of America that emerged in 1783 was both a political product of the Enlightenment and, in its republican and representative government complete with senate, a positive acknowledgment of Classical political structures.

The final revolution had the most immediate impact. The outbreak of revolution in France in 1789 and the overthrow of the monarchy in favor of a republic in 1792 soon engulfed the whole of Europe in war. The turmoil led in turn to the dictatorship and imperial rule of Napoleon Bonaparte, the leader of the republican armies who crowned himself Emperor of France in 1804. Napoleon consciously used Neoclassical imagery to boost his power and prestige, at the same time introducing an influence based on ancient Egypt, the remains of which he had explored during his expedition to the country in 1798.

COALPORT TEAPOT
A spout and handle that terminate in grotesque's heads, together with hand-painted panels and gilt borders and highlights, are typical of the English Neoclassical style. *Early 19th century. H:6¼ in (16 cm).*

OSTERLEY PARK, MIDDLESEX The interior of the house was designed in Neoclassical style by Robert Adam. The wallpaper of the Etruscan Dressing Room was handpainted with arabesques.

ELEMENTS OF STYLE

Reacting against the excesses of the Baroque and Rococo styles, designers began to look back to antiquity for inspiration, spurred on by the rediscovery of ancient sites. Rather than simply imitate ancient forms, they sought to create a timeless and authentic style using Classical rules of proportion and composition. In time, these noble aspirations were swallowed up by the eclectic and disorderly historicism of the 19th century.

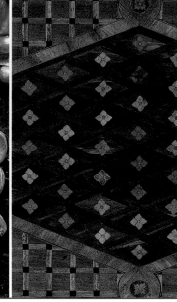

GILDED COALPORT VASE
CLASSICAL URN SHAPE
The urn, or vase, shape was used for glassware, ceramics, and metalware. It became ubiquitous across all disciplines of the decorative arts—carved as a finial atop a longcase clock, surmounting the fluted column of a silver candlestick, or inlaid in an oval panel on a *secrétaire à abattant*.

LION'S MASK DETAIL ON SIDE TABLE
LION'S HEAD
Used in antiquity to represent majesty and power, the lion's mask was a popular Neoclassical feature. It is found on armrests, friezes, and corners of furniture and is also depicted in prunts (applied glass decoration). Mythological beasts such as the griffin are also widely used Neoclassical motifs.

PARQUETRY DETAIL ON COMMODE
PARQUETRY
As veneering increased, English and French craftsmen perfected parquetry (geometric patterns) and marquetry (figurative patterns) techniques. The increased availability of exotic woods with rich colors and strong grains encouraged cabinet-makers to make complex parquetry designs on commodes.

BIEDERMEIER GOBLET
COLORED GLASS
Pigments developed by Bohemian manufacturers for creating new colors of stained glass were adopted widely across Europe. Transparent tints, often featuring multiple colors or combined with gilding, were used to decorate glass with landscapes and armorial themes.

SCENE ON DERBY COFFEE CAN
TOPOGRAPHICAL SCENES
In architecture, Neoclassicism brought about a renewed interest in Classical notions of the relation between natural landscape and the built environment. Scenes depicting the integration of buildings, artificial landscaping, and wild nature explored this theme.

ORMOLU SWAG ON CENTER TABLE
SWAGS
Originally used to decorate Roman altars, swags are also seen carved into ancient stone architecture. Neoclassical swags often feature bundled laurel leaves—emblematic of honor and victory—tied with ribbons. In the example above, the swag is draped from a rosette stud.

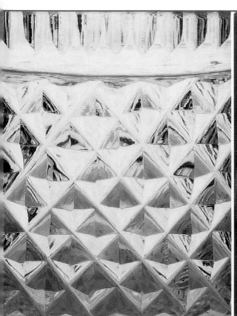

DIAMOND-CUT GLASS
CUT GLASS
Cut glassware grew far more sophisticated after the development of lead glass in the 1670s. Popular Neoclassical treatments include fluting, diamond cutting, and hobnail, a kind of diamond cutting with stars at the center of the diamonds. These elaborate designs had not been possible in the past.

DETAIL OF WEDGWOOD BASALT WARE
NEW CERAMICS
Developments in the ceramics industry included pearl ware—an earthenware with a white finish made by many factories in the Staffordshire area. Inspired by the discovery of ancient ceramics at sites such as Pompeii, Josiah Wedgwood perfected his black basalt ware during the 1760s.

GILT BEADING AND GUILLOCHE
ARCHITECTURAL MOLDINGS
Many devices used as architectural decoration in the ancient world were adopted by Neoclassical craftsmen. Popular examples include various forms of beading, and shapes like guilloche, a pattern of twisting bands, linked chains, spirals, or double spirals.

BOSTON MAHOGANY CARD TABLE WITH LYRE PEDESTAL
LYRE SUPPORTS
The ancient Greeks attributed the invention of the lyre to Hermes, messenger of the gods, who gave it to Apollo, the sun god. The motif is frequently seen on Neoclassical chair backs. Apollo's association with the sun means that lyres are often found on clocks, too.

NANTGARW VASE PAINTED BY WILLIAM BILLINGSLEY
NATURALISTIC FLORAL PAINTING
The development of porcelain in Europe prompted decorators to use the material for fine painting. Floral painting of the Neoclassical period tended to be naturalistic, as exemplified by William Billingsley's work for firms such as Swansea, Derby, Nantgarw, and Coalport.

PLATE WITH GREEK KEY DESIGN
GREEK KEY
One of the most common variations of the Classical fret motif, the Greek key pattern was revived by Neoclassical craftsmen. It is most often seen as a continuous band. It was used in everything form architectural moldings to furniture and ceramics in place of the fanciful fretwork popular during the Rococo period.

WEDGWOOD JASPER WARE CANOPIC VASE
EGYPTIAN MOTIFS
Napoleon installed himself as Emperor of France right after his conquest of Egypt. His retinue returned to France laden with ancient Egyptian artifacts, sparking an obsession with Egyptian design that spread across Europe. Hieroglyphs, scarabs, obelisks, and lotus leaves permeated the decorative arts.

ROBERT ADAM MARQUETRY DESIGN
ARABESQUES
One of Robert Adam's favored motifs, the arabesque is a linear, interlaced pattern based on foliage and tendrils. When human figures are included, it is called a grotesque. Arabesques were used across the decorative arts—for vertical wall decoration, marquetry, painting on ceramics, and etching on glass.

THE ANCIENT WORLD

THE TERM "NEOCLASSICAL," FIRST COINED IN 1861, APTLY DESCRIBES THE STYLE THAT EMERGED IN REACTION TO THE FRIVOLOUS EXUBERANCE OF THE ROCOCO AGE. THE YEARS 1760 TO 1840 SAW A REVIVAL OF CLASSICAL ARCHITECTURE AND DESIGN, WHICH PERVADED ALL AREAS OF THE DECORATIVE ARTS.

REGENCY MAHOGANY STOOL The X-frame chair or stool was based on the Roman folding campaign chair. This stool has a subtly shaped seat with scrolled ends and light carving on the surface. *c.1810. W:20 in (51 cm).*

The discovery of ancient Roman sites at Herculaneum (1738) and Pompeii (1748) and the Greek site of Paestum (1750s) generated renewed enthusiasm for the Classical age, and a number of scholars published works illustrating the ancient world. Among them was Giovanni Battista Piranesi, whose publications *Antichità Romane* (Roman antiquities) and *Vedute di Roma* (Views of Rome) had a lasting impact on artists and architects throughout Europe.

Rome and Naples—home to Herculaneum, Pompeii, and Paestum—became a focus for Grand Tourists. Aristocrats returning home wanted to emulate the Classical architecture and interiors they had seen. Stirred by the antiquities that had been on display during their travels, they returned with a host of ancient-world souvenirs.

THE DAWN OF NEOCLASSICISM

Inspired by the wall paintings at Herculaneum and Pompeii, early Neoclassical designers introduced similar color schemes: red, blue, green, and white became popular colors for painted furniture in Italy. German architect Leo von Klenze created fine Pompeiian interiors for his clients, and Classical scenes, resembling those of Piranesi, began to appear in European design—from marquetry panels in fine furniture to painted scenes on enameled *objets de vertu*.

Furniture designers applied the rules of Classical architecture to their pieces, adopting more rectilinear forms, and including architectural

SPODE STONEWARE VASE This flared potpourri vase of Classical form has a flat, pierced cover. It was common for Neoclassical designers to incorporate ancient Greek or Roman scenes in their works, as here with the applied white putti. *c.1810. H:6¼ in (16 cm).*

SNUFF BOX Many pieces of the time popularized the Grand Tour, embellished with scenes of ancient Rome. This snuff box depicts the Forum in Rome with Trajan's Column and the Colosseum. *c.1760. L:2¾ in (7 cm).*

motifs. Fluted columns, volutes, festoons, and paterae were all common. New materials were produced in an attempt to recreate those of the ancient world: Wedgwood developed new ceramics in rosso antico and black basaltes (*see pp.64–65*), and in Germany Count von Buquoy developed black and red-marbled Hyalith glass (*see pp.74–75*).

INCREASING AUTHENTICITY

As the style developed, so did a fashion for producing more accurate renditions of ancient forms. Driven by the imperial tendencies of Napoleon, designers began to produce furniture and ornaments that were almost exact copies of original forms, such as the *klismos* chair, the Warwick vase, and the urn shape. Motifs also became more closely associated with the military overtones of a growing empire and included laurel wreaths and fasces (an authority symbol of a bundle of rods bound around an ax). The eagle—emblem of the legions of Rome—appeared in American Classical and Austrian Biedermeier designs, in particular.

CLASSICAL ORDERS

All public buildings in ancient Greece were built according to the three Orders of Greek architecture—Doric, Ionic, and Corinthian—best represented by the columns of their temples. The Orders were used in various ways throughout the decorative arts.

The Doric column was the simplest, with a plain, circular capital, a fluted shaft, and no base. It tended to be short and wide, and generally massive in form. The Ionic column was taller than the Doric, and also fluted. At the base were a number of graduated rings, while the capital featured two volutes, front and back, which flanked the top of the shaft. Corinthian columns were the most decorative, with flutes and bases similar to those of the Ionic column. They had elaborate capitals carved with acanthus leaves.

Some buildings used all three orders: the simple Doric on the ground floor, Ionic on the first floor, and elaborate Corinthian on the top floor.

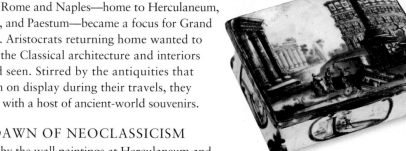

Corinthian capital

Ionic capital

Doric capital

GRAND TOUR CANDELABRA Classical influences are evident in the stylized Corinthian columns of this pair of bronze and gilt candelabra. The orb knop and acanthus pedestal, the tripod base with lion's feet, and the concave marble plinth with leaf cast moldings all speak of the ancient world. *H:28¾ in (73 cm).*

SCHLOSS CHARLOTTENHOF Designed in 1826, Germany's greatest Neoclassical architect, Karl Friedrich Schinkel—also a painter, stage designer, and interior designer—masterfully integrated the interior, exterior, and landscape setting of this royal pleasure house with his blend of Prussian Hellenism.

FURNITURE

THE LATE 18TH CENTURY SAW A MOVE AWAY FROM ROCOCO TOWARD A FURNITURE STYLE THAT WAS STEEPED IN THE CLASSICAL ORDER OF THE ANCIENT WORLD.

A CLASSICAL STYLE

Buoyed by travel through Europe, and in particular Italy, designers and aristocrats were eager to create interiors inspired by Classical Greece and Rome. They adopted a simpler, more elegant look in furniture: serpentine forms became linear; cabriole legs were replaced with straight, tapering ones; and chair backs progressed from ovals to rectangles.

EMERGING NEOCLASSICAL

Signs that a new style was emerging were evident in the *Goût grec* furniture that developed in France toward the end of Louis XV's reign. Inspired by architecture, and akin to the British Palladian style, furniture was large, rectilinear, and decorated with Classical motifs such as Vitruvian scrolls, Greek key, and guilloche bands.

The spread of the new style was not instant, however, and furniture design underwent a transitional phase. During the early years of Louis XVI's reign (1774–89), pieces often retained their Rococo form—chests with serpentine fronts and chairs with cabriole legs—but were decorated with typical Neoclassical motifs, including acanthus leaves, palmettes, and lion's masks.

The Neoclassical style that eventually emerged under Louis XVI and spread throughout Europe was one of pure symmetry, arbitrated by skilled cabinet-makers including Martin Carlin and Adam Weisweiler. Forms were rectilinear, light, and well proportioned. Designers abandoned heavy ormolu mounts and turned to carving for decoration. Inspired by English cabinet-makers of the previous half-century, they made much of the wood— usually mahogany—relying on its grain for the success of a piece. Tapering chair and table legs were often fluted, imitating Greek and Roman columns, while Classical ornament included cameos, laurel swags, Greek urns, and anthemia.

Marquetry continued to be popular. Instead of naturalistic floral displays, it was now common to see Classical scenes or motifs— urns, trophies, and stylized fans. French *ébénistes* used trellis marquetry and parquetry to striking effect on large, flat surfaces. Some designers incorporated ceramic plaques by Sèvres or Wedgwood into their pieces, adding a cameo detail.

SECRÉTAIRE À ABATTANT The tall fall-front desk became a seminal form of the Neoclassical period. This Parisian version has marquetry panels depicting Classical ruins with figures highlighted in inlaid ivory. *c.1775. H:55¼ in (140 cm).*

The table stands on eight ebonized and ormolu channeled, tapering legs, which terminate in sabots chased with laurel leaves

Each leg is headed by ebony blocks outlined in ormolu; the inner ones are each applied with a large foliate rosette

The laurel swags appear to run through each block and hang down from each outer leg

EBONIZED AND ORMOLU CENTER TABLE The massive proportions of this table, attributed to Joseph Baumhauer, accentuate the architectural nature of its design. Classical motifs include the molded guilloche and foliate outer border to the ormolu band that surrounds the writing surface, the use of the Greek key pattern, and the large swags of laurel leaves tied with ribbons suspended from the apron. *c.1760. H:31½ in (80 cm).*

Giltwood Adam-style open armchair. c.1775.

NEWBY HALL, NORTH YORKSHIRE The interior of the house was redesigned by Robert Adam. In the entrance hall the pale tones of the wall and ceiling are offset by Chippendale furniture. The house also boasts a Gobelins tapestry room and a gallery of Classical statues.

which incorporated a range of Classical motifs. The refined and elegant result was much sought after and copied—so much so that the Neoclassical look became known generally as Adam style in Britain.

DESIGN INGENUITY

It was during this era that designers used springs and levers to add novel uses to pieces: sections of a table that could be raised to reveal hidden drawers, or pull-out slides that provided additional useful surfaces. In France, Jean-François Oeben developed a *bureau à cylindre*, where the roll top disappeared from view when opened. David Roentgen was particularly adept at creating mechanical pieces,

among them architect's and writing tables. Writing desks for ladies continued to be popular. A new form emerged in the *bonheur-du-jour*, a small table with a raised back, almost like a mini-cabinet, containing shelves or pigeonholes and a writing surface above a frieze drawer. First made in the 1760s, they became widespread as the century progressed, and were often used as dressing tables.

The *secrétaire à abattant* was first designed in 1760 by Oeben. This writing desk took the form of a tall fall-front cabinet, housing a writing surface and fitted interior above an arrangement of cupboards or doors. Such was the popularity of the piece that it was made throughout Europe.

MAHOGANY ARCHITECT'S TABLE The rectangular top has a gilt tooled-green leather writing surface and can be raised with a winding mechanism. Stamped A. Weisweiler. c.1790. H:51 in (129.5 cm).

ADAM STYLE
Robert Adam was the leading Neoclassical architect and designer in Britain. He had studied and traveled in Italy and, although influenced by developments in France, he was also inspired by the work of Piranesi and the Palladian movement in Britain. He designed complete interiors, matching colors, tones, and decoration in furniture, walls, and ornament alike. His designs for furniture, carried out by Sheraton and Hepplewhite among others, tended to use light-colored woods, including harewood and satinwood, together with delicate painted designs,

The chair advertised in *Country Life Annual*

UMBRELLA-BACK CHAIR The wavy back of this mahogany chair has a central floral medallion and carved top rail. The chair stands on cabriole legs. c.1780. H:36 in (90 cm).

CHIPPENDALE SIDE CHAIR The serpentine crest rail, carved open splat, cabriole legs, and claw-and-ball feet are typical Chippendale. The style prevailed in the United States until the 1780s. c.1760.

LATE NEOCLASSICAL

Toward the end of the 18th century, furniture designs became more austere: linear, geometric forms were even more slender and delicate, and rectangular backs replaced ovals on chairs. The use of ornament declined, and carving made way for inlays of wood imitating carved detail. Lighter woods—satinwood, tulipwood, and ash—were used, often contrasting with darker woods—ebony and mahogany—for decorative effect.

AMERICAN FEDERAL

American design had remained predominantly Chippendale in style, but this changed when the Revolutionary War ended in 1783. In Britain, designers George Hepplewhite and Thomas Sheraton had done much to popularize the Neoclassical style with their pattern books, *The Cabinet-Maker and Upholsterer's Guide* (Hepplewhite, 1788) and *The Cabinet-Maker and Upholsterer's Drawing Book* (Sheraton, 1791–94). Their simplified versions of dominant forms were much copied in Britain and now, with the continued influx of immigrant craftsmen, they were also interpreted in the American Federal style.

New forms included the shield-back chair, the sideboard, and the Pembroke table. Hepplewhite's shield-back chair had a double-carved shield-shaped crest rail and tapering uprights. The back was often pierced and decorated with Classical motifs such as urns and wheatsheaves. A typical Sheraton-style sideboard was an elegant *demi-lune* piece, on tall, slender legs. The Pembroke table, with two drop leaves and two frieze drawers, became a salon addition. Usually raised on casters, it was portable and suited to card games, writing, and dining.

EUROPEAN INTERPRETATIONS

Much of Europe followed the fashions in France, with delay in some regions. In Germany, David Roentgen produced rectilinear furniture that relied on the grain of the wood—typically mahogany—for decoration, often married with fine gilt-bronze or bronze mounts. He is noted for his outstanding marquetry skills as well as his mechanical pieces.

The drawers have simple oval cast-bronze plates with bail handles

AMERICAN SHERATON SECRETAIRE The upper case of this mahogany and figured birch Federal secretaire has a cornice with foliate carved panels below turned and gilded urn finials. The lower section has a hinged fall-front with a banded edge over three drawers with flanking bottle drawers and stands on ring-turned legs. *L:40 in (101.5 cm).*

NEW YORK SIDEBOARD This Hepplewhite inlaid mahogany sideboard has a subtly bowed front and square, tapering legs. Decoration is minimal, with rope-twist geometric inlay on each of the drawers and diamond-over-oval stringing in the stiles. *L:73¼ in (186 cm).*

A central flap lifts to reveal six internal drawers and is flanked by additional graduated drawers

Ornament is limited to a simple three-quarter brass gallery and the square drop handles on each of the six external drawers

The reeded decoration at the top of each leg is a Sheraton feature

BRITISH CARLTON HOUSE WRITING TABLE The simple linear shape of this Sheraton-period desk and slender, turned legs are characteristic of the more refined late Neoclassical style. *c.1800. H:37 in (93 cm).*

GUSTAVIAN FURNITURE

Swedish designers copied the work of their French counterparts but produced a style of their own, with light-colored painted pieces, ornamented with gold-painted decoration instead of gilt. *Table: H:33½ in (85 cm).*

This late-Gustavian table displays early examples of the use of Egyptian motifs

Roentgen enjoyed commissions from a number of prestigious clients, among them Louis XVI, Catherine the Great of Russia, and Frederick William II of Prussia.

While much of the furniture produced in Italy was larger in scale and less refined than that made in France, one designer, Giuseppe Maggiolini, produced works to rival any in France. Austere in form, Maggiolini's furniture rarely had mounts or carving. Instead, he decorated pieces in exquisite marquetry, using many different colors to create dazzling displays.

In Sweden, cabinet-maker Georg Haupt emulated the Louis XVI style, producing exceptional pieces with exotic veneers, Classical-motif marquetry, and fine ormolu mounts. Gustav III, enamored of what he had seen on a visit to Versailles before being crowned, invited French craftsmen to Sweden. The result was the Gustavian style, an elegant interpretation of French taste, painted in light colors—pastel blue, green, and gray—to match the decor of a room.

GUSTAVIAN ARMCHAIR One of a pair by J. Lindgren, stamped "ILG."

HYLINGE, SWEDEN The Gustavian style emphasized the quality and fitness for purpose of the furniture. In this admiral's house, the grouped furniture contributes to the elegant proportions and light color scheme.

THE EMPIRE LOOMS

By the turn of the 19th century, furniture design in much of Europe was moving in a new direction. With their publication *Recueil des Décorations Intérieures* (Collection of Interior Decorations) in 1801, French architects Charles Percier and Pierre-François-Léonard Fontaine foreshadowed the Empire style that developed under Napoleon. Both men had studied and traveled extensively throughout Italy. Furniture in the Directoire period (1795–99) had been smaller and simpler, while now, during the Consulat period (1799–1804), forms began to copy slavishly ancient Greek and Roman models. Georges Jacob and his sons were leading cabinet-makers of the Consulat period.

The marquetry design features flowers and flowing ribbons

The legs are screwed into place

GERMAN MARQUETRY TABLE This mahogany, rosewood, and maple table would have been used as a writing desk or dressing table. The superb floral marquetry was probably by Johann Michael Rummer, the leading marqueteur in Roentgen's workshop. *c.1770. H:48 in (122 cm).*

AUSTRIAN LYRE-SHAPED SECRETAIRE This desk-cabinet is decorated with partial inlay and has an arched pediment flanked by gilded Classical figures. The lyre form is echoed in the stringlike decoration. *c.1807. H:55½ in (139 cm).*

THE EMPIRE STYLE

Such was Napoleon Bonaparte's personality that, once crowned Emperor in 1804, he dominated social and artistic trends in the whole of Europe, except Britain, cultivating an all-pervasive Empire style. In appointing family members to seats of power as the Empire grew, he vouched that his was the style of choice for Europe's fashion-hungry elite.

Employing the services of architects Percier and Fontaine, and cabinet-makers Jacob-Desmalter (run by Georges Jacob's son), Napoleon moved toward a more masculine form of Neoclassicism, and one that was closely tied in with the sentiments of Roman imperialism. Furniture was more strictly rectangular and symmetrical, often relying on architectural devices—columns, plinths, and pediments—for visual effect. Motifs remained Classical in inspiration, but now included those associated with warfare and victory—fasces and trophies of weapons. Animal motifs were also popular—rams' heads and lions' paws among them—as were all things Egyptian.

Mahogany remained the wood of choice, and much was made of its figuring. However, blockades on imports from British colonies made it scarce, so native woods were also used, including bird's-eye maple and walnut. Fabrics were widely used in interiors, bold in color and striped or with a recurring motif.

FRENCH EMPIRE FORMS

Empire designers tried to recreate ancient furniture accurately. New forms emerged—the *klismos* chair, a Greek form with saber legs; the *guéridon*, a small Roman table on tripod legs or a columnar base; and heavy console tables with monopodia legs and a plinth base.

The *fauteuil* (armchair) became more rectangular, with an upholstered back and scrolled top. The open arms had straight supports often carved with sphinx heads. A typical Empire commode was rectangular with flanking columns and a projecting frieze drawer above two or three drawers on a heavy plinth base with gilt-bronze mounts. The *lit en bateau*—essentially a daybed with scrolled ends and raised on a dais—was widely interpreted.

DEVELOPMENTS IN BRITAIN

As in France, design was driven by one person—the Prince of Wales (later George IV, 1762–1830). With exuberant taste, he commissioned works from a number of designers and architects, resulting in the

FRENCH EMPIRE CANDLESTICK Made of gilt brass, the urn-shaped candleholder rests on a fluted, leaf-decorated column. The column stands on a tripod base with lion's-paw feet. *H:11½ in (29 cm).*

The table top is centered by a rosette and circled by starlike points in a marble band

The ormolu and black-patinated base is centered by a small pedestal

The ormolu has matte and burnished highlights

CHÂTEAU DE COMPIÈGNE Tented areas, particularly in bedrooms, captured the spirit of Napoleon's military campaigns. Here, the canopy frames a *lit en bateau*, the focal point of this sumptuous room.

EMPIRE *GUÉRIDON* A table of majestic proportions, it is made of ormolu and specimen marbles. The circular inlaid marble table top is edged with an ormolu band and supported on the wings of three sphinx monopodiae, forming a tripod, on a triangular base. *c.1815. H:30 in (76 cm).*

AMERICAN CLASSICAL SIDE CHAIR This mahogany chair was designed by Duncan Phyfe. It has a curved and rolled crest rail above incurved *demi-lune* splats, flanked by reeded stiles. The over-upholstered seat is raised on saber legs with claw feet. *NA*

Regency style. It had much in common with Empire—clean, symmetrical lines; richly colored wood veneers; gilt mounts; and ancient motifs such as paterae, laurels, and anthemia—but was a lighter, more elegant, simplified, and feminine version.

While design was dominated by imperial Roman ideals, its designers also sought inspiration from afar. Brighton Pavilion, remodeled for the Prince Regent by John Nash between 1815 and 1823, epitomizes the prevailing fashion for the exotic with Indian-style domes, minarets, Islamic arches, and Chinese-inspired bamboo suites, lacquered panels and furniture, and Indian-style pierced screens.

Popular forms included the side cabinet, or chiffonier, a Regency interpretation of the commode with a pair of doors that had brass grilles backed with colored silk; the sofa table, with drop ends and designed to stand in front of a sofa for reading or writing; and the chaise longue, a daybed with scrolled ends, similar to the *lit en bateau*.

STYLE FOR THE BOURGEOISIE

Napoleon's brother, Jérôme, introduced the Empire style to Germany, where it met with approval among the aristocracy. Elsewhere, however, a

secondary style found favor with the middle classes. Originating in Austria, what later became labeled Biedermeier furniture was smaller than its Empire counterparts, strictly geometric, and with architectural features for ornament. Mahogany was the wood of choice, but lighter, local woods were also used, including cherry, birch, and ash. The grain was paramount and many pieces featured large areas of flat veneer. Inlaid borders on pediments or decorative columns made from darker, often ebonized, woods accentuated the grain of the lighter wood.

FAR-REACHING INFLUENCES

Around 1800 the elegant American Federal style became more bulky. Heavy, geometric furniture was produced, often with high-relief carving. Typical forms, the *klismos* chair and scroll-end sofa, were Regency inspired, while Duncan Phyfe was a leading Classical exponent, producing a range of fine furniture for New York's elite.

AMERICAN EMPIRE SOFA Upholstered and with outscrolled arms and bolster cushions, the heavy, symmetrical form of this sofa and high-relief-carved seat rail are typical features of the American Empire style. W:64 in (162.5 cm).

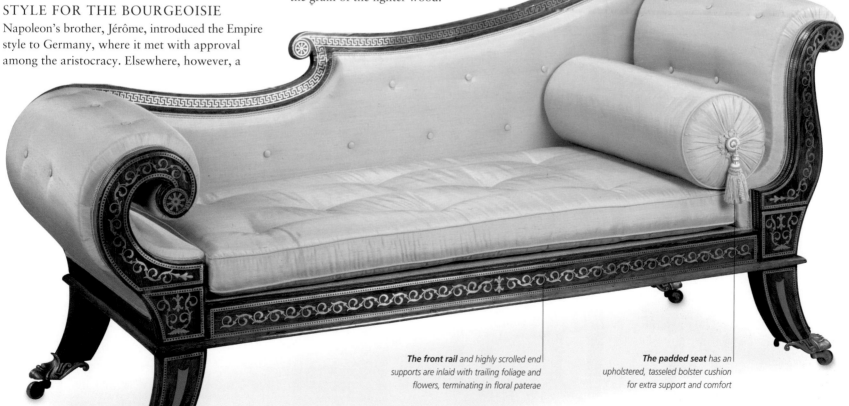

The front rail and highly scrolled end supports are inlaid with trailing foliage and flowers, terminating in floral paterae

The padded seat has an upholstered, tasseled bolster cushion for extra support and comfort

ENGLISH REGENCY CHAISE LONGUE This rosewood chaise longue is inlaid throughout with brass marquetry and supported on outswept saber legs terminating in lion's-paw feet. c.1810. H:34 in (86 cm).

FURNITURE GALLERY

Neoclassical furniture was characterized by a return to furniture forms of ancient Rome and Greece, and architectural elements such as columns or pediments were common. Shapes became more rectilinear. Ornament included marquetry and rich flame veneers and porcelain insets. Marble was often used to top tables and cabinets. Decorative motifs such as sphinxes and urns were borrowed from Greece, Rome, and Egypt.

KEY

1. Classical figured mahogany gondola chair. c.1830. ② **2.** Gustavian armchair. ② **3.** Mahogany saber-leg chair. c.1810. H:34 in (86.5 cm). ③ **4.** Armchair with white-lacquered beech frame. H:33 in (84 cm). ③ **5.** Rosewood curricule chair by Gillows of Lancaster. c.1811. H:34¼ in (87 cm). ③ **6.** George III mahogany rent table with rotating top by Gillows of Lancaster. c.1790. H:30¾ in (88 cm). **7.** Regency coromandel sofa table with satinwood crossbanding. W:57½ in (146 cm). ④ **8.** Regency rosewood sofa table. c.1820. H:30 in (76 cm). ⑤ **9.** French sycamore, kingwood, and floral marquetry table with porcelain Sèvres-style inset. H:29 in (73.5 cm). ⑦ **10.** Swedish parcel -gilt center table sup-

1 Gondola chair

2 Gustavian armchair

3 Saber leg chair

4 Beech armchair

5 Rosewood chair

6 George III rent table

7 Regency sofa table

8 Regency sofa table

9 French table

10 Swedish center table

ported on sphinxes. c.1820. H:34 in (86.5 cm). **11.** Empire mahogany secretaire with marble top. H:55 in (140 cm). ④ **12.** Dutch mahogany marquetry secrétaire à abattant. Early 19th century. H:64 in (163 cm). ④ **13.** Louis XVI hardwood parquetry secrétaire à abattant. c.1780. H:48¾ in (124 cm). **14.** Gustavian chest of drawers by N. P. Stenström. H:33½ in (83.5 cm). ⑤ **15.** German Empire cherrywood secretaire. c.1805. H:65 in (165 cm). ⑤ **16.** George III mahogany chest-on-chest. H:76½ in (194 cm). ⑤ **17.** Louis XVI commode by G. Dester. c.1775. H:36¾ in (93 cm). **18.** Louis XVI marble-topped mahogany commode. W:54½ in (136 cm). ⑤ **19.** George III ormolu-mounted, painted, and gilt commode, attributed to George Brookshaw. c.1790. H:33¾ in (89 cm). **20.** Italian walnut and marquetry commode. c.1800. W:53 in (132.5 cm). ④ **21.** Mahogany secretaire. c.1800. H:65½ in (165.5 cm). ⑦

13 *Secrétaire à abattant*

12 Dutch *secrétaire à abattant*

11 *Empire secretaire*

16 *Chest-on-chest*

15 *German secretaire*

14 *Gustavian chest of drawers*

18 *Louis XVI commode*

17 *Louis XVI commode*

19 *George III commode*

20 *Italian commode*

21 *Secretaire*

CERAMICS

THE SECOND HALF OF THE 18TH CENTURY WAS A PERIOD OF DEVELOPMENT
IN CERAMICS, AS PORCELAIN-MAKERS HONED THEIR SKILLS AND POTTERY
FACTORIES VIED WITH EACH OTHER TO COMPETE WITH THE "WHITE GOLD."

PEARL WARE PLATE The Etruscan trophies pattern on this Spode plate reflects an early-19th-century interest in Etruscan style. It is printed in underglaze blue with details in iron red and yellow. c.1825. D:8¼ in (21 cm).

BRITISH POTTERY

The Industrial Revolution brought the English pottery industry to prominence. Traditionally, the potteries around Staffordshire in the Midlands had made lead-glazed earthenware using brown clays. Now, however, they were experimenting with whiter clays that might be able to compete with porcelain, and created creamware, cream-colored earthenware with a thin, smooth, and transparent lead glaze that made it nonporous.

Josiah Wedgwood perfected the art of creamware, adding cobalt to the earthenware to make it whiter. In the 1770s he found even paler clays. By using a combination of calcium, flints, and cobalt oxide, he changed the light honey tinge of creamware to an ice-blue white, which was called pearl ware.

At first the opportunities for colored decoration were limited. F. & R. Pratt pioneered the use of colors such as green, yellow ocher, blue, and brown, that could be fired at high temperature,

often over relief decoration. Popular subjects were topical or Classical figures, and Neoclassical motifs such as lion masks and paws, swags, husks, and the Greek key pattern. Similar pieces, called pratt ware, were made by other Staffordshire factories.

Creamware and its variants were used for all kinds of household pieces. Commemorative items were popular, and could be ordered from the local potter. Dinner services, basins, and ewers were all made. By the 1760s creamware was such a success that it was copied on the Continent, leading to the near demise of tin-glazed earthenware by 1800.

WEDGWOOD

The self-styled "vase maker General to the Universe," Josiah Wedgwood was born in the heart of the Staffordshire potteries, in Burslem, now known as Stoke-on-Trent. Apprenticed at the age of 14, he left the family firm in 1754 and joined forces with Thomas Whieldon, who was known

for making creamware with mottled glazes on marbled light and dark clays. Wedgwood was lame and found it difficult to use a kick-wheel, so he concentrated on making pottery in molds and improving the quality of the ceramic body. His creamware even found favor with Queen Charlotte, the wife of George III, who allowed him to call his range Queensware.

By the early 1770s Wedgwood was making vases in the Neoclassical style, inspired by archaeological discoveries in Greece. Not content with leading the field in creamware, Wedgwood developed a fine-grained stoneware called basalt ware, or black basaltes. He imitated severe Classical styles for this

Floral decoration is applied where the ribbon-style handle joins the body of the jug

The pilasters are headed by lion's masks and end in stylized lion's-paw feet

Strap handle

CREAMWARE JUG This baluster-shaped jug has simple ribbed decoration around the lower section. Much of the creamware made during this time is unmarked and difficult to attribute to specific makers. c.1780. H:6 in (15 cm).

PRATT WARE JUG A commemorative naval jug from the turn of the 19th century, one side is molded with an image of Captain Berry, the other with Admiral Nelson. Each is set between two ships and titled. c.1800. H:6 in (15 cm).

JASPER WARE VASE In this Wedgwood three-color jasper ware vase, the tapering body is decorated with typical Neoclassical motifs, including oval paterae and floral swags hung from fluted pilasters. c.1794–1800. H:5 in (12.5 cm).

range of black wares, which he made into vases, busts, and tableware. In 1775 he produced a jasper ware range, made from white stoneware that could be tinted different colors. It was often made in blue, the color most associated with Wedgwood. Decoration—usually white—was applied on top by shaping clay in a mold, then applying it to the body of the piece. Although machinery was used, skill was still required, especially for the finer details, such as drapery. The decorative motifs were similar to those used by designers such as Robert Adam—lyres, anthemia, toga-clad figures—so the vases would sit comfortably in any Neoclassical interior.

Red stoneware had a history dating back centuries. Wedgwood updated the designs,

using engine-turned decoration. Called rosso antico, the unglazed background was decorated in black, in the style of Greek black-figure vases. As well as Classical forms and motifs, Egyptian themes were adopted after Napoleon's invasion of Egypt at the end of the 18th century. Other factories in the area, such as Spode, mimicked Wedgwood's red ware and jasper ware with varying degrees of success.

Wedgwood died in 1795 after a prolific lifetime including 50 years as a potter, during which he paid homage to Classical art. He said he had "endeavored to preserve...the elegant simplicity of the antique forms." He was also blessed with an astute business sense.

RED WARE TEAPOT This squat, globular Spode teapot is decorated with black hieroglyphs above a meander band. The ribbed cover has a crocodile finial. *1815. H:4½ in (11.5 cm).*

DESSERT PLATE This Mason's Ironstone plate features Neoclassical decoration: a landscape surrounded by a gilt foliate-decorated rim. *c.1820. W:9¼ in (23.5 cm).*

TRANSFER-PRINTING

Developments in technology led to the mass production of ceramics, which then became affordable to the expanding middle classes. Transfer-printing was a cheap, quick, and efficient way to decorate homeware. The subject matter could be as complex as a painting, with Classical or topographical scenes. Until the 1820s the color was usually cobalt blue, the only one that could cope with firing. The design was engraved on a copper plate, using hatching (parallel lines) for shading. The copper was warmed, rubbed with ink, and pressed onto paper, which was placed on the porous, biscuit-fired earthenware. The design was then transferred to the body, ready for glazing and firing.

The blue of the jasper ware is a byword for Wedgwood

The urn shape is ubiquitous, one of the ancient forms Neoclassical designers emulated

The vase is raised on a spreading foot, impressed "Wedgwood V"

WEDGWOOD VASE This rare Wedgwood blue jasper ware vase has a lift-out lid and three laurel leaf-bulb holders. The body is decorated with applied figures of Apollo and the nine Muses above a band of trophies. *c.1785–95. H:8¾ in (22.5 cm).*

SPODE MEAT DISH A Caramanian-series meat dish of the later indented shape, transfer-printed with the design "Antique Fragments at Limisso." *L:16½ in (42 cm).*

TIN-GLAZED EARTHENWARE

"Every man of any status or consequence turned within a week to faience," said Saint-Simon in 1709, after France had melted down silverware to help fund her wars. But by the mid-18th century, porcelain was a threat to tin-glazed earthenware. Delft was still being made in Holland, but its popularity was waning. The development of creamware in England posed yet more competition. Some manufacturers on the Continent copied it, while others stuck to tin-glazed earthenware—known as faience in France, fayence in Germany, and maiolica in Spain and Italy—paying lip service to the Neoclassical trend.

FRENCH RUSTIC FAIENCE

The factory of Moustiers in southern France rivaled that of Rouen and began a new lease on life in 1738 when Joseph Olerys went into business with Jean-Baptiste Laugier. Olerys had been working at the Spanish factory of Alcora, and brought with him the techniques for polychrome high-temperature decoration. Tableware such as *bouillabaisse* (fish soup) bowls was decorated with garlands and medallions, little figures and flowers, grotesques inspired by the engravings of Callot, and arabesques taken from the designs of Jean Bérain. Complete services were made for the middle classes, copying Sèvres styles. Sometimes the decoration was in a single color, usually green or yellow, but occasionally mauve.

The factory of Quimper in Brittany, like faience-makers throughout France, followed the Rouen *style rayonnant*, which had been popular under Louis XIV. Its lambrequins, decorative Baroque lacy swags, were the ceramicist's

PAIR OF EWERS This pair of Quimper ewers is decorated in the Rouen style with blue and red lambrequins. *H:18 in (46.5 cm).*

Decoration extends to the handles, where it is complementary but simpler

Lambrequins are a deeply scalloped fringelike ornament

The base flares to balance the height of the ewers

MOUSTIERS PLATE The plate is decorated in high-temperature green with motifs based on flowers and leaves, centered by a Commedia dell'Arte–style Punch figure. *Late 18th century. D:9½ in (24 cm).*

FAIENCE KRUG The surface of the oval jug is decorated in strong colors, depicting large bunches of grapes and the tools of the viticulturist, surrounded by floral garlands. *1796. H:11 in (28 cm).*

SPANISH MAIOLICA FLASK The ring molding on the ovoid body defines bands of figures and animals. The handle stretches the full height of the flask and is in the form of a green lizard. *H:10¼ in (26 cm).*

Despite the rustic imagery, the flask displays Neoclassical-style geometry in the colored banding

Blue, green, and yellow were the dominant fayence colors in northern Europe

Geometric bands of arches and ovals containing flowers at the top and bottom

FAIENCE TANKARD This Austrian pear-shaped tankard has a pewter lid and stand. Geometric borders frame the depiction of a maiden holding a letter. *Late 18th century. H:8½ in (22 cm).*

equivalent of festoons of drapery. Quimper used more exuberant colors than Moustiers. Nevers, famous for its *bleus de Nevers* solid colored grounds in the 17th century, stayed in business by producing wares with witty inscriptions known as *faiences parlantes,* pragmatically switching to political slogans during the French Revolution.

Niderviller near the German border specialized in trompe-l'oeil decoration of a print pinned on to a background that looked like grained wood. It also made beautiful figures in faience. And, using the local Lorraine clay, it produced *faience fine,* which resembled English creamware. Niderviller kept using original 18th-century molds into the 19th century and is still in production today.

GERMAN FAIENCE

Faience factories had sprung up all over Germany after 1700 as the country was divided into numerous principalities, all of which wanted to be self-sufficient. Since Böttger discovered how to make hard-paste porcelain in Meissen around 1709, they had to compete. By the second half of the 18th century they were copying the Neoclassical designs used on porcelain, successfully providing a cheaper alternative. But porcelain did not cause the demise of tin-glazed earthenware. English creamware, which was just as cheap, had a harder body and did not chip as easily.

Bérain's delicate designs were used for *Laub- und Bandelwerk* (leaf- and strapwork) decoration in

Austria and Germany. *Indianische Blumen* (India flowers) from Meissen were the inspiration for naturalistic Strasbourg *deutsche Blumen* (German flowers), whose influence percolated through the states. In Nuremberg a motif of a curling stem with feathery leaves and stylized flowers developed but, partly because Germany was splintered into tiny states, faience decoration varied hugely. It was often the product of an individual potter's fancy.

PAIR OF *ALBARELLI* Each of these pharmacy jars has the typically thin waist for ease of lifting off a shelf. The geometric banding and blue and white pattern is a late 18th-century style. *H:8¾ in (22 cm).*

ITALIAN MAIOLICA

Alongside customary *albarelli* (waisted drug jars), Italian factories adopted Neoclassical forms such as urn-shaped vases. Blue and white borders and Chinoiserie decoration were popular, influenced by Chinese porcelain. The workshops in Savona continued the *istoriato* (narrative) tradition, with lively freehand painting. As in Spain, factories continued to work in earlier styles after 1800.

MAIOLICA TAZZA Made in Savona, Italy, the tazza is painted in green, yellow, manganese, and blue and decorated with images of birds, trees, and ruins. *Late 18th century. D:13½ in (34 cm).*

NEOCLASSICAL PORCELAIN

In 1764, Madame de Pompadour, Louis XV's mistress and Sèvres' biggest patron, died, and the style of Sèvres porcelain began to change. Vases were now made in the Neoclassical urn shape, even though they were still painted with sweet pastoral Rococo subjects including children, lovers, and flowers. The designs became symmetrical and shapes were adorned with applied and molded Classical decoration such as acanthus leaves, laurel garlands, guilloche, swags, and rosettes. The sides were fluted or reeded, like the ridges on Classical columns. New colors were introduced, such as the overglaze *bleu nouveau*, developed in 1763.

In 1769, Sèvres began to make hard-paste porcelain. Many of its ground colors did not work on the harder porcelain so new ones were developed. Colors became more muted, including purple, brown, and soft green. There was a brief vogue for pearling—applying blobs of enamel over metal foil, which raised the color like pearls. Rich gilding was used. Medallions (oval or circular panels), often featuring *grisaille* (gray) figures and scenes based on the ancient Roman frescoes at Pompeii, were popular.

ENGLISH FOLLOWERS

By the 1770s the Neoclassical style was well established in porcelain. English factories such as Worcester and Derby copied Sèvres, using oval panels and straight sides in flat colors enlivened with fluting. Bands of gilding separated areas of decoration, and borders featured Classical patterns such as guilloche, Greek key, Vitruvian scrolls, or Sèvres-style pearling. Chelsea-Derby was founded in 1769 when William Duesbury of Derby bought the Chelsea factory, and continued production until 1784. Its Neoclassical tableware was immensely fashionable. Pale yellow, pink, or green grounds were left plain or were painted with Classical or floral motifs.

FLARED BEAKER This Chamberlain's Worcester beaker is decorated in gilt with panels. The central titled oval panel is finely painted in colored enamels with a portrait of Sappho and Phaon. *1795–1800. H:3½ in (9 cm).*

The cover for the cup has a marigold-shaped finial

SÈVRES COFFEE CUP AND SAUCER The cup and saucer are painted in enamels with birds in landscapes, within gilt oval panels. The rims are painted with bands of birds and laurel garlands. *1793.*

SÈVRES CHOCOLATE CUP SET This set comprises a two-handled cup with cover and stand. It is painted with garlands of flowers and gilt leaf fronds within gilt-decorated blue borders. *1761. Cup: W:7½ in (18.5 cm).*

DERBY TEAPOT This oval fluted, straight-sided teapot has a wishbone handle and loop knop. It has banded decoration, painted in black and gray and picked out in gilt, on a pink ground. c.1790. H:6 in (15 cm).

In Germany, Meissen had virtually ceased production during the Seven Years War (1756–63). The French sculptor Michel-Victor Acier was brought in to help it compete with Sèvres, but Meissen had lost its earlier preeminence. Factories such as Berlin and Vienna came to the fore, especially at the turn of the century.

THE NEW CENTURY

After the French Revolution, the Republic took over and Sèvres lost royal privilege, but the factory never stopped production. In 1800 Alexander Brongniart took charge and abandoned soft-paste porcelain. The huge dinner service that Louis XVI had ordered in 1783, the last big soft-paste project, was never finished. Vases became larger and larger as hard paste was less likely to collapse during firing; and elaborate grounds such as agate gray and simulated tortoiseshell were introduced.

MEISSEN COFFEE POT The pear-shaped pot has a volute handle and domed lid with a ball knop. The ribbed surface is painted with floral decoration. There is partial gilding. c.1800. H:9½ in (24 cm).

EMPIRE STYLE

Under Napoleon, porcelain had to be rich and colorful to fit the integrated style of the tentlike draperies and sumptuous furnishings that Percier and Fontaine had designed for Napoleon's palace at Malmaison. The Empire style, similar to Regency in Britain, Biedermeier in Germany, and Empire in Scandinavia, was characterized by massive and more elaborate shapes. As Napoleon modeled himself on a Roman emperor, these were embellished with elaborate ornament in the Classical mode, such as imperial eagles, swans, lions, and caryatid handles. Extensive gilding completed the look of opulence. After Napoleon's Egyptian campaigns, sphinxes, lotus leaves, and other Egyptian imagery were used on porcelain as well as on furniture.

In Britain, stoneware was popular in the last quarter of the 18th century, but by 1800 porcelain was once

again in demand. The naturalistic flower painting typical of Rococo had remained popular in England. William Billingsley developed a way of making flowers, especially roses, look particularly lifelike, by applying pigment and then wiping the color off, leaving the white porcelain for highlights. He was hired to work in Wales on Nantgarw porcelain bodies, renowned for their whiteness, a perfect foil to his delicate painting.

The tapering form reflects the new style, while the floral decoration remains Rococo

The cup has an angular handle, characteristic of the Empire style

The geometric shapes alternate with panels of fine-painted gold arabesques

BERLIN EMPIRE CUP AND SAUCER This set has strong geometric patterning and gold details. Diamond panels contain paintings of Classical figures. It is marked KPM. c.1800. Cup: H:2¼ in (6 cm).

WELSH PORCELAIN CAMPANA VASE The form of this vase is a copy of the ancient Greek Borghese vase in the Louvre. William Billingsley painted the flowers. 1813–23. H:10¾ in (27.5 cm).

CERAMICS GALLERY

Neoclassical ceramics are more symmetrical and less patterned than Rococo ceramics. Cups and beakers are designed with straighter sides and patterning itself becomes geometric. Bands of decoration are balanced with areas of plain color. Forms and motifs are taken from the ancient worlds of Rome and Greece, and pieces are based on typical Classical forms such as the urn.

KEY

1. Cozzi figure of a young man, with tricorn hat at his side. c.1770. H:4¼ in (11 cm). ① **2.** Sèvres hard-paste cup and saucer, with tooled gilding and platinum. Late 18th century. ② **3.** Paris coffee can and saucer. c.1810. Coffee can: H:3 in (7.5 cm). ① **4.** Pair of Sèvres porcelain cups and saucers. Saucer: D:6 in (15.5 cm). ④ **5.** White-glazed figure of Hygeia, Greek goddess of health. Late 18th century. H:11½ in (29 cm). ① **6.** Miniature figure by Johann Adam Bauer. H:3½ in (9 cm). ① **7.** Marcolini Meissen part tea and coffee service, painted with fruit and flowers. ④ **8.** Cozzi group of figures, picking grapes. ② **9.** Pair of figures by John Jacques Louis. c.1775. H:9½ in (25 cm). ② **10.** Coalport two-handled, enamel-painted sauce tureen and cover, with ball knop. c.1800. ②

1 Cozzi figure

2 Sèvres cup and saucer

3 Paris coffee can and saucer

4 Sèvres cups and saucers

5 Figure of Hygeia

6 Miniature figure

7 Meissen service

8 Cozzi figures

9 Pair of figures

10 Coalport tureen

11. Derby botanical enamel-painted plate, the pink ground border with gilt bands. c.1795. D:9 in (23 cm). ① **12.** Derby plate from the Gosling Service, with gilt initial G. c.1795. D:9 in (23 cm). ① **13.** Paris porcelain plate by Dagoty. D:9½ in (24 cm). ① **14.** Worcester fluted ovoid gilt tea canister and domed cover, with flower knop. c.1772. H:6¼ in (16 cm). ① **15.** Derby plate, painted in Paris style with gilt laurel bands and flowerheads. c.1785. D:9¼ in (23.5 cm). ① **16.** Nymphenburg plate with relief decoration and painted flowers. c.1765. D:9 in (23 cm). ① **17.** Pair of Sèvres-style English porcelain vases and covers. c.1840. H:11¾ in (30 cm). ③ **18.** Pair of Coalport ice pails with gilt handles and feet. 1810. H:11 in (28 cm). ④ **19.** Coalport campana-shaped, two-handled vase, painted with flowers within C-scroll borders. c.1820. H:9¼ in (23.5 cm). ② **20.** Spode porcelain campana-shaped pastel burner. c.1820. H:4¾ in (12 cm). ③

13 *Paris plate*

12 *Derby plate*

11 *Derby plate*

15 *Derby plate*

16 *Nymphenburg plate*

14 *Worcester tea canister*

20 *Spode pastel burner*

17 *Sèvres-style vases*

18 *Coalport ice pails*

19 *Coalport vase*

GLASS

THE UNSETTLED POLITICAL SITUATION IN CONTINENTAL EUROPE
DURING THE SECOND HALF OF THE 18TH CENTURY GAVE BRITAIN
AN OPPORTUNITY TO TAKE THE LEAD IN GLASSMAKING.

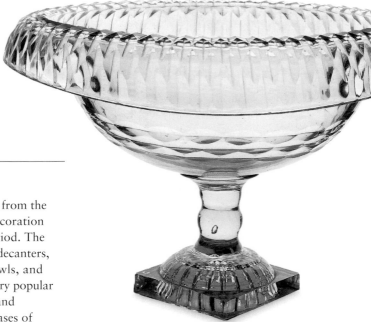

CUT AND ENGRAVED GLASS

British designers, looking back to the ancient
world, found inspiration in the engravings of
Piranesi (see p.54) and in the Roman and
Greek antiquities they saw on the Grand Tour.
The drawings of the architect Robert Adam
also inspired designers in many media.

DOMINANT STYLES

The decoration on earlier Baroque and Rococo
glass had tended to be superficial and restrained.
Neoclassical glass began to reflect the style in form
as well as ornament; claret jugs and decanters, for
example, were often fashioned as baluster shapes. A
seminal form of the era was the rummer wine glass,
with its wide bowl, short, knopped stem, and
square "lemon-squeezer" base, derived from the
urn shape. The Neoclassical style of decoration
reached its pinnacle in the Regency period. The
forms and decoration were evident on decanters,
claret jugs, sweetmeat dishes, fruit bowls, and
candlesticks. Deep-profile cutting was very popular
and various cuts such as pillar, prism, and
strawberry diamond dominated. The bases of
decanters were often cut with fan shapes or stars.

MECHANIZATION

A new steam-cutting process was introduced to
Britain in 1789, which revolutionized the world of
cut glass, making deep-profile cuts possible. This
made the most of the lead-based crystal that had
been discovered by Ravenscroft in the late 1670s.

PEDESTAL BOWL The turnover rim of this cut-glass pedestal bowl is typical
of glass made in Ireland around 1800. The rim is cut with three lozenge-fluted
bands and the bowl with a central three-strand lozenge band. It is raised on a
knopped stem and square lemon-squeezer foot. c.1800. W:12 in (30 cm).

Pieces sparkled as they reflected and refracted the
light. Similar techniques were used elsewhere in
Europe. In France both the Baccarat Glasshouse,
founded in 1764, and the Saint-Louis Glassworks,
established in 1767, became well known for their
cut-glass tableware from about 1800.

Ireland was given free-trade status in 1780, which
reinvigorated its glass industry. The most common
decorative techniques were shallow cutting and
engraving. Irish cut glass was also popular. Claret
decanters with extended spouts, piggin cream bowls
with one raised side, and stemmed bowls with deep
turnover rims are typical Irish forms.

The jug is of a large size,
which would have made
blowing more difficult

Hops were usually
used to decorate
beer jugs

LARGE JUG This baluster-shaped jug has a
heavy strap handle and is engraved with sprigs
of hops. The base is engraved with initials and
dated. 1828. H:8¼ in (21 cm).

MEDICI CUT-GLASS VASES This pair of glasses have ornate gilt-bronze
mounts that display typical Neoclassical motifs: cupids playing cymbals
supported on palmettes and vine branches. c.1820. H:22¼ in (56.5 cm).

REGENCY RUMMERS These three commemorative dated rummers are inscribed with the monogram "JB" and engraved with shields and paterae suspending swags. The lower section of each bowl is fluted. Each has a lemon-squeezer plinth base. *1823. H:5¼ in (13.5 cm).*

INKSTAND This blue opalescent and clear-pressed glass inkstand with inkwell and sander was made by the Boston and Sandwich Glass Company. *1830–35.*

ENGRAVING

Engraving glass was still fashionable, especially in early Neoclassical pieces. Engraved ornament was more restrained, leaving large areas of plain glass. However, the popularity of symmetrical, geometric designs was evident in borders of swags and paterae, both common Neoclassical motifs. An engraved medallion might bear an inscription or a client's monogram. Diamond-point engraving was particularly suited to thin-walled glass. Shallow cutting was also popular and included shallow flutes around the base of a decanter, for example, or oval printies on its shoulders.

AMERICAN GLASSMAKING

The early 19th century saw the development of pressed glass in the United States, first made at the New England Glass Company, which was established by Deming Jarves in 1818. The process, which involved pushing molten glass into a plain or patterned brass or cast-iron mold with a plunger, revolutionized glass manufacture. Cheaper than cut glass, it made more styles available to more people. It proved an ideal technique for Neoclassical design, allowing easy production of symmetrical shapes for a wide range of domestic glassware.

A number of glass factories was established. The New Bremen Glass Factory in west Maryland was founded in 1787 by German immigrant Johann Friedrich Amelung. A few surviving pieces feature engraved decoration in the Germanic style.

The company Bakewell, Pears & Co. was founded in 1808 by two Englishmen in Pittsburgh, Pennsylvania. It is credited with making the country's first chandelier in 1810. Pressed glass was made here from 1825.

The Boston and Sandwich Glass Company, established in 1825 in Massachusetts by Deming Jarves, also founder of the New England Glass Company, produced sandwich glass and flint glass of exceptional quality—America's answer to British lead-based crystal. From 1828 pressed glass formed most of the company's output.

The stopper has been bevel-cut to create a flower shape

The pseudo label is a trompe l'oeil effect rather than an actual label

WHITE WINE

The top of the bowl has a shallow decoration around the rim

The stem is faceted

WINE GLASS The bowl was engraved in the workshop of James Giles, an outside decorator. The engraved motifs include a stag's head and Neoclassical paterae amid interlaced swags and bellflowers. *c.1770. H:4½ in (11.5 cm).*

WINE DECANTER This shape, known as a shoulder decanter, is one of several developed during the early Neoclassical era. It is engraved with a pseudo wine label for white wine. *c.1765. H:11½ in (29 cm).*

LACY COMPOTE The decoration on this clear, pressed glass compote by the Boston and Sandwich Glass Company was created with a mold to imitate the diamond cutting and fluting often seen on cut glass. *1830–35.*

COLORED GLASS

Toward the end of the Neoclassical period, new developments in the field of colored glass brought French and, in particular, Bohemian glassmakers back to the forefront of glassmaking in Europe.

The creation of opaline glass in France in the mid-1820s heralded a new direction for European glassmaking. The semi-opaque glass looked like fine porcelain and was well suited to the Neoclassical forms and gilded mounts that dominated the French Empire style. The glass was made by adding bone ash to the mix, together with metal oxides for color, producing a range of soft white, blue, and pink tones. Opaline glass was sometimes referred to as "fire" glass because of its translucent color when held up to the light. The contemporary German equivalent—principally from Bohemia and Thuringia—was known as *Beinglas* or *Milchglas*.

MIMICKING THE ANCIENTS

While the French excelled in their production of opaline glass, manufacturers in Germany—

especially Bohemia—were constantly experimenting with new types of colored glass during this era, primarily in a bid to recreate glass that had been discovered at ancient Roman sites in the first half of the 18th century. Two major pioneers of such glass were Count von Buquoy and Friedrich Egermann.

Inspired by developments in the field of ceramics at the Wedgwood factory in Britain, and in the creation of new materials such as basalt ware and antico rosso, which emulated Roman stoneware (*see pp.64–65*), von Buquoy created red-marbled opaque glass in 1803 and a dark red and sometimes jet-black Hyalith in 1817. This was the first truly successful black opaque glass ever made.

In 1828 Friederich Egermann patented his Lithyalin glass. Also opaque, this marbled glass was the result of staining the surface of colored—usually red or black—glass with a second color such as yellow in order to create the desired effect. The idea was to recreate the types of "agate" glass made by the ancient Romans. Agate glass, itself,

PERFUME BOTTLE The top section of this turquoise opaline Charles X perfume bottle and its round, fluted stopper have been decorated with gold-painted floral motifs. *c.1825. H:5¼ in (13.5 cm).*

This shade of pink is known as gorge de pigeon (pigeon's breast)

The central panel is decorated with elegant columns below a Moorish-style frieze

The heavy bases are decorated with the laurel leaf motif

CHARLES X VASES These rare opaline and bronze vases have several Empire features: their urn shape, the restrained ornament, and the architectural pedestals. *c.1825. H:10 in (25.5 cm).*

BLACK HYALITH GLASS TANKARD This piece has fine gold-painted decoration and a faceted knop. There are bands of decoration and the bulbous section is ornamented with very fine rosettes. *c.1830. H:8 in (20 cm).*

had been made by combining two or more colors of molten glass, so producing a glass that resembled semiprecious stones such as agate, jasper, and chalcedony.

Also imitating ancient Roman glass, a third Bohemian glassmaker, Johann Joseph Mildner, revived the *Zwischengoldglas* technique popular in Germany during the 1730s and 1740s (*see p.39*). His designs featured medallion-shaped ovals on the sides and base of a piece—typically beakers and tumblers. Such pieces are now referred to as Mildner glass.

FLASHED AND CASED GLASS

Additional coloring techniques used at this time included flashing and casing. Flashed glass involved producing a piece in clear glass and dipping it while hot into molten glass of another color. This was an effective and less costly way of producing glassware that appeared to be one consistent color. The second, thinner layer of glass was often engraved or cut. Cased glass, particularly popular in Germany, involved producing a clear-glass form and pouring molten glass of another color into it. The two layers fused when the piece was reheated. Cased glass tended to be heavy, as several colors could be added. Pieces were often deep-cut in order to reveal the different layers for decoration.

PREVAILING TRENDS

Despite innovations in color, shapes were still influenced by the designs of the late 18th century.

BOHEMIAN GOBLET The central panel of this Biedermeier cut-glass goblet, made of clear glass flashed with amber, depicts a Persian figure with a horse. *1840. H:6¼ in (16 cm).*

Popular forms were urn-shaped or taper decanters; short, knop-stemmed goblets; and jewel-like boxes and perfume bottles. The beaker or tumbler with a recessed lip and straight, tapering sides was common throughout Germany. Sometimes the beaker had a slight waist and a domed base; often the sides would be faceted as well. Such pieces might be cased or flashed with engraved or cut decoration. They might also be enameled (*see below*) or gilded. Common Neoclassical motifs included medallions and recurring geometric designs.

ENAMELED BEAKER This Viennese drinking glass, decorated by Anton Kothgasser, features a view of Karlsbad within gilded borders. *c.1825. H:4½ in (11.8 cm).*

Selective gilding *of the finial is augmented with two bands of gilding to the cover and bowl*

BOHEMIAN GOBLET WITH COVER Decoration of this tall, cobalt-blue drinking glass is in the form of faceting to the foot, knops, base of the bowl, cover, and finial. *c.1850. H:8¾ in (19.5 cm).*

BIEDERMEIER TANKARD This Bohemian tankard has a pewter lid with a glass insert and deep-cut ornament. The colorless glass is flashed deep red in parts. *c.1840. H:6¾ in (17 cm).*

The D-shaped handle *is clear glass and has been cut to match the decoration on the tankard*

A star motif *has been cut in the base of the tankard*

ENAMELING

A popular technique during the early 18th century, enameling continued to find favor with Neoclassical designers, and it was during the early 19th century that the skills of the glass painter reached new heights. With the grandeur of the Empire style came a fashion for glassware decorated with topographical scenes and Classically inspired portraits. The majority of these were skillfully handpainted in transparent enamels. The best-known exponent of enameled glass during this period was the Austrian glass and porcelain decorator Anton Kothgasser, who created a number of enameled city- and landscapes and portraits on beakers and tumblers.

ENAMELED BEAKER This elegant beaker was designed by Friedrich Egermann. The tapering, faceted sides have enamel decoration in red, blue, and black, highlighted with geometric and floral patterning. There are two bands of geometric cut-glass ornament. *c.1837. H:4 in (10.5 cm).*

GLASS GALLERY

Neoclassical glassware borrowed the urn and goblet shapes from Classical Greece and Rome. Decanters and claret jugs were also popular forms, with mushroom, lozenge, or ball stoppers. Decoration was added by cutting. The diamond-cut pattern, slicing, and star-cut bases were common. Engraving was also used to add decoration, and many pieces feature heavy gilding.

KEY

1. Claret jug with flat-cut flutes, pillar-cut neck rings, and mushroom stopper. c.1830. H:10½ in (26.5 cm). ① **2.** Pair of cut piggins, with fan-cut handles and serrated rims above a diamond band. c.1825. D:6 in (15 cm). ① **3.** Austrian painted glass beaker with gilt rim. c.1815. H:3 in (7.5 cm). ④ **4.** Pair of Boulton-style glass and gilt campana wine coolers cut with strawberry diamonds. H:7¾ in (20 cm). ④ **5.** Sliced and flute-cut claret jug, with ball stopper. c.1800. H:11½ in (29 cm). ① **6.** Decanter with cut neck rings, flute-cut base, and lozenge stopper. c.1800. H:11¼ in (28.5 cm). ① **7.** Claret jug with flute-cut body and star-cut base. c.1820. H:16 in (23 cm). ② **8.** Mallet-shaped decanter and stopper, with gilt inscription "Brandy". H:12 in (30 cm). ① **9.** Engraved liqueur

2 Cut piggins with serrated rims

3 Austrian painted glass beaker

4 Boulton-style wine coolers

1 Claret jug with mushroom stopper

9 Engraved liqueur glass

5 Flute-cut claret jug

6 Decanter with lozenge stopper

7 Claret jug with star-cut base

8 Mallet-shaped decanter

10 English airtwist wine glass

glass with gilt rim. H:4½ in (11.5 cm). ① **10.** English wine glass, the stem with airtwist cable encircled by twin opaque white threads. c.1760. H:6 in (15.5 cm). ② **11.** Beaker by Friedrich Egermann. H:3¾ in (10 cm). ① **12.** Biedermeier beaker by Friedrich Egermann. H:5½ in (13.5 cm). ① **13.** Molded goblet with incised twist stem and conical foot. c.1800. H:6 in (15.5 cm). ③ **14.** Beaker by Anton Kothgasser with cherub motif within gilding. c.1825. H:4¼ in (11 cm). ⑤ **15.** Airtwist wine glass, the ogee bowl molded with broad flutes, the stem with a gauze core within spiral tapes. c.1760. H:7½ in (18.5 cm). ① **16.** Bonnet glass, the honeycomb-molded ogee bowl on a conical foot. c.1790. H:3¼ in (8 cm). ① **17.** Rummer engraved with a band of swags and stars. c.1830. H:7¾ in (19.5 cm). ① **18.** Engraved and polished rummer with an egg and tulip band. c.1810. H:5¾ in (14.5 cm). ①

11 Friedrich Egermann beaker

12 Biedermeier beaker

13 Goblet with twist stem

14 Anton Kothgasser beaker

15 Airtwist wine glass

16 Honeycomb-molded bonnet glass

17 Rummer with swags and stars

18 Engraved and polished rummer

METALWARE

THE RESTRAINED SURFACE DECORATION OF PLAIN AND
PATTERNED BANDS THAT CHARACTERIZED NEOCLASSICAL
SILVERWARE ACCENTUATED THE REFLECTIVE QUALITIES OF THE METAL.

FORMAL GRANDEUR

Enormous table services were commissioned
at the end of the 18th century, when dinner for the
aristocracy was a serious, formal, and often public
affair. Centerpieces were as much sculpture as
wrought silver.

To keep up with the latest fashions, many people
had their old silver melted down to make new
pieces or refashioned into the new style, and so old
designs have not survived. However, the Orloff
service, made for Catherine the Great's lover by
Jacques-Nicolas Roettiers, shows that some French
silversmiths were working in the massive, Classical
style of Lalive de Jully's furniture, known as *Goût*

PAIR OF CANDLESTICKS Made by John Carter of London,
these candlesticks have ornate knopped stems and bases with
swirling flutes. Each stands on a raised, square, gadrooned plinth.
1779. H:10½ in (26.5 cm).

The finial is in
the shape of a
pine cone

The spoons are made
of silver and vermeil

CONFITURIER This silver *confiturier* (jam pot) by Joseph-Gabriel Genu has
12 spoons. The bowl stands on four uprights with griffin heads and feet, and
the base has a frieze of palmettes. *1798–1809. H:10¼ in (26 cm).*

Grec (Greek style). Between 1750 and 1770
France was turning away from the Rococo style,
but it lingered on in Scandinavia and Germany
until the 1780s.

ROBERT ADAM

Although *Goût Grec* was fashionable for a while in
France, Robert Adam was the biggest influence in
Britain. Britain never really took to Rococo, except
in direct copies of the French, and moved fairly
smoothly from the solid, Classical Palladian style
to the lighter Classicism of the Adam style. Like
many designers, Adam masterminded every aspect
of his interiors, including the main items of silver,
which were often displayed on a table set into a
niche in the dining room. Adam considered the
ancient world as "a magazine of common
property...whence every man has a right to

SILVER EWER Thought to have belonged to Napoleon, this
ewer has a beaded rim and shoulders, a central band of applied
grotesques, a chased acanthus base and stem, and is set on a square
pedestal base. *Early 19th century. H:7½ in (19 cm).*

BIEDERMEIER BASKET This silver basket by Ferdinand Aloysius Hartmann has a boat-shaped, engraved silver body with a cobalt-blue glass liner and a domed foot. *W:6¾ in (17 cm).*

The twisted silver handle is movable and can be laid flat

SHEFFIELD PLATE

Around 1742, Thomas Boulsover of Sheffield discovered that copper could be sandwiched between sheets of silver and the two metals fused together. The resulting plate was much cheaper than silver and became very popular, displacing pewter. Exported all over Europe and to the United States, its widespread use by the 1780s spread the Neoclassical style. Matthew Boulton used Sheffield plate for coffee- and teapots, applying extra silver at any edges that were likely to wear through to the copper. It is referred to as Old Sheffield plate, and remained popular until the even cheaper method of electroplating was discovered around 1840.

THREE-LIGHT CANDELABRA This pair of Sheffield-plated three-light candelabra by Matthew Boulton & Co. has torch finials, reeded scroll branches, and circular bases with gadrooned borders. *1810–20. H:17¾ in (45 cm).*

take what material he pleases." Adam led the fashion for forms based on Grecian urns, tripods, and Roman sarcophagi. From 1760 to 1790, favorite motifs were paterae (ovals or circles with a rosette in the middle), ram's heads, often for handles, Vitruvian scrolls (wave patterns), festoons, and husks. Stylized plants in the form of palmettes, anthemion flowers, or trails of leaves abounded, as did spiral fluting and other forms of ridged surface. Bright-cut engraving—cutting an angled groove—made any surface decoration highly reflective. After Napoleon's Egyptian campaigns, sphinxes and eagle heads were added to the Classical repertoire.

This wealth of ornament was limited to bands separated by plain surfaces that formed a contrast to the decoration. Candlesticks were a popular vehicle for banded ornament,

especially as they resembled Classical columns in shape. Tea urns, which were ideally suited to the form of the Neoclassical vase, were also popular, since they catered to the fashion for drinking hot beverages.

MASS PRODUCTION

Few people were wealthy enough to commission Robert Adam and other leading architect-designers. Steam-powered machines made it possible to roll out silver objects more thinly and cheaply, so silverware came down in price just as the middle classes became more affluent and wanted to buy it. The patterns of repeated motifs were suited to mass production. By the late 1770s the Adam style was firmly established in Britain. In France, *Goût Grec* evolved into the more delicate Louis XVI style.

Matthew Boulton, a Birmingham silversmith, helped to make metalware more affordable for the general public. He teamed up with the architect James Wyatt and manufactured his top-quality designs for thin silver candlesticks, jugs, and snuff boxes. Boulton wrote: "Fashion hath much to do in these things, and as that of the present age, distinguishes itself by adopting the most elegant ornaments of the most refined Grecian artists...I am humbly copying their styles and making new combinations of old ornaments."

British and French styles spread throughout Europe. After an interruption during the American Revolution, they also reached the United States. Silver imports, pattern books, and catalogs made the styles available to a wider public. Philadelphia and then Baltimore were centers for fashionable silver. In Boston, Paul Revere adapted Classical forms for silver tableware, using sparing decoration to emphasize the elegant shapes he used.

Pierced and galleried rim

The front of the urn bears the script monogram "GCC"

SUGAR URN This Philadelphia silver sugar urn by George Drewry has very little ornamentation. The body has a circular lid with a finial and it stands on a circular foot with a square base. *1763. H:10½ in (26.5 cm).*

SILVER COFFEE POT The grandeur of this Eames and Barnard silver coffee pot is characteristic of the British Regency style. The high-relief ornament is balanced with areas of plain silver. *1825. H:9 in (22.5 cm).*

CLOCKS

AS A HIGHLY ARCHITECTURAL STYLE, NEOCLASSICISM WAS EMINENTLY

SUITED TO CLOCK CASES. LONGCASE CLOCKS LOOKED PARTICULARLY

ELEGANT ADORNED WITH FEATURES INSPIRED BY THE CLASSICAL WORLD.

LONGCASE CLOCKS

As grand pieces of furniture housing the most important timepiece in the home, longcase clocks enjoyed the attention of some of the best cabinet-makers of the period. The wood of choice through most of Europe was mahogany, and this was frequently inlaid with specimen woods. From simple stringing to complex marquetry and parquetry designs, these decorative embellishments accentuated the fine figure of the dense mahogany case. Some examples feature intarsia panels with depictions of animals or human figures.

CLASSICAL FEATURES

Wooden longcase clocks typically borrowed a number of features from Classical Greek architecture. Swan-neck pediments, for example, were a variation of the triangular top that adorned ancient temples such as the Greek Parthenon. The pediment might be transformed into a pair of facing S-scrolls, but remained firmly rooted in the Classical world.

The front edges of longcase clocks were often set with pilasters or columns—another basic component of ancient temple architecture. The three main architectural orders developed by the Greeks—Doric, Ionic, and Corinthian (*see p.54*)—can all be seen in the Neoclassical style. Many 18th-century designers regarded the Corinthian order as the most desirable. Its influence on clock design can be seen in the form of columns capped with acanthus leaves. A more

REGENCY LONGCASE CLOCK This mahogany clock is charged with Neoclassical features: the broken arch bonnet; the use of fluted columns either side of the clock face and flanking the door; and the two large inlaid cartouches of Britannia. *c.1800. H:95 in (241.5 cm).*

FEDERAL LONGCASE CLOCK The bonnet has a swan's neck crest with knopped terminals and three brass finials, the center one with an eagle, above colonettes with contrasting inlaid stringing. *98 in (249 cm).*

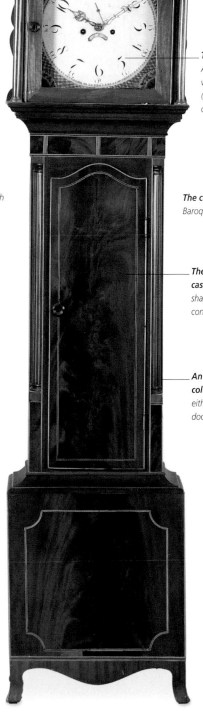

The broken arch bonnet is inlaid with delicate floral rosettes

The clock face is brass and has a musical works with seven bells and a moon phase

MARQUETRY LONGCASE CLOCK This Austrian clock has a walnut-veneered softwood body inlaid with maple and plumwood. The rectilinear lines of the case are accentuated by those of the marquetry. *H:93¼ in (237 cm).*

The square clock face is metal with Roman numerals

The dial has Arabic numerals within diapering (checks) and floral corner spandrels

The clock has an original Baroque brass movement

The waisted case has a shaped door with contrasting inlay

An inlaid quarter-column lies on either side of the door

An amphora vase supporting a large crown tops the clock

The clock face has Arabic numerals for both the hours and minutes, and pierced brass hands

The central panel is ornamented with fine-carved flaming hearts

The pendulum is visible through a small window in the case

BIEDERMEIER MANTEL CLOCK The enameled face of this clock has Roman numerals and is housed in a mahogany case with maple inlay and crowned with an eagle. A sun-shaped pendulum hangs from the case, which arches down to a plinth above four bronzed paw feet. *c.1825. H:20½ in (52 cm).*

example. Clock cases made in the Biedermeier style that originated in Austria tended to be less cluttered than other Neoclassical examples. This lightness of touch was accentuated by the paler woods, including some fruit- and nutwoods, which were popular in northern Europe.

CLOCK DEVELOPMENTS

More general developments in clock design included the round face. In contrast to the square and then arched clock faces that had previously been preferred, more and more longcase clocks were made with circular faces. From around 1790 many clock faces in France were equipped with gilded brass hands instead of the blued steel that had hitherto been the norm.

Other forms that date from this time include the cartel clock—a highly decorative French wall clock—and the Act of Parliament clock, which is a type of tavern clock made to hang on a wall and popularized by a tax levied on timepieces by the British government in 1797.

BRACKET CLOCKS

Neoclassical bracket clocks are generally made from mahogany and tend to be larger than their earlier walnut or ebony cousins. Many of them are highly elaborate and feature typically Neoclassical decorative touches such as finials in the shape of flaming urns or pine cones. But these were frequently replaced as fashions changed and so are not a reliable indicator of age.

Balloon bracket clocks, with cases that hug the contours of the round dial, are a less prevalent variation of the typical square-case bracket style; they are often found with satinwood veneers.

Biedermeier designers in particular were drawn to the architectural bracket clock form. French bracket clocks of the period exhibited greater variety and more lavish decoration than those made elsewhere.

understated homage to antiquity might take the shape of fluting or a decorated frieze separating the hood from the body of the case.

NATIONAL VARIATIONS

The American Federal style was as enthusiastic as French Empire and other European Neoclassical movements in its deference to ancient forms. Defining Federal touches include patriotic American emblems—the finial centering a swan-neck pediment might be topped with an eagle, for

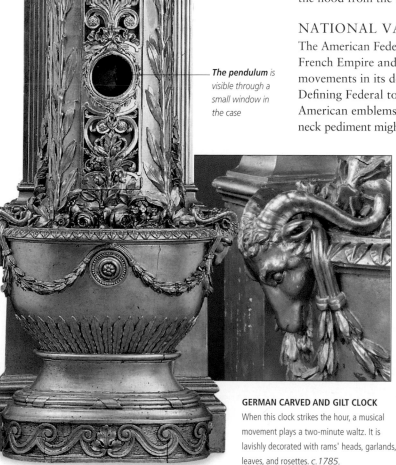

GERMAN CARVED AND GILT CLOCK When this clock strikes the hour, a musical movement plays a two-minute waltz. It is lavishly decorated with rams' heads, garlands, leaves, and rosettes. *c.1785.*

CARRIAGE CLOCKS

The carriage clock was a 19th-century French innovation. As suggested by the name, it was designed as a portable timepiece, suitable for carriage. Most examples have brass cases and are of eight-day duration. To mark the passage of time, many carriage clocks repeat the last hour after striking the quarter-hour—these are known as *grande sonnerie* clocks. Additional features found on the best examples include *cloisonné* decoration, subsidiary dials for seconds, days, or an alarm, repeat buttons, and fine engraving. Carriage clocks remained popular throughout the 19th and 20th centuries. While most were made in France, there are some English examples.

GRANDE SONNERIE STRIKING CLOCK This A. L. Breguet clock has spring detent chronometer escapements. *Early 19th century. H:6¾ in (17.5 cm).*

OBJETS DE VERTU

THE MAIN REQUIREMENTS FOR AN *OBJET DE VERTU*—A SMALL DECORATIVE

ACCESSORY SUCH AS A SNUFF BOX, PERFUME BOTTLE, OR SEWING KIT—WERE

RARE OR LUXURIOUS MATERIALS AND THE FINEST CRAFTSMANSHIP.

SNUFF BOX The surface of this circular French two-color gold snuff box and cover has engine-turned decoration and chiseled foliate borders. *1780–90. D:2½ in (6.5 cm).*

PRECIOUS GIFTS

At the top end of the market, snuff boxes were presented as diplomatic gifts. Gold was the obvious material—Frederick the Great of Prussia had 300 gold snuff boxes. They could be decorated in gold, most simply by engine turning, or engraved to reflect the light. Contrasting colors were created by adding another metal such as silver or iron to the gold, but pictures were often painted in enamels or gouache on inset panels. Hunting or mythological scenes were popular, as were portraits.

Other materials, such as mother-of-pearl, porcelain, micromosaics, ivory, or Japanese lacquer, were used as inlays, and precious stones might also feature. Tortoiseshell might be molded into the shape of a small box or veneered onto a wooden box covered in white gesso. Sometimes the gesso was colored to create a green or red tinge. Any decoration was deliberately kept simple so as not to detract from the striking markings of the shell.

Snuff boxes were not just made for royalty and the aristocracy. Silver was elegant enough for a Regency buck to cut a dash, especially when combined with shell or quartz, and all the porcelain manufacturers made snuffboxes as well as tableware.

EXOTIC INFLUENCES

From 1750 papier-mâché became increasingly fashionable as the European alternative to Asian lacquer. It was made by laminating sheets of paper and varnishing them, but by the early 1800s factories had discovered how to pulp paper, and papier-mâché was often used to make snuff boxes. They were painted with

Chinoiseries, landscapes, portraits, or Classical motifs, and sometimes incorporated Wedgwood cameos.

For wooden boxes, novelty shapes such as shoes were popular. Boxes of local hardwoods with ivory inlays were imported from Vizagapatnam in India. In England, prisoners of the Napoleonic Wars improved their lot by making and selling pine boxes decorated with natural and dyed pieces of straw.

CHANGING STYLES

Robert Adam drily observed, "To understand thoroughly the art of living, it is necessary, perhaps, to have passed some time among the French." As always,

GEORGE III SNUFF BOX The rectangular form of this elegant tortoiseshell and silver snuff box has serpentine edges and a hinged lid. *c.1780. W:3½ in (8.5 cm).*

The painting of the demure lady has a motto reading Elle Attend (She Is Waiting)

STOBWASSER SNUFF BOX The japanner Johann Heinrich Stobwasser was particularly renowned for his papier-mâché. Here the lid of the snuff box is painted with a picture of a reclining lady. *c.1830. W:3¾ in (9.3 cm).*

ANGLO-INDIAN LAP DESK
This ivory-veneered sandalwood lap desk has bands of tambour paneling, alternately stained black. The flowerhead- and leaf-engraved top acts as a writing slope and opens to reveal a partitioned interior. *c.1820. W:15 in (38 cm)*.

French high society was the arbiter of taste. So decoration showing "pagodas and fantastic fripperies"—the artist William Hogarth's description of Chinoiserie—Gothic ruins, and pastoral scenes gave way to Classical ruins and sarcophagus shapes. The rest of Europe carried on in the Rococo vein—Chelsea continued making porcelain toys, as adult accessories were then called, in imitation of Sèvres' Louis XV style until it merged with Derby in 1769.

By then, France had moved on toward the next style. In 1756 the philosopher Denis Diderot commented on the vogue for *Goût Grec*: "Everything is now made in the Greek manner. The taste has passed from architecture into the milliners' shops...our dandies would think it a disgrace to be seen with a snuff box not in the Greek style." Soon, the lighter Louis XVI style was fashionable, and after about 1820, shapes became serpentine or *bombé* as the Rococo style was revived.

WOMEN'S FANCIES

Women had a wider choice of fashionable accessories. *Nécessaires* contained miniature kits, often for sewing. *Étuis* were similarly useful cases for small items such as writing equipment, sewing accessories, or tiny sets of cutlery. *Bonbonnières* were little sweet boxes. Vinaigrettes were silver boxes, small enough to be tucked into a glove, that contained smelling salts a sponge soaked in aromatic vinegar. In an era of unpleasant smells including open sewerage, such items were essential for the fairer sex.

SNUFF-BOX EROTICA

Snuff boxes were beautifully made and had no fastening mechanism, but relied on the lid fitting the box perfectly. They had to fit smoothly so that snuff would not spill out when the box was opened. This precise workmanship had another use for boxes that were more for show—or concealment—than function. Some boxes had hidden panels that unscrewed to reveal miniature paintings of erotic boudoir scenes, a lock of hair, musical automata, or the face of a loved one. One such box in London's Wallace Collection has a secret panel, only found in 1976, showing gouache portraits of Voltaire and his mistress.

TORTOISESHELL SNUFF BOX This gilt-metal-inlaid snuff box is decorated with a vase of flowers. The interior unscrews to reveal a painting on ivory of a boudoir scene. *c.1785. D:3 in (8 cm)*.

Perfume was another way to ward off body odors. At the time, perfume was not prepackaged and had to be decanted into small bottles. Perfume bottles were usually made of glass, which could be cased, colored, and decorated with techniques such as cutting, pressing, cameo, and frosting. Chelsea, Sèvres, and Wedgwood also made perfume bottles out of nonporous ceramics.

Gorge de pigeon (pigeon's breast) pink opaline glass

PERFUME BOTTLE The deep-cut body of this perfume bottle is in the extremely rare *gorge de pigeon* glass, which was only made in France between 1815 and 1835. It has a three-color gold mount. *1815–25. H:2¼ in (6 cm)*.

IVORY *NÉCESSAIRE* This gold-mounted ivory *nécessaire* contains gold-handled scissors, an ivory memo, tweezers, a snuff spoon, a thimble, and a bodkin. *H:3¼ in (8.25 cm)*.

ENAMELED *ÉTUI* This gilt-metal mounted case has a screw cover shaped like a thimble. The case is inscribed *Sincer en amitie* (Honesty in friendship) and contains a glass perfume bottle. *Early 19th century. L:3 in (8 cm)*.

TEA AND SNUFF

BENEATH THEIR RIGIDLY FORMAL EXTERIORS, OUR
18TH-CENTURY ANCESTORS WERE JUST AS SUSCEPTIBLE
TO VICE AS WE ARE TODAY. THE TWIN TEMPTATIONS
OF TEA AND SNUFF WERE A RICH SEAM FOR THE SINS
OF GREED AND COVETOUSNESS.

Snuff had been known in elite European circles since the 16th century, when the French ambassador to Portugal cured one of Queen Catherine de Medici's interminable headaches with a pinch of powdered tobacco leaf.

THE POWER OF SNUFF

Snuff was first introduced to the nobility in Britain when large quantities of it were seized from Spanish ships captured at the beginning of the 18th century. As with any addictive substance, the use of snuff soon spawned a range of conventions and peculiar habits. A carved wooden Scottish Highlander was used as a shop sign by many snuff retailers. Many devotees of snuff took to toting

their powdered tobacco around in specially made boxes, although Dr. Johnson, one of the most well-documented snuff-takers, carried his loose in his coat pockets. The wide variety of snuff boxes on the market included metal ones decorated with scenes in Staffordshire enamels, engraved silver boxes, boxes studded with precious stones, and countless treen (wooden) examples. Larger snuff mulls, designed to stand on a table for communal use, were often decorated with rams' horns or even fashioned from an entire ram's skull.

TEA-DRINKING NATION

The popularity of tea in Europe, and especially in Britain, rocketed during the 18th century. In 1685 the British East India Company imported nearly 12,000 lb (5,500 kg) of tea; by 1750 it was bringing in about 4.5 million lb (2 million kg) every year. The monopoly enjoyed by the East India Company, combined with an extortionate tax, made tea expensive enough to encourage a thriving smuggler's market. In fact, the value of tea was so great, usually 70 percent of the cargo's worth, that porcelain tea bowls and other ceramics were included with shipments of tea as ballast, just to make up the weight.

The word "caddy" comes from the Chinese for a 1-lb weight, which is exactly what the first tea caddies were designed to hold. They were often equipped with locks to safeguard their contents from servants. As with snuff boxes, no expense was spared in the decoration of a tea caddy. The rarest woods and luxury materials such as tortoiseshell, mother-of-pearl, and ivory housed the precious commodity. Elaborate decorative techniques including penwork and painted enamels added an exotic touch. Even the caddy spoons were wrought from silver and decorated immaculately.

TAX ON TEA

Tea even took on a political importance in the United States. The citizens of Boston, incensed at what they saw as an illegal tax of three pence a pound levied on their supply of tea, refused to let the East India Company

ENAMEL TEA CADDY The sides of this squared caddy are enameled with Classical myths depicting Pyramus and Thisbe and Perseus and Andromeda and scenes from *The Ladies' Amusement. c.1760. L:3½ in (8.5 cm).*

ENAMEL SNUFF BOX The decoration on such items was often inspired by the works of famous Italian and French artists. Here the image is titled *Les Poussins* after Boucher and is on a powder blue ground. *c.1770. L:3 in (8 cm).*

COWRIE SHELL SNUFF BOX The smooth surface and exotic patterning of the cowrie shell made a luxurious material for a snuff box. The silver cover is engraved with a coat of arms. *c.1770. L:3 in (8 cm).*

REGENCY TEA CADDY This tortoiseshell and mother-of-pearl tea caddy is square with canted corners. The case has a geometric lozenge design; the front has a silver escutcheon and initialed mount. *W:6 in (15 cm).*

dock and unload one fateful day in 1773. The standoff culminated in the Boston Tea Party, when a mass of townspeople dressed as American Indians stormed the boats and threw the cargo of tea into the sea.

Demand for tea reached such an extent in the early 19th century that the East India Company resorted to illegally smuggling opium into China to exchange for huge quantities of the leaf. The result was the loss of an entire Chinese generation to opium addiction, and eventually a war in 1840.

SOCIAL WHIRL British cartoonist Thomas Rowlandson parodied the fashionable tea parties of the time.

AMERICAN FOLK ART

The late 18th century ushered in a golden age of American folk art, perhaps linked to the newly won sovereignty of the 13 original colonies. Although diverse, folk art is characterized by a lack of formal training on the part of the artists and craftsmen. It also tends to follow the artistic traditions of the immigrant communities that forged it, making it the ideal medium through which American citizens could assert their individuality and independence while remaining true to their roots.

ANONYMOUS CRAFTSMEN

Different areas specialized in different art forms, although Pennsylvania counties have emerged as the most prolific in many spheres. While some folk artists have become famous in their own right, most of the artifacts described as folk art were made by anonymous individuals. Occasionally a body of particularly fine work is attributed to a single unknown craftsman who is given a title such as "The Hannovertown Artist." Folk art takes many forms, from the functional to the purely decorative, and examples practiced by American communities have encompassed media as diverse as ceramics,

wood, tin, and paper. Popular subjects include animals, often carved in wood. These range from decoy birds with naturalistic painting, used by hunters to lure their prey, to portrait carvings, of either generic animals or favorite pets. Animals such as turkeys, dogs, and horses, important to the livelihoods of early Americans and commonly found on homesteads, were frequently depicted on painted wood.

PAINTERLY SKILLS

Painted decoration can transform an ordinary item into an extraordinary piece of folk art. Itinerant painters such as the prodigiously talented Rufus Porter traveled over large areas, accepting commissions to decorate anything from walls to boxes. At a local level, a villager known for his skill with a brush would attract the attention of his neighbors and often earn a supplementary income by painting prized possessions.

Certain motifs occur time and again throughout American folk art. The tulip, loaded with significance for early settlers, is particularly prevalent. The flower had associations with contented home life and was also a symbol

CARVED AND DECORATED TURKEY Animal carvings have always been a popular folk art theme. This Pennsylvanian turkey is brightly colored and has a stylized fantail and beak. *Late 18th century. H:7 in (18 cm).*

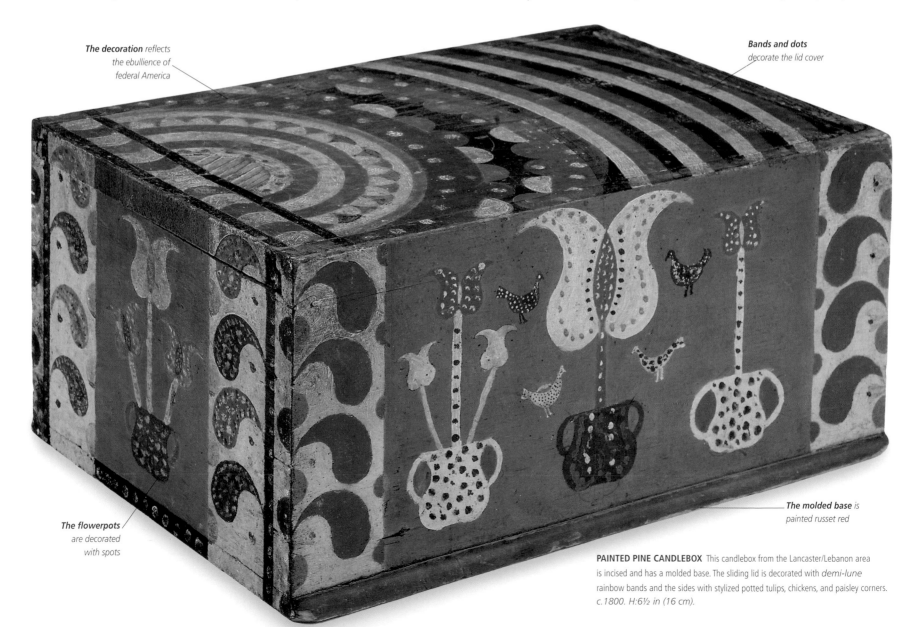

The decoration reflects the ebullience of federal America

Bands and dots decorate the lid cover

The flowerpots are decorated with spots

The molded base is painted russet red

PAINTED PINE CANDLEBOX This candlebox from the Lancaster/Lebanon area is incised and has a molded base. The sliding lid is decorated with *demi-lune* rainbow bands and the sides with stylized potted tulips, chickens, and paisley corners. *c.1800. H:6½ in (16 cm).*

PIE PLATE This earthenware sgraffito pie plate is from Pennsylvania. It is decorated with naive drawings of a horse, two birds, and a tulip, and has green and yellow slip glazing. *c.1800. D:9 in (23 cm).*

TOLEWARE COFFEE POT This gooseneck coffee pot is decorated with fruits and flowers in earthy tones. Most toleware had a black background, so this piece, probably from New England, is rare. *H:10¼ in (26 cm).*

RED WARE INKWELL Most red ware—glazed red earthenware—was made before 1840 by northern European immigrants. This example is a heart-shaped inkwell with pierced sides. *Early 19th century. W:5½ in (14 cm).*

of the Holy Trinity. This religious symbolism is never far from the surface of American folk art of this period. The peacock, another favorite motif, was associated with the resurrection of Christ, while the red rose signified God's love.

EUROPEAN TRADITION

Folk art ceramics already had a long European history before they were first produced in the United States. Pennsylvania red ware is based on German folk ceramics, and other American slip-decorated wares had similar roots in the European tradition. The application of slip is one of the most

straightforward ways of waterproofing and decorating earthenware vessels and was employed extensively by American settlers. More sophisticated potters created sgraffito wares by incising designs into the slip clay. Common themes include the wildflowers and animals of the American landscape as well as the abstract wavy lines of Pennsylvania slipware. These ceramics were instrumental in forging the early American domestic style and continue to exert an important influence on contemporary American ceramics.

Painted tinplate, known as toleware, was decorated using a method similar to the imitation

lacquer technique known as japanning. The base coat is usually made of asphaltum, a naturally occurring tarlike substance that provides a glossy, opaque black ground. Rarer examples have red or even yellow base colors. Oil paints were then stenciled or handpainted on top of the base coat, depicting flowers or abstract patterns. Decorating toleware was difficult and time-consuming, so these pieces were often reserved for special occasions and given as wedding gifts. Toleware items such as coffeepots, candlesticks, and trays would probably have been valued as decorative display objects and would only have been used rarely, if at all.

STORAGE BOX The heart-shaped motifs on this mahogany-veneered and inlaid storage box are typical of American folk art, while the geometric patterning and shield motifs are characteristic of the Federal era. *c.1820. W:14¾ in (37.5 cm)*

FRAKTUR

The German immigrant population in Pennsylvania began to produce *Fraktur*—illuminated manuscripts—in the 18th century. These fall into several distinct categories, the most prevalent of which are the *Taufschein* documents created to record the birth and baptism dates of children born to these early settlers. Local schoolmasters would draw up these records on behalf of the families living within their communities, using goose-quill pens with steel nibs. The most talented artists were in great demand and sometimes even worked in several different counties.

Devotional motifs such as angels, crowns, and the symbolic tulip were drawn from the Lutheran religion of the German settlers. These were combined with astrological and natural symbols such as hearts and stars as well as pictures—images of the family in formal dress are common. English gradually supplanted German as the dominant language for *Taufschein* documents in the 19th century.

Other types of Fraktur include *Vorschriften*—handwriting samplers, bookplates, and house blessings. They are all characterized by extensive use of brightly colored inks and careful script. Fraktur dwindled in popularity as printing became more common in the United States during the 19th century.

BIRTH CERTIFICATE A watercolor and ink on paper birth certificate for Joseph Horner, by Henry Young, Pennsylvania. The two central figures of husband and wife hold hands, while the gentleman presents a bouquet of flowers. *1841. H:10¼ in (26 cm).*

TEXTILES

WHETHER THEIR DESIGNS WERE INCORPORATED IN THE WEAVE OR
PRINTED ONTO THE FABRIC, FRENCH TEXTILES WERE THE MOST
INFLUENTIAL OF THE LATE 18TH AND EARLY 19TH CENTURIES.

THE SILK TRADE

The French city of Lyon has been associated with
the silk trade since medieval times. By the start
of the 18th century, Lyon directed trends and
produced luxurious woven silks, which inspired
designs all over Europe.

The first 18th-century fashion associated with
Lyon was bizarre silks. Used mainly for dresses,
these vibrant asymmetrical patterns combined
Asian-style flowers and foliage with jagged lines
and architectural motifs. The dominant pattern
was usually in gold or silver thread.

From the 18th century onward, the innovative
silk weavers of Lyon positioned their products at
the top-quality end of the market and attracted
leading textile designers to work for them.

FLORAL LAMPAS SILK Made by La Maison Grand Frère, this design has a
naturalistic flower arrangement within a floral laurel wreath. It is a reworking of
an 18th-century model designed by Gaudin. *1788. L:100 in (254 cm).*

KEY DESIGNERS

Jean Revel helped change the look of silk
dress fabrics in the 1730s. He developed a
special weaving technique—*points rentés*—to
create shading and three-dimensional effects.
He used this technique to make realistic
designs: flowers, fruit, shells, and architectural
ruins were among his favorite motifs. The
images were woven into the silk entirely by
hand. These naturalistic designs dominated
silk patterns until the end of the 19th century.

Lyon silk designer Philippe de Lasalle
trained under François Boucher, the painter.
Like Revel, he was a weaver who improved
silk-production techniques. His fabric designs
bridge the gap between delicate Rococo and
the simpler Neoclassical look. He specialized
in furnishing fabric with detailed naturalistic
decoration of flowers and motifs of bows,
swags, and vases. He sometimes included

LYON LAMPAS SILK This length of red silk is decorated with a repeating pattern of
eagles, pheasants with their nests, flowers, torches, and flower-filled urns. The pattern
was created in 1785. *L:63¾ in (160 cm).*

animals and birds. Lasalle's textiles were the height of luxury and quality. He supplied fabrics to Louis XVI and European monarchs such as Catherine the Great and Charles III, King of Spain.

The French Revolution was a blow to the Lyon silk trade, which received so much patronage from the monarchy. Fortunately, in the early 1800s, Napoleon took up the role. He commissioned vast quantities of furnishing fabric for his residences. Jean-François Bony designed many of these textiles. His Neoclassical style had the right political connotations, associated with the Roman Empire. Bony used motifs like laurel wreaths, trophies, shields, and Napoleon's personal symbol—the bee— for woven silks in strong blues, reds, and yellows.

TOILES

Indian printed cottons were so popular in the late 17th century that the French government banned them to protect France's wool and silk industry. When the government lifted this law in 1759, Christophe-Philippe Oberkampf founded a cloth printing works in Jouy. As a result, this style of printed fabric is called *toiles de Jouy* (cloth from Jouy) even though other cities like Nantes also produced it. The earliest toiles were multicolored floral prints similar to Indian fabrics. The monochrome printing associated with toiles came later. Classic designs feature chinoiseries, contemporary vignettes, and images from Greek and Roman mythology, printed in red, sepia, mauve, or blue on white or yellow grounds. Immensely influential, toiles still inspire fabric designers today.

COTTON FURNISHING FABRIC Manufactured by Petitpierre Frères et Cie of Nantes, the design was printed using copper plates. It shows scenes from a comedy by Rabelais. *1785–90. L:71¼ in (181 cm).*

WALLPAPERS

Many consider the 18th and early 19th centuries a high point in wallpaper design. At the beginning of the 18th century, handpainted wallpapers from China took Europe by storm. Decorated with blossoming trees, long-tailed birds, and exotic scenes, they helped raise wallpaper from a humble substitute for tapestry to something even aristocrats would want. Wallpapers decorated with floral sprays were also popular, while other fashionable designs imitated marble columns or swags of fabric.

French manufacturer Jean Bapiste Réveillon introduced Neoclassical wallpapers in the 1770s. Some of his papers imitated the ancient wall paintings found in Pompeii. He employed leading designers including Jean-Baptiste Huet, also celebrated for his *toiles* designs. Jacquemart and Bénard manufactured papers inspired by Roman wall paintings. During the Revolutionary period, they produced designs decorated with republican tricolor ribbons and caps of liberty. In the early 1800s the French firms Zuber and Dufour made wallpaper panels, which formed panoramic views of towns and landscapes such as the Swiss Alps.

ROYAL LAMPAS SILK This pattern was created by Michel for Queen Marie Antoinette's games salon at Versailles. The striking yellow-gold ground is decorated with oak boughs and flowers. *1784–86. L:55 in (140 cm).*

WALLPAPER PANEL This design imitates drapery and is charged with Neoclassical motifs: elaborate columns topped by busts of Classical figures, swags, paterae, and griffin motifs. *c.1800. H:100 in (255 cm).*

DIRECTOIRE WALLPAPER This piece of wallpaper was printed using wood blocks. The central bust of Barras *en grisaille* is framed by wheatsheaves and sprigs of laurel leaves on a blue ground. *c.1798. W:21½ in (55 cm).*

SAMPLERS

In an age when aristocratic girls' lives were confined to pursuits such as books and music, the embroidered sampler was a testament to their needlework skills and the leisure time available to them. Such skills were important, and women produced examples of stitches on cloth scraps for practice and guidance. In the 16th and 17th centuries, these samples began to be worked into textile samplers. Many bore their maker's name, age, and the date they finished. Some took years to make.

Sampler-making was a social activity that bound the generations together. Mothers helped daughters make these pretty as well as useful guides. Families handed down cherished samplers and proudly displayed them in frames.

The earliest samplers were made by professional needlewomen or well-to-do ladies, who had time to embellish their clothing or beautify their homes.

Samplers were immensely popular in Britain. Pilgrims, the early settlers in the United States, took this custom with them and made them equally popular. The Dutch, Germans, Spanish, and Mexicans also produced samplers in great numbers.

VERSES ON SAMPLERS

The increased inclusion of text such as the maker's name charts the rise in literacy among the population as a whole in the second half of the 17th century. In the early 18th century, samplers were a way of teaching basic reading and mathematical skills as well as giving religious instruction. By the mid-18th century, making samplers was a primary educational exercise for girls, and it became rare not to incorporate letters, numerals, or some form of text. Girls began working on a simple sampler with the alphabet and numerals at age five or six. As they grew older, teenage girls of about 13

ALPHABET SAMPLER Centered beneath the alphabet is a verse within a panel supported by crowned cherubs. Adam and Eve stand beneath the Tree of Life with other home-life designs, all within a floral border. *1809. H:22 in (56 cm).*

produced more sophisticated samplers embroidered at length with motifs and verses that showed off the skills they had acquired. Biblical quotations and pious prose were popular, as were mottoes and rhymes. *"All you my friends who now will see this little piece that has been work'd by me,"* is a typical example.

PICTORIAL SAMPLERS

Makers carefully and symmetrically arranged images on samplers in the 18th and 19th centuries, unlike the randomly embroidered 17th-century examples. They finished later samplers with decorative borders. The embroidery style on samplers is usually charmingly naive, with no attempt at perspective. Typical motifs include fruit, flowers, trees, birds, animals, and geometric designs. Because of their role in religious education, many of these images have Biblical symbolism. Adam and Eve with the snake in the apple tree began regularly appearing as a focal point from the 1740s onward. The needleworker's own home was another favorite subject. As the antislavery movement gathered momentum in the early 19th century, related imagery also appeared on samplers.

NEEDLEWORK SAMPLER Within a bold floral border is a panel of pious verse and inscriptions above a hillock with ducks, sheep, rabbits, a horse, and a snake. The sampler was worked by Lydia Ann Beales of Chester County, Pennsylvania, in colored silk threads on a gauze ground. *1832.*

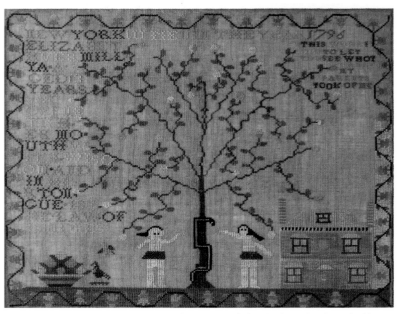

NEW YORK SAMPLER This silk-on-linen sampler features a Tree of Life with Adam and Eve by a Federal house, with a strawberry border. By Elizabeth Vermillya, aged 13. *1796. H:17½ in (44.5 cm).*

GEORGE III SAMPLER Worked in colored silks on linen, this sampler depicts verse above a Tree of Life with figures, itself above a country landscape. By Ann Carr, aged 15. *1806. H:15¼ in (39 cm).*

WILLIAM IV SAMPLER Below an alphabet row, a tree is flanked by plants, figures, birds, and animals, with a strawberry border. Worked in colored silks by Elizabeth Ambridge, age 9. *1836. H:13½ in (34 cm).*

DARNING SAMPLERS

Before the mid-20th century, women mended rather than threw away costly sheets, stockings, and dresses when they became worn or damaged. Learning to darn with near-invisible stitches was a practical skill much in demand. In the late 18th and early 19th centuries, women who mastered this skill sometimes turned their fine stitches into art. They created darning samplers, working darning stitches into patterns: usually bold squares, but sometimes floral motifs and trees. A lady's maid looking for work would show her darning samplers as evidence of her ability to care for her mistress's outfits.

After 1850 samplers began to decline in quality and quantity. The sewing machine meant women no longer had to be proficient at basic stitching. Girls' education became more academic, so less time was given to needlework. But, most important, colorful, naturalistic images in wool on square meshed canvas were now the height of fashion. This technique, called Berlin wool work, dominated embroidery for the rest of the 19th century.

TEMPLE OF SOLOMON This George III sampler is worked in colored silks. Two jardinières sit amid birds, figures, and trees above the Temple of Solomon and verse, within a strawberry border. *1792. H:12¼ in (31 cm).*

MAP SAMPLERS

British women began making map samplers in the 1770s. They usually chose to depict the British Isles and sometimes Continental Europe, often in an oval-shaped design. By the late 18th century it had become easier and safer to travel long distances for work or pleasure and geography became an increasingly important part of a young lady's education. British sea power was a source of pride, and many women had family and friends in the navy. Map samplers often included naval motifs like compasses and sailing ships. British immigrants to the United States spread the fashion. Map samplers remained a popular embroidery subject until the mid-19th century.

MAP OF ENGLAND, SCOTLAND, AND WALES A fascinating record of the contemporary geography of the United Kingdom, this sampler is worked in black silks with the various counties highlighted in reds, greens, ochers, oranges, and blues. *1778. H:19¾ in (50 cm).*

SCULPTURE

NEOCLASSICAL SCULPTURE AIMED TO PORTRAY BUSTS AND FIGURES WITH
THE "NOBLE SIMPLICITY AND CALM GRANDEUR" THAT THE GERMAN
ARCHAEOLOGIST J. J. WINCKELMANN SO ADMIRED IN THE ANCIENT WORLD.

RETURN TO THE CLASSICAL

The work of Jean-Antoine Houdon and his French
peers marked a "return to good taste" after the
Rococo "jumble of shells," as a disparaging critic
termed it. By the 1750s in Paris—where designers
led continental fashion and were quick to change
it—there was already nostalgia for the days of
Louis XIV and the formality of the palace at
Versailles. The imposing medium of marble
could be used both for figures from antiquity
such as the Olympian gods or Roman emperors,
and for prominent people of the day, elevated
with a Classical bearing.

Antonio Canova, famous for his Three Graces,
standardized the method for working in marble,
whether on a large or small scale (only Michelangelo
could work straight to marble). From drawings,
one or more clay maquettes would be made, then a
plaster model would be molded from wet clay. This
could be scaled up to a full-size model by sticking
in lead nails, and measuring the distances with
calipers, helped by a pointing machine. Successful
sculptors had apprentices to hew the marble,
working closely to the model. The maestro would
then add the finishing touches.

REINTERPRETING THE ANCIENTS

Marble could end up looking cold in the austere
Neoclassical style. In the hands of those who
simply made inferior copies of ancient statues,
it was lifeless, but the best sculptors, such as
Houdon and Canova, were able to
bring marble to life.

The French sculptor
Étienne-Maurice

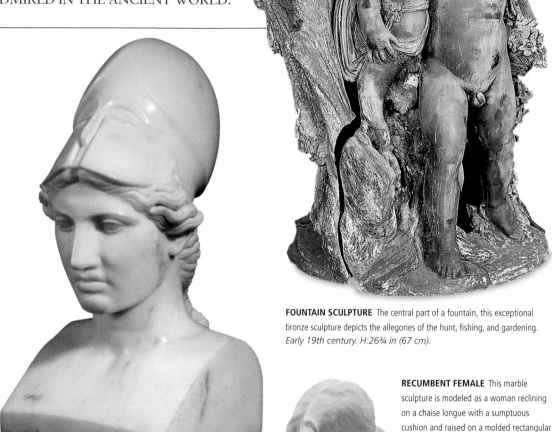

FOUNTAIN SCULPTURE The central part of a fountain, this exceptional
bronze sculpture depicts the allegories of the hunt, fishing, and gardening.
Early 19th century. H:26¾ in (67 cm).

MINERVA This bust of the Roman goddess of wisdom and war,
known as Athena by the Greeks, was sculpted by Johann Heinrich
Dannecker in Rome. Here the goddess is represented in the armored
helmet she is said to have been born with. *1785–86.
H:12 in (30 cm).*

RECUMBENT FEMALE This marble
sculpture is modeled as a woman reclining
on a chaise longue with a sumptuous
cushion and raised on a molded rectangular
base. *H:22 in (56 cm).*

Falconet spent the early part of his career making mildly erotic boudoir-style nymphs that resembled those of the Rococo painter François Boucher. But then he created a massive bronze equestrian statue in a more serious, imposing style for Peter the Great in St. Petersburg in 1778.

He shocked his contemporaries by claiming that modern sculptors were better at lifelike portrayals than the ancients. He wrote: "In attempting the imitation of the surfaces of the human body, sculpture ought not to be satisfied with a cold likeness, such as man might be before the breath of life animated him...It is living nature, animated, passionate, that the sculptor ought to express." Jean-Antoine Houdon, who was based in Paris but had trained in Rome, came closest to fulfilling Falconet's ideal. His portrait busts of the rich and famous captured the individual personalities, gestures, and expressions of his sitters.

NEW MATERIALS

Both bronze and marble could be used on any scale, whether for outdoors or inside buildings, but new ceramic materials could also be used for sculpture indoors. Wedgwood's black basalt was hard and imposing, making it the ideal material for a Classical bust. John Flaxman, one of the few English sculptors whose name was known in Europe, started his career designing low-relief plaques and medallions for Wedgwood. Spode, which was known as Copeland and Garrett after 1833, had discovered a recipe for stone china, an extremely hard earthenware, which it started using in 1805. This proved a good material for busts of leading contemporary figures.

As recipes for hard-paste porcelain spread across Europe, this more stable formula enabled factories to make larger examples of ceramics, often as sculptural centerpieces for the dining table. Falconet designed statues for Sèvres that were made in biscuit porcelain and left unglazed to show off the sculptural detail better. His statue of Cupid, with a finger to his lips, was highly popular. By 1780 mythological and Classical subjects had replaced pastoral themes, under Louis-Simon Boizot, who was in charge of the modeling workshop at Sèvres from 1773.

Maurice Falconet's designs were copied by other factory modelers, such as Johann Carl Schönheit at Meissen. Meissen adopted the Neoclassical style under the directorship of Count Camillo Marcolini from 1774. He approved of biscuit porcelain for allegorical and Classical figures, as the material resembled the marble sculptures being excavated in Greece and Italy.

DUKE OF WELLINGTON This Copeland and Garrat feldspar porcelain bust of the Duke of Wellington gives Wellington the noble bearing of a Roman general. *c.1835. H:9½ in (44 cm).*

BUST OF THE MARQUIS DE MÉJANES This bust by Jean-Antoine Houdon sits on a pedestal; the style of it predates the French Revolution. *c.1786. H:34 in (86 cm).*

YOUNG WOMAN Made of marble and alabaster, this French bust of a young woman wearing a scarf over her hair is signed A. Aurili. *Early 19th century. H:9¾ in (25 cm).*

The young woman has the small facial features characteristic of Classical sculpture

MEISSEN MARCOLINI BUST The bust is a model of Johann Daniel Schöne, sculpted from biscuit porcelain. It is marked "Guttenberg," and has the blue sword mark. *1810. H:5 in (12.5 cm).*

The dress, in a pale red color, has a square neckline, ornamented with a geometric design

AGE OF EXCESS

1840–1900

19TH-CENTURY REVIVALS

DURING THE 19TH CENTURY, MANY ARTISTS, ARCHITECTS, AND DESIGNERS TURNED THEIR BACKS ON THEIR OWN CENTURY AND BEGAN TO EXPLORE THE STYLES OF EARLIER AGES. IN PARTICULAR, THEY TURNED THEIR ATTENTION TO THE MEDIEVAL WORLD.

MEISSEN CLOCK This porcelain mantel clock has applied decoration of exotic birds and flowers, with a brass dial. *19th century. H:11½ in (29 cm).*

THE RISE OF NATIONALISM

The various stylistic revivals of the century can best be understood as an expression of national feeling, for they represented a nostalgic return to long-forgotten or neglected forms of art that gave continuity and substance to newly emerging nations. In seeking inspiration from the past, they were also rejecting the mass production and commercialism of the industrial age in favor of a supposedly purer, more idealistic, Utopian age.

Throughout Europe at this time, nationalism became the dominant theme. Subject peoples—Greeks, Serbs, and Romanians in the Ottoman Empire, Poles in the Russian Empire, Hungarians in the Austrian Empire—struggled for independence and nationhood, while both Italy and Germany emerged as united nations at this time: Italy in 1859–61, and Germany in 1871. Revivalist styles bolstered this nationalist tide.

THE GOTHIC REVIVAL

The main revivalist style was neo-Gothic, or the Gothic Revival, which took various forms. In Britain, as in Germany, the Gothic style was a continuation rather than a revival, for it had always remained popular. It became closely linked with the revival of Catholicism within the Anglican Church and the renewed strength of Roman Catholicism itself. Many medieval churches were restored in the Gothic style, while Keble College and other buildings in Oxford—the spiritual home of the Anglo-Catholic movement—were built in this style.

In Germany the revival was linked with anti-French sentiments and was heavily nationalistic: one of the major projects of the time was the restoration of Marienburg Castle, the medieval seat of the crusading Teutonic Knights. In Bavaria, an independent kingdom until it joined the German empire in 1871,

Ludwig II built fairy-tale Gothic castles as his personal escape from the modern world. In Italy the return to medievalism was part of the push toward Italian unification, with many Italian cities adopting the style as an echo of their former medieval glory: work was resumed on Milan Cathedral and the facade of Santa Maria del Fiore in Florence, among other projects.

FRENCH AND OTHER REVIVALS

In France the neo-Gothic style was used to identify the monarchy, which was restored after the defeat of Napoleon in 1815, with its medieval past, and to link national identity with Catholicism: Gothic cathedrals and abbeys were restored and extended in the new revivalist style. Furniture-designers in France, as elsewhere in Europe, also looked back

NEUSCHWANSTEIN CASTLE The reclusive Ludwig II of Bavaria had this castle built in Gothic style in the 1860s. Inside, the decor illustrated the medieval legends that inspired composer Richard Wagner.

DUTCH SILVER BASKET The undulating Rococo-style shape of the rim is teamed with elaborate decoration including a diamond-cut pattern and Neoclassical swags and medallions. *c.1890. W:10¼ in (26 cm).*

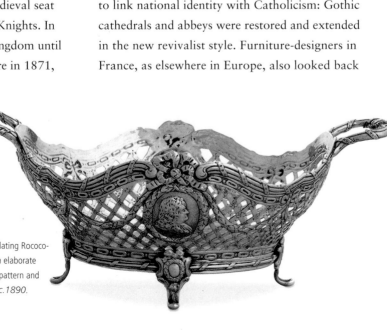

CHÂTEAU DE GROUSSAY This French castle was completed in 1825. The rich, dark interior decor of the library, its heavy furnishings, and its eclectic, lavish display of ornaments and pictures are typical of the 19th century.

to the Renaissance, making large, architectural pieces with deep-carved decoration. They also returned to the Baroque styles of Louis XIV's reign, combined with forms and motifs from the Rococo designs of Louis XV's and the Classical styles of Louis XVI's reigns. These influences were seen elsewhere in Europe and the United States and led to increasing clutter: walls were hung with layers of tapestries or numerous paintings; chairs and sofas were richly upholstered and button-backed; rooms were crammed with palms and other exotic plants; and bibelots or knickknacks were placed on tables, sideboards, and mantelpieces.

The increase in nationalism also brought about a renewed interest in folk motifs and crafts, depicting people in traditional dress or engaged in rural pastimes. Ceramicists revived the rustic folk designs of faience of the late 17th and early 18th centuries. The decorative arts of the East continued to influence Western designers. Chinese and Japanese ceramics and furniture, Middle Eastern motifs from Persian carpets, Iznik pottery from Turkey, and ancient Egypt were all inspirations. A final revival took place in the United States, where furniture-makers returned to the colonial styles that had been popular in the 18th century.

TRIPOD TABLE Made of papier-mâché and decorated with mother-of-pearl, the central panel on the tabletop is painted with a mountainous landscape. c.1860. H: 26 in (65 cm).

ELEMENTS OF STYLE

A FLURRY OF REVIVAL STYLES dominated 19th-century decorative arts. Designers focused on demonstrating their expertise, sometimes at the expense of decorative cohesion, which resulted in a mix of wildly disparate styles on the same piece. A mania for accumulating and displaying collections of scientific specimens and ornamental trinkets was reflected in a generally cluttered and varied style of interior decoration. Advances in manufacturing technology and the aspirations of the rapidly growing middle class fueled an unprecedented demand for decorative arts and furniture.

FRENCH PORCELAIN VASE
EXCESSIVE ORNAMENT
Eager to show off their technical virtuosity, craftsmen cluttered their wares with a wealth of decorative techniques. Ceramics, furniture, and glassware groaned under the weight of enameling, gilding, and all manner of intricate applied ornament, often obscuring the basic form of the piece.

SILVER GILT GRAPE SCISSORS
REPRESENTATIONALISM
The 19th-century obsession with natural science had a huge impact on the decorative arts. The study of botany and zoology was boosted by new discoveries in far-flung countries. Depictions of animal and plant life became less stylized and more realistic than ever before in a bid to replicate faithfully even the smallest details.

ENGLISH DINING CHAIR
GOTHIC
Especially prevalent in Britain, the Gothic Revival was a romanticized reworking of the great church architecture of the Middle Ages. Designers used architectural features such as pointed arches, trefoils, tracery, and pinnacles on heavy-set oak furniture. Stained glass also enjoyed a revival.

PENWORK SIDE CABINET
NEW TECHNIQUES
Penwork was often applied to furniture that had been covered with faux lacquer, or japanned. The decoration was applied in white shellac, and detail and shading were added with a quill pen. Papier-mâché was used to make everything from trays to furniture. Items were painted black or lacquered, then decorated with paint, gilding, and inlays, including mother-of-pearl and shell.

ENGLISH ROCOCO REVIVAL VASE
ROCOCO REVIVAL
Alongside the influence of archaic Gothic, Classical, and Renaissance forms, this period also saw renewed interest in 18th-century French design. New technologies paved the way for more economic reproductions of the curled scrolls and intricate foliate applications associated with high Rococo style.

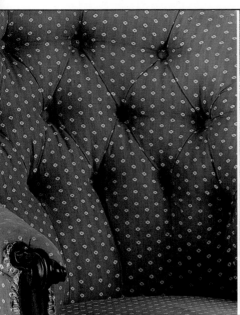

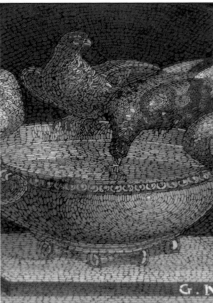

BUTTON-UPHOLSTERED ARMCHAIR
BUTTONED UPHOLSTERY
Chesterfield sofas and club chairs, with their stuffed and buttoned leather upholstery, became fixtures of exclusive establishments in the 19th century. The increasing importance of comfort prompted upholsterers to use luxurious fabrics such as velvet and damask in the same way.

MICROMOSAIC SNUFF BOX
REDISCOVERING OLD TECHNIQUES
The rise of nationalism came with a nostalgia for old techniques. Micromosaic—using miniature colored glass cubes to build up intricate images—became popular for decorating furniture and jewelry. Glassmakers also replicated historic glass from ancient Venetian soda glass to medieval German glass.

GRAMMAR OF ORNAMENT ELIZABETHAN DESIGN
PATTERN BOOKS
The development of color printing allowed pattern books to bring historical and modern styles to design studios and factories. As a result, common themes such as Japan, the Celts, and botany developed. The most influential pattern book was Owen Jones's *Grammar of Ornament* (1856).

RENAISSANCE REVIVAL TABLE
RENAISSANCE REVIVAL
The 16th-century flowering of Italian art and science was first called the Renaissance by 19th-century scholars. Designers began to incorporate details such as caryatid pillars and broken arch pediments into their work as an homage to Renaissance art and architecture.

HUNGARIAN MOON FLASK
INFLUENCE OF JAPAN
Sir Rutherford Alcock's display at the 1862 London International Exhibition was the first major public showcase of Japanese decorative arts. It sparked a wave of interest in Japanese forms, techniques, and motifs that transformed every sphere of European and North American decorative arts, from ceramic glazes to furniture design.

APPLIQUÉ QUILT
HANDCRAFTS
Even in the age of industrialization, traditional handcrafting techniques continued to flourish. Examples ranged from Italian master craftsmen producing micromosaic furniture to American homesteaders sewing appliqué textiles. The support of social reformers such as John Ruskin eventually burgeoned into an entire movement in the later half of the 19th century.

WESTERN PERSIAN RUG
ORIENTAL INFLUENCE
The decorative arts of Asia continued to exert an important influence on Western designers. As well as Chinese and Japanese ceramics and furniture, 19th-century designers were inspired by Middle Eastern motifs seen on artifacts like Persian carpets, Iznik pottery, and the art of ancient Egypt.

QUIMPER FAN VASE
FOLK REVIVAL
An increase in nationalistic feeling in many countries brought about a renewed interest in folk motifs and crafts. Depictions of figures in traditional dress or engaged in customary pastimes became more widespread. Vernacular traditions were practiced by cottage industries and also appropriated by industrial manufacturers.

FURNITURE

FROM THE MID-19TH CENTURY, FURNITURE-MAKERS INCREASINGLY SOUGHT
INSPIRATION FROM THE PAST, WHILE THE MECHANIZATION OF MANY
PROCESSES INTRODUCED PRODUCTION ON A SCALE NEVER SEEN BEFORE.

ITALIAN COURT CUPBOARD Made in walnut, in the Renaissance Revival style, this cupboard has deeply carved animal-paw feet and corner pilasters incorporating Classical figures and lions. *c.1850. H:80¾ in (205 cm).*

AN AGE OF REVIVALS

The air of nationalism that swept across Europe during this era provoked furniture-makers—in Italy and Germany, in particular—to look back to the former glories of furniture design. The highly skilled craftsmen of the Renaissance era were their main reference.

RENAISSANCE REVIVAL

Originating in 14th-century Italy, the Renaissance style had been inspired by the architecture of ancient Greece and Rome. The 19th-century interpretations of the style included large-scale, heavy, architectural pieces laden with deep-carved panels and friezes. Center tables were of simple construction, with well-proportioned tops raised on legs joined by stretchers. The settle returned as a form, often with galleried backs or arms incorporating rows of fine spindles, and sometimes raised on short, spiral-turned legs. Renaissance-style court cupboards, with various arrangements of small drawers, niches, and cupboards, were also popular. Broken pediments, molded cornices, arched doors, and pilasters—all features taken from Classical architecture—were common on such pieces.

Woods of choice were dark, predominantly oak and walnut, both of which lent themselves well to the prolific, deep carving that epitomized the style. Motifs were also inspired by the Classical world

The decoration includes harpies, which were monsters with wings and claws but the head and breasts of a woman

GERMAN ARMCHAIR An upholstered leather seat and back are stuffed-over within an oak and walnut frame incorporating bulbous, turned supports and richly carved figures and scrolls. *1890s. H:54¾ in (139 cm).*

FRENCH TABLE Elaborately carved in the Renaissance Revival style, this walnut table features dense figural and foliate imagery in the frieze, feet, and stretcher. This is further enriched with pairs of banded columns, two human figures, and six winged harpies from Classical mythology. *c.1870. L:43¼ in (110 cm).*

Dense foliate carving within a scrolling form on a claw foot

and included cherubs, grotesques, and semi-nude figures. In Italy there was a fashion for using blackamoors, which had been popular in the 1700s. In Germany, Renaissance Revival pieces often featured elaborate porcelain mounts set into an ebony-veneered or black-painted ground. The finest examples were produced by Meissen and handpainted with Classically inspired or folk scenes taken from 17th-century paintings.

The Renaissance style was also adopted in France, where it was referred to as the Henri II style, and in the United States following the Civil War.

ROCOCO REVIVAL

Having originally developed in France during the first half of the 18th century, Rococo produced furniture with asymmetrical, curvaceous lines and richly ornamented with naturalistic motifs—shells, rockwork, and elaborate scrolls—as well as gilt-metal mounts, porcelain plaques, and intricate floral marquetry. Furniture-makers operating within the Rococo Revival framework produced furniture that was altogether more feminine than that made under the Renaissance Revival banner.

As well as the return of the Louis XV *fauteuil*—with its shaped back, upholstered seat and arms, and serpentine crest and seat rails—this period saw new Rococo-inspired forms in the balloon-back chair and the conversation seat, a sofa with a number of "sections," in which groups of people could talk almost facing each other. Buffets and sideboards had arched tops, asymmetrically carved fielded panels, and shaped aprons.

New techniques introduced innovative materials in laminated and bent woods. The mechanization of a number of processes meant that veneer cutting, carving, and the making of gilt-metal mounts could all be achieved at a fraction of the cost of the previous century. The Rococo style was therefore no longer a style for the wealthy few, but one that was also available to the aspiring middle class.

INTERPRETATIONS OF ROCOCO

The Rococo Revival style found particular favor in Italy, where slightly larger interpretations of the original version were prominent. Richly carved, often heavily gilt pieces included side tables with pierced and scrolled aprons and marble tops. In Britain, a more restrained version emerged, with elaborate decoration in the structure of a piece rather than applied to the surface.

The refurbishment of Palais Lichtenstein in Vienna, by Michael Thonet and Peter Hubert Desvignes between 1837 and 1849, exemplified the style in Austria. In the United States, where serpentine forms began to replace the heavy geometric pieces of the Empire style, John Henry Belter's laminate veneers provided the ideal medium for the florid designs that found favor.

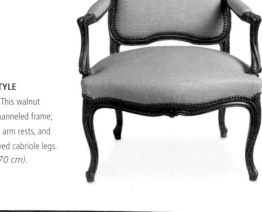

LOUIS XV-STYLE FAUTEUIL This walnut chair has a channeled frame; padded back, arm rests, and seat; and carved cabriole legs. *W:27½ in (70 cm).*

FRENCH VITRINE The Rococo Revival form of this vitrine includes cabriole legs, a serpentine pediment and apron, floral and foliate cresting, gilt-metal mounts, and the romantic *vernis Martin* painting. *1870s. H:73½ in (187 cm).*

LOUIS XV-STYLE BOW-FRONT COMMODE Veneered with palisander wood, rosewood, and violet wood, this commode is decorated with floral marquetry and metal mounts and has a marble top. *W:51½ in (131 cm).*

JOHN HENRY BELTER

A German immigrant who went to the United States in 1833, John Henry Belter had been trained in the art of woodcarving. While in the United States, Belter began experimenting with thin sheets of wood, which he used to make laminate panels. His technique involved gluing one sheet to the next, each time with the grain perpendicular to that of the sheet below. With eight, sometimes 16, sheets of laminate in a single board, the result was a very strong yet pliable material. Belter made furniture from his product in the fashionable Rococo style, using predominantly rosewood, but also oak and mahogany. The nature of the wood enabled Belter to make pieces with intricately carved and pierced ornament incorporating naturalistic flower and vine motifs. He also bent the boards under steam to produce panels with dramatic curves, and these subsequently became a hallmark of his style.

GILTWOOD CONSOLE TABLE The serpentine marble top of this Rococo Revival table is raised on a fluted, scrolling frame. *c.1860. W:48 in (122 cm).*

AMERICAN SOFA The Rococo Revival rosewood frame of this Belter sofa is raised on cabriole legs and incorporates serpentine cresting and seat rails with finely carved floral and foliate motifs. *1850s. W:62 in (157.5 cm).*

BATTLE OF THE STYLES

The neo-Gothic style that emerged in the 1830s was not a true representation of original medieval Gothic, but rather a pastiche of it. This is true, to some extent, of all the various interpretations of neo-Gothic style in Europe at the time: the work of Pierre Cuypers in the Low Countries; the French Gothic Troubadour, or "cathedral," style of the 1830s and 1840s; and the American interpretation in the second half of the 19th century. All of these styles saw the widespread use of architectural motifs—pointed arches, trefoils, and latticework on otherwise-contemporary forms, typically carved from dark, solid wood such as oak. The style was predominantly masculine in appearance.

As the style developed, however, one exponent in particular was responsible for a movement toward a more accurate rendition of Gothic furniture. A. W. N. Pugin was commissioned to provide furnishings for the refurbishment of the Houses of Parliament in London in the mid-1830s. His designs for furniture were based on existing medieval pieces, and he paid considerable attention to the methods of construction that had been used. This quite often meant that pieces reflected the exposed construction of joints, for example—a concept that was embraced by Arts and Crafts furniture-makers toward the end of the century.

NEOCLASSICAL REVIVAL

The second half of the 1800s brought renewed interest in Neoclassicism. In France, Napoleon III was a driving force behind the style, which advocated a return to the designs of Louis XIV's reign, perhaps combined with forms and motifs from the Classical revivals of Louis XVI's reign. Woods of choice tended to be dark—mahogany and ebony—which contrasted well with the decorative details in gilt-bronze and ivory and mother-of-pearl inlays that were fashionable, as well as new materials such as cast iron and papier-mâché. The revival of Boulle marquetry became a hallmark of this era.

Britain and the Low Countries saw a return to the designs of Adam, Hepplewhite, Sheraton, and Chippendale during the 1870s. Furniture-makers had a host of pattern books at their disposal and were successful in making exceptional copies of a number of pieces. Furniture tended to be small-scale, often made from satinwood, with slim, tapering legs, metal mounts, and stringing made from contrasting wood. Pieces might be decorated

ENGLISH CABINET The perpendicular Gothic Revival form of this cabinet is accentuated by parcel-gilt and brass Gothic tracery, including cusps and foils. *c.1870. H:84 in (213.5 cm).*

Bands of Gothic quatrefoil motifs are repeated up the facade

The multifoil tracery with plain cusping is framed by the lozenge shapes

Tudor flower finials augment brattishing or ornamental crestings of similar form

ENGLISH DINING CHAIR The Gothic Revival pitch-pine frame of this "king" carver (one of six) has a floral quatrefoil beneath foliate trefoil carvings on a back with brattishing details. *c.1880. H:55½ in (141 cm).*

OAK ENGLISH HALLSTAND This Gothic Revival hallstand has an angular pediment with stylized floral cutouts, butterfly fretwork, and a row of tiles by Christopher Dresser. *c.1880. H:97 in (246 cm).*

with fine marquetry panels or Wedgwood plaques featuring typical Classical motifs: fans, acanthus leaves, and the ubiquitous urns.

The Biedermeier style that developed in Germany and Austria in the early 1800s continued to be popular for much of the 19th century, both there and in Scandinavia, with pieces featuring architectural elements such as columns and pediments—the only ornament on mostly rectilinear forms—with richly figured veneered surfaces.

COLONIAL REVIVAL

In the United States, from the late 1870s, a number of furniture-makers returned to furniture styles that had been popular in the 18th century.

Dubbed Colonial Revival, the style reintroduced forms such as the gate-leg table. Dominant forms included large buffets and sideboards for dining rooms—the former a two-tiered piece for displaying all manner of household crockery; the latter used for storing cutlery and wine, perhaps even as a side table for serving food. Buffets tended to be rectangular and architectural in shape, usually made

from oak or mahogany and decorated in low relief with Classical motifs such as pilasters, urns, and laurel swags. The Sheraton-style sideboard was also a popular form—*demi-lune* in shape, and with slim, tapering legs. Hardware remained simple—typically brass plates with ring pulls.

A number of chair styles returned, including the archetypal "Chippendale" chair, Adam-style chairs, the shieldback, and the chaise longue. Ornament was spare, furniture-makers preferring to rely on the grain of the wood for visual interest. Where motifs did feature, they were subtle renditions of Neoclassical examples and included geometric inlay, parquetry panels, marquetry medallions, and paterae.

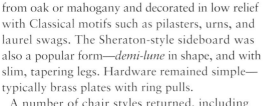

CHARLES LOCKE EASTLAKE

In 1868 the English architect Charles Locke Eastlake published a work entitled *Hints on Household Taste in Furniture, Upholstery and Other Details*, in which designs for furniture included a number with Gothic-inspired examples. Eastlake pioneered the use of authentic materials and methods of construction in representing the Gothic style, but the style that developed as a result of his publication was not truly representative of Gothic forms. Instead, pieces were made with ornate materials, including ebonized cherrywood, and incorporated motifs from a wide range of sources, such as Moorish and Arabic.

HOUSES OF PARLIAMENT, LONDON
The New Palace of Westminster was built between 1840 and 1850. It is the seat of the British government and the finest expression of the 19th-century Gothic Revival "national style."

The turned, tapered legs
are typical of the Sheraton Revival style

SHERATON REVIVAL SATINWOOD CHAIR Painted all over with flowers and leaves, this chair bears an ivorine plaque for Edwards & Roberts of London.

The top features a plum-pudding veneer

LOUIS XVI–STYLE MAHOGANY TABLE Designed by Henri Dasson, this table has fluted, octagonal legs with cast mounts. *H:28¼ in (72 cm).*

AMERICAN CHIFFONIER The marble-topped walnut carcass, doors, and drawer-fronts of this chiffonier in the Eastlake Style are carved in shallow relief with floral and foliate motifs. *c.1880. H:81¾ in (207.5 cm).*

FURNITURE GALLERY

In the Age of Excess, a period of revivals and extremes, Rococo, Gothic, Neoclassical, and Renaissance design elements were mixed together without restraint, resulting in heavily ornamented pieces of furniture. Decoration was exaggerated and taken to extremes, with large metal mounts and twisted columns. This was also an era that relished comfort, so upholstered furniture was popular, especially overstuffed and button-backed chairs and sofas.

2 Breakfront armoire

3 Louis XV-style cabinet

1 Miniature mahogany cabinet

4 Marquetry commode

5 Ebonized credenza

6 Rosewood tea table

7 Walnut whatnot

8 Ebonized settee

supports. W:26¼ in (67 cm). ② **8.** Ebonized settee with buttoned upholstery. W:62½ in (156 cm).
② **9.** Mahogany-framed easy armchair with a buttoned and upholstered back above molded
supports. ② **10.** One of a pair of mahogany library chairs with a padded and upholstered back.
⑦ **11.** Walnut-framed gentleman's easy chair, with a leather buttoned back and seat. ③ **12.** One
of a set of eight oak dining chairs, with foliate carved top rails above and leather overstuffed seat.
③ **13.** One of a set of six walnut balloon-back dining chairs with pierced scroll spars on cabriole
legs. ① **14.** Walnut and tapestry upholstered prie-dieu, the back flanked by twist columns. H:39 in
(99 cm). ① **15.** Carved walnut nursing chair on cabriole legs. ① **16.** Louis XV-style beech open
armchair, with shieldback and padded woodwork seat, back, and armrests. W:24½ in (62 cm). ①

11 Walnut-framed easy chair

10 Mahogany library chair

9 Mahogany-framed armchair

12 Oak dining chair

13 Walnut balloon-back dining chair

14 Walnut prie-dieu

15 Walnut nursing chair

16 Beech open armchair

CERAMICS

TRADITIONAL POTTERY STYLES OF THE PAST ENJOYED A REVIVAL IN THE
LATE 19TH CENTURY, FINDING FAVOR WITH A MIDDLE CLASS LOOKING
FOR DECORATIVE ITEMS WITH WHICH TO FURNISH THE HOME.

FOLK CERAMIC REVIVAL

Looking back to previous eras for inspiration, European ceramicists revived the vibrant, rustic folk designs of tin-glazed earthenware pottery typical of the late 17th and early 18th centuries. Known as faience in France and Germany, and as maiolica in Italy and Spain, such pieces had been made with tin oxide added to the glaze, which gave a characteristic opaque-white finish.

REPLICATING THE STYLE

Bearing in mind the shapes and styles of the originals that they sought to copy, late 19th-century designers produced pieces that were painted in strong colors derived from natural pigments—yellow, green, orange, purple, and blue. Decorative designs ranged from small-scale repeats of delicate leaves and flowers, to Rococo-style scrolling floral patterns. Animal and bird motifs were also popular, especially domestic fowl, and a number of pieces depicted romantic rural scenes featuring figures in local costume.

REVIVING FAIENCE

In France the earlier works of Nevers, Rouen, and Moustiers were reinterpreted at factories such as Quimper and Desvres. The former had a long-established history of producing traditional-style faience and, from the late 1800s became renowned for pieces depicting local flora and fauna and decorative figures in customary Breton clothing—typically baggy pantaloons and high lace collars.

QUIMPER FAN VASE Decorated in a naive style with a lady and a gentleman in traditional clothing, this fan-shaped vase is marked "Alfred Pourquier." c.1875. H:4¾ in (12 cm).

The wares emerging from Desvres had a characteristic creamy-white background. Designs were applied in the Rouen style, using a vibrant palette of Delft blue, yellow, red, and sage green.

Exotic flowers, birds, and figures recall 18th-century imagery

Rope moldings are painted in a floral palette of yellow, blue, manganese, and green

NEVERS POTTERY URN This polychrome earthenware urn is decorated with architectural ruins. The tap is in the form of a lion's head. H:21¾ in (55 cm).

FRENCH WINE COOLER One of a pair, this cooler is in a Classical Revival form. Its exotic floral and figural polychrome decoration recalls Moustier's earthenware designs of the late 1700s. c.1870. W:12¼ in (31 cm).

The 18th-century faience pieces produced in Nuremburg, Magdeburg, and Schrezheim were among the principal sources of inspiration for German potters in the Revival era. In German faience, designs were rendered in more subtle colors than those of France, and fairy tales were popular themes for decoration.

MAIOLICA'S COMEBACK

At the Cantagalli factory in Italy, pottery-makers were inspired by the maiolica traditions of 14th-, 15th-, and 16th-century Spain and Italy. Among the pieces produced were a number that copied the style of Renaissance della Robbia

ware. High-relief models of fruit and foliage were a common feature of such designs. Copies of the early 16th-century Istoriato style were also popular. In these pieces, most often decorative plates or chargers, a central design represented a Biblical, mythical, or allegorical story.

In Portugal, the Caldas da Rainha, a major producer of tin-glazed earthenware, was inspired by the 16th-century French Huguenot glass-painter and potter Bernard Palissy, whose pottery often featured motifs from nature, including snails, foliage, and lizards, in high relief.

TRADITIONAL SHAPES

Nineteenth-century ceramicists looked to the past for more than just techniques and decorative ideas. They were also instrumental in reviving pottery shapes that had been popular in earlier times.

These tended to be simple and peasantlike, especially since they were mostly designed for utilitarian rather than decorative

purposes. Among the most common were pear-shaped jugs, baluster-shaped vases, simple bowls, and, specific to Germany, the traditional beer tankard. Plates were popular for decoration, the edge providing an ideal opportunity for a delicate floral border or for high-relief ornamentation.

Apothecary jars were also in great demand. Largely unchanged since the 16th century, apothecary jars came in two shapes: straight-sided *albarelli* for dry medicines, and more bulbous forms with spouts for wet drugs.

In a bid to satisfy the demands and tastes of a growing market, a number of new forms emerged, such as fan-shaped and asymmetrical vases. Other popular forms included candlesticks, ink stands, figures, and jardinières.

ROCOCO-STYLE ITALIAN MAIOLICA VASE This molded vase is decorated with a gentleman and a lady on a country walk. It is marked with a crowned "M." *Late 19th century. W:10 in (25 cm).*

GERMAN TANKARD Made at the Mettlach factory, this tankard has a pewter-mounted stoneware body. The handle is relief-molded with leaf forms and a dwarf's head thumb rest. *c.1880. H:7½ in (19 cm).*

MAJOLICA

Minton's majolica was first seen at London's Great Exhibition of 1851. Developed by Frenchman Leon Arnoux, majolica took inspiration from early faience pieces, and is particularly associated with strong sculpted forms and thick glazes in bright colors. Arnoux was influenced by the work of Palissy, and

early pieces were in the Renaissance style, although more contemporary styles also developed, including those inspired by Chinese, Japanese, and Islamic motifs and forms. Typical themes reflected an interest in horticulture and the countryside, while popular forms included jardinières, umbrella stands, garden seats, pie dishes, and tureens. Majolica became extremely popular in Britain following the Great Exhibition and subsequently in Europe and the United States. By 1860 there were more than 30 major majolica manufacturers throughout the world.

MINTON MAJOLICA HERON Modeled by French sculptor Paul Comolera, this piece displays the highly naturalistic style for which he was known. *1876. H:39½ in (100 cm).*

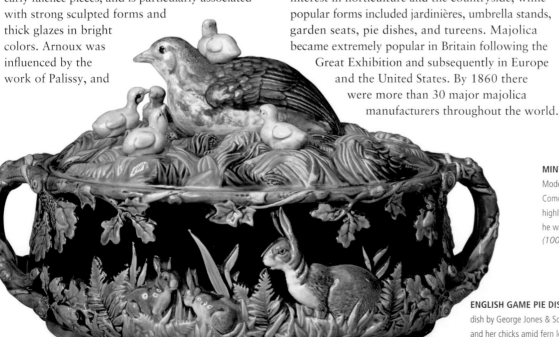

ENGLISH GAME PIE DISH The cover of this pie dish by George Jones & Sons features a woodcock and her chicks amid fern leaves; the sides are decorated with rabbits. *1873. D:14¼ in (36 cm).*

ENGLISH CERAMICS

In the course of the 19th century, several favorable circumstances conspired to make England one of the largest and most renowned pottery-producing centers in the world. England was well placed to earn such a reputation. The Industrial Revolution had brought mass production on a scale never seen before; a healthy social climate provided a growing middle class hungry for the latest fashions, whether in tableware or colorful ornamental figures; and Britain benefited from an expanding empire looking for goods to import in considerable quantities.

STAFFORDSHIRE POTTERIES

Leading England's pottery production on a large scale was the county of Staffordshire. The "Staffordshire potteries" were originally based in and around the six towns—Tunstall, Burslem, Hanley, Stoke, Fenton, and Longton—collectively known as Stoke-on-Trent.

The area owed its success to a number of factors. Primarily, the land was rich in raw materials for the production of pottery—clay for modeling, salt and lead for glazing, and coal for firing

the kilns. As a result of this natural wealth, the area could already boast several well-established, reputable potteries with leading figures at the helm, including Minton, Wedgwood, and Spode.

Already pioneers in the field, the larger companies were ready to embrace industrialization and adapted quickly to mass production. Their switch to mechanization received a further boost in terms of staffing: because of the Industrial Revolution, large numbers of agricultural laborers from the surrounding countryside were looking for new employment in the towns.

The final element that contributed to the Staffordshire potteries' prominence in the ceramics industry was that the area had a reliable transport system in place—a network of canals and the ports of Hull and Liverpool, which guaranteed the swift and widespread exportation of goods to the rest of the world.

BATTLE BETWEEN A BUFFALO AND A TIGER The transfer-printed underglaze blue pattern is from Spode's Indian Sporting series. This was inspired by Samuel Howitt's illustrations in Captain Thomas Williamson's early-19th-century publication *Oriental Field Sports*. c.1830. L:9¼ in (23.5 cm).

TRANSFER-PRINTED DISH Made by Ralph and James Clews of Cobridge, Staffordshire, this dish features a transfer-printed underglaze blue Romantic Ruins pattern set within a floral border. It portrays Don Quixote– and Sancho Panza–like figures in front of Classical ruins. 1820–30. L:11 in (28 cm).

BLUE-AND-WHITE POTTERY

Particularly successful were the blue-and-white wares mass-produced in Staffordshire using transfer-printing methods developed from the mid-18th century. The middle classes demanded dinner services in the latest styles, and a fascination with Britain's expanding empire promoted designs featuring Classical, mythical, and topographical scenes. Motifs from China and India were also popular, as were those depicting royal events such as the wedding of Queen Victoria to Prince Albert in 1840, and her various jubilees.

A good number of pieces exported to the United States bore designs specifically suited to that market—for example, the Beauties of America series, which featured notable American landmarks. In 1891 the American McKinley Tariff Act saw the introduction of country of origin appearing on wares for exportation, which helps with dating particular pieces today.

STAFFORDSHIRE FIGURES

Since the late 1700s, Staffordshire potters had been emulating the porcelain figures produced by factories such as Bow, Derby, and Chelsea. As the 19th century

TRANSFER-PRINTED PITCHER The Landing of General Lafayette at Castle Garden, New York, is one James & Ralph Clew's patterns intended for export to North America. c.1825. H:17 in (43 cm).

TRANSFER-PRINTED TUREEN The Cambridge College, Massachusetts, pattern is from the Beauties of America series made for export by John and William Ridgway. 1820s. W:15¼ in (39 cm).

TRANSFER-PRINTED PLATE Part of a series of 13 for export to North America, this Thomas Mayer plate has a pattern called Arms of New York. 1825–30. D:10 in (25.5 cm).

progressed, they started to create their own designs, which could be mass-produced at a fraction of the cost of the earlier figures. The factories made them in vast quantities and in all manner of styles, satisfying the demands and eclectic tastes of their ever-growing market.

These pottery figures tended to be flat-backed, so that they could be displayed with pride on a mantelpiece, and portrayed anything and everything—from domestic animals and pets, such as that perennial favorite, the King Charles spaniel, to portraits of contemporary figures. There was a fashion for renditions of famous people—leading politicians, sports figures, military heroes, and royalty—as well as a huge interest in everyday figures, including soldiers, sailors, courting couples, and country folk in regional costume.

Initially, the figures were relatively well molded, colorfully painted, and very decorative. Toward the end of the 19th century, however, as demand grew and figures were also made for the working classes, quality tended to deteriorate.

Flowering trees, or bocage, are a feature of many Staffordshire figures

FIGURAL GROUP Set under bocage, this polychrome-painted pearl ware composition of a performer, tethered bear, and lion displays in the latter a naivety of form characteristic of earlier Staffordshire figures. c.1830. H:9 in (23 cm).

THE RAILWAY CHILDREN These spill-holders portray figures dressed in fantasy tartans and sitting above stylized trains. They are mementos of the surge in tourism to Scotland in the second half of the 1800s. c.1860. H:9½ in (24 cm).

STAFFORDSHIRE HEARTH SPANIELS Also known as "comforters" because of the sense of companionship they provided their owners, this pair may have been inspired by Queen Victoria's pet King Charles Spaniel, Dash. c.1860. H:16¼ in (41 cm).

AMERICAN CERAMICS

In the early 1800s the introduction of post-Revolutionary tariffs made it easier for American ceramics to compete with foreign wares. The industry began growing rapidly, but vast quantities of ceramics were still imported to keep up with American needs, especially in the first half of the 19th century. Spatter ware, with sponge-decorated borders, and mocha ware, decorated using liquid clay called slip to resemble mocha stone or moss agate, were two of the most popular products that Staffordshire made for the American market.

RED WARE

One of the earliest American ceramics was red ware, a form of earthenware made from widely available red clay. During the 18th and 19th centuries in the US, this was used for everything from mugs and dishes to chamberpots. Red ware pieces are frequently decorated with creamy-colored slip, applied like icing. Curly designs and wavy lines were the most popular form of decoration. Some potters produced pieces with names and dates or uplifting messages written in slip, like "Temperance, Health, Wealth" or "A Good Pie." The Pennsylvania Dutch community was renowned for its slip-decorated red ware.

ROCKINGHAM-STYLE POTTERY

American ceramics manufacturers made a wide variety of mottled brown, glazed earthenware throughout the 1800s. Usually called Rockingham ware after the English ceramics manufacturer that developed it, this glaze was used mainly for everyday items such as teapots and baking dishes, but also for ornamental pieces such as Toby jugs of famous Americans. Though Rockingham ware was made across the country, the Norton & Fenton factory in Bennington, Vermont, was usually associated with its production. In 1849 Norton & Fenton patented flint enamel glaze, a streaked yellow, orange, blue, or brown version of Rockingham glaze.

STONEWARE

Nonporous stoneware was ideal for jugs, crocks, jars, and other storage vessels for homes and businesses such as breweries. It had been made in North America since colonial times, but production

PENNSYLVANIA RED WARE LOAF DISH This rectangular dish is decorated with trailed yellow slip in the form of a series of waves. *W:18 in (45.5 cm).*

CANADIAN RED WARE JUG This Ontario jug has a slightly bulbous form and is covered with a mottled dark red glaze. *c.1875. H:9¾ in (25 cm).*

PENNSYLVANIA STONEWARE HARVEST JUG
Decorated with overall floral patterns in blue on an off-white ground, this jug is impressed "George Renerbel." *H:12 in (30.5 cm).*

SPATTER WARE BOWL AND PITCHER The polychrome stripe-pattern spatter decoration is applied to white earthenware forms copied from mid-18th-century Rococo silverware. *c.1850. Pitcher: H:13 in (33 cm).*

increased dramatically after the Revolution. This hard ceramic was glazed by throwing salt into the kiln. Stoneware was typically decorated with naive cobalt-blue motifs, including birds, flowers, and grapes. Handmade stoneware pieces are sometimes stamped with the maker's name and town.

CHALKWARE

Many rural homes in 18th- and 19th-century America were brightened up by chalkware ornaments, usually in the shape of an animal. Pieces were sold for pennies at fairs and peddled door to door. Made from molded, air-dried plaster of Paris rather than fired pottery or porcelain, they were hand-decorated with dashes of oil paint or watercolor, and their name derives from their matte chalky appearance. Chalkware ornaments from the 19th century often imitated pricier Staffordshire dogs or farmyard groups prized by wealthier Americans.

AMERICAN BELLEEK

In the second half of the 1800s many Americans admired the decorative porcelain designed by the Irish Belleek factory. This firm specialized in eggshell-thin ceramics that looked like shells or woven baskets decorated with lifelike flowerheads.

A number of American ceramic firms such as Ott & Brewer and Ceramic Art Company began producing their own American Belleek pieces in response to demand. In fact, these delicate ceramics were so popular that some firms even

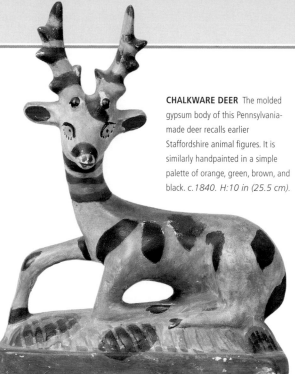

CHALKWARE DEER The molded gypsum body of this Pennsylvania-made deer recalls earlier Staffordshire animal figures. It is similarly handpainted in a simple palette of orange, green, brown, and black. c.1840. H:10 in (25.5 cm).

FLINT-ENAMEL LION Essentially a Classical composition, this lion was made in Bennington, modeled with tiny parings simulating the mane, and decorated with a mottled brown-blue flint-enamel finish. c.1840. H:10 in (25.5 cm).

incorporated the name "Belleek" into their trademark or replicated Belleek's designs. Knowles, Taylor & Knowles produced a notable range of American Belleek, called Lotusware, predominantly in cream or white, just like Irish Belleek. This range was often molded into forms that resembled real leaves, or decorated with raised flowers and beaded ornament. Others were pierced to imitate basketwork. Many Lotusware pieces had a touch of gilding to highlight their naturalistic shapes and relief decoration.

JOHN BENNETT

Originally trained as a ceramics decorator at Coalport, the British porcelain factory celebrated for its tableware, John Bennett emigrated to New York in the 1870s. Here he taught porcelain decoration at his Lexington Avenue studio. Painting decoration on blank porcelain was a fashionable hobby for ladies at the time. They tended to paint realistic fruits and floral designs. Bennett's own work, generally painted on Oriental-shaped vases, often features blossoming branches. Though relatively naturalistic, his simplified motifs show a Japanese influence and can be associated with the Aesthetic Movement that had such an effect on late 19th-century British and American design.

COVERED JAR This Bennett Jar's ovoid form and cover are handpainted with red roses and branches of yellow dogwood, strongly contrasted against a black ground. 1881. H:15¼ in (39 cm).

GOURD-SHAPED PITCHER Made by Ott & Brewer in exceptionally delicate Belleek-style porcelain, this pitcher features alternate panels handpainted with blossoms in pink and gold, and has a gilded water-lily handle. c.1880. H:9 in (23 cm).

LOTUSWARE VASE Raised on gilded ball feet and handpainted with delicate polychrome flowers, this Belleek-style porcelain vase was made by Knowles, Taylor & Knowles of Liverpool, Ohio. c.1890. H:7¾ in (20 cm).

PAIR OF COMFORTS Imported as white blanks from England, this pair of comforts are handpainted by Bennett with a parrot and a parakeet, in a style that was fashionable at the time. c.1880. H:8¾ in (22.5 cm).

MEISSEN

The first European factory to create hard-paste porcelain, Meissen had fallen on hard times when Heinrich Gottlieb Kühn became director in 1833. Lucrative export markets had declined, and the economic situation in Saxony was dire. In an effort to rekindle Meissen's fortunes, Kühn focused on modernizing production techniques and developing new colors.

Ernst August Leuteritz, Meissen's head modeler between 1849 and 1886, was responsible for the factory's finest work. The success of his tenure was favored by the fact that a prosperous business class was emerging. These wealthy industrialists and merchants were competing in the style stakes with the old aristocracy and wanted to furnish their homes in a similar fashion. Leuteritz reintroduced porcelain figurines in the Rococo style based on 18th-century models by Johann J. Kändler and Peter Reinicke. Neoclassical figures were also put back into production. In response to consumer demand, Meissen ceramics of the mid-19th century became the most flamboyant ever produced by the firm.

LAVISH DECORATION

At the Great London Exhibition of 1862, the French firm of Sèvres displayed wares decorated with layers of slip clay. At the same exhibition, Worcester exhibited porcelain painted in the style of Limoges enamel work. Both techniques catered to the public demand for lavish decoration, and Meissen was quick to follow suit.

Having recently moved to new, custom-built premises with larger kilns, the company was able to produce greater quantities of ceramics at a

CROSSED-SWORDS MARK Meissen's crossed-swords mark was frequently copied by unscrupulous manufacturers.

MEISSEN STAND AT THE 1851 GREAT EXHIBITION IN LONDON Like other leading manufacturers of the decorative arts, Meissen exhibited specially made pieces at the large trade exhibitions held in Europe and the United States. The pieces shown were larger and more spectacular versions of their normal range of ceramics.

The spout is shaped like a seashell and has a gilded lip

The main handle resembles ribbons and vines, grasped at one end by a cherub

Neptune, the sea god, watches over his watery domain

Sailing ships, mermaids, and jumping horses decorate the body of the jug

PORCELAIN WATER JUG One of a series of Rococo Revival jugs on the theme of the four elements, this jug is glazed, gilded, and painted, and shows Meissen's mastery of scrolling forms and applied detail. The handle and base of the jug are molded to look like seaweed. c.1850. H:25½ in (65 cm).

The base is almost bell-like

Applied dolphins convey a sense of movement typical of the Rococo Revival style

better quality than ever before. The *Schneeballen* (snowball) technique, involving the application of dozens of tiny flowers, was particularly well suited to Meissen's new production methods. First developed in the mid-18th century, the *Schneeballen* technique enjoyed a large-scale revival and was widely imitated. Leuteritz also devised theatrical new motifs such as handles in the form of snakes. Gilding became more lavish, and the range of colors available to Meissen's painters was expanded. As the 19th century progressed, Meissen carved out a successful niche supplying Europe's wealthy industrialists with the status symbols that they coveted.

CROSSED-SWORDS MARK

The famous blue crossed-swords mark found on much Meissen porcelain is based on the coat of arms of the Prince Elector of Saxony. The Electoral Swords, as they are known, were first used on Meissen porcelain in 1723. Meissen's reputation for outstanding quality proved to be the downfall of the crossed-swords mark as a guarantee of authenticity. It is the most frequently imitated mark in the history of porcelain. Dozens of firms, particularly in the area around Dresden during the 19th century, copied the famous trademark in an attempt to pass off their own inferior wares as Meissen.

MEISSEN PLATE OF FLOWERS This mid-19th-century latticework plate has a fluted edge and is covered with naturalistic relief flowers and leaves painted with colored enamels. It bears the crossed swords mark. c.1860. D:10½ in (27 cm).

MEISSEN SNOWBALL VASE Made of glazed and painted porcelain, this crater-shaped vase has a round base. It is decorated all over with tiny applied snowballs and snowball flowers, overlaid with scrolling branches and a bullfinch. c.1860. H:13¾ in (35 cm).

DRESDEN FACTORIES

As the capital of Saxony, situated not far from Meissen, the city of Dresden became a center of porcelain production in its own right from the second half of the 19th century. A steady trickle of Meissen workers who decided to go into competition with their former employer founded their own factories. More than 40 ateliers were active in Dresden by the end of the 1800s, but many continued production for only a limited period of time, and most are unknown today.

Decorating ateliers thrived on a steady supply of blanks and seconds. Many of these establishments unscrupulously used the blue crossed-swords mark on their wares in an attempt to pass them off as genuine Meissen products, although a blue crown mark was also in widespread use.

Among the most accomplished ceramicists was Helena Wolfson, who specialized in replicating Meissen's celebrated Watteau figures.

PALE IMITATION

Although made in the style of Meissen, most of the ceramics made and decorated in Dresden were of inferior quality. The modeling and application of motifs were less refined than on Meissen examples, and the colors and styling more crude. As such, they catered to the aspiring middle classes who coveted the trappings of success but could not afford the high prices commanded by Meissen.

Since styles and marks were copied with impunity for so long, the only way to make sure that a Meissen piece is authentic is to compare it with examples known to be genuine.

DRESDEN POT AND COVER Based on an 18th-century Meissen model, this baluster-shaped pot with gilded edges by Carl Thieme is painted on both sides with scenes in the style of Watteau. It is covered with applied, naturalistically painted flowers, leaves, and fruit, and the cover is decorated with a bird. c.1880. H:13 in (33 cm).

EVOLUTION OF STYLE

One of Meissen's great successes was with Johann J. Kändler's charming Rococo figures in the mid-18th century. Flowing robes with realistic folds gave his figures a sense of movement for which they are still celebrated. The painting was also very fine, although areas were often left white to show off the superb quality of the hard-paste porcelain.

Meissen's mid-19th-century Rococo Revival figures had many of the same features as the earlier work but were more lavish. Scrolled bases, more complex poses, and a greater emphasis on applied, painted, and gilded decoration made for a more extravagant product altogether. Improvements and refinements to modeling and production processes helped Meissen preserve its reputation for outstanding quality.

GARDENER WITH A BASKET This 18th-century Johann J. Kändler porcelain figure is glazed, painted, and gilded. It stands on a simple round base decorated with flowers. H:8 in (20 cm).

AUTUMN Glazed, painted, and gilded, this 19th-century Meissen porcelain figure is elaborately decorated and has an more extravagant Rococo-style base. H:11 in (28 cm).

DRESDEN SPIRIT BURNER One of a pair, this gilded spirit burner has a light turquoise ground and a pierced lid. Shaped like a two-handled urn, it is decorated with pastoral scenes in the style of Watteau and has Berlin scepter marks. c.1880. H:6¾ in (17 cm).

SÈVRES

From 1800 to 1815 Sèvres created hard-paste porcelain in the Empire style, decorating Classical shapes with elaborate gilding and large painted areas. The factory continued to produce such wares after the Napoleonic Wars and through the reigns of Louis XVIII, Charles X, and Louis-Philippe (the last three French monarchs, who ruled between 1814 and 1850). Although technically brilliant, designs before 1848 could lack originality and included ultra-thin cast porcelain mimicking Chinese eggshell wares and accurate imitations of oil paintings.

SÈVRES IMITATORS

The large-scale, showy Empire style also prevailed in Russia. During the reign of Czar Nicholas I, the Imperial Porcelain Manufactory in St. Petersburg copied oil paintings in the Hermitage museum as faithfully as Sèvres reproduced the Old Masters. Military themes were also popular after the Russian

defeat of Napoleon. As at Sèvres, porcelain wares copied other shapes and decorative styles, from Chinese vases to Greek oil jars. Sumptuous gilded wares also featured in Germany and Scandinavia, where Biedermeier was in its golden age.

BRITISH ROCOCO REVIVAL

Due in part to a reaction against the French Directoire and Empire styles—and their associations with the Revolution and Napoleon—thoughts in Britain returned to Rococo, and a revival was in full swing by 1830. The bone china used was more stable in the kiln, leading to less waste; more durable once fired; and cheaper to make, helping firms such as Minton to emulate early Sèvres.

While the late Neoclassical style promoted majestic sizes and symmetrical forms that left large areas plain for skilled painters to cover, now shapes swirled and surfaces undulated with applied decoration. Painting was swamped by asymmetrical *rocaille* in relief and often gilded, combined with applied flowers. The Great Exhibition of 1851 showed porcelain that wildly embellished the restrained elegance of early Sèvres.

SÈVRES BACK TO ITS ROOTS

Several French factories followed a similar pattern. Sèvres revived some of its molds from the 18th century and recreated accurate versions of its original Rococo wares, down to the earlier turquoise and pink grounds decorated with pastoral panels in the style of Watteau and Boucher. In an

PAIR OF CANDELABRA Renaissance and Rococo forms are evident in this Sèvres composition. Gilt-bronze floral and foliate bouquets and garlands are centered on baluster-shaped blue-porcelain vases. *c.1880. H:28¾ in (73 cm).*

COVERED BOWL Recalling 16th-century Limoges enamels, this Sèvres bowl features polychrome putti musicians on a royal-blue-enameled ground, and gilt-bronze foliate, scrolling leaves, pineapple, and mask mounts. *1845–48.*

The gilt-bronze mounts on the cover, neck, and shoulder echo the base

Areas of white porcelain remain visible

The gilt-bronze base recalls Classical Greco-Roman forms

MOUNTED VASE On a gilt-bronze base with female busts, scrolling leaves, and cloven-hoof feet, this Sèvres vase features romantic-historical imagery. The main scene is of Columbus, attended by a winged cherub, discovering the New World; the other side (*see detail above*) depicts a cherub with the flag of the United States. *Late 19th century. H:22 in (56 cm).*

earlier financially stricken phase, Sèvres had sold off blank wares to French and German factories that now copied the Rococo Revival decoration. The French factory Samson et Cie sold reproductions of early Sèvres porcelain that looked as genuine as the 18th-century originals—apart from the use of hard instead of soft paste.

PORCELAIN FIGURES

Sèvres had been making biscuit figures since the 1700s. However, the Classical and allegorical subjects that had been popular in the Neoclassical period were replaced by dandies, children, and allegorical groups in sentimentalized Rococo costume, as well as figures in contemporary dress decorated with C- and S-scrolls. Figures in folk costume were also popular, especially in Russia, where modelers were strong in tradition. As well as the Imperial Porcelain Manufactory, the private company of Gardner, started up by an Englishman of the same name, had great success with similar wares.

PÂTE-SUR-PÂTE

By 1850 a change in fashion and new technology combined to help popularize a revival in Classical style and the porcelain made at Sèvres in the 1750s and 1760s. In the 1860s Sèvres turned its attention to Marc Louis Solon's new method of building decoration *pâte-sur-pâte*, which was ideally suited to Classical figures. The image was built up like a sculpture, by applying several layers of clay slip to produce a relief image. This hand process could take up to 50 days' work before firing, and it achieved great subtlety of texture, from diaphanous drapery to full solidity. Solon came to Stoke-on-Trent and brought the technique to Minton. The Imperial factory in Russia also used *pâte-sur-pâte*, though no one could do it as well as Solon, who retired in 1904.

Scrolling floral and foliate
Rococo Revival forms

The gilded decoration is over a Limoges enamel-like colored ground

ENGLISH VASE The baluster-shaped body is encrusted with flowers and foliage in relief and polychrome-painted. Along with the scrolling foliate feet, handles, and neck, it displays the English Rococo Revival style at its most extravagant. *1850s. H:10¾ in (27 cm).*

REGIMENTAL PLATE The rim of this Russian plate has an Imperial black eagle and a wreath. The center depicts His Imperial Highness Grand Duke Nikolai Nikolaievich and His Royal Highness Virtembergsky. *1875. D:9¾ in (24.5 cm).*

PARIAN WARE

In the 1840s, Britain's answer to Sèvres's biscuit figures was Parian porcelain. This hard, white material, developed by Copeland and Minton by adding feldspar to the mix, had a texture that looked like marble and did not need glazing or dusting. It was the perfect material for small-scale statues and brought sculpture to the masses. A 10-ft- (3-m-) high sculpture could be reduced to 12 in (30 cm). Parian statuettes by Copeland and Minton were a runaway success at the 1851 Great Exhibition. Even Queen Victoria had Parian images of all her children made after Thorneycroft marbles. Later in the century, when excitement at its resemblance to marble had worn off, Parian began to be colored.

Highly vitrified soft-paste porcelain made in imitation of Paros marble

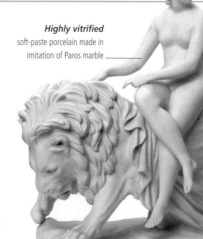

UNA AND THE LION The subject of this Parian figure modeled for Minton by John Bell was taken from Edmund Spencer's *Faerie Queene*. Una represents Truth and Purity, and the lion, Britain. *c. 1850. H:14¼ in (36 cm).*

FRENCH VASE This Parisian-made piece is essentially Rococo Revival in both form and decoration, but it also incorporates Gothic elements such as the foliate cresting at the rim. *c. 1845. H:13½ in (34 cm).*

GLASS

THE LAST THREE-QUARTERS OF THE 19TH CENTURY SAW GREAT REFINEMENT
AND EXPERIMENTATION IN GLASS TECHNIQUES AND, AS WITH ALL THE
DECORATIVE ARTS, A REVIVAL OF EARLIER STYLES.

SURFACE TECHNIQUES

Glassmakers continued to decorate glass with enamel and gilding and to make flashed glass, but they also revived two ancient Roman glassmaking techniques: cased (overlaid) and cameo glass.

To make cased glass, a bubble of colored glass was blown into shape, then a second color was applied on top. The process could be repeated to create several layers, then the vessel was reheated to fuse the layers together—a highly specialized process, as each layer had to expand and contract at identical rates or the glass would crack. The result was a thick glass that could be cut or engraved to reveal the layers for decorative effect.

While Bohemia was at the forefront of the revival of cased glass, it was British glassmakers who

inspired the return of cameo glass. The Romans used cameo glass to imitate hardstone cameos. The glass was made in the same way as cased glass, usually with a blue body covered with one or more layers of glass in contrasting colors, one of which was often white. The layers were then cut back to show the base color with the contrasting design standing out in relief (*see p.206*).

STRONG COLOR

In the early 1800s, Bohemian glassmakers experimented with yellow and green uranium glass. This was mainly used for decorative items such as vases, beakers, and scent bottles. Black Hyalith glass and marbled Lithyalin glass were also developed.

French glassmakers perfected a translucent opaline glass at the Baccarat Glassworks in about 1823. A range of pastel shades was subsequently developed, including pink, turquoise, and pale green. The glass was used at French glassworks, including Baccarat and St Louis, to make jugs, vases, and decorative dishes. Opaline glass provided a perfect canvas for the enameling and gilding techniques for which the French were renowned. Toward the end of the century these

The scrolling floral imagery is handpainted

CRANBERRY GLASS VASE
Made in the United States, this transparent Cranberry glass vase, with its distinctive raspberry-pink tint, is further embellished with handpainted floral, scrolling tendrils and leaves. *c.1850.* *H:8¾ in (22 cm).*

CAMEO GLASS

As the second half of the 19th century progressed, glassmakers and decorators were spurred to ever-greater virtuosity by the possibilities offered by the new techniques. And the great exhibitions being staged in capital cities around the world provided them— and their employers—with a growing and appreciative audience for their skills. The result was heavily yet exquisitely decorative pieces that often formed the centerpiece of a display. They were quite literally displays of the glassmakers´ virtuosity.This vase (*right*) was exhibited at the 1867 Paris Exhibition.

Naturalistic floral imagery was fashionable in the mid-19th century

BACCARAT CAMEO GLASS This baluster-shaped vase is exquisitely hand-cut and wheel-carved with bands of Moorish stylized flowers and leaves and four large medallions of naturalistic bouquets. *1867.* *H:24 in (61 cm).*

The applied gilding contrasts with the turquoise opaline ground

OPALINE VASE Probably produced at the St Louis Glassworks in Lorraine, this opaline glass vase has been colored with metal oxides to produce a turquoise shade, contrasted with naturalistic gilded flowers. *1850–60. H:10 in (25.5 cm).*

were used to embellish glass with Japanese-inspired designs featuring animals, birds, and flowers.

Bohemian glassmakers, who had been decorating glass with enameling since the 16th century, continued to do so. Ludwig Moser & Sons and J. & L. Lobmeyr were among its greatest exponents.

In the 1870s the British firm of Thomas Webb & Sons developed Vaseline glass, which has a characteristic green-blue, greasy tinge. It also experimented with using chemical fumes to create a replica of the iridescent finish seen on ancient Roman glass—a technique that

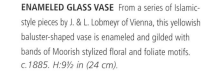

ENAMELED GLASS VASE From a series of Islamic-style pieces by J. & L. Lobmeyr of Vienna, this yellowish baluster-shaped vase is enameled and gilded with bands of Moorish stylized floral and foliate motifs. c.1885. H:9½ in (24 cm).

was later used by Bohemian and American glassmakers working in the Art Nouveau style (*see pp.210–11*).

Cranberry (ruby) glass was first made in Stourbridge, but the glass—with its rich pink tinge—was copied widely in the United States, particularly at the Boston and Sandwich Glass Co.

GLASS IN THE NEW WORLD

As the 19th century progressed, American glassmakers produced more and more innovative colored glass. By the 1880s they had developed highly demanding techniques, which created art glass with subtle gradations of color.

At the Mount Washington Glass Co., new developments included Burmese glass—a glass with a satin finish that shaded from pale yellow to pink—and the opaque white Crown Milano. These were used to make vases, brides' baskets, and dressing table sets, and were often enhanced with enameled floral decoration. The company also created the Royal Flemish range, which was expensive due to the amount of applied decoration.

Peachblow—a cased glass that shaded from yellow to purple and had a white opaline lining—was developed by Hobbs, Brockunier & Co. in 1883. The style was imitated by other glass factories, including the New England Glass Co., which named its range Wild Rose. New England (later Libbey) patented Amberina glass, which was shaded from pale amber to fuchsia, in 1883. It was also made under license by Hobbs, Brockunier & Co.

PEACHBLOW VASE Lined with white opal glass, this long-necked, gourd-shaped vase is in a form of cased glass known as Peachblow, which shades from a buttery yellow at the base to a purplish-red at the top. Made by the Mount Washington Glass Co. 1886–88. H:5 in (12.5 cm).

FOOTED OVERLAY GLASS GOBLET This goblet was made by F. P. Zach of Munich in red and clear overlay glass engraved with a hunting scene amid scrolling, interlaced foliage. c.1850. H:8¾ in (22 cm).

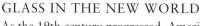

The rim is engraved with the number of the Masonic lodge for which the glass was commissioned

BOHEMIAN OVERLAY GLASS BEAKER Made in pale blue and clear overlay glass, this beaker has a gilded rim and an applied central band engraved with a diaper pattern. c.1860. H:6¼ in (16 cm).

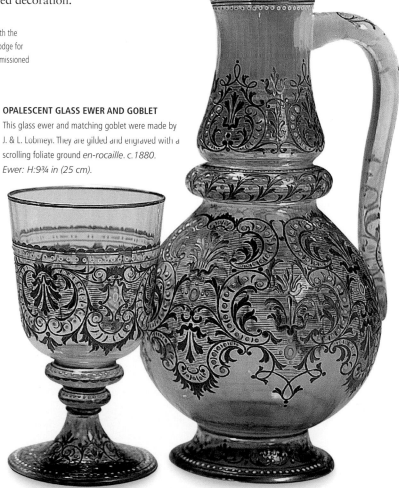

OPALESCENT GLASS EWER AND GOBLET This glass ewer and matching goblet were made by J. & L. Lobmeyr. They are gilded and engraved with a scrolling foliate ground en-rocaille. c.1880. Ewer: H:9¾ in (25 cm).

CUT GLASS

Cut glass, particularly suited to the qualities of lead glass, had been popular in Britain from the early 18th century. The repeal of tax on glass in Britain in 1845 led to a surge in production. The Crystal Palace that housed the Great Exhibition of 1851 was itself made of glass and inside, F. & C. Osler of Birmingham exhibited a huge fountain made entirely out of cut and molded glass.

Popular cut patterns include Van Dyck points fanning out like lace cuffs at the tops of glasses, as well as diamonds, points, and flutes. Flutes were slender vertical bands in the 1820s, but were cut more broadly in the late 1830s. By 1840 luxury glass was deeply cut with simple, bold designs. One was the Gothic arch; another was the broad hollow,

a circle or oval cut out of a broad flute. By the 1850s, relative simplicity had given way to ornate mixed patterns.

John Ruskin disliked cut glass. In *The Stones of Venice*, published in 1853, he wrote: "All cut glass is barbarous, for cutting conceals its ductility and confuses it with crystal." The greatest exponent of this "barbarous" glass was the Waterford Glass factory, but fashions changed and the factory closed in the mid-1850s.

ENGRAVED AND ACID-ETCHED GLASS

Still popular, engraving had two distinct styles: Neoclassical, with ornamentation derived from ancient Greek pottery, and naturalistic floral decoration. Neoclassical engraving reached its peak between the 1851 Great Exhibition and the Exhibition of 1862, and dominated the luxury end of glassmaking.

Acid etching was patented in 1857 by the English glassmaker Benjamin Richardson. John Northwood developed a template machine in 1861. He devised a similar machine for geometric linear patterns and a technique for frosting the design so that it looked like an engraving. By 1867 Grecian designs were popular again and the published work of the sculptor John Flaxman was used as a source book. Large quantities of acid-etched glass were made at the end of the century by Holmegaard

BRISTOL-BLUE GOBLET Press-molded in Britain with stylized floral medallions (front and reverse), this goblet was tinted with cobalt oxide to produce the royal blue color known generically as Bristol blue. *c.1860. H:8 in (20.5 cm).*

PEACHBLOW PITCHER Produced by the Phoenix Glass Company, this pitcher was press-molded in relief with a "hobnail" pattern, in warm Peachblow glass. *1880–90. H:4½ in (11.5 cm).*

of Denmark, Val Saint Lambert in Belgium, Stuart and Sons of Stourbridge, and many other factories.

ICE GLASS AND ROCK CRYSTAL

Many other techniques were revived, such as the 16th-century Venetian technique of ice, or crackle, glass (called overshot glass in the United States). The hot glass was

Typically bold mid-19th-century floral and foliate imagery decorates the body

American cutting is typically deep and sharp to the touch

Swagged forms acknowledge Classical Greco-Roman ornament

CUT-GLASS DECANTER Attributed to Stevens & Williams of Stourbridge, this decanter is cut in green over Cranberry glass with an undulating floral and foliate pattern. It has an applied loop handle in clear glass and a sterling-silver stopper with repoussé floral decoration. *c.1870. H:9 in (23 cm).*

CUT-GLASS DECANTER This ovoid Tiffany decanter is cut with a diamond pattern. The silver stopper is chased with 18th-century-style putti heads, flowers, ribbons, and a trumpet. *1875–91. H:9 in (23 cm).*

plunged into cold water to craze it. When reheated, it retained a finish like cracked ice. In London, Apsley Pellatt marketed it as Anglo-Venetian glass.

Thomas Webb & Sons revived the medieval technique of rock crystal—brightly polished cut and engraved glass. From 1879 Stevens & Williams also made it, appealing to sophisticated tastes by engraving the glass with naturalistic Japanese-style designs. The technique was adopted by the Baccarat glass company in France and Thomas G. Hawkes & Co. in the United States.

PRESSED GLASS

The greatest technical innovation of the century was pressed glass, invented in the United States in the 1820s. Pressing lead glass into metal molds by machine made production cheap, and factories sprang up, particularly in New England and the

Midwest. The Boston & Sandwich Glass Co. in Massachusetts was one of the most prolific. Between 1850 and 1900 there were over 70 factories making pressed glass in Pittsburgh alone. To begin with, all-over stippled patterns masked the lines left by the mold. Soon, table services were made to look like cut glass. Competition fostered color production and a wide range of designs. The mold-makers initially used many historical styles but then developed distinctly American designs such as the ubiquitous eagle.

In Britain the success of the cut glass at the Great Exhibition encouraged manufacturers to make pressed glass. Cut glass was expensive, but pressed glass, made to imitate it, was cheaper. Several firms made frosted pressed glass, and colored and marbled glass was made in the 1870s. Since molds were expensive, styles continued with little change into the 1880s and 1890s.

ROCK-CRYSTAL VASE Made in France, this vase is enameled and engraved with marine-life imagery, and finely etched to create the subtle mottled appearance of rock crystal. *c.1880. H:8¾ in (22 cm).*

CRANBERRY GLASS JUG The distinctive raspberry-pink tint of this Cranberry-glass jug made in Stourbridge, England, is augmented with a crackle pattern and contrasted with a rope-twist handle in clear glass. *c.1880. H:10 in (25.5 cm).*

BRILLIANT CUT GLASS

The displays by John Gillander & Sons and Christian Dorflinger's factory and others at the influential Philadelphia Centennial Exhibition of 1876, which was visited by 10 million people, fascinated the public with a new "rich cut glass." Subsequently known as the Brilliant style, this glass was cut deeply and polished, with a mass of intersections that fractured bold patterns based on stars, diamonds, and scallops into myriad secondary shapes.

The American Brilliant Period lasted from the late 1870s to the early 1900s. Skilled immigrant cutters worked for the American glasshouses, enabling them to develop a product good enough to rival the finest cut glass from England, Ireland, and France.

CUT-GLASS WATER JUG Made by W. H., B. & J. Richardson of Stourbridge, this jug has a clear glass body that is frosted inside, miter-cut with stylized foliate decoration, and has an applied rope-twist handle. *c.1860. H:9¼ in (24 cm).*

BRILLIANT-PERIOD PITCHER One of a pair, this pitcher was made during the Brilliant Period. The high lead content of the crystal gives the glass a gemstone-like quality. *c.1890. H:10¾ in (27.5 cm).*

HISTORICAL STYLES

Over 150 glassmaking firms took part in the Great Exhibition of the Works of Industry of All Nations, held in Hyde Park, London, in 1851. Manufacturers from the United States, Germany, Italy, Austria, and Bohemia displayed glass in exciting new colors and a range of extravagant revival styles, whetting the appetite of increasingly prosperous middle-class clients. In particular, the Bohemian exhibitors, the Counts Buquoy and Harrach, were highly praised for their exhibits of colored glass. Glassmakers were inspired by the medieval and ancient art on display and started experimenting in an attempt to revive the decorative techniques of the past.

The Great Exhibition was immensely influential and was soon followed by others: New York in 1853, London in 1862, Paris in 1867, Philadelphia in 1876, and Paris in 1878.

REVIVALS

During this period there was no one coherent style, as glassmakers had access to a wealth of historical styles, forms, and decorative motifs, which they borrowed, mixed, and matched freely. Following the unification of Germany in 1871, German manufacturers tried to forge a sense of national identity by reviving "Old German"-style glass, especially the numerous forms of traditional drinking glass,

including the *Pokal*, a Baroque beaker with a lid. This was often decorated in the colorful Bohemian enameling tradition with spurious coats of arms or light, playful Renaissance-style motifs.

Alternatively, traditional shapes were made from clear glass cased in two or more colors and skillfully wheel-engraved with romanticized landscapes or hunting scenes by master Bohemian engravers such as August Böhm.

Glassmakers like Salviati & Co. of Murano reinterpreted the hot glass tradition to produce fanciful shapes, such as serpent vases, combined with the strong,

brilliant colors that are characteristic of Venetian glass of this period. Salviati's glass found approval with the influential architect Charles Eastlake in his book *Hints on Household Taste*, published in 1868. Salviati was also commissioned to produce the elaborate glass mosaic tiles for the Albert Memorial in London, which was completed in 1876—an inescapable mark of Royal approval.

BOHEMIAN OVERLAY GLASS This lidded goblet made in ruby red over clear overlay glass was wheel-engraved by August Böhm with a fashionable forest landscape with a deer on the bowl, and featuring grapevines around the lid. *c.1850. H:21 in (53 cm).*

Pastoral imagery was popular in the mid-19th century

The engraving cuts through the overlay to reveal clear glass below

The polychrome glass rods are set in clear glass

The faceted baluster stem is in ruby red over clear glass

Renaissance Revival figures include Cupid, Bacchus, and Pan

RENAISSANCE REVIVAL JUG Of baluster form with a loop handle, this cobalt-blue jug by J. & L. Lobmeyr is handpainted with Renaissance-style motifs in bright enamels. *c.1870. H:8 in (20.5 cm).*

VENETIAN REVIVAL PITCHER Hand-blown in the form of a dolphin in clear glass with polychrome glass rods, this Salviati & Co. pitcher is in the style of 17th-century Venetian glass. *1880s. H:9½ in (24 cm).*

RENAISSANCE REVIVAL CUP Produced in clear glass by Adolf Meyr of Vienna, this cup is delicately black lead-enameled by hand with flora, fauna, and images from Classical mythology. *c.1880. H:12¼ in (31 cm).*

STAINED GLASS

A renewed interest in stained glass was initiated by A. G. W. Pugin's buildings and studies of Gothic architecture. Many churches had been stripped of their stained glass windows by Henry VIII in the 16th century, but fired with enthusiasm for the 19th-century Gothic Revival, many churches wanted to replace them. William Morris brought stained glass to greater prominence by commissioning the great Pre-Raphaelite painters Dante Gabriel Rossetti and Edward Burne-Jones to design magnificent new church windows. This resurgence of interest in stained glass led to people commissioning stained-glass windows for private homes. Powell of Whitefriars was one of the most prolific producers.

HISTORICAL TECHNIQUES

Renewed interest in the ancient cameo technique was sparked by the Portland Vase, which was displayed at the British Museum. English glassmakers, such as John Northwood and George Woodall, were masterly exponents of the time-consuming and expensive technique, which was used on either small pieces such as vases and scent bottles or large, dramatic exhibition pieces.

INFLUENCE OF NATURE

The natural world was a huge influence on Victorian designers. The inspiration for this came from diverse sources: some designers, such as Christopher Dresser, had initially trained as botanists, and Owen Jones's seminal pattern book, *Grammar of Ornament* (1856), included detailed plates based on leaves and flowers.

Inspired by books like Moore and Lindley's *The Ferns of Great Britain and Ireland*, published in 1855, and J. K. Colling's *Art Foliage*, published in 1865, ferns became one of the main decorative motifs, especially in some of the Scottish glassworks. Firms such as Richardson's of Stourbridge used elaborate, naturalistic enameling to decorate many glass forms, and Stevens & Williams often used plant imagery to create illusions of the natural world. Many of Webb's less expensive "commercial cameo" pieces, introduced in the 1880s, were decorated with flowers and leaves, as were the wares of many American firms, including Mount Washington and C. F. Monroe's Wave Crest.

CLARET JUG Made in clear and green tinted glass by Stevens & Williams, this jug is further embellished with scrolling plants and a similarly fashioned silver mount. *1890s. H:14¼ in (36 cm).*

SILVER-MOUNTED BARREL An example of Mount Washington's Royal Flemish line, this barrel features tinted and enameled roses outlined with gilt piping. *c.1890. H:7¼ in (18.25 cm).*

INSPIRED BY THE EAST

Japan opened its borders to the West in 1853, and in 1862 London hosted the International Exhibition—the first showcase for the arts of that country. The Japanese ceramics, carved ivory, prints, and textiles had a profound influence on European designers and created a passion for all things Asian that became known as *japonisme*. Motifs such as blossoms—notably in the work of the French designer Jules Barbe for Thomas Webb & Sons—chrysanthemums, fish, dragons, and exotic creatures appeared in high-relief enameling on Oriental-style vases. The fashion for exotic flowers spurred designers into creating a huge number of different styles of vase to hold them.

Nineteenth-century "Islamic" glassware was inspired by the forms and decoration of 13th- and 14th-century Islamic glass mosque lamps. At the 1878 Paris Exhibition, the first prize was awarded to the French glassmaker Philippe-Joseph Brocard for his ewers, individual and pairs of vases, and dishes, all of which were richly decorated with elaborate

symmetrical motifs carried out in a mixture of enameling, gilding, and jeweling. His fellow countryman, I. J. Imberton, also produced superb "Islamic" glass. The Austrian firm of J. & L. Lobmeyr, established in 1823, won prizes for its magnificent gilded and enameled jugs and vases, decorated with dense, vividly colored enameling and gilding that resembled cloisonné work. The flat, nonrepresentational patterns of Islamic wares were also adapted, less ambitiously, as a motif by English manufacturers such as Stevens & Williams.

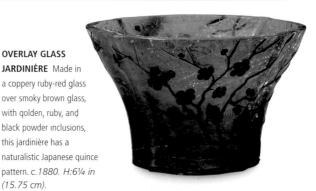

OVERLAY GLASS JARDINIÈRE Made in a coppery ruby-red glass over smoky brown glass, with golden, ruby, and black powder inclusions, this jardinière has a naturalistic Japanese quince pattern. *c.1880. H:6¼ in (15.75 cm).*

ARABIAN VASE J. & L. Lobmeyr's richly enameled glass vases were inspired by French imitations of 13th- and 14th-century Islamic lamps with their arabesques, scrolls, and stylized floral imagery. *c.1875. H:10¼ in (26 cm).*

Intricate arabesques are applied in polychrome enamels

The body is in a semi-matte pink crystal

DRAGON VASE This vase's ovoid body is gilded in relief with an Oriental winged dragon, the focal point of a large-scale, Oriental diaper pattern. From Mount Washington's Royal Flemish line. *c.1890. H:7½ in (19 cm).*

METALWARE

INCREASINGLY SOPHISTICATED MACHINERY ENABLED MANUFACTURERS
TO REPRODUCE ALMOST ANY FORM OR TYPE OF DECORATION. THIS
TRANSLATED INTO A WEALTH OF CHOICE FOR CONSUMERS.

SILVERWARE

In the 1840s the increasing refinement of dining habits and the Victorians' love of ostentatious display signaled the beginning of a golden age for silver tableware, which was helped along by new technological advances. In both Europe and the United States, machine-produced parts led to massive production of domestic wares such as cruets, candlesticks, cutlery, tea and coffee services, and dining accessories.

HISTORICAL REVIVAL STYLES

At times, it was a matter of quantity over quality; however, some manufacturers, including Tiffany & Co. (est. 1837), successfully combined mass production with superb quality. German firms produced luxurious silverware, copying the forms and decoration of the Baroque and Renaissance Revival styles. The "plastic" nature of silver could be shown to full advantage in the swirling, asymmetric forms typical of the Rococo Revival (or Louis XV style). Alternatively, designers simply embellished the plain surfaces of traditional forms with a plethora of chased decoration.

A growing interest in antiquarianism prompted the mid-century revival of Italian Renaissance-style silverware, loosely inspired by sculptor and goldsmith Benvenuto Cellini. These pieces sat side by side with Gothic Revival tea and coffee services; jugs and flagons inspired by the harsh philosophy of A. W. N. Pugin; or Neoclassical amphorae and vases.

Starting from the 1860s, when Japanese art flowed into Europe, a new repertoire of motifs became available. Designers such as Christopher Dresser reinterpreted Japanese designs to produce a strikingly modern range of silver domestic wares, including teapots and toast racks. The Arts and Crafts movement also revived and reinterpreted historical styles, decorating items with restrained naturalistic floral patterns or motifs inspired by Celtic scrollwork.

FRUITING VINES Grapevines have been a popular decorative form in many vocabularies of ornament, from ancient Egyptian, Classical Roman, early Christian, Celtic, and Renaissance, to diverse 19th-century revival styles.

The four-footed base is applied in the form of scrolling branches

ROCOCO REVIVAL CANDELABRA Made in the style of Louis XV, each of these American silver candelabra has seven branches of scrolling foliate form above a similarly decorated stem and circular base. c.1850. H:26¼ in (66.5 cm).

GERMAN CENTERPIECE Cast in silver, this centerpiece combines decorative motifs such as a guilloche, grapevines, scrolling tendrils and branches, and a putto in a typically eclectic 19th-century style. 1875. H:12½ in (32 cm).

INSPIRED BY NATURE

By 1851, improved industrial methods made it possible for manufacturers to produce almost any form in silver, including elaborate naturalistic pieces. Large-scale exhibition and presentation pieces featured realistic fruit and flowers, animals, and birds.

Sometimes the form itself imitated nature: shell-shapes made natural containers for food, condiments, or other objects; water lilies became inkwells; and bears became honey pots. Decoration might echo function: fish and shell motifs were often used on sauce boats that accompanied fish dishes; and grapes and foliage, accompanied by idealized putti, became standard decoration on a wide variety of drinking accessories, from bottle and decanter labels to goblets. Natural forms such as shells, flowers, plants, and animals were also liberally added as applied decoration or used as chased, engraved, or repoussé motifs.

REPOUSSÉ DECORATION

The versatility of the repoussé technique made it an ideal vehicle for elaborate decoration in a wide range of styles. Repoussé could create the fruit and flowers, swags, and garlands of the Baroque, Neoclassical figures, Rococo asymmetric swirls and scrollwork, Celtic motifs, the restrained naturalism of the Arts and Crafts movement, and the grotesques and arabesques of the Renaissance Revival.

Also known as embossing, repoussé creates relief designs on the surface of a metal object. The silversmith works from the back or underside of the sheet of metal, hammering out the motif with plain or decorative punches. The design stands proud of

SPOON WARMER In the shape of a large nautilus shell, this spoon warmer made in silver by H. Wilkingson & Co. has a hinged lid and is supported on a *rocaille* base. *1870. H:5½ in (14 cm).*

PAIR OF SALTS Shell forms had been a popular and apt choice for salts from the Middle Ages to the 18th century. This elaborate French example in Continental silver recalls Baroque prototypes. *1880. H:4¼ in (11 cm).*

the surface, creating a three-dimensional effect that was an essential feature of naturalistic decoration. The resulting surface decoration can then be further embellished with engraving and/or chasing to create more intricate details such as veining on leaves. Engraving, which involves cutting into the surface and removing tiny amounts of metal, was

used for delicate details such as monograms. With chasing, the silversmith uses a small hammer and chasing tools to create the design on the outside surface using small indentations but without actually cutting or removing any metal. The American firm of S. Kirk & Son of Baltimore was famous for its skillful chased work.

ELECTROPLATING

Promoting mass production of plated silverware in fashionable styles at affordable prices, electroplating was pioneered and patented in 1840 by the Birmingham firm of Elkington & Co. (est. 1830s). It involved coating a base-metal object with a thin layer of pure silver, using an electric current to deposit the silver particles. The resulting piece, like the tea kettle on the right, looked like silver but had a whiter, slightly harsher appearance without the soft sheen found on Old Sheffield plate or sterling silver. One of the major advantages of electroplating was that the silversmith could create whole pieces with complex decoration that could then be plated as a whole, covering any seams or joins. The new technique could also be used to gild and replate pieces. By the 1850s and 1860s electroplate manufacturers were producing a whole range of household wares in fashionable styles, as well as impressive exhibition pieces.

WATER GOBLETS The bell-shaped bowls and trumpet feet of these goblets (from a set of six) are embellished with an all-over floral repoussé decoration. By S. Kirk & Son of Baltimore. *1835–50. H:6¾ in (17 cm).*

SALTCELLAR Made by Fouquet-Lapar in the Rococo Revival style, this cellar is covered with chased and repoussé scrolling foliate decoration, and has an engraved monogram. *1880. H:6 in (15.5 cm).*

TEA KETTLE AND STAND Made in England, probably in Birmingham, this kettle has a silver-plated body and stand that are essentially Rococo Revival in form and decoration. The latter includes repoussé flowers, scrolls, and cartouches, and an applied bird-of-prey finial. *1850.*

VICTORIAN INGENUITY

The Industrial Revolution that had begun in England in the 18th century was given a strong technological boost by the inventive Victorians. An era that had initially relied mainly on candlelight and horsepower ended with inventions such as electric lighting, railroads, the steamship, and automobiles firmly established.

New artistic styles and materials proved irresistible to craftsmen and designers whose originality swept away the restraint of Georgian design. This was, after all, the period that produced the plant houses at Kew Gardens and the Crystal Palace for the 1851 Great Exhibition.

BRONZE'S VERSATILITY

In the 19th century, in an attempt to satisfy the wealthier consumers' continued demand for exquisite workmanship, new techniques crept into some aspects of handmade work. Craftsmen took simple, everyday items—the humble andiron (*chenet* in French), for

The candelabrum terminates in a flowering urn finial

The spool-shaped sockets are cast with fluting

example—and wrought them into veritable works of art. An andiron is a horizontal bar supported on feet, used to hold burning logs above the hearth. It often features an upright decorative frieze at the front.

Pairs of andirons are called firedogs. In the 18th century, the Sun King, Louis XIV, had *chenets* of silver. Now the utilitarian version was made of iron, although great houses sometimes had bronze or brass firedogs.

An alloy of copper and tin, bronze is a more fusible material than pure copper and eminently suitable for casting. It is also harder than copper, and more durable. In the 18th and 19th centuries the best work in bronze design and making—much of it from France—was remarkable for its fine hand-finishing and

The stems are wrapped in curling laurel leaves

Shells surmount the grotesque head

PAIR OF GILT-BRONZE *CHENETS* Also known as andirons or firedogs, these *chenets* are modeled in the Louis XVI style in the form of recumbent lions on foliage-decorated bases. They were cast by the Bouhon Frères foundry of Paris. *c.1880. W:12½ in (32 cm).*

The ram's head was a recurring motif in Greco-Roman ornament

GILT-BRONZE CANDELABRUM One of a pair made in the Louis XVI style by G. Durand et Fils of Paris, this candelabrum has a three-branch form raised on a tripod marble and ormolu base. It incorporates many Neoclassical motifs, including a flowering urn finial, laurel and stiff leaves, paterae, cloven-hoof feet, and, as in the detail above, ram's heads. *c.1890. H:23¼ in (59 cm).*

WALL SCONCE One of a pair made in gilt bronze by the Parisian foundry of Henry Dasson, this wall sconce is cast with a horned grotesque mask issuing forth three scrolling acanthus branches with leafy drip trays. *1887. H:23¼ in (59 cm).*

GERMAN GILT-BRONZE TUREEN Made in the Rococo-Revival style, this tureen is decorated with two monogram medallions flanked by flowers with scrolling tendrils. It has scrolling foliate feet and handles. *c.1860. L:45½ in (108 cm).*

gilding. After casting, sculptors and metalworkers decorated the object. They would do this by hammering thin panels or vessels from the back, punching the surface to produce a textured finish, and gilding the surface—a technique that became known as ormolu.

GOLDEN ORNAMENTS

Ormolu, or gilt decoration, was very popular in Georgian and early Victorian design. The word derives from the French *bronze doré d'or moulu*, meaning "bronze gilded with ground gold." The term is often applied to gilded-bronze objects in general but, in fact, many ormolu pieces were cast in brass, which is easier to work with than bronze. Purists usually reserve the term for fire-gilded objects from the 18th century onward.

Traditionally, craftsmen used an amalgam of gold and mercury to gild an object; they then fired the piece to drive off the mercury, leaving the gold adhering to the metal. By the 19th century they used a gold-colored alloy of copper, zinc, and sometimes tin—mixed in various proportions but usually containing at least half copper— which gave objects a rich and golden appearance. Craftsmen gilded objects such as clock cases, chandeliers, frames, and candlesticks. They designed ormolu mounts to protect the corners of furniture and for decorative items like bowls and dishes, aiming to achieve a subtle balance between matte and burnished finishes.

GILT-BRONZE *CHENETS* Probably French, these andirons are modeled in the Rococo Revival style in the form of black-painted cherubs—one is painting, the other carving—within scrolling leaf forms. *c.1870. H:16¼ in (41 cm).*

CAST IRON

By the mid-19th century, cast iron had almost entirely replaced wrought iron, which requires more time and labor, for practical products. Craftsmen started to use it architecturally for fireplaces and surrounds, hall stands, and garden furniture.

The innovative Shropshire firm of Coalbrookdale used iron for bedsteads, until then traditionally made of wood. Initially, they disguised the iron as brass, by covering it with brass foil and varnish. Coalbrookdale produced garden benches, tables, and chairs, often casting highly ornate pieces decorated in relief with trailing ivy leaves. They also made the quintessential pub table: round with central pedestal supports.

Cast-iron pieces such as stoves, kitchen utensils, coal bins, and stick stands made their way into the home. The English

GARDEN URNS Made in painted cast iron by A. Bendroth of New York, these garden urns with *faux-marbre* bases recall Renaissance and Neoclassical models. Decorative motifs include scrolling dragon handles and portrait medallions. *1880s. H:24½ in (62.5 cm).*

designer Christopher Dresser typified the move toward making objects beautiful, championed by the Aesthetic Movement, simplifying their design and integrating form with function. His work included designs for Perry, Son & Co., a Birmingham-based lighting manufacturer.

WEATHER VANES

The first weather vanes that appeared in the United States were imported from Europe, but American designers soon adapted traditional designs for local consumption. They added new motifs, including arrows and geometric shapes; American Indians with bows and arrows; and symbols of significance such as the fish—a Christian emblem and New England's main trade. By the middle of the 19th century, thanks to mass production, the market started to offer a plethora of designs. The first commercial manufacturer, Alvin A. Jewell of Waltham, Massachusetts, began in 1852. By the 1880s, mass production and marketing meant that every trade had its own specific design—a pig or horse for farmers, for example. Popular motifs that almost every manufacturer made can still be seen today: the cockerel, the horse, an eagle with spread wings perched on a ball, and the goddess of Liberty holding a flag.

NEOCLASSICAL WEATHER VANE Made in the United States, this weather vane is modeled in copper as an American Indian firing a bow. His feathered headdress is fashioned from sheet copper. *c.1880. L:44¼ in (112.5 cm).*

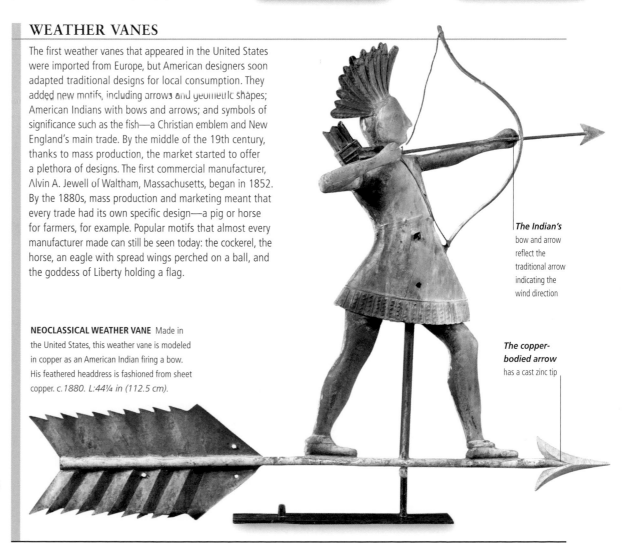

The Indian's bow and arrow reflect the traditional arrow indicating the wind direction

The copper-bodied arrow has a cast zinc tip

METALWARE GALLERY

Metalware of this period drew inspiration from the past and mixed various design elements to create a new style. There was an interest in Neoclassical motifs, which in turn were influenced by Classical Greece and Rome, and forms such as urns and vases were popular. Ornamentation was often heavy, incorporating a variety of decorative elements. Natural motifs were common, and many pieces were decorated with flora or fauna.

KEY

1. Louis Jacques Berger silver sugar bowl decorated with blackberries. D:6¼ in (16 cm). ② **2.** Sterling silver coffee pot by Dominic & Haff in a Classical urn form with an acorn finial on the hinged top. H:12¼ in (31 cm). ① **3.** London silver condiment stand by Edward Barnard. 1868. L:8¼ in (21 cm). ③ **4.** Victorian twin-handled silver desk stand raised on four scroll feet. c.1850. W:12¼ in (31 cm). ② **5.** Japanese ladle made by Koonoike with the handle modeled as a dragon. c.1860. L:15¾ in (40 cm). ④ **6.** Japanese silver and enamel vase decorated with irises. c.1890. H:5½ in (14 cm). ③ **7.** Dutch silver bowl with foliate pierced shaped sides and scroll-cast rim. D:6¼ in (16 cm). ② **8.** London silver

1 Silver sugar bowl

2 Urn-shaped coffee pot

3 Silver condiment stand

4 Silver desk stand

5 Japanese ladle

6 Japanese vase

7 Dutch silver bowl

8 Silver toast rack

9 Silver-plated biscuit box

10 Silver cup

toast rack by Robert Harper. 1869. H:5½ in (14 cm). ② **9.** Silver-plated biscuit box. c.1860. W:8¾ in (22 cm). ② **10.** Silver cup decorated with floral motifs and flutes. H:8¾ in (22 cm). ① **11.** Pair of silver candelabra in the style of Louis XV. H:21¼ in (54 cm). ⑥ **12.** One of a pair of candelabra on four leaf feet, with a winged putto holding the arms. c.1890. H:11½ in (29 cm). ② **13.** Sheffield silver sweet tray by James Dixon & Sons. c.1900. H:3½ in (8.5 cm). ① **14.** Full-bodied copper cow weather vane with cast head and remnants of gilding. L:26 in (66 cm). ⑤ **15.** American metal eagle-shaped weather vane. H:10¼ in (26 cm). ① **16.** Patchen horse weather vane with gilding, full-bodied copper with cast head, mounted on a metal base. L:41¼ in (105 cm). ④ **17.** Silver pheasant. L:23 in (58 cm). ⑤ **18.** Detail of no. 12.

11 Silver candelabra

12 Candelabrum

13 Silver sweet tray

14 Copper cow weather vane

15 Eagle weather vane

16 Patchen horse weather vane

17 Silver pheasant

18 Winged putto detail

PATTERN BOOKS

THE PREDOMINANCE OF SOME DECORATIVE MOTIFS WITHIN CERTAIN PERIODS CAN BE ASCRIBED TO THE POPULARITY OF PATTERN BOOKS. THROUGH TIME, THESE RESOURCES HAVE ACTED AS GUIDES, ESPECIALLY FOR THOSE DESIGNERS WHO HAVE BASED THEIR WORK ON HISTORICAL STYLES.

GRAMMAR OF ORNAMENT This plate from Owen Jones's book shows samples of decorative stone carving that might be applied to fretwork, wallpaper, or any number of other media.

EARLY JAPANESE INFLUENCE

Designs and motifs based on Japanese decorative arts are conspicuous by their absence from many 19th-century pattern books. The reason for this is that it was not until the Meiji period (1868–1912) that Japan opened itself up to the wider world. Japanese artifacts were, however, present in the West—the Netherlands had shared a limited trade agreement with the Tokugawa Shogunate for many years, and discerning European collectors were well aware of the outstanding quality of Japanese art. It is possible to see this influence in Western decorative art even before the great surge in interest in all things Japanese that characterized the Aesthetic Movement.

IMARI WINE POT This wine pot has decorative panels featuring lotus flowers and geometric patterns. It is the kind of artifact that Owen Jones used as source material.

The earliest text dealing with ornament is *De Architectura*, written in the 1st century BCE by Vitruvius, whose examples of architectural beauty served as templates for generations of builders. During the Renaissance, Andrea Palladio published *Quattro Libri dell'Architettura*, spawning a distinct style of architecture named after the author.

The 18th century saw a proliferation of pattern books by English cabinet-makers. Matthias Lock and Henry Copland published *New Book of Ornaments* in 1746. This was followed by tomes from three greats of English furniture design: Chippendale, Hepplewhite, and Sheraton. In France Percier and Fontaine published *Palais, Maisons et Autres Édifices Modernes Dessinés à Rome* in 1798. These books had a huge influence, even reaching the New World.

GRAMMAR OF ORNAMENT

The 1851 Great Exhibition held at London's Crystal Palace was, in effect, another manifestation

COLOR AND PATTERN By following his own "propositions" regarding pattern and color, Owen Jones made the lavish color plates of his *Grammar of Ornament* into works of art in their own right.

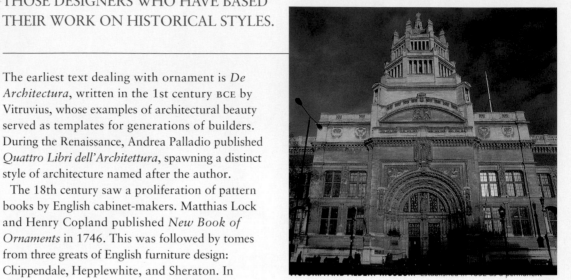

VICTORIA AND ALBERT MUSEUM Established in 1852 as a permanent home for objects from the Great Exhibition, the Victoria & Albert Museum acts as a depository for original designs to this day.

of the pattern book. By collecting examples of the "works and industry of all nations" under one roof, the exhibition's organizers were helping to disseminate the vocabulary of ornament.

Owen Jones, superintendent of works for the Great Exhibition, also designed the Egyptian, Greek, Roman, and Alhambra Courts within the Crystal Palace. His 1856 *Grammar of Ornament* was a pictorial guide to the history of design from the ancient world to the 19th century. Jones's remarkable book included more than 3,000 images, arranged in patterns on pages themed by color and style. The accompanying text comprised a list of 37 "propositions" governing the proper and tasteful application of pattern and color. It quickly became the most widely used source book in the world.

In France in 1876, Auguste Racinet published an exhaustive study of the history of costume. This book was especially useful for designers working in the historic revival styles that dominated 19th-century decorative art and design. Other works such as M. P. Verneuil's *Étude de la Plante* were more explicitly linked to the representation of natural forms within the decorative arts. The popularity of source books continued unabated throughout the 20th century with the publication of volumes such as Édouard Benedictus's *Relais* and Sonia Delaunay's *Compositions, Couleurs, Idées*.

GREAT EXHIBITION AT CRYSTAL PALACE The Medieval Court was one of the focal points of the Great Exhibition. Designed by Augustus Pugin, who also worked on the Palace of Westminster, the court was a celebration of the Gothic Revival that was so popular in Britain at the time. One of the main aims of the exhibition was to raise the public's appreciation of good design.

CLOCKS

AS CONSUMERS STARTED TO TAKE FOR GRANTED THE ABILITY OF CLOCKS
TO KEEP TIME, THE FOCUS OF CLOCKMAKERS SHIFTED TOWARD NOVELTY.
REVIVAL STYLES, HOWEVER, STILL INFLUENCED MUCH OF THE PRODUCTION.

REVIVAL-STYLE CLOCKS

The revival styles that monopolized 19th-century furniture also dominated clock-case design of the period. This was especially true for the florid Rococo taste. The association between this style and the magnificently ornamented French clocks of the 17th and 18th centuries helped perpetuate its popularity among horologists and the buying public alike.

RICH STYLE, CHEAP PRODUCTION

While in the past reliable and accurate clock movements had been a challenge to engineer, by this time they were easy to manufacture. As a result, clockmakers were able to make enormous quantities of clocks housed in elaborate cases

and at affordable prices. They used intricate decorative touches, including Boullework and scrolling brass mounts, to recreate the Rococo style, often replacing costly handcrafted work with cheaper machine-production techniques.

Elaborate clock garnitures that combined a timepiece with a pair of urns, or pairs of candelabra, obelisks, or vases, became staple fixtures of mantelpieces in smart 19th-century homes. They were frequently produced in a combination of materials, including porcelain, bronze, wood, and ormolu. Each component often had an individual base, and vases usually had removable lids, so that a single garniture might be made up of a dozen pieces. Makers lavished attention on the elaborate painted scenes, foliate decoration, and other adornments—

STEEPLE SHELF CLOCK Housing an eight-day movement by Birge & Fuller of Bristol, Connecticut, the mahogany case has a pointed gable flanked by pinnacled pillars. c.1845. H:25½ in (65 cm).

FRENCH MANTEL CLOCK The red tortoiseshell Boulle marquetry case of this clock has scrolling foliate, fruit, and vase mounts of gilt cast brass in the Rococo Revival style. c.1840. H:14¼ in (36 cm).

such as finials—with which they decorated their creations. The clock face, usually plain white enamel or painted metal, was invariably the least decorative component of the entire ensemble.

AMERICAN CLOCKMAKING

The first American clocks had wooden mechanisms, but around the 1830s clock factories started producing sophisticated brass movements.

LOUIS XVI CLOCK GARNITURE Neoclassical elements are revived in this mantel clock with an urn surmount and two matching ewers. Raised on giltwood plinths, the porcelain bodies of the ewers are transfer-printed with Sèvres-style romantic vignettes. c.1870. H:18½ in (47 cm).

The Sèvres-style enameled porcelain dial has black Roman numerals on white porcelain plaques

Transfer-printed vignettes recall late-18th-century Romanticism

ROCOCO REVIVAL MANTEL CLOCK The ornate Louis XV–style case of this clock is cast in gilt bronze and surmounted by a winged cherub holding a songbird. c.1880. H:21 in (53.5 cm).

LOUIS REVIVAL MANTEL CLOCK Incorporating elements of Louis XV Rococo and Louis XVI Neoclassical ornament, this clock is raised on a marble plinth with gilt-bronze foliate and beaded mounts, and is flanked by a winged cherub and a globe. *c.1880.*

Eli Terry's shelf clock, developed in the 1820s, resembled the hood of a longcase clock and kept time just as accurately, but at a fraction of the cost. Soon other factories all across Connecticut were making shelf clocks in the popular styles of the day.

By the 1860s American makers were also imitating the fashionable French clock styles, but using iron or wood, painted to look like marble, or white metal, painted to look like bronze. Gilt highlights were often used to embellish the decoration.

MYSTERY MOVEMENTS

The 19th-century predilection for novelty led to the development of the so-called mystery clocks. These timepieces confounded the observer by having no obvious connection between the mechanism and the hands on the clock face. Parisian horologist Robert Houdin devised an ingenious example in which the base, which houses the mechanism, is attached to the face only by a seemingly empty clear-glass cylinder. In actual fact, this cylinder encases a second glass cylinder that rotates slowly, thus transferring the movement up to the clock face via a series of gears. Another variation uses a clear-glass dial with no visible wheels or cogs driving the hands. In this case, the entire dial revolves, driven by a toothed wheel concealed within the bezel and taking the hour with it.

Other novelty clocks relied less on illusion and more on confounding the viewer's expectation of what a clock should look like. Globe clocks, held aloft on a base by putti or naked maidens, sometimes had numerals in a band around the globe and marked the hours with a hand that traveled around the circumference. These were driven entirely from within the globe, with no moving parts in the base.

The gilt-bronze cherub berates the world below

The celestial aspect is enhanced by the cherub sitting on a cloud

The face is white enamel with contrasting black Roman numerals

LOUIS XV–STYLE MANTEL CLOCK Made in Paris in gilt bronze, this clock has a case draped in foliage and surmounted by a cherub. It rests above a bronze elephant on a *rocaille* and scrolling foliate base. *1855. H:17½ in (44.5 cm).*

LYRE MANTEL CLOCK This clock incorporates a French movement within a Louis XVI–style green-onyx frame and base elaborately embellished with ormolu garlands, rosettes, and torches. *Late 1800s. H:19¼ in (49 cm).*

LOUIS XVI–STYLE GLOBE CLOCK The spherical case of this clock, with an ormolu cherub surmount, is held aloft by garlanded female nudes in the Classical style. *c.1880. H:24 in (61 cm).*

SOUVENIRS

JUST LIKE TODAY, 19TH-CENTURY TRAVELERS BROUGHT HOME MEMENTOS
AND LITTLE TOKENS AS GIFTS FOR LOVED ONES, OR AS REMINDERS FOR
THEMSELVES OF PLACES THEY HAD VISITED.

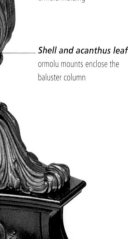

MICROMOSAIC SNUFF BOX Centered in a gilt frame on a granite lid and
base, the micromosaic plaque on this snuff box depicts Pliny's Doves, also
known as Rome's Capitoline Doves. *Early 19th century. D:2½ in (6.25 cm).*

THE RISE OF SOUVENIRS

Throughout the 18th century, members of the
upper classes rounded off their education with a
visit to Europe's cultural capitals—principally
Rome. These wealthy young tourists collected
souvenirs on a grand scale: marble sculptures,
paintings, and rare books by the crateful. Known
as the Grand Tour in Britain, the fashion was
prevalent throughout Europe. Other European
cities such as Paris—as well as the spa towns of
Germany—were included in a trip that could
take months, or even years, to complete.

By the early 19th century, travel had become less
hazardous and less expensive. More people began
to visit places of interest at home and abroad,
including wealthy travelers from the United States.
They all took home souvenirs that were less costly
than their predecessors' works of art, but no less
striking or unusual.

MICROMOSAICS FROM ITALY

During the first half of the 19th century, Italy was
a favorite tourist destination. Micromosaic is a
version of the ancient technique of mosaic and was
developed in the Vatican workshops in the second
half of the 18th century. It was soon being copied,
to various standards, in private workshops across
Italy. Craftsmen placed minute threads of glass
about ¼ in (3 mm) long and a little thicker than a
human hair vertically onto a resin-coated copper
or glass backing, to form a mosaic picture. The

threads were made in a variety of cross-sections,
including rectangular, triangular, circular, and
oval, as well as leaf-shaped or S-shaped to mimic
animal hair. The finest examples contained up to
5,000 tiny pieces of glass (or
microtesserae)

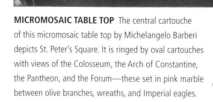

MICROMOSAIC TABLE TOP The central cartouche
of this micromosaic table top by Michelangelo Barberi
depicts St. Peter's Square. It is ringed by oval cartouches
with views of the Colosseum, the Arch of Constantine,
the Pantheon, and the Forum—these set in pink marble
between olive branches, wreaths, and Imperial eagles.

The rim of the table
is an egg-and-dart
ormolu molding

Shell and acanthus leaf
ormolu mounts enclose the
baluster column

MINIATURE TARTANWARE BOX Signed by Lamme Cumnock, this box is inked
around the sides with a Robertson tartan. The lid is handpainted with a rare view of
Balmoral Castle before Prince Albert had it modified. *c.1850. W:1¼ in (3 cm).*

MICROMOSAIC TABLE The micromosaic
table top (*see detail above*) is raised on an
ebonized-oak baluster column and triform
base with shell, acanthus leaf, winged griffin,
and animal-paw ormolu mounts. *c.1845.
D:40¼ in (102 cm).*

TUNBRIDGEWARE WRITING BOX The sides and lid of this box, housing a pen and inkwells, stamp divisions, and a paper knife, display perspective cube and floral and foliate mosaic work. *c.1870. W:12½ in (32 cm).*

TUNBRIDGEWARE SEWING CLAMP Particularly ornate, this clamp incorporates various sewing tools—including a waxer, a winder, tape measure, thimble holders, and a needle case—in stickware and painted sycamore "houses." *c.1830. L:8 in (20.5 cm).*

per square inch, creating the level of detail seen on a typical computer screen. Tiny micromosaic pictures were often set into jewelry or the lids of snuff boxes, but vases, and even pieces of furniture were also decorated using this delicate technique.

By the mid-19th century, micromosaic was being replaced by miniature glass mosaics, which were cheaper to produce as they often used tesserae containing two or more colors, eliminating the need to arrange several single-color microtesserae together in order to create a particular color or effect.

TUNBRIDGEWARE

In the late 1600s craftsmen in Tunbridge Wells, a spa town in southeastern England, developed a distinctive form of parquetry that became popular for game boards, tea caddies, writing boxes, and needle cases. They glued together strips and rods of multicolored wood to create complex geometric and pictorial designs. The solid blocks were cut into thin veneers that could be used to decorate a number of pieces identically. At the height of Tunbridge Wells's popularity as a spa in the early 19th century, Tunbridgeware pieces depicted views and buildings in and around the town.

SCOTTISH GIFTS

Queen Victoria and her husband, Prince Albert, loved the Highlands so much that in 1848 they bought Balmoral Castle. Royal endorsement and easy travel on the new railroads helped make Scottish vacations immensely fashionable in Britain during the second half of the 19th century. The Scottish souvenir industry also benefited from the numbers of visitors to the area. W. & A. Smith, in the Scottish town of Mauchline, had been making snuff boxes since the 1820s. In the 1850s it had a huge success with its tartanware—sycamore wood items covered in "woven" tartan, specially created designs on paper. By the 1860s the firm also made sycamore items decorated with engraved transfer pictures. At first, W. & A. Smith concentrated on Scottish souvenirs decorated with images like Robert Burns's Cottage, but it was soon producing pieces with engraved views of other tourist destinations such as the Isle of Wight. By the 1870s the factory had cornered the international market for inexpensive wooden souvenirs, with a varied production that included boxes, book covers, cups, and buttons.

MAUCHLINEWARE MONEY BOX The turned sycamore body is transfer-printed with London views: on one side, the New Chelsea Suspension Bridge; on the other, Horseguards from St. James's Park. *c.1860. H:3¾ in (9.5 cm).*

MAUCHLINEWARE SPECTACLE CASE This early Scottish Mauchlineware piece is hand-decorated with flora and fauna imagery in brushed and penned ink. *1820–30. W:4¾ in (12 cm).*

BOHEMIAN GLASS

Mid-19th-century visitors to middle European spas such as Baden-Baden, Karlsbad, and Marienbad often purchased heavy glass tumblers engraved with views of these resorts. They reminded their owners of the good times they had at these fashionable spa towns and the health-giving benefits of the mineral water that they drank.

Spa glasses were a specialty of the various Bohemian glassworks whose cut and engraved colored glass was prized throughout Europe at the time. As well as an engraved townscape, these tumblers were also decorated with deep cuts and flashes of brilliant color such as ruby and amber. These popular souvenirs were made in large quantities for numerous spas. As a result, the engraving and cutting varies enormously in quality and detail. The cheapest examples were decorated with acid-etching rather than wheel-engraving, which is done by hand. Engravers sometimes proudly signed and dated finely crafted spa glasses.

BOHEMIAN GLASS TUMBLER Engraved with a view of a French spa town, this tumbler, entitled *La Fontaine Elise*, was produced in ruby flashed glass. It has a delicate floral border under the rim. *c.1875. H:5 in (13 cm).*

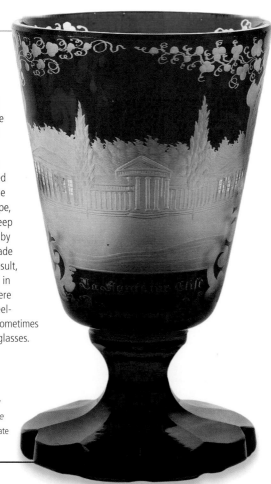

TEXTILES

DURING THE LATE 19TH CENTURY, A FASHION-CONSCIOUS EUROPEAN MIDDLE CLASS DEVELOPED AN ALMOST-INSATIABLE APPETITE FOR BRIGHT, COLORFUL RUGS AND CARPETS, FAVORING THOSE FROM THE "EXOTIC" EAST.

EASTERN CARPETS

Carpets had been imported from the East since the 17th century, but by the mid-1870s carpet-makers along the now long-established trade routes found themselves producing wares on an unprecedented scale. Interest was further buoyed in 1876, when the Shah of Persia, Nasir al-Din Shah, eager to promote his country's textile industry abroad, made a gift to Queen Victoria of 14 Persian rugs (now in the Victoria & Albert Museum). He also sent several to the Vienna Exhibition in 1891, where they were seen by an admiring public.

PERSIA SETS THE EXAMPLE

Having excelled in rug-weaving in the 16th century, the Persian carpet industry once again dominated the field. Looking back to earlier designs, rug-makers produced carpets that borrowed motifs and colors from Classical examples. Urban workshops in major cities such as Tehran, Kashan, and Tabriz produced vast numbers of richly patterned carpets, curvilinear in design and featuring floral motifs, arabesques, and palmettes, often arranged around a central medallion and enclosed within ornate borders. Dominant colors were bright, jewel-like reds and blues drawn from natural pigments, sometimes contrasted with ivory.

SOUTHWEST PERSIAN RUG Woven by the Kashkouli, one of the tribes within the Qashqai confederacy, this woolen rug has three diamond-shaped medallions set within a larger hexagonal one. *Late 19th century. L:80¼ in (204 cm).*

The borders include a sophisticated floral design

Stylized floral motifs are scattered over the field

Geometric animal (or bird) figures commonly appear in Khamseh patterns

WESTERN PERSIAN RUG A tribal rug from the Khamseh confederacy, this example is woven in wool with a typically angular Tree of Life design set within characteristic elaborate floral borders. *Late 19th century. L:81 in (206 cm).*

SHOPPING FOR SOUVENIRS British soldiers stationed in Egypt in 1882 shop in Cairo's bazaar, buying carpets and other local goods to take home. Souvenirs such as these helped boost the fashion for Oriental carpets in the West.

Rural or tribal communities such as the Afshar and Khamseh also made carpets—generally on a smaller scale—where designs tended to be more rectilinear and geometric, though color schemes were similar.

MIDDLE-EAST PRODUCTION

The influence of Persian designs was also evident in Turkey and the Caucasus (a region between the Caspian Sea and the Black Sea), where similar carpets were being produced, mainly by village communities and nomadic tribes. Carpets from these areas tend to be more boldly geometric than curvilinear.

Dagestan in the Caucasus and Ghiordes in Turkey became particularly known for the production of prayer mats. Made throughout the Middle East, these rugs often featured a Tree of Life motif and were always directional—the *mihrab* (an arch pointing to Mecca) on them indicating to the kneeler in which direction to pray.

CARPETS FROM CHINA

Hailing from Beijing and Ningxia, in the northwest of the country, Chinese carpets were quite different from Middle Eastern ones. Instead of a design filling the field to capacity, motifs tended to be more sparse, spread out over a single-color background. Typical designs were neither geometric nor curvilinear, but achieved a balance between the two. Dominant colors were blue and yellow, representing the sky and the earth, respectively, and popular motifs included the peony (wealth) and lotus flower (purity). Borders might feature frets, swastikas, and other geometric shapes.

Common layouts included the "four-and-one medallion," in which a cluster of motifs—animals, flowers, or geometric shapes—formed a central "medallion" and each of the four corners featured subsequent medallions. Full-field layouts in which the decorative motifs filled the central space in an apparently random order were also popular.

FRENCH CARPETS

In keeping with the fashion for revival styles in Europe, French carpet-makers, in particular, looked back to past designs for inspiration. Among

the resulting trends was a revival of the Savonnerie and Aubusson carpets produced under Louis XIV in the 17th century. Typical designs featured floral swags, acanthus leaves, or mythological scenes rendered in rich and luxuriant colors within strong, often wide, and architectural borders.

CHINESE CARPET Typical of the Oriental carpets that became popular in the United States in the late 1800s, this has a scattered peony design over and within rectilinear borders. *Late 19th century. L:147½ in (375 cm).*

CHINESE CARPET Chinese rugs incorporate symbolic motifs with specific meanings. Here the scattered peonies represent nobility and wealth, while the lotus blossoms symbolize purity. *Late 19th century. L:114½ in (290 cm).*

PAISLEY SHAWLS

The fashion for paisley shawls in Europe began in the late 1700s, when wealthy merchants first started to return home from their travels in the East with a luxuriously warm material.

The shawls originated in the mountainous region of Kashmir, in northern India, where they had been made from as early as the 1400s using fine, warm wool sourced from the underbelly of the local Kashmir (cashmere) goat. The term "paisley," however, derives from the eponymous Scottish town, which started imitating Kashmir shawls on hand looms from 1805. The town of Paisley went on to become the most prolific producer of such shawls as the century progressed. The woven shawls bore designs

epitomized by a stylized, cone-shaped motif known as the *boteh*, which is now recognizable as an elongated curve.

Traditional European designs were woven from silk or wool, which made them heavier than their Kashmir counterparts. Advances in technology, however, soon meant that designs could be printed onto wool/cotton and wool/silk fabrics rather than woven, making the production of lighter versions in a more exciting range of designs and colors a reality. Demand grew in the 19th century, when technologically advanced manufacturing methods meant that paisley shawls could be produced on a large scale for the masses. They proved so popular that millions were printed.

FRENCH CARPET This *tapis-ras* carpet (flat-woven using the tapestry technique) is patterned with the elaborate floral bouquets typical of Aubusson weaves of the late 19th century. *L:115¼ in (292.5 cm).*

SCOTTISH SHAWL Inspired by the formalized representations of pine cones found on handwoven Kashmiri shawls, this paisley pattern is machine-woven in silk and wool. *c.1860. W:126 in (320 cm).*

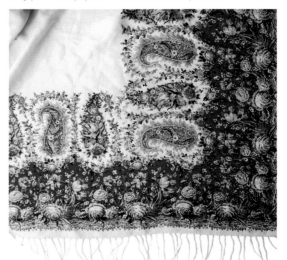

SCOTTISH SHAWL In addition to the pine-cone motif, paisley patterns also incorporate stylized vegetation based on palms, cypresses, and other plant forms, as on this printed woolen shawl. *c.1880. W:61½ in (156 cm).*

NEEDLEWORK

Needlecraft played an important role in women's lives in the 18th and 19th centuries. In bygone eras, sewing was often a communal activity offering women the chance to catch up with friends over some mending or embroidery. Women generally worked on more elaborate items, such as quilts, together, each bringing their own design ideas and skills to the piece.

QUILT DEVELOPMENT

Some of the most intricate and inventive textiles homemade by women are quilts. Early examples from the 18th century were made of three pieces of material: a top; an inner layer of wool, or flock; and a back held together with fancy stitches, usually called "whole-cloth" quilts.

Patchwork quilts—thriftily made from leftover scraps of material—were common by the early 1800s. They were usually made from similar types of material—for example, a combination of cotton patches—pieced together in geometric patterns. There are more than 400 named quilt patterns, the same pattern often having a different moniker in different places. Many have intriguing names such as Tumbling Block, Jacob's Ladder, and Churn Dash. "Crazy quilts" were various types of material like cotton, silk, and velvet all sewn together at random and embellished with embroidery. This popular variety of patchwork quilt was introduced in the 1870s.

Appliqué quilts had a whole cloth base decorated with stitched-on fabric pieces. This technique enabled quilters to create pictorial designs: favorite motifs include flowers, hearts, and pineapples for friendship. Many quilts combine both patchwork and appliqué techniques.

Pioneer women traveling to North America's western frontiers often received quilts as a goodbye present from their friends back east. This form of giving led to a fashion for album, or friendship, quilts, pieced together from separate squares created individually and embroidered with the date and name of their maker.

NORTH AMERICAN RUG CRAFT

Immigrants from Europe brought their needlework skills—and understanding of the need for thrift—with them. By the mid-1800s hooked rugs were being made throughout North America. They were made from narrow strips of wool or cotton hooked closely together through linen or burlap backing.

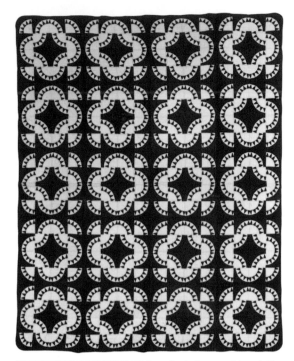

PENNSYLVANIA PATCHWORK This Pennsylvania German quilt has a bold geometric pattern composed of blocks of saw-tooth-bordered fans, in white against a red ground. *Mid-19th century. L:79½ in (202 cm).*

OHIO APPLIQUÉ Of immigrant German origin, this appliqué features a bold stylized floral, berry, and foliate pattern. This is geometrically configured in red and near-black dyed calico, sewn to a contrasting ivory-white flat ground. *Mid-19th century. Sq:74¾ in (190 cm).*

NEW YORK EMBROIDERED PATCHWORK The patchwork fans and peacock feathers are embroidered with diverse sprigs of flowers, within a border of embroidered morning-glories, all in silk-on-silk. *c.1880. W:72 in (183 cm).*

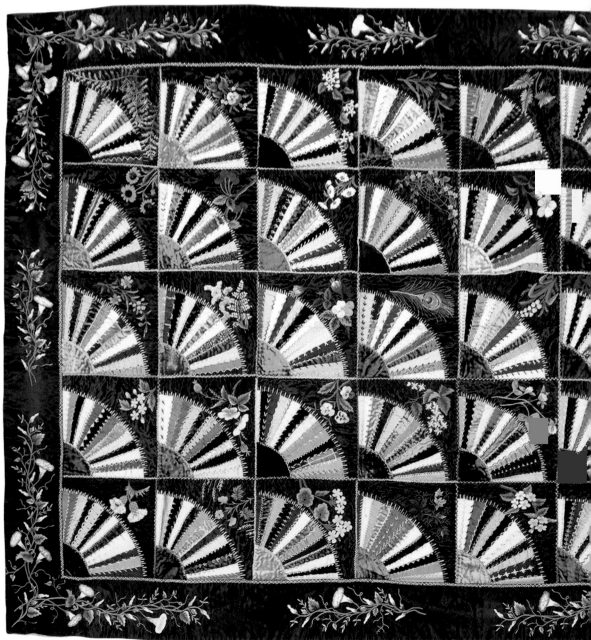

Some hooked-rug makers occasionally cut the loops for a more pilelike effect. Hooked-rug designs were often original and highly imaginative: they ranged from simple images—animals, flowers, geometrics, and stripes—to complex scenes such as Fourth of July picnics and sleighing through the snow.

As interest in hooked rugs grew in the 1860s and 1870s, patterns became available. The enterprising Edward Sands Frost from Maine sold designs stenciled on burlap door to door and through mail-order catalogs. He produced 150 patterns, including birds, flowers, and geometric motifs. Hooked-rug making is still a popular craft today.

NEEDLEWORKED PICTURES

In the early 1800s embroidering pictures was considered a suitable occupation for young women, who had gained proficiency in stitching by producing samplers. In some cases, the embroiderer followed a design sketched by a professional artist or teacher. Prints or pattern books were often used as a source of more elaborate embroidered pictures. Typical subjects included still lifes of fruits and flowers, the girl's home or school, pastoral scenes, and figures in a landscape.

Mourning embroidery, created to commemorate departed loved ones, usually had a figure weeping in a graveyard. They included poignant Classical symbols such as funeral urns and weeping willows, as well as the departed's name and dates. In the United States, many of these were made in memory of George Washington; in Britain, of Nelson.

Production of embroidered pictures declined as girls started receiving a more academic education in the mid-19th century.

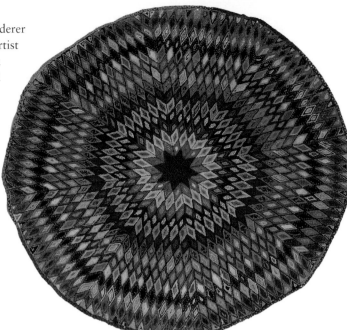

AMERICAN HOOKED RUG The hooked geometric pattern of this rug suggests Shaker origin. It is made up of polychrome diamond forms radiating out from a red eight-pointed star. *Late 19th century. D:77¾ in (197.5 cm).*

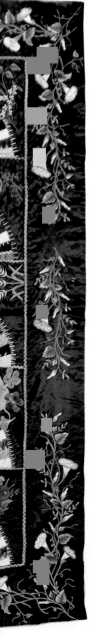

Woolwork predates the brighter but cruder coloring of aniline dyes

AMERICAN BERLIN WOOLWORK
This framed woolwork still life of a bowl of fruit within a wreath of roses is by Elizabeth Swartz, who was probably from Chester County, Pennsylvania. *1839. W:17¼ in (44 cm).*

BRITISH BERLIN WOOLWORK
Incorporating long and short stitchwork, this maple-framed picture of a first-rate man o' war flying the White Ensign exemplifies the bold, nationalistic imagery popular in Victorian England in the mid-1800s. *W:22¼ in (56.5 cm).*

GREENFELL RUGS

British doctor Wilfred Grenfell moved to Newfoundland in 1894 to set up a medical mission. He came up with the idea of supplementing impoverished women's incomes by paying them to make hooked rugs that he would sell. He gave rug-makers kits that included everything they needed—from materials to burlap backing printed with a pattern. Early Grenfell rugs were made of wool and cotton; later examples from donated damaged silk stockings. Designs such as fishing scenes and dog teams reflect Newfoundland's craggy environment. Select stores in North America, such as Eaton's department store in Toronto, sold Grenfell rugs from 1910 to the late 1940s.

GRENFELL HOOKED RUG Typically tightly hooked, thin, and durable, this rug depicts a map of Newfoundland enhanced with a compass and numerous indigenous motifs, including seals, whales, boats, and settlements. *Late 19th century. L:21¼ in (54 cm).*

SCULPTURE

IN THE 19TH CENTURY THE POPULARITY OF SMALL BRONZES OF REALISTICALLY
PORTRAYED ANIMALS SPREAD SWIFTLY FROM FRANCE TO THE REST OF
EUROPE AND THE UNITED STATES. A NEW GENRE OF SCULPTURE WAS BORN.

EQUESTRIAN BRONZE This repatinated Coalbrookdale cast is of *Djiin—Cheval à la Barrière*, by French sculptor Pierre-Jules Mêne, widely acknowledged as the leading equine animalier. *c.1890. H:11½ in (29 cm).*

FRENCH BRONZES

Bronze sculpture in 19th-century France enjoyed an acclaim that Europe had not seen since the work of Cellini in Renaissance Italy 300 years before. The Industrial Revolution had as much of an effect on sculpture as on the other decorative arts. For the first time, it was cheaper to make bronze than marble sculptures; as a result, bronze foundries became more numerous, and more efficient and consistent in quality.

The improvement coincided with the rising wealth of the middle classes, and a new appreciation and study of nature. In Paris there was the thrill of seeing wild animals from the colonies in Africa and Asia up close at the museum in the *Jardin des Plantes*. Sculptors tapped into this vibrant market by making small, affordable bronzes of animals of all species.

LES ANIMALIERS

As with Impressionism, the term "animalier" was first used by a hostile critic to deride the work of Antoine-Louis Barye and other like-minded sculptors. In previous centuries, animals in art had taken supporting roles to humans or had been presented as allegories. Like people, animals were idealized to conform to Classical notions of proportion and beauty. Barye flouted all the conventions. He showed nature in the raw, including subjects such as lions attacking and devouring prey, and stags locking horns.

Barye, an artist as well as a sculptor, had worked under painter Baron Goss, who specialized in romantic views of battle, with rearing horses and conquering heroes. Captivated by the portrayal of animals in action, and eager to produce anatomically correct replicas, Barye observed the big cats in the *Jardin des Plantes* and drew the skeletons and muscle systems of dead ones. Meanwhile, by working for a goldsmith for eight years, he learned how to model on a small scale.

Barye exhibited his first sculpture, *Tiger Devouring a Gavial*, at the Salon in 1831. Despite mixed reactions from the critics—not all saw natural beauty in instinctive animal behavior—it was bought for the Luxembourg Gardens. Two years later, Barye exhibited *Lion and Serpent*, which was also purchased by the state. His career as a sculptor had taken off.

EAGLE BRONZE Cast by the Barbédienne foundry, Antoine-Louis Barye's *Aigle, les Ailes Déployées* displays the aggression, in this case latent, for which Barye's wild-animal sculptures are known. *Late 1800s. H:5½ in (14 cm).*

DOMESTIC ANIMALS

Some of Barye's disciples followed in his footsteps and chose to capture moments of predatory violence, but most toned down the subject matter.

The bronze castings are finished in a black patina

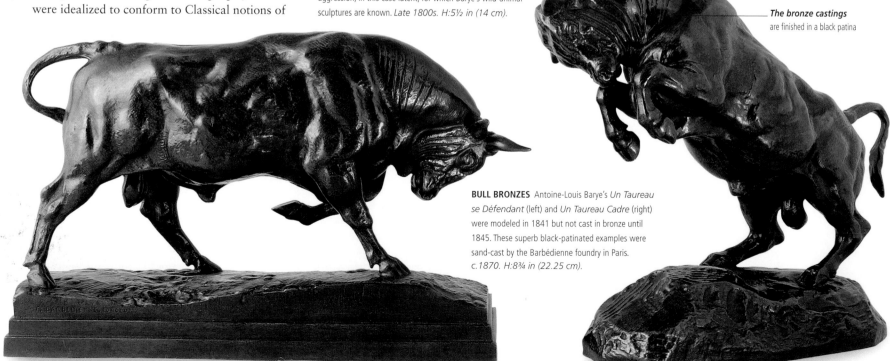

BULL BRONZES Antoine-Louis Barye's *Un Taureau se Défendant* (left) and *Un Taureau Cadre* (right) were modeled in 1841 but not cast in bronze until 1845. These superb black-patinated examples were sand-cast by the Barbédienne foundry in Paris. *c.1870. H:8¾ in (22.25 cm).*

EQUESTRIAN BRONZE French animalier Pierre-Jules Mêne created numerous racing equestrian sculptures. This *Vainqueur du Derby* depicts the winning horse and jockey of the English racing classic. *c.1860. H:9¾ in (25 cm).*

HUNTING DOG BRONZE After horses, Pierre-Jules Mêne's favored subject was dogs. This *Chien Braque, Anglais Pur-Sang, Gardant du Gibier* depicts a pointer guarding game by a tree stump. *c.1860. H:11 in (28 cm).*

VIENNESE BRONZES

In the mid-1800s the trend for small animal bronzes spread to Vienna, where Franz Bergmann started to produce miniature bronze animals and birds.

Over time, bronze acquires a natural patina, which can be chemically induced by the artist. However, Bergmann chose to cold-paint the bronze, a technique usually applied to ceramics or glass. As the name suggests, the paint is not fired to fuse with the body, so it tends to peel or rub off. The tiny naturalistic replicas looked even more realistic with their true coloring. Their size made them affordable, and they were avidly bought. Bergmann's work can be identified by a stamp with his name, sometimes spelled backward, or a monogrammed "B."

BIRD STUDY This European jay in cold-painted bronze is highly naturalistic and characteristic of the bronzes produced by the Bergmann factory in Vienna. *Late 1800s. H:4½ in (11.5 cm).*

Domestic animals lent themselves to being presented more tamely. Pierre-Jules Mêne specialized in horses and dogs at work and play. By studying animals at the *Jardin des Plantes*, as Barye had done, Mêne managed to create anatomically accurate works that showed animals behaving naturally. He made large editions of his work and was obsessive about quality, making sure that the last in a series was as perfect as the first.

As the middle classes aspired to traditional aristocratic pursuits, sporting art also became a genre, with portrayals of hunting, game shooting, racing, and polo playing. Mêne exhibited at the Great Exhibition of 1851 and was highly popular in Britain. He made some editions specifically for the British market; his *Horse and Jockey*, a portrait of a Derby winner exhibited at the Salon in 1863, was a bestseller.

The work of Isidore-Jules Bonheur was so naturalistic that his Normandy cow was recognized as a standard for the breed. He also made racing bronzes and animal groups, all characterized by sympathetic realism.

DOG STUDY Like many of Bergmann's naturalistic, cold-painted figural bronzes, this study of a Great Dane would have originally found a British or an American owner. *Late 1800s. L:5½ in (14 cm).*

Equestrian studies, like this one, were partly inspired by Buffalo Bill's traveling Wild West Show

POLO PLAYER French animalier Isidore-Jules Bonheur's brown-patinated study of a mounted polo player was cast in bronze by the Hippolyte Peyrol foundry. This is where most of Bonheur's, and his sister Rosa's, casts were made.

BULL STUDY One of a pair by Isidore-Jules Bonheur, *Taureau Beuglant* was cast by Hippolyte Peyrol. Originally retailed by Tiffany & Co. in New York, both studies have a distinguished deep-brown patina. *H:15½ in (39.5 cm).*

AMERICAN SCULPTURE

THE OLD WEST PRODUCED A DISTINCT SCHOOL OF ART INFORMED BY THE TOUGH REALITIES OF LIFE BEYOND THE FRONTIER. COWBOY ART WAS BORN OUT OF HARD EXPERIENCE AND KEEN OBSERVATION OF THE ORDINARY PEOPLE AND EVERYDAY EVENTS THAT SHAPED THE AMERICAN WEST.

THE MEDICINE MAN This figure was cast in bronze by Roman Bronze Works of New York from an original model by Charles M. Russell. *H:7 in (18 cm).*

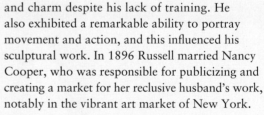

COUNTING COUP Documents suggest that this group was the second of Charles M. Russell's sculptures to be cast. From an original model by Russell himself, it was cast in bronze by Roman Bronze Works of New York. *c.1925.*

Toward the end of the 19th century—during the years between the end of the Civil War and the closure of the frontier—the American West was a territory of open range and trails, peopled by railroad workers, buffalo hunters, and cowboys, with scant local law enforcement. It was a period of gunfights between gamblers and skirmishes with American Indians—in short, the era of the Wild West. The romance of these heady days was not lost on the residents of "civilized" America, where news from the frontier was always greeted with excitement.

CHARLES MARION RUSSELL

Born to wealthy parents in Missouri in 1864, Charles M. Russell found the pull of the West irresistible, and he moved to Montana to work on a sheep ranch at the age of 16. Legend has it that his first successful painting was of an emaciated beef bull being stalked by wolves. It was sent by Russell's employer to a ranch owner in response to an inquiry about the effects of the bitter 1886 winter, and it eventually ended up on display. Russell's ability to capture the spirit of his environment is characteristic of his paintings, which are full of atmosphere

THE LAST DROP Cast in bronze by Roman Bronze Works of New York from an original model by Charles Schreyvogel, this sculpture depicts a cowboy giving his horse water from his hat. *c.1900.*

and charm despite his lack of training. He also exhibited a remarkable ability to portray movement and action, and this influenced his sculptural work. In 1896 Russell married Nancy Cooper, who was responsible for publicizing and creating a market for her reclusive husband's work, notably in the vibrant art market of New York.

CHARLES SCHREYVOGEL

A struggling painter trying to eke out a living through his art when he first went West in 1893, Charles Schreyvogel quickly became an excellent horseman and learned to communicate with American Indian nations in an effort to persuade them to pose for his paintings and sketches. However, he still had trouble finding patrons. In despair, Schreyvogel sent a painting to the National Academy of Design in 1901 and won the Thomas B. Clarke prize. Interest in his works immediately soared as a result of this accolade, and Schreyvogel joined Russell as a leading exponent of Western art. By the beginning of the 20th century the Old West was already a thing of the past, but this only served to increase public appetite for Western art. The detailed depictions of frontier life in the sculpture and painting of Schreyvogel, Russell, and others helped satisfy a kind of nostalgia.

20TH-CENTURY EXAMPLES

The tradition of the original frontier artists has been kept alive, and there exists a vibrant community of cowboy artists to this day. James Nathan Muir worked at ranches in Texas during the 1980s before settling in Arizona and embarking on a career as a sculptor. His militaristic themes show the influence of Frederic Remington, a war correspondent who began sculpting in bronze around the turn of the 20th century. Muir specializes in cavalry subjects—in particular, figures from the Civil War and the Old West. With his attention to detail and his intuitive grasp of movement and action, Muir is the heir of Charles M. Russell.

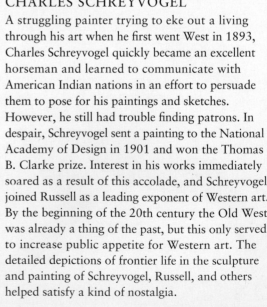
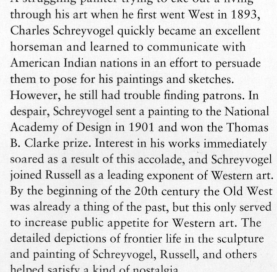

SAVING THE FLAG From a limited edition of 24 cast in bronze from an original model by James Nathan Muir, this group depicts a fallen cavalryman holding a standard up from the ground.

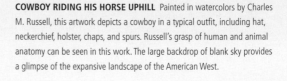

COWBOY RIDING HIS HORSE UPHILL Painted in watercolors by Charles M. Russell, this artwork depicts a cowboy in a typical outfit, including hat, neckerchief, holster, chaps, and spurs. Russell's grasp of human and animal anatomy can be seen in this work. The large backdrop of blank sky provides a glimpse of the expansive landscape of the American West.

ARTS AND CRAFTS

1880–1920

TRADITIONAL VALUES

THE ARTS AND CRAFTS MOVEMENT AIMED TO RECAPTURE THE PURE DESIGN AND CRAFTSMANSHIP LOST TO MASS PRODUCTION. IT BEGAN IN BRITAIN BUT GAINED A WIDER AUDIENCE IN THE UNITED STATES, WHERE EXPONENTS COMBINED HAND AND MACHINE TECHNIQUES.

TECO VASE The American firm Teco was known for its green glaze and architectural forms. This bulbous vase has eight leaf-shaped handles buttressed to the base and a lobed rim embossed with lotus blossoms. *W:11½ in (29 cm).*

REVIVALS GONE MAD

The late 19th century was a powerhouse of industrial and military might, and wealthy citizens enjoyed the benefits of unparalleled economic success. The Great Exhibition of 1851 in London had shown that no scheme was too elaborate for British craftsmen; variety and novelty drove architecture and design.

There were, however, dissenting voices. A. W. N. Pugin argued that the Gothic architecture of the Middle Ages had been the product of a purer, more godly society, and that to replicate it faithfully it was first necessary to adopt medieval working practices. John Ruskin took up his plea. A highly influential figure, Ruskin acted as a sort of universal conscience for the cultural and artistic philosophies of Victorian England. Like Pugin, he held the medieval craftsman in particularly high regard, believing him to have been free to express himself through his art. He considered the lives of Victorian craftsmen wretched by comparison, maintaining that they were industrial servants, acolytes of the "Goddess of Getting-on."

WILLIAM MORRIS

A tireless campaigner, William Morris spread his romantic vision of a golden age in which artist-craftsmen found personal fulfillment through their work. He encapsulated the principles of the Arts and Crafts movement when he said, "Have nothing in your houses that you do not know to be useful, or believe to be beautiful." Utility was fundamental to his vision, as he rejected tawdry decoration. Beauty, it followed, must be wrought by other means—including the careful design of interiors so that every element formed part of a harmonious whole and, on individual pieces, by a visible understanding of and respect for the raw material.

HANDMADE VERSUS MACHINE

As the movement spread from London to provincial cities and, crucially, the countryside, it acquired stylistic influences from elsewhere. The Celtic Revival added pagan ornament to the Catholic medieval tradition, and the pastoral strain that had always been part of Morris's vision matured as it absorbed vernacular craft traditions from all over the country and abroad.

C. R. Ashbee made the most successful shift from city to country, but even he eventually found that cheaper manufactured versions of the handcrafted goods made by his Guild of Handicraft forced him out of business.

AMERICAN INTERPRETATIONS

The entrenched interests of large-scale manufacturing were less of a threat in the United States, where there was a tradition of skilled European migrants establishing small workshops.

THE RED HOUSE Philip Webb designed William Morris's home in Kent with Arts and Crafts principles in mind. Even the well is unique, inspired by Gothic architecture.

GUSTAV STICKLEY TABLE This luncheon table shows American Arts and Crafts at its purest: plain and simple, with visible structure and joinery. *c.1900. H:27¼ in (69 cm).*

RODMARTON MANOR Ernest Barnsley and the Cotswold Group built and furnished the house to Arts and Crafts ideals for Claud and Margaret Biddulph, beginning in 1909. With local craftsmen, they worked by hand using local stone and timber. Most of the furniture was made in the Rodmarton workshops or by the Barnsleys.

During the second half of the 19th century, American society consigned Civil War divisions to the past and took notice of the indigenous community, so long sidelined. Designers developed a national style to define all aspects of America's cultural makeup.

Even before the first Arts and Crafts exhibition was held in London in 1888, the architect Henry Hobson Richardson visited William Morris and began to evangelize on his behalf, recommending Morris & Co. furnishings to his own clients. He was followed by others, notably Elbert Hubbard and Gustav Stickley, whose artistic reconnaissance took them to leading department stores such as Liberty & Co. and Heal & Son. They returned to the United States impressed by both the honest craftsmanship of William Morris and the high volume of sales achieved by main-street retailers. The American vision of Arts and Crafts combined both factors, and managed to reach a far wider audience than its English antecedent. Despite his revolutionary socialist politics, Morris's detestation of machinery can be seen as an elitist stance that stunted Arts and Crafts in Britain. Only once this bar had been removed could it reach its potential.

MORRIS AND CO. TAPESTRY
Designed by John Henry Dearle, the *mille-fleurs* (thousand flowers) tapestry is woven in colored wools and mohair to show a woodland glade with rabbits, a fox, and fallow deer. *1892. W:184½ in (460 cm).*

ELEMENTS OF STYLE

As a reaction against the fussy revivalist styles of the day, Arts and Crafts designers often sought inspiration in the past. They aimed to strip away artifice and return to simple craftsmanship. In Europe, designers revered the preindustrial age as a feudal utopia, while Americans held up the art of native peoples as an ideal. Other cultures perceived to have preserved their artisan heritage, such as Japan and Persia, were similarly admired.

DETAIL OF WILLIAM MORRIS TAPESTRY

MEDIEVAL INFLUENCE

Like John Ruskin, William Morris harbored a romanticized concept of the medieval period as a golden age of honest craftsmanship. The Gothic style provided a starting point for many Arts and Crafts designers. Gothic features such as oak furniture, simple natural forms, and stained glass are prominent in work of the period.

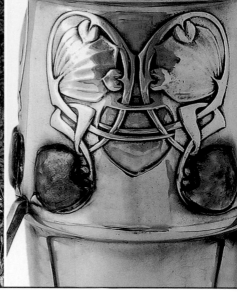

TUDRIC PEWTER VASE

CELTIC INFLUENCE

Archibald Knox brought the Celtic heritage of his Isle of Man homeland to artistic prominence. Celtic motifs were enthusiastically followed up in Scotland. Entwined knots, Celtic crosses, and complex entrelac (interlaced) designs featured heavily, especially on metalware of this period.

ROOKWOOD VASE

HANDCRAFTSMANSHIP

The point of Arts and Crafts philosophy was to restore joy in craft. The movement created a rebirth in vernacular handcraft traditions. Artisans invested time and effort in handcrafting objects rather than using cheaper and quicker molds.

ARTIFICER'S GUILD COPPER WALL SCONCE

STYLIZED NATURE

Nature was a vital source of stylistic inspiration, with plant and animal motifs influenced by medieval stone- and metalwork. Wallpapers and textiles made prominent use of large, repeating flat patterns featuring stylized floral designs. These were colored with natural plant and vegetable dyes.

DETAIL OF SILVER BOX WITH ENAMEL TOP

ENAMELING

The revival of this ancient technique as a popular decorative device was largely the work of London-based painter and silversmith Alexander Fisher. As an affordable alternative to precious stones, enameling gave a splash of color to metalware and furniture. Specialists created painterly enamel panels that were inset into jewelry and boxes.

STRAP HINGES
HANDCRAFTED HARDWARE
To relieve the plain oak finishes of much Arts and Crafts furniture, many manufacturers made features of their applied metal hardware. A number of successful metal workshops were founded to make strap hinges, drop handles, and metal studs used to affix leather upholstery.

DETAIL OF CREWELWORK
NEEDLEWORK
William Morris sparked a revival of traditional weaving and needlepoint crafts after he was captivated by medieval tapestries in France. His two-dimensional repeating designs featuring stylized foliage and birds were widely imitated. Elsewhere, needlework societies kept up their folk traditions by practicing the craft.

WILLIAM DE MORGAN TILE PANEL
ISLAMIC ORNAMENT
The Islamic world was a fund of inspiration, especially after The Arab Hall in Leighton House in London aroused interest in Islamic decoration. Monochrome and luster glazes owed a debt to Persian ceramics. Complex pierced aprons and galleries on furniture of the period also came from Islamic sources.

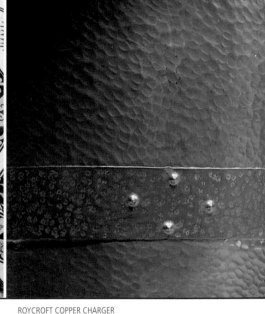

ROYCROFT COPPER CHARGER
HAMMERED METAL
As proof of honest construction, the hand-hammered finish was characteristic of Arts and Crafts metalware, whether on silver, copper, or brass. Some workshops even applied hammer marks to machine-made items purely for their aesthetic appeal.

BRANDED ROHLFS MARK
CRAFTSMEN'S MARKS
One of the effects of releasing the working man from the tyranny of the factory was to reinstate pride in craftsmanship, and many craftsmen marked their work with prominent initials and ciphers as a way of demonstrating this pride. Shrewd business minds also saw marking as a way of advertising their brands.

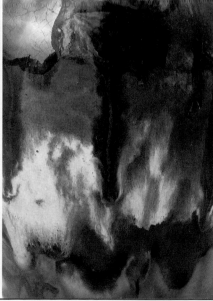

DETAIL OF GEORGE OHR GLAZE
INNOVATIVE GLAZES
An explosion in the range and number of glazes available invigorated the ceramics industry. From Rookwood's high-gloss Standard glaze to Grueby's trademark matte green, via a wealth of Chinese-inspired glazes such as *sang-de-boeuf* and flambé, never before had the Western ceramic tradition been so innovative.

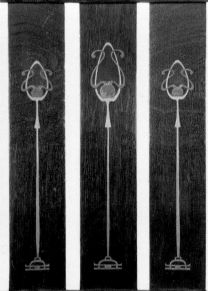

EXOTIC INLAY ON A CHAIR BACK
INLAYS
Although Arts and Crafts craftsmen tended to avoid complicated decorative techniques, some of them used exotic woods, base metals, and leather as ornamental inlays. A labor-intensive technique, using intricate inlays not only lightened dark stained oak, it gave craftsmen a chance to flaunt their considerable skills.

DETAIL OF STAINED-GLASS WINDOW
STAINED GLASS
The ecclesiastical Gothic roots of the Arts and Crafts philosophy found ideal expression in stained glass. Long-forgotten techniques were revived when new windows were made for church renovations. These techniques were adapted by lighting manufacturers such as Tiffany to stunning effect.

THE AESTHETIC MOVEMENT

THE AESTHETIC MOVEMENT FLOURISHED IN BRITAIN DURING THE 1870S AND 1880S, INSTIGATING A LIVELY DEBATE ABOUT THE NATURE OF ART. IT HAD A CONSIDERABLE INFLUENCE ON THE EMERGING ARTS AND CRAFTS MOVEMENT.

JAMES MCNEILL WHISTLER An expatriate American artist, Whistler was a leading figure of the Aesthetic Movement, rejecting realism in favor of decorative paintings characterized above all by harmony of color.

At the heart of the Aesthetic Movement was a rejection of the link between art and morality claimed by thinkers such as John Ruskin, and a reaction against the French Revival styles of the high Victorian period. Led by the artists Frederic Leighton and James McNeill Whistler, the Aesthetes firmly believed in the notion of art for art's sake, namely that the form, color, and decorative features of a work of art were more important than its subject. This pursuit of beauty linked the many strands of the complex movement.

JAPANESE INFLUENCE

One of the main pillars of the Aesthetic style was the influence of Japan. After years of self-imposed isolation, Japanese ports had reopened for trade in 1859, creating a huge demand for all things Japanese. The first global showcase of Japanese decorative arts was the 1862 International Exhibition in London. Up until then, most people had had very little exposure even to the export lacquer or Kakiemon wares coveted by wealthy collectors. The exhibition created a great clamor, and ceramicists, cabinet-makers, and metalworkers across Europe and North America were soon producing work in the Japonaiserie style. It was characterized by Japanese-influenced glazes and spare, rectilinear construction. The best craftsmen avoided simply applying Japanese motifs to Western forms and instead tried to fuse the Asian tradition with their own work.

Meanwhile, Gothic Revival was becoming the English national style in the late 19th century, due partly to the influence of Charles Barry and A. W. N. Pugin's Gothic Revival design for the Houses of Parliament in London. This also strongly influenced the Aesthetic Movement.

AESTHETIC INTERIORS

The typical Aesthetic interior was decorated in tertiary greens, blues, gold, and white. The furniture was simple in line and ebonized, with

SATIRICAL TEAPOT Modeled by James Hadley for Royal Worcester, with Oscar Wilde on one side, a fashionable lady on the other, the mutual limp wrists form the handle and spout. c.1882. H:6 in (15 cm).

JAPANESE VASE Slender ovoid forms, gilding, and dense polychrome painting, here of Asian figures in a landscape, characterize Satsuma earthenware of the Meiji period. 1868–1912. H:12¼ in (31 cm).

spindle legs, often based on the work of E. W. Godwin, one of the most influential designers of the day. Cabinets were made from strips of ebonized wood or sometimes bamboo arranged in a symmetrical, rectilinear form. They were often inlaid with marquetry or ceramic panels and displayed objects, usually Gothic Revival trinkets or Japanese-style porcelain.

Peacock feathers and sunflowers—both archetypal Aesthetic motifs—were displayed alongside handcrafted items, and further decoration was provided by Japanese prints, screens, and fans.

A growing distinction between utilitarian and art furniture was reflected in other areas of the decorative arts. The field of ceramics in particular enjoyed an explosion of creativity. Firms such as Doulton championed a revival of interest in the decorative possibilities of earthenware and stoneware, while Worcester and Minton developed glazes and new decorative techniques for porcelain that demonstrated the influence of Japanese ceramic, lacquer, and cloisonné wares.

Bamboo is a common Asian motif

Exotic plants echo Asian blue and white export porcelain

JAPONAISERIE JARDINIÈRE Made by Pinder Bourne & Co., the porcelain frame is molded to look like bamboo, while the underglaze-blue and white porcelain panels depict Asian-style plants and birds. c.1880. H:8 in (20 cm).

Japanese-style painted floral panels flank the mirror glass

Marquetry in stained red fruitwood contrasts with the ebonized carcass

Legs are ring-turned and gilded

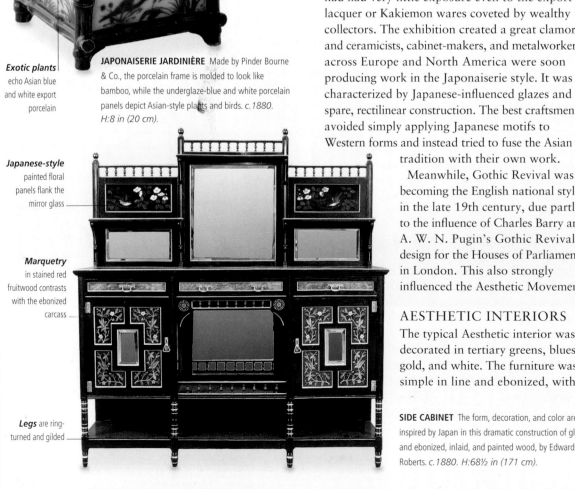

SIDE CABINET The form, decoration, and color are inspired by Japan in this dramatic construction of glass and ebonized, inlaid, and painted wood, by Edwards & Roberts. c.1880. H:68½ in (171 cm).

PEACOCK ROOM This room was designed by Thomas Jeckyll and was originally in the London home of Frederick R. Leyland, a wealthy shipowner, where it displayed his collection of blue and white porcelain. Whistler retouched the room in Aesthetic taste as a suitable setting for his painting. The walls bore gilded shelves and huge gold paintings of fighting peacocks, and the ceiling was painted with gold leaf and peacock feathers.

FURNITURE

AFTER THE GREAT EXHIBITION OF 1851, A NEW WAVE OF CRAFTSMEN TOOK
AUGUSTUS PUGIN'S REWORKING OF ENGLISH GOTHIC AS THE STARTING POINT
FOR FURNITURE WITH LESS PAGEANTRY AND MORE SUBSTANCE.

MORRIS AND CO.

Inspired by the task of furnishing the Red House—his new Kent home designed by Philip Webb—William Morris founded Morris, Marshall, Faulkner & Co. in 1861 with members of his inner circle. As a reaction against poor industrial design, the aim was to coordinate a range of furniture using local woods such as oak and ash and other natural materials like rushes for seating. At first, oak was often ebonized in the Aesthetic Movement style, easing country-style furniture into the drawing room. Alternatively, it was polished to a warm brown yellow. Decoration was minimal, taking nature or medieval legend as inspiration or emphasizing the structure with large hinges and exposed dowels securing extended tenons.

Webb gradually took responsibility for the firm's furniture as William Morris concentrated on textile design. Chairs and settees by the company were often upholstered with fabrics designed by Morris as part of an attempt to create a harmonious, integrated interior. In sympathy with influential campaigners such as Bruce Talbert and Charles Eastlake, Webb had nothing but scorn for the machine-cut veneers that covered so much 19th-century furniture and advocated the use of plain wood surfaces that exposed the structural beauty of his designs.

Philip Webb was responsible for much of the firm's most enduring work, including the redrafting of the original designs discovered in a Sussex carpenter's shop that became the celebrated adjustable Morris Chair. He resigned his full-time position within the company in 1875 when it was restructured to become Morris & Co.

Many of the brightest creative lights of the day became involved with the cabinet-making side of Morris's company, including W. A. S. Benson and

OAK HALL CHAIR An early and rare example by C. F. A. Voysey, this chair has five vertical back splats, paddle arms, tapering legs and posts, and a (new) leather seat. c.1885. H:55 in (21.5 cm).

painter-poet Dante Gabriel Rossetti. Morris & Co. furniture was marketed in two distinct tiers, referred to by Morris as "necessary workaday" tables and chairs and "state" nonessential items such as sideboards and cabinets. Unlike the plain furniture, these

MORRIS CHAIR This classic Morris & Co. design includes original upholstery and an ebonized walnut frame in which the elegant parallel curves of the back legs and arms are characteristically united by ring-turned spindles. c.1866. H:40 in (101.5 cm).

DRAWING ROOM AT STANDEN Built 1892–94 in West Sussex for James Beale by architect Phillip Webb, Standen was decorated throughout by Morris & Co. Its original furniture, fabrics, and wallpapers were made with the traditional craftsmanship that underpinned the Arts and Crafts movement.

THE VERNACULAR TRADITION

As part of the manifesto that celebrated the rustic and the ancient, the Arts and Crafts movement embraced vernacular tradition—conventional practice built up over time and centered around a local area. Furniture-makers in each British region had their own idiosyncrasies and expertise.

The Sussex Chair of Morris & Co. was influenced by cottage chairs in the county of its name. There were several versions, including a round-seated one by Rossetti. Ernest Gimson also learned how to manufacture rush-seated chairs, from a Worcestershire rather than Sussex maker. Gimson and Barnsley incorporated vernacular motifs not traditionally associated with furniture, using pitchfork shapes and modeling headboards for beds after wagon backs.

SUSSEX CHAIR This chair was designed by Ernest Gimson and made by Edward Gardiner. Curvaceous, horizontal back splats and delicate spindle work make the rush-seated ash frame more sophisticated than its original rustic model. c.1890. H:33½ in (85 cm).

"state" pieces could be made "as elaborate as we can with carving, inlaying, or painting."

Architect Charles Voysey had little sympathy for such luxury or for decorative baubles. His furniture had elegant, mannered lines that relied on the beauty of oak and minimal pierced decoration. Trademarks of his furniture include tapered square-section legs that continue as uprights and terminate in flat caps.

REGIONAL VARIATIONS

After leaving London, architect-designers Ernest Gimson and Ernest and Sidney Barnsley moved to the Cotswolds in Gloucestershire in 1892. Sidney Barnsley, in particular, took to cabinet-making and became the archetypal solitary artisan

craftsman. He used oak, with little if any ornament. Any work he could not cope with he referred to his brother Ernest and Ernest Gimson, who created a thriving furniture-making business. They designed for walnut and ebony as well as oak, and used inlays of holly alongside exotic materials such as ivory and abalone shell. Known as the Cotswold School, the work of these craftsmen had a lasting influence.

The vortex of the Arts and Crafts movement in Scotland was in Glasgow. Students at the School of Art received intensive practical training in their craft in on-site studios. The firm of Wylie & Lochhead prospered on the proceeds of Glasgow's shipping industry, fitting the luxury liners built on the Clyde with good-quality furnishings.

CRAFTSMEN'S GUILDS

Gimson and the Barnsley brothers moved to the Cotswolds to escape city life and fulfill a rural dream of community involvement, just as Charles Ashbee did some years later. Both moves established rural guilds, set up for a community of craftsmen to work together and learn from each other. Although the foreman of Gimson & Barnsley's furniture workshop was a migrant Dutchman, the labor they employed was drawn overwhelmingly from the area around Sapperton, where they were based, and they apprenticed a number of local boys. Provincial expertise was crucial to the success of the Cotswold School—Richard Harrison, Sapperton's resident wheelwright, took on the task of sourcing locally available woods such as ash, deal, and oak and supplying them to Gimson's workshop.

Guilds flourished in the capital, too. The Art Worker's Guild, to which Voysey belonged, was founded at the Charing Cross Hotel in London in 1884. It was a forum where designers of anything from buildings to sculpture and furniture met to exchange ideas under the motto "Art is unity."

Whether urban or rural, the concept of the guild—with its connotations of skilled craftsmanship and a respect for the artisan tradition—was very important within the Arts and Crafts movement.

REVOLVING BOOKCASE Designed and made in walnut and fruitwood by Cotswold School craftsman Sidney Barnsley, the bookcase is raised on a triform base and characteristically incorporates exposed dovetail joints. 1920s. W:15 in (38 cm).

MAHOGANY DINING TABLE Designed by Philip Webb, made by Morris & Co., and almost identical to a table at Standen, this has an incised-edged oval top above a central support encircled by six ring-turned legs, linked by ring-turned stretchers. 1860s. L:70¼ in (176 cm).

OAK CASKET The abalone, mother-of-pearl, and coromandel wood inlays in this pigeonholed and multiple-drawer construction are typical of Sidney Barnsley's more elaborate work. 1920s. W:21 in (53.5 cm).

THE STICKLEY DYNASTY

Born to German migrant parents in Wisconsin, the five Stickley brothers—Gustav, Charles, Albert, Leopold, and John George—achieved various degrees of artistic and financial success as manufacturers of Arts and Crafts furniture. When Gustav Stickley dedicated the first issue of his design magazine *The Craftsman* to William Morris, he was consciously allying himself with the father of the British Arts and Crafts movement. Yet, like his brothers, his interpretation of it was distinctly American. The Mission style that came to be associated with the Stickley family had a profound effect on American living, influencing architecture and interiors across the country from New York to Washington state.

Mission became a general term for American Arts and Crafts furniture, but its roots were in Gustav Stickley's statement that "a chair, a table, a bookcase or bed [must] fill its mission of usefulness as well as it possibly can...the only decoration that seems in keeping with structural forms lies in the emphasizing of certain features of the construction, such as the mortise, tenon, key, and dovetail." In keeping with this assertion, Stickley furniture was made from natural materials such as oak with seats and upholstery made of leather or rush. The grain of the quarter-sawn oak was brought out with a finish of fumed ammonia. Forms were mostly

ILLUSTRATION FROM *THE CRAFTSMAN* MAGAZINE Gustav Stickley spread Arts and Crafts principles in this influential monthly publication. The notion that design begins with a room is evident in this extract, as is his belief that furniture should suit "the place it had to occupy and the work it had to do". *1910–12. H:11 in (28 cm).*

rectilinear, based on 17th- and 18th-century settles and trestle tables.

Gustav Stickley, the most prolific of the brothers, originally trained as a stonemason before starting work at his uncle's chair factory in Pennsylvania at the age of 17. During the late 1890s, Gustav traveled to England, where he met the key players in the Arts and Crafts movement. Already an

admirer of John Ruskin and William Morris, Stickley reaffirmed his own conviction in the beauty of simplicity. A visit to the 1900 Exposition Universelle in Paris, which featured among other things a full-size replica of a medieval French town, only confirmed his distaste for clumsy reproduction and overwrought decoration. These considerations did not, however, prevent Stickley

Exposed circular dowel ends are a recurring feature of Stickley joinery

Square-section posts exemplify the solid, linear forms used by the Stickleys

The figuring of quarter-sawn oak is distinctive, accentuated by the hallmark fumed finish

Stickley hardware ranged from copper to pewter to, as with these pulls and strap hinges, wrought iron

FUMED OAK SIDEBOARD Gustav Stickley's design is raised on six posts and has four central drawers flanked by cupboards set under a plain, rectangular top with a plate-rack backsplash, and wrought-iron hardware. *W:70 in (178 cm).*

from using machinery to maintain consistent high quality. Stickley spurned the exclusive use of labor-intensive handcraftsmanship of British Arts and Crafts in favor of a pragmatic American blend of traditional craft and machine technology.

CRAFTSMANSHIP EXCELLENCE

On returning to the United States, Stickley was flushed with a new enthusiasm for his craftsman ideal. His furniture business was booming and he acquired and refitted Crouse Stables near Syracuse. He christened his new premises the Craftsman Building, using it to house not only his furniture workshops but also a metalwork studio, lecture hall, and publishing offices for *The Craftsman*, the most important contemporary periodical of the American Arts and Crafts movement.

Ostensibly a marketing tool for Stickley's furniture, *The Craftsman* grew to cover philosophy and architecture, and published house designs by Harvey Ellis. Ellis did much to temper Stickley's austere taste with a more delicate edge. Although their working relationship lasted for little over a year, cut short by Ellis's untimely death in 1904, the influence on Stickley was profound. Craftsman furniture designed by Ellis has decorative touches such as inlaid marquetry that owe much to British designers, including C. R. Mackintosh and Baillie Scott.

DROP-FRONT DESK Designed in oak by architect Harvey Ellis, it features floral inlay work, in nickel and stained fruitwood, that characterizes Ellis's lighter touch. *c.1903. W:30¼ in (77 cm).*

L. & J. G. STICKLEY

Following the success of their Onondaga shops (*see below*), Leopold and John George renamed their firm L. & J. G. Stickley and unveiled their first line of furniture at a 1905 trade show in Grand Rapids, Michigan. They marketed their product as "simple furniture built along mission lines," clearly influenced by the work of their brother Gustav. Unlike Gustav, however, they had little time for costly handcraftsmanship and opted instead to produce their furniture mechanically. L. & J. G. Stickley were financially successful in a way that Gustav never was, thanks to their better business acumen. In the early 1920s the firm used traditional New England and Pennsylvania furniture designs as inspiration for a new range called the Cherry Valley Collection. They married vernacular American form with Native American wood by using black cherry sourced from the Adirondack Mountains.

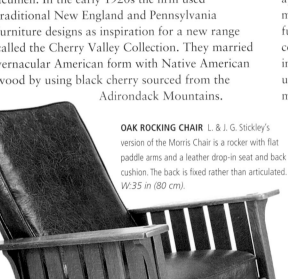

OAK ROCKING CHAIR L. & J. G. Stickley's version of the Morris Chair is a rocker with flat paddle arms and a leather drop-in seat and back cushion. The back is fixed rather than articulated. *W:35 in (80 cm).*

STICKLEY BROTHERS

The first furniture company founded by members of the Stickley family was Stickley Brothers, based in Binghamton, New York, in the 1880s. This early venture involved Charles, Albert, and Gustav, although Charles left to work with John George in Michigan during the early 1890s. After Gustav's departure, Albert was left at the helm of the original family firm. The features that define Stickley Brothers furniture are similar to those used by other members of the family, including plain oak and mahogany surfaces.

Albert's Quaint Furniture trademark was also applied to more decorative items inspired by members of the Scottish School. Albert Stickley's furniture is generally rigidly rectilinear, with conspicuously exposed structural elements including through-tenoned stretchers and rails. He used a variety of stained finishes ranging from rich mahogany red to a yellow-tinged limed oak color.

LAMP TABLE English and Scottish forms are evident in this Stickley Bros. oak table, notably the cutout spade motifs at the sides, the gently curved stretchers, and the defined feet. *1890s. H:30 in (75 cm).*

ONONDAGA SHOPS

When Leopold and John George Stickley set up business together in Fayetteville, New York, in 1904, they used the name Onondaga Shops for two years before rebranding themselves as Handcraft. Onondaga was the name of an American Indian nation from the upstate New York area. Leopold and John George became successful by producing more economical versions of the Mission furniture made by Gustav Stickley. They took advantage of their brother's relaxed attitude to issues of copyright—Gustav often encouraged architects and designers to customize and so appropriate his plans. Leopold and John George scaled down Gustav's designs, to make them more cost-effective. They also turned out work from designs by Frank Lloyd Wright *(see pp.260–61).*

OAK SERVER Raised on square posts, with an undershelf, a back-splash, and drawers with copper ring pulls, the simple form is typical of the Onondaga Shop. *1904–06. W:44 in (110 cm).*

LARGE CHANDELIER A hammered and pierced domed iron ring supports nine pendent copper and amber-yellow glass lanterns in this rare Onondaga Metal Shops light fixture. *1904–06. H:32 in (80 cm).*

AMERICAN WORKSHOPS

Following in the footsteps of the Stickley brothers, American cabinet-makers began to take a keen interest in the Arts and Crafts style around 1900. Like Gustav Stickley, they often took a pragmatic approach to industrialization, considering it to be liberating rather than constricting if used well. Although anathema to William Morris's ethic, machine production actually enabled American manufacturers to come closer to the ideal of supplying good-quality furniture to the masses than Morris ever did. The idealism that spawned the English guild revival was also at work in the United States, and a number of rural craft communities were founded.

SOLID AND SPARTAN

The city of Grand Rapids in Michigan became something of a center for the American furniture industry from the 1880s. As well as L. & J. G. Stickley, it was home to Charles Limbert, founder of the Limbert Furniture Co. in 1894. His work owed as much to the early modernity of Charles Rennie Mackintosh as it did to the English and American Arts and Crafts movements. Sparsely

decorated with keyed-through tenons and unobtrusive metalware, Limbert's furniture was mostly made of oak, often stained and sometimes with combinations of contrasting stained finishes. Cutout patterns relieve the plain oak surfaces on many of his designs, varying from simple squares and circles to half-moons and hearts.

AMERICAN CRAFT COMMUNITIES

The oldest surviving artists' community in the United States, the Byrdcliffe Arts Colony, was established by an Englishman—Ralph Radcliffe Whitehead—and his American wife Jane Byrde McCall. Centered around their home at White Pines near Woodstock, New York, the Byrdcliffe community included craftsmen from many different fields, so ideas flowed between disciplines. Furniture was handmade on the site— often using poplar as a cheaper alternative to oak—and was sometimes painted by artists in the colony. Jane McCall contributed landscapes painted in oils.

The most ambitious and successful American craft community of the period was Elbert Green Hubbard's Roycroft in East Aurora, New York. Inspired by the Kelmscott Press, run by William Morris, Hubbard established the Roycroft Print Shop in 1895 as a publishing venture, but cast his brief wider as the years passed. His band of Roycrofters began to attract tourists, and a small woodworking operation was set up to create gifts and trinkets to sell them. This part of the business expanded and by 1910 the Roycroft presses were

OAK CHIFFONIER Attributed to Jane Byrd Whitehead (née McCall) of the Byrdcliffe Arts colony, it is raised on square corner posts and features a pair of cupboard doors, each with an oil-painted rural landscape. *1904. H:27¼ in (68 cm). 1904.*

The top rail is in a rectilinear style

The composition of the drawers and door is symmetrical

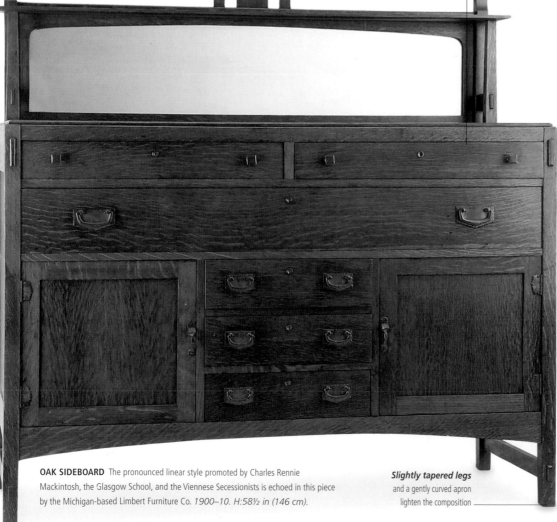

OAK SIDEBOARD The pronounced linear style promoted by Charles Rennie Mackintosh, the Glasgow School, and the Viennese Secessionists is echoed in this piece by the Michigan-based Limbert Furniture Co. *1900–10. H:58½ in (146 cm).*

Slightly tapered legs and a gently curved apron lighten the composition

MORRIS CHAIR The quarter-sawn oak frame with flat-plank arms, legs, and stretchers, and an arched apron, is upholstered in leather. It bears the Limbert Furniture Co.'s branded "Arts & Crafts made in Grand Rapids and Holland" mark. *c.1910. W:28½ in (72 cm).*

busy producing mail-order catalogs for the huge range of furniture made on site.

The furniture produced by the Roycrofters was made from solid oak to a high standard. Early pioneers of the flat pack, the Roycrofters dispatched furniture in pieces, to be assembled at its destination. For this reason they relied heavily on pegged through-tenon joints, which could be dismantled and reassembled without tools or glue. Every aspect was handcrafted—the on-site metalworking shop produced hand-hammered iron and copper hinges, studs, handles, and locks. Roycroft furniture was stamped with a crossed orb encircling an R, a mark based on that of a medieval monastic scribe. Hubbard died aboard the ocean liner *Lusitania* when it was torpedoed in 1915, but his community continued to thrive under his son's direction until 1938.

SHOP OF THE CRAFTERS

After seeing Arts and Crafts furniture at the Louisiana Purchase Exhibition in 1904, retailer Oscar Onken founded the Shop of the Crafters in Cincinnati, Ohio, to give shape to his own vision of the style. In partnership with a Hungarian designer named Paul Horti, Onken imported Austrian woods, which he used to create contrasting colored panels and marquetry designs. Horti brought a European flavor to the Shop's furniture—like Charles Limbert, he was influenced by Scottish School and Secessionist designs and relied heavily on rectilinear members with cutouts for decorative effect. The attention given to metalware as part of the integrated design was as close here as at other establishments. Strap hinges and beveled knobs complemented the rich fumed finishes of the stained oak. Promoted nationally in newspapers and magazines, the Shop of the Crafter's Arts and Crafts furniture remained popular until it was discontinued around 1920.

INLAID CABINET Made from quarter-sawn oak with a raised drawer, open shelf, and cupboard, this cabinet displays fruitwood marquetry typical of the Shop of the Crafters. 1905–10. H:51 in (129.5 cm).

OAK ARMCHAIR Dark stained and of solid, mortise-and-tenon, flat-plank construction, this Shop of the Crafters' piece has a shaped top rail and fruitwood marquetry. c.1910. H:37 in (92.5 cm).

OAK TABOURET The plank sides have keyhole cutouts. One is carved with the primary Roycroft mark: a double-barred cross and orb enclosing an "R," adapted from a 14th-century European monastic manuscript. 1900–10. H:20½ in (52 cm).

PYRAMIDAL BOOKCASE Cut into graduated shelves, flanked by flared sides scalloped at the base and secured with pegged-through tenons, the oak displays a warm, nut-brown patina often favored by Roycroft. It is carved with his decorative mark: an oak leaf. 1900–10. W:20 in (51 cm) at base.

GOTHIC REVIVAL STYLE

British and American craftsmen returned time and again to the Gothic roots of the Arts and Crafts style. Scotsman Bruce Talbert had been among the first to praise and popularize the honest construction of Gothic-style furniture in his 1867 book *Gothic Forms Applied to Furniture*.

In the United States, Charles Rohlfs made furniture with pierced and decorated Gothic motifs and drew on Moorish and Scandinavian traditions. Gothic arches and metal accessories show Rohlfs's sympathy with Gothic design—he described his own work as having "the spirit of today blended with the poetry of the medieval ages."

Based in Buffalo, New York, Rohlfs established his own studio in 1891, eventually employing a team of craftsmen to execute his designs. He exhibited to great critical acclaim and won many prestigious commissions, including work at Buckingham Palace in England.

Carved flame finials emphasize the height of the desk

Fretwork motifs, echoed in the carving, include quatrefoils and fleurs-de-lys

Typical intricacies of construction include a side cabinet with shelving

DROP-FRONT DESK This Charles Rohlfs desk is made of dark oak carved with Gothic motifs, and bears his branded shopmark: an "R" set within a fretwork saw. 1900. H:55 in (139.5 cm).

FURNITURE GALLERY

These Arts and Crafts pieces celebrate the vernacular traditions of country and Mission furniture. Typical stylistic features include exposed structural elements such as dowels and mortise-and-tenon joints. Combined with prominent handles and chunky metal hinges, these are often the only forms of decoration on display. Other marks of craftsmanship include inlays of contrasting woods or metals and adzed surfaces.

KEY

1. Hallstand with stylized tubular motifs and a tiled panel by Harris Lebus. c.1905. H:82½ in (210 cm). ③ **2.** Aesthetic Movement sideboard with Japanese lacquer panels attributed to E. A. Godwin. c.1880. W:50 in (127 cm). ⑧ **3.** Oak side table with a lattice back by Sidney Barnsley. W:27 in (68.5 cm). ③ **4.** Display cabinet attributed to E. A. Taylor, with repoussé fenestration and marquetry inlay. c.1905. H:69 in (175 cm). ② **5.** Glasgow School cabinet with stained glass windows. W:42¼ in (107 cm). ① **6.** Guild of Handicraft music cabinet on bracket feet, designed by C. R. Ashbee. c.1899. H:49 in (124.5 cm). ① **7.** Magazine stand with demi-lune cutouts by Charles Limbert. c.1910. H:37 in (94 cm).

3 Barnsley side table

7 Limbert magazine stand

2 Aesthetic Movement sideboard

6 Pine music cabinet

8 Limbert lamp table

1 Harris Lebus hallstand

4 E. A. Taylor display cabinet

5 Glasgow School cabinet

9 Shop of the Crafters library table

③ **8.** Lamp table with corbels and cutout sides, by Charles Limbert. W:45 in (112.5 cm). ④
9. Library table with slatted legs and spade feet by the Shop of the Crafters. c.1910. ③
10. Stained oak settee with unusual carving, by Charles Rohlfs. 1900. W:45 in (114 cm). ①
11. Oak hall settle with an arched slat back and a hinged seat. W:48 in (122 cm). ① **12.** Walnut armchair with a heart cutout, by E. Punnet. c.1903. H:32 in (82 cm). ① **13.** Clissett-type elm ladderback chair, designed by Ernest Gimson. ③ **14.** Desk chair with a leather seat by Robert "Mouseman" Thompson. c.1910. H:31½ in (80 cm). ① **15.** Mahogany elbow chair, the broad back splat with marquetry floral motif. **16.** English oak armchair with a tall carved and paneled back. c.1900. H:51½ in (130.5 cm). ②

10 *Rohlfs stained oak settee*

11 *Oak hall settle*

13 *Ladderback armchair*

12 *Walnut armchair*

16 *English oak armchair*

14 *Oak desk chair*

15 *Liberty chair*

CERAMICS

THE LINK BETWEEN MOST SUCCESSFUL ARTS AND CRAFTS CERAMICISTS WAS

A TIRELESS QUEST TO DEVELOP NEW AND BETTER GLAZING TECHNIQUES.

IN THE UNITED STATES, ROOKWOOD SET A HIGH STANDARD.

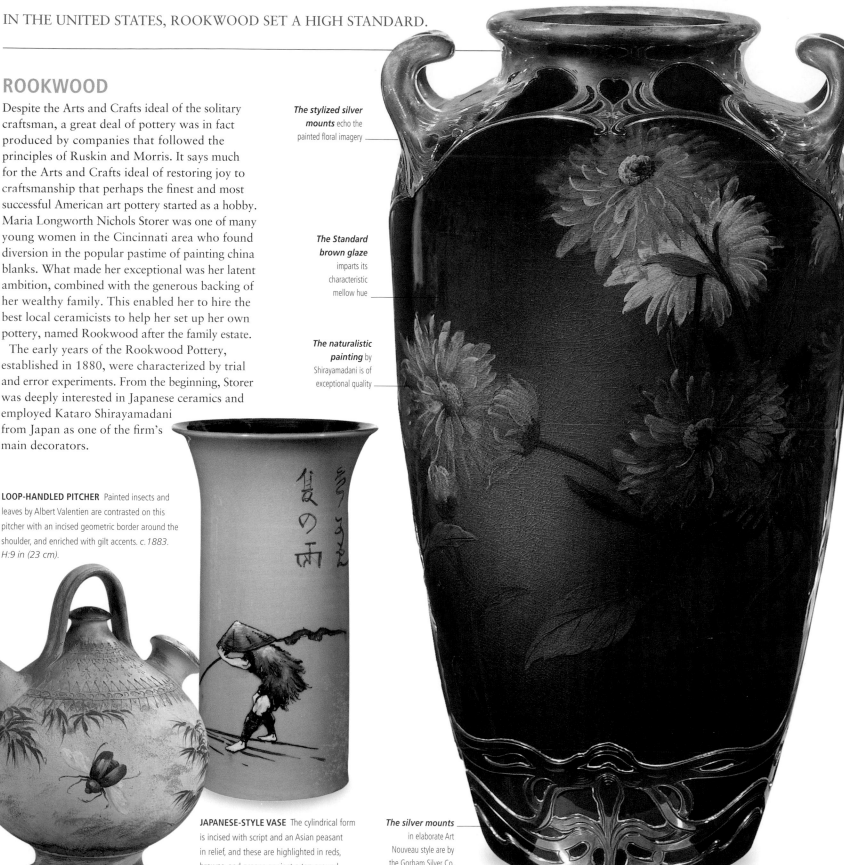

STANDARD GLAZE VASE The slender, shouldered oviform body was designed by Kataro Shirayamadani and painted with naturalistic chrysanthemums in shades of orange, yellow, and green under Rookwood's Standard brown glaze. *1898. H:12 in (30.5 cm).*

ROOKWOOD

Despite the Arts and Crafts ideal of the solitary craftsman, a great deal of pottery was in fact produced by companies that followed the principles of Ruskin and Morris. It says much for the Arts and Crafts ideal of restoring joy to craftsmanship that perhaps the finest and most successful American art pottery started as a hobby. Maria Longworth Nichols Storer was one of many young women in the Cincinnati area who found diversion in the popular pastime of painting china blanks. What made her exceptional was her latent ambition, combined with the generous backing of her wealthy family. This enabled her to hire the best local ceramicists to help her set up her own pottery, named Rookwood after the family estate.

The early years of the Rookwood Pottery, established in 1880, were characterized by trial and error experiments. From the beginning, Storer was deeply interested in Japanese ceramics and employed Kataro Shirayamadani from Japan as one of the firm's main decorators.

The stylized silver mounts echo the painted floral imagery

The Standard brown glaze imparts its characteristic mellow hue

The naturalistic painting by Shirayamadani is of exceptional quality

LOOP-HANDLED PITCHER Painted insects and leaves by Albert Valentien are contrasted on this pitcher with an incised geometric border around the shoulder, and enriched with gilt accents. *c.1883. H:9 in (23 cm).*

JAPANESE-STYLE VASE The cylindrical form is incised with script and an Asian peasant in relief, and these are highlighted in reds, browns, and greens against a tan ground. *1882. H:11¼ in (29.25 cm).*

The silver mounts in elaborate Art Nouveau style are by the Gorham Silver Co.

THE CHEMISTRY OF SUCCESS

When William Watts Taylor was appointed manager in 1883, Rookwood became more commercial. The following year, decorator Laura Fry began to apply colored slip and, later, background colors with an atomizer, producing the phenomenally smooth finish for which the pottery is renowned. The ceramicist Artus van Briggle catered to the continued preoccupation with Asian forms and motifs. During his 13 years with the pottery, he took working vacations in Paris, where he studied, among other things, the Asian collection at the Musée des Arts Décoratifs. In 1889, Rookwood was awarded a gold medal at the Exposition Universelle in Paris and the firm recorded a profit for the first time. Maria Storer retired the next year, in 1890.

Among the most celebrated wares produced by Rookwood are the vessels and plaques decorated with underglaze portraits. Leading artists employed by the company, such as Grace Young and Matt Daly, painted a series depicting African Americans and American Indians. Other designs were drawn from nature, featuring forest and sea landscapes resplendent with flowers, fungi, birds, and fish. The common theme was the beauty and abundance of the American landscape. Some of the more prestigious pieces had sinuous silver overlays.

Rookwood pottery has a whole range of factory marks and features artist's ciphers, process marks, shape numbers, and even clay marks.

AMERICAN INDIAN SERIES The Chief High Hawk Standard Glaze plaque (*above*) was painted by Grace Young in 1903, and the red clay charger (*right*) by Henry François Farny in 1881. H:14¼ in (37.5 cm).

Painted pressed red clay charger D:11 in (28 cm)

ROOKWOOD GLAZES

Two chemists, Karl Lagenbeck and Stanley Burt, ushered in a golden age when the Rookwood Pottery perfected many of the outstanding glazes that made it such a success. The first great accomplishment was the Standard glaze, developed in 1884. A translucent high gloss with a yellow tinge, Standard glaze makes the underlying artwork look darker and heavier. Production of the glaze ceased in 1909 as it was becoming less popular.

Also developed in 1884, Iris is a clear lead-based glaze with a high sheen. It was named after the painted irises that decorate so many of the pots coated with the glaze. A variation known as Black Iris also exists.

Another high-gloss glaze, Sea Green gives the underglaze decoration a blue-green color and an impression of depth. It was particularly suited to seascapes and fish, but also used for flowers.

Noting the success of Grueby's matte glaze, Rookwood devised its own version, simply called Matte, around 1900. Flat and opaque with a relatively coarse texture, it was made and applied in a wide variety of tones.

Vellum, considered to be the link between Rookwood's gloss and matte glazes, was introduced in about 1900. It creates a hazy effect on the underglaze decoration, as if it were viewed through a film. Vellum was generally clear, although it was also available with green and yellow tints. Flowers and landscapes were usual subject matter.

One of Rookwood's later creations, the Jewel Porcelain glaze was first used in 1916. A clear gloss glaze, it is remarkable for its tiny air bubbles that produce an effect similar to the Vellum glaze, but without the same waxiness.

LIMOGES-STYLE VASE The French ceramics–inspired imagery of birds in flight and perched on branches was handpainted by N. J. Hirschfeld, and is enriched by a glossy glaze. 1882. H:7¾ in (19 cm).

VELLUM GLAZE VASE The wild mushroom decoration was painted by Carl Schmidt in shades of brown, orange, yellow, green, and gray, against a blue-graduating-into-celadon ground. 1906. H:7 in (18 cm).

JEWEL PORCELAIN GLAZE VASE Also painted by Carl Schmidt, this vase depicts lavender, irises, and leaves in characteristically soft pastel tones of lavender, white, and green on a shaded blue-green ground. 1925. H:11¾ in (30 cm).

IRIS GLAZE VASE Carved in high relief by Matthew A. Daly, hyacinths and leaves are painted in subtle shades of blue and green, set against a mottled and graduated indigo and violet ground. 1901. H:8 in (20.5 cm).

MATTE GLAZE VASE Designed by Kataro Shirayamadani, this vase is modeled with branches of ginkgo leaves and berries in shallow relief under a typically soft and hazy green and yellow Matte glaze. 1905. H:10½ in (26.5 cm).

SEA GREEN GLAZE VASE Designed by Anne Marie Valentin, this vase features an overlaid, languid, verdigris-bronze nude above the typically opalescent Sea Green glazed ground. 1900. H:5¼ in (13 cm).

GEORGE OHR VASE This corseted vase is glazed in four panels: brown and green speckled, caramel speckled, gunmetal, and bottle green, all over a marbleized clay body. *1890s. H:8¼ in (21 cm).*

The gaping neck recalls young birds feeding in the nest

The scrolled handles suggest tendril-like forms

GEORGE OHR TEAPOT The large, C-handled vessel with a serpentine spout is finished in one of Ohr's flambé glazes, here dynamically streaked and mottled from blood red to emerald green. *1890s. W:9 in (22.75 cm).*

AMERICAN ART POTTERY

The work done at the Biloxi Art Pottery in Mississippi by George Ohr between about 1880 and 1910 remains unique in the world of art pottery. Known to many as the "mad potter of Biloxi," Ohr was an inimitable artisan firmly in the Arts and Crafts mold.

GEORGE OHR'S MUD BABIES

Not only did Ohr dig his own clay and formulate his own glazes, but he also built his own pottery and throwing wheel—all this with just the occasional help of his son Leo. Complete freedom from organized industry at every level of his operation allowed Ohr to develop a highly personal relationship with his craft. He thought of his prolific stockpile of vessels as his "mud babies." After a fire destroyed his workshop in 1894, he referred to the charred pots rescued from the wreckage as "burnt babies."

GEORGE OHR POT With a folded petal rim and a whimsical pinched and applied face, the pot is made of scroddled clay bisque. Like most of Ohr's bisque vessels, it bears his signature in script on the underside. *c.1905. W:5½ in (14 cm).*

Innovative glazing is a feature of Ohr's earlier pieces

Scroddled describes the mottled appearance that comes from scraps of different-colored clays

Ohr's virtuosity at the wheel is evident in the eggshell delicacy of his vessels. It is still unclear how he managed to contort such thin clay into the bizarre twisted, folded, and dented forms that characterize his work—it has certainly never been replicated. Many of Ohr's contemporaries, although exasperated by what they considered his stubborn disdain for the principles of good design, were full of praise for his glazes. Ohr created matte and luster glazes as well as a wide range of vibrant hues including yellow and pink, but was always more interested in form and left more and more of his work unglazed as time went by.

ECCENTRIC EXPERIMENTERS

As extravagantly eccentric as he was gifted, Ohr cultivated an enormous waxed mustache and was a consummate self-publicist. Like many a neglected genius, he was firmly convinced that he would one day be revered as a visionary. He put up signs at exhibitions proclaiming himself "the greatest art potter on Earth" and even delivered a selection of his work to the Smithsonian Institution, including an umbrella stand inscribed with a rambling and prophetic dedication ending, "This pot is here, and I am the potter who was." Ohr's legacy— thousands of unsold mud babies packed and crated in his old pottery—was discovered in the late 1960s, some 50 years after his death, and led eventually to a reappraisal of his work.

Another precursor of the studio pottery movement was Theophilus Brouwer. Like Ohr, Brouwer was personally involved in every stage of the production process, from sourcing the clay right through to decorating the finished pots. He was another eccentric with a talent for self-promotion: the entrance to his Middle Lane Pottery in East Hampton was marked with the jawbones of

CHELSEA KERAMIC ART

The Chelsea Keramic Art Works was established in 1872, one of the first dedicated American art potteries. Early innovations included a fine redware burnished with linseed oil, made for two years from 1876. In 1877, Chelsea began to produce glazed faience pieces, eventually inspiring Rookwood and Grueby. Although the firm sometimes opted for the pick-and-mix approach to historicism so hated by Morris and other Arts and Crafts purists, the quality of its glazes was outstanding.

Chelsea is notable for sacrificing commercial success in favor of artistic experiments and expression. Interesting effects were achieved by hammering the surface before firing, applying real flowers, and exploring the possibilities of slip decoration. Hugh Robertson, son of Chelsea Keramic's founder, spent the 1880s obsessed with replicating the deep red Asian oxblood glaze. He developed many glaze tones, finally perfecting his Robertson's Blood to great critical acclaim in 1888.

PILLOW VASE The bird is painted in barbotine (relief) by Hugh Robertson of the Chelsea Keramic Art Works, and set against a marbleized black and gray ground. *1880s. H:5¼ in (13.5 cm).*

an enormous whale. Brouwer usually worked on his own, sometimes with the help of American Indian assistants.

His most celebrated achievement was the Fire Painting technique, perfected around 1900. This involved applying glaze to a biscuit-fired pot with a brush and then exposing the pot to an open furnace. Once cooled, the process resulted in a high-gloss finish with wonderful variegated tones.

POTTERY AS THERAPY

Arequipa Pottery was steeped in the warm climate of the San Francisco Bay area, where Henry E. Bothin sponsored a sanatorium for the rehabilitation of young women suffering from tuberculosis. The Englishman Frederick Rhead, formerly art director at Roseville, was invited to join the community as ceramicist in 1911, instructing the convalescing women in every aspect of his craft.

Inspired by the lush wooded setting of his new workplace, Rhead began to experiment with the local California clay before Albert Solon succeeded him as director of the pottery in 1913. The rapid turnover of patients meant that new decorators were constantly being trained and then lost, so Arequipa's output was variable in quality. Some of the decorative work is outstanding, including luster glazes and experiments with squeezebag ornament, in which tubes of slip are applied as though a baker were decorating a cake.

AREQUIPA VASE Squeezebag-decorated with branches of fruits and leaves, this vase is handpainted in a pale matte blue against a mottled indigo ground. *1911–18. H:6 in (15 cm).*

AREQUIPA VASE The baluster shape of the vase is decorated with a carved pattern of leaves finished with a green and lustrous turquoise glaze. *1913–18. H:13½ in (34.5 cm).*

BURNT BABY VASE Some of Ohr's vases—the "burnt babies"—survived the fire in his workshop in 1894. The bulbous body and torn neck of this vase emerged covered in shards and extensively charred. *1894. H:4½ in (11 cm).*

BROUWER VASE Bands of dark brown glaze are dripped over a streaked and mottled orange and yellow ground. The lustrous finish was achieved in the kiln by the technique known as Fire Painting. *1890s. H:12 in (30.5 cm).*

NEW GLAZES

Toward the close of the 19th century, a growing demand for art pottery prompted a number of American ceramics firms to venture into uncharted territory. With the materials, equipment, and skilled staff already in place, many of these companies found new success with their artware, often thanks to innovative approaches to glazing.

The Grueby-Faience Company of Boston, noted for its fine tiles, began to market a range of art pottery in 1897. Designer George Prentiss Kendrick was inspired by the French potter Auguste Delaherche, but found his true muse in the native flora of New England. Grasses, flowers, and above all leaves feature prominently on Grueby pots of this period, often incorporating handles into an overall organic form. The

company blended traditional handcraft with factory production, employing teams of potters—often students from art colleges—to throw pots to specified designs. Decorative elements were then incised, applied, and molded precisely by hand. The result was a product that was entirely made by hand but to a preapproved standard.

THE COLOR OF NATURE

Proprietor William Henry Grueby was personally responsible for developing his firm's most important asset—its glazes. He concocted a range of matte colors including yellow, blue, and gray, usually used alone but sometimes combined. These were among the first matte glazes available in the United States, after those developed by Chelsea Keramic Art Works and Rookwood (*see p.159*), and they were well received.

It was, however, Grueby's matte green glaze, which he described as being "like the smooth surface of a melon, or the bloom of a leaf," that established the reputation of his firm. The soft variations in leafy green tone are all the more remarkable because they were achieved simply by controlling the kiln environment carefully, without any post-firing treatments.

In 1899 the company was divided into two separate concerns—Grueby Faience (later Grueby Faience and Tile Company), which produced architectural ceramics, and Grueby Pottery, which concentrated on artwares. After enjoying great success with the matte green glaze in particular for several years, the art pottery business began to falter. Despite appointing Karl Lagenbeck from Rookwood superintendent in 1908, the firm stopped production in 1911.

The glass shade, in mottled green and yellow, complements the soft green of the base

The Tiffany shade is secured above the base with a brass frame

The flowerheads, like their trailing stems, are handmolded

Grueby's matte glazes range from pale yellowish green to a rich dark cucumber-skin green

GRUEBY-TIFFANY LAMP The color of the Grueby base is echoed in the glass tiles of the made-to-match Tiffany shade. *c.1905.* H:21¾ in (55.25 cm).

CUENCA-DECORATED TILE Mounted in a bronze trivet (not shown), this Grueby tile by Marie Seaman features a red tulip with speckled green leaves against a mottled, darker green matte ground. *c.1905.* Sq:6 in (15 cm).

VASEKRAFT VASE With a pair of long, pierced, buttressed handles, the inverted trumpet shape of this vase is finished with Fulper's Leopard's Skin crystalline glaze in subtle shades of green, brown, and black. *1909–15.* H:11 in (27.5 cm).

FROM HOMEWARE TO ARTWARE

Farther down the eastern seaboard, the Fulper Pottery Company of New Jersey launched its Vasekraft art pottery after experiments in 1909. Fulper was known for its heavily set homeware and used the same clay mix for this new line, so the art pottery is relatively coarse. Here, too, the crowning achievement was the glaze, or more accurately the staggering variety of glazes, used to finish the pots. Fulper marketed a range of gloss and luster glazes, as well as fashionable matte, in colors with evocative names such as Cat's Eye and Elephant's Breath.

Fulper's most prestigious line was named Famille Rose, with a glaze claimed to be an authentic reproduction of the ancient Asian technique. The glaze was made in six tones, including one called Peach Bloom after the famous antique Chinese vase bought for $18,000—then a small fortune—by the banker J. P. Morgan.

The Chicago lawyer William Gates had built up a sizable business manufacturing ceramic pipes and bricks when, in 1901, he began to design art pottery. His trademark, Teco, was derived from Terra Cotta, the name of the Illinois town in which his company was based. Although original and striking, these forms were for the most part molded rather than thrown, which had the advantage of keeping the prices down. The real craft of the operation was in the mottled earth-tone glazes.

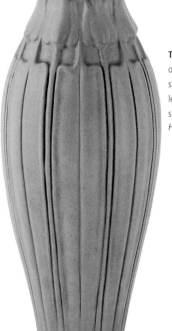

DEDHAM POTTERY VASE Hugh Robertson's abstract composition comprises a thick, curdled, streaked, and mottled semigloss glaze. *1900–10. H:7½ in (19 cm).*

Following the phenomenal success of Grueby's matte green glaze, Teco developed a similar product and concentrated on this to the exclusion of all else for almost a decade. This Teco Green can be distinguished from Grueby's matte green by its slight silver luster.

TECO POTTERY VASE The organic form is molded with stylized tulips above a curled leaf base, and finished with a smooth, matte glaze. *1903-10. H:13¾ in (35 cm).*

MARBLEHEAD POTTERY VASE The tapering cylindrical body is painted with stylized chestnut trees in muted green and pale pink against a rich, tobacco-brown ground. *1910–15. H:11½ in (29 cm).*

A GALAXY OF GLAZES

Other notable achievements were chalked up by Dedham, a Massachusetts firm that formulated a thick, flowing lava glaze and a mysterious crackle glaze achieved by using lamp black. Chemist Cadmon Robertson formulated almost 1,000 distinct recipes for Hampshire Pottery. Marblehead, originally conceived as a therapeutic workshop for convalescing patients, primarily decorated in monochrome but also marketed complex multicolored pieces.

The Pewabic Pottery was founded by Mary Chase Berry, who was initially interested in decorating ceramics and then started her own business. Nothing if not experimental, Pewabic developed dozens of glazes, among which the iridescent hues are especially prized.

FLAMBÉ VASE Its large, squat, ovoid form is streaked and mottled with one of Fulper's Asian-inspired glazes: a frothy Chinese Blue flambé. *1909–15. W:10 in (25.5 cm).*

CLIFTON

The Clifton Art Pottery, established in 1905, came closer to Morris's Arts and Crafts ideal than most American ceramics firms. Employing scarcely more than a dozen staff, the firm used the local New Jersey red clay in its unglazed state for a range of vessels named Clifton Indian Ware. The shapes and decorative motifs found in this line were directly inspired by American Indian pots. Substituting the indigenous American people for Morris' romanticized medieval past, Clifton's craftsmen drew on a vision of a bygone age more in touch with the simple rhythms of nature. The range extended to kitchenware as well as more decorative objects. For these, the porous raw clay was sealed with an application of gloss black glaze to the interior. Other Clifton Art Pottery lines included Crystal Patina, decorated with a pale green glaze and blended tones of other colors, including yellow, green, and brown.

Gourd-shaped Indian Ware vase W:6½ in (16.5 cm)

Tapered oviform Indian Ware vase H:9½ in (24.5 cm)

CLIFTON VASES Both pieces are modeled in red clay and incised with geometric and eagle (*above*) motifs inspired by American Indian designs. *1905–08.*

PEWABIC POTTERY VASE A slender and elongated baluster form is covered in one of the company's iridescent glazes, in this case a spattered abstract pattern in shades of green indigo. *c.1910. H:12½ in (32 cm).*

BRITISH CERAMICS

The vigorous market for handcrafted ceramics around 1900 was led in Britain by small art potteries. Larger, more established companies followed with artware alongside their existing mass-produced ranges.

DOULTON

Already a successful producer of architectural stoneware, the Lambeth firm of Doulton & Co. turned to its local art school for its new

LAMBETHWARE VASE Decorated by Hannah Barlow, a sgraffito band of cows and donkeys lies between grapes on the shoulder and waves on the foot. *1880–1900. H:12¼ in (31 cm).*

art pottery venture in the 1870s. Henry Doulton, son of the firm's founder, gave his designers an extraordinarily free reign, and the success of his artware can largely be ascribed to individual artists such as George Tinworth and Frank Butler. The firm pioneered the employment of female staff, who enjoyed the same autonomy as their male colleagues. Women such as Emily Edwards and Hannah Barlow produced much of Doulton's most celebrated work in this period.

Hannah Barlow worked for the factory for more than three decades from 1871. Her sgraffito designs featuring horses, goats, and other animals came from the sketches she had made since she was a child. The sgraffito technique itself, involving scratching away at a slip glaze to reveal the contrasting ground beneath, was firmly within the Arts and Crafts tradition. Even after firing, the incised lines retain their original precision, so not only is each pot unique but they all also bear the indelible stamp of the potter's hand.

The owl's head forms a push-fit stoneware lid for the jar

LAMBETHWARE JAR The footed-owl body is influenced by much earlier 17th-century German examples. The jar is molded in stoneware and decorated with the greens, blues, browns, and grays typical of Doulton's Lambeth palette. *1883. H:7¾ in (19.5 cm).*

THE MARTIN BROTHERS

Another famous graduate of Lambeth School of Art, Robert Wallace Martin worked freelance for Doulton before going into business with his brothers in 1873. They were a close-knit team, and each of the Martin brothers specialized in a particular aspect of their craft.

Robert Wallace had the greatest creative input and was responsible for the extraordinarily characterful birds, armadillos, salamanders, and other fantastical creatures that still define the firm's work. Edwin, also trained at Lambeth School of

Art, designed seascapes and murky aquatic vistas that, like Robert's models, owed a debt to the Italian grottoesque tradition. Walter Frazer was in charge of throwing pots—work that was carried out entirely by hand, at a wheel. He also contributed glaze recipes and was adept at decorating with incised marks.

Charles was in charge of the administration side of the business. He garnered much favorable press attention as well as prominent clients including Queen Victoria. From 1877 the pottery was based in Southall, where it remained until it closed in 1914.

BIRD GROUP Modeled in salt-glazed stoneware by Robert Wallace Martin, each of the three grotesque birds has a detachable head and is glazed in shades of blue, green, and ocher. *1914. H:7¾ in (19.5 cm).*

STONEWARE VASE The oviform body of this Martin Brothers vase is decorated with incised pomegranates and caterpillars in shades of ocher and brown. *1896. H:10½ in (27 cm).*

THE BROTHERS Walter Frazer Martin (*left*), Robert Wallace Martin (*center*), and Edwin Bruce Martin (*right*) photographed working in the studio of their Southall Pottery, in London. *1912.*

RUSKIN ART POTTERY

William Howson Taylor, founder of the Ruskin art pottery in 1898, was better placed than most to tap the pool of talent nurtured by Britain's art schools. His father, Edward Richard Taylor, was the principal of Birmingham School of Art and a pioneer of craft teaching. William persuaded his father to contribute a number of designs for simple vessels inspired by Chinese forms to the Ruskin Pottery during its early years, and Edward had a lasting association with the business.

William Taylor relied almost entirely on local talent to keep his operation afloat, concentrating his own efforts on developing glazes. With superlative results, he joined the vigorous pursuit of the perfect flambé glaze—a challenge that had been occupying the minds of many of Europe's leading ceramicists since the 1870s. First developed in Ming-dynasty China, flambé glazed wares have a lustrous crimson finish with streaks of turquoise.

The output of the Ruskin Pottery was true to its namesake, avoiding the clutter of so much 19th-century ceramic work. Simple shapes carried little surface adornment, drawing attention to the carefully worked glazes. Taylor's firm found further success supplying ceramic cabochons for department stores such as Liberty & Co. that were looking for a cheaper alternative to precious and semiprecious stones. The cabochons were mounted on mirrors and furniture.

Different reds, such as crimson and *sang-de-boeuf*, recur in the high-fired flambé glazes

Chinese shapes and forms are echoed in many Ruskin pieces

Streaks and graduations of color, as well as mottling and speckling, are a feature of Ruskin wares

RUSKIN POTTERY VASE The elegant, Chinese-inspired shape of the vase is complemented by a high-fired Chinese-style flambé glaze of rich crimson with hints of turquoise. *1910. H:11 in (28 cm).*

RUSKIN POTTERY VASE The shouldered oviform body is finished in a high-fired flambé glaze speckled with crimson, purple, and turquoise. *1912. H:9 in (23 cm).*

RUSKIN ONION POT The squat body of this pot is finished in a high-fired glaze, producing speckled bands of colors ranging from *sang-de-boeuf*, through turquoise and green, to pink. *c.1905. H:9½ in (24 cm).*

CERAMICS GALLERY

The inventive use of specialty glazes, both matte and gloss, was a key characteristic of Arts and Crafts ceramics. Underglaze was often used to apply artwork that was then covered in layers of sheer glazes to add depth and texture. Decoration was sometimes added in the form of colored slips. Flowers and leaves were popular motifs, and some pieces depicted whimsical animals.

KEY

1. Adelaide Robineau porcelain tile. W:6½ in (16.5 cm). ④ **2.** Batchelder tile. H:8¾ in (22 cm). ①
3. W. J. Walley bowl. W:9 in (22.5 cm). ② **4.** Minton charger decorated by Louis J. Rhead. c.1880. D:16¼ in (41.5 cm). ⑤ **5.** C. H. Brannam sgraffito jug. 1898. H:11¾ in (30 cm). ① **6.** C. H. Brannam Puffin jug. H:6½ in (16.5 cm). ① **7.** Bernard Moore ruby luster punch bowl. c.1910. D:18 in (45.5 cm). ③ **8.** Della Robbia ceramic jug. H:7½ in (19 cm). ② **9.** Salt-glazed stoneware punch bowl by Susan Frackelton. 1902. D:14 in (35.5 cm). ⑤ **10.** Stoneware charger by Alfred Powell. D:13 in (33 cm). ②

1 Robineau tile

2 Batchelder tile

3 W. J. Walley bowl

4 Minton charger

5 Sgraffito jug

6 C. H. Brannam jug

7 Bernard Moore punch bowl

8 Della Robbia jug

9 Stoneware punch bowl

10 Stoneware charger

11 Earthenware plate

11. Earthenware plate by J. Selwyn Dunn. D:12 in (31 cm). ② **12.** Clifton Crystal Patina vase. 1906. W:7 in (18 cm). ② **13.** Hancock & Sons Morrisware vase by George Cartlidge. H:7 in (17.5 cm). ③ **14.** Niloak Mission Ware vase. H:7½ in (19 cm). ① **15.** Elton vase decorated in colored slips. H:10¼ in (26 cm). ① **16.** Adelaide Robineau porcelain vase. H:4 in (10 cm). ③ **17.** Overbeck vase decorated by Elizabeth and Hannah Overbeck. H:8½ in (21 cm). ⑥ **18.** Walrath vase with a speckled green glaze. H:6 in (15 cm). ③ **19.** C. H. Brannam vase decorated with sgraffito fish. 1902. H:7 in (18 cm). ① **20.** Hancock & Sons Morrisware vase by George Cartlidge. H:9¾ in (25 cm). ③

12 *Clifton vase*

13 *Hancock & Sons vase*

14 *Niloak Mission Ware vase*

15 *Elton vase*

16 *Robineau vase*

17 *Overbeck vase*

18 *Walrath vase*

19 *C. H. Brannam vase*

20 *Hancock & Sons vase*

EXOTIC INFLUENCES

OUTLINING HIS VISION OF IDEAL INTERIOR DECORATION IN AN 1895 LECTURE, FREDERIC, LORD LEIGHTON SAID: "IT WILL NOT BE FALSE AND PALTRY LUXURY; IT WILL BE OPULENCE, IT WILL BE SINCERITY." THE GREAT CITIES OF THE WEST WERE CERTAINLY CRYING OUT FOR A TOUCH OF TRUE DAZZLE AND SPLENDOR.

WALNUT PLANT STAND Made for Liberty & Co. in the Anglo-Moorish style, the stand has ebonized Moorish brackets and mashrabiyya (bobbin turnings), on angled kickout legs. *c.1890. H:33 in (84 cm).*

Heavy industry had brought progress and prosperity to the West, but carried soot and dirt in its wake. Those with enough money to travel returned home struck by the riot of color they had seen in exotic places such as Persia, India, and Morocco.

Owen Jones's *Grammar of Ornament*, written after wide travel in Spain and the Middle East, gave extensive coverage to Moorish and Persian style. This illustrated guide had a lasting influence and many interior decorators used it as a source book. In the South Kensington Museum, founded to house artifacts from the 1851 Great Exhibition, the public could see ancient Iznik ceramics at first hand. Designers allied to the Aesthetic Movement looked to Japan for artistic influence, while Eastern architecture had been fashionable since John Nash completed his extraordinary Royal Pavilion at Brighton on the English south coast in the "Hindoo" style.

EASTERN ALLURE AND LUSTER

Eager to learn from the craft traditions of other countries, Arts and Crafts designers studied exotic antiques in the hope that they might unearth their secrets. William de Morgan was more successful than most, rediscovering the lost technique of luster glazing in 1873. Originally used in Persia and spreading as far as Italy before being lost, this technique produced vivid colors. De Morgan used a Persian palette of turquoise, lemon yellow, purple, green, and red enamels over a white ground to create fresh and lively tiles and other ceramic wares after the Eastern tradition.

Glass-maker Thomas Webb introduced a range of cameo glass decorated with intricate repeating tendrils in symmetrical patterns inspired by Moorish designs. George Woodall's finest design for Webb was a cameo plaque entitled "The Moorish Bathers." Department stores, too, responded to demand and soon began to stock exotic furnishings. Liberty & Co., for example, retailed a galleried side table with fretwork panels inspired by Moroccan design.

LEIGHTON HOUSE

The epitome of exotic style in late Victorian London was Leighton House, the home of Frederic, Lord Leighton. His position as a respected artist had visitors flocking to see the opulence of his Arab Hall, completed in 1881 to designs by George Aitchison.

Modeled closely on the banqueting room at La Zisa, an ancient Saracen palace in Sicily, the Arab Hall's main features include a domed ceiling, numerous carved marble columns, elaborate paintwork, and mosaics. A golden mosaic frieze by Walter Crane encircles the walls, and the floor is covered with a mosaic designed by Aitchison. The frieze features exotic creatures, although it was modified from Crane's original design after Leighton told him to "cleave to the sphinx and the eagle, they are delightful. I don't like the duck women." A fountain in the center of the room is surrounded by a shallow pool, into which guests would apparently inadvertently plunge. Latticework wooden mashrabiyya (bobbin-turned) screens line the galleries. Unfortunately, Leighton did not have enough money to commission Edward Burne-Jones to decorate the domed ceiling as originally planned.

IZNIK TILE Potters in Iznik, near Istanbul, made wares with swirling, scrolling designs in blue, turquoise, green, and red. These wares had a huge influence in the late 19th century on designers such as William de Morgan. *c.1570. H:7¾ in (19.5 cm).*

Stylized flowers and leaves are inspired by Islamic pottery

"IZNIK" VASE AND COVER The color scheme and bold, all-over decoration of this William de Morgan vase look directly to Iznik wares. *c.1890. H:10¾ in (27.5 cm).*

CAMEO GLASSWARE English glass-maker Thomas Webb made a range of glasses covered with Moorish-style decoration of semi-abstract patterns. *1890. D:4½ in (11.5 cm).*

LEIGHTON HOUSE The Arab Hall is the centerpiece of the house. It was designed to display the vast collection of Islamic tiles that Lord Leighton bought on his travels through Syria, Egypt, and the Greek islands.

GLASS AND LAMPS

THE ARTS AND CRAFTS GENERATION UNDERSTOOD THE IMPORTANCE OF LIGHT IN INTERIOR DESIGN. LEADED GLASS FILTERED AND ENHANCED SUNLIGHT, WHILE LAMPS WERE INCREASINGLY A SOURCE OF ARTIFICIAL LIGHT.

MEDIEVAL LOOK Inspiration for much Arts and Crafts stained and leaded glass came from medieval examples, such as this round window depicting a horned devil on horseback. *14th century.*

LEADED GLASS

The use of leaded and stained glass owed much to William Morris's passion for medieval Gothic churches, noted for their colorful windows that provided decoration and stylistic harmony as well as light. His admiration for Gothic architecture led him to sites such as York Minster, the chapel at Merton College in Oxford, and Chartres Cathedral in northern France. All boast outstanding decorative leaded glazing. Taking his lead from Augustus Pugin, father of the Victorian Gothic Revival, Morris established the early reputation of Morris, Marshall, Faulkner & Co. for stained glass.

The Pre-Raphaelite painters Edward Burne-Jones and Dante Gabrielle Rossetti provided a wealth of designs for the stained glass of Morris, Marshall, Faulkner & Co. These men never strayed far from their 14th-century religious inspiration, drafting designs with

BIBLICAL IMAGERY This stained and leaded glass panel by Morris and Co. depicts St. Peter with the keys to heaven, set against lozenge-shaped lights of British wild flowers—the latter a favorite Morris motif. *1870s–80s.*

verdant backgrounds and biblical subject matter. So accurate was Morris's re-creation of medieval stained glass that his competitors accused him of fraud, arguing that his prize-winning exhibit at the 1862 International Exhibition consisted of restored glass from the Middle Ages.

TIMELESS WINDOWS

Morris's company outsourced much of its manufacturing work to Powell & Sons, experts in flashed glass, in which the clear body of the glass is coated with a translucent colored husk. Other manufacturers who kept traditional methods alive included Britten & Gibson, who made glass for Walter Crane and E. S. Prior. By blowing liquid glass into flat molds, they managed to imitate medieval glass, in which the panes were thicker at the center and distorted the light in an intriguing way. This bona fide medievalism was applauded by Christopher Whall, a professor at the Central School of Arts and Crafts in London, who was at the forefront of the stained glass renaissance in Britain. One of his principles was that figures in colored glass should be drawn from life not from paintings.

The British guilds turned to stained glass as the Arts and Crafts movement matured. Mackmurdo's Century Guild was supplied with designs by clergyman Selwyn Image, while

Cherish some flower
Be it ever so lowly

Work for some end
Be it ever so slowly

PRE-RAPHAELITE STYLE Inspired by the Italian style of painting before the influence of Raphael, this stained and leaded glass panel depicts a medieval maiden gathering flowers. The accompanying romantic verse is by the Pre-Raphaelite artist and poet Dante Gabriel Rossetti. *1860s–80s. H:10½ in (26.5 cm).*

AMERICAN FLORAL Depicting stylized blossoms among a border of small pave-set tiles, around a field of larger tiles with scattered petals, this American window is stained in tones of amber, blue, and pink, and black and white. It survived the 1906 San Francisco earthquake and fire. *1880s. W:58 in (145 cm).*

TIFFANY STYLE Set in oak and iron frames, with protective glass to one side, this pair of leaded glass windows depicts a rural landscape in the style of Louis Comfort Tiffany. They incorporate blown, mottled, striated, and confetti glass in many vivid colors. *c.1905. H:66 in (165 cm).*

Ashbee's Guild of Handicraft employed the manufacturer Paul Woodroffe. Traditional stained glass workshops were set up all over Britain, with particular success in Scotland and Ireland. Sarah Purser founded Au Túr Gloine (The Tower of Glass) in Dublin in 1903. Like Burne-Jones and Rossetti, she brought her experience as a painter to bear on her new career as a glazier.

GLASS IN THE HOME

In the mid-19th century, the glass tax was abolished and domestic glaziers began using larger panes of glass, often installed in bay windows. While enjoying the lighter interiors created by larger windows, homeowners could still subscribe to the Arts and Crafts aesthetic by using colored glass panels as wall hangings or inset into furniture.

There was a reaction against windows with large glass expanses in some circles by those who considered broken, latticed panes more homelike. William Purcell and George Elmslie, American architects of the Prairie School, installed over 80 glass panels in Purcell's Minneapolis home. Mostly decorated with simple rectangular and diamond grid geometric motifs, the main virtue of these panes was to harmonize the interior color scheme.

FROM LA FARGE TO TIFFANY

The American oil painter and watercolorist John La Farge carefully followed the progress of the Pre-Raphaelite movement and through it was introduced to the leaded glass of Morris, Marshall, Faulkner & Co. Combining these influences with his fascination for two-dimensional Japanese prints, La Farge set about developing his own brand of leaded glass. His church commissions made use of many different types of decorative work within the same window, from cloisonné to confetti glass, a complicated technique that involved embedding tiny flakes of color within the molten batch of opalescent glass.

La Farge's experiments with opalescent art glass provided a starting point for the most celebrated American designer of leaded glass—Louis Comfort Tiffany. His leaded glass products included screens as well as the widely imitated Tiffany lamps. These ranged in complexity from simple geometric designs to intricate designs of stylized leaves and flowers in many different colors.

Along with leaded glass panes above the front door, leaded glass lampshades became the most common way in which Arts and Crafts principles were applied in the home.

TABLE SCREEN This small, trifold, leaded glass screen made by the Tiffany Studios depicts stylized trees and leaves in rich fall colors. *1905–10. H:8¼ in (21 cm).*

LAMPS

Artificial lighting became more efficient toward the end of the 19th century. The messy kerosene lamp was already being phased out in favor of gas lamps when Thomas Edison patented the light bulb in the 1880s. Although not in common use until about 1900, this invention had a huge effect on lighting design, especially in the United States, where people were quicker to adopt new technology.

BEATEN METAL AND GLASS

W. A. S. Benson was an early English pioneer in designs for electric light. He intuitively understood how best to harness the properties of copper and brass—his favored materials—to create soft lighting. Whereas gas lamps had invariably been directed up toward the ceiling, Benson used reflective metal to deflect electric light back down toward the floor. In his Chelsea home, C. R. Ashbee used fixtures made from beaten metal and hung with enamel shades to color and soften his electric lights.

Many American designers such as Dirk van Erp and members of the Roycroft community also favored beaten metal. Both of them had established reputations for fine hand-hammered copperware in the Arts and Crafts style. Van Erp's signature lamps often have bases converted from milk cans and other everyday items. His conical shades are usually made from stretched mica—a shiny, translucent silicate mineral that mottles the light

source beneath. Roycroft lamps sometimes have hammered copper shades that match their bases, giving them an austere decorative unity. Others have shades made out of stained and leaded glass—an ornamental feature that became very popular in the United States as more households converted to electricity.

The copper-domed glass shade terminates in a decorative conical finial

Pumpkin-orange glass is contrasted around the lower rim with small panels of periwinkle-blue glass

Ring handles hang from a copper band secured with a typical Arts and Crafts device: exposed rivets

ROYCROFTERS COPPER SHOP LAMP Designed by Dard Hunter, this lamp has a flared shade and leaded glass. The shade is raised on a hand-hammered, brass-washed, baluster-shaped base with three sockets and a pair of ring handles. 1905–10. H:22 in (55 cm).

The finish of hand-hammered, patinated copper is highly characteristic of Arts and Crafts metalware

DIRK VAN ERP LAMP This early example of Erp's work has a large milkcan-shaped base hand hammered from copper and finished with a warm brown surface patina. Riveted arms from the neck support the shade with its original mica panels secured in a copper frame. c.1910. H:24 in (61 cm).

ROYCROFT LAMP The hand-hammered shade has a ball finial and is raised above a candlestick-like copper base with ring-shaped knops, a circular foot, and a copper-bead pull. c.1910. H:20½ in (52 cm).

The shade is topped with a vented bronze cap in the form of a lotus flower

A lead framework, as with most Tiffany shades, secures the glass panels

The panels are made from Tiffany's Favrile iridescent glass

TIFFANY STUDIOS CHANDELIER The turtleback shade covers a six-socket fixture and displays two rows of Favrile glass medallions of blue-green luster. c.1905. W:22 in (56 cm).

Of all the American firms that produced decorated glass lamp shades, Handel was one of the most innovative. Founded in Connecticut in 1885 by Philip J. Handel, the firm is most famous for reviving the old English craft of mirror painting and adapting it to lighting. Handel's reverse-painted and leaded glass designs feature scenes from the natural world. Soft colors and flowing shapes reminiscent of draped fabric give Handel lamps a more feminine look than those of Tiffany, the company's biggest rival. With a record of success with stained glass, Louis Comfort Tiffany bought a glass furnace at Corona near New York in 1892 and began to manufacture lampshades. Ideal for softening electric light, his colored leaded glass shades were a huge success and inspired many imitators. Former employees of Tiffany Studios founded both Quezal Art Glass and Steuben Glass Works, and both became successful in their own right. Tiffany's continued experiments with glass resulted in Cypriote, which mimics the pitted finish of ancient Roman glass. Many Tiffany lamps incorporate glass turtlebacks into the base or the shade. Made from iridescent Favrile glass, these decorative elements have an uneven finish that diffuses light in an unusual manner and gives the lamps a handcrafted appearance. Tiffany combined his glass shades with exquisitely detailed matching metal bases, making the lamps unique works of art in their own right.

STURDY WOOD

Gustav Stickley made much plainer lamps than those of Tiffany and his rivals. Combining solid wooden structures with hand-forged matte metal fittings, Stickley's standing Newell post lamps bear a resemblance to his furniture in their simplicity of form and structure as well as their architectural design. At the Roycroft in East Aurora, Elbert Hubbard sold similar simple wooden lamps alongside his hammered-copper creations.

Influential American architects such as the Greene Brothers and Frank Lloyd Wright began to take a keen interest in lighting, recognizing it as a key feature of their building designs. At the Gamble House in Pasadena, the Greenes used light to help define different areas within an interior, and Frank Lloyd Wright experimented with recessed lighting to make it an integral part of his buildings.

HANDEL CO. LAMP The domed shade has curved panels of marbled, honey-colored glass. Set under an overlaid lead framework, it is reverse-painted around the rim with an oak-leaf border. c.1910. H:13¾ in (35 cm).

The bronze base is chemically finished with a rich brown patina

The urn-shaped base incorporates a band of iridescent Favrile glass turtlebacks

TIFFANY STUDIOS LAMP Its domed leaded-glass shade is composed of graduated panels of marbled green glass, and a border of lozenge-shaped turtlebacks in iridescent green Favrile glass. c.1905. H:20¾ in (53 cm).

GUSTAV STICKLEY LAMPS Designed as staircase newel posts, these two lamps have four-sided, hammered-copper lanterns lined with mica glass. These are raised above stained cedar posts with square bases. 1904–15. H:29½ in (74 cm).

METALWARE

INSPIRED BY WILLIAM MORRIS AND THE CELTIC REVIVAL, ARTISAN

METALWORKERS SOUGHT TO MAKE HIGH-QUALITY HANDCRAFTED SILVER. BUT

THEY STRUGGLED TO COMPETE WITH CHEAP FACTORY GOODS.

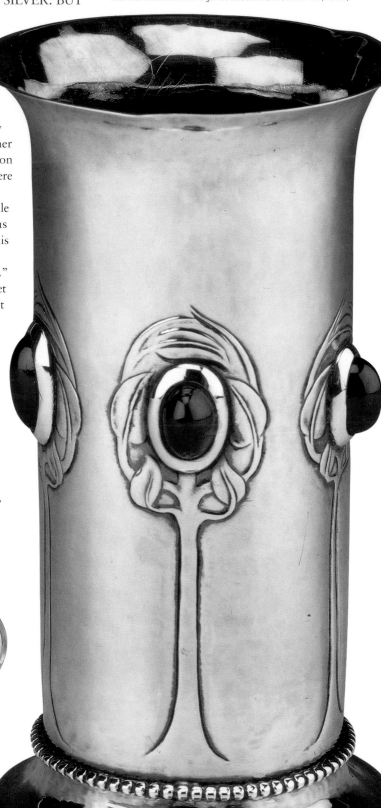

SILVER VASE Designed by C. R. Ashbee for the Guild of Handicraft, the vase is decorated with four embossed stylized trees above a ring of bead molding. Each tree is centered with a garnet cabochon. *c.1900. H:7 in (18 cm).*

THE NEW GUILDS

In 1871, John Ruskin had pleaded the importance of redeveloping rural industry in his *Fors Clavigera*, a series of letters to the working men of England. William Morris agreed with his romantic notions of a benevolent feudal society. Reviving the medieval guild system saved the skill base of British metalware. More than just workshops, these guilds were training grounds for raw talent, where master craftsmen could pass on their skills to a new generation. Spreading knowledge was central to Arts and Crafts philosophy, undermining the tyranny of the urban factory by empowering local communities to keep their traditions going. In Surrey, Godfrey Blount founded The Haslemere Peasant Industries as part of his proposal to return England to a preindustrial economy.

FROM CITY TO COUNTRY

In 1888, C. R. Ashbee, a London-trained architect and friend of Blount, founded the Guild of Handicraft following a series of lectures on Ruskin he had delivered at Toynbee Hall in London. As the enterprise grew, the Guild moved to larger premises at Mile End in East London. A smithy was constructed in the yard. The first metalware produced by the Guild of Handicraft included copper and brass dishes decorated with embossed

motifs of foliage and fish. Ashbee's architectural commissions kept the smithy busy producing door hardware and other fixtures. Metalworker John Pearson worked at the Guild and taught there until he left in about 1893.

When the lease on the Guild's Mile End premises expired, Ashbee was seized by the notion that he and his band of workers should "leave Babylon and go home to the land." The semi-derelict Cotswolds market town of Chipping Campden might have been custom-built for him— stately but neglected, it was ripe for an injection of new life.

Around 150 Londoners were settled in Chipping Campden and the Guild's workshops installed at the Old Silk Mill, renamed Essex House in honor of the Mile End property they had left behind. The Guildsmen overcame the initial hostility of some of the locals by becoming active in the community, organizing social events, classes, and lectures.

TEAPOT AND MILK JUG These Birmingham Guild pieces have a hand-hammered, electroplated silver finish, and were probably designed by Arthur Dixon. *c.1900. W:6½ in (16 cm).*

Newlyn School charger

COPPER BOWL AND CHARGER The large Newlyn School charger is the work of John Pearson, and is repoussé hammered with birds set among foliage. 1896. D:25¼ in (63 cm). WW. Also from Newlyn, the bowl is unattributed, but its repoussé fish frieze is inspired by Pearson's use of aquatic imagery. c.1900. W:11½ in (29 cm).

Newlyn School bowl

ENAMELING

The humility of form implicit in the strictest interpretation of Arts and Crafts style meant that silver- and metalworkers avoided decoration of precious stones. Alongside cabochon and uncut semiprecious stones such as garnets, the use of enamel escalated and became a fine art in its own right. Against a foil of plain or hammered silver, bright polychrome enamel plaques provided fresh and lively embellishment to silver in particular. Galleons in sail and natural landscapes were popular themes. Many silversmiths, such as Omar Ramsden, carried out their own enamel work, although others brought in specialists. One such was Fleetwood Charles Varley, a watercolorist whose landscapes can be seen on silver by the Guild of Handicraft.

SILVER AND ENAMEL BOX From the London workshop of Omar Ramsden and Alwyn Carr, its silver carcass is chased with wave-scroll motifs to complement the seascape imagery of the polychrome enamel panel set into the lid. 1907. W:3¾ in (9.5 cm).

The move caused quite a stir, and a number of skilled local men were inspired to join. The range of silver- and metalware produced by the Guild of Handicraft developed in scope to include elegant, loop-handled bowls and vases, and boxes set with semiprecious stones and enamel plaques. The outstanding quality of the work—mostly designed by Ashbee himself—was especially remarkable considering many of the Guildsmen were trained entirely on the job. After more than 20 years in business, the Guild of Handicraft was dissolved in 1908. Ashbee laid the blame for his project's demise on department stores such as Liberty and Heals. They could offer similar products at a much lower cost by using machine production methods.

REJECTING THE MACHINE

Under the motto "by hammer and hand," the Birmingham Guild of Handicraft avoided the use of machinery as much as its namesake in the Cotswolds. Aside from lathing, every process used to work the metal was done by hand. The Guild was established in 1890 and had close ties with Birmingham Art School. It spread its ideas through *The Quest*, a quarterly, hand-printed magazine. Silverware by the Birmingham Guild was sparsely decorated, inspired by churchware and Celtic design. Pieces often had the hand-hammered finish so typical of Arts and Crafts metalware. They were stamped with the Guild hallmark—individual designers and artists remained largely anonymous.

Montague Fordham, a director of the Birmingham Guild, took over the reins of the London-based Artificer's Guild in 1903 and began to display products by its members at his Maddox Street gallery. His appointment of Edward Spencer as chief designer took the Artificer's Guild in a new direction, producing functional homeware in copper,

brass, and silver, with stylized patterns drawn from natural forms. The hand-hammered finishes, particularly on silverware, are a tribute to the ideals that underpinned the Guild's work.

GOTHIC AND CELTIC INFLUENCE

Not every metalworker of this period rejected machinery as the new guilds did. Despite his growing belief in Arts and Crafts values, W. A. S. Benson was an unashamed fan of the machine, which helped his commercial success. Benson's work was inspired by the Gothic goblets and lanterns of Augustus Pugin and, later, by Christopher Dresser's strikingly geometric metalwork (*see pp.242–43*).

The Celtic influence that had proved such a hit for Liberty & Co. was much in evidence in Scottish metalwork. Alexander Ritchie and others took stylistic cues from the ancient Celtic carvings on Iona, incorporating knots and *entrelac* designs into their work. Phoebe Traquair and Marion Henderson championed this Scottish School style, which found a unique expression among students of the Glasgow School of Art (*see pp.244–45 and 262–63*).

COPPER AND BRASS BOWL
Designed by W. A. S. Benson, the copper, fluted petal bowl is raised on a foliate-form brass base with handle. c.1900. H:6 in (15 cm).

A naturalistic leaf shape creates a handle

The copper petals show signs of individual handcrafting

BRASS CANDLE SCONCE
By Agnes Bankier Harvey of the Glasgow School, the backplate is repoussé decorated with a girl's head among poppies. c.1900. H:11¾ in (30 cm).

LIBERTY & CO.

Arthur Lasenby Liberty's store in central London's Regent Street was founded in 1875, selling ornaments, fabrics, and objets d'art from East Asia. The fashionable emporium soon became a favorite source of decorative furnishings and knickknacks for people who valued good design.

During the 1880s, Liberty began to foster commercial ties with those members of his circle involved with the Arts and Crafts movement. In the work of Archibald Knox, Liberty & Co. unearthed a fresh new style and kick-started the Celtic revival.

HIDDEN TALENT

Liberty & Co. developed a policy of commissioning work from prominent designers and outsourcing production to firms around the country. These products were then sold under the Liberty banner, both designer and manufacturer remaining uncredited. Such an approach drew scorn from those who struggled to eke out a living while avoiding any concession to the perceived evil of organized mass-production—the antithesis of the Arts and Crafts manifesto. C. R. Ashbee was particularly vehement in his criticism, calling Liberty & Co. "Messrs. Nobody, Novelty & Co." Irreconcilable business methods frequently pitted Arthur Liberty and William Morris against one another. When Morris bought a paintworks farther down the Wandle River from Liberty's own contractor, Liberty quipped "we send our dirty water downstream to Morris."

The formula was, nonetheless, a successful one, and Liberty found willing collaborators in many of the Arts and Crafts movement's finest talents. In the process, the store also helped buoy the fortunes of many small workshops and individual designers. On the shop floor, furniture by Baillie Scott was sold alongside glass by John Couper & Sons (Glasgow) and James Powell & Sons (Whitefriars), and textiles designed by C. F. A. Voysey and Jessie M. King. The business of printing fabrics was undertaken by Thomas Wardle, an early associate of William Morris. The Silver Studio, run by Arthur Silver, devised many of Liberty's most popular fabric patterns. Arthur's son, Rex, later became involved with what proved to be Liberty's greatest success.

SILVER LINING

Unveiled in 1899, the Cymric line of gold- and silverware was an instant hit. The range of jewelry, tea sets, candlesticks, clocks, vases, and other assorted objects was manufactured by the

CYMRIC VASE Unattributed but probably by Archibald Knox, this vase incorporates Celtic motifs offset by red and mottled bluish-green enameling. *c.1905. H:9½ in (24 cm).*

Birmingham firm W. H. Haseler using industrial methods, keeping costs within the reach of middle-class families. Rex Silver, Arthur Gaskin, and Jessie M. King contributed designs, but it was Archibald Knox who created most for the Cymric range.

Knox's designs bore the stamp of his Isle of Man background. In the island's capital, where he attended the Douglas School of Art, he carried out extensive research into Celtic ornament. It culminated in published works such as *Ancient Crosses on the Isle of Man*. Knox became friends with Baillie Scott, who first brought him to the attention of Liberty & Co. around 1895. His first drafts for the firm included patterns for fabrics and wallpapers, but it was his metalware that caused a sensation.

CYMRIC FLOWER VASE The design is attributed to Archibald Knox. The vase is cast with stylized leaf forms and supported by three curved brackets raised on a dished circular base. *1903. 5½ in (14 cm).*

TUDRIC ICE BUCKET An Archibald Knox Liberty Tudric design, the tapering cylindrical form is flanked by angular D-shaped handles, and is embellished in relief with interlaced Celtic flora. *c.1903. H:7½ in (19 cm).*

SILVER PICTURE FRAME Possibly by Archibald Knox, although more fairytale than Celtic in style, this Liberty & Co. frame is in the form of a canopy of leaves above two tree trunks flanking a pair of copper-hinged, red-enameled doors with blue-enameled floral motifs. *c.1905. H:6¼ in (16 cm).*

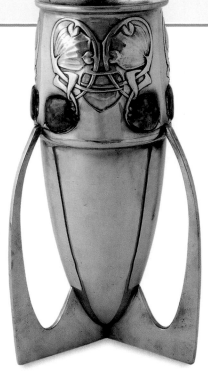

TUDRIC VASE This Knox design has a bullet-shaped body with three looped bracket feet, and is embellished with entrelac flowers and six cabochon-like bluish-green enameled plaques. c.1905. H:11½ in (29 cm).

ARCHIBALD KNOX

Archibald Knox's designs were suffused with Celtic ornament—interwoven knots, intricate entrelacs, and stylized foliate motifs feature heavily. Knox never replicated the ancient devices he had studied on standing stones and in illuminated manuscripts, but invented new permutations of their tangled mystery.

Later in his career, Knox took up teaching and eventually returned to the Isle of Man. His work for Liberty & Co., encompassing carpets, ceramics, and garden ornaments as well as metalware and jewelry, was the vanguard of the Celtic revival that became popular in other areas of the Arts and Crafts movement, particularly in Scotland.

Archibald Knox

ANCIENT ORIGINALITY

For the Cymric line and the Tudric range of pewterware that came out in 1900, Knox drew heavily on his Manx heritage and Celtic roots. John Llewellyn, who Liberty employed as manager of the two projects, was entirely sympathetic to Knox's decorative vocabulary and encouraged him to contribute as much to both lines as possible.

Cymric silverware had a hammered finish and was left unpolished to give it a handcrafted look. The plain surface of the silver was tempered through the use of vivid blue, red, and green enamels, and cabochons of semiprecious stones. The Tudric range was cast in pewter to be a more affordable alternative to silver, and had quite distinct designs.

The overall forms and decorative details of Tudric wares were die-stamped, then individually hammered for a handmade finish

Copper numerals, like enameling, provide color contrast with the pewter

Enameling injects vibrant color into many pewter Tudric wares

TUDRIC MANTEL CLOCK
Designed by Archibald Knox for Liberty & Co's Tudric range, it has a pewter case with stylized leaf decoration, and a circular, polychrome-enameled dial with berry motifs and copper Arabic numerals. c.1905. H:8¼ in (21 cm).

PEWTER AND CLUTHA GLASS BOWL Designed by Archibald Knox, the mount is pierced and embellished with simple leaf forms. The glass liner is suffused with bubbles and has milky streaks and copper-colored aventurine inclusions. H:6 in (15.5 cm).

AMERICAN METALWARE

American craftsmen did not share William Morris's dislike of machinery, but along with salesmen, they enthusiastically adopted the idea of the integrated interior. To preserve the quality of his meticulously handcrafted furniture, Gustav Stickley added a metalwork shop to his Craftsman Workshops rather than resort to the use of machine cut-and-stamped accessories. Other more business-minded producers saw the potential in offering consumers a range of beaten-metal products to complement the Mission-style furniture that was in vogue.

One such entrepreneur was Louis Comfort Tiffany, founder of the interior decorating firm Tiffany Studios. The Studios' metalworking arm was initially set up to make metal bases for the stained glass lampshades of Tiffany & Co. It grew to encompass desk accessories, candelabras, jugs, and vases. These were mostly brass, with gilt and gold doré finishes on the most expensive pieces. Silver was used only for custom commissions.

STYLISH SIMPLICITY

Dirk van Erp in San Francisco made a similar range of pieces, although they were made of copper. Van Erp was originally from the Netherlands, but settled in California in 1885.
He began working in metal as

a hobby, hammering hollowware from the spent artillery shells that littered the naval yard where he worked. He collaborated with Canadian Eleanor D'Arcy Gaw, who had trained at Ashbee's Guild of Handicraft in England. Their working relationship lasted little more than a year but it had a lasting influence on van Erp, who stuck rigidly to the plain look they developed. Surface decoration barely extended beyond a hand-hammered finish or the occasional flash of structural riveting. Lampshades made from stretched mica integrated style and material in his wide range of lamps. To vary the finish of his metalware, van Erp perfected formulae for patinas in deep green, red, and amber. In his experiments, he used materials as diverse as brick dust and driftwood. He was so successful that he inspired imitations, notably the machine-made lamps of Old Mission Kopperkraft of San Jose.

Sensing that consumers had developed a taste for hammered copper, Elbert Hubbard opened the Roycrofters Copper Shop in 1903 as part of his growing craft community at East Aurora in New York. Utilitarian wares, including plates and bowls, were supplemented by more decorative pieces such as lamps and bookends.

Karl Kip helped Hubbard's new venture when he moved from the community's bookbinders to the metalwork shop in 1908. The decorative techniques Kip had learned transferred surprisingly well to beaten copper. Relief borders crafted to resemble stitched leather lent a distinctive edge to

COPPER PLATE Hand-hammered at the Roycrofter's Copper Shop, the plate was also chemically treated to produce an instant aged patina. It bears the distinctive Roycrofters "R" within a cross and orb mark. *1905–15. D:8 in (20.25 cm).*

the Roycroft's metalware. As with the furniture and printed material produced on the same site, Hubbard promoted and sold his copperware through his popular mail-order catalog. All his copperware bore the impressed orb and cross stamp of the Roycrofters.

INNOVATION AND TRADITION

Otto Heintz was another talented entrepreneur who caught on to the market for Arts and Crafts metalware. Originally a jeweler with the family business in Buffalo, Heintz bought The Arts & Crafts Co. in 1903, renaming it Heintz Art Metal Shop. Foremost among Heintz's achievements was a process he developed to affix silver overlay to a

COPPER VASE Made by Dirk van Erp, this broad, baluster-shaped vessel has a slightly planished surface and is finished with one of van Erp's surface patinas: here, a mottled reddish-amber hue. The underside bears van Erp's windmill mark. *c.1910. H:7½ in (19 cm).*

COPPER PITCHER Of bulbous form with a leaded interior, hinged domed cover, riveted loop finial, and an ear-shaped handle, this van Erp vase has a planished surface, finished in a reddish-brown patina. *c.1910. H:11¾ in (30 cm).*

bronze ground without the use of solder. Like van Erp, Heintz was interested in patina and came up with a wide range of finishes, including an iridescent red he called Royal and a silver tone known as French Gray.

ESOTERIC INFLUENCE

The exoticism that influenced many spheres of Arts and Crafts decoration—notably the early textiles of William Morris and the luster-glazed ceramics of William de Morgan—also found favor among some metalworkers. Tiffany Studios launched a range of desk accessories with patterns based on the 12 signs of the zodiac. The exotic roots of this and other ranges produced by Tiffany sets them apart from much of the Arts and Crafts metalware produced by other studios. In contrast to the plain hammered surfaces that dominated this period, Tiffany metalware often has intricate filigree surface decoration and is more opulent.

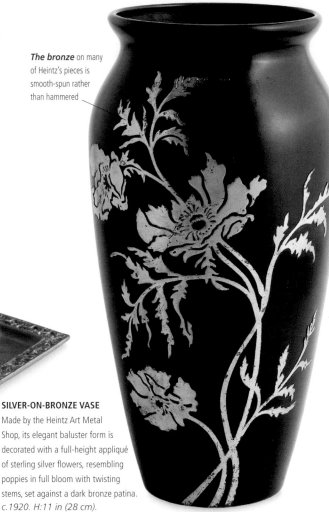

The bronze on many of Heintz's pieces is smooth-spun rather than hammered

SILVER CHALICE Made as a trophy by the Jarvie Shop, this chalice has a hand-wrought hemispherical bowl raised on a tapering stem above a circular foot. It has a lightly hammered surface, and is chased with floral and leaf decoration by George Grant Elmslie. *1915. H:7¾ in (19.5 cm).*

GILT BRONZE INKWELL This octagonal well made by Tiffany Studios is centered in a square tray, retains its original lead liner, and is chased with a Venetian-inspired pattern of stylized leaf motifs. The gilt finish is also known as gold-doré. *c.1905. W:9½ in (24 cm).*

SILVER-ON-BRONZE VASE Made by the Heintz Art Metal Shop, its elegant baluster form is decorated with a full-height appliqué of sterling silver flowers, resembling poppies in full bloom with twisting stems, set against a dark bronze patina. *c.1920. H:11 in (28 cm).*

KALO SHOP

Taking a cue from the guild revival led by C. R. Ashbee in England, Clara Barck Welles founded a rural craft community in Park Ridge near Chicago in 1900. The great emphasis she placed on apprenticeships certainly paid dividends—the master silversmiths who made the Kalo Shop such a success were drawn largely from a migrant Scandinavian population and trained on the job. The name of the enterprise was taken from the Greek word *kalos*, which translates as "beautiful." This sentiment found further expression in the shop's motto—"beautiful, useful and enduring." Offsetting the cost of labor-intensive handcrafting by selling its products direct through its own outlet, the Kalo Shop had a loyal following for its understated, elegant silverware with fluted and hammered decoration.

STERLING HAND WROUGHT AT THE KALO SHOP G 152 H

STERLING-SILVER BOWL This Kalo Shop bowl is raised on a ring foot and has angular D-shape handles and a lightly hammered surface with four out-pressed, hourglass-shaped lobes. An interlaced "GH" monogram is applied to one side. *1905–14. W:10 in (25.5 cm).*

SILVER CANDLESTICKS This pair of candlesticks is hand-wrought with broad-flanged, tulip-shaped sockets, rising from slender club-shaped stems, raised on broad, stepped circular feet. The hand-wrought mark on the underside indicates manufacture after 1914. *1920–25. H:14 in (35.5 cm).*

METALWARE GALLERY

Arts and Crafts metalworkers made extensive use of base metals such as copper, brass, and pewter as well as more expensive silver and gold. They avoided precious stones in favor of simpler embellishments such as enamel decoration and uncut or cabochon semiprecious stones. The handcrafted look was fundamental—even machine-made pieces were frequently given a hand-hammered finish. Recurring decorative themes include stylized plants and flowers as well as motifs inspired by ancient Celtic design.

KEY

1. Roycroft brass-washed, hammered copper American Beauty vase. H:18½ in (47 cm). ③
2. Artificer's Guild goblet, the design attributed to Edward Spencer. 1926. H:6 in (15 cm). ③
3. W. A. S. Benson muffin dish. W:10 in (25.5 cm). ① **4.** Two Scottish School brass vases in the style of Alexander Ritchie. H:12¼ in (31 cm). ③ **5.** Newlyn Arts & Crafts copper rose bowl. W:15¾ in (40 cm). ② **6.** Silver vase by C. R. Ashbee. c.1900. H:7 in (18 cm). ④ **7.** Arts and Crafts plated brass vase, designed by Edward Spencer. H:6¾ in (17.5 cm). ① **8.** Guild of Handicrafts inkwell, with a foiled enamel boss on the cover. 1906. H:2½ in (6.5 cm). ③ **9.** Artificer's Guild Edith & Nelson Dawson silver bookmark. 1905. L:5 in (12 cm). ① **10.** Heintz sterling-on-bronze trophy cup. H:11¼ in (28.5 cm). ① **11.** Liberty & Co. Tudric pewter candlesticks, designed by Archibald Knox. c.1905. H:9 in (23 cm). ③

3 W. A. S. Benson muffin dish

2 Artificer's Guild goblet

4 Pair of brass vases

7 Plated brass vase

8 Guild of Handicrafts inkwell

9 Artificer's Guild bookmark

1 Roycroft vase

5 Copper rose bowl

6 C. R. Ashbee silver vase

10 Trophy cup

11 Liberty & Co. Tudric candlesticks

12. Artificer's Guild copper wall sconce, design attributed to Edward Spencer. H:10½ in (27 cm). ③
13. Liberty & Co. Tudric pewter and enamel clock designed by Archibald Knox. H:8¼ in (21 cm). ⑦
14. Liberty & Co. Tudric pewter mantle clock. H:7¾ in (20 cm). ④ **15.** Cotswold School brass fender.
W:49¼ in (123 cm). ④ **16.** Guild of Handicraft silver cigar box with enamel panel, by Fleetwood
Varley. c.1904. L:8 in (20 cm). ⑤ **17.** Guild of Handicraft silver and enamel cigar box. 1903. H:3 in
(7.5 cm). ④ **18.** Artificer's Guild copper and silver box, designed by Edward Spencer. 1931. H:4¾ in
(12 cm). ② **19.** Birmingham Guild copper plate. c.1920. D:8¼ in (21 cm). ① **20.** Scottish School Arts
and Crafts brass planter with repoussé-decorated sides. W:20 in (51 cm). ① **21.** Artificer's Guild
copper tray, the design attributed to Edward Spencer. L:21½ in (55 cm). ① **22.** Ramsden and Carr
silver vase set with agates. 1913. H:11 in (28 cm). ⑤

14 *Liberty & Co. Tudric clock*

13 *Liberty & Co. Tudric clock*

17 *Silver and enamel box*

12 *Copper wall sconce*

18 *Copper and silver box and cover*

16 *Silver cigar box*

15 *Cotswold School brass fender*

20 *Brass planter*

19 *Birmingham Guild copper plate*

21 *Artificer's Guild copper tray*

22 *Ramsden and Carr silver vase*

CLOCKS

ASSOCIATIONS WITH THE DAILY CYCLE OF LABOR AND REST RAISED THE STATUS OF THE CLOCK DURING THE ARTS AND CRAFTS PERIOD. CLOCKS WERE DESIGNED AS PART OF AN OVERALL DECORATIVE SCHEME.

MANTEL CLOCK Made by the Hamburg American Clock Co. for export, this clock has a copper dial set in a wooden carcase. The architectural copper facing has Arts and Crafts style exposed riveting. c.1900. H:12 in (30.5 cm).

METALWORK CLOCKS

Clocks took on aspects of design appropriate to the materials from which they were made. Consumers began to see the appeal of unified interior furnishings and removed the clutter of the 19th century. In response, clock manufacturers started to model their cases in the dominant styles of the day. At one end of the spectrum, individual artist-craftsmen designed and produced clock cases as custom commissions, while at the other, multinational companies such as the Hamburg American Clock Co. mass-produced fashionable clocks. Bridging the gulf between these two extremes came retailers such as Liberty in London and Tiffany in New York.

DECORATIVE DEVICES

Decorative elements on clock dials and cases ranged from structural flourishes to labor-intensive embellishments such as repoussé or embossing (hammering on the reverse side to create relief patterns). As well as beautifying the clock face while remaining faithful to the material, this technique allowed artisans to display their skill at both embossing and chasing—defining the decoration by impressing outlines from the front. After the Celtic revival peaked around the turn of the 20th century, repoussé decoration frequently took the form of entwined knots and similar devices. Repoussé work was suited to silver and brass, and firms such as Keswick and Newlyn specialized in

The angular bends of the entrelac border decoration are characteristically Celtic

Arabic numbers rather than Roman numerals were favored for Arts and Crafts clocks

Spiral motifs were much used in Celtic art. These three-lobed examples may represent the Trinity in Christian iconography

BRASS WALL CLOCK Made by a metalworker of the Scottish School, the clock's octagonal form incorporates a circular dial with Arabic numbers, within a band of repoussé Celtic interlacing and spiral motifs reserved on a hammered ground. c.1900. D:14 in (36 cm).

ORIVIT MANTEL CLOCK Designed by Albin Müller for the German manufacturer Orivit, the chased silvered-pewter case is a stylized plant form raised on tendril-like supports. c.1900. H:9¼ in (23.5 cm).

ZODIAC DESK CLOCK Made by Tiffany Studios, the cathedral-shape case has a gold-doré finish. Both the front and sides have polychrome enameled signs-of-the-zodiac medallions linked by entrelac work. *c.1905. H:5¼ in (13.5 cm).*

AESTHETIC CLOCKS

Aesthetic designers were more concerned with the visual impact of individual items than their place as part of a coherent whole. Their clocks therefore had more decorative embellishment than those made by adherents to Arts and Crafts principles. This example displays features typical of Aesthetic Movement trends, the most obvious being the strong Japanese influence. The Satsuma ceramic plaques that surround the clock face are drawn indirectly from the Japanese tradition. The intricate turning of the wooden frame serves no structural purpose and would be rejected by an Arts and Crafts designer as frivolous decoration. The wood has been ebonized, whereas Arts and Crafts woodwork was often stained more subtly, allowing the grain to show through.

MANTEL CLOCK The turned and carved, ebonized wooden case is in the Anglo-Japanese architectural style of the Aesthetic Movement, and is inset with floral polychrome Satsuma-style tiles. *c.1880. H:16 in (40.5 cm).*

embossed copper. Exposed rivets on some metal mantel clocks displayed a sympathy with the idea of structural honesty, making a feature out of fixing the component pieces together.

APPLIED ORNAMENT

As well as features integral to the structure of the clock, many manufacturers applied ornament to achieve the decorative effect they wanted. Enamels, cabochons, and patinas enhanced the metal and wooden ground of the clock case. Popular motifs included galleons and other devices traditionally associated with timepieces.

Of particular note were the many clocks of the period that bear admonitory inscriptions—variations on the theme "Time Flies." These mottoes reflected the work ethic of the Arts and Crafts philosophy, which valued honest toil and frowned upon idle pursuits and wasted time.

The silver and pewter clocks that Archibald Knox designed for Liberty & Co. as part of the store's Cymric and Tudric ranges often had bright enamel dials picked out in primary colors. Across the Atlantic, Tiffany & Co. produced bronze desk clocks with scrollwork designs as part of the Zodiac range. Less orthodox materials were used to create timepieces by companies branching out from their traditional areas. Doulton, for example, produced ceramic clocks as part of its art pottery range.

LONGCASE CLOCKS

Longcase clocks of this period tended to be similar in style to cased furniture. They had plain wooden surfaces, sometimes stained to emphasize the natural grain of the wood. Surface decoration was scarce, and when it was present was usually restricted to subtle use of contrasting inlay.

In keeping with the doctrine of structural honesty, pendulums and weights were often visible, through either a glass door or structural gaps in the case.

EBONIZED MANTEL CLOCK Designed by Charles Rennie Mackintosh in characteristically linear style, its ebonized wooden case is inlaid with erinoid (an early type of plastic). *c.1917. H:13 in (33 cm).*

LONGCASE CLOCK The clean, straight lines softened with subtle curves of Richard Riemerschmid's designs are evident in this German clock with a fruitwood frame and a hammered-copper face. *c.1905. H:84 in (213.5 cm).*

TEXTILES

FABRICS WERE A KEY ELEMENT OF THE INTEGRATED ARTS AND CRAFTS INTERIOR. LIKE LEADED GLASS, FABRIC PRINTING, AND WEAVING, THEY PROVIDED THE CHANCE TO RESURRECT NEGLECTED TECHNIQUES.

UNPICKING THE PAST

Before taking rooms at Red Lion Square in London during the 1850s, William Morris and Edward Burne-Jones toured northern France's Gothic cathedrals. This reinforced Morris's admiration for medieval leaded glass, and the pair were awed by the Lady and the Unicorn tapestries at Cluny.

Back at home in London, Morris sat at a traditional wooden embroidery frame for hours and taught himself stitches by unpicking and reworking old samples. Later, he had his wife Jane and her sister Bessie produce a series of appliqué and embroidery wall hangings that he had designed for the Red House, his new marital home.

LINEN PILLOW American made and decorated, the pillow is stenciled and embroidered along three sides with a formalized dogwood flower and leaf pattern in shades of blue, green, reddish brown, and yellow, against an oatmeal ground. *c.1900. W:19½ in (49.5 cm).*

NEEDLECRAFT

Passing the baton to his female relatives proved prophetic, as Arts and Crafts textiles came to be dominated by women more than any other area. Candace Wheeler, a colleague of Louis Comfort Tiffany and the foremost American practitioner of

Arts and Crafts needlework, ascribed this to the willingness of polite society to let women create and even sell handcrafted goods with the proviso that "she must not supply things of utility—that was a Brahmanical law." Nonetheless, many women achieved positions of prominence through needlework. Morris passed control of his firm's embroidery production to his daughter May in 1885. The wife of Thomas Wardle, with whom Morris had collaborated to create many of his early

BIRD PATTERN This woolen textile is woven on a Jacquard loom with one of William Morris's most popular patterns: Bird. Here seen in a predominantly red colorway, it was also produced in blue and in green. *c.1880. L:29 in (73.5 cm).*

CREWELWORK SEAT COVER One of a set of eight, the William Morris–style pattern of flowering sprays and foliage was worked in colored wools by Lady Phipson Beale on an unbleached linen ground. She learned her needlework skills from her sister-in-law, Margaret Beale, who in 1872 helped found the Royal School of Art Needlework with Princess Helena's patronage. *1880s. L:17½ in (44 cm).*

EMBROIDERED SCREEN Made by Morris & Co., this screen has a trifold mahogany frame enclosing three needlepoint panels with different flower and foliage patterns. The center panel displays the Parrot Tulip pattern, primarily in shades of red and green, and one of Morris's best-known designs. *c.1900.*

MORRIS & CO. The photograph shows craftsmen hand-block-printing chintz patterns in the home crafts workshops of Morris & Co.

STRAWBERRY THIEF PATTERN Presenting thrushes among strawberry plants, this was one of William Morris's most popular designs. This detail is from a pair of printed cotton curtains, 1890s. L:112¼ in (280 cm).

Needlework was formed in Massachusetts in 1896. Its aim was to preserve the embroidery techniques of the first settler Pilgrims.

AN EMERGING PATTERN

Like the wallpapers for which Morris remains famous, his fabric designs are primarily made up of large, repeating patterns featuring two-dimensional representations of plant and animal life. A master of the mirror-repeat, Morris's best-known works still include block-printed textile patterns such as "Strawberry Thief," "Acanthus," and "Bird."

The Silver Studio became a prolific supplier of fabric patterns to Liberty & Co., which counted them among its bestsellers. Established and respected designers such as Walter Crane and Charles Voysey also became involved with fabric design, indicating how far the Arts and Crafts movement had elevated the status of this often dismissed art form.

ESSEX A.17 PATTERN C. F. A. Voysey's stylized floral design was commissioned by Scott Morton & Co. for their Essex range of fabrics and wallpaper. It is shown here as a framed and glazed woodblock proof. c. 1900. L:29¼ in (74.5 cm).

patterns and dyes, established an embroidery school in Staffordshire. Its members embarked on a re-creation of the Bayeux Tapestry in 1885. The Scottish School produced many skilled female needleworkers—Phoebe Traquair and Jessie Newberry, in particular, had a huge influence on the direction of textile design with work soaked in Celtic myth. Bessie Burden was head instructor at the Royal School of Art Needlework for a time.

Women up and down the country set themselves to work stitching designs bought from Morris, Marshall, Faulkner & Co., and other companies to decorate their own homes. This was the Arts and Crafts ideal in action, taking industry away from the factory and restoring it to the hearthside.

REINVENTING TRADITION

Printed and embroidered Arts and Crafts textiles were produced by traditional methods. Morris was opposed to the use of artificial or chemical dyes and experimented with a wide range of plant products to achieve his Aesthetic palette of indigo, sage green, peacock blue, yellow, red, and brown.

Many of the recipes he devised with Thomas Wardle were derived from Elizabethan models. The Hammersmith range of hand-knotted carpets was indebted to ancient Persia in terms of both design and manufacture. Indeed, so labor-intensive was this process that only the wealthiest industrialists and aristocrats could afford them. Textiles presented one of the biggest challenges in making quality crafts affordable.

To make his work more widely available, Morris engaged the Wilton Royal Carpet Factory to produce high-quality machine-made versions that sold at a fraction of the price. This was a significant compromise for Morris, and was a tacit admission that factory production could be put to good use.

Traditional Flemish methods were the basis for much of the tapestry production, and leading designers such as John Henry Dearle created some superlative examples. Many firms experimented with Eastern techniques for applying patterns to fabric such as wax resist, also known as batik, and discharge printing. The Society of Blue and White

ART NOUVEAU
1880–1915

SINUOUS CONTOURS

FEMININE AND LUXURIOUS, WITH WHIPLASH CURVES AND SEMI-CLAD
MAIDENS, ART NOUVEAU WAS A REACTION TO THE HISTORICAL REVIVALS
THAT HAD DOMINATED FOR DECADES. IT TRANSFORMED THE DECORATIVE
ARTS AS THE 19TH CENTURY CAME TO A CLOSE.

ALPHONSE MUCHA PLATE Advertising a mythical product for teaching purposes, this poster by Mucha has the favored Art Nouveau subject matter of an idealized woman with stylized hair and a flowing gown. *c.1902. H:17¾ in (45 cm).*

NATURE AS INSPIRATION

Art Nouveau is one of the most easily recognized
design styles, with its use of exotic materials, rich
colors, curves, asymmetrical lines, and shapes
inspired by nature. A great success in its time,
it inspired architects and designers and continues
to capture the imagination today.

Art Nouveau was the result of intense activity by
visual artists that began in the studios, workshops,
and galleries of the art world but then quickly
moved out across the whole of late 19th-century
culture. It was both elitist and popular, loved and
hated, and occurred not just as architectural
decoration for new museums and official buildings
and in beautiful furniture and jewelry, but
also on biscuit tins, posters, menus, and
children's toys. It was high art, but also
provided the imagery for erotic theater
and pulp pornography.

MODERN STYLE

Despite its disparate and often conflicting
nature, Art Nouveau was defined by
modernity. It was the first self-conscious,
internationally based attempt to transform
visual culture according to modernist
ideas. The world was changing fast at
the end of the 19th century, with
technological, economic, and political
developments reshaping the physical
environment. Rapid industrialization,
the growth of cities at the expense of
the countryside, the invention of the
automobile, the electric light bulb, the
typewriter, and much more besides were
all transforming people's lives across
Europe and in the Americas. A new
aggression in international trade and
the European competition to acquire
colonies in Africa and the Pacific were
remodeling the world on imperialism.

These changes did not affect every country in the
same way, which partly explains the differences
in Art Nouveau from place to place. But wherever
they came from, Art Nouveau artists all rejected
the idea of a hierarchy—with fine art at the top
and the decorative arts at the bottom—in favor
of an equality of the arts so that they could all be
made accessible to everyone. When *Les Six* group

**EUGÈNE FEUILLÂTRE
CUP** This silver and enamel
cup and cover is based on
an azalea. The bud terminal
tops the azalea-decorated
cover and body and the
stem curls into roots on
the pedestal foot. *1901.
H:10 in (25 cm).*

PARIS DOORWAY The whiplash tendrils
that appear to grow out of the figurehead
and engulf the entrance and first floor
exterior are typical of French Art Nouveau.

ART NOUVEAU DINING ROOM Integrated interiors are the epitome of Art Nouveau design. This dining room in the Musée de l'Ecole de Nancy was designed by Eugène Vallin in 1903 and features carved wooden paneling, fireplace, and dresser. The ceiling and leather-upholstered furniture are by V. Proute.

of artists exhibited in Paris in 1898, they stressed this: "It is necessary to make art part of contemporary life, to make the ordinary objects that surround us into works of art."

Art Nouveau designers drew on a wide range of natural, historical, and symbolic references, combining them in surprising ways, sometimes to produce complete interiors. The ideas behind it were formulated in the 1880s but found public expression in 1893, in the drawings of Aubrey Beardsley and the architecture of the Belgian Victor Horta, and in 1895 in the manifesto *Déblaiement d'Art* (A Clean Sweep for Art) written by another Belgian, the polemicist Henry van de Velde.

UNIVERSAL EXHIBITIONS

After 1895 Art Nouveau quickly spread to the major cities of Europe and North America and, after 1900, around the world. This wide success can be traced to the international exhibitions, those hugely popular world fairs of industry, commerce, and the arts held at regular intervals in the great cities of the world. Art Nouveau made its first appearance at the Brussels exhibition in 1897 and was far more in evidence in Paris in 1900. Two years later, in Turin, almost every pavilion and its contents reflected the new style.

Yet Art Nouveau was little in evidence at the Brussels exhibition in 1910 or the Glasgow and

Turin exhibitions the following year. By then, its role as a modern style had come to an end and its commercial viability was in steep decline. By the time World War I began in August 1914, Art Nouveau had almost disappeared.

DAUM FRÈRES GLASS VASE The Daum brothers, Antonin and Auguste, produced blown and cased glass and cameo glass, and used cutting, engraving, painting, and enameling. This vase is etched with a peacock-feather decoration. c.1905. H:10¼ in (25.5 cm).

ELEMENTS OF STYLE

ART NOUVEAU ARTISTS AND CRAFTSMEN self-consciously developed their own vocabulary of motifs adapted from nature. Plants, animals, and sensuous women were the main sources of inspiration, often metamorphosing from one to another. In the best examples, form and decoration complement each other to create a unified whole. Although they claimed to have turned their backs on tradition, especially Classical sources, craftsmen also borrowed techniques and ideas from the past but reinterpreted them to create their own, new decorative style.

E. BARRIAS BRONZE FIGURE
THE FEMALE FORM
The nude was a time-honored staple of the fine arts, but now sensual female figures, often semi-clad in diaphanous robes or turning into animals or plants, were popular for small-scale sculptures. They also adorned all types of decorative objects, from jewelry to furniture and lamps.

EMILE GALLÉ CAMEO GLASS VASE
CAMEO GLASS
Cameo glass is made by using several layers of colored glass. Carving or etching away areas of the top layer reveals the underlying glass and creates an image in relief. This technique was adopted enthusiastically by Art Nouveau glassmakers, who used up to five sheets of different-colored glass.

BRASS FIRE SURROUND
WHIPLASH MOTIF
The key linear motif of Art Nouveau was based on the shapes of swirling plant roots and was similar in look to that of an unfurling whip. As early as 1882, Arthur H. Mackmurdo used the whiplash motif in a distinctive chair back. Hermann Obrist's whiplash embroideries became iconic emblems of the style.

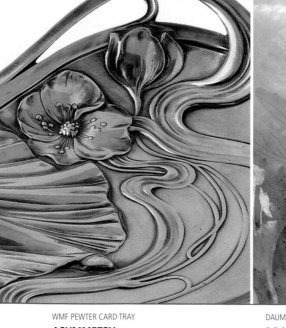

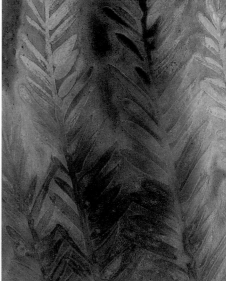

WMF PEWTER CARD TRAY
ASYMMETRY
A characteristic feature of Art Nouveau, asymmetry owed a debt to the art of Japan. The frothy asymmetry of 18th-century Rococo, which was revived in the 19th century, was also influential. Both shape and decoration could be asymmetrical, often reflecting organic forms found in nature.

DAUM FRÈRES CAMEO GLASS VASE
DRAGONFLY
The distinctive shape and bright colors of the dragonfly, a familiar sight in the French countryside around Nancy, were used on Art Nouveau glass vases and inspired René Lalique's iconic dragonfly-woman brooch. Émile Gallé even adorned furniture with the dragonfly form, complete with bulbous eyes.

WELLER POTTERY VASE
INNOVATIVE GLAZES
New, experimental glazes were a striking feature of Art Nouveau ceramics, from Bohemia and France to the United States. Red glazes fired at high temperatures were used on stoneware. Crystalline glazes that produced a speckled finish and lustrous metallic glazes were also commonly used.

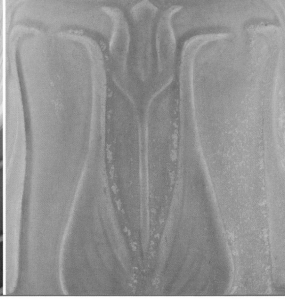

TIFFANY LABURNUM LAMP
LEADED GLASS
Pieces of stained glass enclosed in a metal framework were not only used in window panels but also made into lampshades, so the colors of the glass glowed when the lamps were turned on. Lead was traditionally used for windows, but the more flexible copper was often favored for lampshades.

LOUIS MAJORELLE CABINET
MARQUETRY
Elaborate marquetry—making a picture or pattern out of different-colored pieces of wood—was a form of craftsmanship beautifully revived by the furniture-makers of the Nancy School in France. The natural world—from local wildflowers to insects— was the main source of inspiration.

STEUBEN AURENE VASE
IRIDESCENT GLASS
Contemporary excavations of ancient Roman glass with a pearly sheen inspired Art Nouveau glassmakers to try to re-create the effect themselves, making iridescent glass. They used metal oxides when firing glass to create pieces with gently shimmering, multicolored surfaces.

ARTUS VAN BRIGGLE VASE
TULIP DECORATION
The theme of nature unified all aspects of Art Nouveau and was based not only on local flora and fauna, but also on the exotic species often seen in botanical publications. A popular decorative motif, especially for vases, was the tulip, sometimes influencing the shape as well as the decoration of a piece.

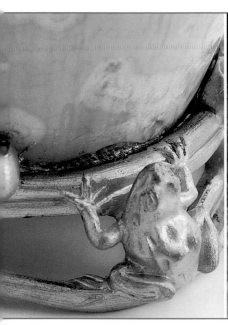

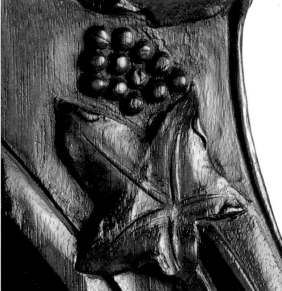

SÈVRES PORCELAIN VASE WITH A GILT-BRONZE MOUNT
GILDED BRONZE
As in many late 17th- and early 18th-century French pieces, bronze was often molded into mounts and gilded to create a shiny gold surface that framed and complemented a piece of porcelain or glass. Most mounts, such as the one shaped like a frog and lily pad above, were based on natural motifs.

DAUM FRÈRES WINTER LANDSCAPE GLASS VASE
ETCHED AND ENAMELED GLASS
Much early French Art Nouveau glass, especially that of Gallé and Daum, was elaborately patterned or bore pictures made by acid-etching, which creates a look similar to that of an etching. The graphic effect of the picture was then strengthened by painting on glowing colors with enamels.

JOHANN VON SCHWARZ PANEL
FEMME-FLEUR
Quintessentially French Art Nouveau, the femme-fleur is half-woman and half-flower. The image of a dreamy maiden with flowing hair, much loved by Symbolist poets and artists, was usually entwined with swirling plant tendrils and appeared on metalware, posters, and ceramics.

EDMUND DIOT WALNUT STAND
HANDCARVED WOOD
As the division between fine and decorative arts became increasingly blurred, sculptors used the forms of furniture to display their skills, and furniture-makers carved wood like sculptors. Motifs included leaves, fruit, flowers, the undulating lines of stems and roots, insects, and the female form.

FURNITURE

FRENCH FURNITURE-MAKERS WANTED TO BREAK FREE
FROM TRADITIONAL CONSTRAINTS, AND NANCY AND
PARIS BECAME LEADING CENTERS OF INNOVATION.

A FRENCH REVOLUTION

The town of Nancy in eastern France was brimming with creativity in the 1890s, and Émile Gallé and his protégé Louis Majorelle were its stars. Many of the style aspects adopted by the school founded by Gallé can be seen in his famous vitrine (*see right*). These include the use of glossy wood, with exotic species for the marquetry (applied small wooden shapes) that covers every flat surface; pierced carvings of Japanese cherry blossoms; and asymmetrical elements.

NANCY AND NATURE

As a botanist and symbolist, Gallé turned nature into furniture—not just in decoration, but in form, too, with rails shaped like dandelions, headboards resembling moths, frog table feet, and butterfly handles. Dragonflies also abounded, with their bulbous eyes gleaming out of dark, sumptuous woods at the corners of little tables. Marquetry was a traditional technique, but few were as masterful in its use as Gallé, who integrated it into his pieces beautifully, creating delicate plant and animal designs out of different woods for vitrines, table tops, chairs, and bedsteads.

Majorelle was also an exponent of marquetry, but he found its intricacy time-consuming. Familiar with the widespread gilding of

**Detail of marquetry
on the top tier**

Elegant C-scrolls
support the top tier

TWO-TIER TABLE The two tops of this rosewood table are inlaid with fine floral marquetry. Designed by Émile Gallé, this rare and important piece was made for the 1900 Paris *Exposition Universelle*. H:32½ in (83 cm).

*Carved, out-swept
legs* are in keeping with
contemporary sinuous forms

WALNUT VITRINE Designed by Émile Gallé, this vitrine is glazed at the front and sides and has an asymmetrical two-tier interior and exquisite marquetry panels. With a carved, pierced cresting and apron, the piece is raised on carved, outswept legs. H:58¼ in (148 cm).

MARQUETRY TABLE This two-tier mahogany table was designed by Louis Majorelle. It has bronze foliate handles to the sides and is raised on carved and molded "W" end supports. *W:35¼ in (89.5 cm).*

GILTWOOD SIDE TABLE The mottled marble top of this table is set within a carved molding above a frieze. The tapering, stretchered legs have pierced tops. It was designed by Louis Majorelle. *H:30½ in (78 cm).*

18th-century furniture and its 19th-century reproductions, he came to favor gilt-bronze mounts over marquetry. The region of Lorraine, of which Nancy is the capital, was an iron-smelting area, and Majorelle also used wrought iron for decoration.

In order to attract buyers from farther afield than Nancy, Majorelle established *ateliers* (workshops, or studios), in which an assembly line of workers produced multiple identical pieces of furniture to be sold throughout France. Quality and prices were high, and the materials used were deliberately rich to appeal to the luxury market. Dark hardwoods such as mahogany were often incorporated into his pieces.

COMPLETE INTERIORS

This new generation of designers was not content to design only furniture: they wished to create entire interiors and, since many among them were architects, the exteriors of buildings as well. They believed that everything should go together, as a *Gesamtkunstwerk*, or total work of art. Many of these designers were trained in other artistic disciplines, so they bypassed the traditional French furniture stages of a design being implemented by an *ébéniste*, a master craftsman who controlled the making of a piece. This idea of a united creative picture governed by a single designer came to fruition with the Art Nouveau designers of Paris.

ELEGANT AND STYLIZED PARIS

These wishes for autonomy on the part of the designers coincided with the vision of entrepreneur Siegfried (also called Samuel) Bing, who opened his shop La Maison de l'Art Nouveau in Paris in 1895 and gave the style its name. He envisaged whole salons of interior design in the latest fashion and hired leading cabinet-maker Léon Jallot to oversee furniture production. Bing commissioned Georges De Feure, Edward Colonna, and Eugène Gaillard to design the furniture. Colonna and De Feure

designed sitting rooms for Bing's pavilion at the 1900 Paris *Exposition Universelle*, choosing a restrained mode between Louis XV and XVI, with sophisticated carpets, embroidery, and upholstery to complement the furniture. De Feure's—featuring gold-leafed furniture and a butterfly-backed sofa—earned him a gold medal. Colonna's creations incorporated the Parisian stylized use of decoration, suggesting and abstracting nature, rather than proclaiming it. Decoration took a back seat to form, instead of the exuberance of Nancy motifs. Colonna also designed silver mounts for Tiffany glassware, shown at the same Exposition.

Gaillard designed the bedroom and dining room for Bing's pavilion, molding wood into stemlike forms that took their inspiration from plants. Bends and curves dominated, and one particular armoire featured undulating mirror plates. The native woods used at the beginning of the 19th century were out of favor; Gaillard used exotic woods such as mahogany, amaranth, rosewood, and dark walnut, lightening the panels of the pavilion's bed with figured ash. He sculpted with wood, squeezing it into the required shapes. But while Bing picked the best of the young Parisian designers, another name stands above them all: Hector Guimard.

ROSEWOOD-FRAMED FIRESCREEN This rare piece was designed by Edward Colonna and features distinctive, stylized floral fabric. The frame is raised on dual standard ends. *H:31½ in (80 cm).*

The crest of the chair is pierced and carved with sinuous plant forms

The frame features delicate floral scrolling carving

The plant theme is echoed in carvings on the chair legs, which terminate in square feet

CARVED WALNUT CHAIR The floral, embossed leather upholstery of this chair is original. It sits within a pierced, carved frame with bronze mounts at the tops of the legs. Designed by Eugène Gaillard. *H:42 in (107.5 cm).*

THE STYLE EVOLVES

Visitors who arrived at the 1900 Paris *Exposition Universelle* via the city's subway system would have passed through the still-startling landmark Metro entrances designed by Hector Guimard. Their vegetal, writhing, cast-iron lines gave rise to the alternative name for the Art Nouveau movement: *Le Style Métro*. As an architect-designer in no doubt of his own talents, Guimard put his stamp on every aspect of a commission. His furniture was majestic and architectural, charged with linear swirls, contorting wood as if it were metal. Designers such as Léon Benouville soon followed suit.

CLEAN, SWEEPING LINES

Like Eugène Gaillard, Guimard owed something to the streamlined forms of the Belgian designer Henry van de Velde. Originally a painter in Antwerp, van de Velde built himself a house in 1894, designing everything, from the exterior to the furniture, plates, knives, and forks—right down to the clothes that his wife was to wear in it.

Passionate about the decorative arts, in 1895 van de Velde published the pamphlet *Déblaiment d'Art* (A Clean Sweep for Art). Like Eugène Emmanuel Viollet-le-Duc in France and John Ruskin and William Morris in Britain, he campaigned for an end to the hierarchy of fine arts (architecture, sculpture, and painting) above design and to the tiers of decorative arts. He demanded equality for all—be it building exterior or interior, large or small sculpture, metalware, ceramics, furniture, or graphic art. "Suddenly they were called arts of the second rank, then decorative arts, and then the minor arts... None of [the arts] had been independent; they were held together by a common idea, which was to decorate...We can't allow a split that aims at single-mindedly ranking one art above the others, a separation of the arts into high art and a second-class, low industrial art," wrote Van de Velde in his pamphlet.

Siegfried Bing visited van de Velde's house and commissioned him to design four rooms in his Paris shop. Sweeping forms give van de Velde's furniture a sense of movement that is sympathetic to the natural curves of wood. The extreme distortion of wood

MIRROR The gilded plaster frame of this mirror was designed by Hector Guimard, and the curved foliage is reminiscent of his designs for the Paris Metro. *H:54 in (137 cm).*

that characterized some Parisian examples was not for van de Velde: he chose light-colored native woods such as beech, walnut, and oak, and his decoration was minimal. Around 1900 he moved away from the organic base of nature as inspiration, toward a Classical, plainer style.

SIDE TABLE Léon Benouville designed this mahogany side table with mixed-wood marquetry. Below the inlaid table top is a single drawer above a narrow cupboard. The table has four supports and handmade brass hardware. *c.1900. W:34 in (86.5 cm).*

WHIPLASH HORTA

Guimard was quick to acknowledge the influence of another Belgian architect-designer, Victor Horta. Horta also designed his own house from top to bottom, as well as those of several other wealthy Brussels inhabitants. But while van de Velde was influenced by the refined simplicity of the Arts and Crafts style, Horta opted for an airy exuberance

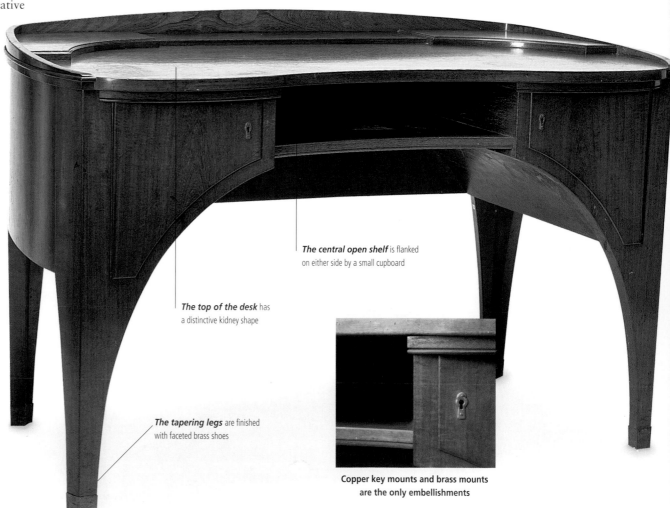

The central open shelf is flanked on either side by a small cupboard

The top of the desk has a distinctive kidney shape

The tapering legs are finished with faceted brass shoes

Copper key mounts and brass mounts are the only embellishments

LADY'S BUREAU Designed by Henry van de Velde, this mahogany desk has an organic, sweeping shape that is characteristic of his streamlined style. *c.1905. W:48½ in (123 cm).*

Detail of pull on cabinet drawer

DOUBLE BED The paneled head- and footboards of this light-brown-stained mahogany bed have profiled edges and are joined by graduated side panels. The bedside cabinets are integral to the design, which is by Victor Horta for the house of Solvay in Brussels. *1894. L:80 in (200 cm).*

MUSÉE HORTA, BRUSSELS The Brussels home of Victor Horta has been turned into a museum. The exuberant whiplash motif of this staircase is typical of the Belgian architect's decorative style.

unmatched since Louis XV. The center of his house—and of others he designed—was an iron cage, with windows at the top so that light flowed down the stairwell. In his hands, a staircase became a place in its own right—somewhere to linger and enjoy rather than a mere passageway from one floor to the next. Horta liked open spaces where people, air, and light could circulate.

He manipulated daylight by using subtly colored leaded glass in skylights and windows, so that his clients could enjoy the play of light and colored shadows and reflections to the fullest. He exploited electric as well as natural light in interesting shapes such as bells, flowers, and showers of stars, always with a particular focus—to illuminate a dining table, or to embellish the colors of a stained-glass window.

The whiplash was Horta's leitmotif—energetic and vital. The sinuous wooden rail of the banisters in his houses was combined with frenetic swirls of

iron that cast shadows on the wall. In many houses he decorated the walls at banister level with a similar whiplash pattern.

Like many Art Nouveau designers, Horta was influenced by the Gothic and Rococo revivals, as well as by the asymmetry and light touch of Japanese art, but he added an individual Brussels flavor to these elements. He played with contrasts of material, juxtaposing cold metal with warm wood and smooth marble with rough stone. He favored the use of warm colors, reflected in the walls and carpets of his house and the light brown stain of his mahogany furniture. As well as mahogany, Horta used fruitwoods and maple, combined with rich upholstery in materials such as velvet or silk, set on thick carpets or marble floors. Horta's furniture was designed for specific houses, and it often had a dual purpose: the double bed (*see above*), for example, has integrated bedside tables and cupboards.

CARLO BUGATTI

Like other European designers, Italian Carlo Bugatti (1856–1940) was looking for a new artistic direction—although his own route was unconventional. He was a craftsman with workshops in Milan, and his furniture was handmade and sometimes handpainted.

Heavily influenced by Middle Eastern and North African architecture and Japanese art, Bugatti incorporated keyhole arches, Egyptian latticework, and decorative inlays based on Arabic writing into his furniture. As well as exotic motifs, he drew on materials such as the silk tassels used on Persian rugs, or used leather and vellum for upholstery and table tops. He often featured inlays of metal, ebony, bone, and mother-of-pearl, too. Bugatti liked to mix wood with brass and pewter, and used quirky decorative devices such as wheel-shaped leg supports and dragonfly handles.

Although his pieces were not particularly comfortable or usable, Bugatti was commissioned to supply the Egyptian royal family with furniture and won first prize for his Moorish interior at the 1902 Turin World Fair.

Wheel-segment supports are characteristic of Bugatti's work

CORNER ARMCHAIR The chair by Bugatti is inlaid with brass and pewter, and the curved arm and back rail is covered with embossed copper and encloses circular totems tied with ropes. The square seat is upholstered with vellum.

BUGATTI DESK This walnut gilt-bronze-mounted desk strung in brass and pewter has two small shelved cupboards above a skiver inset writing surface. *H:36½ in (92.5 cm).*

GERMAN JUGENDSTIL

In Germany, furniture and other decorative arts had their own renaissance centered around a breakaway band of young designers in Munich. The exhibition in 1897 at the Glaspalast—Munich's answer to London's Crystal Palace—devoted three rooms to the decorative arts. These included glass by Gallé and Tiffany but also showcased the work of Munich designers such as Richard Riemerschmid, Hermann Obrist, and Bernhard Pankok. Designs submitted had to "fulfill the requirements of our modern life," as well as being original, rather than simply new versions of historical styles. However, anything that "overstepped the limits of artistic decorum" or was "exaggerated and misguided through a disregard for materials or through a striving for originality" was to be excluded. So the excesses of French Art Nouveau were not for the Munich Secessionists. Jugendstil ("New Style," derived from the name of the contemporary literary and artistic publication *Jugend*), as Art Nouveau was called in Germany,

was a more sober affair, hovering between British Arts and Crafts and the Wiener Werkstätte, with the occasional continental flourish.

Riemerschmid, among other organizers of the Applied Art Section, consolidated the aims of the exhibition by setting up the *Vereinigte Werkstätten für Kunst im Handwerk* (United Workshops for Art in Handicraft) the same year. Despite the title, handicraft was less important than division of labor, using the latest technology, and bringing modern designs to a wide public, so that everyone involved could make a living.

RECTILINEAR RESTRAINT

Originally a painter and architect, Riemerschmid first designed furniture in 1895 when he could not find any that she liked for his new marital home. As with his exhibits at the Glaspalast in 1897, he drew on the Arts and Crafts movement for form and Art Nouveau for decorative brasswork and carving; his ornamentation, however, was abstract rather than

MAHOGANY ELBOW CHAIR Each arm is carved from a single piece of mahogany, and the tapering legs have block feet. Designed by Richard Riemerschmid. *1897. H:32½ in (83 cm).*

Each door panel has a square inset, echoing the rectilinear form of the piece

Applied wrought-iron bands on the top two sections are the only decorative detail

The rectilinear form is in keeping with the German Jugendstil movement

THREE-PIECE PINE CUPBOARD The top two sections of this cupboard each have two two-part hinged doors, while the lower section has three doors. Designed by Richard Riemerschmid and made by the *Dresdner Werkstätten*, this pine cupboard has a silky, matte polish. *1902. H:83 in (211 cm).*

LEMON-MAHOGANY CUPBOARD Jugendstil references can be seen in the simple, organic relief carving and ornamental copper mountings. The cupboard was designed by Patriz Huber. *1902. H:80 in (200 cm).*

CHERRY ARMCHAIR Designed by Bruno Paul for the *Vereinigte Werkstätten für Kunst* in Munich, this elegant chair is polished and upholstered. *1901. H:36 in (90 cm).*

parts and to designs by Bruno Paul. Riemerschmid fulfilled both elaborate commissions at the top of the market and purely functional furniture designs similar to those of van de Velde, with clean, straight lines softened by slight curves. This "semi mass production" was a huge financial success, and the two workshops amalgamated. Other designers such as Patriz Huber also produced bold, functional designs. Huber carved linear motifs and patterns that offered a more subtle decoration than the continental whiplash. But many German designers ignored all modern styles, and continued producing plain Neoclassical or solid, heavily carved Baroque furniture.

AUSTRIAN STYLE

Austria had a success story similar to that of Germany. Thonet's bentwood chairs, first produced in the 1840s, were a household name throughout Europe and even in the United States. The technique of steaming solid or laminated wood so that it could be bent naturally produced the curves characteristic of Art Nouveau. Other Vienna firms, including J. & J. Kohn, built their reputations on bentwood furniture, employing designers such as Marcel Kammerer.

naturalistic. Riemerschmid's furniture was praised by contemporary critics for its spatial awareness and because "its structure is rendered wholly transparent," with simple construction and "modest materials." Emphasizing structure highlighted rather than hid how the furniture was made.

One of Riemerschmid's big commissions was for "The Thieme House" in Munich. Each room had a unified design: formal for the drawing room, with golden motifs and mother-of-pearl inlays repeated

on chairs and cabinets; simpler for family rooms. He also designed carpets, light fixtures, and cutlery for the house, and gained a separate commission from Meissen for a porcelain service.

Most of his furniture was made in the Dresden, later German Workshops of Munich, as well as the German Workshops of Dresden-Hellerau. From 1907 the Berlin branch of the United Workshops concentrated on serial production, making *Typenmöbel* (type furniture) from standardized

ARTS AND CRAFTS CROSSOVER

In Britain and the United States, most new furniture stayed within the Arts and Crafts mold, contemporary with continental Art Nouveau. Many designers worked across two ranges: one simple and plain in local woods, and the other more luxurious, with hardwoods and exotic inlays. Some manufacturers such as Wylie & Lochhead and Shapland & Petter used Art Nouveau motifs in their work. But their solid architectural forms were more akin to the Glasgow School than the Continental Art designers.

MAHOGANY HALLSTAND The rectangular, beveled mirror sits below a repoussé copper panel with inscription above a pierced frieze of plant motifs. The base incorporates a walking-stick stand and seat. *W:42 in (107 cm).*

SALON SUITE The seating in this suite consists of a settee and two armchairs. The chairs have solid, bentwood beech frames and button-back leather upholstery. Designed by Marcel Kammerer, and produced by J. & J. Kohn, Vienna. *c.1910. Settee: W:29½ in (75 cm).*

CERAMICS

WHILE MANY PORCELAIN MANUFACTURERS CONTINUED WITH THEIR TRADITIONAL OUTPUT DURING THE ART NOUVEAU PERIOD, WORKERS IN STONEWARE SET A TREND FOR EXPERIMENTING WITH NEW SCULPTURAL SHAPES, PARTICULARLY IN FRANCE.

The budlike shape reflects the designer's interest in natural forms

BUD-SHAPED STONEWARE CACHEPOT Featuring three molded nymphs around the rim, this Delphin Massier vase has a green, red, and golden luster glaze. c.1900. H:17½ in (44 cm).

INNOVATIVE GLAZES

Nonporous and durable, stoneware had previously been used mostly as a utilitarian medium for containers. It was Théodore Deck who started the movement of French artist pottery when he set up a studio in Paris in 1856 making decorative earthenware. His followers were at the vanguard of the new art, experimenting with innovative, often lustrous glazes that glinted with different colors as they caught the light. Usually fired only once, at *grand feu* (high temperature), stoneware was glazed by adding salt to the kiln. For the first time, potters could call themselves artists. Their status rose, as did that of their materials: stoneware became as popular as porcelain.

In Germany, designers such as Richard Riemerschmid and Peter Behrens introduced new colors and decorative motifs—including stylized flowers—to stoneware tankards and flagons. But it was French ceramicists who really brought out the sculptural qualities of the hard material. A sculptor named Jean (Joseph-Marie) Carriès was inspired by the Asian stoneware at the 1878 Paris *Exposition Universelle*. He started working in stoneware to create figures of Christ, pagan gods, fauns and other mythical beasts, and waifs and strays on the street. Carriès triggered a reappraisal of stoneware, and other artist-potters started to work with the material, trying out new glazes that emphasized form.

The fact that stoneware was fired only once added uncertainty and meant that each piece was unique. As the painter Paul Gauguin, who worked extensively in unglazed and red-glazed stoneware, said: "Nature is an artist. The colors achieved in the same firing are always in harmony."

COMBINING ART AND SCIENCE

For many ceramicists, the glaze became more important than the vessel itself. Artists looked to science for new chemicals that would produce new effects. Deck disciple Ernest Chaplet and Auguste Delaherche experimented with iron-red flambé glazes for stoneware, creating rich reds speckled or streaked with other colors such as green, blue, or white. They later applied flambé glazes to porcelain, too. Pierre-Adrien Dalpayrat perfected a glaze of saturated red speckled with green that came to be known as *Rouge Dalpayrat*.

Chaplet, Delaherche, and others also revisited the techniques of Renaissance luster-glazed Hispano-Moresque wares. They would spray metal oxides into the kiln and cut off the oxygen by blocking the air vents at a key moment. The result was an explosion of gases reacting with the oxides. Once the sooty surface of the vessel was polished, the glaze gleamed like metal. In the past, lead, tin, copper, and iron oxides had been used, but now the repertoire extended to chromium, titanium, and uranium (banned in the 1920s).

In Great Britain these experiments were carried out by the likes of William De Morgan. In 1892 he said of the mystique attached to luster glazes: "In spite of reproductions, an impression continued to prevail that the process was a secret. I used to hear it talked about among artists, about 25 years ago, as a sort of potters' philosopher's stone."

TAPERING BELGIAN POTTERY VASE This circular vase by Henry van de Velde features a twisting, sinuous abstract decoration in green and honey-colored glazes. H:11¼ in (28.5 cm).

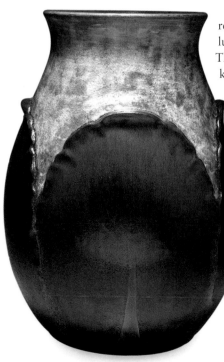

STONEWARE VASE This Pierre-Adrien Dalpayrat stoneware vase with blue and beige glaze is signed "Dalpayrat 1008." c.1905. H:12¾ in (32.5 cm).

DELAHERCHE VASE Glazed in blue on a brown ground, this stoneware vase bears the maker's mark. c.1890. H:14½ in (36.5 cm).

The vase is decorated with a lustrous, iridescent glaze

LA NUIT MAJOLICA VASE
The tapering form of this vase by Jean-Baptiste Massier rises to a poppy-seedhead rim, while at the neck of the vase is the figure of an owl. Both elements are associated with and symbolic of the night. *H:10¼ in (26 cm).*

The vase is adorned with an owl in relief

SYNERGIZING SHAPE AND GLAZE

If any ceramics can be described as essentially Art Nouveau, it is arguably those produced by the Massier company. This sculptural stoneware decorated with plant forms and semi-clad females typifies the style. Pots were decorated with a luster glaze developed by Clément Massier, who ran the family factory near Nice in the south of France. His brother, Delphin, who had his own pottery, specialized in sculptural detail, such as owls, applied beneath the overall luster glaze.

In Belgium, Henry van de Velde was as creative as his French counterparts, coming up with organic shapes, sinuous decoration abstracted from nature, and glazes with colors that flowed seamlessly into one another. Adding boric acid to the recipe created streaky glazes with running colors.

EASTERN EUROPEAN INNOVATIONS

France was not the only country with exciting developments in ceramics. In 1879 Hungarian manufacturer Vilmos Zsolnay came to study ceramics and Asian art in London and Paris. He had bought his company from his brother in 1865, when it made stoneware in traditional Hungarian peasant style, and built it up to employ 1,000 workers by 1900.

He courted ceramic pioneers to come up with new glazes and aesthetics, and in the 1890s one of his chemists, Vince Wartha, invented a new luster glaze called eosin. It flooded iridescent color across the ceramic body, which now often took a floral, asymmetrical form. Low-relief molded detail was a feature of Zsolnay wares. Wartha became artistic director in 1893, and the company specialized in painted decoration created with lustered glazes.

The Zsolnay factory also produced a range of crystalline glazes. Mineral salts added to a colored glaze formed crystals that looked like frost or ice.

Original maker's mark clearly visible on the base of the vase

The sinuous outline is modeled with tendrils

The flowers are vividly colored

RARE VASE WITH STOPPER Produced by the Hungarian manufacturer Zsolnay, this vase has a purple-red and iridescent blue glazed body with a berry-molded stopper. The pierced body of the vase is decorated with vibrant relief-molded flowers. *H:10½ in (27 cm)*

ACROSS THE OCEAN

Throughout the history of ceramics, new ideas and techniques have been passed on as experienced workers moved from one factory or country to another, either out of choice or because they had to. Former employees would take their knowledge with them, and new recipes for ceramic bodies and glazes, ideas for shapes, and techniques quickly spread around Europe and to North America. The luster glazes of the Weller Pottery in Ohio demonstrate this perfectly. They were very similar to European glazes because their maker, Jacques Sicard, had originally trained as a potter in France under Clément Massier, before going to work at the Weller Pottery in 1901. He eventually returned to France in 1907.

TAPERING VASE With a molded rim and an iridescent copper ground, this vase is decorated with brightly colored leaf and branch motifs. It was designed for Weller by the French potter Jacques Sicard. *c.1905. H:9 in (22.5 cm).*

TRADITION AND INNOVATION

While the pottery industry was given a new lease on life by the Art Nouveau movement, traditional porcelain factories hesitated to abandon the successful formula of the previous 100 years and continued making high-quality reproductions of 18th-century designs.

In some cases, however, conventional vases and other objects were manufactured alongside items displaying more contemporary shapes and motifs. The big factories employed new designers for the change in look. The German company Meissen, for example, commissioned Henry van de Velde, among other leading designers, to produce tableware. In France, Sèvres, with its royal backing and the inspirational Théodore Deck as director

from 1897 until his death in 1901, was also vigorously progressive in strands of its output. The factory commissioned Hector Guimard, who provided Art Nouveau forms in his distinctive fluid sculptural style for stoneware and porcelain.

REMARKABLE DEVELOPMENTS

Sèvres and Royal Copenhagen in Denmark sparred over their own development of crystalline glazes, using zinc and quartz oxides. The Swedish company Rörstrand produced pieces similar to Royal Copenhagen. Taxile Doat, a disciple of Deck, developed a *pâte-sur-pâte* range for Sèvres, using a technique where he built up a design in relief with layer upon layer of slip. He applied the decoration to porcelain vases and plaques with female figures.

Doat also had his own works, where he experimented with glazes. He wrote in 1903: "The ceramicist does not exist without his kiln any more than a violinist without his violin." With his hands-on approach, taking responsibility for the whole

process rather than handing a design over to a thrower and decorator, Doat was a great influence on American studio pottery.

Meanwhile, as well as its new glazes, Royal Copenhagen developed high-temperature underglaze colors. The soft, hazy blues, greens, and browns, used to paint Danish landscapes influenced by Japanese art, invited a deep look into the glaze.

FLORAL DECORATION

For many ceramic factories the Art Nouveau style was translated into rich floral motifs, whether applied, incised, or painted. Royal Copenhagen's fellow Danish factory, Bing & Grondahl, also used smoky underglaze colors. They applied naturalistic plant forms to their vases with metal mounts that harmonized with the painted decoration. Both Danish factories were praised for their ceramics at the 1900 Paris *Exposition Universelle*.

The Amphora range of vases made by Riessner, Stellmacher & Kessel (RSK) in Bohemia, in what

RÖRSTRAND PORCELAIN VASE The pale grey-blue ground of this urn-shaped vase is decorated with swirling sea currents and stylized red manta rays. The base of the vase bears the factory stamp. *H:9 in (23 cm).*

The handles are shaped like the tails of stylized manta rays

SILVER-MOUNTED PORCELAIN VASE The narrow neck and base of this teardrop-shaped vase by Bing & Grondahl of Copenhagen are adorned with pierced silver mounts. The body of the vase is decorated with clover leaves in muted colors. *c.1900. H:6¾ in (17 cm).*

The silver mounts bear poppy motifs

Thistles and spiky foliage are molded in relief

AMPHORA VASE The sinuous handles of this ovoid vase are the stems of the thistles and foliage that decorate the vessel. Marked "Amphora, Made in Czechoslovakia." *H:17 in (43 cm).*

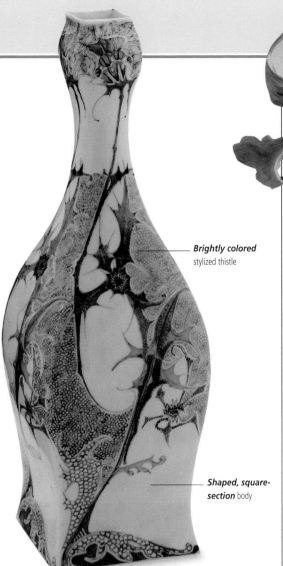

Brightly colored stylized thistle

Shaped, square-section body

EGGSHELL-PORCELAIN VASE The body of this extremely thin, lightweight vase is decorated with stylized thistles in yellow and orange. The vase is marked "Rozenburg, den Haag". *1902. H:10½ in (27 cm).*

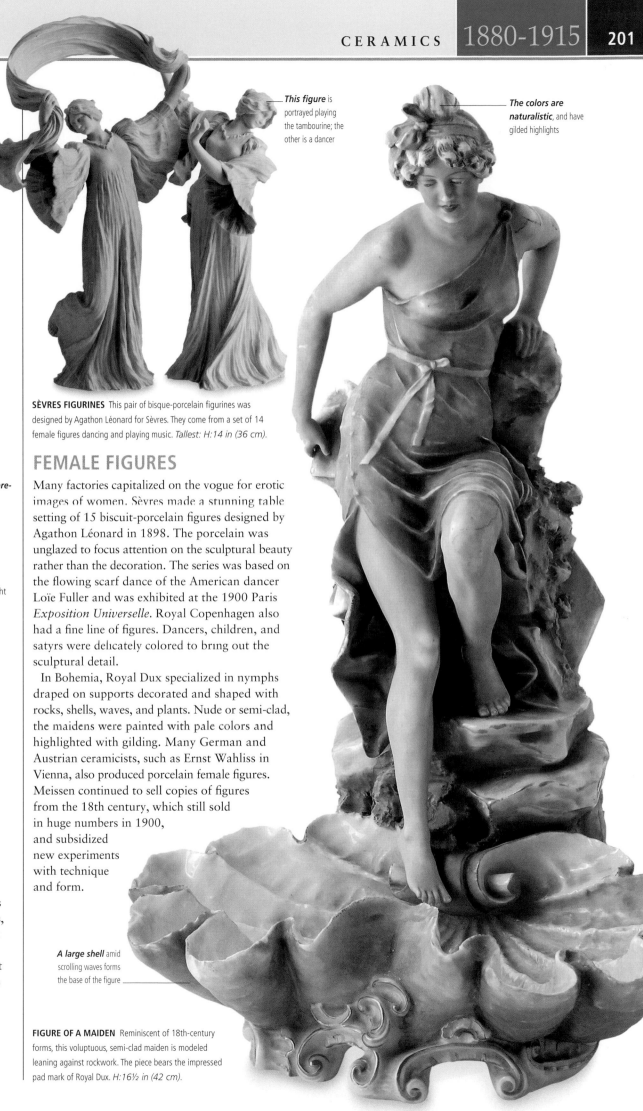

This figure is portrayed playing the tambourine; the other is a dancer

SÈVRES FIGURINES This pair of bisque-porcelain figurines was designed by Agathon Léonard for Sèvres. They come from a set of 14 female figures dancing and playing music. *Tallest: H:14 in (36 cm).*

The colors are naturalistic, and have gilded highlights

A large shell amid scrolling waves forms the base of the figure

FIGURE OF A MAIDEN Reminiscent of 18th-century forms, this voluptuous, semi-clad maiden is modeled leaning against rockwork. The piece bears the impressed pad mark of Royal Dux. *H:16½ in (42 cm).*

FEMALE FIGURES

Many factories capitalized on the vogue for erotic images of women. Sèvres made a stunning table setting of 15 biscuit-porcelain figures designed by Agathon Léonard in 1898. The porcelain was unglazed to focus attention on the sculptural beauty rather than the decoration. The series was based on the flowing scarf dance of the American dancer Loïe Fuller and was exhibited at the 1900 Paris *Exposition Universelle*. Royal Copenhagen also had a fine line of figures. Dancers, children, and satyrs were delicately colored to bring out the sculptural detail.

In Bohemia, Royal Dux specialized in nymphs draped on supports decorated and shaped with rocks, shells, waves, and plants. Nude or semi-clad, the maidens were painted with pale colors and highlighted with gilding. Many German and Austrian ceramicists, such as Ernst Wahliss in Vienna, also produced porcelain female figures. Meissen continued to sell copies of figures from the 18th century, which still sold in huge numbers in 1900, and subsidized new experiments with technique and form.

was to become Czechoslovakia, also received international acclaim. These vases were organic in shape, down to details such as the rim opening out like a flower or handles shaped like stems. Nature also inspired the decoration of the vases, such as embossed waterlilies and lily pads, in an exuberant manner similar to the School of Nancy. Flowers and foliage were painted and molded in relief and highlighted with gilding. As well as adopting the Art Nouveau idiom by fusing naturalistic form and decoration, Bohemian Amphora ware also featured dreamy women with flowing hair and the whiplash motif of curved lines.

In the Netherlands, the Rozenburg and Gouda Ceramic factories painted stylized flowers in a unique Dutch manner. Gouda's abstracted plants in strong colors were inspired by the printed cloths, or batiks, typical of their colony, the Dutch East Indies (now Indonesia). By contrast, Rozenburg made exquisite "eggshell porcelain" in flamboyant shapes. Not true porcelain, its fragile thinness was matched by the delicate floral painting floating across the white surface.

Sèvres also painted naturalistic decoration by hand, generally onto traditional shapes, and entwined flowers into patterns in delicate pink, green, blue, and yellow on a white ground.

EARLY NEWCOMB COLLEGE VASE The elegant yellow and light blue blossoms on this exceptional vase were carved by Leona Nicholson, against a stylized cobalt and deep-green ground. *H:12½ in (32 cm).*

AMERICAN ART POTTERY

In the United States, the tradition of art pottery, which had begun with the Arts and Crafts movement, continued during the Art Nouveau period. Some large commercial works such as S. A. Weller and Roseville rapidly caught on to the international style or copied the originality of firms such as Rookwood. Others, such as the Newcomb Pottery, developed their own distinctive line of Art Nouveau vases with a regional flavor.

SOUTHERN FLAIR

The American Civil War of 1861–65 decimated the male population in the United States, and meant that women had to take on jobs formerly held by men, such as pottery-making. In 1895 the New Orleans-based Sophie Newcomb College for Women set up a pottery department. Mary G. Sheerer, a ceramic painter who had trained with Rookwood, taught design. Along with director Ellsworth Woodward, Sheerer led a team of eager students, and together they developed some of the finest American art pottery. Each piece was unique, hand-thrown and handpainted, or modeled.

Woodward's aim was to create "a Southern product, made of Southern clays, by Southern artists, decorated with Southern subjects." The decoration was based on Louisiana flora and fauna, including tobacco and cotton plants, jonquils, lizards, and waterbirds, as well as more abstract motifs indirectly inspired by Japan. Plant drawing was a required course, and many students kept gardens in which to study nature at first hand.

The earliest vases had glossy glazes, with stylized flower patterns incised in outline and painted underglaze. Later wares were covered with matte, muted glazes and soft pastel colors—yellow, blue, green, and black gave way to pale blue, white, and

OVOID VASE Thick green stems emerge from the base of this matte blue vase, rising to the delicate narcissus flowers that decorate the vase's neck. They were carved by Henrietta Bailey at Newcomb College. *1918. W:6¾ in (17.25 cm).*

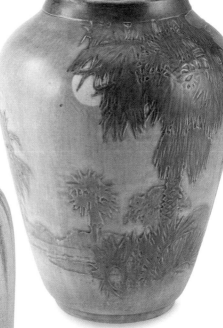

LARGE NEWCOMB COLLEGE VASE This blue, white, and soft cream vase carved by Sadie Irvine depicts a nighttime landscape with palm trees and a full moon. *H:9¾ in (25 cm).*

Detail of the star-shaped heads of the narcissus flowers

CUERDA SECA POTTERY These two pieces are typical of the work produced at the Paul Revere Pottery of the Saturday Evening Girls' Club: a simple, brightly colored bowl depicting a landscape scene with large white geese and green trees; and a bullet-shaped wall pocket with yellow poppies on a white and lime-green ground. The colors and *cuerda seca* technique used for decorating these pieces are reminiscent of early Spanish works. *Bowl: W:11½ in (29 cm); Wall pocket: H:6 in (15 cm).*

Artus Van Briggle's mark

VAN BRIGGLE VASE This early vase features embossed leaves under a matte raspberry glaze. *1904. H:9¾ in (25 cm).*

VAN BRIGGLE

Uniquely in the United States, the ceramics of Artus Van Briggle were directly influenced by French Art Nouveau.

cream. Decoration became freer. Sadie Irvine, a student who later ran the department, produced one of Newcomb's most famous designs: a dreamy bayou landscape of oaks covered in Spanish moss, with a pale yellow moon half-hidden by the trees.

Students could sign their own work and sell their best pieces to help fund their tuition. As well as Irvine, key names that emerged from Newcomb include Harriet Joor, Anna Frances Simpson, and Henrietta Bailey.

After Ellsworth Woodward's retirement in 1931, quality declined, and Newcomb College's pottery department closed in 1940.

A NEW SKILL FOR WOMEN

In 1906 James J. Storrow and Edith Brown set up the Saturday Evening Girls' Club in Boston. The aim of this concern was to teach underprivileged girls, often from immigrant families, a craft they could both enjoy and earn money from. The workers learned how to glaze, fire, and decorate thrown pots. The club flourished and soon moved to a bigger site, renaming itself the Paul Revere Pottery after the local silversmith hero of the Revolutionary War.

The club produced earthenware breakfast bowls, nursery sets, and other useful items. The decoration—flowers, animals, witches on broomsticks, sailboats, windmills, and landscapes—was often outlined in black, setting off the colorful palette. It was frequently drawn on to the vessel using the *cuerda seca* technique, which involved creating a wax outline to prevent the glaze from running during firing. Instead, the glaze would bead up, subtly flooding the delineated area with color.

Although the founders set up the club for benevolent rather than commercial reasons, the enterprise flourished and moved again in 1915 to custom-built premises based on those of Rookwood. Output expanded to include candlesticks, lamps, book ends, and paperweights, but the children's bowls decorated with animals remained a popular line. The Saturday Evening Girls' Club closed in 1942.

BUD VASE This Paul Revere vase is covered in an unusual, thick, green mottled glaze dripping over a blue-gray ground. *H:7 in (17.5 cm).*

While working at Rookwood, Van Briggle was sent to Paris to study sculpture and painting. Learning to model in clay helped him both at Rookwood and at his own pottery works, which he and his wife Anna set up in Colorado Springs in 1901. Van Briggle's best-known range, Lorelei, displays a typically sculptural feel, with the hair and arms of a languid woman curving around the neck of the vessel, fusing form, function, and decoration. Other decorative motifs include embossed stylized plant patterns or American Indian designs. Van Briggle also perfected the use of matte glazes. He often employed an atomizer for spraying on colored glazes, green being most common, though blue and maroon were also favored.

Van Briggle died of tuberculosis at 35 in 1904. His wife continued to run the company, only selling it in 1912, and today it is still in production, largely making copies of Van Briggle originals.

SIREN OF THE SEA BOWL The rim of this center bowl is decorated with a molded recumbent mermaid figure and has a flower frog in its center. The bowl is covered in a shaded, matte turquoise glaze. *1920s. H:7½ in (19 cm).*

DINNER PLATE The center of this Paul Revere blue-gray plate features a landscape medallion. The plate also has an "FG" circular stamp on the rim. *D:12 in (30.5 cm).*

CERAMICS GALLERY

Floral forms are a common theme on these ceramics—the flowers featured tend to be in full bloom, softening the contours of the designs. Young, beautiful women, usually portrayed with long, flowing hair, are another popular motif. These curvy lines are typical of the liberated, naturalistic aesthetic that characterized Art Nouveau. Decoration was often molded in relief to give a greater feeling of depth and texture. Art Nouveau ceramicists favored a naturalistic palate of greens and browns, although brighter colors and gilding were sometimes added as decorative highlights.

KEY

1. Salvini faience plate with a woman's head in polychrome on a white ground. D:6 in (15 cm). ① **2.** Foley Intarsio circular wall plaque depicting two maidens within a band of waterlilies. D:15 in (38 cm). ① **3.** Amphora pottery vase painted with stylized tulips. H:7¼ in (18.5 cm). ① **4.** Johann von Schwarz vase decorated with sword lilies. H:22 in (56 cm). ③ **5.** Dutch eggshell-porcelain vase with a single handle. H:6 in (15.5 cm). ④ **6.** French pottery plate based on a design by Alphonse Mucha. D:12 in (31 cm). ② **7.** Charlotte Rhead for Bursley Ware bowl with tube-lined Glasgow Rose decoration. D:10¾ in (27.5 cm). ② **8.** Utzschneider & Co. Sarreguemines vase, with tulip decoration in violet and blue. H:8½ in (21.5 cm). ① **9.** Eichwald Pottery vase molded with flowers and with stylized handles. H:9¾ in (25 cm). ① **10.** A. Stuchly tapering vase, embossed with a lady's

[1] Salvini faience plate

[2] Foley Intarsio wall plaque

[3] Amphora pottery vase

[4] Johann von Schwarz vase

[6] French pottery plate

[5] Dutch porcelain vase

[7] Bursley Ware bowl

[8] Sarreguemines vase

[9] Eichwald Pottery vase

[10] A. Stuchly vase

head covered in a brown and green matte glaze. H:12 in (30.5 cm). ② **11.** Nippon vase decorated in Coralene with yellow and orange lilies on a shaded ground. H:8¾ in (22 cm). ② **12.** Frainersdorf ceramic vase by P. A. Wranitzki. H:5¾ in (14.5 cm). ① **13.** Nippon vase decorated in Coralene with pink and russet peonies on a shaded ground. H:8¼ in (21 cm). ① **14.** Royal Bonn floor vase slip-decorated in matte glazes with thistles and acanthus. H:22¼ in (55.5 cm). ② **15.** Teren vase embossed with large gold flowers and cabochon hearts on a green ground. H:14 in (35.5 cm). ①
16. Moorcroft bulbous vase in the Orchid pattern. H:17½ in (44.5 cm). ① **17.** Rare Weller Fru Russet vase embossed with flowers under a pale blue-gray and green glaze. H:14 in (35.5 cm). ③
18. Macintyre squat vase painted with stylized poppies and foliage in the Imari palette. H:6¼ in (15.5 cm). ① **19.** Johann von Schwarz vase with stylized floral imagery. H:3¾ in (9.5 cm). ① **20.** Two-handled Foley Intarsio vase by Frederick Rhead, decorated with stylized poppies. H:11 in (28 cm). ①

11 Nippon lily vase

12 Frainersdorf vase

13 Nippon peony vase

14 Royal Bonn floor vase

15 Teren vase

16 Moorcroft vase

17 Weller vase

18 Macintyre vase

19 Johann von Schwarz vase

20 Foley Intarsio vase

ÉMILE GALLÉ

REJECTING THE MID-19TH-CENTURY TASTE FOR HEAVY CUT-CRYSTAL GLASS, GALLÉ EXPLOITED THE TRANSLUCENT AND PLIANT QUALITIES OF THE MEDIUM. HE WAS A PIONEER IN THE FIELDS OF CERAMICS, FURNITURE, AND, ABOVE ALL, GLASS, DISPLAYING ARTISTIC FLAIR AND A WIDE RANGE OF TECHNIQUES.

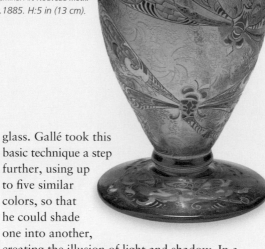

AUX LIBELLULES VASE Made by Gallé, this pale amber vase was designed by Eugène Kremer. It is etched, enameled, and gilded with dragonflies—a seminal Art Nouveau motif. *c.1885. H:5 in (13 cm).*

Born in Nancy, the heartland of French Art Nouveau and a renowned glassmaking area, Émile Gallé (1846–1904) was the son of a glass and faience factory owner. As well as learning the family business, he studied botany, drawing, and landscape painting and traveled throughout Europe. In 1874 Gallé took over his father's factory, and four years later he exhibited at the Paris *Exposition Universelle*. Here, seeing how other avant-garde glassmakers were molding and treating the material inspired him to embrace innovative designs. In turn, Gallé's own exhibits, which included enameled decoration with gracefully stylized plant motifs interpreted from Japanese art, were an inspiration to others.

CAMEO GLASS TABLE LAMP Wildflowers decorate the domed shade and base of this lamp. The organic shape and fascination with nature are typical of Gallé's work. *Early 1900s. H:13¾ in (35 cm).*

CHRYSANTHEMUM VASE Of tapered ovoid form, this cameo vase is etched with chrysanthemum blossoms, buds, and branches in dark ruby-red glass over an amber ground. *c.1900. H:12½ in (31.5 cm).*

LOVE OF NATURE

Gallé saw nature as the underlying force of life. The organic shapes of his designs and decorations found a parallel in the natural world, and his depictions of plants, insects—especially his favorite, dragonflies—and other animals were scientifically accurate.

Gallé chose to depict natural motifs for more than just random aesthetic reasons. He used them symbolically, sometimes including lines of Symbolist poetry by Stéphane Mallarmé or Charles Baudelaire, leading to the tag *verres parlantes* (talking glass). When Gallé helped found the School of Nancy in 1901, he educated his pupils in the theory of symbols.

Beetles stood for hard work; thistles for his home region of Lorraine and its separation from Germany; roses for France and love; poppies for sleep; and pine trees he called "a metaphor of energy in repose."

Gallé also drew heavily on the swirling asymmetry of Rococo designs—Nancy's central square has a superb example of Louis XV ironwork—and dizzyingly reinterpreted medieval, Islamic, Asian, and Classical sources.

TECHNICAL VIRTUOSO

Gallé used a medieval Syrian enamel painting technique to work on glass as freely as if he were using watercolor on paper. He also adopted the internally crackled and colored glass that fellow glassmakers were using, originally inspired by Chinese carved rock-crystal and Japanese lacquerwork. He manipulated light within and without glass using clear, colorless, colored, and painted glass.

Cameo glass is perhaps Gallé's best-known legacy. In this ancient Roman technique, two layers of different colored glass are fused together. The top layer is then carved, so that the image stands out from its surrounding, lower layer of

glass. Gallé took this basic technique a step further, using up to five similar colors, so that he could shade one into another, creating the illusion of light and shadow. In a lamp, lit from within, the effect was even more subtle and glowing.

Instead of carving the outer layers of glass, acid-etching could be used to eat away the areas around the relief image. Other technical innovations saw Gallé placing metal foil between the glass layers to provide highlights, or pressing small pieces of hot colored glass into the molten glass body—a glass adaptation of marquetry. Once the glass cooled down, the pieces could be carved.

THE WORKSHOP

By 1890 Gallé employed more than 300 workers. Only occasionally did he have the time to make the piece himself, so he would usually hand his designs over to trusted glassblowers and decorators. He also allowed his team of designers artistic freedom, so long as they represented botanical and animal motifs with realistic precision.

After Gallé's death in 1904, a star was added to his signature engraved on glass as a mark of respect. For a time the factory was run by his widow and his lifelong friend Victor Prouvé. After World War I, however, Gallé's son-in-law Paul Perdrizet took over, producing mainly cameo glass with floral designs. The factory closed in 1936.

GALLÉ AT WORK Émile Gallé shown in his studio, surrounded by botanical specimens and drawings.

OVAL VASE This vase is decorated in marquetry style with daffodils, each element individually carved. The vase is engraved with Gallé's signature. *1900. H:7in (18 cm).*

GLASS

ART NOUVEAU FOUND ITS IDEAL MEDIUM IN GLASS. NOT ONLY COULD IT

BE MOLDED INTO FLUID SHAPES, IT ALSO LENT ITSELF TO THE STYLE'S

RICH COLORS AND MULTILAYERED DECORATION.

CAMEO GLASS

Research into ancient techniques combined with innovative industrial methods allowed designers to push the boundaries of glass decoration. At the forefront of the glass revolution was Émile Gallé (*see pp.206–07*), closely followed by the Daum brothers, who in 1887 had taken over their father's glassworks in the French decorative-arts capital of Nancy in the Lorraine region. Cameo glass was a specialty of both factories.

After seeing Gallé's glass at the 1889 Paris *Exposition Universelle*, the Daum brothers were inspired to make their own versions. They also drew on the flora and fauna local to their region for motifs; but while Gallé had invested them with symbolic fervor, the Daum brothers were mostly concerned with the accurate rendition of the natural world.

INNOVATIVE TECHNIQUES

In order to make plants, animals, and their background setting look even more realistic, the Daum brothers developed a series of complex decorative techniques.

In some instances, the decoration on a vessel would be acid-etched. This process could also be done by a machine, in which case the glass was defined as "faux cameo" to distinguish it from handcarved cameo glass. Once the glass was cold, enamels—powdered colored glass bound in an oil medium—would be applied over the decoration to give it a natural sense of depth. Enameled vessels could be sold as they were, without another firing, or reheated to fuse the design to the body and make them more hard-wearing.

BARREL-SHAPED VASE Decorated with freshwater plants and dragonflies, this cameo vase is etched and enameled in subtle shades of blue, green, yellow, and purple. The mottled effect of the glass is characteristic of much glass produced by Daum Frères. Signed "Daum, Nancy." *1904. H:9 in (23 cm).*

SPIDERWEB VASE This rare Daum vase has cameo decoration of green iris blossoms and leaves on a frosted chipped-ice background. A cameo green spider rests on a gold enamel spiderweb (*inset, right*). The vase sits in its original embossed silver holder and is signed "Daum Nancy" in gold lettering on the base. *H:9¼ in (23.5 cm).*

TWIN-HANDLED VASE The pink ground of this cameo-glass vase is decorated with green trailing-vine motifs. The green of the foliage and swirling tendrils is repeated in the base of the vase and in the handles. It is signed "Daum Nancy." *H:8¼ in (21 cm).*

Other techniques perfected by the Daum brothers included the *martelé*, or hammered-metal, effect, borrowed from silversmithing to give the surface of a vessel texture and depth; and intercalaire (literally "between the layers") decoration. In this technique, a decorative layer is applied, then covered with a sheet of colored glass, which acts as the surface for another layer of decoration. Daum Frères also applied high-relief foil-backed decoration and, like Gallé, used *marqueterie-sur-verre* (marquetry on glass), mainly on the Nancy theme of dragonflies over lily ponds.

THE ELECTRIC REVOLUTION

The advent of electric light meant that the Daum brothers could apply their creativity to a new range of items such as lamps and lampshades. Their collaboration with Louis Majorelle, Gallé's protégé and Nancy's leading metalworker, led to a series of lamps that combined decorated glass shades with metal mounts. Some of the best pieces are those that mirror nature in both form and decoration, such as lamps shaped like mushrooms or zucchini flowers.

In other instances, a glass shade and base would be integrated by using the same decoration for both. The stem of the lamp was sometimes left hollow so that it, too, could be lit from within, creating a stunning effect.

OTHER CAMEO MAKERS

In other parts of Lorraine, the Müller Frères were inspired by Émile Gallé to specialize in cameo glass. Like their mentor, they also illustrated natural themes of flowers, birds, and landscapes, and dark brown and yellow were their favored colors. Like Gallé and the Daum brothers, the Müller Frères used the technique of fire polishing, which involved melting the surface of the glass a second time to smooth out any imperfections caused by acid-etching.

Another set of brothers, Ernest and Charles Schneider, based in Épinay-sur-Seine, produced an acid-etched cameo range known as *Le Verre Français*, as well as carved, layered, and applied glass. In Paris, Auguste Legras simplified the style to appeal to as wide an audience as possible.

Cameo glass had been popular in Britain 100 years earlier, in the Neoclassical era, when its success had been fanned by the Portland Vase from Roman antiquity. However, in the late 19th century most British designers disregarded Art Nouveau, which they saw as too florid and decadent a style. A handful of artists, though, did embrace the style, including Thomas Webb & Sons. This firm made some remarkable ranges of cameo glass, often combining clear glass and a color, or using white on a colored ground.

In the United States, the Honesdale firm specialized in decorating, and brought in blanks from other companies.

THOMAS WEBB VASE Featuring cameo floral decoration of roses and leaves, this three-color cameo vase (white over red over citron) is signed "Tiffany & Co. Paris Exposition 1889 Thomas Webb & Sons Gem Cameo." *1889. H:7½ in (19 cm).*

NARROW BALUSTER VASE This ovoid vase with a flared rim and a circular foot has a milky opalescent luster and is decorated with acid-etched chrysanthemums in coral and green. Designed by Henri Müller, of Croismare, near Nancy. *c.1900. H:10½ in (27 cm).*

The opalescent body is overlaid with amber- and green-colored glass

HONESDALE VASE This cameo-glass vase has a narrow, tapering waist and flared rim and foot. The clear-glass ground is overlaid with acid-etched fall leaves. There is also gilded decoration at the rim and base. *1915–20. H:9¾ in (25 cm).*

The bell-shaped shade resembles a zucchini flower

ZUCCHINI-FLOWER TABLE LAMP The arched brass stem and leaves rise from a leaf-shaped base and terminate in a colorless shade decorated with yellow and green matte-etched enamel. *c.1905.*

The brass base and stem are likely to be by Louis Majorelle

FROSTED CAMEO-GLASS BOWL Made by Auguste Legras, this bulbous bowl is decorated with fruiting vines. The narrow neck has a silver band around the top. *H:5½ in (14 cm).*

IRIDESCENT GLASS

In the 19th century, excavations of ancient Roman sites yielded glass that had turned lustrous from being buried in damp soil. The rebirth of interest in iridescent glass heralded an explosion of creativity in the previously stagnant glassmaking world. Iridescence makes a glass vessel gleam and catch the light with a vast array of colors. Most iridescent glass in existence today was made in the Art Nouveau era. At the same time, the invention of electric light gave rise to new forms and showed off the sparkling color. Famously associated with Louis Comfort Tiffany (*see pp.212–13*), iridescent glass was widely made in the United States, Europe, and Britain.

METALLIC FINISHES

Methods and recipes for obtaining iridescent glass varied but, as with ceramic luster glazes, they all involved metal oxides. Some glassmakers exposed the glass to the fumes of metallic oxides and varied the degree of heat and cooling across the glass; others preferred to spray the glass with a metal-oxide mist. Tiffany developed a complex technique that demanded precise timing. The salts of metal oxides were dissolved in the molten glass, making the colors luminous. Different metals produced different colors: silver, for example, created a straw color, and copper a ruby red. The glass was then sprayed with chloride while held in a reducing flame. The chloride left minute lines on the surface that refracted light, making the colors appear to change.

HOT COMPETITION

Tiffany, however, was not the first to experiment with iridescent glass. The British firm Thomas Webb & Sons in Stourbridge exhibited "bronze glass" at the Paris *Exposition Universelle* in 1878. Three years later, Tiffany took out a patent; then in 1893 he harnessed the Stourbridge expertise by employing Arthur J. Nash, a talented glass-blower who had made iridescent glass at Webb's. The rich luster that Tiffany and his team perfected would inspire many others.

Among Tiffany's rivals was the Steuben Glassworks, established in 1903 in Corning, New York, by Frederick Carder, another former Stourbridge worker. Carder was the driving force behind some 6,000 shapes and more than 100 finishes. His gold Aurene glass, patented in 1904, usually has a brighter iridescence than Tiffany's, while the Blue Aurene range of 1905 has a bright-blue luster, and *verre de soie* (silk glass) is clear, with a silvery appearance. Red, brown, green, and other colors followed, used either on their own or in combination, sometimes decorated. Carder was experimenting with *pâte-de-verre* and lost wax techniques when he retired at 96.

THE AUSTRIAN TIFFANY

Bohemia had long been a center of cut and engraved glass enjoying royal patronage,

STEUBEN DECORATED VASE The stylized heart-and-vine decoration on this blue Aurene vase is similar to that seen in European Art Nouveau pieces. The iridescent blue finish has purple highlights. *H:10¼ in (26 cm).*

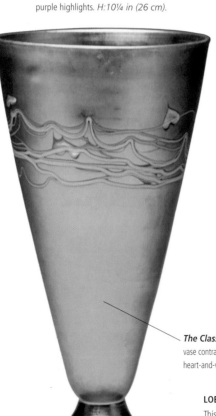

The Classical shape of the vase contrasts with the random heart-and-vine decoration

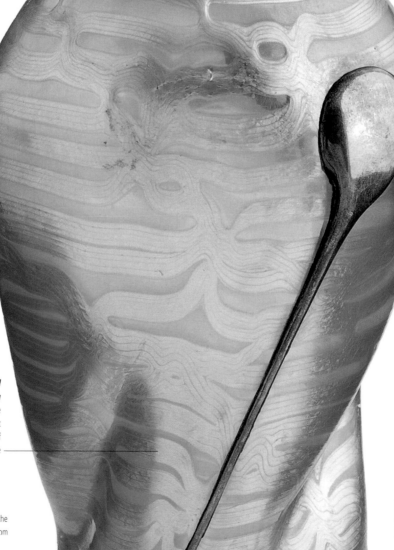

Applied silver trailing emphasizes the tapering, almost twisted shape of the vase

LOETZ IRIDESCENT VASE This glass vase of organic form is decorated with gold and gasoline-blue bands, as well as applied silver trailings. Signed "Loetz Austria." *H:6½ in (16.5 cm).*

STEUBEN VASE In this Gold Aurene vase with blue and purple highlights, the leaf-and-vine decoration is interspersed with flowers. The piece is signed "Aurene 582." *H:6¼ in (16 cm).*

but the area's fortunes had waned in the course of the 19th century. Iridescent glass provided Bohemian glassworks such as Loetz with a new lease on life. In the wake of Tiffany's success, in 1897 Loetz launched a spectacular iridescent range with wavy decoration called Phänomen. Another popular pattern was Papillon, which aimed to recreate the delicate patterns of a butterfly's wings in red, gold, or blue.

Loetz director Max Ritter von Spaun experimented with iridescent spots, ribbons, and streaks, and his vessels were sometimes overlaid with open silverwork. Vase shapes were as startling as the color effects, often with wavy or ruffled rims or swan-necked, like Persian rosewater sprinklers. The factory also employed some of the most progressive designers of the day, including Viennese Josef Hoffmann and Koloman Moser, and the Prague glass designer Marie Kirschner.

Loetz's iridescent glass was so similar to that of Tiffany's that the American artist took out a lawsuit against the Bohemian factory, preventing the import of unsigned Loetz pieces to North America.

THE INSPIRATION OF ROMAN GLASS

In the late 19th century archaeologists excavating ancient Roman sites discovered glass that had been buried for at least 1,700 years. Metal oxides in the soil had reacted on the surface of the glass to make it textured, corroded, and iridescent. With new technology, and a good deal of experimentation, late 19th-century glassmakers managed to speed up the chemical process to create a similar surface sheen in a fraction of the time. While some designers came up with entirely new shapes, many copied not just the surface effects but also the ancient Roman forms.

OINTMENT BOTTLES These Roman *unguentaria*, or ointment bottles, exemplify the look that Art Nouveau designers were trying to recreate with their iridescent glass. The aim of the luster glazes was to achieve the effect of glass that had been worn by years of being buried underground. *1st–3rd century CE. Blue bottle: H:2½ in (6 cm); Honey-colored bottle: H:3¼ in (8.5 cm).*

A BRIGHT NEW WORLD

In the early days of electricity, many light fixtures still bore a striking resemblance to traditional oil lamps, shaped as if for an oil-containing base with a domed cover above. Soon, however, it dawned on manufacturers and designers that they were no longer bound to the old shapes and they could exploit their creativity to the fullest.

Combining glass with metal, and integrating form and decoration, Art Nouveau artists began to flood the market with innovative and colorful lamps in the shape of plants, flowers, or animals, such as that perennial Art Nouveau favorite, the dragonfly. The peacock, which had appeared in Roman, Persian, Indian, and Byzantine ornament, was also adopted by Art Nouveau glassmakers as the ultimate symbol of beauty and was incorporated into many designs.

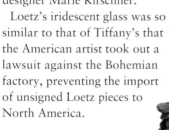

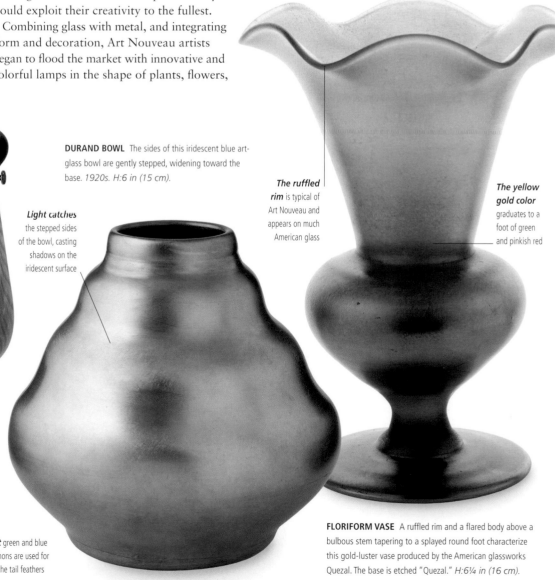

The amber shade is decorated with a feather pattern

PEACOCK LAMP The bronze base of this lamp is in the shape of a peacock holding the shade ring in its beak. The eyes of the tail feathers are set with iridescent green and blue glass that matches the "pulled" feathers in the art-glass shade made by Loetz. *c.1900. H:19½ in (49.5 cm).*

Iridescent green and blue glass cabochons are used for the eyes of the tail feathers

DURAND BOWL The sides of this iridescent blue art-glass bowl are gently stepped, widening toward the base. *1920s. H:6 in (15 cm).*

Light catches the stepped sides of the bowl, casting shadows on the iridescent surface

The ruffled rim is typical of Art Nouveau and appears on much American glass

The yellow gold color graduates to a foot of green and pinkish red

FLORIFORM VASE A ruffled rim and a flared body above a bulbous stem tapering to a splayed round foot characterize this gold-luster vase produced by the American glassworks Quezal. The base is etched "Quezal." *H:6¼ in (16 cm).*

LOUIS COMFORT TIFFANY

ART NOUVEAU FLOURISHED AS THE CAREER OF NEW YORK–
BASED TIFFANY MATURED. HE MASTERED A NUMBER OF
DISCIPLINES—NOTABLY SILVERWARE, JEWELRY, AND
GLASSWORK—AND HIS PIECES ARE BYWORDS FOR AMERICAN
ART NOUVEAU, OFTEN CALLED THE "TIFFANY STYLE."

America's answer to Émile Gallé (*see pp.206–207*), Louis Comfort Tiffany (1848–1933) had all the credentials to become a superb designer—and the zeal to match. His father owned a successful jewelry company in New York called Tiffany & Co. The firm's art director, Edward C. Moore, was an important formative influence on the young Tiffany: he had a huge collection of Classical, medieval, Asian, and Islamic decorative arts, and an extensive library including Owen Jones's *Grammar of Ornament*. Tiffany studied glass-blowing in Venice, met William Morris in London, and traveled to North Africa and Spain, where he painted watercolors of Moorish architecture.

SOURCES OF INSPIRATION

At the beginning of his career, Tiffany set up an interior-design business called Louis C. Tiffany & Associated Artists, starting an unprecedented collaboration with furniture and textile designers. Like many designers of the time, Tiffany's inspirations were wide-ranging: he was interested in Celtic and American Indian art, as well as the exotic. He looked to nature and to historic sources, and his glass, jewelry, ceramics, enameled copper, furniture, wallpaper, fabrics, and mosaics were frequently decorated with natural motifs such as dragonflies, flowers, and grapes.

Form and decoration were often more important than function—a vase, for example, could become an excuse for a glass sculpture of a single flower and its stem, dispensing with the purpose of holding fresh flowers. Among such floriform vases, the most distinctive is arguably the Jack-in-the-Pulpit vase, shaped like the North American wildflower of that name. Other pieces were swan-necked, inspired by the slender, undulating shape of Persian rosewater sprinklers.

EXPERIMENTAL TECHNIQUES

In 1894 Tiffany launched his Favrile (from "fabrile," Old English for "handcrafted") range of iridescent glass, which was an instant success. Another bestseller was the Lava range, with trails of molten glass oozing like lava down the iridescent surface of a vessel.

Tiffany also made vases in the so-called paperweight-glass style, with a magnifying dome of clear, faceted, or cased glass often enriched with a lampwork

PEACOCK LAMP Twenty peacock eyes decorate the orange, amethyst, and teal-green shade of this table lamp. The scalloped base is decorated with a raised peacock-feather design in bronze relief, each feather with a single peacock eye made of mosaic glass. *H:25 in (63.5 cm).*

design or millefiori decoration. In this technique, brightly colored canes (tiny glass rods) are arranged in patterns and embedded in clear glass. Such glass was difficult to make into vases, and few pieces were ever produced.

METAL AND GLASS

When art dealer Siegfried Bing opened his prestigious Paris shop La Maison de l'Art Nouveau in 1895, he bought many Favrile pieces. Then he commissioned Edward Colonna to design mounts for Tiffany vases, so that light would play over the gleaming surfaces of both the glass and the silver bases.

In 1900 Tiffany set up Tiffany Studios to make the lamps that would become his best-known legacy, embodying the marriage of metal and glass. Where the stand was an integral part of the lamp, the two elements always worked in harmony, so a flower lamp would have a base in the shape of a stem, for instance. Tiffany also made a positive feature of the metal linking the pieces of glass in the shade—it might be used, for example, to create the outlines of a dragonfly's wings or the petals of a flower.

Despite the name "leaded glass," Tiffany actually used copper rather than lead, as it was more flexible, enclosing small pieces of sheet glass colored with some possible 5,000 variations.

PAPERWEIGHT VASE This rare Tiffany carved cameo vase is inlaid with different colors and engraved. c.1910. H:7 in (18 cm).

LILY LAMP Produced by Tiffany Studios, this three-light lily lamp has one Tiffany-style shade and two Quezal shades. Each is shaped like a blooming lily and has an iridescent finish. The piece is signed, and the base is impressed "Tiffany Studios New York 313." H:12 in (30 cm).

MAXIM'S, PARIS Once dubbed "the Museum of Art Nouveau," Maxim's was the place to be seen during the Belle Époque. Tiffany's luxurious interiors epitomized his talent for creating a harmonious, integral look. The stained-glass ceiling and organic-framed mirrors create a magnificent, jewel-like atmosphere.

GLASS GALLERY

The organic forms that feature so prominently as decorative designs on Art Nouveau glassware are often echoed on the rims of vases and other vessels. Molded or pinched rims and handles with whiplash curves extend the floral motifs. Decorative themes are overwhelmingly botanical—vistas of trees or parts of plants such as petals, tendrils, and leaves predominate. Iridescent finishes, wrought by exposing the glass to metal oxide fumes, were also in vogue.

KEY

1. Ernest-Baptiste Léveillé vase with carved cinnabar-red glass, decorated with four of the eight Chinese Scholars of Wisdom. 1893. H:6¼ in (16 cm). ⑦ **2.** Pair of English Art Nouveau twisted tear vases. c.1900. H:10 in (25 cm). ① **3.** Auguste Jean globular smoky glass vase with flared trefoil neck and blue rim and feet. 1880. H:6¾ in (17 cm). ③ **4.** Footed vase, attributed to Charles Schneider, with etched and enameled decoration on frosted ground. c.1900. H:5¼ in (13 cm). ② **5.** Harrach decanter and two glasses. c.1900. H:11¼ in (28 cm). ② **6.** Wilhelm Kralik Sohn glass vase in elaborate metal mount. 1900–05. H:4 in (10 cm). ③ **7.** Austrian bottle-shaped vase of lustered green and purple glass in pewter mount. H:7 in (18 cm). ② **8.** Steuben acid-cut ivory vase. H:10½ in (26.5 cm). ③

1 Carved glass vase

2 English vases

3 Auguste Jean vase

4 Footed vase

5 Harrach decanter and glasses

6 Metal-mounted vase

7 Austrian vase

8 Steuben vase

9. Wilhelm Kralik Sohn glass bowl with etched decoration. 1900. H:3¾ in (9.5 cm). ① **10.** Amédée de Caranza vase decorated with cherries and leaves on a mustard ground. H:6¼ in (16 cm). ③ **11.** Loetz vase of organic form, with trailed iridescent decoration. H:8 in (20.3 cm). ① **12.** Pallme-König glass vase. c.1905. H:8¼ in (21 cm). ① **13.** English glass light shade with short neck and rim and ruffled base. c.1900. H:7¼ in (18.5 cm). ③ **14.** Elisabeth Glass Factory vase of pinched form with threaded iridescent decoration. H:4½ in (11.5 cm). ① **15.** Josef Rindkopf's Söhne vase with a trefoil lip and lappet decoration on a red ground. H:6¾ in (17 cm). ③ **16.** Handel Teroma covered jar painted with birds flying in a bamboo thicket, in polychrome on dark green. H:7½ in (19 cm). ③ **17.** Cameo glass vase by De Vez, acid-etched with red poppies on a lemon-yellow ground. H:6¼ in (16 cm). ① **18.** Villeroy & Boch cameo glass vase by Edmund Rigot. c.1930. H:12¼ in (31 cm). ③

9 *Etched bowl*

10 *Caranza vase*

11 *Iridescent Loetz vase*

12 *Pallme-König vase*

13 *English light shade*

14 *Pinched-form vase*

15 *Trefoil-lip vase*

16 *Handel Teroma jar*

17 *De Vez cameo vase*

18 *Cameo vase*

LAMPS

DOMESTIC ELECTRICITY REVOLUTIONIZED LAMP DESIGN. IT WAS AMERICAN GLASSMAKERS WHO LED THE FIELD, EXPERIMENTING WITH FINISHES AND THE OPPORTUNITY TO COMBINE GLASS WITH METAL.

BEAUTY AND FUNCTIONALITY

While many creative disciplines of Art Nouveau followed the Aesthetic Movement's credo of "art for art's sake," electric lamps proved that it was possible to be useful as well as beautiful. Lamps could be a pleasure to look at and touch, as well as supremely useful items, providing light at the mere flick of a switch.

REVERSE-PAINTING

As electricity became more commonplace in homes throughout the United States, glass manufacturers came up with shades designed to enhance the beauty and effects of lamplight.

One of the most popular techniques used to decorate the shades was reverse-painting, in which artists painted the inside of the lamp,

where the design would be better protected and therefore less subject to wear and tear.

Transferring a design onto a lampshade was not as simple as transferring it onto a flat surface, and it involved several laborious stages. The starting point was a watercolor design with precise notes on what colors to use where. First the image was transferred to steel-engraving plates. A thin, transparent piece of paper was then put over the plates, and the image was traced by piercing holes with a fine metal point. The paper tracing was then fixed to the inside of the shade, where it was wiped over with a swab dipped in charcoal to reproduce the dotted lines of the original image. The decorator filled in the outline dot to dot and applied the color following the instructions given with the original master design.

The riser terminates in a cluster of three sockets

A lava glass ball supports the riser

LAVA GLASS TABLE LAMP The shade of this rare Handel lamp has an amber-colored textured background over which white and turquoise "lava" flows. The three-legged bronzed spelter base supports a matching lava glass ball. Signed "Handel Lamps." *H:25 in (63.5 cm).*

The lamp stands on a gray-white marble foot

Reverse-painting looks dramatic when the lamp is lit

HANDEL TABLE LAMP
The autumnal landscape on the lamp's hemispherical glass shade has been reverse-painted. The painted shade is marked as model number "Handel 7039," and the rim is stamped "Handel Lamps Patent." *H:23½ in (59.5 cm).*

The bronzed base is embossed with trees

A Japanese theme reflects the Asian influence on Art Nouveau

REVERSE-PAINTED LAMP
The design of this Handel lamp features a Japanese scene of pine trees, mountains, and a pagoda. The bronzed metal base stands on a molded foot. *H:23½ in (59.5 cm).*

The metal base is ribbed

HANDEL HYDRANGEA TABLE LAMP The shade of this lamp is painted with large pink and white clusters of flowering hydrangeas on a light green background. The lamp stands on a bronzed-metal, pear-shaped base in an unusual acid-finished patina. H:23¼ in (59 cm).

The shade has a frosted, chipped ice finish

The base has two flying scroll handles and a circular foot

HANDEL DESK LAMP The yellow-orange, reverse-painted shade of this desk lamp is held within a metal overlay frame. The curved, sinuous lamp stem rises from a deep, rounded foot.

Exquisite detail is shown in the metal overlay

The rich colors give the lamp an almost tropical feel

HANDEL LAMPS

One of the biggest makers of reverse-painted lamps was the Connecticut-based company Handel, which bought in ready-molded shades of various shapes—domed, hemispherical, or cylindrical, for example. These shades were then decorated with a vast range of subjects: floral patterns, colorful butterflies and birds like macaws and flamingos, and landscapes and seascapes, whether local or exotic, the latter often inspired by Asia. Sunset scenes looked particularly effective when the light was turned on. The curve of the shade also gave the opportunity to show depth and the effects of perspective, as objects grew paler, hazier, and smaller in the distance. In typical Art Nouveau fashion, the bases were designed to integrate perfectly with the shades, reflecting the theme of the lamp with unusual designs or figures.

TEXTURED FINISHES

As well as painting the lamps, manufacturers textured the outer surface of the shade to diffuse the light. Ribbing was one such common effect. The more unusual finish known as frosted glass was created by a technique called chipped ice, in which glue was applied to the surface and heated. When the glue dried, it flaked off, leaving a textured finish.

LEADED GLASS

Instead of painting or texturing a lampshade, some glassmakers preferred to use colored glass. Inspired by the richness of medieval stained glass, Tiffany and other American manufacturers created mosaics out of glass and metal that came to

life and changed color when the light was turned on. The subject matter, as with reverse-painted lamps, was taken from nature and included stylized flowers, insects, landscapes, and sunset scenes.

The success of the final product lay in the hands of the glassmaker, who graduated the color even within a single tessera of glass and textured it to suit its subject matter. Glass was fibrillated and striated for the sky, rippled for the sheen of an insect wing, and fractured for a sunset or a flower. The purpose was to recreate nature in its subtle infinity of color, light and shade, and texture.

Each piece of glass had to be cut with minute precision to slot into its allotted space in the metal framework. The base, as always, was crucial to the success of the lamp's aesthetics. The shape was naturally reminiscent of a tree trunk, and decoration on this theme was particularly apt when the lampshade was patterned with flowers or a woodland landscape.

PUFFY LAMPS AT PAIRPOINT

The Pairpoint Corporation in New Bedford, Massachusetts, had an interesting line in top-quality lampshades. Whereas most shades were cast in a mold, this company produced blown ones, called Puffy table lampshades. Some were decorated with high-relief flowers and foliage, with naturalistic details taken to such an extent that there might be bees and butterflies alighting on the blooms. Puffy lamps were painted in pastel tints of pink, yellow, blue, and green. Pairpoint also made bases in copper, bronze, brass, silver plate, and wood. The base was designed to go with the shade, although buyers could choose from other, interchangeable styles—plain, patterned, or "tree trunk"—if they wished.

The company used a full repertoire of other decorative techniques for their lampshades including reverse painting, acid-etching, ribbing, and frosting for texture, and scenic pictures, sometimes signed by the artist. Scenes included rural local landscapes, Roman temples, and follies in landscaped parkland, sometimes combined with Neoclassical shapes on the base, and seascapes. Like Handel, Pairpoint produced other items as well as lampshades, made with cut, etched, molded, and blown glass and quadruple-plated metal.

PUFFY BOUDOIR LAMP The design of this lamp is characteristic of the Pairpoint brand, with puffy roses in pink and yellow decorating the shade. The lamp has its original tree-trunk base in a silver finish. Signed "PAIRPOINT." H:10½ in (26.5 cm).

METALWARE

METALWORK PLAYED A KEY ROLE IN SPREADING ART NOUVEAU WORLDWIDE.

FRENCH DESIGNERS TARGETED THE ELITE, WHILE GERMANY, THE UNITED

STATES, AND BRITAIN MADE PIECES FOR MIDDLE-CLASS HOUSEHOLDS.

FRENCH LUXURY

Even more so than other craftsmen, silversmiths and metalworkers had spent the 19th century working in historical styles. Mass production gave little scope for individuality or change. Architect-designer Hector Guimard was an avid proponent of iron, and he created his own prefabricated range, writing: "Why condemn architects for using outmoded decorative devices, when component manufacturers can only supply Louis XVI models?" The same applied to domestic wares.

SILVER WATER JUG Simple in form and decoration, this rare piece by Maurice Dufrène has a leaf-shaped cover and a sinuous thumbpiece. The leaf motif is repeated in other places. Stamped "Leverrier." *H:7¾ in (20 cm).*

TECHNIQUES AND MATERIALS

Designers at the cutting edge despised factory methods such as die-stamping and pressing; instead, they aimed to raise standards by reviving traditional techniques and using them in the modern style. Planishing—smoothing out the surface with a hammer—left a surface that could be polished and made shiny. Decoration could be raised by embossing (called *repoussé* in French). For this effect, the piece would be hammered from the inside—or the back for something flat like a tray—to push out the decoration. Chasing sharpened up the design from the front, without removing any of the silver, unlike engraving, which cut into the surface.

Like many Parisian designers, Guimard and jeweler Lucien Gaillard worked in an organic Rococo manner that was tauter and less frilly than the original style. They simplified Rococo's organic naturalism, appealing to the wealthy with extravagant materials kept simple. Guimard also let the metal speak for itself in his sculptural bronze vases. He would have agreed with artist Paul Gauguin, who asked: "Why repaint iron so it looks like butter?" However, gilding still appealed to many designers and their buyers. Although metal acquires a natural patina over time, the process can be sped up with chemicals.

Many metalware designers crossed disciplines and mixed media with confidence. Materials combined

RARE BRONZE VASE The sides of this tapering vase by Hector Guimard are decorated with vertical sinuous bands that culminate in high-relief whiplash curves and leafy fronds around the shoulders and neck. *H:11 in (28 cm).*

TEA AND COFFEE SERVICE This Paul Follot silvered-metal service comprises a tray, coffee pot, teapot, sucrier, and cream jug. Each piece features arcing, fluted decoration. Signed "Follot." *c.1900. Coffee pot: H:7¾ in (20 cm).*

with gold and silver included ivory from the Belgian Congo colony, horn, and enamels. Lucien Gaillard made exquisite Art Nouveau horn combs. Paul Follot was also an interior designer; Maurice Dufrêne, later a key Art Deco figure, was chief designer for the German art critic and dealer Julius Meier-Graefe. Dufrêne's porcelain tableware, similar in style to his silverware, sold at La Maison Moderne, Meier-Graefe's gallery outlet in Paris.

DECORATIVE SOURCES

It was nature, the root of Art Nouveau, that inspired the shapes and decoration of silverware. With spare restraint, Dufrêne could link the handle of a jug to its body with a leaf, and more foliage would decorate the cover. Other motifs might include shells, their linear emphasis matched by whiplash curves, leafy fronds, and vertical sinewy bands. By contrast, other makers were producing works with a veritable forest of foliage, poppy flowers, and plant tendrils.

Gaillard also drew inspiration from ancient Egypt, with a scarab beetle, the symbol of sun, life, and regeneration. Taken up in the 19th century, the scarab was a good-luck charm on necklaces, bracelets, and belts. René Lalique (see pp.286–87) had a similar penchant for beetles. He created hybrid creatures with the coloring of European beetles and the distinctive shape of a North Indian species. Their distinctive, life-size appearance raised questions as to whether he cast them from nature, like the French 16th-century ceramicist Bernard Palissy. Some of his hybrids were more obvious fantasy figures, such as his iconic dragonfly-woman brooch.

Gaillard had a passion for all things Japanese, even bringing craftsmen from Japan to teach him their techniques, such as painting metal. Many of the Art Nouveau motifs filtered through to the West from Japan after the country reopened for trade in the 1880s. Insects, birds, flowers (including cherry blossoms and chrysanthemums), bamboo, and fans all found their way on to silver- and metalware. The asymmetry of Japanese designs fused with that of Rococo to inspire Art Nouveau designers.

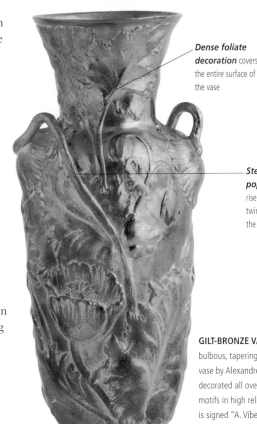

Dense foliate decoration covers the entire surface of the vase

Stems of poppy flowers rise up to form twin handles at the shoulders

GILT-BRONZE VASE The bulbous, tapering body of this vase by Alexandre Vibert is decorated all over with poppy motifs in high relief. The piece is signed "A. Vibert." H:9½ in (24 cm).

Each handle is created from a scarab proboscis

SCARABÉES VASE

This striking vase designed and signed by Lucien Gaillard has a thin, tapering neck above a shaped, bulbous body. The base is cast with four applied scarab beetles, each with an exaggerated proboscis that extends to form a loop handle. H:9½ in (24 cm).

The scarab beetles are life-size and highly detailed

CAST-BRONZE VASES Made by François-Raoul Larche, each of these exceptional vases is finely cast with four allegorical female figures standing among relief-molded lilies. The vases are inscribed with Larche's signature and the foundry mark "Siot Fondeur Paris." H:16 in (41 cm).

PLIQUE-À-JOUR ENAMEL

Some of the best luxury pieces of French metalware were small items and jewelry using enamel. Technically challenging, enameling involves fusing vitreous paste to metal at extremely high temperatures, uniting materials that expand and contract differently. The most skilled practitioners revived the ancient technique of plique-à-jour—enclosing translucent enamel within a fragile unbacked metal frame so that the light can shine through. It was just right for the representation of dragonflies, peacock feathers, and other such colorful but delicate motifs. Eugène Feuillâtre was chief enameler in Lalique's studio until 1897. His work proved hugely popular when he exhibited enameled objects in his own name in 1898, as did the stunning Norwegian plique-à-jour enamelwork shown at the 1900 Paris Exposition Universelle.

EUGÈNE FEUILLÂTRE VASE This exquisite, silver-and-enamel twin-handled small vase, or coupe, takes the form of an artichoke. It has a green petal pattern around the ribbed base and plique-à-jour foliage handles. W:3 in (7.5 cm).

NORTHERN EUROPE

Handmade silver- and metalware at the top end of the market was extremely expensive. Most silversmiths continued making pieces in the traditional styles on which their reputations had been based throughout the 19th century. Other manufacturers, however, saw an opening for mass-produced ranges, using less precious metals such as pewter and electroplated brass, and working with a new look. WMF (*Württembergische Metallwaren-Fabrik*) in Germany was at the forefront of this less luxurious but still quintessentially Art Nouveau style of metalware.

AFFORDABLE QUALITY

The designers at WMF might have been working with less precious metals, but they still adopted the florid, luxuriant forms typical of the Art Nouveau style. Some of the items they created became true icons of the French decorative style. Metal (usually pewter) vases might be decorated in relief with long-haired maidens wearing flowing robes or intricate floral and foliate patterns. The decoration was not limited to the body of the vessel but extended to the handle. Some examples have handles that mirrored the whiplash motif, while others represented female figures, such as mermaids or *femmes-fleur*.

The sinuous French and Belgian idiom was not to everyone's taste. Germany, Austria, and Britain preferred a more restrained and geometric style

(*see* The Birth of Modernism, *pp.236–63*). WMF also made wares to suit this taste. The German firm created every type of household object, from toast racks to candlesticks, mirrors to trays, and cigar boxes to fruit stands. Small wonder that its workforce escalated from 16 workers in 1853, when it first opened, to 6,000 by 1914, with factories in Germany, Poland, Austria, and outlets in London, Paris, Hamburg, and Berlin. Other manufacturers of boxes and biscuit tins distributed the style to an even wider public, making metalware second only to posters in terms of disseminating Art Nouveau.

SILVER-PLATED WMF VASE Made from Britannia pewter alloy and green glass, this baluster-form vase has high relief decoration of a boy emerging from flowers and holding a rose out to a draped nude. The base has stamped marks. H:20½ in (51 cm).

Naked boy emerging from iris flowers

WMF PEWTER CENTERPIECE VASE The elongated baluster-shaped body of this vase with glass liner is decorated with a pair of *femmes-fleur*, their flowing robes forming the splayed foot of the vase. A floral pattern adorns the neck of the item, which is flanked by two whiplash handles. c.1900. H:13¾ in (35 cm).

Togalike robes flow to the base of the vase, creating a splayed foot

JEWELRY

René Lalique (*see pp.286–87*) set a lasting trend for making the craftsmanship of jewelry more important than the value of the gold and precious gems used. Firms such as Unger Brothers in the United States specialized in mass-producing small items and affordable jewelry. They used sterling silver a lot, sometimes finished with matte gold plating. Much of their jewelry depicted the ubiquitous beautiful, languid maiden with whiplash hair. Their Floradora and Gibson Girl lines were made into brooches, bracelets, necklaces, pendants, and even earrings.

BELT PIN This Unger Brothers belt pin features a classic Art Nouveau motif of a girl with billowing hair. The brooch is sterling silver with selected matte ("French") finish gold plating. 1904–05. W:1¾ in (4.5 cm).

BRITISH OUTPUT

A handful of British designers made metalware in the Art Nouveau style, but their treatment of form and motif differed from the lavish continental look. Avant-garde silver designers such as C. R. Ashbee and Archibald Knox had an allegiance to the Arts and Crafts movement and found inspiration in the Middle Ages rather than in whiplashes and dreamy maidens. However, Ashbee's Guild of Handicraft became more flamboyant in its output around 1900, with exaggerated loop handles and swooping lines.

Each country was influenced by its own past, and Celtic devices—which Owen Jones described in his book *The Grammar of Ornament* as "strange, monstrous animals and birds with long top-knots, tongues, and tails, intertwining in almost endless knots"—were the dominant inspiration in Britain and Ireland. This knotty work, also known as entrelac (interlaced), was used in metalwork with great technical skill. The whole surface was often covered with curvilinear designs, achieved by applying spirals of gold wire. The Celtic wheel cross, the Christian cross on a circle, was another frequent motif.

INDIVIDUALS AND ORGANIZATIONS

Architect W. A. S. Benson was the leading metalworker of the Arts and Crafts movement, excelling in brass and copper. He designed in the Art Nouveau idiom, making great use of asymmetry and motifs from nature. His domestic wares were on sale in London and in Siegfried Bing's shop in Paris.

Alexander Fisher was a sculptor turned enamelist who trained in France. His silver and enamel plaques with Celtic decoration made his name and influenced the next generation of silversmiths, such as Nelson and Edith Dawson, who set up the Artificers' Guild in 1901.

Companies such as William Hutton & Sons and Hukin & Heath were the exceptions to the Arts and Crafts dominance. They created Art Nouveau silverware with sweeping lines and entwined tendrils, mixing them with the peacock feathers beloved of the Aesthetic Movement and other Japanese-inspired decoration. Christopher Dresser (*see pp.242–43*) designed restrained silverware for Hukin & Heath that reflected the influence of Japan, while Omar Ramsden, in partnership with Alwyn C. E. Carr, blended Art Nouveau with medieval ornament and forms.

AMERICAN SILVERWARE

The Gorham Silver Company in Providence, Rhode Island, was the largest American silver factory and one of the first to use machinery. It adopted Japanese motifs such as dragons, butterflies, bamboo, fans, fish, and Asian bird for wares in silver and copper in the 1870s and 1880s. In the 1890s, British director William Colman allocated a workshop to make Art Nouveau silver by hand. In fact, its output was only a hair's breadth away from the mainstream Rococo revival style that most American manufacturers continued to produce.

Gorham used the trade name of Martelé for its new range, meaning hand-hammered, influenced by the attention to craftsmanship of the Arts and Crafts movement as much as by Art Nouveau. The Martelé range was made to the Britannia standard, containing more silver than sterling. Launched at the 1900 Paris *Exposition Universelle*, it was phased out after 1910 as sales dropped.

Another American company, Roycroft, based in East Aurora, New York, also deliberately kept the hammer marks naturally left by planishing—hand-raising a piece from a flat sheet. In a twist of irony, the company even enhanced the marks of the hammer mechanically—using a machine to make their wares look more handmade. Unger Brothers and William B. Kerr in New Jersey both worked in the French Art Nouveau style, incorporating *femmes-fleur* and leaf patterns into their silver.

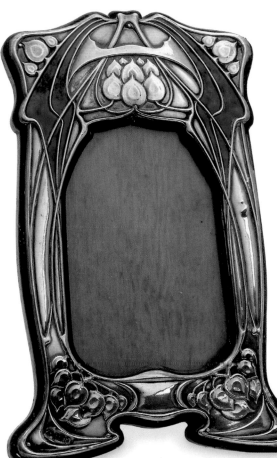

PHOTOGRAPH FRAME Produced by William Hutton & Sons Ltd., this silver easel-back frame is embossed with stylized peacock feathers and trailing tendrils. There is some blue and green enameling to the arched cresting of the piece. *1904. H:8¾ in (22.5 cm).*

W. A. S. BENSON CANDLESTICKS In these English counterweighted candlesticks, the candle holder sits on a copper, leaf-shaped base, which is joined by a curved stem to a copper leaf and brass fruit-shaped weight. *c.1890–1900. L:11¾ in (30 cm).*

Leaves were a common Art Nouveau theme. Benson also used them to refract the light

The addition of weighted fruit was novel and practical

GORHAM VASE The spiraling sides of this vase of slender baluster form are embossed with a lily-of-the-valley decoration. The everted rim of the vase and its lobed base are composed of overlapping leaf petals. Monogrammed beneath the base. *1902. H:14½ in (39 cm).*

The lily-of-the-valley gives an Art Nouveau slant to Gorham's standard design

Overlapping leaves on the base and rim were central to the range

GEORG JENSEN

Self-styled as an *orfèvre sculpteur* (goldsmith-sculptor), Danish designer Georg Jensen (1866–1935) worked briefly but brilliantly in a unique Art Nouveau style. He intended to pursue a career as a sculptor but was apprenticed at the age of 14 to a goldsmith. While an apprentice, he went to art classes, and once qualified, he studied sculpture at the Royal Danish Academy of Fine Arts. In 1897 Jensen's wife died, leaving him with two small children (his son, Soren Georg Jensen, eventually became chief designer for the firm from 1962 to 1974). After working briefly as a modeler for Bing & Grondahl, Jensen set up a porcelain firm, which went bankrupt. His checkered career as a porcelain-maker was mitigated by two years traveling around Europe on a grant from the Danish Academy, during which Jensen witnessed the growth of Art Nouveau.

STYLE DEVELOPMENT

Jensen also worked with Mogens Ballin, a Danish painter and silversmith who made jewelry with simple curved shapes and abstract patterns. Jensen was 37 by the time he started his own silver firm in Copenhagen. He began by making jewelry rather than silver because the materials were cheaper. By 1906 he embarked on designs for coffee and tea services, bowls, tureens, candlesticks, and flatware. In the early stages of his career Jensen kept his majestic rounded shapes free of any distracting ornament. He gradually introduced bunches of fruit and bouquets of flowers to finials, stems, and bases, tendril-shaped handles, and paw feet. The ornament, however, never distracted from the cleanness of the shape but contributed to its elegant formality.

A TYPICALLY DANISH LOOK

Jensen was quoted as saying: "Do not follow fashion, but be guided by the present if you want to stay young in the struggle." Following his own

GEORG JENSEN FLATWARE Jensen's decoration was often inspired by nature, as in these servers (*right*) and fish knife and fork (*near left and far left*). Note the shell and fish motifs on the knife and fork—a play on the function of the flatware. *c.1920. Servers: L:7¾ in (20 cm); Fish knife: L:8¾ in (22 cm).*

Spiraling stems and grapes decorate the tall pedestal

TRAINING AND SUPPORT This picture, taken in Georg Jensen's silversmithy in 1908, shows Jensen next to his female trainee Alba Lykke Andersen. Kay Bojesen, who was also a trainee, is shown on the left.

SILVER TAZZA The shallow, flared bowl of this elegant tazza is raised on a slender twisted stem that terminates in a spreading circular foot. Design No. 263. *c.1920. H:7½ in (19 cm).*

advice, he created designs that looked contemporary but were distinctive, original, and Danish. Their simple lines drew on both recent Danish trends and the 18th-century French traditions. The naturalistic motifs that characterized Art Nouveau and Arts and Crafts (called *skonvirke*, meaning "aesthetic work" in Danish) inspired the decoration. Jensen's statuesque shapes came from his training as a sculptor, combined with his instinctive feel for the malleable medium of silver.

As well as for the uncluttered look and pleasing proportions of his pieces, Jensen became renowned for his satin finish. He created the shiny look by annealing the piece (heating it to remove stresses and make it workable), submerging it in sulfuric acid, and then buffing it, leaving slight oxidization on the surface.

When it came to designing flatware, Jensen produced forks with more widely spaced prongs and knives with shorter blades than usual. As in his hollow ware, the functional areas are plain and the handles decorated with motifs such as grapes, spiraling stems and tendrils, berries, and blossoms. The handles of tea and coffee services were often in ivory, contrasting with the satin surface of the silver. Occasionally he incorporated semiprecious stones such as amber.

GROWING SUCCESS

The popularity of Jensen's wares spread to the rest of Scandinavia and Europe. His work was also successful in the United States, where the publishing billionaire William Randolph Hearst bought a whole exhibition of Jensen silver. Still in operation today, Jensen's empire now has 85 outlets worldwide. His studio is still famed for its dedication to traditional techniques, with handmade pieces. After his death in 1935, the *New York Herald* described Jensen as "the greatest silversmith of the last 300 years."

JEWELRY DESIGNS

Jensen's first jewelry range under his own name was created in the Danish Arts and Crafts style and exhibited in the Danish Museum of Decorative Art. It won him international recognition and gave him the freedom to expand his output.

Like other Danish jewelers of the time, Jensen worked mainly in silver. He usually left the surface unplanished, with a visible patterning of hammer marks. Sculptural like his tableware, his jewelry pieces had high-relief decoration on themes taken from nature, such as plump birds and stylized soft, round berries, foliage, flowers, and fruit. For color, he embellished his jewelry with cabochons of semiprecious stones such as amber, amethyst, agate, and lapis lazuli, rather than the enamelwork so exquisitely executed by his fellow Scandinavians in Norway. All Jensen's work has an exceptionally high standard of craftsmanship.

SILVER BROOCH Acorns were a popular motif for Jensen. Here an amber acorn is central to the design of this drop-pendant brooch. *c.1905. L:4½ in (11.5 cm).*

JENSEN AND HIS COLLEAGUES

Georg Jensen designed many pieces himself, but as his reputation and business grew, he also employed other designers. Mindful of his own humble beginnings and difficult youthful career, and with a sociable, generous nature, he encouraged creativity in his employees and allowed them artistic freedom. Jensen also acknowledged the individual contributions of his

FIVE-LIGHT CANDELABRUM Designed by Johan Rohde, one of several designers working for Jensen, this candelabrum is raised on a baluster-form stem and faceted foot. Design No. 472. *c.1925. H:17 in (43 cm).*

BALL BONBONNIÈRE Designed by Johan Rohde, this bonbonnière has a bowl and lid with the unornamented, satinlike patina of many of Jensen's designs. Design No. 43. *1920s. H:6 in (15.5 cm).*

designers, so it is usually possible to tell the exact provenance of a piece. Most pieces are marked with a design number or the initials of the designer.

Painter Johan Rohde was a key member of the silverware team. Far ahead of their time, Rohde's designs typically had streamlined shapes even simpler than Jensen's, with the emphasis on form rather than decoration. In 1906 Rohde asked Jensen for help putting his designs into practice and in 1913 agreed to an exclusive design contract with the company. So began a creative collaboration that lasted until their deaths, in the same year. Both Jensen and Rohde went on to become leading Art Deco figures.

Other prominent designers who helped ensure the longevity of the Jensen studio were Harald Nielsen, a pioneer of Art Deco and, later on, Henning Koppel and Vivianna Torun Bulow-Hube.

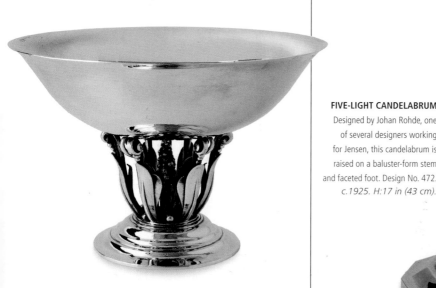

GRAPE GOBLET The stem of this simple drinking goblet of clean, rounded form is ornamented with grapes and vines—recurring motifs in Jensen's work. Design No. 296. *c.1920. H:3¾ in (9.5 cm).*

METALWARE GALLERY

ART NOUVEAU DESIGNERS favored curves, with an emphasis on sensual vitality and fertility. The whiplash curve, suggestive of plant tendrils, is often seen on metalware of the period. The same curve is generally used to depict the flowing hair of maidens in the bloom of youth. Pierced decoration is another common design feature, giving metalware an intricate complexity that again represents a stylized vision of nature.

KEY

1. WMF champagne bucket designed by Albert Mayer. c.1900. H:13 in (33 cm). ④ **2.** Elkington & Co. set of four silver candlesticks. 1906. H:12½ in (32 cm). ⑦ **3.** Kayserzinn pewter candelabrum designed by Hugo Leven. c.1900. H:19½ in (49.5 cm). ⑤ **4.** WMF visiting card tray. c.1900. W:7½ in (19 cm). ② **5.** Kayserzinn bonbonnière, with a bud finial. H:4¼ in (11 cm). ② **6.** French silver-plated mermaid dish. c.1900. L:7¾ in (19.5 cm). ① **7.** Weighted silver vase of organic design with tendrils. 1906. H:9 in (23 cm). ① **8.** WMF electroplate photograph frame. H:10 in (25.5 cm). ②

2 Silver candlesticks

3 Pewter candelabrum

1 WMF champagne bucket

4 WMF visiting card tray

8 WMF photograph frame

5 Kayserzinn bonbonnière

6 Silver-plated mermaid dish

7 Silver vase

9 Gilded centerpiece

10 Silver-plated picture frame

9. Orivit centerpiece, with original gilding and liner. c.1900. L:10¾ in (27.5 cm). ② **10.** WMF silver-plated picture frame. c.1905. H:7¾ in (19.5 cm). ② **11.** G.A. Scheid silver cigarette case, the enameled lid with a picture of a young woman. 1901. H:3¼ in (8 cm). ② **12.** WMF double-handled silver-plated tazza. W:9½ in (24 cm). ① **13.** WMF silver-plated claret jug. c.1900. H:16 in (41 cm). ② **14.** Albert Edward Jones two-handled silver comport. 1910. L:12½ in (32 cm). ④ **15.** Albert Edward Jones silver tea and coffee service. 1928–30. Coffee pot: H:7½ in (19 cm). ⑤ **16.** Kayserzinn pewter liquor set designed by Hugo Leven. c.1905. H:8½ in (21.5 cm). ① **17.** WMF silver-plated and glass claret jug. c.1905. H:17 in (43 cm). ③ **18.** *Repoussé* vase with foliate decoration. ①

| 13 | *WMF claret jug* |

| 11 | *Cigarette case* |

| 12 | *Silver-plated tazza* |

| 14 | *Silver comport* |

| 15 | *Silver tea and coffee service* |

| 17 | *WMF claret jug* |

| 16 | *Pewter liquor set* |

| 18 | *Repoussé vase* |

CLOCKS

IN THE ART NOUVEAU ERA, EVERY FUNCTIONAL OBJECT WAS RESTYLED.
THE HUMBLE CLOCK WAS TREATED LIKE A SCULPTURE: STRAIGHT LINES
AND GEOMETRIC SHAPES WERE REPLACED BY CURVES AND ASYMMETRY.

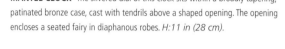

THE NEW METAL

The response to public demand for cheaper metalware led to the revival of pewter, an alloy of tin and lead, putting well-designed household objects within the reach of the many. Pewter had a slight softness that made it suitable for decoration. Firms such as WMF in Germany produced machine-made clocks in silver-plate of a high quality. Instead of angular contours, the sides of the clock were often gently curved, reflected in the decoration, and a female bust might grace the top. In some extreme examples, the form and decoration were wildly asymmetrical. London's Liberty & Co. also sold pewter clocks in its Tudric range designed by Archibald Knox, often with an enameled dial in contrasting bright colors.

The tall proportions of a longcase clock lingered on even in a small mantel clock. But instead of a slender rectangle, the framework softened to curves, without a single straight line. Silverwork was often embossed with Art Nouveau organic decoration such as interlaced tendrils and flowers.

SHAPES AND FINISH

Designers created ingenious shapes such as oval hollows that made use of negative space as well as positive form. Often the purpose was to introduce a female figure, whether a nymph or fairy, either semi-clad or with artfully arranged diaphanous robes. Sometimes the figurative element extended to a couple. Mottoes on the theme of time often featured somewhere on the clock and were usually relevant to the decoration. French sculptors draped beautiful maidens over clocks in which both the shape and decoration used the organic motifs of nature.

Metal could be patinated to give it an attractive surface sheen and the appearance of age. The large ceramics firm of Goldscheider in Vienna specialized in making earthenware look like

MANTEL CLOCK The silvered dial of this clock sits within a broadly tapering, patinated bronze case, cast with tendrils above a shaped opening. The opening encloses a seated fairy in diaphanous robes. *H:11 in (28 cm).*

metal by enameling it with a bronze patination. The voluminous robes of their terracotta women were used to conceal wiring and bulbs in lamps as well as to adorn clocks.

Ceramics could mimic other materials, too (*see Foley Intarsio ware box, opposite*). But one designer who had no wish to disguise the material he was using—nor, indeed, to opt for figural representation—was the Belgian Victor Horta.

METAL TOUR DE FORCE

Horta gloried in metal. In his architecture as well as in his interiors, he exploited both the structural and ornamental potential of iron in particular. Even in delicate forms, metal could imply its strength and power. The asymmetrical whiplash that supports and decorates Horta's bronze clocks has the same verve that he brought to his ironwork banisters and balustrades.

SILVER-PLATED CLOCK This WMF-style clock combines the rectilinear lines associated with the Jugendstil movement with the Art Nouveau motifs of the female figure and flowing drapery, here rendered with more restraint. *c.1900. H:13 in (33 cm).*

SILVER-FACED CLOCK The wooden frame of this clock has a sinuous outline and a silver panel to the front. In keeping with the shape of the piece, the silver is embossed with interwoven tendrils and florets. The clock has Birmingham date marks. *1910. H:14 in (36 cm).*

The enamel dial is painted with flowers

MANTEL CLOCK This patinated mantel clock has a circular enamel dial painted with flowers. The case, of flowering organic form, is molded with leaves and dragonflies and surmounted by the figure of a young girl in diaphanous robes. The base is signed by Aristide de Ranieri. *H:22¾ in (58 cm).*

While fellow Belgian Henry van de Velde leaned toward the abstract, nature's life force is always visible in Horta's designs. His clocks look as though they have legs and feet, which give them a firm foundation, but seem as though they want to spring into action like a caged animal—quivering yet controlled energy. The whiplash motif was plant rather than animal in origin, inspired by roots, leaves, and shoots, and Horta's clocks seem to grow up toward the sun, with tendrils of bronze escaping from the framework. Horta uses the clock form to translate the whiplash into three dimensions, and his treatment of metal differs from Italian sculptor Aristide de Ranieri's use of curve.

THE LINEAR LOOK

Critical opinion at the time, even within Belgium and France, was divided as to whether the whiplash was a mishmash of free-form curves or an artistic expression of nature's beauty. Whichever, the whiplash was typical of early Art Nouveau before about 1900 and pervaded all possible decorative art forms. Like its fellow ornament of the time, the arabesque, the success of the whiplash relied on the designer's sensitivity of line. The English designer Walter Crane, while disparaging of Art Nouveau's excesses, understood the importance of line. He wrote: "Line is

FRIENDSHIP CONQUERS TIME In this brown-colored stoneware clock by Friedrich Goldscheider of Vienna, two young lovers stand on either side of the curved, outswept case. Below the dial is the Latin inscription: *Amicitia vincit horas* (Friendship Conquers Time). *1900–02. H:15¾ in (40 cm).*

all important. Let the designer, therefore, in the adaptation of this art, lean upon the staff of line—line determinative, line emphatic, line delicate, line expressive, line controlling and uniting." Belgian Art Nouveau designers followed this creed, although Horta's frenzy of line might not be quite what Crane had in mind. Van de Velde summed up the key to design strength, saying: "Line is a force."

FOLEY INTARSIO WARE

The British ceramics manufacturer Foley made a range of Intarsio wares, with areas of flat color that looked like marquetry in wood. The clock below may have been wittily designed to look like a house, complete with pitched roofs and canted sides. Foley also used pretty girls for decoration, often with stylized patterns of flowers and countryside scenes. As well as clocks, Foley made vases and table services in Intarsio, and the range was featured in Liberty & Co.'s catalogs. Trading as Shelley from 1925, the company had even greater success with Art Deco tableware.

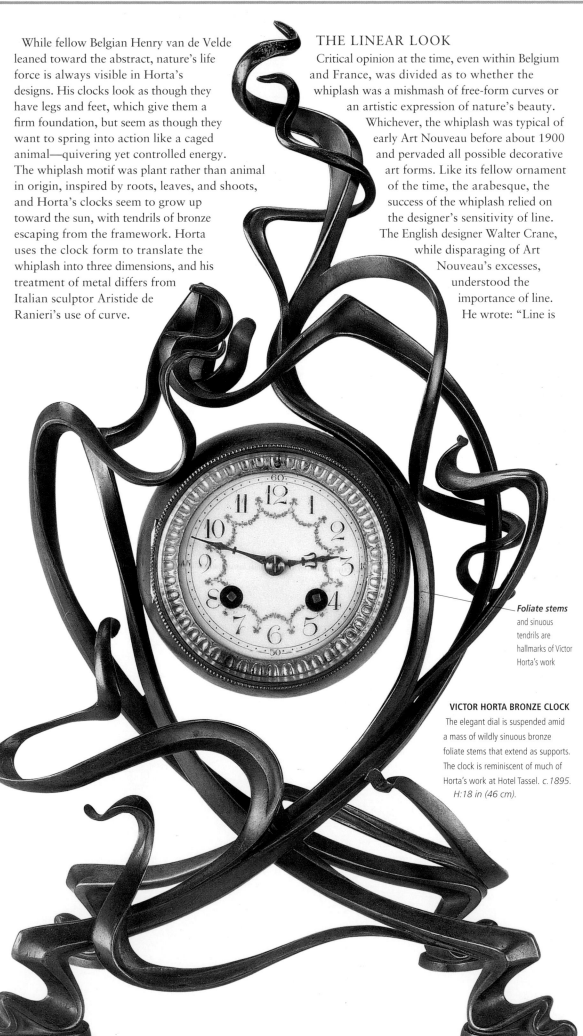

Foliate stems and sinuous tendrils are hallmarks of Victor Horta's work

VICTOR HORTA BRONZE CLOCK
The elegant dial is suspended amid a mass of wildly sinuous bronze foliate stems that extend as supports. The clock is reminiscent of much of Horta's work at Hotel Tassel. *c.1895. H:18 in (46 cm).*

INTARSIO MANTEL CLOCK The circular, enamel dial of this Foley clock has Arabic chapters and sits within a rectangular case with a pitched roof and canted sides. The case is printed and painted in bright colors, features Art Nouveau maidens, lilies, and boats sailing on a river, and bears the inscriptions *Carpe Diem* (Seize the Day), *Dies* (Day), and *Nox* (Night). *H:11½ in (29.5 cm).*

TEXTILES

THE SOFT FURNISHINGS, CURTAINS, AND RUGS PRODUCED IN THE

LATE 19TH CENTURY WERE DECORATED WITH THE STYLIZED FLOWERS,

FOLIAGE, ANIMALS, AND BIRDS TYPICAL OF THE ART NOUVEAU STYLE.

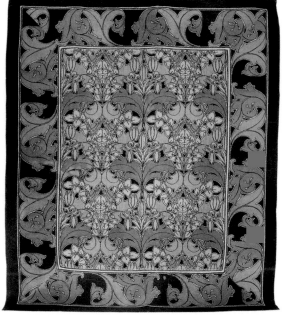

WILTON RUG This large rug, with a luxuriant, all-over flowering design within a deep scrolling foliate border, was designed by C. F. A. Voysey and woven by Tomkinson and Adam for Liberty & Co. *L:106½ in (271 cm).*

THE TEXTILE REVOLUTION

In the last decade of the 19th century, the eclectic mass of unrelated knickknacks that cluttered the typical Victorian room gave way to a lighter, more streamlined interior where each element worked in conjunction with the next to create an overall harmonious effect. Textile furnishings played a fundamental role in these interiors. As in other Art Nouveau disciplines, France and Belgium soon took a place at the forefront of textile design, but in each country, traditional textile crafts were reinterpreted and brought up to date.

ARTS AND CRAFTS INFLUENCE

The British Arts and Crafts movement, active at the same time as continental Art Nouveau, was heavily influential. An 1896 Arts and Crafts exhibition in London was a showcase for the latest developments in textiles. By this time William Morris had stopped designing textiles, but his influence remained strong. He had shown Britain, Europe, and the United States how textiles brought color and texture into the interior, and raised the profile of tapestry, embroidery, carpets, and printed material.

C. F. A. Voysey, one of the leading lights of the band of Arts and Crafts designers a generation younger than Morris, is credited with the first repeating pattern. Some of his nature-inspired patterns were humorous, such as the punningly titled *Let Us Prey*, showing the food chain as rows of cats looking up at birds looking up at tulip flowers.

"CONTINENTAL EXCESS"

The Belgian artist Henry van de Velde said of Voysey's fabrics: "It was as if spring had come all of a sudden." The compliment was not returned, however. Voysey disapproved of the florid Art Nouveau style and was quoted in *The Studio* magazine as saying: "It is not necessary for artists to...be crammed to overflowing with the knowledge of the products of foreign nations," and, later, that the Continental trends had "brought into our midst foreign styles of decoration totally out of harmony with our national character and climate." Such xenophobia was typical of many Arts and

PEACOCK PRINT Typical of so many Art Nouveau textiles, this cotton print bears a formalized repeat pattern of natural forms: a peacock sitting among a field of sunflowers. *1890–1900. L:34 in (86.5 cm).*

Crafts designers, for Art Nouveau had neither their socialist ideals nor any trace of British understatement, even though it shared the same concept of the integrated room. However, many designers in France, such as Georges de Feure and Edward Colonna, used British textiles in rooms created for Siegfried Bing, as did Victor Horta and van de Velde himself.

INFLUENCED BY PAINTING

Textiles had the same two-dimensional quality as a picture, so it was a logical conclusion that textile designers would follow current trends in painting. One of van de Velde's celebrated wall panels, *La Veillée des Anges*, displays complete confidence with embroidery skills and a painter's eye for composition and color. It shows the influence of Gauguin in its flat areas of color, which are used expressively rather than realistically. The patches of color are darkly

outlined in the cloisonné enameling technique that Gauguin himself had translated into paint. The Nabis ("prophets" in Hebrew) group of artists who worshiped Gauguin used color for its own sake and for symbolic purposes, emphasizing rather than disguising the flatness of the painting surface.

REPEATING PATTERNS

Flat, repeated patterns were the order of the day. Foliage and flowers became so stylized in the flattening process as to be unrecognizable, abstract, and increasingly geometric. So textiles, of all the decorative arts, paved the way for the emergence of Art Deco and Modernism.

PRINTED COTTON The poppy-flower pattern of this printed cotton was available as both upholstery and curtain fabric, in keeping with the prevailing desire for integrated design. It was also printed on either a red or pink ground. *L:65½ in (166.5 cm).*

THE SILVER STUDIO

Not all British designers were as insular as Voysey in their outlook. The Silver Studio, run from 1880 until 1963, commissioned designers to come up with patterns for textiles and wallpapers in Art Nouveau and Arts and Crafts styles, which it supplied to shops such as Liberty & Co. In total, including designs for other decorative arts, the company produced some 30,000 designs. Open to the commercial opportunities of continental art, the Silver Studio created designs that featured seed pods, thistles and teasels, bindweed, and hemlock. This acknowledgment of French floral motifs was acceptable to the cautious British taste and also sold well abroad. By 1906, 40 percent of the Silver Studio's designs were sold on the Continent, mostly to weaving firms in the French town of Lille. The company had excellent artists on its books, such as Celtic-inspired Archibald Knox and Harry Napper. Napper was comfortable with the exuberance of French and Belgian textiles and designed in a distinctly continental style himself.

POPPY PRINT This Silver Studio printed cotton bears a repeat flower-and-scrolling-leaf pattern in red and pink on a black ground. *L:90 in (228.5 cm).*

THE WHIPLASH MOTIF

After it was exhibited at the 1896 Arts and Crafts exhibition, Swiss-born Hermann Obrist's (1862–1927) whiplash embroidery was described by *The Studio* magazine as "the lightning-like flick of a whip...the endless continuity of line and spring of curve of some fascinating monster orchid." Its stylized stems, lashing back and forth on themselves, and flowerheads ending in a tangle of roots broke all the rules of artistic depiction of nature.

Obrist's embroidery was the blueprint for a mass of textile patterns. In all, he exhibited six embroideries and one hearth rug, part of a much larger collection of his work that toured Munich, Berlin, and London. Each of the panels was embroidered by Berthe Ruchet, who managed Obrist's workshop. She serrated the stems and shaded them with the utmost delicacy. Her use of gold and brightly colored thread on dark lustered backgrounds made the patterns of the embroideries stand out all the more richly.

In Germany, Obrist's work was hailed as "the birth of a new applied art." A multidisciplinary man of the age, he designed furniture and ceramics as well as textiles and won gold medals at the 1889 Paris *Exposition Universelle*.

Other important textile designers of the era included the Czech Alphonse Mucha, better known for his posters, and Gerhard Munthe of Norway. Like van de Velde, Munthe was influenced by the Nabis and his group of artists; his compositions illustrate the folklore of his native country. The judging panel at the 1900 Paris *Exposition Universelle*

OBRIST'S DESIGNS This exquisite and iconic silk on wool *Peitchenhieb* (whiplash) embroidery is based on organic plant forms and depicts flowers, stalks, and roots in a fluid, swirling pattern. It was created by Berthe Ruchet, the manageress of Hermann Obrist's workshop. *c.1895.*

credited him with triggering "a truly national style in the modern art of Norway."

Other countries took textile art in their own national directions: the Netherlands learned the batik technique used in the Dutch East Indies colonies (now Indonesia), while Hungary used its traditional lace-making industry to make startlingly modern patterns.

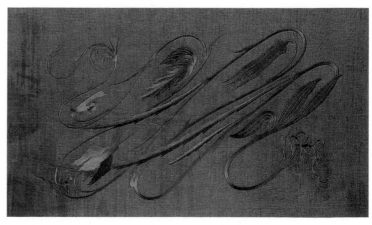

SCULPTURE

FOR A VISUAL DEFINITION OF ART NOUVEAU, ONE NEED

LOOK NO FURTHER THAN THE SMALL SCULPTURES

MADE IN PARIS BETWEEN ABOUT 1890 AND 1910.

A NEW MARKET

In mid-19th-century France, sculpture was very much run by the state, which commissioned clichéd, Classical-style works that were considered the acceptable model. Auguste Rodin, however, revived the moribund Salon, opening the door for other avant-garde sculptors. The invention of the pantograph in 1838 had made it possible to scale sculpture down to a domestic size and reproduce it in series. Now an artistically aware public was eager to buy sculpture in the form of statuettes. Foundries capitalized on the new market and commissioned sculptors to work in the Art Nouveau style. France, especially Paris, was the acknowledged center of sculpture, and Siegfried Bing put together an international array of sculptures in the modern style in 1895.

FEMALE SENSUALITY

Nature, symbolism, and, above all, erotic women were uppermost in the fin-de-siècle French mind. For sculpture, figures and female curves gave the perfect opportunity for myriad poses—from a straightforward bust, to a dancing

woman, or a more pensive mood. Women were depicted nude or with clinging drapery, often metamorphosing into plants as the Art Nouveau *femme-fleur*, who draws strength from nature. The dancer Loïe Fuller was an inspiration (*see box, opposite*), ingeniously depicted by Raoul Larche in the form of a lamp. Her diaphanous dress swirled into the lampshade above her head, and rippled around her body to hide all the wiring and the bulb. Her hair, typically of Art Nouveau women, trailed into plantlike forms.

EXOTIC MATERIALS

Ivory was often combined with the more traditionally used metals for dramatic contrast, and Belgian designers in particular incorporated ivory because their king promoted trade in the material with its African colony, the Congo. Both exotic and ancient, ivory paid homage to the traditional craft process and advertised the wealth of

DANCER With her dress caught by her movement, this cast-bronze dancer in the style of Loïe Fuller is a perfect snapshot. Made by Rudolf Küchler, it has both light and dark patination and stands on an oval base. *c.1900.* *H:23 in (58.5 cm).*

REVERIE BY PODANY Dreamy, pensive maidens were a popular motif for Art Nouveau designers. Here the bronze figure is seated on a rocky outcrop with legs pulled up and looking down to see her reflection. The piece is signed and marked "1869." *H:23½ in (60 cm).*

LOÏE FULLER Designer Raoul Larche was particularly well known for his sculptures of contemporary dancer Loïe Fuller. As here, the gilt-bronze forms often doubled as lamps and light fixtures. The piece bears the mark "Siot, Paris." *H:12½ in (32 cm).*

GILT-BRONZE FEMALE BUST The smiling face of this maiden, turned slightly to the right, is surrounded by her long, boldly modeled flowing hair. The bust is signed by the maker, Léopold Savine. *H:12½ in (32 cm).*

the Belgian empire. Nautilus shells were another wonder of nature that was used in sculpture, such as in the ingenious bronze table lamp produced by Austrian Gustav Gurshner (*see right*).

Sculptors also worked in biscuit porcelain, which, as an unglazed medium, was perfect for showing off the intricacy of their handiwork. The sculptural possibilities of stoneware and earthenware were explored, too, as the hierarchy of sculpture over ceramics was questioned.

In the hands of Rupert Carabin, furniture became a vehicle for bound and otherwise subjugated women carved from wood. Sadistic overtones aside, when he submitted a bookcase carved with female figures to the *Société des Indépendantes* in 1890, it was refused on the grounds that it was not a sculpture. The outcry over the snobbery of even this supposedly independent body—let alone that of the official Salon—forced a rethink of the artistic hierarchy, and unity was called for within the art world.

CYCLE OF FASHION
After a decade of must-have popularity, the French appetite for sensual female figurines was shifting. What had once been fresh now seemed as stale as the hackneyed sculpture that it had replaced. But the female form as sculptural subject matter was unlikely to go away. Indeed, it found itself back in vogue in a new decorative style in the years following World War I.

LOÏE FULLER

The greatest inspiration for Art Nouveau dancing figurines was an American dancer named Loïe Fuller, who came to Paris in 1892. In her unique dances, performed at the Folies-Bergère, she used electric light to illuminate the swirls of her billowing drapery; at one point she seemingly transformed into a bat. In 1897 there were no fewer than nine bronze sculptures of the idolized dancer at a single exhibition, including studies by Raoul Larche and Rupert Carabin. At the 1900 Paris *Exposition Universelle* there was a Loïe Fuller Theater, the entrance topped by a sculpture of her by Pierre Roche. Loïe Fuller figures and lamps epitomize French Art Nouveau.

FOLIES-BERGÈRE POSTER Designed by Jules Chéret, this striking poster captures Loïe Fuller in full flight. The rich colors and play on light and dark convey the pure drama of her performances. *1893.*

HOUSEHOLD OBJECTS
Part of the French Art Nouveau policy was expressed in the tenet *l'art dans tout* (art in everything). Household objects—whether bowls, inkwells, vases, candlesticks, or mirrors—had to be functional, but they could still be beautiful. Raoul Larche subscribed to the philosophy with his table lamps, as did his fellow sculptor Maurice Bouval, whose pewter planter (*below*) is entwined with leaves. In contrast to the dark metal, the gilt-bronze nude female perched on the edge gleams brightly. Bouval is said to have given his maidens enigmatic and even sad expressions that reflected the soul-searching visions of Symbolist painters and poets and the beautiful but serious women depicted by Pre-Raphaelite painters such as Dante Gabriel Rossetti and Edward Burne-Jones.

Lamps were the ideal art form for sculptors—a new type of object for a new look. The figure of a woman or her trailing robes could easily conceal the mechanics of the light fixture. She often held the lampshade in her

hands, as in the bronze table lamp with a nautilus-shell shade (*below*) by Austrian Gustav Gurschner. When the light was turned on, the glow picked out the delicacy of modeling on her face and body. Gurschner's mermaid figure is much more spare, abstracted, and elongated than the curvaceous, idealized sensuality of the French models. Public taste was turning in favor of the lean, geometric look coming out of Vienna and Glasgow (*see pp.236–63*) and, ultimately, it became a more lasting style than French Art Nouveau.

BRONZE TABLE LAMP The form of this lamp is fashioned as a sinuous mermaid, supported on her tail. She clutches a pale nautilus shell, which acts as a pearlized shade. The lamp was designed by Gustav Gurschner for K. K. Kunst-Erzgiesserei, Vienna. *c.1900. H:11 in (28 cm).*

ART NOUVEAU PLANTER Maurice Bouval's pewter open planter has a leaf-molded handle and foot. To one side sits a gilt-bronze reclining nude. Signed by the maker. *W:13 in (33 cm).*

BRONZE VASE This bulbous vase is decorated in relief with a female face set among scrolling waves. The piece is signed "F. Madurelli." *H:5½ in (14 cm).*

POSTERS

AS NEW PRODUCTS CAME ONTO THE MARKET, MASS ADVERTISING CASHED
IN. ADVANCES IN PRINTING TECHNOLOGY LED TO A DELUGE OF POSTERS,
MAGAZINES, AND PRINTS, QUICKLY SPREADING THE STYLE OF ART NOUVEAU.

FRENCH STREET ART

Alphonse Mucha, who was born in South Moravia
but spent most of his career in Paris, used all the
Art Nouveau ingredients to perfection in his poster
work. His sophisticated use of beautiful women,
selling a way of life rather than a product, launched
a trend that is still a mainstay of the marketing
world today. Women, doyennes of consumerism,
could appreciate the pleasure principle as much as
men. The woman in Mucha's *Les Arts* panels has
whiplash hair and elaborate Art Nouveau jewelry
and is reverently haloed by a zodiac. Mucha often
used Eastern symbolic forms in his posters.

Mucha had a meteoric rise in 1895 when he
designed a poster for the play *Gismonda*, with
legendary actress Sarah Bernhardt. With its
attenuated figure in a format to match, soft colors,
and integral decorative motifs, Mucha's poster

was an overnight success. He collaborated with
Bernhardt on her next 13 plays, designing costumes,
jewelry, and posters. The imagery he used worked
up an insatiable appetite for his posters, which sold
out the moment they were printed.

Mucha's printed designs included postcards,
stamps, biscuit barrels, bank notes, menus, fabric,
and magazine covers. He also designed the interior
of Georges Fouquet's Paris jewelry shop, using
carved wood, glass, and metal in peacock motifs
and foliate whiplashes; the Bosnia-Herzegovina
Pavilion for the 1900 Paris *Exposition Universelle*;
and murals and stained-glass windows in Prague.

The posters of Jules Chéret featured more blatantly
sexy women. Throughout his career he designed
almost a thousand posters, which advertised
everything from coffee to cough drops, cigarettes

LES ARTS One of four decorative panels by Alphonse Mucha
(*below*), each of which depicts one of the four seasons with a
Muse as the central motif. Each Muse is inscribed within a highly
decorative circle with seasonal floral ornamentation above and
wears a light, flowing gown. *1898. H:22 in (56 cm).*

DIVAN JAPONAIS One of Henri de Toulouse-Lautrec's best-known posters
(*right*), in the style of Japanese woodblock prints, this shows dancer Jane Avril
seated next to literary critic Edouard Dujardin. *1893. H:32 in (81 cm).*

LE SILLON This was the first poster designed by Belgian artist Fernand Toussaint. It is a Symbolist work and was created for a circle of decorative realists known as *Le Sillon*. 1895. H:40 in (101.5 cm).

ELDORADO The bright colors and lively imagery of this rare poster are hallmarks of its creator, Jules Chéret. It is an advertisement for the king of Parisian music halls, Eldorado, and the allegory of dance and music perfectly sums up this mecca of performing arts. c.1895. H:46½ in (118 cm).

LE CHAT NOIR This rare poster by Théophile Steinlen was designed for the cabaret club Le Chat Noir. The clever positioning of the huge, wide-eyed black cat allows for a lot of text. It is a simple, powerful image rendered in only a few colors; many text versions exist. c.1895. H:24¼ in (61.5 cm).

to cabaret, and were also available to buy commercially. The Parisian music hall Eldorado inspired one of Chéret's classic posters (*above*), which incorporates the use of a powerful perspective gleaned from sources such as the ceiling allegories of Old Master painter Giovanni Battista Tiepolo.

THE JAPANESE INFLUENCE

Henri de Toulouse-Lautrec was captivated by the Japanese prints coming into the West. A contemporary critic described the blueprint: "Take any representative Japanese print…and it will be

SALON DES CENT Depicting a woman with red hair holding flowers, a pen, and a pad, this is considered one of the best images by Eugène Grasset. A 100-copy limited edition without lettering. 1899. H:24¾ in (63 cm).

found to embody all that a good poster should. One dominant idea is presented graphically, beautifully. The detail does not weaken, but actually enforces the motif. There is not a superfluous line. The color scheme…is fresh and striking, but always harmonious. The composition gives an idea of balance and breadth, but affords no hint as to how these qualities have been obtained…The general effect is decorative in the highest degree, may be humorous, and is certainly pervaded by the 'hidden soul of harmony'." Toulouse-Lautrec's flat silhouettes, asymmetrical composition, elongated figures, and firm outline all recall Japanese art. However, for his neutral portrayals of hedonistic modern life, he set his figures in real places, rather than in the symbolic, decorative settings that were so beloved of core Art Nouveau artists.

Eugène Grasset was mainly influenced by William Morris and the Pre-Raphaelites, but his thick, black outlines are reminiscent of the woodcuts that were coming from Japan, as well as of Paul Gauguin's cloisonné painting technique. Grasset's portrayal of the feminine form, linked closely with nature, was more delicate than the provocative Chéret women, idealized Mucha maidens, or worldly Toulouse-Lautrec sophisticates.

Théophile Steinlen's well-known poster for the Symbolist cabaret Le Chat Noir (*above left*) fused Art Nouveau's symbolic and decorative motifs. A contemporary critic wrote: "The walls of Paris have been dignified by the presence of this haloed cat, hieratic, Byzantine, of enormous size, whose thin fantastic silhouette hangs high above the crowd in the streets."

LE STYLE MUCHA

The French poster style spread to Belgium, where designers such as Privat-Livemont and Fernand Toussaint took up the baton. Following Mucha's lead, they used decorative women to imply the beauty of a product.

LITHOGRAPHY AND TYPOGRAPHY

Advances in color lithography allowed artists to work directly on the lithographic stone, which was then inked for transfer to paper. Jules Chéret's technical refinements made it possible to produce a rainbow of colors. His designs, brighter than Mucha's muted palette, were sometimes produced in several different color combinations.

Words were a key element of posters, magazine covers, and advertisements, and they were treated increasingly as an integral part of the design. Paul Berthon, a pupil of Eugène Grasset, made a frame for his Folies Bergère poster (*right*) out of the name of both the cabaret and the dancer, lessening the severity of the tall, thin format. He used a fleshy, flowing typeface that suited the floral motifs and female figure, haloed with a spider's web. Austrian Secession artists (*see pp.236–63*) went much farther, designing typefaces that were more stylized than legible—an abstracted element that dominated the decorative surface.

FOLIES BERGÈRE A rare masterpiece of the French Art Nouveau movement, this poster was designed by Paul Berthon for Liane de Pougy's first appearance at the famed Folies Bergère cabaret. The image of the performer is flanked, top and bottom, by the typography. c.1895. H:58½ in (148.5 cm).

EUROPE AND BEYOND

The craze for posters spread from France to the rest of Europe and the United States. With it went the Art Nouveau style, which, as with all the decorative arts, each country adapted in its own way.

GERMAN FLAVOR

All over Europe artistic magazines were springing up, due partly to more efficient printing and distribution. Britain's *The Studio* journal had its German equivalent in the Munich-based magazine *Die Jugend*, launched in 1896. It gave the name Jugendstil (New Style) to Art Nouveau in Germany. On the whole, German Art Nouveau was more geometric, closer to the styles of the Austrian Secession and the Glasgow School. Multidiscipline designer Peter Behrens turned his hand to posters in the 1890s, with stylized entwined couples, flowers, and butterflies. His industrial designs for AEG electricity, however, were more severe and geometric, suited to the 20th century's machine age.

The Low Countries made fascinating contributions to the poster industry. In Belgium, Privat Livemont returned from painting stage sets in Paris and began producing posters. He made 30 between 1896 and 1900, all with dreamy Belle Époque flower-strewn maidens. They were as popular in Belgium as in France. The Dutch Symbolist artist Jan Toorop also made posters, with attenuated women with skeletal fingers, rhythmic coils of hair, and billowing dresses. He had made several visits to England during the 1880s, and his work bears similarities to that of Aubrey Beardsley.

BRITISH CONTRIBUTIONS

Apart from the Glasgow School and Aubrey Beardsley, both with their own unique twists and interpretations, British designers made few forays into Art Nouveau graphic design. In John

DELFTSCHE SLAOLIE Characteristic of the work of its designer, Jan Toorop, this Dutch advertisement for salad oil combines a symbolic, mystic mixing of the Javanese puppet influence with frantic arabesques. *1895. H:34 in (86 cm).*

JUGEND A lithograph in pink, yellow, turquoise, and black, this poster was designed by Josef Rudolf Witzel for the Munich-based illustrated magazine *Jugend*. The image is of a young maiden draped in a garland of flowers and sitting beneath a tree surrounded by butterflies. *1896–97. H:44½ in (113 cm).*

THE GIRL & THE GODS This poster by British designer John Hassall draws on imagery from the Classical period, rendered in the Art Nouveau style. *H:30 in (76 cm).*

PARIS Beautifully rendered in shades of pale green, blue, red, and pale brown, this image of peacocks in Paris was designed by Louis J. Rhead. The scene depicted shows a male peacock wooing a female, with a full display of his tail feathers. *1897. W:60½ in (153.5 cm).*

L. PRANG & CO.'S HOLIDAY PUBLICATIONS Designed by Louis J. Rhead, this advertisement shows a woman in lavender seated at a green desk, holding up Christmas books. It features red and green lettering against a yellow background. *1895. H:22 in (56 cm).*

WOMEN'S EDITION COURIER Here the depiction of the "Art Nouveau woman" is less rigid than in many other American images of the time. One of only two posters designed by Alice Russell Glenny. *1895. H:27 in (68.5 cm).*

Hassall's poster (*opposite*), all the elements are Classical, but the swirl of steam emanating from the teapot and linking the various parts of the composition is distinctly Art Nouveau in style.

AMERICAN POSTER PARTIES

Louis John Rhead was born in Britain and trained in London and Paris before moving to New York. Most of his work was on posters for New York newspapers such as the *Herald* and the *Sun*, but he also created advertisements for scent, soap, and cigarettes. He favored a bold palette and contrasting color schemes. His poster for Prang Holiday Publications shows the influence of the Pre-Raphaelite painters, and his portrayals of demure women with striking looks and manes of hair suited the American market. Rhead was also in thrall to the work of Eugène Grasset, whose images had inspired him to become a poster designer himself. Like Grasset, he used a thick, dark outline to make the clear statement needed in a graphic image. Grasset's work in stained glass and his knowledge of Japanese woodcuts both influenced his own style.

Edward Penfield used strong outlines in his 1897 poster calendar, made bolder by the contrast of complementary colors. However, Rhead was versatile and could work in a more intricate style, as in his Parisian peacock scene (*above left*).

A NEW SCHOOL

Female designers, such as Alice Russell Glenny, also played a part in the poster movement. Another key American graphic designer was Will Bradley, who worked in a more dynamic, organic, and linear style than Rhead. He wrote: "I think the American poster has opened a new school whose aim is simplicity and good composition. One can see its effect in all directions, especially the daily papers." Bradley's greatest inspiration was Aubrey Beardsley, who had an acute instinct for composition, especially with Japanese asymmetry, even if simplicity was not always his aim.

POSTER CALENDAR 1897 This image was designed by Edward Penfield and featured as the cover for this deluxe-edition calendar. It depicts an artist setting to work, accompanied by his cat. Male figures were a relatively rare feature in Art Nouveau design. *1896. H:14 in (35 cm).*

AUBREY BEARDSLEY

In 1893 *The Studio* journal was launched with a feature on Aubrey Beardsley, which catapulted the illustrator to fame. Notoriety followed when he illustrated Oscar Wilde's play *Salome* with a predatory elongated femme fatale hawkishly clutching the head of John the Baptist, complete with arabesques of blood. The combination of decorative and grotesque, especially pronounced with his graphic use of black and white, both in flat areas and linear ornament, sparked accusations of depravity. Beardsley died of tuberculosis in 1898, at the age of 25.

KEYNOTES SERIES Designed by Aubrey Beardsley, this poster depicts various figures promoting a series of books. Bold and simple images, rather than florid, elaborate designs are characteristic of Beardsley's work. *1896. H:18¾ in (47.5 cm).*

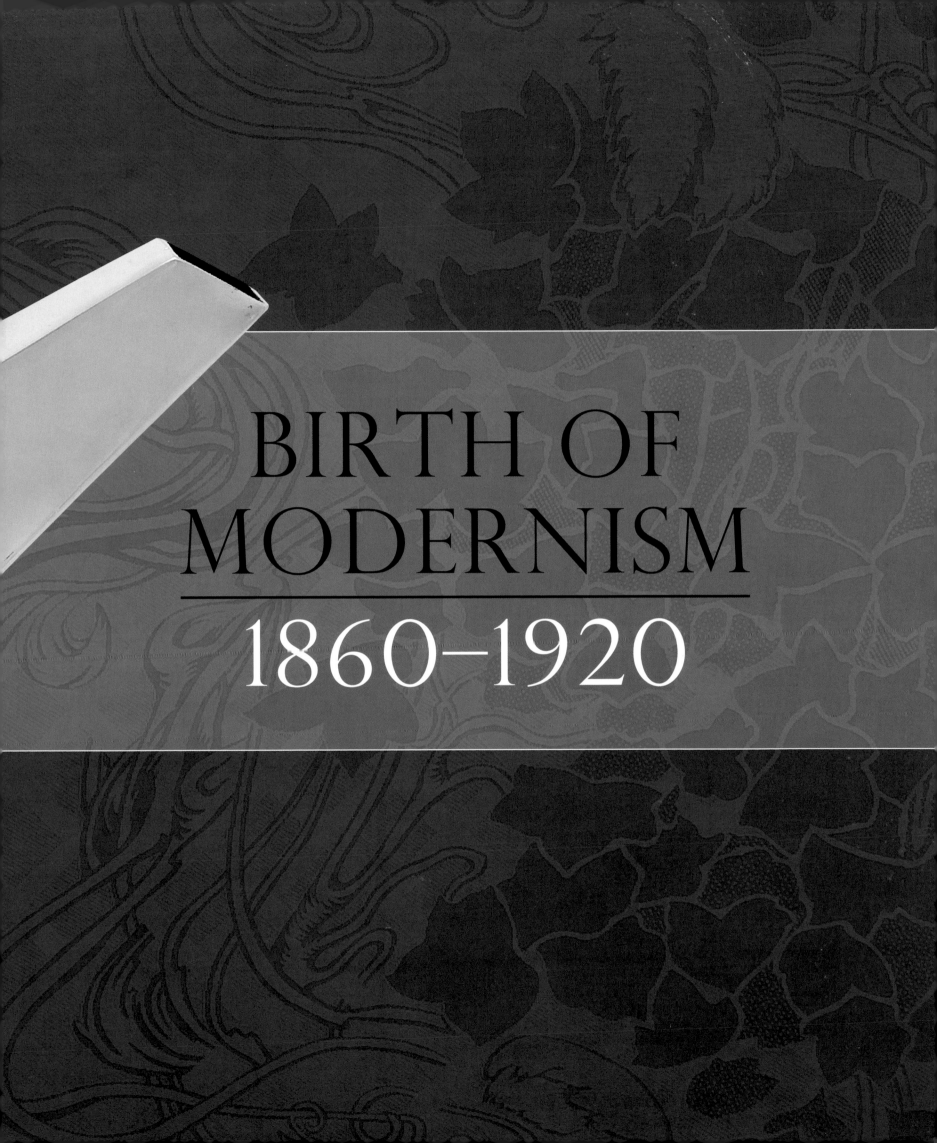

BIRTH OF
MODERNISM

1860–1920

DYNAMIC DESIGNERS

IT IS DIFFICULT TO DATE THE BIRTH OF MODERNISM WITH ANY
PRECISION, BUT FROM THE 1860S ONWARD, THERE WERE CERTAIN
DESIGNERS WHOSE WORK STOOD OUT FROM THE PREDOMINANT
TRENDS OF THE DAY AND LOOKED FORWARD IN STYLE AND CONCEPT.

STIRRUP VESSEL Christopher Dresser's design for Ault Pottery is
decorated with a distinctive streaked and dribbled glaze, which is far
removed from the historical revival trends of the time. *c. 1890.*

EARLY MODERN THINKERS

In Vienna the German designer Michael Thonet
designed a bentwood chair in 1859 that, when
mass-produced, sold 50 million copies by 1930.
It was included by architect Le Corbusier as a
prime example of modernist design in his 1925 Paris
exhibit *Pavillon de L'Esprit Nouveau*. In England
Christopher Dresser set out a theory of aestheticism
that combined nature with designs from disparate
cultures and periods into a new, harmonious whole
in *The Art of Decorative Design* (1862).

The Scottish designer Charles Rennie Mackintosh
developed a new rectilinear style with gentle curves
and geometric decoration to produce elegantly
attenuated furniture, as well as interiors and whole
buildings. Three Viennese designers—the painter and
book illustrator Koloman Moser, the architect Josef
Hoffmann, and the painter Carl Otto Czeschka—set
up the Wiener Werkstätte (Viennese Workshops) in
1903 to produce simple, functional and well-
designed furniture, textiles, metalwork, and other
items. Like Mackintosh, they rejected the sweeping
curves and floral motifs of Art Nouveau in favor of
straight lines and geometric shapes.

What these and other designers had in common
was that, while they were often placed within
existing stylistic movements, their work displayed
a more modernist approach. Modernism was never
conceived as a single style but was more a loose
collection of related ideas covering a range of styles
and movements in different countries. In rejecting
history and tradition, modernism embraced the
new, having an almost utopian desire to create a
better world, sometimes from scratch. It rejected
decoration and embraced abstraction. Most
important, it believed in the power and potential of
the machine and industrial technology to change the
world. Modernism was often allied with left-wing
social and political beliefs, as both held that art and
design could transform society.

CONTINUING THE TREND

Such radical design continued in Europe,
flourishing alongside Art Deco and motivated by
the belief that the world needed to be rethought
and reshaped after the carnage of the trenches.
The Russian Revolution of 1917 offered a model
of how that new society might look. In the
Netherlands a group of designers and artists led by
Piet Mondrian founded the De Stijl group, which
promoted a rigorous, abstract approach to art and
design. In 1918 one of their members, Gerrit
Rietveld, designed a red and blue chair that was
not only a three-dimensional equivalent of

SCHRÖDER HOUSE
Gerrit Rietveld designed
this house in Utrecht
in the Netherlands as a
series of abstract planes,
with projecting roofs
and balconies but no
historical ornament.

**EBONIZED
SYCAMORE CHAIR**
Designed by Charles
Rennie Mackintosh, the
emphasis is on verticals
softened by a slightly
curved back. Crosspieces
form a panel of squares
like a stylized tree.
*1904. H:28½ in
(72 cm).*

BEDROOM BY WALTER GROPIUS Functional, light, and airy with a window the width of the wall, the room is as conducive to reading and relaxing as to sleeping. The room is furnished with pieces made from the new materials pioneered by Gropius and his contemporaries: bent and molded plywood, tubular steel, glass, and laminated wood.

Mondrian's geometric paintings but also a physical statement of what modernism itself was all about.

The undoubted powerhouse of early modernism was the Bauhaus, an art, architecture, and design school founded by the architect Walter Gropius in Weimar, Germany, in 1919. The school initially handcrafted items but became more of a research center producing machine-made prototypes for industry. Among its most famous products was Marcel Breuer's tubular-steel-framed chair and a glass and nickel desk lamp designed by Wilhelm Wagenfeld, which so closely embodied the theories of the school it became known as the Bauhaus lamp.

MASS MODERNISM

This shift from the individually crafted to the mass-produced product reflected the move away from the theoretical, and from the enclosed world of private exhibitions and small-circulation magazines, toward a practical, industrial mass application. Modernist architects were involved in the vast new housing projects in Germany, Austria, and the Netherlands designed to solve the postwar housing shortage, while modernist ideas influenced everything from typography to tea sets and chairs.

By the 1930s, modernism had lost its social and political beliefs and become a recognizable design style, based on abstract, rectilinear geometry using industrial production techniques and materials, notably chrome, steel, and glass. It also became more national, with different styles appearing in Britain, Czechoslovakia, the United States, the Soviet Union, and, despite extreme political differences, in Fascist Italy and Nazi Germany.

EXHIBITION POSTER This poster by Herbert Bayer for a retrospective exhibition captures the spare, geometric spirit of Bauhaus design. *1968. H:25 in (66 cm).*

ELEMENTS OF STYLE

The first modernist designers had completely different philosophies from each other but were united by a desire to break new ground. Drawn away from naturalistic representation by the perceived freedom of abstract forms and the possibilities of new materials, they created decorative arts untrammeled by history. There was a conflict between affordability and exclusivity, as well as debate about how far natural forms should be rejected.

KEITH MURRAY VASE
SIMPLICITY
To break away from decorative tradition, the early modernists rejected 19th-century fussiness and demanded a minimalist approach. In favor of reductionism, they pared down design to its essential elements. Function was more highly regarded than ornament, which was considered regressive.

CHRISTOPHER DRESSER VASE
NEW SHAPES
Strange new forms were a blend of organic and geometric shapes. The highly stylized "art botany" of Christopher Dresser had a huge influence on modernists who turned 19th-century naturalism into ever more extreme and abstract forms.

PIET MONDRIAN POSTER
GRAPHIC DESIGN
Modernists absorbed influences from painting and graphic design. Bolshevist propaganda posters in the Constructivist style helped spread abstraction through Europe. Typographers at the Bauhaus rejected heavy German black letter type in favor of a simpler sans-serif style, free of ornament.

MIES VAN DER ROHE BARCELONA CHAIR
LUXURY MATERIALS
Modernist designers working on custom commissions used animal hides and leather for coverings and upholstery to satisfy their clients' taste for luxury. Designers such as Frank Lloyd Wright and Josef Hoffmann produced grand, integrated interiors with the finest materials.

CHARLES RENNIE MACKINTOSH CHAIR
GEOMETRY
As the influence of abstract art spread, geometric motifs and forms increased. Designers allied to the De Stijl movement attempted to reduce every plane to a straight line. The rigid geometric look of the Glasgow School was admired and emulated in Germany and Austria.

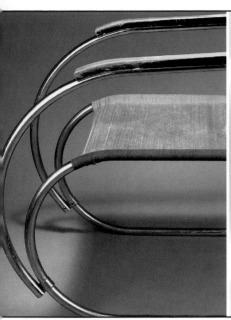

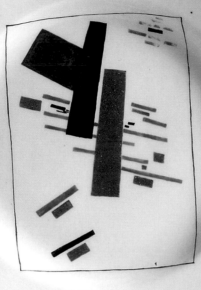

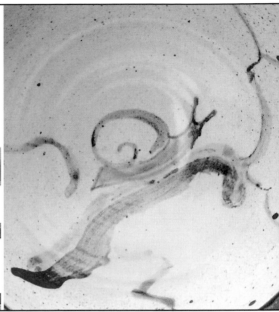

CHRISTOPHER DRESSER VASE

MIES VAN DER ROHE CHAIR
CANTILEVERED STEEL
The properties of tubular steel—affordable, versatile, durable, and lightweight—were ideally suited to the modernist agenda. The cantilevered design fused form and function, doing away with the need for sprung upholstery and reducing the number of chair legs from four to two.

KASIMIR MALEVICH PLATE
ABSTRACT DECORATION
Cubism in France, Futurism in Italy, Russian Constructivism, and English Vorticism all dismissed representational art. Instead of nature ruling supreme, designers celebrated the triumph of the machine with abstract shapes and patterns.

MARCEL BREUER CHAIR
PLYWOOD AND LAMINATED WOOD
Building on the work of Michael Thonet, modernists made the most of bent plywood and laminated wood. Bentwood reduced the components of furniture, which meant fewer joints and a smoother overall design. These were the first steps toward producing furniture from single pieces of material.

BERNARD LEACH BOWL
HANDCRAFT
The paradox of modernist decorative art was that, in the age of the machine, so much supposedly industrial design was made by hand. Many of the Bauhaus handcrafted prototypes, for instance, were never mass-produced.

CHRISTOPHER DRESSER VASE
GLAZES
Interest in the raku tradition of Japan led Western ceramicists to experiment with wood-fired climbing (stepped) kilns for the first time. The result was a huge variation in glaze tones and colors. This led to continual creation of new colors and effects. Matte glazes complemented smooth surfaces.

BAUHAUS SOFA BY WALTER GROPIUS
COLOR
To modernists, form was more important than ornament, so solid blocks of color were often used to mask texture and throw shape into sharp relief. Designers tended to favor primary colors and monochrome black and white rather than more subtle and varied tones.

BERNARD LEACH VASE
JAPANESE INFLUENCE
Frank Lloyd Wright was a great admirer of Japanese woodwork, and Christopher Dresser was beguiled by the simplicity of Japanese design. The sparseness of Asian ceramic design—particularly early Chinese blue and white and Japanese Kakiemon porcelain— was a precursor of modernist minimalism.

CHRISTOPHER DRESSER FACSIMILE SIGNATURE ON VASE
BRANDING
Designers worked with industry to mass-produce attractive, functional homeware for the general public. Christopher Dresser introduced the concept of branding by having his facsimile signature stamped on the products he designed. Graphic artists experimented with the first logos.

CHRISTOPHER DRESSER

IN HIS POPULAR *MANUAL OF BOTANY*, CHRISTOPHER DRESSER
IMAGINED HIS ERA AS "THE EARLY MORNING OF THE LONG
HOPED-FOR DAY." HIS WORK WAS THE ROOT OF A
REVOLUTION IN ART AND DESIGN.

LARGE BRASS EWER Manufactured by Benham
& Froud to a design by Dresser, its bulbous, conical
body is raised on a circular foot and tapers to
an angled tubular spout also linked by a hooped
handle. *1880s. H:2 in (5 cm).*

PROPELLER VASE Designed
while Dresser worked with the
Ault Pottery, the form is fluid
and dynamic, with a shimmering
blue and green aventurine glaze.
1890s. H:13 in (33.5 cm).

PAIR OF VASES Also designed for
the Ault Pottery, their form is of Islamic
inspiration. The glaze is splashed
and streaked in an abstract pattern.
1890s. H:10¼ in (26 cm).

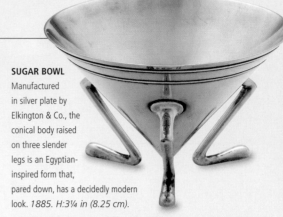

SUGAR BOWL
Manufactured
in silver plate by
Elkington & Co., the
conical body raised
on three slender
legs is an Egyptian-
inspired form that,
pared down, has a decidedly modern
look. *1885. H:3¼ in (8.25 cm).*

Dresser's audacious talents were apparent from a
young age, and he was enrolled in the Government
Design School at Somerset House in London when
he was just 13. Born in 1834, he was an exact
contemporary of William Morris and had an equal
influence on the decorative arts, albeit in a totally
different direction. Many of his designs stood
radically apart from those of his contemporaries.

Dresser's studies at Somerset House included
botany, and he continued to specialize in this
field, receiving his honorary doctorate from the
University of Jena in Germany in 1859. When his
application for Chair of Botany at the University
of London was rejected, Dresser resolved to forge a
career as a designer, setting up his studio in 1860.

ART BOTANY
In 1857 Dresser had contributed drawings of plants
to Owen Jones's *Grammar of Ornament*, the
leading sourcebook for Victorian designers. He
fused his great skill as a botanical draftsman
with his interest in geometry and pattern to
produce a new stylization of nature that he
referred to as "art botany." The distinction
between representational (imitative) and
imagined (ideal) art was important to Dresser.
He considered decorative art, as opposed
to pictorial art, the more noble pursuit, as it was
more likely to be ideal. This contention boldly
challenged the entrenched interests of the artistic
establishment. In voicing it, Dresser played a key
role in raising the status of the designer.

At his studio, Dresser would repeat favorite
maxims to his students. One of the most common
was "maximum effect with minimum means,"
instilling an economy of style. A voyage to Japan
in 1876 as the representative of the South
Kensington Museum—later to become the Victoria
and Albert Museum—strengthened Dresser's
preference for form over ornament. It reaffirmed
his view that "fitness for purpose" was the basis
of good design. The European avant-garde later
championed these same principles—particularly the
Bauhaus, although that organization did not enjoy
the same industrial success as Dresser.

THE DRESSER BRAND
The list of firms that carried the Dresser brand
in the late 19th century reads like a roll call of
the cream of Victorian industry. Some of
Dresser's most radical work was for metalware
manufacturers Elkington & Co.—pioneers of the
electroplating process. In the 1880s, his designs for
James Dixon & Sons rivaled even De Stijl's in their
geometry. Dresser put his belief that free-blowing
was the best way of manipulating glass into
practice through his Clutha range for Couper and
Sons of Glasgow, which featured deliberate
imperfections, bubbles, and irregular handles and
rims. With John Harrison and Henry Tooth,
he founded Linthorpe Pottery in 1879, and
experimented with ceramic glaze and form. After
the venture failed, Ault Pottery acquired many of
the molds and persuaded Dresser to contribute new
designs. Dresser died in 1904, having made his
proto-modernist vision available to the masses
by working with industry to create attractive,
functional, and affordable household objects.

EXOTIC INFLUENCES
Dresser traveled in Japan, the United States,
Europe, and the Middle East, constantly adding to
his mental inventory of color, form, and ornament.
By refusing to restrict himself to specific design
conventions, he fused local, exotic flavors into
something new. His Egyptian designs included
creations for Wedgwood and Minton, a chair that
appeared in his book *Principles of Decorative
Design* (1873), and another that retailed through
the Art Furnishers' Alliance as well as a design
commission for Bushloe House in Leicester.

EGYPTIAN REVIVAL SOFA With its sphinx carvings, this sofa
was originally attributed to Dresser, but is now thought to have
been bought by him on a trip to Egypt. *W:56½ in (144 cm).*

GRAMMAR OF ORNAMENT This plate was Christopher Dresser's first
published work. Owen Jones's book of decorative motifs spanning time and
continents had a huge influence on the young designer.

Nº 13. OLOSOCOMIA CLEMATIDEA

Nº 5. ONION

Nº 3. DAFFODIL

Nº 8. HONEYSUCKLE

Nº 4. NARCISSUS

Nº 11. SPEEDWELL

FURNITURE

RADICAL DESIGNERS FROM ACROSS EUROPE AND THE UNITED STATES CAME UP
WITH STARTLING NEW 20TH-CENTURY FURNITURE DESIGNS THAT WERE SLEEK,
GEOMETRIC, AND SOMETIMES SEVERE IN THEIR SIMPLICITY.

THE GLASGOW SCHOOL

Under the directorship of Francis Newbery from 1885, the Glasgow School of Art expanded quickly, building on its already formidable reputation as one of the foremost government design schools.

It was around this time that a group of four young designers, brought together through their association with the school, formed a loose alliance that would stimulate a creative revolution across Europe. Known as the Glasgow Four, the group was made up of Charles Rennie Mackintosh and James Herbert MacNair, with their respective wives, sisters Margaret and Frances Macdonald.

THE FAMOUS FOUR

Together they took elements from the Arts and Crafts and Art Nouveau styles that were popular at the time and passed them through the filter of the Celtic Revival to produce something new. Mackintosh himself designed new premises for the Glasgow School of Art in 1896 using the archaic Scottish Baronial style as his base, embellished with restrained and functional decorative details. Although considered his masterpiece today, at the time the building attracted little if any press attention outside Glasgow.

The elongated elements that characterize much of Mackintosh's furniture were a trademark of the Glasgow style, dubbed the Spook School by some commentators in reaction to its exaggeratedly stretched lines and ghostly figures. Mackintosh often obliterated the wooden grain of his furniture by applying glossy black lacquer or colored painted finishes. His use of white and pale green echoed the palette used by other members of the Glasgow Four in their painting, needlework, and gesso panels. Mackintosh saw his dark color schemes as masculine, contrasting with his light feminine schemes.

The decorative motif most commonly associated with Mackintosh's work is the Glasgow rose. His representation of the flower is so acutely stylized that it is almost abstract—a series of curved and straight lines within a roughly circular border. Similarly, the pierced motifs cut into the oval top

THE WHITE BEDROOM Mackintosh designed and furnished the Hill House in Helensburgh, near Glasgow, for the publisher Walter Blackie in 1904. The furniture in the guest room, including a ladderback chair, is embryonic modern in its predominantly linear and geometric form and decoration.

The bird-in-flight cutout is typical of Mackintosh's stylized organic motifs

Wide spacing of the back splats creates a light and airy quality

The back legs change from round to oval to square—an extremely complex piece of carpentry

The elegant arches of the seat rails echo the oval top above and an arched apron below

The front legs are thin, tapering, and square-sectioned to underpin the composition, at once robust and delicate

ARGYLE CHAIR Designed for the Argyle Street Tea Rooms in Glasgow, this was Mackintosh's first high-back chair, and remains one of his most striking designs. *1897. H:54 in (137 cm).*

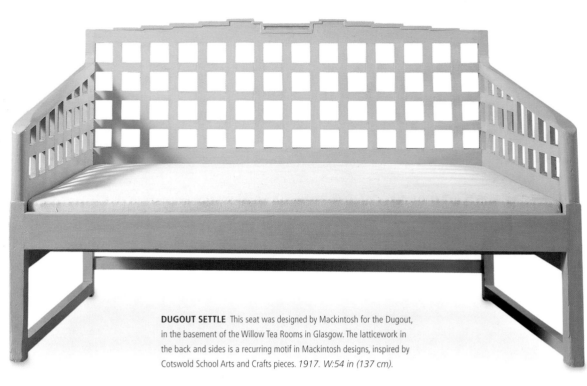

MUSIC ROOM CHAIR Designed by Mackintosh for Miss Cranston's Hous'hill in Glasgow, the vertical back splats instantly convey his rectilinear style. As often in his earlier work, it is softened by gentle curves, here seen in the front seat rail. *1904. H:30 in (75.5 cm).*

DUGOUT SETTLE This seat was designed by Mackintosh for the Dugout, in the basement of the Willow Tea Rooms in Glasgow. The latticework in the back and sides is a recurring motif in Mackintosh designs, inspired by Cotswold School Arts and Crafts pieces. *1917. W:54 in (137 cm).*

rails of Mackintosh's tall Argyle chairs, designed for Miss Cranston's Tea Rooms in 1897, are just recognizable as birds in flight. This bold move toward abstraction is all the more remarkable for occurring more than a decade before the Cubist movement gained momentum.

The furniture designed by both MacNair and Mackintosh is rigidly geometric, comprising horizontal and vertical members that intersect to produce repeated square spaces. Ovals and arcs complement and temper these perpendicular lines without sacrificing any of their stark simplicity.

Mackintosh's Hill House chair is one of the most striking examples of this style—ostensibly a heavily stylized version of a traditional ladder back chair, it features more than two dozen horizontal bars, augmented toward the top with vertical members to create a grid section behind the sitter's head.

FEMININE INPUT

This unconventional approach was the vanguard of a movement that would sweep the European mainland. When Mackintosh collaborated with Frances and Margaret Macdonald to create a room

for the 1900 Vienna Secession Exhibition, key figures of the Secessionist movement such as Gustav Klimt and Josef Hoffmann were so impressed by the exhibit that they began to incorporate the Glasgow School aesthetic into their own work.

So synonymous is the name of Charles Rennie Mackintosh with the Glasgow style that the contribution made by the Macdonald sisters and the many other women who followed in their footsteps is too often overlooked. Francis Newbery actively encouraged women to enroll in the Glasgow School of Art, and many of them came to excel in the design and creation of mural panels, screens, and embroidery.

Margaret Macdonald contributed her own designs to Mackintosh's decorative scheme for Miss Cranston's Tea Rooms. Looking back on their work, Mackintosh declared: "I had talent, Margaret had genius." The Glasgow School was diverse and its adherents created an integrated style that was more than the sum of its parts.

Stylized roses are a recurring motif in Mackintosh's earlier designs

The wood is painted white for one of Mackintosh's feminine color schemes

Tapering, pilaster-like forms soften a rectilinear carcass

WHITE CABINET Originally designed by Mackintosh as one of a pair for Kingsborough Gardens, Glasgow, this is painted white with inlaid glass panels. The panels have stylized imagery of a woman holding a rose ball—a feminine touch attributed to the influence of Mackintosh's wife. *1902. H:61 in (154.5 cm).*

HOUS'HILL WRITING TABLE Made of ebonized mahogany inlaid with mother-of-pearl, ceramic, and ivory, and further embellished with leaded glass and metal, this was designed for the blue bedroom at Hous'Hill, and is recognized as one of Mackintosh's most accomplished pieces.

THE WIENER WERKSTÄTTE

Josef Hoffmann and Koloman Moser left the Vienna Secession in the first years of the 20th century, frustrated by their peers within the movement who were in thrall to the florid Art Nouveau style. Together they drew up a manifesto for a pioneering, integrated decorative art idiom relevant to the modern age. Having secured the financial backing of wealthy industrialist and patron of the arts Fritz Wärndorfer, they founded the Wiener Werkstätte in 1903.

Based upon the same medieval model that had inspired C. R. Ashbee's Guild of Handicraft, the Wiener Werkstätte anticipated the Bauhaus in that its members were taught practical crafts alongside the theory of design. In common with many of the groups that reacted against the historical revivals of the 19th century, the Wiener Werkstätte believed that every element of a building's architecture and interior fixtures should follow a single theme. Unlike the modernists who followed in their wake, Hoffmann and his disciples made few concessions to the mass market, recognizing that the fruits of their intensive labor would be available only to the wealthy. Among the many maxims Hoffmann instilled at his workshop was "better to work ten days on one product than manufacture ten products in one day"—a sentiment far closer to the values of William Morris than Le Corbusier.

INTEGRATED DESIGN

Hoffmann took the Wagnerian concept of *Gesamtkunstwerk* (synthesis of the arts) and applied it to the architectural commissions he took on behalf of the Wiener Werkstätte. The first of these was the Purkersdorf Sanatorium, intended as a luxury refuge and spa. The spartan cleanliness

VIENNESE APARTMENT Baroness Magda Mautner-Markhof's apartment was furnished by Josef Hoffmann in 1902. It reveals his move away from sinuous Art Nouveau to the elegant linear style promoted by Charles Rennie Mackintosh.

UPHOLSTERED ARMCHAIR This beech reclining chair was designed by Josef Hoffmann for J. & J. Kohn. It has openwork decoration and spherical motifs. *c.1905. W:19¾ in (50 cm).*

NEST OF TABLES Designed in overtly geometric form and detail by Josef Hoffmann at the Wiener Werkstätte, and designated model number 968, the tables (three here from a set of four) were made in mahogany-stained beech by J. & J. Kohn. *1905. Largest: H:29¾ in (75.5 cm).*

demanded by this kind of environment later became a feature of much modernist design. The unified design scheme included dozens of fixtures to provide soft, even lighting.

This first commission was followed by an opportunity in 1905 to develop a grand private residence in Brussels for Baron Stoclet, who gave the workshops extraordinary freedom to appoint the interior with everything from furniture to cutlery. The designer-craftsmen of the Wiener Werkstätte developed and expanded the range of wares made for the Palais Stoclet for their first exhibition, entitled *Der gedeckte Tisch* (The laid-out table), in 1906.

SIMPLE LINES

Hoffmann became an admirer of the elongated lines expressed by the Glasgow Four when they exhibited at the Secession House in 1900. The steamed wood pieces are a follow-on from the early bentwood pieces perfected by Michael Thonet. Josef Olbrich—who later designed a number of significant modernist buildings—and Koloman Moser often made a feature of front risers that ascend from a base rail and curve backward to form armrests. This geometric simplicity was most eloquently expressed by Hoffmann's Cabaret Fledermaus chair, designed for the café of the same name in Vienna.

Unusually for Wiener Werkstätte products, furniture was usually made by other Vienna workshops rather than carried out on site. Preferred contractors included Thonet and J. & J. Kohn—both venerable firms with expertise in bentwood construction. J. & J. Kohn produced Hoffmann's adjustable reclining chair, model no. 670, from around 1905. With its rectangular openwork decoration and radial bentwood members, the chair is rigidly geometric in form. The round knobs are functional as well as decorative, providing a mechanism that allows the back of the seat to recline. By applying his rigid design aesthetic to the Morris chair developed by Philip Webb in 1866, Hoffmann had created something entirely new.

Moser left the Wiener Werkstätte in 1907. World War I deprived the workshops of talent and resources. When it ended, the defeated Austrian nation was less able to support such a lavish venture. Attempts to open branches in other cities, including New York in 1922, met with some success, but Hoffmann had to shut down his project in 1932.

Geometric forms in the Hoffman style are evident in the glazed doors

Decoration is typically understated and includes annular (ring-shaped) ribbing on the spindle supports

The marble top is characteristically both practical and decorative

The escutcheons and ring-pull handles are made of brass

WALNUT-VENEERED SIDEBOARD Designed in the style of Josef Hoffmann, its marble-topped base with cupboards and a drawer supports a mirror-glass panel and, with a pair of spindles, a raised cupboard. *1902. H:70 in (178 cm).*

UPHOLSTERED ARMCHAIR This chair is one of the many variations of the J. & J. Kohn 714 series. It was inspired by the 19th-century English smoker's chair. The traditional design was supervised by the Kohn design director, Gustav Siegel. *c.1902. H:30½ in (76 cm).*

WRITING DESK Designed by Koloman Moser, and made by J. & J. Kohn in mahogany-stained beech with a mirror and brass hardware, the composition of the desk is rectilinear. Its subtly undulating back acknowledges the existence of a more curvaceous Art Nouveau style. *c.1900. W:45¼ in (113 cm).*

THE BAUHAUS

Founded in 1919, the Bauhaus was inevitably shaped by the aftermath of World War I. The Treaty of Versailles had crushed Germany, forcing it to give up valuable tracts of land and imposing restrictions on its economy. In the wake of such a humiliating defeat, the designers at the Bauhaus turned their backs on the past, ignoring tradition and convention, and reassessed the fundamental nature and purpose of good design.

VISION FOR THE FUTURE

The vision of Walter Gropius, the first Bauhaus director, found expression in the Haus am Horn, the 1923 exhibition home by Georg Muche furnished by Bauhaus students. The inside of the building provides a glimpse of domestic interiors that are true to the Bauhaus ideals of economy, durability, fitness for purpose, and aesthetic merit.

The principle that underpinned all of the work done under Gropius's direction was close collaboration with industry—Bauhaus products were designed as archetypes that could be made cheaply by machine. While the Bauhaus was at Weimar, its remit expanded to embrace architecture, stone, metal and woodworking, pottery, painting, weaving, graphic design, and, of course, furniture. Students were encouraged to learn how to work with confidence in as many design spheres as possible.

NEW CHAIR DESIGNS

The furniture of the early Bauhaus was often far removed from the sleek chromed steel pieces with which it is most commonly associated. Marcel Breuer started a woodwork apprenticeship there in 1920 and constructed his Slatted Chair, inspired by the angular designs of Gerrit Rietveld, from maplewood and horsehair cloth. The integration between the arts that the Bauhaus strove for found a neat expression in Breuer's African Chair, made from stained oak painted and upholstered in fabric by the weaver Gunta Stölzl.

A year after completing his course, Breuer returned in 1925 as a young master at the second incarnation of the Bauhaus, based at new premises in Dessau designed by Walter Gropius. It was here that he developed the tubular steel furniture that has become synonymous with the modular International Style. Breuer was attracted to tubular steel as a furnishing material because it was cheap and versatile. It provides recoil without the need for springs and is easy to clean.

His Wassily chair and Thonet shelving unit show how he applied a similar tubular frame to a range of design briefs. Breuer continued to teach at the Bauhaus until 1928, eventually leaving at the same time as Walter Gropius.

DESSAU BAUHAUS The concrete monolithic structure has glass curtain walls, which were a complete innovation in the 1920s.

The upholstery is made from black leather straps

The tubular steel frame was inspired by Breuer's bicycle

MARCEL BREUER CHAIR Originally designed for Wassily Kandinsky's quarters at the Dessau Bauhaus, the iconic Wassily B3 was revolutionary in its use of a bent steel frame for residential furniture. *1925–27. W:27½ in (69.75 cm).*

SOFA TABLE Designed by Marcel Breuer, the nickel-plated frame has a crystal glass top. It was reissued by Tecta in 2004. *H:23½ in (60 cm).*

MIES VAN DER ROHE

Ludwig Mies van der Rohe is mainly remembered for his work in the United States, yet his early career in Germany produced some of his finest achievements. He believed that chair design was a challenge equal to that of skyscraper architecture because of its "endless possibilities and many problems." His MR10 chair was a close relative of Breuer's Wassily model, although the cantilevered construction was indebted to the S33 chair designed by Mart Stam, another star of the Bauhaus.

While working on a 1929 commission from the German government to design the German pavilion at the Barcelona International Exhibition, Mies van der Rohe devoted as much time to the furnishings as he did to the building itself. Not yet involved with the Bauhaus and certainly not a believer in its iconoclastic manifesto, he based the designs for his Barcelona chair and ottoman on a classical Roman form. They were nonetheless thoroughly modern in conception, although their high construction cost made them unsuitable as models for cheap mass production. Faced with growing opposition from conservatism and the rising Nazi party, the Bauhaus was dissolved in 1933, just a year after it had moved to Berlin under Mies van der Rohe's directorship. In the turbulent years that followed, many of the figures associated with the school fled Germany. Gropius and Breuer worked on the modernist Isokon project in London during the 1930s before eventually settling in the United States. Mies van der Rohe crossed the Atlantic in 1937 and forged a successful career designing high-rise buildings and teaching.

ERICH BRENDEL TABLE Tecta's 2004 reissue of Brendel's design incorporates the original four-flap octagonal top above a shelf and cupboard, raised on a plinth with casters. *1924. W:57¾ in (147 cm).*

The colorway of ash white is one of several choices: others are black, red, or natural ash

BARCELONA OTTOMANS Designed by Mies van der Rohe to accompany his best-known chair, the Barcelona MR90, and originally made by Joseph Müller, their chromed X-frame was derived from the classical *sella curulus*—a Roman magistrate's stool—but given a decidedly modern twist. *1929. W:25 in (63.5 cm).*

MR20 CHAIR Designed by Mies van der Rohe, it has a then-revolutionary cantilevered, chromed tubular steel frame. Here the seat and back are leather, but woven equivalents remain an option. *1926–27. W:21 in (53.5 cm).*

DE STIJL IN THE NETHERLANDS

After the end of World War I, a small band of artists developed an extremely strict template for utopian design that they spread through the journal *De Stijl*, Dutch for "The Style." The goal of De Stijl was to restrict both color and form so much that their compositions included only vertical and horizontal lines and primary colors. Diagonal lines were sometimes permissible. Adherents included the painter Piet Mondrian and the architect Gerrit Rietveld, who also produced furniture to De Stijl principles. The most complete realization of De Stijl is the Rietveld Schröder house in Utrecht. Like the philosophy that underpinned the Bauhaus, De Stijl rejected historicism, making a clean break with the past.

Painted decoration is restricted to a primary color, red, on the chair back

RED-BLUE CHAIR Rietveld's design classic, here reproduced under license by Cassina, is the three-dimensional equivalent of an abstract painting by Piet Mondrian. *1917.*

The oblique angle modifies the tension between vertical and horizontal lines

ZIGZAG CHAIR A stark assertion of function and visual simplicity, incorporating the De Stijl movement's desire for oblique diagonal lines, Gerrit Rietveld's cantilevered, modular chair is structurally complex in its use of dovetail joinery, and nuts and bolts through each of the horizontal, vertical, and oblique panels. *1922.*

LE CORBUSIER

European avant-garde design was not confined to the Bauhaus. Le Corbusier, probably the most influential modernist figure, was born in Switzerland and spent most of his career in France. Le Corbusier was a phenomenon. Largely self-taught—and self-named—he designed his first house at just 18, under his real name, Charles-Edouard Jeanneret. He laid out his manifesto for furniture in his 1925 publication *L'Art Décoratif d'Aujourd-hui* (Decorative Art Today), in which

he argued that furniture designers should create objects that worked like extensions of the human body.

Like Frank Lloyd Wright before him, Le Corbusier was in favor of open-plan living spaces and often designed his housing units with free-standing interior walls that the owner could rearrange at will. Wright, however, was not won over by Le Corbusier's style, describing his Villa Savoye units as "big boxes on sticks." Corbusier's furniture has proved less controversial than his

architecture, providing a model of corporate modernism years ahead of its time. He was influenced by Adolf Loos's polemic *Ornament and Crime*, which linked surface decoration to decadence, dishonesty, and waste.

MACHINE FOR LIVING

Le Corbusier's first forays into furniture design were made in 1928 after he invited Charlotte Perriand to join his studio. Despite having rejected her initial job application with the remark "We don't embroider cushions here," Le Corbusier relied on Perriand to provide him with furniture designs for almost a decade. Aiming to fulfill three distinct briefs, the pair produced three very different chairs—one for conversation, one for sleeping, and one for relaxation—for the Maison la Roche in Paris. The relaxation model, otherwise known as the LC2 *Grand Confort* armchair, demonstrated

LA JAOUL, PARIS Designed by Le Corbusier, the vaulted brick ceiling unites the open-plan living and dining areas, providing a view through to the staircase.

TABLE 1852 Here in square rather than rectangular form, the Le Corbusier/[his cousin] Paul Jeanneret/Charlotte Perriand design has chromed legs and a linoleum-covered wooden top with aluminum edging. *c.1929. H:30¾ in (78 cm).*

Tubular steel recurs as a functional motif in early modernist furniture

The leather upholstery was conceived as black, but is now produced in other colors, including tan and, as here, burgundy

LC2 LOVESEAT Also known as the *Petit Confort*, the prototype was designed by Le Corbusier in 1929, but was not put into production until 1959. This example was made by Cassina under license. *1980s. W:66 in (167.5 cm).*

that functional modernism need not be cold and hard. All three chairs had frames of tubular steel, the material of choice for the early modernists. Parallels with Bauhaus designs of the same period did not end with the use of materials—Perriand remarked of working with Le Corbusier that "the smallest pencil stroke had to...fulfill a need, or respond to a gesture or posture, and to be achieved at mass-production prices."

Harnessing the machine to provide the masses with good design unified the European trendsetters, but Le Corbusier went further, seeing domesticity itself as an extension of industry. In his key work *Vers une Architecture* (Toward One Architecture), he meditated on the beauty of the airplane and car and their compatibility with mass production—the 10 millionth Ford automobile was built in 1924. He concluded that the home must become "a machine for living."

Le Corbusier and Perriand helped found the *Union des Artistes Modernes* (UAM) in Paris in 1929. The group channeled the many streams of leading French design at the time. Like the Bauhaus experiment in Germany, the UAM was committed to promoting unity within the decorative arts and creating prototypes for mass production.

Perriand exhibited work for the movement under her own name. She was foremost in a new generation of female designers that included Eileen Gray, an Irish exile who settled in Paris in 1907. Gray's Nonconformist chair, with its single armrest, is a witty interpretation of the functional rationale of modernism. Like many of her peers, Gray worked mainly in metal but was more sympathetic to surface decoration than most early modernists—she had long been interested in Asian lacquer techniques.

ALVAR AALTO

Avant-garde functionalism influenced designers elsewhere in Europe. One of the greatest was Alvar Aalto, a Finnish architect who began to design furniture in 1925. In deference to his Scandinavian roots, Aalto used bent birchwood rather than steel, finding that it had similar properties. His Tank armchair was the first wooden chair to echo the cantilevered design of Mart Stam's groundbreaking S33 model. Aalto's trademark feature—legs that curve underneath seats and table tops—fused elegance and function.

TEA CART Designed by Alvar Aalto for Artek, the birchwood frame encloses a tile panel top and a wicker basket. *1936. L:35¾ in (91 cm).*

TANK CHAIR Formally known as Easy Chair 400, the iconic cantilevered birchwood frame is in this example upholstered in amber and ivory tweed. *1940s. H:29½ in (74 cm).*

René Herbst was another prominent member of the Union, and a pioneer of the witty adaptation of new industrial and functional materials to furniture design. For the frame of his Sandows chair, he followed the tubular steel standard set by his contemporaries, but chose to make the seat and backrest out of bicycle bungees.

METALLIC CURTAIN An industrial look is evident in Eileen Gray's four-fold design in which geometrically perforated metal panels are enclosed within a similarly black-lacquered metal frame. *1929. H:66 in (168 cm).*

The headrest is adjustable

B306 CHAISE LONGUE Designed by Le Corbusier and Charlotte Perriand in 1928, this day bed is made from chrome-plated tubular steel with rubber stretchers and black leather upholstery. *L:64 in (160 cm).*

SANDOWS CHAIR Designed by René Herbst, this chair has a nickel-plated tubular steel frame slung with a seat and back of bluish-gray, elasticated sprung straps. *1928–30. H:32 in (81.5 cm).*

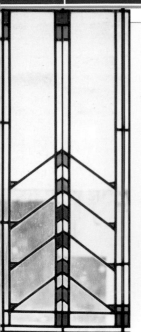

FRANK LLOYD WRIGHT

WRIGHT'S ARCHITECTURAL CAREER SPANNED MORE THAN 60 YEARS. RATHER THAN SEEING THE ROOMS OF A HOUSE AS A SERIES OF BOXES, HE AIMED TO LET SPACE FLOW, INTEGRATING FURNITURE, BUILDING, AND LANDSCAPE.

In 1887, Wright left the University of Wisconsin and went to Chicago to find work at Adler & Sullivan, the best architectural practice in the city. Despite his lack of training, he began to develop and promote his own Prairie House style, which was similar to the Craftsman model of Gustav Stickley and Harvey Ellis.

PRAIRIE HOUSE STYLE

So called because a building should "begin to associate with the ground and become natural to its prairie site," Wright chose materials to make his Prairie House style homes blend into the landscape. Robie House was typically arranged around a central hearth with open-plan interiors fully integrated down to the art glass windows, recessed lighting, and custom cupboards. Wright believed that "every chair must be designed for the building it will be in"—an extension of the Arts and Crafts integrated interior and a precursor of modernism.

Wright based his wooden furniture on Japanese models, having come to the conclusion that "with the exception of the Japanese, wood has been misused and mishandled everywhere." His Barrel chair, designed in 1937 for the Johnson house, displays Japanese influence in its galleried vertical slats and intersecting horizontals. Wright's many variations of his high-backed chair anticipated the strict geometry of Gerrit Rietveld. Unlike Hoffmann, who clung to circular and rectangular forms, Wright was more flexible, incorporating hexagons and octagons into his furniture design.

THE TALIESIN FELLOWSHIP

Work was scarce during the Depression, and Wright, with an outspoken personality and scandalous private life, found few commissions. But young architects flocked to Wright's home after he published his autobiography in 1932. About 30 apprentices lived and worked with him under the Taliesin Fellowship, reinvigorating his career in the process. In 1936, Wright completed designs for Fallingwater—arguably his most famous work. Built directly over a rocky waterfall, horizontal levels of smooth concrete set at different angles are supported by stone verticals. The luxury house fulfills the ideal of living in nature.

The next year Wright made plans for Taliesin West in Arizona, to be a winter base for the Fellowship. One of Wright's most enduring bequests is the Usonian model, a system for designing and building affordable homes that could be adapted for different families. This organic design, while undoubtedly modern, was a far cry from the strict modular Bauhaus standard.

BARREL ARMCHAIR Evolved from a 1904 prototype, it was designed by Frank Lloyd Wright c.1937 with a cherry frame and an upholstered seat, and has been reissued by Cassina since 1986. *H:32 in (81 cm).*

OCCASIONAL TABLE Fashioned in metal with an octagonal top, this is probably a prototype for tables which Frank Lloyd Wright designed for the Biltmore Hotel in Arizona. *c.1926. W:26 in (66 cm).*

EXECUTIVE CHAIR Designed by Frank Lloyd Wright for his only skyscraper, the Price Tower, in Oklahoma, it has an aluminum hexagonal seat and back, raised on a faceted aluminum and wood base. *c.1952. H:36 in (91 cm).*

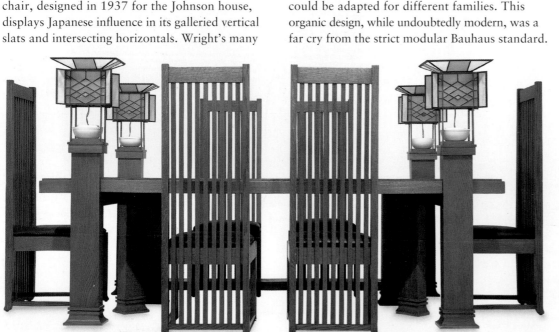

DINING SUITE Incorporating illuminated corner posts, this suite was designed by Frank Lloyd Wright for the dining room at the Robie House, in Chicago. The high slatted chair backs help to keep the dining and living areas distinct. *c.1909. Chair: H:52¼ in (133 cm).*

ROBIE HOUSE The living room displays the Prairie House style open floor plan, dramatic overhangs, stretches of glass, and sweeping horizontal lines that revolutionized 20th-century architecture. The furniture echoes the horizontal emphasis. The house was designed in 1908 and completed in 1910.

CERAMICS

CERAMICS CREATED AT THE FORWARD-LOOKING DESIGN COLLECTIVES OF
EARLY-20TH-CENTURY EUROPE WERE DISTINCT FROM THE STUDIO POTTERY
MOVEMENT, BUT MODERNIST NOVELTY AND FUNCTION PERMEATES THEM ALL.

EUROPEAN MODERNISM

After World War I, Dagobert Peche rather than
Josef Hoffmann became the guiding influence at
the Wiener Werkstätte. From around 1915, Peche
introduced a more playful style to the workshops,
with more color and freer surface decoration.
Ceramics designed by Peche for Wiener Keramik
combine restrained formalism and liberated
experimentation. His colorful use of geometric
decoration coincided with Art Deco,
which was emerging.

The fusion of organic and geometric shapes
happened throughout the early modern period.
The work of Hilda Jesser, who designed ceramics
and glassware for the Wiener Werkstätte, provides
a typical illustration. Her ceramic vase has flared
sides, concave corners, and a fitted lid set beneath
the rim of the vessel, all of which combine to give
a Cubist impression of a ripe fruit on a branch.

Albin Müller, from the Art Nouveau artist's
colony in Darmstadt, came from the same Secession
background as many of the designers allied to the

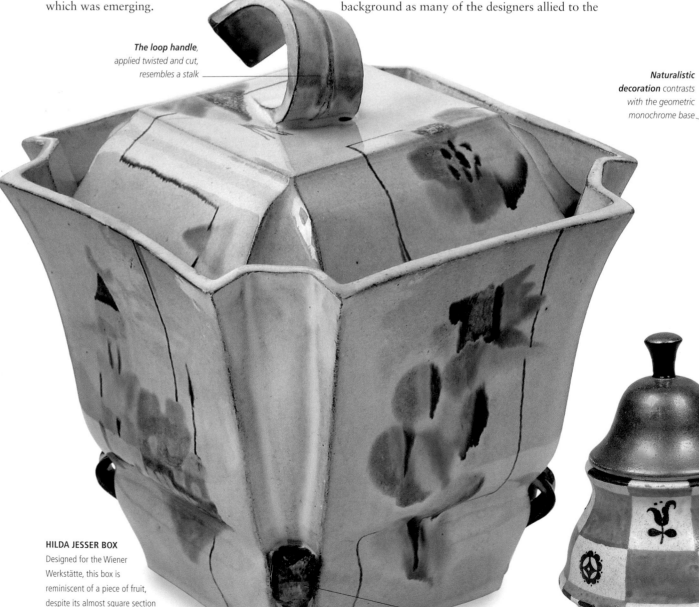

The vase is handpainted
with a geometric pattern

**WIENER WERKSTÄTTE
VASE** Gudrun Baudisch
designed this vase with a
footed ovoid body, asymmetric
handles, and a trumpet-
shaped, flared neck. *c.1920.
H:10 in (25 cm).*

The loop handle,
applied twisted and cut,
resembles a stalk

*Naturalistic
decoration* contrasts
with the geometric
monochrome base

KERAMOS FOOTED VASE Inspired by
Dagobert Peche, the bell-shaped body is
handpainted with a stylized branch and
a geometric pattern on the foot. *1925.
H:8¼ in (21 cm).*

HILDA JESSER BOX
Designed for the Wiener
Werkstätte, this box is
reminiscent of a piece of fruit,
despite its almost square section
and its abstract imagery. *c.1920.
H:7½ in (19 cm).*

Highly glazed applications
mimic droplets of juice

DAGOBERT PECHE BOWL
Of squat, bulbous form under
a bell-shaped cover, the bowl
is handpainted with a checker
pattern and motifs that include
flowers and crowns. *c.1912.
H:4 in (10 cm).*

JUTTA SIKA COFFEE POT
Designed for the Jos. Böck porcelain company in Vienna, the tapering cylindrical body has a circular pattern. The angular handle of both pot and lid is pierced with a hole as a finger grip. *1900–05. H:7 in (18 cm).*

The matching cover has a ball finial

ALBIN MÜLLER LIDDED JAR Made of glazed earthenware by Villeroy & Boch, Müller's design has an octagonal foot. The geometric form is accentuated with vertical bands of blossoms and leaves against a white ground. *c.1912. H:18½ in (46 cm).*

RUSSIAN CONSTRUCTIVISM

Taking their lead from abstract, machine-minded European art movements such as Cubism and Futurism, Russian designers began to reject representational art after the Russian Revolution. Constructivism and Suprematism, founded by Vladimir Tatlin and Kasimir Malevich, respectively, aimed to reflect the dominance of the machine and its triumph over nature. They were among the first to renounce any depiction of natural form, however stylized. Their compositions relied on precisely arranged geometric shapes, sometimes using mathematical tools and formulae. The Soviet establishment commissioned Constructivist artists to create propaganda for the state.

The Suprematists' aim of making Suprematism part of everyday life for the masses came closest to being realized by Nikolao Suetin, a pupil of Malevich, who worked at the State Porcelain Factory from 1923 to 1924. His geometric designs continued to be made into the 1930s. However, a proportion was sold abroad to bring in much-needed foreign currency.

Wiener Werkstätte. He created ceramic forms that went well beyond Art Nouveau, highly stylized like the art botany of Christopher Dresser.

THE BAUHAUS

The pottery workshop at the Bauhaus was separated from the rest of the school both physically and ideologically. The studios were based at Dornburg an der Saale, just outside Weimar, under the direction of Gerhard Marcks. His idea of the school as a forum for free experiment and learning sometimes put him at odds with other Bauhaus masters such as Walter Gropius, who saw the school as a powerhouse of industrial design.

Ceramics students trained under master potter Max Krehan, who instilled in them the local vernacular pottery tradition of Thuringia. Once they were adept at this, they could experiment with freely modeled sculptural receptacles. Krehan's star students included Otto Lindig, who became master of the school in 1924, and Theodor Bogler, who developed a modular system for designing ceramics entirely in tune with avant-garde philosophy. Bogler devised teapots that could be constructed from a series of basic elements.

GERMAN FACTORIES

Despite these efforts to comply with industrial needs, attempts by Bauhaus ceramicists to forge links with German factories were only moderately successful. Big-name firms such as KPM Berlin and Velten-Vordamm did take on some Bauhaus designs, but they were reluctant to risk investing heavily in anything too new.

The Bauhaus had to leave Weimar in 1925, and the ceramics studios did not survive the move to Dessau but it continued to influence ceramic design—former pupils of the pottery school took jobs within Germany's mainstream ceramic industry and founded their own studio potteries. Walter Gropius went on to design one of the most famous modernist ceramics—his sleek and functional TAC1 teapot is still made by Rosenthal today.

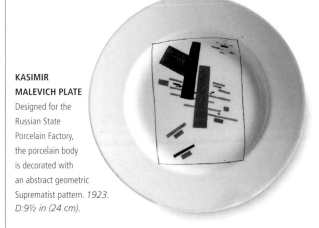

KASIMIR MALEVICH PLATE Designed for the Russian State Porcelain Factory, the porcelain body is decorated with an abstract geometric Suprematist pattern. *1923. D:9½ in (24 cm).*

STONEWARE VASE This vase, designed by J. K. Liehm at the Herrsching Workshops near Munich, has a glazed pattern of dense tendrils in green and black on a slightly crackled white glazed ground. *1912. H:5¾ in (14 cm).*

R. HANKE VASE Designed by Henry van de Velde and made in Höhr, the vase has two handles and is decorated with a crystalline glaze. *c.1902. H:7 in (17.5 cm).*

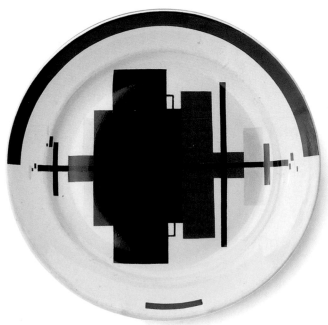

ILJA TSCHASCHNIK PLATE The white-glazed earthenware ground is decorated with Tschaschnik's Constructivist geometric pattern. *1924. D:13½ in (34 cm).*

THE BIRTH OF STUDIO POTTERY

One of the most enduring legacies of the Arts and Crafts movement and its veneration of the solitary artisan was the beginning of studio pottery. The pioneering approach taken by figures such as George Ohr and Auguste Delaherche was to merge form and decoration—aspects of the trade that factory ceramicists had traditionally separated.

Often called the father of studio pottery, Bernard Leach was inspired by the raku wares used in the Japanese tea ceremony. His link with Japan started when he spent part of his childhood with his grandparents, who were teachers in Kyoto. It was while working as a teacher in Japan that Leach became fascinated by traditional raku ceramics. Captivated by the transformations wrought by the heat in the kiln, Leach looked for a tutor and was taken on by the raku master Ogata Kenzan VI. It was only after his mentor's death in 1920 that Leach returned to England, accompanied by his friend Shoji Hamada.

Hamada familiarized himself with aspects of the English ceramic tradition such as slipware by studying exhibits at the British Museum. He settled with Leach in Cornwall, where they founded the St. Ives pottery and built the first wood-fired climbing (stepped) kiln in Europe. Burning wood creates fly ash in the kiln, helping to produce the delicately textured glazes for which Leach's work is known. As well as Asian methods, Leach worked with Western techniques such as salt glaze and slip decoration. In *A Potter's Book*, published in 1945, Leach discussed his methods in detail. He set forth his thoughts on proportion, decoration, and function, expressing among other things a very

BERNARD LEACH BOTTLE Japanese influence is evident in the shape of Leach's design. A flat-sided vessel with a narrow waisted neck and a spreading oval foot, it is also decorated with Japanese-style calligraphy against a two-tone checker-pattern ground. *c.1923. H:7¾ in (19.5 cm).*

The distinctive glaze is Leach's emulation of a traditional Japanese rust-black temmoku

BERNARD LEACH CHARGER
Made in stoneware, its center was hand-painted by Leach with impressionistic zodiac imagery: the Gemini twins rendered in the temmoku glaze also applied as the overall finish. *c.1927. D:15 in (38 cm).*

SHOJI HAMADA BOWL Thrown by Hamada at Bernard Leach's studio in St. Ives, the footed stoneware bowl is finished with a traditional Japanese iron temmoku glaze, which runs from black to a rusty hue where it thins. *1920–23. D:6 in (15 cm).*

modern fondness for minimalism: "Overstatement is worse than understatement."

LEACH'S DISCIPLES

With Leach's growing reputation as a master of his art, the St. Ives pottery attracted an entire generation of studio potters. Michael Cardew, Leach's first student, left to pursue a career crafting traditional slipware. Katharine Pleydell-Bouverie and Norah Braden, both educated at the Central School of Arts and Crafts, met while working for Leach at the St. Ives pottery in 1925. Inspired by Leach's methods, Pleydell-Bouverie built a wood-fired kiln on her family's estate at Coleshill. Braden joined her in 1928, and they set about experimenting with the dozens of varieties of wood on the estate, each of which produced subtly different glaze effects when burned in the kiln.

Their partnership, which lasted until 1936, produced a range of simple thrown vessels in a gamut of glazes. As a woman of independent means, Pleydell-Bouverie was able to keep the cost of her pottery low, making it accessible to a wide audience.

LUCIE RIE

Leach also influenced Lucie Rie's work, persuading her to extend her craft to include stoneware and porcelain as well as earthenware. Rie was born in Vienna and studied at the Kunstgewerbeschule, the art school associated with the Wiener Werkstätte. She settled in London in 1938 and began to make ceramic buttons for the Bimini Glass and Jewellery Workshop.

KEITH MURRAY

In 1933, the John Lewis department store exhibited a new range of Wedgwood ceramics that thrust their designer, Keith Murray, who was an architect from New Zealand, into the international spotlight. At a time when many leading ceramicists were turning out Art Deco designs—dismissed by Le Corbusier as "the final spasm of a predictable death"—Murray was conspicuous in his restraint. His plain forms were minimally adorned, often with little more than a series of lathe-turned grooves interrupting an otherwise perfectly smooth surface. The matte glazes developed for Murray by Norman Wilson were a perfect match for the uncluttered lines of his pots.

VASE AND BOWL With their lathe-turned ribbed and fluted decoration, these pieces are typical of the elegant, machinelike, earthenware forms Keith Murray designed for Wedgwood. *Early 1930s. Vase: H:7½ in (19 cm); Bowl: D:13¾ in (35 cm).*

After the war, she resumed her experiments with art pottery, drawing on arenas as diverse as Scandinavian modernism, Asian ceramics, and the British decorative tradition. Infused with her bold spirit, Rie's work appears less derivative and more modern than Leach's pottery. It is dominated by functional forms such as stem bowls and bottles and has a strong architectural presence. Rie's glaze work is extremely varied, ranging from pitted volcanic glazes to intricate sgraffito filigree.

From the late 1940s she worked with Hans Coper, who became a partner in her studio. Coper would often shape his pots by hand after throwing the basic form on a wheel. His work is more sculptural and less functional than Rie's.

The rise of art pottery to the status of fine art was a slow process, gradually achieved through the work of key figures such as Leach. William Staite Murray, another British studio potter who made large vases with brush-painted decoration, put pottery on a par with sculpture and painting. He began to title his works in 1925 and stage annual exhibitions in conjunction with modern painters. Along with the high prices he charged, this tactic encouraged the art establishment to take notice of studio pottery.

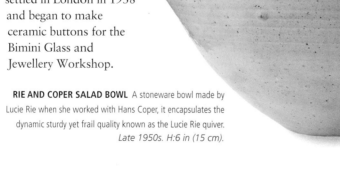

RIE AND COPER SALAD BOWL A stoneware bowl made by Lucie Rie when she worked with Hans Coper, it encapsulates the dynamic sturdy yet frail quality known as the Lucie Rie quiver. *Late 1950s. H:6 in (15 cm).*

LUCIE RIE SAUCE BOAT AND BOWL Both stoneware vessels display a favorite Rie finish: bleeding and/or dripping bands of manganese or copper oxide glaze contrasted against a white tin glaze ground. *1950s. Sauce boat: L:8 in (20.25 cm); Bowl: D:5 in (12.75 cm).*

GLASS AND LAMPS

GLASSMAKERS IN BOHEMIA TRADITIONALLY FOLLOWED THE LATEST TRENDS FROM THE FASHIONABLE CITY OF VIENNA. THEY WERE QUICK TO ADOPT THE NEW MODERN STYLE IN THE EARLY 20TH CENTURY.

GLASS AND LAMPS

Once again the Glasgow Four acted as a catalyst. While Josef Hoffmann's 1899 Ariel vase rests in a modern frame, the glass component itself is organic, with languorous curves more a product of the Secessionist Art Nouveau style than anything else. The elongated stems and straight decoration of Otto Prutscher's 1907 wine glasses, by comparison, betray the unmistakable influence of the Glasgow School. Bohemian factories excelled at cutting glass, although they were used in naturalistic or jewel-like designs rather than grids and other geometric structures. Josef Hoffmann continued a long-standing association with Loetz in the years leading up to World War I, but his designs changed dramatically. His experiments with color led him to combine milky white opaque glass with contrasting red, blue, or pink. In shape, Hoffmann's glass moved toward the formalism of the Constructivists, incorporating disks, cylinders, and rods.

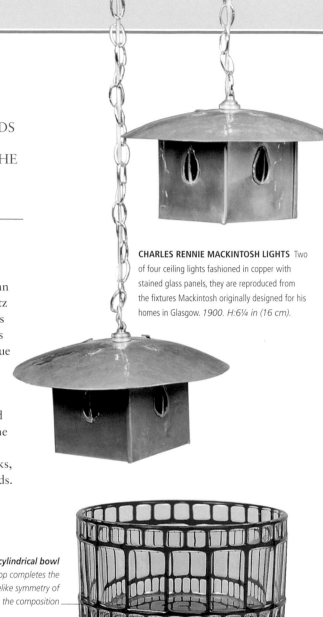

CHARLES RENNIE MACKINTOSH LIGHTS Two of four ceiling lights fashioned in copper with stained glass panels, they are reproduced from the fixtures Mackintosh originally designed for his homes in Glasgow. *1900. H:6¼ in (16 cm).*

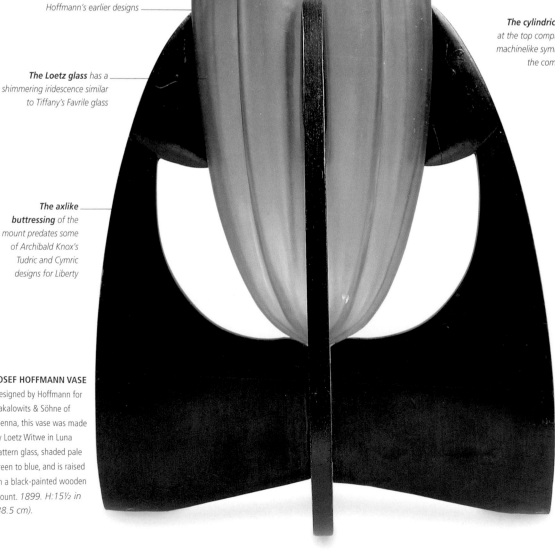

Gadrooning with vegetal curves is a recurring motif in Hoffmann's earlier designs

The Loetz glass has a shimmering iridescence similar to Tiffany's Favrile glass

The axlike buttressing of the mount predates some of Archibald Knox's Tudric and Cymric designs for Liberty

JOSEF HOFFMANN VASE
Designed by Hoffmann for Bakalowits & Söhne of Vienna, this vase was made by Loetz Witwe in Luna pattern glass, shaded pale green to blue, and is raised on a black-painted wooden mount. *1899. H:15½ in (38.5 cm).*

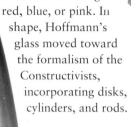

The cylindrical bowl at the top completes the machinelike symmetry of the composition

Cut checker-pattern decoration reinforces the geometric form

OTTO PRUTSCHER GLASS
Commissioned by Bakalowits & Söhne, Prutscher's design was manufactured by Meyr's Neffe in blue-on-clear overlaid glass with geometrical cut decoration. *1907-12. H:8½ in (21 cm).*

BAUHAUS CLASSICS

The Wiener Werkstätte look softened with the arrival of Dagobert Peche after World War I, and the modernist cause was championed by avant-garde designers elsewhere, notably at the Bauhaus. Of all its departments, the metal workshop came closest to fulfilling Walter Gropius's original vision by becoming a "laboratory of modernity" through its association with lighting manufacturer Körting & Mathiesen.

One of the first lamp designs produced by the school was the 1924 MT8 table lamp by Wilhelm Wagenfeld and Carl Jucker. It was an instant classic and remains in production to this day. Its form has been pared down to the bare essentials of a disk base, cylindrical shaft, and domed shade. Made from glass and metal, it presages the favored materials of International Style architects.

The director of the metal workshop at this time was Christian Dell, credited with designing the basic form of the modern desk lamp. Originally trained as a silversmith, Dell went on to design iconic lamps for large German companies throughout the 1930s and 1940s.

Dell left the Bauhaus in 1925, but the metalwork program continued unabated. After the move to Dessau in 1925, Bauhaus students designed and manufactured all of the light fixtures for Gropius's new building in the improved metal shop. In 1928, the start of a working relationship between the Bauhaus and Körting & Mathiesen's Kandem lighting brand represented the pinnacle of the school's cooperation with industry. Tens of thousands of Bauhaus-designed Kandem lighting units had been sold by 1930, and many models are still popular into the 21st century. Marianne

TABLE LAMP Employing a near-hemispherical, multi-rotational shade, this lamp is one of many eminently functional designs by Christian Dell, who was master of the metal workshop at the Bauhaus Weimer from 1922 to 1925. *H:17 in (43 cm).*

TABLE LAMP Designed by Marianne Brandt and Hin Bredendieck for Kandem, this lamp was made by Körting & Mathiesen with a hemispherical, enameled shade and a curved steel stem. The foot is pressed glass, but other versions had a steel foot. *c.1928. H:18½ in (47 cm).*

Brandt and Hin Bredendieck, among others, worked alongside Kandem technicians to ensure that the designs were in keeping with Bauhaus principles and suitable for factories.

STUDIO GLASS IN FRANCE

Originally a Fauve painter, Maurice Marinot reinvigorated French glass design throughout the 1920s and 1930s. He started by decorating blown glass with enamels. Later, he taught himself to blow glass, and his interest shifted to bringing out the decorative possibilities of the material itself. He experimented with air bubbles and metals, creating streaks, veins, and trails, crackling and bubbling. He inspired sculptor Henri Navarre to mold vases with internal decoration sandwiched between two layers of glass.

While Marinot's glass was highly acclaimed at the 1925 Paris International Exhibition, it was

Scandinavian glass that starred at the 1937 Paris Exhibition. Inspired by the peasant dress of his native Finland, Alvar Aalto designed the prize-winning Savoy vase for Karhula-Iittala glassworks in 1936. It is still made today.

MOSER'S LOETZ DESIGNS

Like Josef Hoffmann, Koloman Moser designed glassware for Loetz. His contributions, including a series of ten electric lamps, show the influence of Christopher Dresser in their bulbous organic forms with geometric components.

Moser's original sketches for these lamps suggest more restrained decoration than on the finished article, indicating that Loetz may have altered his submissions to conform to their house style.

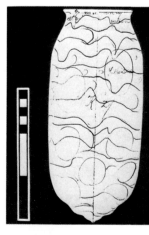

KOLOMAN MOSER DESIGN Hanging from a brass mount, this lamp was made by Loetz Witwe from Moser's drawing, in clear and colored iridescent glass with a mottled and striated pattern. *1900. L:9½ in (24.5 cm).*

MAURICE MARINOT BOTTLE Of flattened oval form, the bottle has a typically imaginative, swirling marblelike pattern in tones of gray, green, and black, with white enameling to the rim. *1910-20. H:6¼ in (16 cm).*

ALVAR AALTO SAVOY VASE Made by Karhula-Iittala, Aalto's design is of undulating, slightly flared free-form section. This example is mold-blown in green tinted glass. *c.1936. H:6 in (15.25 cm).*

METALWARE

NATURALLY LINKED TO MACHINES, METAL WAS THE IDEAL VEHICLE FOR
MODERNISM. FUNCTIONAL DESIGNS WITH LITTLE DECORATION ENABLED
DESIGNERS TO SHOW A RESPECT FOR THEIR RAW MATERIAL.

MAN OR MACHINE

After Christopher Dresser's extraordinary experiments in the late 19th century (*see p.242*), the earliest metalware designers to show modernist tendencies were linked to Charles Rennie Mackintosh in Glasgow and Josef Hoffmann in Vienna. Mackintosh designed flatware to go with his tea room interiors in Glasgow. Plain and simple, his cutlery often has trefoil terminals, slender stems, and elongated tines, blades, or bowls. Hoffmann uses the same ball motif on his *Sitzmaschine* chair for his metalware.

Koloman Moser of the Wiener Werkstätte took the length and geometric symmetry of the Glasgow School and fused them with architectural innovations in the United States. The result was polished metal skyscraper vases, inspired by structures such as the Flatiron Building in Manhattan, New York.

Work at the metal studios of the Wiener Werkstätte was handcrafted to look as if it was machine-made—the opposite of what many other firms were doing with the fashionable Craftsman look. Its symmetry and simple details emphasized balanced proportions,

WIENER WERKSTÄTTE VASE
Designed in silver by Koloman Moser, its skyscraper-like body, pierced on four sides with bands of square apertures, is typical of Moser's vertical, architectural forms and geometric pattern decoration. *1905. H:8 in (20.25 cm).*

and indicated how much this new breed of designers venerated the machine.

MARIANNE BRANDT

The work of Marianne Brandt is similar to that of Christopher Dresser. In 1924 she became the first woman to enroll at the metal workshop of the Bauhaus. Although initially sidelined by her male colleagues, she instantly took to the medium. Items she crafted in her first year are still classics today. She was influenced by her Hungarian tutor László Moholy-Nagy, who was an enthusiast of the Constructivist movement.

Among Brandt's iconic designs is her functional MT49 teapot—so famous that it has appeared on a postage stamp in Germany. Although intended as an archetype for mass production, fewer than ten were ever made. When the Italian designer Alberto Alessi revived selected designs from the Bauhaus archive, he reluctantly rejected Brandt's

C. R. MACKINTOSH CUTLERY The knife, fork, and spoon are from an 18-piece suite of electroplated cutlery designed for Miss Cranston's Tea Rooms in Glasgow. Their trefoil terminals may echo Gothic ornament, but their overall clean, uncluttered lines preempt modernism. *c.1905. Knife: H: 8 in (22.5 cm).*

teapot as, even with contemporary production technology, it presented too many problems. A common misconception among members of the Bauhaus was that simple, geometric shapes were bound to be suited to factory production. Like metalware made at the Wiener Werkstätte, much

MARIANNE BRANDT COASTER HOLDERS
Made by Ruppelwerk, these are good examples of Brandt's enameled metal designs—in this case, one of the pair is enameled in off-white with a red trim, the other in green with a black trim. *c.1930. D:5 in (13 cm).*

Enameled metal comes in different colorways

PEWTER CANDLESTICKS Designed by Joseph Maria Olbrich for the German firm Metallwarenfabrik Eduard Hueck, the pair of candlesticks have wide, flared bases and Art Nouveau–style decoration. They are marked with the artist's initials. *c.1901. H:14 in (36 cm).*

The curving decoration is in low relief

The flared bases balance the candle holders at the top

JAN EISENLOEFFEL TEA SERVICE Made by Sneltjes of Haarlem, Eisenloeffel's brass, wicker, and glass composition has functional features such as long, nondrip spouts and an insulating handle. The form is inspired by European and Japanese designs. *c.1905. D:12 in (30 cm).*

An angled neck gives the composition an organic harmony

PETER BEHRENS KETTLE This hammered-brass electric kettle has a canework handle. Designed for AEG, it is a groundbreaking example of individualized mass production in the burgeoning electrical appliance industry. *1909. H:8½ in (21.5 cm).*

The insulator handle is in the more traditional ebony, rather than an early plastic such as Bakelite

of the Bauhaus metal shop's output was custom craftsmanship masquerading as industrial design. Brandt left the Bauhaus in 1929 and was employed by Ruppelwerk. In her three years with the firm, she designed a range of mass-produced functional metalware, including ashtrays and napkin holders.

Some architects in Germany provided competition as well as inspiration. Peter Behrens, a hugely influential planner within the modern movement, designed a range of hammered-metal electric and traditional kettles.

DUTCH DESIGNERS

The architect H. P. Berlage preached the honest use of materials and inspired a purity of form among modernist Dutch designers, especially Frans Zwollo and Jan Eisenloeffel. Zwollo specialized in furniture mounts with an Asian touch. Eisenloeffel's sleek and practical tea sets made a major contribution to Dutch modernism and he established a workshop for handcrafted silver services and machine-made copper sets.

SCANDINAVIAN SILVER

While Norway made a name for itself with *plique-a-jour* enamelwork, Danish silversmiths dominated the modernist Scandinavian scene. Mogens Ballin handmade metalware and jewelry decorated with abstract organic shapes. In 1901 Georg Jensen went to work for him. The sleek silverware produced by Jensen generally owes more to the flowing lines of Art Nouveau than the functional demands of modernism. But from 1906 his colleague Johan Rohde designed silver that helped propel Jensen's workshop into the international spotlight. Some of it was so modernist that it was pulled from production until consumer taste caught up.

GEORG JENSEN WATER JUG The smooth, baluster-shaped silver body and bowlike handle with an ebony insulator fuse form and function. Design No. 432 by Johan Rohde was far ahead of its time. *c.1925. H:8¾ in (22.5 cm).*

TEXTILES

IN THE EARLY 20TH CENTURY FORWARD-THINKING DESIGNERS

CHALLENGED TRADITIONAL NATURALISTIC IMAGERY ON TEXTILES

WITH THEIR STYLIZED MOTIFS AND GEOMETRIC PATTERNS.

JULIUS ZIMPEL SILK Designed by Zimpel for the Wiener Werkstätte (and printed WW in the selvage), Zimpel's Bahia pattern comprises polychrome, interlocked rectangular forms, and is characteristic of his machinelike compositions. *1925. L:29 in (73.5 cm).*

GLASGOW SCHOOL TEXTILES

At the Glasgow School of Art, Jessie Newbery, the wife of the principal, began offering embroidery classes in 1894. Since many of her students were young beginners, intending to become teachers themselves, Newbery favored inexpensive materials and easier techniques like appliqué. *Educational Needlecraft*, the popular book she co-authored with Margaret Swanson in 1911, demonstrated new ways of teaching embroidery as a means of self-expression.

Newbery's embroideries were characterized by simplified Art Nouveau motifs. Her influence can be seen in several of her ex-students' textile designs including Jessie Marion King and the McDonald sisters, Frances and Margaret. In 1902 Margaret contributed embroidered hangings, with elongated figures and geometric components, to her husband Charles Rennie Mackintosh's booth at the Turin Exhibition and his decoration schemes for the Willow Tea Rooms and Hill House in Glasgow.

WIENER WERKSTÄTTE

The textile division was the most successful part of Austria's Wiener Werkstätte. It exerted a major influence on textile design over the course of a quarter century, on everything from table linens

and embroidery to lace and even clothing. Some were made by hand; others were manufactured. More than 80 designers worked on textiles. Best known are Josef Hoffmann, Maria Strauss-Likarz, Mathilde Flögl, Max Snischek, Koloman Moser, Dagobert Peche, Carl Otto Czescheka, Bertold Löffler, and Kitty and Felice Rix.

Early Wiener Werkstätte textiles and rugs feature uniform rows of geometric motifs or linear

DAGOBERT PECHE SILK Peche's Wiener Werkstätte Liszt pattern is a now-iconic combination of stylized organic and geometric imagery, in which formalized flowerheads are compartmentalized within vertical ropelike and plain horizontal borders. *1911–13. L:17¾ in (101.5 cm).*

JOSEF HOFFMANN COTTON The *Luchs* (Lynx) pattern comprises stylized, wreathlike plant forms with triple leaf or petal centers, joined by interlaced scrolling stems to form an overall geometric pattern, and is printed in black on a parchment-colored ground. *1910–12. L:37 in (94 cm).*

forms—mostly printed in black on white. They introduced stylized floral patterns inspired by folk art around 1910, and by the 1920s their textiles had become increasingly colorful and capricious.

OMEGA WORKSHOPS

Captivated by French post-Impressionist art, English art critic Roger Fry and artists Duncan Grant and Vanessa Bell founded the Omega Workshops in 1913, to create home products that reflected this bold new way of painting. They painted plain furniture, pottery, and fabrics by hand, as if they were blank canvases, their work characterized by improvisation and spontaneity. Many of their colorful, striking designs feature abstract forms outlined in black for definition.

EILEEN GRAY

Eileen Gray, an Irish-born designer who worked in Paris, used rugs decorated with striking angular patterns to offset the radical minimalism of her interior designs. Many of Gray's rugs were made for her at a studio directed by Evelyn Wyld. She also produced furnishing fabrics. Originally, she designed on commission for clients' homes. However, Gray began creating limited-edition rugs for the shop she opened in 1922.

THE BAUHAUS

Until it was closed by the Nazis in 1933, Germany's revolutionary Bauhaus Art School promoted simple, unadorned designs for mass

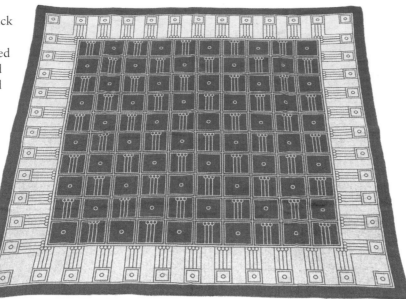

OTTO PRUTSCHER TABLECLOTH Made in linen by Herrburger & Rhomberg of Austria, and distributed by the Wiener Werkstätte, the repeat geometric motifs recall the ornament on a Classical frieze. *c.1919. Sq:52½ in (131 cm).*

GUSTAY KALHAMMER FABRIC Printed as cotton dress fabric, Kalhammer's Schönau design for the Wiener Werkstätte is a polychrome riot of stylized flowers against an equally abstracted foliate ground. *1910–12. W:46 in (117 cm).*

manufacturing. Ironically, few Bauhaus designs were actually put into production—they were considered too radical at the time. From 1926 to 1931, under the direction of weaver Gunta Stadler-Stölzl, the textile workshop was one of the few Bauhaus departments to take design prototypes through to mass production on a regular basis.

The teaching of abstract artist Paul Klee, a Bauhaus tutor, greatly influenced Bauhaus textile design, which often featured geometric forms and vivid color contrasts. There was an emphasis on color, texture, and tactility. Decorative effects were frequently integral to the fabric weave rather than printed on it. The careers of Stadler-Stölzl and other designers associated with the Bauhaus, like weaver Anni Albers, went on to flourish following World War II. The Bauhaus had a marked impact on textile design for the next 30 years.

BAUHAUS FABRIC Printed on cotton and rayon, the unattributed Bauhaus pattern is abstract-geometric with a pronounced three-dimensional quality. It comprises a diagonal repeat of quadrant forms in shades of gold and brown. *1920s. L:90¾ in (227 cm).*

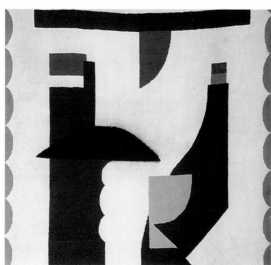

EILEEN GRAY WOOLEN RUG The central abstract-figural pattern is entitled Solidadi: Nude/Torso, and is woven in gray, brown, and black on a cream ground, and set within gray, repeat crescent borders. *Late 1920s. L:125 in (312.5 cm).*

GLASGOW SCHOOL DESIGN This watercolor design for a batik is by Jessie M. King. The repeated stylized fuchsia blossoms give a sense of movement. *H:10½ in (26 cm).*

ART DECO
1920–1940

STYLISH MODERNITY

FOR A STYLE SO CLOSELY ASSOCIATED WITH THE 1920s AND 1930s, IT IS SURPRISING THAT THE NAME "ART DECO" WAS USED FOR THE FIRST TIME ONLY IN 1966. IN THAT YEAR, AN EXHIBITION CALLED *LES ANNÉES "25": ART DÉCO/BAUHAUS/STIJL/ESPRIT NOUVEAU* WAS HELD IN FRANCE.

THE INTERWAR YEARS

The 1966 exhibition distinguished French decorative arts of the 1910s and 1920s from other modernist styles such as Bauhaus and De Stijl. Two years later, the British design historian Bevis Hillier published *Art Deco of the 20s and 30s*, defining Art Deco as "an assertively modern style, developing in the 1920s and reaching its high point in the 1930s...a Classical style in that, like Neoclassicism but unlike Rococo or Art Nouveau, it ran to symmetry rather than asymmetry, and to the rectilinear rather than the curvilinear; it responds to the demands of the machine and of new materials...[and] the requirements of mass production."

The ending in 1918 of the Great War, as World War I was known at the time, led to profound changes in society. The war had been so lengthy, and so costly in human life and physical, social, and economic destruction, that people were determined the world must never again go to war. There was also a belief that it should be possible to construct a new, better world out of the ruins of the old. So the war and its immediate aftermath represented a break from the failed past and a move into modernity, into the future.

Art Deco neatly spans the end of World War I in 1918 and the start of World War II in 1939. It began in the tumult of revolution in Russia and defeat in Germany and Austria-Hungary, continued through the rise of fascism in Italy and the worldwide Great Depression of the 1930s, and ended with Nazism in Europe and totalitarianism and militarism in Japan and elsewhere.

BERGÈRE This chair by Paul Follot has a ribbed, upholstered, arched back and ebonized, fluted, tapering feet, which are typical of his elegant reinterpretation of 18th-century Classicism. *c.1920. H:32 in (81.5 cm)*.

But Art Deco also spanned an age of social and economic advance, in which women received the vote in many countries and some of the old political and economic inequalities were removed. For the first time ever, working people had leisure time, and the money to enjoy it, while light industries mass-producing cheap domestic appliances such as telephones, radios, and electric irons transformed daily life. This was the age of the flapper and the Hollywood movie, of the skyscraper and the luxury ocean liner, the cheap car, and, in Germany, the *Autobahn* or specially built freeway.

CHRYSLER BUILDING Architect William Van Alen designed the New York skyscraper in stainless steel with automobile-derived ornamental details. Completed in 1930, it was the world's tallest manmade structure at the time.

PERFUME BOTTLE Ancient Egypt was one of the inspirations of Art Deco. This English glass perfume bottle has a silver stopper in the style of an Egyptian sarcophagus head. *H:6½ in (16.5 cm)*.

THE INFLUENCE OF ART DECO

Art Deco reflected all these changes in society. It was essentially a pragmatic rather than a utopian style: it had no belief in the redemptive value of art, as did the designers of the Arts and Craft movement or Art Nouveau, or indeed the modernists. It was also increasingly democratic and popular, delivering high-quality, often mass-produced artifacts at affordable prices, even if it did have strong associations with high fashion and elite tastes.

Art Deco drew on a range of influences. Historic European styles, the pictorial inventions of contemporary avant-garde art, and the urban imagery of the machine age combined to form the mature style. So did a romantic fascination with ancient Egypt and pre-Columbian Meso-America, as well as the arts of Africa and Asia and a vogue for the exotic or *l'art nègre*, as personified by the dancer Josephine Baker.

Art Deco's influence on the modern world was immense, affecting the design of skyscrapers and movie theaters, trains and cars, furniture and domestic appliances, silverware and jewelry, book design and typography, posters and postage stamps.

DAILY EXPRESS NEWSPAPER'S ENTRANCE HALL Designed by Robert Atkinson, the former London offices of the newspaper are modernist on the outside and Art Deco on the inside, with battered gold and silver flowing over exploding geometric shapes.

AN INTERNATIONAL STYLE

In some parts of the world Art Deco was largely associated with European elites: the princely courts in India; the Anglo-American business community in Shanghai; and the white elite of South Africa. But it reached a mass audience through the 1925 *Exposition Internationale des Arts Décoratifs et Industriels Modernes* in Paris, an international exhibition attended by over 16 million people.

From here it spread to the United States where, later, manufacturers affected by the Depression developed an innovative style known as streamlining. They saved money by producing contoured forms that best lent themselves to mass-production processes using new, cheap materials such as plastics, Bakelite, aluminum, and chrome. The style transformed small towns all over Depression America, reshaped the cities of Latin America, and finally achieved worldwide success through Hollywood movies.

GLASS VASE The geometric pattern on this Schneider vase is acid-etched. The contrasting black pedestal base is signed "Le Verre Français." *c.1925. H:9 in (23 cm).*

ELEMENTS OF STYLE

MANY PEOPLE CONSIDER Art Deco to be the first truly international design movement—and with good reason. Not only did Art Deco affect design on every continent, it also drew on inspiration and ideas from around the globe. Influences range from Classical antiquity and African sculpture to Aztec ziggurats and new technology. Designers used an eclectic range of exotic materials—from rare ebony to new, inexpensive plastics.

H. G. RICHARDSON VASE
GEOMETRIC
Many Art Deco designers wanted to create a style stripped of all historic references and naturalistic ornament. A design vocabulary based on nonrepresentational motifs, clean lines, and pure geometric forms is more typical of later Art Deco.

CLUTCH BAG IN THE STYLE OF SONIA DELAUNAY
CUBISM
The 20th-century abstract art style Cubism was developed in the first decade of the 1900s by artists such as Pablo Picasso and Georges Braque. By the mid-1920s progressive design incorporated characteristics of Cubism such as distortion, faceted forms, and geometric arrangements.

ARGY-ROUSSEAU *PÂTE-DE-VERRE SCARABÉES* VASE
EGYPT
The 1922 discovery of Tutankhamun's tomb by archaeologist Howard Carter sparked off a taste for Egyptian designs. Ancient Egyptian-style images of pharaohs, eagles, and scarabs, as well as hieroglyphs, appeared on everything from jewelry to movie theater walls. The craze had largely died out by the late 1920s.

RAYMOND SUBES CONSOLE TABLE
JAZZ
In the 1920s and 1930s, the fast-paced sound of jazz swept young people around the globe on to the dance floor. Portraits of jazz performers such as Josephine Baker symbolized the good times. Designers took the swinging tempo of the genre and translated it into rhythmic linear motifs and bold color harmonies.

CLARICE CLIFF CIRCULAR CHARGER
SUNBURST
From architecture to ceramics, there are countless variations on the sunburst in 1920s and 1930s design. This classic Art Deco motif—especially in bright gold or glowing reds, oranges, and yellows—radiates warmth and energy. The sunburst expresses the excitement of the modern age and optimism for the future.

FIRESCREEN ATTRIBUTED TO EDGAR BRANDT
FLOWERING DESIGN
Colorful, exuberant, and semi-naturalistic floral imagery is mainly associated with early Art Deco design. Motifs such as garlands, swags, and baskets of blossoms, which harked back to the 18th century, had a stylized twist. Designers were particularly fond of roses, hollyhocks, palms, ferns, and orange trees.

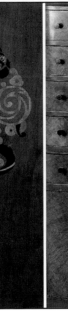

JEAN MAYODON OVOID VASE

ANCIENT GREEK AND ROMAN ART

The elegant poses and muscular proportions of Classical figures from ancient Greek and Roman art appealed to Art Deco designers, who also freely imitated and applied Classical ornaments such as swags. They revived and reworked sculptural facades of buildings and adapted imagery from Classical mythology.

GOLDSCHEIDER FIGURINE BY STEFAN DAKON

WOMEN

In Art Deco design, women are more animated than their languid Art Nouveau counterparts, reflecting their growing independence after World War I. They are seen on the go, dancing, and participating in sports—their physiques gamine and supple, their hair and skirts fashionably short.

MAURICE DUFRÊNE MAHOGANY DRESSING TABLE

INLAYS

The Art Deco love of fine craftsmanship and exotic materials is embodied in inlaid furniture decoration. Designers composed floral, figurative, and geometric patterns in contrasting veneers of rare woods like ebony, mahogany, and satinwood, or materials like mother-of-pearl, ivory, and shagreen, a type of sharkskin.

LÉON JALLOT SECRETAIRE

SLEEK DESIGN

Clean, uncluttered lines are a common design theme throughout the Art Deco era. By the 1930s the Classicism popular in the previous decade gave way to streamlined, curving forms. Most typical of American Art Deco, streamlining was a feature of industrially produced technology, as well as traditional homeware.

KARL HAGENAUER-DESIGNED MASK

AFRICAN INFLUENCE

African art had a powerful effect on artists and designers in the early 20th century. The features of tribal masks and ancestral figures influenced the representation of both faces and people, and there was an increase in the use of exotic African materials such as ivory, Macassar ebony, and leopard skin.

DUNHILL ALUMINUM HUMIDOR

MACHINE AGE

Art Deco designers drew inspiration from contemporary urban life and modern industry and embraced new materials such as plastic, tubular steel, and plywood. They seized on the dynamism of new technology and streamlined features of the automobile, airplane, and ocean liner to produce glamorous motifs.

FRENCH BRASS VASE

STEPPED OR ARCHITECTURAL FORMS

The stepped forms and solid blocks characteristic of some Art Deco design are derived from the temples and pyramids of the Aztecs, Incas, and other ancient American cultures. Art Deco designers also borrowed imagery such as lightning flashes, sun rays, and zigzags from these ancient sources.

FRENCH PRESSED-AMETHYST GLASS VASE

STYLIZED ANIMALS

Exotic beasts popular in the Art Deco era included elephants, parrots, zebras, and panthers. Frolicking deer and graceful doves also featured prominently in Art Deco design. In the 1920s and 1930s designers were almost as partial to greyhounds and terriers as 1950s designers were to poodles.

FURNITURE

THE ART DECO ERA WAS AN INCREDIBLY FRUITFUL PERIOD FOR
FURNITURE DESIGN. MANY OF THE 20TH CENTURY'S MOST ENDURING AND
INFLUENTIAL SHAPES AND STYLES WERE PRODUCED DURING THIS TIME.

FOLDING SCREEN This decorative room divider, or screen, comprises four
tall, hinged sections. Both sides of each individual section are faced in light-
and dark-wood parquetry—including some fruitwoods—arranged in differing
geometric patterns. *1930s. H:72¾ in (185 cm).*

A CHANGE IN STYLE

It is now generally accepted that the style known as
Art Deco first evolved in Paris before World War I.
Its originators wanted to create a type of design
that was not only identifiably French, but also
capable of launching a new style for a new century.

Many of these early Art Deco designers used
18th- and early 19th-century French furniture as
a starting point for their work. They then removed
all the curls and whiplashes characteristic of Art
Nouveau furniture design and
developed a simpler, more
disciplined look.

PREWAR ART DECO FURNITURE

Paul Follot was one designer who created furniture
with this new look. He used simple traditional
furniture shapes from the 18th century for his
exotic-wood pieces. He often embellished his
designs with flattened, stylized carvings—usually
fruit, flowers, and leaves. Follot was responsible
for the basket of flowers, which became a favorite
Art Deco motif. His early prewar furniture was
more richly decorated than his later work.

The 18th- and 19th-century furniture that
fascinated early Art Deco designers such as
Follot was derived from ancient Greek and

Roman designs and is defined as Neoclassical.
Maurice Dufrêne also designed fairly plain
furniture based on Neoclassical style before
World War I. His furniture was more austere
than Follot's, with very little carved detail.
Léon Jallot produced Neoclassical-style furniture

MAHOGANY ARMCHAIR
A variant of Ruhlmann's Napoleon
design, this mahogany armchair has
an oval back above a hexagonal
upholstered seat. The slender,
tapering legs are to the outside of
the seat, rather than beneath it.
1920. W:22 in (56 cm).

Each side door is inlaid in
ivory with connected spirals
of dots; Ruhlmann used this
decorative device often

*Short, fluted,
spindle legs* are
typical of Ruhlmann

ROSEWOOD CABINET Inspired by 18th-century designs, this rosewood
cabinet by Ruhlmann is of *demi-lune* form with two curved side doors flanking a
central pull-out shelf, a shelved recess, and a drawer. The back of the cabinet bears
the coveted "Ruhlmann Atelier A" branding. *c. 1920. W:50¾ in (129 cm).*

The central drawer front is carved in medium relief with a bowl of flowers

BIRD'S-EYE MAPLE TABLE Designed by Süe et Mare, this table has a *demi-lune* form and cabriole legs that betray the 18th-century inspiration in much of their work. The piece has a broad cross-banded top above a thumb-molded edge and a single frieze drawer. *W:48 in (122 cm).*

with large, flat surfaces, which he veneered, lacquered, or applied shagreen and parchment to. Often he enlivened his pieces with geometric designs. His furniture was influential and inspired the work of leading manufacturers such as De Coene Frères in Belgium.

THE BALLETS RUSSES

The formative period of Art Deco, before World War I, was greatly influenced by a dance company called the Ballets Russes. Under its spell, designers fell for bright hues, striking geometric patterns, and sumptuous exotic materials. Furniture designers began using colorful and contrasting veneers such as Macassar ebony and palisander. These rare woods had such dramatic grains that they needed hardly any other decoration. Designs were enriched with exotic ivory, shagreen, and lacquer, which were used to create bold patterns such as checks and sun rays

MAHOGANY SECRETAIRE This elegant secretaire by Jules Leleu is inlaid with rosewood and ivory. The cabinet has a fitted interior behind two doors, and two small drawers flank an arched apron. The whole is raised on tapering, octagonal legs. *c.1930. H:47¾ in (121 cm).*

SÜE ET MARE

The Art Deco style would have dominated design by 1920, had it not been for the onset of World War I. Designers Louis Süe and André Mare had been designing Art Deco furniture since about 1910. They resumed their work together after the war and formed a business to collaborate with colleagues such as Maurice Marinot, Marie Laurencin, and Jacques Villon on interior design and furnishing projects. The official name of the company was *Compagnie des Arts Français*, but any projects they worked on together were usually dubbed Süe et Mare.

The solid Neoclassical style of the early 19th century inspired their furniture designs. They liked massive pieces with a lot of gilding, shiny lacquers, or extravagant cast-metal hardware, and they created numerous show stoppers for exhibitions.

Süe et Mare worked on a number of important commissions, including decoration for the Parfumerie d'Orsay shop and the French embassies in Washington and Warsaw.

RUHLMANN

No furniture designer of the 1920s and 1930s was more famous for his fabulously crafted and luxurious furniture than Émile-Jacques Ruhlmann. Ruhlmann openly admitted that most of his work was inspired by 18th- and early 19th-century Neoclassical pieces. However, he passionately believed that "one ought only to find inspiration in them

[and then] adapt them for our time." He created sleek, elegant furniture with minimal detail using exotic veneers and opulent materials such as lacquer and ivory. Until the 1925 Paris International Exhibition brought him global renown, only his wealthy patrons knew his work.

Other major French designers creating similar Art Deco furniture included Jules Leleu and Pierre Legrain, who combined Neoclassicism with an African style, creating incredibly exotic results.

EBONIZED DINING CHAIR This hardwood dining chair by Léon and Maurice Jallot has a modernist feel to it. The green-leather-upholstered seat has chrome side rails and is raised on tapering, chrome-mounted legs. *1930. W:24 in (61 cm).*

ROSEWOOD COFFEE TABLE With its tubular chrome uprights, the simple design of this rosewood and walnut-veneered coffee table by De Coene Frères veers toward modernism. *Early 1930s. H:24½ in (62 cm).*

EILEEN GRAY

The radical Irish-born designer Eileen Gray lived most of her life in Paris. In the early 1920s she created entirely modern designs, divorced from all past influences, that anticipated 1930s Modernist Art Deco furniture. She based her highly individual style on geometric forms, producing minimalist chairs, couches, stools, and lacquered screens. Interested in new materials for making furniture, Gray was an early convert to tubular steel. Though her pieces were originally created in limited editions for the exclusive use of wealthy patrons, it would have been easy to mass-manufacture her furniture. However, her designs were too avant garde at the time for such consideration.

TRANSAT CHAIR The brown-leather-upholstered sling seat of this chair has an adjustable back rest and is suspended on an unlacquered wooden frame with chrome hardware. *1925–30. L:42 in (106.5 cm).*

SIMPLE DESIGN

After the Wall Street crash of 1929, Americans lost their appetite for luxury goods. Apart from a few exceptions like Eugene Schoen and T. H. Robsjohn-Gibbings, leading American furniture designers were fairly indifferent to specialized craftsmanship and rare materials. Influenced by Germany's Bauhaus art school, they were interested in creating good-quality, practical, mass-manufactured pieces from innovative, industrial materials such as tubular steel. The majority of cutting-edge designers agreed with Paul Frankl, who in 1930 famously said, "Ornament equals crime." They absorbed the Bauhaus passion for design with simple lines, devoid of references to the past or nature. The Depression's onslaught made Bauhaus ideas even more attractive. The production of stylish, affordable goods led to a uniquely American 1930s interpretation of Art Deco.

SKYSCRAPER FURNITURE

Frankl, a key member of New York's progressive design circles, saw the skyscraper as the United States' greatest expression of modern art. In 1925 he introduced a line of stepped wooden pieces

The metal maker's tag reads "Skyscraper Furniture Frankl Galleries 4 East 48th St. New York"

known as Skyscraper Furniture. Other American Art Deco furniture designers and manufacturers imitated Frankl's distinctive skyscraper style. From 1930 he concentrated on designing metal furniture.

ROHDE AND MILLER

Gilbert Rohde did much to popularize Bauhaus furniture design in the United States. He combined a sleek look with solid practicality, using wood, glass, and metal details. The majority of his designs were produced for manufacturers such as Heywood-Wakefield and, most notably, Herman Miller. Indeed, it was Rhode who started Herman Miller's association with modern design.

STREAMLINED FURNITURE

Another uniquely American twist on Art Deco is the so-called streamlined style, popular in designs for furniture from the early 1930s to the late 1940s. Streamlining drew on the machine for inspiration—the power and speed of trains or airplanes—and, crucially, it was highly suitable for manufacture by machine. A 1930s streamlined sofa, for example, might have a trim around its base that resembles the speed trim from a 1930s locomotive. The streamlined furniture style is well represented by the metal pieces of industrial designers such as Warren McArthur and Walter Dorwin Teague. However, this look is more widely

The semicircular, mirrored back is simple and frameless

ROCKEFELLER CENTER NEW YORK This New York Central Lines poster by Leslie Ragan offers a bird's-eye view of the cityscape that inspired much American furniture of the Art Deco period. *c.1935. H:40½ in (102.75 cm).*

The chromed-steel trim and drawer pulls accentuate the table's sleek lines

SKYSCRAPER DRESSING TABLE Inspired by the 1920s Manhattan skyline, Paul Frankl designed a range of furniture under the Skyscraper name. The black-lacquered wood and chrome trim of this dressing table, and the considered asymmetry of its design, are typical of the Skyscraper range. *c.1925. W:44 in (112 cm).*

RADIO CITY MUSIC HALL SOFA The use of curvaceous lines and bold color are typical of Deskey's work. Here the rosewood frame is upholstered in brown vinyl married with a vibrant orange fabric. c.1930. W:72 in (183 cm).

CLUB CHAIR The plush, taupe-colored, fabric-upholstered seat and back of Warren McArthur's Old Point Comfort club chair are encased within a simple tubular aluminum frame. H:23½ in (60 cm).

KNEEHOLE DESK This Widdicomb D-shaped kneehole desk designed by Donald Deskey has a black-lacquered wood top, frieze, and plinth, with rosewood-veneered sides and drawers and chrome-plated banding. c.1935. W:50 in (127 cm).

associated with Donald Deskey, who produced streamlined furniture featuring wood and industrial materials such as plastic and metal. Best known for the Art Deco interiors of New York's Radio City Music Hall, Deskey created a variety of pieces—from one-off luxury suites, to inexpensive designs for mass production by manufacturers such as the Ypsilanti Reed Furniture Company.

BRITISH ART DECO

During the 1920s and 1930s the Arts and Crafts movement was still a strong force in British design. It promoted simple, solid, handcrafted furniture, which was labor-intensive to produce and expensive to buy. Arts and Crafts designers were more interested in rediscovering traditional furniture-making techniques than in being at the cutting edge: they wanted to show that their furniture was handcrafted.

Also in this period, furniture designers Ambrose Heal and Gordon Russell produced pieces that were a hybrid of Arts and Crafts design and the modern Art Deco look. They both rose to prominence by designing and retailing Arts and Crafts furniture that involved some machine work and was aimed at a wider market.

Furniture designer Betty Joel originally designed Arts and Crafts-style pieces inspired by Regency furniture. In the 1930s, however, she changed direction and began producing Art Deco designs characterized by curvilinear geometric shapes and exotic woods. Joel's Art Deco designs were very popular in wealthy circles.

Two London-based reproduction-furniture specialists—Epstein and Hille—moved progressively into Art Deco style at this time, with light-wood furniture based on Classical forms. Hille's pieces in particular show the

influence of French furniture designers such as Paul Follot, while Epstein's capitalized on the very British taste for dining suites, often producing a matching Art Deco table, chairs, sideboard, small server, and bar cabinet.

Manufacturers Isokon and Gerald Summers produced highly innovative and influential plywood furniture in the 1930s. Though British designers produced some experimental tubular-steel furniture at the time, as a rule, the public preferred the warmth of wood—even in an industrially molded form such as plywood.

OAK BOOKCASES Each of these oak bookcases designed by Betty Joel has fluted, square feet and a random arrangement of open shelves and cupboards. The asymmetrical design is reminiscent of Frankl's Skyscraper pieces. 1932. W:36¼ in (92 cm).

Each drawer has a fluted wooden handle

CORNER DESK This large cherrywood-and-walnut corner desk was designed by Gordon Russell. It has a shaped working area above an arched apron flanked on each side by two drawers. Design no. 705. W:45¾ in (116 cm).

EUGENE SCHOEN

Initially an architect, Eugene Schoen switched his focus to furniture and interior design after visiting the 1925 Paris International Exhibition. Unlike many of his American contemporaries, Schoen preferred designing wooden furniture. His clean, classical lines and emphasis on rare woods, exotic veneers, and fine craftsmanship reveal the influence of French Art Deco furniture designers such as Émile-Jacques Ruhlmann. The majority of Schoen's pieces were made by top New York furniture-maker Schmieg & Kotzian (which also traded as Schmieg, Hungate & Kotzian). Featured in numerous magazines of the period, Schoen's Art Deco furniture was both critically acclaimed and popular with well-to-do Americans.

CHEST-ON-STAND Designed by Eugene Schoen for Schmieg, Hungate & Kotzian, this three-drawer solid- and veneered-mahogany chest-on-stand has a cross-hatched parquetry front with circular drawer pulls. c.1935. W:45 in (114.5 cm).

FURNITURE GALLERY

Art Deco furniture is characterized by bold shapes and forms. Architect-designed pieces became popular in this period, with many well-known architects creating custom lines. Advances in engineering were highly influential, and the form of the skyscraper was frequently invoked. Chrome was commonly used, giving furniture a stylish, modern feel. Monochromatic schemes were also popular, with black a particularly fashionable color.

KEY

1. Wolfgang Hoffmann coffee table. 1934. ④ **2.** American cocktail table with chrome banding. c.1935. W:36 in (91.5 cm). ④ **3.** Beresford & Hicks standing mirror with stepped feet. 1935. H:21 in (53 cm). ① **4.** English walnut chest of drawers with black-lacquer banding. 1930s. W:48½ in (123 cm). ② **5.** Russel Wright/Heywood-Wakefield asymmetric server with black-lacquer finish. H:42¼ in (107 cm). ③ **6.** Sideboard by M. P. Davis of London, in bleached mahogany. 1929. H:37¾ in (96 cm). ③ **7.** John Widdicomb commode with stylized inlays. H:44 in (111.5 cm). ② **8.** Skyscraper vanity with rectangular mirror and black enameled trim. H:60¾ in (154.5 cm). ②

1 Hoffmann coffee table

2 American cocktail table

3 Standing mirror

4 Walnut chest of drawers

5 Wright asymmetric server

8 Skyscraper vanity

6 Bleached mahogany sideboard

7 Widdicomb commode

9 Kem Weber chair

10 Modernage lounge chair

11 French armchair

9. Kem Weber American triple-band chair for Lloyd Manufacturing Company. 1937. W:27½ in (70 cm). ④ **10.** Modernage lounge chair in light gray ultra-suede. H:31 in (79 cm). ① **11.** French mahogany armchair (one of a pair). H:31½ in (80 cm). ④ **12.** Norman Bel Geddes vanity with chromium-plated base and trimming. H:71¾ in (182 cm). ③ **13.** Belgian occasional table with a mahogany-colored finish. c.1920. H:31 in (78.5 cm). ③ **14.** Table by Soubrier. c.1930. H:24 in (61 cm). ④ **15.** Side table by Charles Hardy, for Belmet Products of New York. c.1935. W:20 in (51 cm). ③ **16.** Robert Winthrop Chanler three-paneled screen painted with two zebras. 1928. H:78 in (198 cm). ⑤ **17.** Beechwood screen by Bauman. c.1930. W:79 in (201 cm). ② **18.** Circular walnut veneered display cabinet with twin glazed doors. H:73½ in (187 cm). ①

13 *Belgian occasional table*

14 *Soubrier table*

12 *Bel Geddes vanity*

15 *Charles Hardy side table*

16 *Three-paneled screen*

17 *Beechwood screen*

18 *Walnut display cabinet*

EXOTIC INFLUENCES

FROM THE USE OF RARE MATERIALS LIKE SHAGREEN TO THE DEPICTION OF SERPENTS, EXOTICISM PERMEATED ART DECO STYLE. DESIGNERS TOOK IDEAS FROM EAST ASIA AND THE AZTECS, BUT THE MOST IMPORTANT INFLUENCES WERE TRIBAL AFRICA AND ANCIENT EGYPT.

FACETED VASE The stepped sides and partly red-enameled, metal ziggurat mounts on this Boch Frères vase were inspired by the architecture of the ancient Inca and Aztec civilizations. *H:10 in (25.5 cm).*

JOSEPHINE BAKER

From the moment Josephine Baker first danced on the Parisian stage in 1925, she was a big star. Audiences were entranced by the African American entertainer's uninhibited movements, dark beauty, and quick wit. In Europe, Baker embodied the energy of American jazz and the mysteries of Africa, and she played up her exoticism both on and off the stage. Sculpted, photographed, and depicted by many leading artists and designers of the day, Baker helped pave the way for a shift in the perception of African Americans.

LE TUMULTE NOIR The dancer in this stylized drawing by Paul Colin is thought to be Josephine Baker; certainly she was the inspiration. Exotic-looking women had a great impact on American Art Deco design. *1927.*

Western artists and designers discovered Africa at the beginning of the 20th century and began collecting tribal African sculpture, masks, textiles, and other artifacts. They incorporated elements of this tribal art into Art Deco design in the use of simplified, stylized facial features and figures, as well as bold geometric patterns. Art Deco color combinations such as black/yellow/green and red/cream/black had African connotations, as did the use of contrasting light and dark earth tones.

TRIBAL AFRICA

Art Deco designers used exotic African materials for their work, including ivory, snakeskin, zebra hide, and leopard skin. Furniture-makers such as Émile-Jacques Ruhlmann adored the striking grains of rare African woods, producing pieces veneered and inlaid with palisander, Macassar ebony, amaranth, and amboyna. This type of furniture proved so desirable that there was even a special pavilion at the 1931 Paris *Exposition Coloniale* dedicated to promoting the use of these exquisite woods.

The shapes of ceremonial chairs and tribal stools inspired the chaise longues and other seating by designers such as Pierre Legrain and Eileen Gray. They liked the simplicity of African furniture, as well as the newness, in the sense that Western designers had not previously referenced African pieces. Other Art Deco designers chose to depict exotic wild animals. Jean Dunand, for example, used big cats and gazelles on his lacquered screens.

African culture and design also had a huge impact on Art Deco jewelry—from angular stone cuts and geometric bracelet links, to tribal masks and elephant motifs. The fashion for wearing big bangles up to the elbow had African roots, as did the taste for big beads.

CARLTONWARE JAR This ginger jar is printed and enameled with hieroglyphs from Tutankhamun's tomb. The Egyptian influence extends to the large gilt-and-black pharaoh finial on the lid. *H:12½ in (32 cm).*

OWL MASK Art Deco designers were inspired by the primitive designs of African tribal art, such as this mask, with its limited use of color and bold, geometric shapes. *H:22½ in (57 cm).*

ANCIENT EGYPT

Howard Carter's dramatic unearthing of Tutankhamun's tomb on November 4, 1922 was perhaps the biggest media phenomenon of the interwar years. Pictures of the splendid riches found in the young pharaoh's tomb captured the imagination and sparked a craze for all things Egyptian. By February 1923, the *New York Times* was reporting "businessmen all over the world are pleading for Tut-Ankh-Amen designs for gloves, sandals, and fabrics."

Ancient Egyptian-style patterns and motifs such as pharaoh's heads, eagles, cobras, pyramids, sphinxes, and scarabs appeared everywhere. Designers even turned ancient Egyptian writing—hieroglyphs—into decoration. The sheer quantity of golden objects in Tutankhamun's tomb had especially astonished and delighted the public. Designers began splashing gold coloring around with abandon, combining it with white, earth red, turquoise, and ultramarine—colors associated with the pharaohs.

In the 1920s, "Tutmania" had an impact on every conceivable form of design—from sculptures and cigarette packaging, to shawls and movie theater interiors. Even the innovative designer René Lalique (*see p.286*) adopted ancient Egyptian motifs, personalizing them in his glass designs. The taste for ancient Egyptian style resulted in some outstanding Art Deco jewelry and clocks by top jewelers such as Cartier. Just like the pharaoh's possessions, these were made from precious materials and stones, including mother-of-pearl, coral, diamonds, emeralds, and sapphires.

CELEBRATING AFRICA'S CONTRIBUTION

The Salon d'Afrique at the Musée des Arts d'Afrique et d'Océanie in Paris (originally the Musée des Colonies) features murals by Louis Bouquet and furniture by Émile-Jacques Ruhlmann.

CERAMICS

DURING THE 1920S AND 1930S, CLASSIC POTTERY SHAPES AND DECORATION WERE REINTERPRETED IN THE ART DECO STYLE. THE RESULTING CERAMICS LOOKED STARTLINGLY FRESH AND MODERN.

FRENCH CERAMICS

One of France's premier ceramics manufacturers, Sèvres has been associated with high quality since the 18th century. With one eye on the past and the other on the future, in the interwar years director Georges Lechavallier-Chevignard commissioned leading Art Deco designers to inject some modernity into the firm's traditional product range.

CELEBRITY COLLABORATIONS

Lechavallier-Chevignard's beliefs were very much in keeping with the design philosophy of Émile-Jacques Ruhlmann. Fanatical about fine craftsmanship, the Parisian furniture-maker and interior decorator collaborated with Sèvres on several successful ornamental ceramic projects. Lechavallier-Chevignard also persuaded animal sculptor François Pompon to recreate his stylized bronzes—including his celebrated polar bear—in earthenware, to much acclaim. Other important figures in Art Deco design employed by Sèvres included Raoul Dufy, Jean Dupas, and Marcel Goupy.

Witnessing the success of these collaborations, other French ceramics firms, including Haviland of Limoges, soon followed suit, commissioning leading designers to revamp their wares.

JEAN MAYODON

Sèvres's artistic director from 1941 to 1942, Jean Mayodon first worked for the ceramics manufacturer on a freelance basis before World War II. His studio pottery was renowned throughout the 1920s and

1930s. This was due in part to its exciting designs, inspired by traditional Persian, Chinese, and Japanese wares and featuring figurative decoration taken from Greek and Roman mythology. What made Mayodon's ceramics truly distinctive, though, were their earthy, mottled glazes, including lavish amounts of gold.

As well as smaller pieces like vases, bowls, and plates, Mayodon also produced architectural details such as tiles, fountains, and panels. He contributed ceramic designs to a number of distinguished steamship decoration schemes, including the *Normandie*.

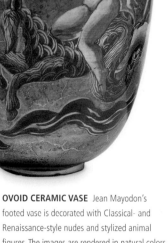

OVOID CERAMIC VASE Jean Mayodon's footed vase is decorated with Classical- and Renaissance-style nudes and stylized animal figures. The images are rendered in natural colors on a mottled and slightly crazed brown- and gold-enamel ground. *c.1930. H:9¾ in (24.5 cm).*

JEAN MAYODON OVOID VASE Classical and Biblical imagery was a source of inspiration for Mayodon. This vase, decorated with polychrome enamels and gold, features images of Adam and Eve with three snakes. It has a wooden base. *1930s. H:22½ in (57 cm).*

The snake was a common Art Deco motif, appealing for the texture and patterning of its skin.

Muted tones and painterly execution of images are typical of Mayodon's work

CIGARETTE BOX Designed by Wilhelm Kåge, this exquisite cigarette box was one of the Argenta line of pottery produced by Gustavsberg. The matte aqua-green pottery has a silver overlay decoration depicting a muscular nude female reclining and enjoying a cigarette. *1930s. W:6 in (15 cm).*

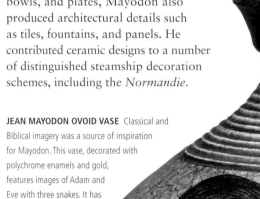

ALL-IMPORTANT FINISH

Boch Frères in Belgium and Longwy in France were industrial manufacturers that hand-finished their ceramics to make them look like studio pottery. Both firms produced decorative vases with innovative crackled glazes that gave their ceramics the appearance of ancient pots found in archaeological digs. The stylized animals, floral motifs, and human figures used for decoration came from a variety of sources, including traditional African vessels and Greek and Roman urns. Boch Frères' ceramics often bear a facsimile of the signature of their principal designer, Charles Catteau.

Upmarket shops and department stores sold Boch Frères and Longwy's vases. Longwy's main retailer was Primavera, the stylish homeware section of Le Printemps department store in Paris. Famous for its chic, modern ceramics, Primavera commissioned pieces from leading firms, as well as manufacturing its own designs at its factory outside Tours.

ITALIAN CLASSICISM

Benito Mussolini's Fascist government gave enthusiastic support to quintessentially Italian design. According to Margherita Sarfatti, organizer of the Italian Pavilion at the 1925 Paris International Exhibition, designers should respond to "the native traditions in each country—which for us means Classicism."

HEXAGONAL VASE Made by the Faiencerie de Longwy, this stoneware vase with a stepped neck is decorated in blue, yellow, and red enamels over a glazed *craquelure* ground. It bears the maker's mark. c. 1925. H: 7 in (18 cm).

The richly colored motifs betray the influence of ancient Egypt

SÈVRES BOX AND COVER The lid is decorated in relief with a geometric gilding design. Along with the additional gilding to the sides of the box, this contrasts well with the vivid blue-green mottled glazed ground. c. 1925. W: 6½ in (16.5 cm).

Many designers, such as Gio Ponti, Angelo Biancini, and Gigi Chessa, used Italian heritage, especially Roman antiquity, as a starting point for their ceramics during the 1920s and 1930s.

SCANDINAVIAN CERAMICS

The simplicity and purity of form of Neoclassicism, a style loosely derived from designs from the ancient, Classical world, had a huge impact on Scandinavian Art Deco. Danish ceramics manufacturers Bing & Grøndahl

and Royal Copenhagen added an angular, stylized Art Deco flourish to Neoclassical designs. In Sweden, Wilhelm Kåge, the artistic director of ceramics firm Gustavsberg, combined traditional East Asian shapes with images from Classical mythology to create a striking range of ceramics called Argenta. Made from mottled-green stoneware with silver-overlay decoration, this popular range featured sculptural figures that were reminiscent of the engraving on Sweden's famous Orrefors glass.

Typical of Boch Frères, enameling in shades of blue and yellow is thickly applied to create pattern in relief

OVOID FAIENCE VASE Made by Boch Frères, this vase is decorated with stylized flying pelicans against a blue sky and flanked above and below by similarly stylized clouds on an off-white *craquelure* ground. H: 13½ in (34.5 cm).

STONEWARE VASE The striking blue, yellow, and green design of this bottle-shaped vase repeats a segmented pattern of stylized sunburst-like forms. It was designed by Charles Catteau for Boch Frères. c. 1925. H: 12½ in (32 cm).

EARTHENWARE VASE The linear design features a central frieze of stylized gazelles—a popular Art Deco motif—painted in green over an ivory *craquelure* ground. By Édouard Cazaux for Sèvres. c. 1925. H: 12½ in (32 cm).

FIGURINES

Many ceramic figurines from the Art Deco era resemble three-dimensional illustrations from contemporary fashion magazines such as *Vogue*. Fashion inspired the way figurines posed, often holding out the fabric of their dresses, which tended to be the latest garments: long evening gowns, bias-cut dresses, sweeping fur-collared coats, sharp suits, and beach pajamas. The figurines also wore their hair in short, modern styles, sporting sleek bobs and Marcel waves. From their cloche hats to the tips of their painted fingernails, these figurines were the height of fashion.

MOLDING A LIFESTYLE

Art Deco fashions and fabrics offered designers the perfect showcase for virtuoso modeling and painting. Incredibly elaborate molds were required to duplicate wide-brimmed hats, wind-blown scarves, and softly draped fabrics. Ceramic decorators skillfully imitated the bright hues and stylized patterns of contemporary fashions. Even nude figurines frequently carried a swath of fabric to show off the designer's technical flair. A group of figurines, the greatest test of a ceramicist's talent, often included a dog, usually the designer's favorite breed: greyhound,

borzoi, or terrier. The canines' distinctive outlines and straining energy nicely set off the slim physiques and elegant dress of the human figures. A writer wryly commented in *Vogue* during the 1920s: "Dogs are now so fashionable that one wonders why they are not sold by the couturier."

As well as illustrating fashionable clothing, ceramics figurines also depict the glamorous lifestyle many women aspired to. Most Art Deco figurines portray lively, independent young women. Even the exotic dancers are usually playfully seductive rather than predatory. These figurines dress up as Pierrette or a Spanish dancer for a costume ball, flirt at parties with feathered fans, and sophisticatedly smoke cigarettes. Active and animated, they participate in sports such as golf, tennis, swimming, and horseback riding.

GOLDSCHEIDER'S REIGN

Arguably the most popular name in contemporary Art Deco figurines, the Austrian manufacturing firm of Goldscheider was renowned for its attractive designs, high-quality modeling, and

Modern couture— including accessories such as hats, gloves, and shoes—was faithfully copied

LADY WITH BORZOI This female figure in a flowing blue floral-print dress and broad-rimmed hat is portrayed walking a borzoi hound. Designed by Klara Herczeg for Goldscheider, the figure was also available wearing a red dress. *c.1935. H:17 in (43 cm).*

The borzoi hound was a popular Art Deco motif

FEMALE GOLFER Designed by Stefan Dakon, this Goldscheider figurine reflects the Art Deco preoccupation with the modern woman, portrayed here taking part in a predominantly male pastime. *H:10½ in (27 cm).*

detailed decoration. What set Goldscheider apart from other figurine specialists in the 1920s and 1930s was its unique ability to recreate the latest fashions faithfully, down to the last flower on a colorful fabric. Typical Goldscheider figurines depict dancers in flowing skirts or women stylishly dressed in a naturalistic way. Some are recognizable portraits of celebrities and famous performers of the day such as actress Dolores del Rio.

High-profile sculptor Josef Lorenzl and leading ceramics modeler Stefan Dakon were responsible for many of Goldscheider's more popular figurines. The firm also employed designers associated with the Wiener Werkstätte, such as Michael Powolny and Vally Wieselthier, to produce more experimental ceramics.

ENGLISH FIGURINES

Between the two world wars, Leslie Harradine was Royal Doulton's most successful and prolific modeler. He is best known for his traditional china ladies in crinoline, which hark back to the 18th and 19th centuries. However, Harradine also designed a number of figurines that reflected contemporary pastimes, such as Harlequinade, a flapper dressed for a costume ball, and Sunshine Girl, a 1920s bathing beauty under a Chinese parasol.

OTHER NOTABLE MAKERS

Goebel und Hutschenreuther in Germany and Royal Dux in Czechoslovakia also produced a variety of figurines portraying exotic dancers, sailor girls, and other bright young things. Italian ceramic manufacturer Lenci specialized in languid, often nude female figures. Designed by Helen König Scavini or Sandro

PORCELAIN FIGURINE Delicate and exquisitely painted porcelain is characteristic of Rosenthal pieces, as seen in this elegant figurine. *c.1935. H:10¾ in (27.5 cm).*

LADY WITH FAN This model was designed by Paul Scheurich for Meissen. It is polychrome-painted in shades of pink and blue. *1929. H:18½ in (47 cm).*

Vacchetti, many Lenci figurines have a distinctive doe-eyed sweetness about them.

Apart from a few exceptions, in the 1920s and 1930s, venerable figurine manufacturers such as Meissen, Berlin, and Royal Copenhagen mainly focused on designs inspired by their heritage.

WALL MASKS

Probably inspired by the way African art collectors hung tribal masks, wall masks reached the height of their popularity in the interwar years, when they were as ubiquitous as that other iconic Art Deco product for the home, the cocktail shaker. Practically every major name in ceramics—from Clarice Cliff and Beswick, to Goldscheider and Lenci—made wall masks. Most portray chic young women in the latest hairstyles and hats, their accessories often highlighted in jazzy colors like jade green, cherry red, and tango orange.

GOEBEL WALL MASK This ceramic mask portrays a young lady in profile. She wears contemporary makeup and sports fashionably short blond hair in tight, stylized curls. *L:8½ in (21.5 cm).*

Costumes feature in several Royal Doulton figurines

Clowns were popular theatrical figure and sources of inspiration

THE MASK In this Royal Doulton figurine, a young girl in a theatrical pose dressed as a clown or a Pierrot-type figure gazes searchingly into the face of a mask that she is holding.

MARIETTA Designed by Leslie Harradine, this Royal Doulton Art Deco figurine is dressed as if for a ball in a devil-style black-and-red costume. *H:8¼ in (21 cm).*

ANGELA This Leslie Harradine Royal Doulton figurine is dressed in a dancer's clothes. She sits on top of a truncated column, holding a large fan behind her head. *1932–45. H:7½ in (19 cm).*

FEMALE DESIGNERS

During the 1920s and 1930s, a number of creative British women took ceramic production in new directions, setting fashions that put Britain at the forefront of Art Deco ceramic design.

THE CLIFF FACTOR

For many, Clarice Cliff and Art Deco are synonymous terms. Cliff's bold, distinctive interpretation of traditional themes—landscapes, cottages, and floral borders—in her instantly recognizable palette of reds, oranges, yellows, blues, and greens epitomizes the look of Jazz Age ceramics. She called her range Bizarre Ware and gave her patterns names such as Black Luxor, Fantasque, and Ravel.

Cliff used plain mass-produced pottery in traditional shapes and more daring geometric styles as a base for her patterns. The decoration was handpainted on these so-called "blanks"— sometimes by Cliff herself, but mainly by the decorators at her studio. She encouraged her predominantly female decorators to interpret her designs freely. Clarice Cliff became a celebrity in the 1930s and her Art Deco pottery sold in huge quantities in Britain as well as internationally.

COOPER'S MASS APPEAL

Another big name in British Art Deco ceramics was Susie Cooper. She worked for A. E. Gray & Company before setting up her own decorating and design business, Susie Cooper Pottery, in 1930.

At the time, much of the tableware available to people with limited resources had staid, traditional decoration. A talented businesswoman as well as a designer, Cooper realized there was a market for reasonably priced ceramics with a fresh, modern look.

The majority of her designs are for practical tableware, though she also produced some decorative items like candlesticks and wall masks. Some of her handpainted geometric designs are similar to Cliff's, while others feature Cooper's distinctive dots, dashes, bands, and shaded crayon lines. According to the *Pottery Gazette* of June 1931, Cooper had "a unique capacity to achieve the maximum degree of effectiveness in pottery decoration by recourse to the simplest modes of expression."

Stylish, well-executed designs were Cooper's priority. It didn't matter to her if her designs were handpainted or transfer-printed. By the mid-1930s she was producing designs for large-scale transfer-printing on tableware. Her most popular transfer designs from the 1930s— Dresden Spray, Patricia Rose, and Nosegay—had stylized flowers in their centers and pastel borders.

Susie Cooper's ceramics were immensely popular. In recognition of her innovative work, she was appointed Royal Designer for Industry in 1940.

CLIFF AND COOPER'S INFLUENCE

Other British ceramic companies quickly picked up Clarice Cliff and Susie Cooper's jazzy modern look. Some, such as Myott, capitalized on Cliff and Cooper's popularity by imitating their geometric patterns, stylized motifs, and bright colors. Others responded by bringing out their own fresh, modern lines. Shelley Pottery developed a reputation for geometrical tableware with dramatic Cubist decoration, while Wiltshaw and Robinson produced Carlton Ware—a highly successful tableware range resembling green leaves.

WALL CHARGER Designed by Clarice Cliff, this Windbells-pattern wall charger comprises a stylized tree with a black trunk and blue leaves against a red, yellow, and green ground. *1933–34. D:10 in (25.5 cm).*

CONE-SHAPED SUGAR SIFTER The design of this sugar sifter is rendered in Clarice Cliff's typically bold colors. Sifters were produced in a number of patterns; this Summerhouse pattern is extremely rare. *H:5½ in (14 cm).*

SQUARE STEPPED VASE The Latona Tree pattern on this Clarice Cliff vase features a tree with a black trunk and stylized blue, orange, red, purple, and green foliage. Design no. 369A, it bears a painted Latona mark. *H:7¾ in (19.5 cm).*

JUG AND COFFEE POT
Susie Cooper's tableware often reflects her interest in European design. Pieces are primarily functional, and decoration is usually geometric in form, with simple, banded designs in soft colors, such as in these examples. *Jug: 1930. H:6¾ in (17 cm) ; Coffee pot: 1928. H:8 in (20.5 cm).*

AMERICAN JAZZ

Many of the best American Art Deco ceramics were inexpensive and mass-produced. By the late 1930s, for example, nearly every American kitchen had a piece of Homer Laughlin China Company's Fiesta ware. Jazzy colors and streamlined shapes make this tableware range among the most iconic of all American Art Deco designs.

However, some factories also produced daring hand-finished limited-edition ceramics. In 1924 Roseville Pottery introduced Futura, a striking range of angular vases with mottled glazes. This was one of the most advanced American Art Deco ceramic ranges of the day. Cowan Pottery produced a variety of products including studio pottery. Owner Reginald Guy Cowan employed cutting-edge designers—Margaret Postgate, Waylande Gregory, A. Drexler Jacobson, and Viktor Schreckengost among them. Now considered one of America's foremost potters, Schreckengost created a number of seminal Art Deco designs while at Cowan, the most famous of which is the spectacular turquoise Jazz Bowl. Decorated with images of New Year's Eve festivities in New York City, it encapsulate the spirit of the Jazz Age perfectly.

DEVELOPMENTS IN DORSET

Some of the highest awards given out for ceramics at the 1925 Paris International Exhibition went to a pottery in Poole, Dorset—the partnership of Charles Carter, Harold Stabler, and the husband-and-wife team of John and Truda Adams. Today this business is known as Poole Pottery. Poole won acclaim for its striking handmade and hand-decorated Art Deco stoneware, which featured stylized flowers and deer, as well as geometric motifs. The simple shapes of Poole pottery were often inspired by Japanese ceramics and decorated with matte glazes and subdued colors.

Truda Adams (who later married Charles Carter) defined the highly original look of Poole pottery. Stabler's wife, Phoebe, also produced distinctive Art Deco stoneware figures for Poole, as well as for other companies such as Royal Doulton and Ashtead Potters. In the mid-1930s Poole introduced more commercial designs, such as Streamline tableware by John Adams.

PUNCH BOWL This limited-edition bowl was designed by Schreckengost for Cowan. It is known as the Jazz Bowl, although its official name is "New Year's Eve in New York City." *1931. W:14 in (35.5 cm).*

HAND-THROWN VASE The strong, repeated pattern of this barrel-shaped vase with a short, narrow neck is rendered in blue and yellow against a white ground. It was designed by Ruth Pavely.

OVOID STONEWARE VASE From the Poole Pottery, this hand-thrown vase features the Leaping Deer pattern 599/TZ designed by Truda Carter. The decoration is rendered in a polychrome palette beneath a semi-matte glaze. *1934–37. H:8¼ in (21 cm).*

ROSEVILLE TANK VASE The modern, angular form of this vase and the blended orange-to-blue mottled glaze are typical of the Futura range. This rare example still bears a partial paper label. *1920s–30s. H:9½ in (23.5 cm).*

CERAMICS GALLERY

Art Deco ceramics are characterized by strong geometric forms that are often asymmetrical. More traditional shapes tend to distinguish themselves for bold geometric patterns and bright colors. Decoration was frequently added by hand-painting. Many of the ceramics pieces of this period convey a sense of cheerfulness and optimism—sunshine was a recurring theme. Other popular motifs were female figures posing in Jazz Age pursuits and Egyptian-influenced patterns.

KEY

1. Sybille May ceramic of a kneeling female figure holding aloft a gold ball. 1930s. H:8 in (20 cm). ② **2.** Ashtead Pottery Corn Girl figurine by Allan C. Wyon. 1927. H:8 in (20 cm). ① **3.** Czech Goldscheider-style terracotta wall mask. H:11½ in (29 cm). ① **4.** Viktor Schreckengost's Madam Kitty figurine of an acrobat on horseback. 1930s. H:9½ in (24 cm). ④ **5.** Primavera figurine of an ermine, thickly glazed in black and white. H:12½ in (31.5 cm). ③ **6.** Elly Strobach's stylized bust of a red-haired woman holding a cigarette. 1930s. H:7 in (17.5 cm). ② **7.** Maling Anzac-pattern part tea service. ③ **8.** Czechoslovakian handpainted jug by Ditmar Urbach. H:7½ in (19 cm). ①

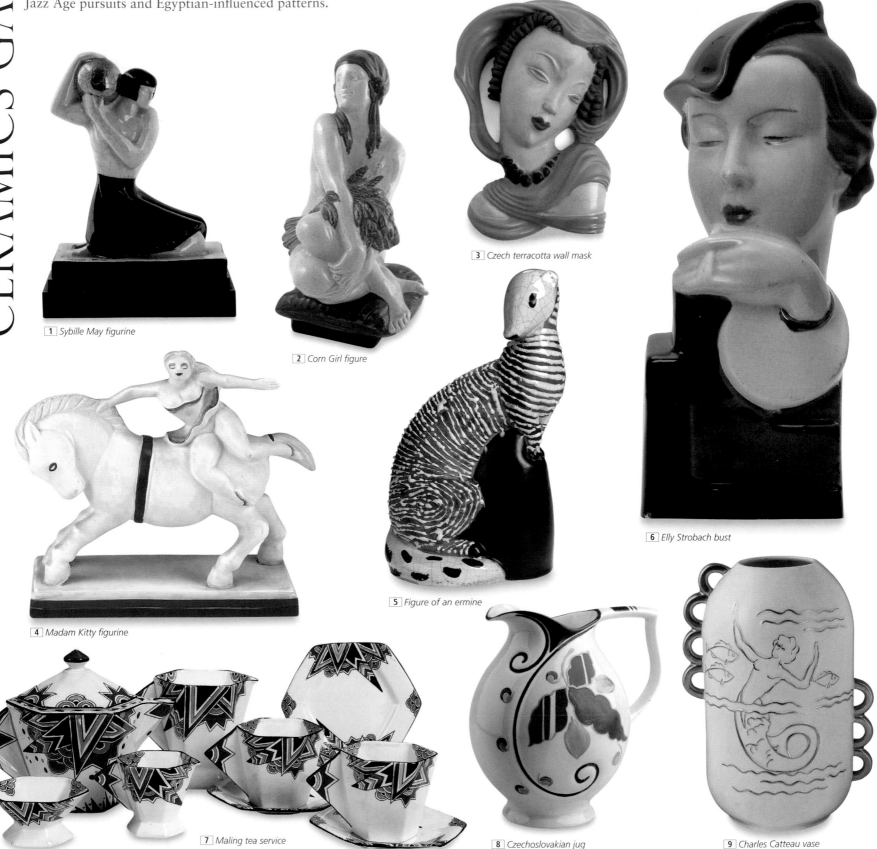

1 Sybille May figurine

2 Corn Girl figure

3 Czech terracotta wall mask

4 Madam Kitty figurine

5 Figure of an ermine

6 Elly Strobach bust

7 Maling tea service

8 Czechoslovakian jug

9 Charles Catteau vase

9. Cylindrical earthenware vase by Charles Catteau. c.1925. H:11½ in (29 cm). ② **10.** Circular wall plaque of a female dancer. 1930s. D:9½ in (24 cm). ① **11.** Stefan Dakon's figurine of a young lady in a dancer's pose. 1930s. H:15 in (38 cm). ③ **12.** Pinecone-range cornucopia-shaped vase. 1931. H:8¾ in (22 cm). ① **13.** Two-handled blue vase. H:15 in (38 cm). ② **14.** Chinese Bird vase by R. Guy Cowan. c.1925. H:11¼ in (28.5 cm). ② **15.** Roseville Futura pink and green rectangular vase. ② **16.** Myott Pottery Pyramid vase with an Orange Flowers pattern. 1930s. H:8¼ in (21.5 cm). ①

16 *Myott Pyramid vase*

10 *Female dancer plaque*

11 *Dakon figurine*

13 *Two-handled vase*

14 *Cowan vase*

15 *Roseville Futura vase*

12 *Cornucopia-shaped vase*

LALIQUE

THE NAME RENÉ LALIQUE IS NOW SYNONYMOUS WITH ART DECO GLASS. LIGHT-YEARS AHEAD OF THE COMPETITION, LALIQUE PROVED THAT IT WAS POSSIBLE TO USE INDUSTRIAL TECHNIQUES TO MASS-PRODUCE WELL-DESIGNED, INNOVATIVE GOODS. HIS STYLISH GLASSWARE APPEALED TO EVERYONE—FROM MILLIONAIRES TO HOUSEWIVES.

A MODERNIST AT HEART René Lalique used modern techniques of mass production—among them hot metal molds, compressed air, and advanced decoration—to create a wide range of glass products.

SUZANNE STATUETTE
Mounted on a bronze peacock-pattern illuminated base, this opalescent-glass statuette is molded as a young female nude with outstretched arms amid flowing drapery. c.1925. H:11 in (28 cm).

René Lalique originally made a name for himself as a jeweler, creating fantastic sculptural orchids, dragonflies, and maidens from enamel and gold in the Art Nouveau style. As part of his jewelry design, he also started experimenting with glassmaking processes. His first glassware commission came from perfumer François Coty, who wanted attractive bottles for a scent he was launching. The perfume bottle was a big hit. Intrigued by the versatility of glass and the idea of replicating the same design, Lalique switched allegiance from jewelry to glassmaking.

TECHNIQUES AND INSPIRATION

Lalique breathed new life into industrial glassmaking techniques including molding and stamp-pressing. Preferring to work in ordinary glass rather than expensive lead crystal, he gave his pieces frosted and opalescent finishes. Sometimes he stained or tinted them in pastel shades, or colored them in striking gem hues such as aquamarine and garnet.

Lalique once said he wanted to "achieve a new result…to create something never seen before." The singular look of his pieces is due to the fact that he treated glass as a sculptural material, taking his glass molds—be they for a statuette or a vase—from wax models. His sources of inspiration were plants and animals, though he increasingly turned to Greek and Roman Classical nudes and draped figures for imaginative glass designs.

ECLECTIC PRODUCTION

By the 1920s Lalique had a flourishing glass-manufacturing business. Incredibly prolific, he created a vast array of tableware and decorative objects such as vases, clocks, statuettes, and jewelry. Lalique also made light

PERRUCHES VASE This ovoid vase is molded with pairs of wooing budgerigars on branches in electric-blue opalescent glass with an enamel-washed patina. The vase has a molded "R. LALIQUE" mark. c.1920. H:10 in (25 cm).

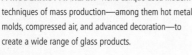

SERPENT PERFUME BOTTLE The snake, or serpent, was a popular Art Deco motif. Here the head of the serpent forms an elaborate stopper, while the scaly body of the snake is coiled on the surface of the bottle. c.1920. H:3½ in (9 cm).

fixtures, panels, doors for interiors, and even glass furniture. Hood ornaments were also among his strengths. These quintessentially Art Deco ornaments decorated car hoods in the interwar years, and Lalique created 28 different types, the most famous being the Victoire, a woman's head with swept-back hair. After his success with Coty, however, perfume bottles became among Lalique's best-known designs. Over the years he produced more than 30 bottles for perfume houses and couturiers, including Houbigant and Worth.

The 1925 Paris International Exhibition was a triumph for Lalique. Not only did he have two pavilions, but he also contributed to other exhibits such as the Hall of Perfume, as well as several displays around the grounds, including a magnificent fountain. The exhibition led to more high-profile architectural and interior-design commissions such as the lighting and decorative panels for France's legendary liners: the *Île de France* and *Normandie*.

A SLEW OF IMITATORS

Lalique's distinctive items were popular internationally and had a far-reaching effect on other glass manufacturers. Sabino and Etling were just two among numerous French firms influenced by Lalique. They used his molded glass and motifs—especially the fish and nudes—as a starting point for their own statuettes. The Belgian glassworks Val Saint-Lambert produced Lalique-style wares called Luxval, while in Britain the Red-Ashay firm specialized in hood ornaments. Some American manufacturers, including the Consolidated Lamp & Glass Company, replicated Lalique's vases and lighting.

L'ÉLÉGANCE PERFUME BOTTLE
This square bottle, made for D'Orsay, is molded with nymphs. The clear frosted glass has been highlighted with a sepia patina. c.1920. H:3½in (9cm).

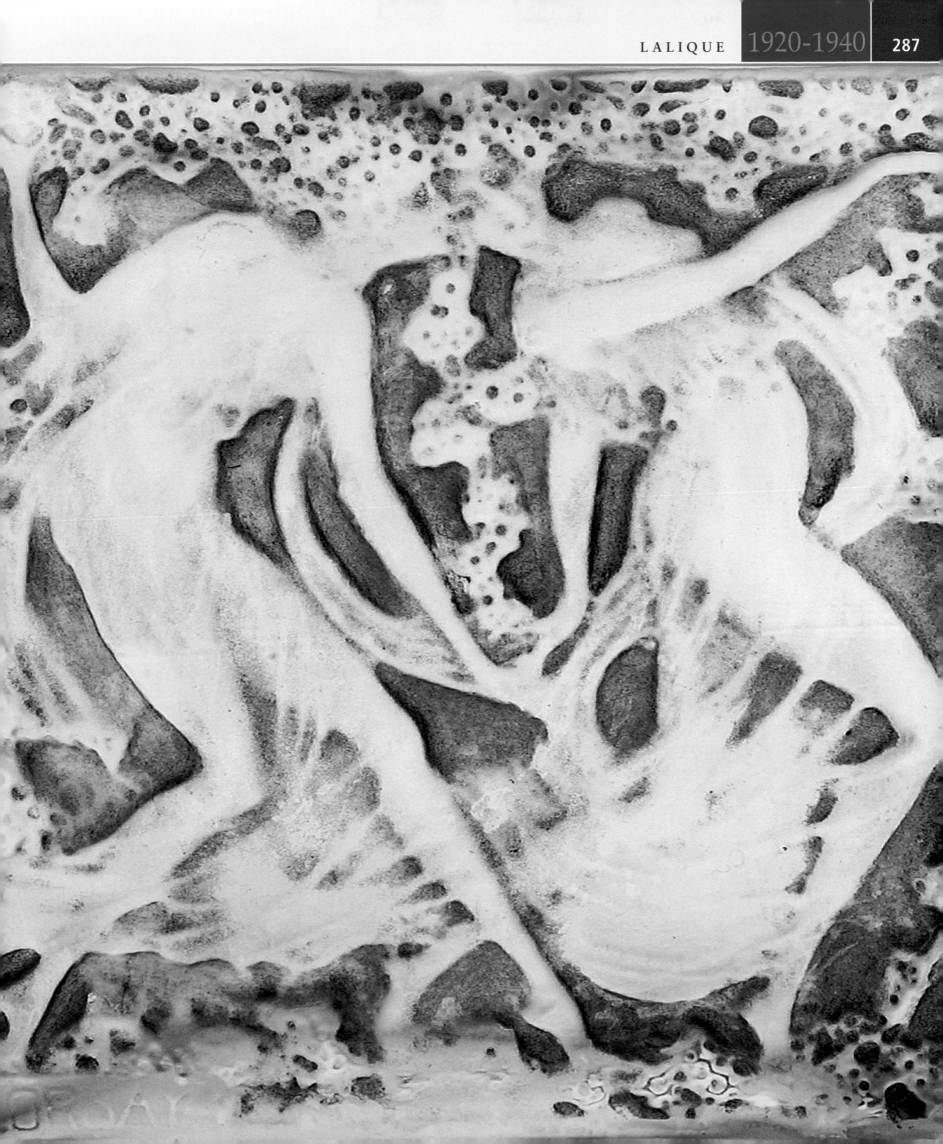

GLASS

GLASS WAS INCREDIBLY POPULAR THROUGHOUT THE ART DECO

ERA. GLASSMAKERS EMBRACED NEW STYLES AND USED THE LATEST

TECHNOLOGY TO KEEP UP WITH PUBLIC DEMAND.

TWIN-HANDLED BOWL Produced by Daum Frères, this footed bowl is made from black and brown glass. It is cut with simple sweeping lines in shallow relief. *c.1925. H:5¾ in (14.5 cm).*

DAUM AND FRENCH GLASS

The Nancy-based firm of Daum, one of the best-known manufacturers of Art Nouveau cameo glass, updated its range after World War I. Its cameo glass vases, lamps, and bowls now came in jazzy colors like tango orange, scarlet, pink, and jade green. They featured the latest decoration such as Egyptian motifs, stylized flowers, and animals, as well as plenty of geometric patterns. In the early 1900s the glassmakers at Daum carved many of their cameo glass pieces by hand, but by the 1920s much of the production was mechanized, which resulted in a striking flattened appearance.

By the early 1930s the public taste for cameo glass was dying out and, accordingly, Daum started moving in a different direction. Its new designs were more abstract in concept and relied on contrasting textured finishes or internal decoration such as bubbles, mottling, and striations, as well as tiny flecks of gold and silver. They came in opaque and opalescent shades of colors, including sea green, gray, turquoise, amber, and pale yellow. The glassmakers often blew their new glass into decorative metal mounts made from bronze or wrought iron. Leading manufacturers—

including Majorelle and Edgar Brandt—produced handsome mounts especially for them. Created with the latest technology, Daum glass—like Lalique's—proved that handcrafting was not the only way of achieving high quality and good design. Many Daum pieces were made in limited editions or as one-of-a-kind items.

SCHNEIDER

Several other French firms, including Muller Frères and Schneider, produced glassware similar to that created at Daum. Schneider specialized in

cameo glass in distinct shades of garnet, bright yellow, orange, and plum, which was developed at the Schneider brothers' factory near Paris. Typical pieces included tall, thin cameo-glass vases etched with naturalistic floral, insect, and animal motifs. Schneider also made undecorated vases and bowls from mottled colored glass, as well as decorative glass items acid-etched with geometric designs. The factory marketed many of its pieces under the name *Le Verre Français*, a range that was sold through major department stores in France and the United States.

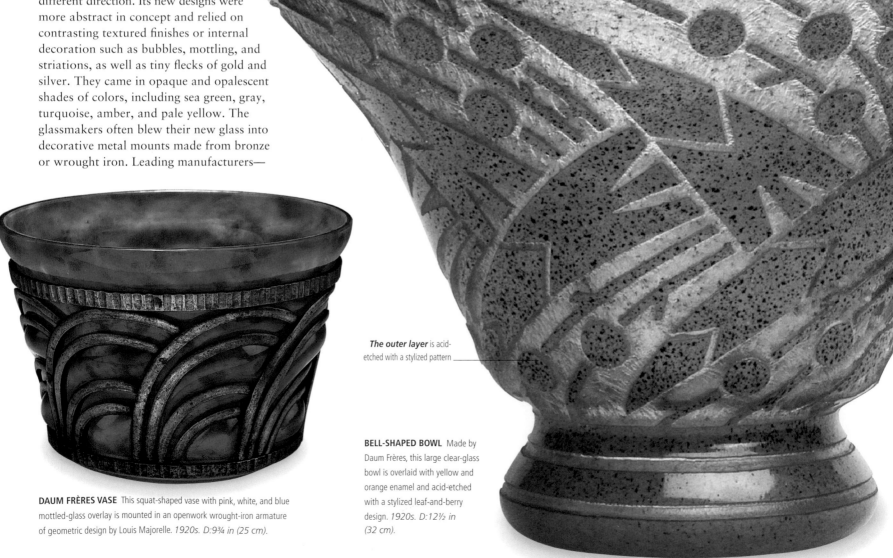

The outer layer is acid-etched with a stylized pattern

BELL-SHAPED BOWL Made by Daum Frères, this large clear-glass bowl is overlaid with yellow and orange enamel and acid-etched with a stylized leaf-and-berry design. *1920s. D:12½ in (32 cm).*

DAUM FRÈRES VASE This squat-shaped vase with pink, white, and blue mottled-glass overlay is mounted in an openwork wrought-iron armature of geometric design by Louis Majorelle. *1920s. D:9¾ in (25 cm).*

VAL SAINT-LAMBERT'S CUT GLASS

Belgium's biggest glassmaker, Val Saint-Lambert, was renowned for its cut-glass production. In the early 1920s the firm began using traditional glass-cutting techniques to create stylish Art Deco geometric patterns on its crystal. At the time, Val Saint-Lambert was one of the few glassmakers outside Bohemia making multicolored cut-glass vases. These pieces usually had a clear body with ruby, cobalt blue, or amethyst on top. This type of hand-cut glassware was extremely expensive to produce, and little was made following the American Depression.

MARCEL GOUPY

As artistic director of Georges Rouard's furnishings gallery in Paris for more than 40 years, Marcel Goupy saw both Art Nouveau and Art Deco come and go. A talented designer, he produced striking designs for ceramics and silverware during the 1920s and 1930s. However, Goupy is most celebrated today for his enameled glassware with brightly colored Art Deco decoration. His tableware and decorative pieces were free-blown from clear or slightly tinted glass and then decorated by hand.

Goupy's enamel glassware often featured images that are considered typically Art Deco, including cypress trees, weeping willows, jazz musicians, stylized flowers, billowing clouds, and cherry blossoms. Glass decorator Auguste Heiligenstein was the man responsible for painting many of these striking designs, even though they bear

Goupy's signature. Heiligenstein went on to enjoy a solo career and won acclaim for his finely detailed enameled and gilt pieces decorated with figures taken from Classical mythology.

Many glass designers used enameled decoration during the 1920s and 1930s. Jean Luce produced glassware decorated with highly stylized enamel floral motifs before moving on to engraving and sandblasting geometric designs.

CASED PEDESTAL FOOT VASE
With a blue exterior and a red interior, this Val Saint-Lambert vase is cut with geometric forms on both the inside and the outside. It has an undulating rim. H:16 in (40.5 cm).

VAL SAINT-LAMBERT VASE Known as a Kipling design, this tapered, cylindrical cased vase stands on a spreading octagonal foot and is cut with a ruby red lozenge pattern over clear glass. 1930s. H:12 in (30.5 cm).

PÂTE-DE-VERRE

At the turn of the 20th century, France saw a revival of the ancient glassmaking technique of *pâte-de-verre* (or *pâte-de-cristal*). Looking like crystalline colored sugars melting together, *pâte-de-verre* involves placing finely ground glass paste in molds and firing it to resolidify the glass. During the Art Deco era, Victor Almaric Walter, the leading *pâte-de-verre* specialist, continued to produce pieces decorated with the same lizards and nudes that first got him noticed in the Art Nouveau period. François-Émile Décorchemont, who was first acclaimed for *pâte-de-verre* in the early 1900s, embraced a more geometric style before abandoning decoration completely in favor of stark shapes.

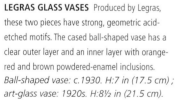

LEGRAS GLASS VASES Produced by Legras, these two pieces have strong, geometric acid-etched motifs. The cased ball-shaped vase has a clear outer layer and an inner layer with orange-red and brown powdered-enamel inclusions. Ball-shaped vase: c.1930. H:7 in (17.5 cm); art-glass vase: 1920s. H:8½ in (21.5 cm).

Ball-shaped vase by Legras

Art-glass vase by Legras

TALL *LE VERRE FRANÇAIS* VASE Decorated with stylized berried branches in green, mottled orange, and brown, this vase has an applied "candy cane" signature. H:19¼ in (49 cm).

PÂTE-DE-VERRE BOWL The shape of this footed, loop-handled bowl by François-Émile Décorchemont was inspired by ancient Roman forms. The decoration is a Classical geometric pattern. 1920s. D:11 in (28 cm).

CUT AND ENGRAVED GLASS

It would be easy to assume that the finest glass made during the Art Deco era came from France, but important developments were also taking place in other European countries and in the United States during the 1920s and 1930s.

BRITISH GLASS

Clear cut glass in Neoclassical designs had been a specialty of British glass manufacturers since the late 18th century. Even in the 1920s and 1930s, most glass produced in Britain was clear, apart from the odd exception such as the bubbly Monart range from Scotland's Moncrieff Glassworks.

In order to keep up with the times, many firms started commissioning cut-glass designs from leading artists. James Powell asked furniture designer Gordon Russell to produce a tableware range, while Clyne Farquharson worked for glass manufacturers John Walsh Walsh, creating a series of plain, shaped tableware with simple cut decoration such as leaves.

One of the most successful and prolific pairings of traditional glass producer and Art Deco designer was that of the firm of Stevens & Williams and Keith Murray. During the 1930s, Murray designed tableware and vases for the firm with simple cut or engraved decoration influenced by Swedish glassmakers Orrefors.

STEUBEN

Founded in the early 1900s by Frederick Carder and Thomas Hawkes, Steuben was one of the few American glass factories to produce finely handcrafted tableware and limited-edition work. Steuben glass from the 1920s often features Asian and Classical imagery. Its jade green glass and bubbly Cluthra range were also popular.

In the 1930s Steuben started specializing in clear engraved glass—for which it is now celebrated. Designer Sidney Waugh's glassware incorporated stylized animals and Classical figures, and it was comparable in quality and

style to the best designs from Orrefors. Waugh's delicately engraved Gazelle bowls are among Steuben's best-loved designs. In the 1930s the firm also commissioned simple engraved tableware, including several drinking glass ranges from leading industrial designer Walter Dorwin Teague.

MURANO GLASS

Renowned since the Renaissance for creating high-quality glass, glassmakers on the Venetian island of Murano specialized in free-blown glass with applied decoration. Paolo Venini, a lawyer interested in cutting-edge design, bought a glass studio in the early 1920s to produce modern pieces featuring bold colors and strong, abstract forms.

ENGRAVED BOWL Designed by Sidney Waugh for Steuben, this near-spherical lead-crystal bowl with thick walls has a central frieze engraved with leaping gazelles. *1935. H:7 in (18 cm).*

FLUTED VASE Cut with horizontal bands of fluting in a repeating pattern that matches its form, this inverted conical-shaped vase was designed by Thomas Webb for the Rembrandt Art Guild, England. *c.1935. H:6¾ in (17.5 cm).*

BUCKET VASE This John Walsh Walsh cut-glass bucket vase features a repeating geometric pattern of ovals and flutes beneath a geometric border. It is marked Walsh Birmingham. *1930s. H:6½ in (16.5 cm).*

The Handkerchief vase was his company's most famous design. Venini employed a number of progressive designers, including Napoleone Martinuzzi, and in the 1930s his studio pioneered many innovative forms of glass and glassmaking techniques.

BOHEMIAN GLASS

Like France, Bohemia (the modern-day Czech Republic) had a thriving, long-established glassmaking industry. By the early 1900s, apart from a few strongly artisanal firms, handcraftsmanship had largely given way to mechanized production. Throughout the 1920s and 1930s, the consumer demand for decorative glass and everyday tableware such as ashtrays was efficiently met by many Bohemian glass manufacturers. If a glass design was successful, they made an inexpensive, mass-produced version. They were responsible for countless perfume bottles, which were sold empty, ready for women to fill with a scent of their choice. Many had fan-shaped stoppers or attached atomizers. Bohemian glassmakers also created decanters and liqueur sets, engraved or decorated with enamel in geometric patterns.

PURPLE GOBLET The bowl of this goblet has an etched and gilded frieze depicting an Amazonian scene. The glass has a hexagonal-faceted stem and conical foot. Base engraved "Moser Karlsbad." c.1920. H:7½ in (19 cm).

ORREFORS

Responsible for revitalizing the traditional art of glass engraving, Orrefors had a huge impact on glass design of the 1930s. One of Sweden's largest glass manufacturers, in the early 1920s the firm opened a small glass workshop under the direction of Simon Gate and Edvard Hald. Distinctive glassware quite unlike anything else available at the time was produced here, with finely detailed motifs and figures inspired by Greek and Roman mythology wheel-engraved on clear lead-crystal vases and bowls. Neoclassicism played an important role in Scandinavian Art Deco design, and the crisp, sculptural images contrasted nicely with the brilliant sparkle of the glass. Orrefors's display at the 1925 Paris International Exhibition brought the firm international attention and won it rave reviews. In the late 1920s and early 1930s, glass designer Vicke Lindstrand introduced new themes to engrave on the firm's glassware, such as underwater scenes. Other innovative and imaginative glass designers employed by Orrefors included Knut Bergqvist and Edvin Öhrström.

ORREFORS JUG The engraving of the female dancer and the use of geometric forms on this clear glass jug are characteristic of Simon Gate's Neoclassical Art Deco style. 1927. H:8¾ in (22 cm).

MASS-PRODUCED AMERICAN GLASS

Apart from limited-edition work by designers such as Victor Durand for Vineland Flint Glasswork, most American Art Deco glass was cheap, even when compared with inexpensive imports from Bohemia.

Molded and pressed glass dominated production by American glass factories during the 1920s and 1930s. Several firms, such as the Phoenix Glass Company and the Consolidated Lamp & Glass Company, copied Lalique designs using cost-cutting techniques. The Consolidated Lamp & Glass Company also produced a more original pressed glass range called Ruba Rombic. Strikingly angular, and in colors such as smoky topaz and jungle green, Ruba Rombic glassware was created by Reuben Haley, who was inspired by Cubist art.

Depression glass put Art Deco design within the reach of those with modest incomes. Its production started in the 1920s but really took off in the 1930s, hence its name. This uniquely American form of pressed glass was sold for pennies in "five and dime" stores across the country. Most pieces of Depression glass tended to be functional everyday wares such as butter dishes and plates. They usually came in clear or pale pastel hues and relied on simple geometric shapes for effect. Ice-cream soda glasses and banana split dishes are among the more iconic Depression-glass designs. Some of the best-known Depression glass manufacturers were Hocking Glass, Indiana Glass, and Jeanette Glass.

DURAND KING TUT VASE Although this pattern had been used by Tiffany and Loetz since around 1900, this blown-glass vase was inspired by ancient Egyptian decoration following the discovery of Tutankhamun's tomb in 1922. 1924–31. H:6¼ in (16 cm).

RUBA ROMBIC VASE Inspired by Cubism, this pale green glass vase was produced by the Consolidated Lamp & Glass Company. The multi-angular, asymmetrical design is visually striking. H:9 in (23 cm).

GLASS GALLERY

The Art Deco period saw a boom in mass-production techniques. In glassware, these were pioneered by Lalique, who used hot metal molds, giving way to new forms and designs. Bold geometric shapes were fashionable, as was Egyptian-influenced styling following the discovery of Tutankhamun's tomb in 1922. Stylized flora and fauna also remained popular. Polychromatic cased glass and iridescent and opalescent glass became fashionable, while the status of cameo glass gradually declined.

KEY

1. Czechoslovakian decanter and three glasses with amber overlay. Decanter: H:10½ in (26.5 cm). ① **2.** Czechoslovakian clear-glass perfume bottle and stopper. H:4½ in (11.5 cm). ① **3.** Czechoslovakian clear-glass perfume bottle with black puffer. H:6¾ in (17 cm). ① **4.** Orrefors glass vase with stylized flowers, by Simon Gate. H:6¼ in (15.5 cm). ⑤ **5.** Schneider mottled-glass vase. H:10¼ in (26 cm). ③ **6.** One of a pair of French pressed black-amethyst glass vases. H:6 in (15.5 cm). ① **7.** Stuttgart School of Applied Art thick glass vase designed by Wilhelm von Eiff. H:8 in (20 cm). ② **8.** Marcel Goupy vase of faceted emerald cut glass. H:5¾ in (14.5 cm). ① **9.** Schneider ovoid vase, acid-etched with a broad geometric pattern. H:12¼ in (31.5 cm). ① **10.** Glass vase with green and gold swirls. H:8¼ in (21 cm). ② **11.** Stuart yellow blown-glass vase. H:7 in (18 cm). ① **12.** Jean Sala bowl for Cristalleries

1 Decanter and three glasses

2 Perfume bottle

3 Perfume bottle

4 Orrefors vase

5 Schneider vase

6 French vase

7 Wilhelm von Eiff vase

8 Marcel Goupy vase

9 Schneider vase

10 Glass vase

11 Stuart vase

12 Jean Sala bowl

13 Saint Louis vase

de St. Louis. H:6½ in (16.5 cm). ③ **13.** St. Louis cut-crystal vase, with stylized floral motifs. H:6½ in (16.5 cm). ① **14.** Marcel Goupy enameled vase, with gilt details. H:9¾ in (25 cm). ④ **15.** Venini *pulegoso* vase by Napoleone Martinuzzi. c.1930. H:14¼ in (36 cm). ⑥ **16.** Vase by Vittorio Zecchin, made by M. V. M. Cappellin. H:9¾ in (24.7 cm). ② **17.** WMF Ikora flared bowl, with a graduated green rim. c.1930. D:10¾ in (27.5 cm). ① **18.** Walsh intaglio Gay Ware bowl with floral design. W:9¾ in (25 cm). ① **19.** Décorchemont glass bowl with stylized flower design. W:11 in (28 cm). ③ **20.** Le Verre Français tall glass vase with stylized Japanese blossoms. H:19 in (47.5 cm). ③ **21.** Daum Frères acid-etched glass vase. H:1 1¾ in (30 cm). ③

14 *Marcel Goupy vase*

15 *Venini vase*

16 Vittorio Zecchin vase

17 *WMF Ikora bowl*

18 *Walsh Gay Ware bowl*

19 *Décorchemont bowl*

20 *Le Verre Français vase*

21 *Daum Frères vase*

LIGHTING

BY THE 1920S, ELECTRIC LIGHT WAS WIDELY ESTABLISHED AND NO
LONGER A NOVELTY. HOWEVER, ART DECO DESIGNERS STILL FOUND
THIS TECHNOLOGICAL LEAP AN INSPIRING CHALLENGE.

FIGURATIVE LAMPS

In the 1920s and 1930s, many glass designers
followed the lead of their Art Nouveau predecessors
by making lamps that blurred the boundaries
between ornament and practicality. In particular,
figurative lamps were enormously popular. They
usually had glass shades, and the bases were made
of brass or the cheaper spelter (a zinc alloy). The
classic Art Deco figurative lamp features a nude
dancing girl holding up a globe of light.

FRENCH GLASS LIGHTS

France's leading glass manufacturers—including
Daum, Müller Frères, and Schneider—had had
a reputation for exciting glass lamps and shades
since the early 1900s. By the Art Deco era,
however, they had moved away from the
earth-toned glass fashionable at the turn of
the 20th century toward vivid colors such

as bright orange. Further visual impact was
provided by marbled, mottled, or textured glass
surfaces, which were often decorated with stylized
flowers, geometric patterns, and Egyptian motifs.
Shapes were simple and elegant.

René Lalique produced vast quantities of
glass lights—from hanging bowls, to his unique
commissions for the ocean liner *Normandie*.
Department stores, hotels, restaurants, movie
theaters, and public buildings around the world
commissioned light fixtures from his famous glass
company. Usually made from opaque or opalescent
glass, Lalique's lights feature his typical shell
shapes, cascading blossoms, and female figures.

BRONZE TABLE LAMP The
stem of this table lamp is in
the form of an archetypal Art
Deco nude female figure. Her
arms are raised to support the
glass-ball shade. *1930s.*

Athletic poses, like this
one, were favored by many Art
Deco designers

The girl's pose is
reminiscent of an
Egyptian dancer's

Scantily clad women
were a popular subject for
Art Deco sculptors

*The chryselephantine
(ivory and bronze)
figure* is taken from a
sculpture by Richard W. Lange
of Rosenthal and Maeder

EGYPTIAN LAMP This lamp by Raymond Guerbe features a young woman
wearing an Egyptian robe. Made from green patinated bronze, she holds an
orange, fan-shaped glass shade. H:20½ in (52 cm).

PARACHUTE LAMP This lamp has a stitched-vellum shade in
the form of a parachute above a bronze-and-ivory base with a
fairylike figure of a female dancer. *1925.* H:34 in (86 cm).

AMERICAN TABLE LAMP
The domed chrome shade of this lamp is suspended on a chrome-and-black-enameled stem with a round, stepped base. *H:18 in (46 cm).*

MACHINE AGE LAMP This brushed-nickel table lamp has a fluted, tapering base and a shade with similar decoration. The shade clips directly on to the bulb. *H:11 in (28 cm).*

MARC EROL LAMP Half frosted glass, half metal cone, the shade of this lamp sits atop a slim stem with a metal ball at the top and stands on a circular base. *c.1925. H:15¾ in (40 cm).*

WOOD-AND-METAL LAMP
The rectangular shade sits above a distinctive medallion-shaped section decorated with carved birds and foliage and a rectangular plinth-type base. *c.1940. H:23¼ in (59 cm).*

FLOOR LAMPS

Often found in pairs, floor lamps are reminiscent of torchères, tall, narrow 18th-century candle and lamp stands. Many leading Art Deco metalworkers, including Edgar Brandt, Paul Kiss, and Albert Simonet, produced Art Deco floor lamps. Brandt teamed up with Daum to produce a variety of lighting. His *La Tentation* floor lamp with a cobra coiling up to a Daum marbled-glass bowl is among his best-known designs.

RUHLMANN'S LIGHTING DESIGNS

By the 1920s and 1930s designers realized that lighting could create a mood or atmosphere. As a result, lighting became an increasingly important element of interior design, whether it was spotlighting, uplighting, directed lighting, or diffused lighting.

Celebrated furniture-designer Émile-Jacques Ruhlmann saw electric lights as an integral part of his decorating schemes. As with all his work, the pared-down Classicism of his chandeliers, wall sconces, and lamps is loosely derived from 18th-century forms. Legendary for his high standards of craftsmanship, Ruhlmann allowed the exquisite properties of materials he used for lights—black marble, alabaster, gilt bronze—to shine through.

Other Parisian designers such as Jacques Adnet, Jean-Michel Frank, and Jean Perzel also produced Art Deco lights with a similar minimal, Classical feel. Parisian firm *La Maison Desny* took this idea a step further with its abstract geometric lights.

AMERICAN LAMPS

The New York-based furniture designer Paul Frankl wrote that "modernity and America have come to mean, in the mind of the world, one and the same thing." It is true that, from the 1930s onward, American designers produced some of the most exciting modern lighting of the Art Deco era. Their designs were Machine Age-sleek, abstract, and made from the latest materials, including aluminum, chrome, and plastic.

Among the most iconic examples of American Art Deco lighting are Walter Dorwin Teague's daring series of streamlined desk lamps for production by the Polaroid Corporation, which were inspired by automobiles, trains, and science fiction. Donald Deskey's custom cherrywood, chrome, and black-plastic desk-and-lamp suite, created for impresario Samuel "Roxy" Rothafel's office at Radio City Music Hall, was also very influential.

FLOOR LAMP Wrought iron, a relative newcomer to interior design, has been used for the elegant, partially gilt stand of this floor lamp, designed by Raymond Subes. *H:59 in (150 cm).*

PAIR OF TORCHÈRES Designed by the American Russel Wright, each of these torchères has a trumpet-shaped shade atop a bamboo shaft with ribbed banding. *H:25¾ in (65.25 cm).*

ANGLEPOISE LAMP

The English automotive engineer George Carwardine, who owned a factory that specialized in vehicle suspension systems, created the Anglepoise lamp in 1932. His highly original lamp had a shade on an articulated spring. It allowed the lamp's beam to move in any direction yet remain rigid when positioned. Carwardine drew inspiration from the "constant-tension principle of human limbs"—the way arms are both flexible and immobile. At first Carwardine thought that his light would be useful in factories, where you might need to focus on a specific area, but he soon realized this could apply to work in offices, too. Carwardine licensed his design to Herbert Terry & Sons. The Anglepoise lamp is still in production today and, much copied, has had a huge impact on lighting design in the second half of the 20th century.

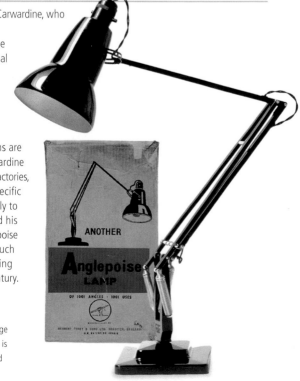

ANGLEPOISE LAMP Designed in 1932 by George Carwardine, the black-lacquered Anglepoise lamp is an iconic piece of the Art Deco era. It was reissued by Tecta in 2004. *1932. H:35½ in (90 cm).*

CHROME AND PLASTIC

ARGUABLY THE MOST INNOVATIVE MATERIALS FROM THE ART DECO ERA, CHROME AND PLASTIC WERE WIDELY USED FOR INEXPENSIVE MASS-PRODUCED ITEMS THAT PUT STYLISH MODERN DESIGN WITHIN THE REACH OF THOSE ON A BUDGET.

OCCASIONAL TWO-TIER TABLE The use of chrome to edge laminate table tops is typical of Art Deco design. This piece has an elegant, clean, almost modernist feel. *H:29½ in (75 cm).*

BULLET RADIO Made from butterscotch, blue, and red Catalin, this Fada radio (model 189) achieves a thoroughly modern look. The sleek design includes smooth knobs. *W:10¼ in (26 cm).*

AVANT-GARDE MATERIAL

Plastic could be easily—and inexpensively—molded into the latest streamlined Art Deco shapes, which made it ideal for stylish yet cost-effective accessories. Ashtrays, dressing-table sets, napkin rings, and handbags were all fashioned from the latest plastics. The material could also be made in a range of fashionable colors to suit every taste.

Even luxury liners such as the *Queen Mary* were home to plastic pieces, since few trend-setting venues were without items made from the new wonder material.

GEOMETRIC ASHTRAY Created for the luxury cruise liner the *Queen Mary*, this ashtray was made in pink on black urea-formaldehyde plastic by the British Buttner Pipe Company Ltd. *1930s. H:4½ in (11.5 cm).*

The word "chrome" comes from chromium, a metallic element rarely seen in its pure, solid form but widely used as a plated finish on objects made of other metals. Chrome-plating protects an object from corrosion and gives it a unique mirror shine.

Art Deco designers were quick to spot the potential of chrome-plating. The French sculptors who made car hood ornaments liked its gleaming, weatherproof durability, while the metal-furniture designers influenced by the Bauhaus ethos liked the fact that this striking finish was an innovative and inexpensive mass-production process.

INEXPENSIVE APPEAL

Chrome-plating was especially popular in the Depression-hit United States, where it was associated with the distinctive machine-styled, streamlined look of American Art Deco. In the 1930s, American metalwork manufacturers saw chrome-plated tableware as an attractively priced, low-maintenance, modern option—a substitute for silverware that would appeal to cash-strapped

DESK FAN The design of this fan, which looks like a propeller, is influenced by the Machine Age. Produced by Ventaxia, it is made from Bakelite, wood, chrome, and metal. *1940s. H:13½ in (34 cm).*

consumers. Companies like Chase and Revere employed leading designers—Peter Müller-Munk and Norman Bel Geddes among them—to create chrome-plated pieces such as pitchers and cocktail sets. The chrome-plated, streamlined look was also used to make domestic appliances such as vacuum cleaners and toasters more enticing to consumers.

MOLDING THE FUTURE

The term "plastic" describes anything that can be molded or shaped, whether natural materials such as amber, wood, and ivory, or synthetic materials such as phenolic resins and Lucite. Many early-20th-century plastics are now dubbed "bakelite," after the first synthetic plastic invented in 1907.

At the start of the Art Deco era, designers used plastics mainly to mimic other materials. They pressed them into imitation ebony knobs and ivory-like boxes. In the late 1920s phenolic resins became available. This combined Bakelite's robustness with a new translucency and unprecedented colors, opening plastic production up to new possibilities.

In the lean 1930s plastics were seen as a Machine Age wonder. These cheap, new materials were simple to cast into streamlined geometric or curvilinear shapes. Plastic products relied on their surface quality and overall form, rather then on decoration, to make them desirable. Müller-Munk recalled that the use of plastic was "the hallmark of modern design…the mysterious and attractive solution for almost any application requiring eye-appeal." Other designers turned plastic into highly original pieces that included jewelry and electrical appliances such as radios. Even everyday 1930s tableware—napkin rings, for example—had an added "jazz" factor when they were made from plastic.

EMPIRE COCKTAIL SHAKER This Revere shaker by William Archibald Welden combines polished chromium with brass. It is finished with a Catalin trim on the spout, lid, and spire finial. *1938. H:12½ in (31.75 cm).*

NICKERBOCKER BAR Guests on board the steamer *The Empress of Britain* enjoy cocktails en route from Southampton to Quebec. The chrome fixtures are archetypal examples of the streamlined Art Deco style.

METALWARE

WHETHER CHARACTERIZED BY LUSH ORNAMENT OR STARK STREAMLINING,
SOME OF THE FINEST SILVER AND METALWORK OF THE 20TH CENTURY WAS
PRODUCED DURING THE ART DECO PERIOD.

JEAN TÉTARD TEA AND COFFEE SET The tea and coffee pots, creamer, and covered sugar bowl in this set are of unembellished cylindrical form, with hardwood handles and finials. *c.1930. Creamer: H:4 in (10 cm).*

EUROPEAN SILVERSMITHS

One of the most innovative silversmiths of the Art Deco period was Jean Puiforcat, who in the early 1920s developed the use of unadorned geometric shapes such as cubes, spheres, and cylinders for tea services, flatware, and other silver pieces.

Puiforcat believed that form should follow function. His silverware is indeed characterized by an absence of any superfluous detail; yet it is incredibly sensuous to look at and touch. Many pieces have sumptuous details like handles and knobs made from rock crystal, lapis lazuli, or exotic woods. Renowned for his use of the best-quality materials and high standards of craftsmanship, Puiforcat was the silversmith counterpart to Émile-Jacques Ruhlmann, the cabinet-maker, with whom he collaborated on a display at the 1925 Paris International Exhibition. He also exhibited and worked with other leading designers of the period, including Le Corbusier.

ABSTRACT ELEMENTS

By the mid-1920s, other silversmiths started to take on elements of Puiforcat's geometric style. At the 1925 Paris International Exhibition, the Belgian Wolfers Frères exhibited an angular tea and coffee set, the Giaconda service, featuring ten-sided forms and bold ivory handles. It was a big hit, and the firm continued to make silverware based on geometric shapes throughout the late 1920s and 1930s.

French craftsman-designer Jean Tétard was interested in creating pieces stripped of all reference to historic styles. He began exhibiting plain silverware produced at his father's metalworks to critical acclaim in 1930. These striking designs, featuring angular and cylindrical forms, look deceptively simple. In reality, they were complicated to make and are a tribute to Tétard's technical skills.

SILVER-PLATED COMPOTE
Designed by Luc Lanel for Christofle and produced for the *Normandie* ocean liner, this simple, shallow compote is raised on a modernist sphere base. *c.1935. D:13 in (33 cm).*

CHAMPAGNE BUCKET Christofle produced most of the silverware for the *Normandie*. Here the simple styling, geometric banding, and solid handles are all characteristic of Art Deco style. Designed by Luc Lanel. *c.1935. H:8 in (20 cm).*

FLÈCHE (ARROW) CANDLESTICKS
This pair of two-flame, Gallia-metal candlesticks was designed for Christofle by Gio Ponti. The piece takes its name from the arrow between the two intertwined cornucopias. *1930s. H:8 in (20 cm).*

BALANCING PAST AND FUTURE

The French firm of Christofle made mainly electroplated silverware, using a process it had introduced to France in the 1840s. During the late 1920s and 1930s, Christofle produced traditional pieces alongside contemporary Art Deco vases, trays, tea services, and other items. Designers such as Carl Christian Fjerdingstad, Gio Ponti, Luc Lanel, Paul Follot, and Maurice Dufrêne were responsible for many of these pieces. Some were specially produced for the Compagnie Générale Transatlantique, which owned the famous *Normandie* and other ocean liners.

A number of other major silver manufacturers reacted to the modern Art Deco style. The British firm Mappin & Webb commissioned several designs for tea services and cocktail sets from leading designer Keith Murray, for example. In the United States, Tiffany created contemporary pieces like cocktail shakers and table lighters and made a splash with its modern designs for the 1939 New York World Fair.

NICKEL-PLATED BRASS CANDLESTICK The candle sockets are raised on a footed, semicircular frame pierced with stylized animal forms. Made by the Hagenauer Werkstätte. *1925. H:9¼ in (23.5 cm).*

HOOD ORNAMENT This large, rare, leaping-lion hood ornament in heavy, chromed bronze was designed by Casimir Brau. *c.1920. L:8¼ in (21 cm).*

HUNGARIAN SILVER SUGAR BOWL The body and lid of this sugar bowl with a circular foot and a slightly domed lid are chased with a geometric pattern. *1930s. W:4¼ in (11 cm).*

WROUGHT IRON IN INTERIORS

Normally associated with garden furniture and gates, in the 1920s wrought iron was put to innovative use indoors. Edgar Brandt, Paul Kiss, and other metalworkers made elevator panels and door frames for grand office and retail schemes. They also created firescreens, radiator grilles, console tables, mirrors, floor and table lamps, and bookends for use in domestic settings. The increased use of wrought iron in homes paved the way for the acceptance of tubular-steel dining-room chairs and other furniture in the 1930s.

AMERICAN WROUGHT-IRON GATE Fashioned in the style of Wilhelm Hunt Diederich, this gate (one of a pair) shows leaping hounds and stags in a stylized landscape. *1930s. H:62¾ in (159.5 cm).*

GEORG JENSEN

The most famous of all the Art Deco silversmiths is the Danish Georg Jensen, whose machine-made metalware is of exceptionally good quality. Jensen designs are very simple, usually based on curvilinear rather than angular forms. The main focus is on shape and, accordingly, Jensen kept decoration to a minimum, even leaving some pieces completely unadorned. His wide range of silverware includes tea and coffee services, candlesticks, and raised bowls, as well as pieces that were emblematic of the Jazz Age, such as cocktail shakers, cigarette boxes, and brush-and-mirror sets for dressing tables. Jensen also produced inexpensive silver jewelry—brooches, bracelets, and earrings—featuring stylized animals and floral motifs. His flatware—in the Pyramid pattern created by his brother-in-law Harald Nielsen, for example—was especially popular.

The firm employed a number of gifted designers. Preeminent among them was Johan Rohde, who designed the bestselling Acorn flatware pattern in 1916 and jug in 1920, which famously anticipated the streamlined designs of the 1930s. Jensen achieved international acclaim and opened shops in Paris, London, New York, and Buenos Aires. His designs were widely imitated by silversmiths throughout Europe, the United States, and Mexico. The Jensen firm is still making many of its celebrated Art Deco designs today.

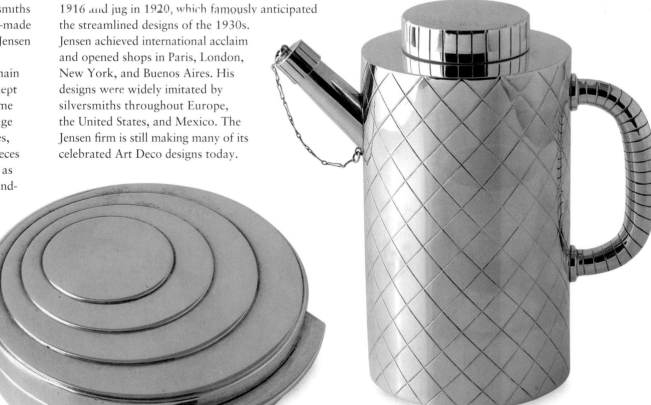

SILVER PILLBOX This simple yet elegant pillbox produced by Georg Jensen features a stepped lid with a series of offset concentric circles—a recurrent Art Deco motif. *c.1930. D:1¾ in (4.5 cm).*

JENSEN COCKTAIL SHAKER The stark, geometric form of this jug-shaped cocktail shaker designed by S. Bernadotte is accentuated by the banding on its lid and handle and the check patterning. *c.1940. H:5¾ in (14.5 cm).*

AMERICAN METALWARE

Throughout the 1920s, handmade or hand-finished European silver had set trends in metalwork design. Machine-made silver was not highly esteemed, and there was very little on display at the 1925 Paris International Exhibition. However, this situation changed when the Depression set in, in the early 1930s.

ALTERNATIVES TO SILVER

By the end of World War I, most American silver manufacturers used the latest technology to mass-produce silverware. As incomes rose during the Roaring Twenties, people wanted to entertain more lavishly, and American silver manufacturers responded to this by churning out traditional designs alongside watered-down Art Deco designs.

The market for silverware dried up almost overnight as a result of the Wall Street stock-market crash of 1929. Already geared up for mass production, American silver manufacturers concentrated on more modestly priced silver-plated pieces, and turned to even cheaper alternatives such as aluminum, pewter, copper, and chrome-plate.

ART DECO DESIGNS

Many companies also employed leading Art Deco designers to tantalize consumers with daring and affordable new designs in these less expensive materials. The Revere Copper & Brass Company commissioned about 17 designs from Norman Bel Geddes, a highly influential American Art Deco

SILVER BUD VASE Of elegant proportions, this Kalo vase rises from a flat bottom to a tapering neck. The slightly flared top has wire applied to the rim. *c.1925. H:6¾ in (17 cm).*

designer who helped popularize streamlining. Bel Geddes's linear Manhattan cocktail set stands out among his designs for Revere. It consists of a cylindrical cocktail shaker, matching stemware, and a stepped tray. Bel Geddes also produced metalwork designs for other manufacturers—for example, aluminum candleholders for the Kensington Company.

Perhaps more than any other metalwork manufacturer, the Chase Brass & Copper Company was determined to bring adventurous Art Deco design to those on a budget. Chase's chrome-plated designs were widely available in department stores at prices comparable to Depression glass, an inexpensive substitute for crystal. The firm employed several major industrial designers including Walter von Nessen, whose best-known work for Chase is the Diplomat tea and coffee service, a modern variant on Neoclassical forms.

Another key name employed by chase was industrial designer Russel Wright, who used spherical and cylindrical forms in chrome-plated brass kitchen utensils and tableware manufactured by the American company.

LEADING THE WAY

Wright also experimented with a new material developed for the aircraft industry: spun aluminum. He turned it into tea services, trays,

TIFFANY BOWL With chased bands below the rim and around the foot, this hemispherical bowl combines a satin finish on the outside with a brilliant-finish interior. *c.1925. D:5½ in (14 cm).*

plates, and tumblers that he had mass-produced by manufacturers such as West Bend Aluminum. These designs proved so popular that soon other manufacturers—the ALCOA company, for example—were producing similar ranges.

Meanwhile, the United States' largest silver manufacturer, the International Silver Company, commissioned cutting-edge designs from the Finnish-born architect Eliel Saarinen. Her most celebrated design for the company was a spherical

LIQUEUR SET This set of six chrome-plated cordial cups on a cobalt-blue glass tray was designed by Russel Wright for the Chase Brass & Copper Company. *1934. Tray: D:6 in (15 cm).*

PANCAKE AND CORN SET A Russel Wright design for the Chase Brass & Copper Company, this set comprises a chrome-plated, sphere-shaped pitcher and shakers on a cobalt-blue glass tray. *1934. Tray: D:6 in (15 cm).*

silver-plated coffee urn on a pierced cylindrical base with a matching tray. These futuristic pieces, exhibited at the 1934 Metropolitan Museum of Art's show devoted to industrial design, influenced many other designers, including Walter von Nessen, who created a similar chrome-plated urn for Chase Brass & Copper Company four years later.

OTHER INDUSTRIAL DESIGN STARS

A few American craftsmen-designers—among them, Peter Müller-Munk—switched successfully from silversmithing to industrial design in order to make a living during the Depression era.

Before opening his own studio in 1927, Müller-Munk had worked for Tiffany. Unlike most handmade American silver from the period, Müller-Munk's studio pieces were not influenced by Danish designs. His studio silver is very angular and geometric. Later, as an industrial designer in the 1930s, Müller-Munk created perhaps the most celebrated of all American Art Deco chrome-plated designs for Revere, the famous *Normandie* pitcher inspired by Cassandre's iconic poster image.

COCKTAIL SHAKERS

Nothing evokes the Art Deco era more than a cocktail shaker. The essential drinks accessory of the 1920s and 1930s was usually made of inexpensive silver-plated or chrome-plated metal, or from glass, with a silver-plated or chrome-plated top. Cocktail shakers inspired leading designers, including Walter Dorwin Teague. Most glass and metalwork manufacturers—from Steuben and Lalique, to Tiffany and Jensen—produced one. The classic form is a graduated cylinder with a bell-shaped top. Other popular designs resemble coffee pots with spouts and handles, or have a sleeve that twists to reveal the ingredients required for a cocktail. Novelty shapes include dumbbells, champagne bottles, penguins, and even airplanes.

MANHATTAN COCKTAIL SHAKER This Bel Geddes cocktail shaker has raised vertical ribs. The clean lines and use of chrome epitomize Art Deco styling. *1936–40. H:13 in (33 cm).*

NEW YORK SPEAKEASY Streamlined metal featured increasingly in interiors. In fashionable bars and clubs, metal railings might encase the cocktail bar, while chrome or silver cocktail shakers were employed to mix drinks.

MARIE ZIMMERMANN

In the 1920s and 1930s, acclaimed silversmith and metalworker Marie Zimmermann had a thriving New York workshop: the National Arts Club Studio. Here she made a variety of pieces, including jewelry, vases, candlesticks, and tableware. An avid gardener, Zimmermann also produced garden gates and furniture.

Her designs feature simple, often fluted forms that rely on patination, color, and texture for effect. She enjoyed working in iron, copper, bronze, brass, and gold, as well as silver, and her pieces often incorporate ivory and cabochon stones such as jade, amethyst, and quartz for an added touch of exoticism.

In her heyday, Zimmermann exhibited across the United States, and institutions such as the Metropolitan Museum of Art collected her pieces. After she closed her workshop in 1944 and

moved away from New York's art scene, she slipped into relative obscurity. A 1985 retrospective at the Metropolitan Museum of Art helped rekindle an appreciation of her craftsmanship and stylish designs.

Along with other American metalworkers such as Robert Jarvie, Margaret Craver, and Clara Barck Welles, the founder of the Kalo workshop, Zimmermann remained faithful to Arts and Crafts principles in the interwar years but gave her designs a modern Art Deco twist.

GOLD-PLATED COPPER VASE This cornucopia-shaped vase in hammered, gold-plated copper has applied chased leaf forms at the end of a curling tail that terminates in another leaf form. *W:10¾ in (27 cm).*

TWO-PIECE CENTERPIECE Both vase and stand are in hammered, gold-plated copper. The three-lobed vase flares out at the top in stylized leaf form, while the stand features heavy wirework with applied leaves and chased detail. *W:17 in (43 cm).*

METALWARE GALLERY

Art Deco metalware is simpler in style than Art Nouveau metalware, with angular and streamlined shapes. Geometric forms were very popular, as was stylized figural imagery. Technological advances at this time brought new materials such as stainless steel, chrome, and aluminum to the fore. There was also a rise in mass production of decorative metalworking. However, fine handcraftsmanship remained prevalent, often used in conjunction with mass-production techniques where pieces were hand-finished.

KEY

1. Chase bud vase in polished chrome. H:9 in (23 cm). ① **2.** Kalo silver candlesticks in tulip form. H:14 in (35.5 cm). ⑥ **3.** Georg Jensen silver candelabra. c.1935. H:6½ in (16.5 cm). ⑥ **4.** Set of Russel Wright box-shaped salt and pepper shakers. 1930. H:1½ in (3.75 cm). ② **5.** Chase centerpiece box marked The Architex, from a set with a pair of candlesticks. W:6 in (15 cm). ① **6.** Set of sterling-silver geometric powder boxes by Eliel Saarinen for International Silver. H:4–5 in (10–13 cm). ③ **7.** One of a pair of chrome Face lamps by the Revere Company. 1930s. H:10 in (25.5 cm). ① **8.** French silver-plated box with Bakelite handles. 1930s. W:10¾ in (27.5 cm). ④ **9.** Georg Jensen silver ashtray. 1930s. D:5 in (12.5 cm). ② **10.** One of a pair of French silver salt dishes. ② **11.** French wrought-iron firescreen attributed to Edgar Brandt. 1920s. H:28½ in (72.5 cm). ⑥ **12.** French

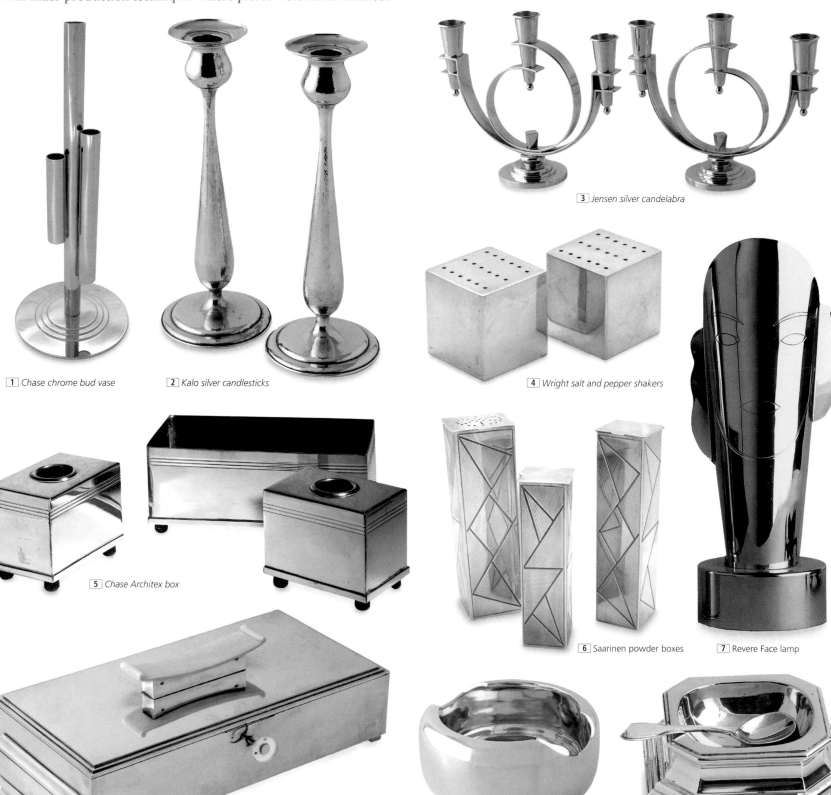

③ Jensen silver candelabra

1 Chase chrome bud vase

2 Kalo silver candlesticks

4 Wright salt and pepper shakers

5 Chase Architex box

6 Saarinen powder boxes

7 Revere Face lamp

8 French silver-plated box

9 Jensen silver ashtray

10 French silver salt dish

iron radiator cover of angular, Modernist design with rosette motif. H:37½ in (95 cm). ④ **13.** Evans leaping gazelle silver compact with copper accents. 1930s. D:3 in (7.5 cm). ① **14.** French brass vases of stepped shape decorated with an embossed panel of floral motifs. c.1925. H:6¼ in (16 cm). ② **15.** One of a pair of copper and brass bookends by Walter von Nessen for Chase. 1930s. W:5¼ in (13.5 cm). ① **16.** Georg Jensen cocktail shaker designed by Harald Nielsen. c.1925. H:10 in (25.5 cm). ④ **17.** French silver Cubist tea and coffee set by Ravinet d'Enfert with Macassar ebony handles. Coffeepot: H:7½ in (19 cm). ④ **18.** German copper and wicker coffee set. Tray: D:11½ in (29 cm). ② **19.** Manning Bowman chrome and Bakelite Connoisseur cocktail shaker. 1936. H:12 in (30.5 cm). ① **20.** Silver martini shaker by Mappin & Webb. H:9 in (23 cm). ②

13 *Leaping gazelle compact*

11 *French wrought-iron firescreen*

12 *French iron radiator cover*

14 *French stepped brass vases*

15 *Copper and brass book end*

16 *Jensen cocktail shaker*

17 *French tea and coffee set*

18 *German copper coffee set*

19 *Connoisseur cocktail shaker*

20 *Mappin & Webb martini shaker*

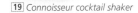

CLOCKS

IN THE 1920S AND 1930S, THE POPULARITY OF THE ART DECO STYLE WAS ALSO REFLECTED IN CLOCK-CASE DESIGN—FROM UNIQUE WORKS BY DESIGNER NAMES TO MASS-PRODUCED ITEMS.

STYLISH TIMEPIECES

People's desire for a coherent "look" for their home or office meant that every object had to fit into their design scheme. Most rooms had a clock, and there was a seemingly endless supply to choose from—from the most expensive examples, like Cartier's, decorated with diamonds, to simple mirror-glass electric wall clocks by Smiths.

DESIGNERS AND SPECIALISTS

Most Art Deco clocks were made by specialist clockmakers such as ATO, Le Coultre, and Omega. Paris-based ATO made its own designs and also sold movements in cases designed by Lalique. There are more than 20 Art Deco ATO models, all highly stylized and usually made in glass, metal, and plastic, with a battery movement. American mass-produced clocks abound, mostly with electric movements in a streamlined case featuring chrome and Bakelite. They were made by firms such as Manning Bowman and Lawson Time, Inc.

Leading French designers such as Jean Trenchant and Albert Cheuret produced custom designs or limited editions, and styles ranged from the highly decorated to the most severe and economical of designs. Meanwhile, celebrated decorators Louis Süe and André Mare produced clocks as part of their interior schemes.

Designers often made clocks with the intention of complementing their other work. Furniture designer Maurice Dufrêne, for example, produced a palisander longcase clock in 1925 to match his furniture. Like many of his

MOLDED GLASS CLOCK The face of this clock has bronze-painted numerals and stands on a stepped, black base. Designed by René Lalique, the piece is signed on the bottom right of the face. *1930s. H:10 in (25 cm).*

The numerals are in a geometric Art Deco style

SQUARE-FACED CLOCK This French Art Deco clock has a carved and frosted-glass square face. It stands on a stepped, black, Bakelite base. *1930s. H:8¾ in (22.25 cm).*

TABLE CLOCK The green-enameled face of this striking table clock is set within a simple chromed frame. The clock features a Jaeger-Le-Coultre movement. *1925. H:10 in (25 cm).*

The clock stands on a circular, black, Bakelite and chrome base

TELECHRON ALARM CLOCK Designed by Paul Frankl, this green catalin clock is architectural in form. A light bulb is set within the silvered ring around the dial. *H:7¾ in (19.5 cm).*

MANTEL CLOCK The square face of this clock is set within a simple alabaster case with stepped sides. On the top is the spelter figure of a scantily clad female. *W:18½ in (47 cm).*

TABLETOP CLOCK This striking clock has a variegated marble case housing a lozenge-shaped clock face. A spelter woman sits on the top balancing a ball. *W:12¾ in (32.5 cm).*

VIKING MANTEL CLOCK The color combination of this catalin clock makes it a desirable collector's piece. The simple round face is mounted on a black base and is flanked on either side by a decorative scroll. *1930s. H:3½ in (9 cm).*

The angular, geometric forms are typically Art Deco

contemporaries, Dufrêne advocated using technology to produce large numbers of machine-made pieces at moderate prices.

INFLUENCES ON CLOCK DESIGN

Designers borrowed widely for inspiration. Following Howard Carter's discovery of Tutankhamun's tomb in 1922, Egyptian motifs began appearing on all sorts of objects. The numerals and green sun-ray enameling on a small mass-produced table clock by Meyrowitz identify it as unmistakably 1920s, but the most striking feature is the pair of scarab wings, one each side of the clock—a sign of the popular Egyptian influence. Paul Frankl's 1928 design of the Skyscraper clock for the Warren Telechron company is made of a combination of polished and textured silver.

LALIQUE'S CLOCKS

René Lalique produced clock cases in his characteristic molded glass. In his search for new uses for decorative glass, he designed a clock set in a semicircular slab of glass with a light bulb in its bronze base. When switched on, the bulb illuminated the two nude figures—male and female—surrounding the clock face with a subtle light, giving a mysterious effect. Lalique managed to maintain the unusually high quality of his design and finish in mass-produced versions of his designs.

HERMAN MILLER

Famous modern furniture manufacturer Herman Miller originally studied clockmaking in Germany. With his son-in-law, D. J. De Pree, he started a subsidiary business, the Herman Miller Clock Company, in 1927, initially to make traditionally designed reproduction wall and mantel clocks. In the early 1930s, looking for a way to save the company's fortunes after the Great Depression, De Pree met Gilbert Rohde, a designer from New York. Rohde convinced De Pree to move away from traditional designs and focus on new products that were more suited to the changing lifestyles of Americans. A Gilbert Rohde design for a clock about 16 in (40 cm) wide, made by the company in the early 1930s, has a self-starting electric movement. The unusual hour hand is characteristic of Rohde's designs. The case is made from solid wood and has exceptionally clean lines, while the grain of the veneer emphasizes its sleek design.

In 1937 Herman's son, Howard, took over the clock business and changed the company name to the Howard Miller Clock Company. The firm continued to have success with its modern clock designs.

ROSEWOOD MANTEL CLOCK This Gilbert Rohde/Herman Miller electric mantle clock has a rosewood case, a circular dial, red-and-black-enameled metal hands, and chrome details. *W:16¾ in (42.5 cm).*

ELECTRIC CLOCK Attributed to Gilbert Rohde, this streamlined clock has a square face with abstract numerals set within a curving burr-walnut-veneered case with three applied chromed bands. *W:13 in (33 cm).*

TEXTILES

DURING THE ART DECO ERA, DESIGNERS FROM ALL FIELDS OF THE DECORATIVE
ARTS TRIED THEIR HAND AT TEXTILE DESIGN. THEIR INTEREST WAS PARTLY
EXPLAINED BY THE DESIRE TO ACHIEVE A UNIFIED LOOK FOR INTERIORS.

WOOL ART RUG The design of this rug is based on a work by the French
Cubist painter Fernand Léger. The asymmetrical arrangement and geometric
shapes are characteristic of Art Deco design. *L:65½ in (166.5 cm).*

NEW IDEAS

Designing textiles gave artists the opportunity to
express radical ideas and have them picked up by
a wider audience, especially since the public has
always been far more receptive to groundbreaking
ideas when these are presented in the decorative
arts than in fine art. In the 1930s, women who had
rejected or been shocked by the industrial scenes
depicted in modern art happily decorated their
homes with textiles covered in similar motifs.

POIRET'S INFLUENCE

The impact of the Ballets Russes' 1909 visit to
Paris on the development of Art Deco in France
was immediately evident in textiles and clothing
design. The celebrated fashion designer Paul Poiret
was responsible for popularizing their colorful,
exotic look in his extravagant couture garments.
Poiret was also an interior decorator. In 1911 he
set up the Atelier Martine, a workshop where
talented girls—often in their early teens—with
no formal training were encouraged to produce
naive artworks that he then used as the basis for
his textiles and furnishings.

Poiret got the idea for the Atelier Martine from
Austria's Wiener Werkstätte, whose Arts and
Crafts workshops he visited in 1911. The Wiener
Werkstätte was especially renowned in artistic
circles for its fabrics, which featured geometric
and stylized floral patterns based on folk designs.

ARTIST'S CREATIONS

It was Poiret who originally encouraged the
Fauve painter Raoul Dufy to design textiles.
Dufy worked on a number of projects for the
Atelier Martine before becoming artistic director
at Bianchini-Férier, a Lyon textile manufacturer.
With designs featuring abstracted figures and
bold colors, Dufy soon developed a reputation
as one of the foremost textile designers of the
Art Deco era.

The Russian-born but Paris-based painter Sonia
Delaunay was also renowned for her textiles.
A set designer for the Ballets Russes, Delaunay
was interested in Cubism and color theory; her

abstract canvases were dominated by geometric
shapes, mainly in primary colors. Delaunay
explored the same visual ideas in her textiles
and patchwork designs.

HARMONIOUS VISIONS

The exquisite quality of Émile-Jacques Ruhlmann's
creations is legendary. No material was too costly,
no detail too small for this French furniture and

SILK GAUZE PANEL Like much of the work produced by Sonia Delaunay, this
panel betrays a clear Cubist influence in its use of contrasting earthy tones and
simple geometric shapes. *c.1925. W:56 in (142 cm).*

interior designer. Ruhlmann not only produced his own designs for fabrics, he also commissioned designs from other artists for unique textiles to use in his luxurious decoration schemes. A real perfectionist, he had these materials produced by the best names in French textiles, such as Aubusson and Cornille Frères, the Lyon silk weavers.

The Irish designer Eileen Gray is best known today for her lacquered screens and tubular-steel furniture, but she also designed fabrics and rugs. Gray lived in Paris for most her life and was a pioneer of the modernist Art Deco movement. Her textile designs, like her furniture, were based on geometric forms. She used her colorful and boldly patterned rugs as a vital accent in her otherwise radically austere interior schemes.

TEXTILES GO GLOBAL

The 1925 Paris International Exhibition confirmed France's obvious lead in textile design, but daring, abstract, woven textiles were being produced by the

Bauhaus art school in Germany. Until this time, these artists had achieved only limited recognition outside their own country. However, by the 1930s, designers all over the western world were catching up and promoting their own versions of the Art Deco style. English designer Marion Dorn developed a name for herself designing luxurious geometric-patterned carpets, while Donald Deskey's famous Swinging Woman carpet in the auditorium of New York's Radio City Music Hall helped popularize Art Deco textiles in the United States.

PARK LANE HOTEL FOYER Elegant arches and stylized fern leaves decorate the carpet in the foyer of the Park Lane Hotel in London. These Art Deco shapes are echoed in the curved wall lights and column decorations.

MOHAIR PANEL The bold use of color and the pattern of this French rug, with its overlapping triangles, quadrants, stripes, and squares, make it a classic Art Deco design. L:118 in (300 cm).

VOIDED VELVET COVERLET The fountain was a recurring motif in the early Art Deco years. It often appeared in stylized form, as in this design woven in wool and silk. L:85 in (216 cm).

RUTH REEVES

Ruth Reeves is one of the best-known American textile designers of the 1930s. She produced designs for W. & J. Sloane, a chic New York interiors shop that promoted the latest styles. Her wall hangings and furnishing fabrics depict scenes from contemporary life, such as families listening to the radio, telephonists at a switchboard, or a tennis game among friends. Reeves's use of earth tones and block printing is indicative of her Arts and Crafts roots, which she developed between 1911 and 1913 while at the San Francisco Institute of Art, a hotbed of the American Arts and Crafts movement. She continued her studies with the Cubist painter Fernand Léger when she lived in Paris in the 1920s. Her stylized tubular figures and everyday urban themes demonstrate her familiarity with avant-garde European painting. Reeves moved to India in 1956 and spent her last decade studying and collecting traditional Indian crafts.

THE AMERICAN SCENE Commissioned by W. & J. Sloane in New York, this block-printed cotton tapestry is one of several in which Ruth Reeves captured the essence of everyday life. c.1930. W:83 in (211 cm).

SCULPTURE

IN THE INTERWAR YEARS, SCULPTURE WAS AN IMMENSELY POPULAR MEDIUM
FOR ARTISTIC EXPRESSION. FROM PREISS'S DANCERS, TO PROST'S SLEEK PANTHERS,
SOME OF THE ERA'S MOST ENDURING IMAGES WERE PRODUCED BY SCULPTORS.

IDEALIZING THE FEMALE FORM

Decorative sculpture was highly popular
throughout the Art Deco period, and women were
by far the favorite subject. In the 1920s and 1930s,
women were far more active and independent than
their predecessors had been. They danced with
abandon, participated in sports, and drove
automobiles. Art Deco sculptures of female figures
capture this dramatic transformation: slim and fit,
the ideal beauty is dressed in short skirts or, even
more daringly, in pants.

NEW AND TRADITIONAL MATERIALS

Sculptors and foundries met the increasing public
demand for sculptures with a plethora of designs
in differing materials and of variable quality.

Many portraits of women were produced using
a special combination of bronze and carved ivory
known as chryselephantine. More affordable,
mass-produced pieces were made from bronze,
white metal, or spelter, a zinc alloy that was
often patinated or painted to resemble bronze
or to produce a silvered or gilt finish. Many
of these mass-produced pieces were unsigned.

Most Art Deco sculptures sit on marble or onyx
bases that are modeled in the stepped style that
was fashionable at the time.

THE LIBERATED WOMAN

Demêtre Chiparus is probably the best known of
the Art Deco sculptors. The Paris-based artist was
famous for his figures of dancers in elaborate,
Asian-style costumes inspired by the Ballets Russes.
His showgirls look as if they have stepped straight
off the stage of the Folies Bergère onto the pedestal.
Chiparus created more than 100 sculptures, mainly
large and impressive figures with tight costumes
highlighted with gold paint and gilt.

Another successful Art Deco sculptor, Ferdinand
Preiss, was renowned for his charming, naturalistic
portraits of newly independent women. Many of
his works depict women performing some kind
of physical activity—swimming or playing golf
or tennis—or dancers and gymnasts in dramatic
poses holding torches, hoops, and balls. A number
of his finely carved and modeled sculptures were
inspired by the female athletes taking part in the
1936 Berlin Olympics. In the ultimate celebration

The ivory face
is intricately carved

The bronze body
is decorated with gold
paint and gilding

*Chiparus used
dancers* on the Paris
stage as his inspiration

JANLE SCULPTURE This chrome figure on a black
marble base is signed by Max LeVerrier. The woman's
pose is reminiscent of a gymnast's. *H:12½ in (32 cm).*

FEMALE EMANCIPATION Athletic female pursuits were becoming
acceptable by the 1920s and 1930s, a liberation celebrated by Art
Deco sculptors, who depicted women in numerous sporting poses.

DANCER OF KAPURTHALA Dancers in elegant poses are characteristic of
Demêtre Chiparus's work. Here the figure wears a headscarf and bodysuit and
stands on a stepped brown and green onyx base. *c.1925. H:21¾ in (55 cm).*

of the liberated woman, Preiss produced a figure of a female pilot based on celebrity pioneer aviator Amy Johnson.

Bruno Zach's sculptures of women are the dark counterpoint to Preiss's wholesome athletes and dancers. The German sculptor specialized in erotically charged portraits of women who were part of the decadent Berlin night scene. His "blue angels" are totally sexually liberated and unabashed about their nakedness.

AUSTRIAN OUTPUT

Austrian sculptor Josef Lorenzl also concentrated on images of women. He stylized his mainly nude figures in a distinct way, elongating their limbs and abstracting the facial contours. His sculptures of women are lively and animated, with outstretched legs and arms and thrown-back heads. His most ambitious design is probably a figure of Diana the Huntress flanked by two hounds and holding a bow aloft.

Lorenzl's models were made in various sizes and from a variety of materials. He also turned his hand to figural clocks, bookends,

and hood ornaments. His diverse output also included models for the ceramics firm Goldscheider. There, his elegant women were dressed in the latest colorful fashions or exotic costumes as Asian dancers.

The Austrian firm of Hagenauer Werkstätte also mass-produced statues in the Art Deco style under the creative guidance of Karl Hagenauer, son of the company's founder. Hagenauer's figures fall into two main categories: Western-influenced and African-influenced. Made from chrome, brass, or bronze, they were particularly popular in the United States. The highly stylized figures include Masai warriors, nude dancers, bellboys, and tennis players.

PREISS FIGURE This patinated-bronze and ivory figure portrays a young contemporary woman in a short-sleeved shirt and slacks, mounted on an onyx base. *H:12 in (30.5 cm).*

GRECIAN WITH TORCH Ferdinand Preiss sometimes created figures in Classical robes, as here with this bronze and carved-ivory Grecian female holding a flaming torch. *H:11 in (28 cm).*

The body is elongated and slim, highlighting the elegance of the pose

Lorenzl's figures often stand on tiptoe

Aphrodite is semi-draped in a robe with a jeweled and turquoise belt

LORENZL FIGURE This stylized figure is cast in bronze from a model by Josef Lorenzl and patinated with a silver finish. It stands on a conelike green onyx base. *H:15 in (38 cm).*

APHRODITE This Preiss bronze and ivory figure of the Greek goddess portrays her with her hands behind her head. She stands on a circular pink marble base. *H:9 in (23 cm).*

DEPICTION OF ANIMALS

Along with women, animals were a favorite subject of Art Deco sculptors. Silhouettes were simplified, and their shapes reduced to curvilinear forms and geometric planes. François Pompon was one of the first to move away from realism in the early 1920s. His smooth, stylized polar bears were a great success. Others, such as Gaston Le Bourgeois, Maurice Prost, Edouard-Marcel Sandoz, and Max Le Verrier, soon followed Pompon's lead. Art Deco sculptors portrayed the elegant dynamism of animals such as deer, doves, and horses. Reflecting Art Deco's fascination with exoticism, they were also drawn to African and tropical wildlife— antelopes, monkeys, and angelfish. Panthers in various poses were arguably the most popular of all animal subjects, though sculptors also captured the cool, calculating instincts of other predators, including foxes, eagles, and cobras.

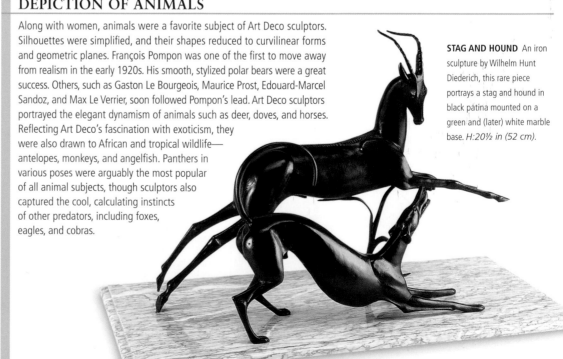

STAG AND HOUND An iron sculpture by Wilhelm Hunt Diederich, this rare piece portrays a stag and hound in black pátina mounted on a green and (later) white marble base. *H:20½ in (52 cm).*

POSTERS

BY THE 1920S AND 1930S POSTER ADVERTISING REACHED UNPRECEDENTED HEIGHTS OF SOPHISTICATION. AS A RESULT, POSTERS OF THE DAY FEATURED SOME OF ART DECO'S MOST EYE-CATCHING AND COLORFUL DESIGNS.

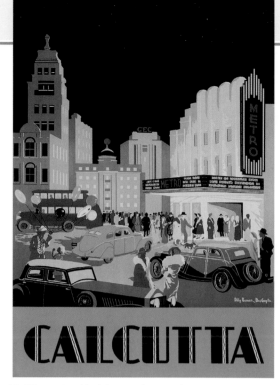

FRENCH VANGUARD

Since Art Deco began in France, some of the most inventive posters of the period were by French designers. Paul Colin employed a bold, simple figurative style to get his clients' message across. He became renowned for his posters of Parisian performers such as Josephine Baker. Jean Dupas explained that he used "a re-creation of nature according to [his] own temperament" to grab attention for the products that his posters were promoting, such as London Underground and the upmarket department store Saks Fifth Avenue.

The Art Deco period was also known as the Machine Age. During this time, modes of transportation, such as automobiles, airplanes, and ocean liners, were celebrated by graphic artists and elevated to new heights in the public's eye. A. M. Cassandre, the master of Art Deco graphics, was responsible for iconic images of locomotives and steamships that transcended the poster world and were readily recognized. Widely admired, he also inspired countless poster designs including Willem Ten Broek's poster for the Holland America Line.

BRITISH POSTERS

Some of the most enlightened British graphic arts patrons were the London Underground and railroad companies such as Great Western, London

CALCUTTA Designed by Philip Kumar das Gupta, this poster advertises a fashionable evening out at Kolkata's first MGM movie theater with its fabulous Art Deco facade. *1938. H:39 in (99 cm).*

AMERICAN AIRLINES Designed by Edward McKnight Kauffer, this advertising poster evokes the splendid grandeur of New York's skyscrapers from the perspective of the pedestrian. *c.1950. H:38½ in (98 cm).*

HOLLAND-AMERICA LINE Characteristic of travel posters of the era, this example by Willem Ten Broek features a stylized luxury liner—a powerful, sweeping image. *1936. H:38½ in (98 cm).*

NORD EXPRESS Strong lines and geometric shapes combine with bold use of color in this striking image by Cassandre, which captures the modernity and speed of rail travel. *1927. H:41¼ in (105 cm).*

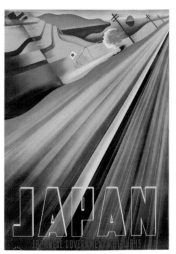

JAPAN This design by Munetsugu Satomi depicts the blurred view from a speeding train as it hurtles through the countryside. Subtle features include the Japanese flag and a cherry tree in full blossom. *1937. H:38½ in (97.5 cm).*

Midland, and Scotland and Southern Railway. They employed leading artists and encouraged imaginative poster designs to advertise events, beauty spots, historic sites, seaside towns, and leisure facilities reached by subway or train. One of the most prolific and best remembered graphic designers to be employed by the Underground was the American-born Cubist, Modernist, and Vorticist designer Edward McKnight Kauffer. He was also commissioned to design work for Shell, American Airlines, and Pan-American Airlines.

AMERICAN POSTERS

Some of the most creative American posters produced in the interwar years were also travel-related, commissioned by railroad companies such as the Pennsylvania Railroad, steamship owners like Matson, and airlines, including Pan American. These posters capture the power of the speeding trains, the awesome skyscrapers of the big cities, and the sizzling nightlife of tropical destinations such as Cuba. Others encourage visitors to come and see the future in science, design, and technology at the World's Fairs in Chicago, New York, and San Francisco.

President Roosevelt's New Deal program, aimed at economic recovery after the Depression, commissioned poster artists to create a series of campaigns to publicize travel and tourism, health and safety issues, cultural and educational programs, and community activities. The artists were given a fairly free hand, and the results were more than 2,000 striking silkscreen, lithograph, and woodcut posters.

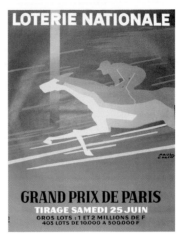

LOTERIE NATIONALE
Designed by Paul Colin, this poster celebrates the Grand Prix de Paris horse race. The horse and rider's streamlined poses suggest a dash to the finish line. *H:61 in (155 cm).*

DECO POSTERS IN OTHER NATIONS

The modernity, fantasy, and glamour of Art Deco also affected poster design outside the West. Despite living relatively traditional lifestyles, people in cities such as Tokyo, Shanghai, and Mumbai were open to the latest technology, design, and fashion trends from abroad. One of Japanese graphic designer Sugiura Hisui's best-known posters, The Only Subway in the East, illustrates this beautifully. He depicted passengers in both kimonos and Western attire in a colorful, stylized manner. Hisui's efforts to promote Art Deco graphic design in Japan included founding *Affiches*, a journal that introduced Japanese audiences to contemporary European and American poster design. Art Deco–flavored posters and advertising material also appeared in South America and even some African nations.

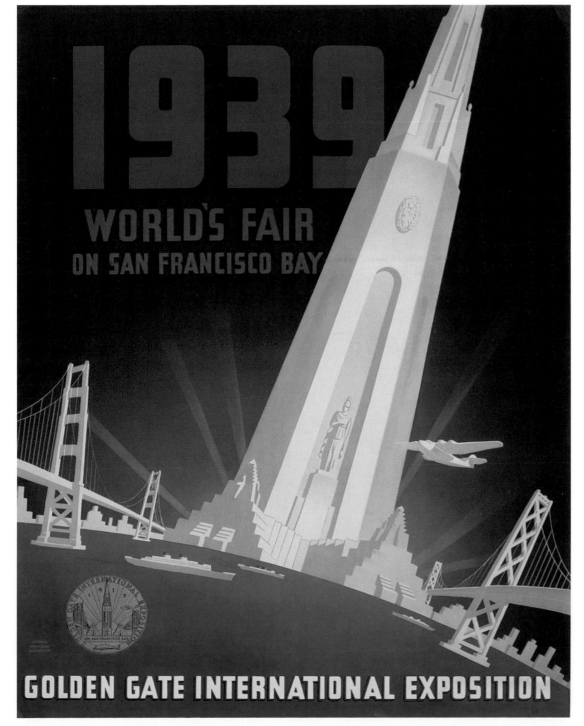

1939 WORLD'S FAIR This poster by Shawl, Nyeland & Seavey shows the Inca-inspired Tower of the Sun flanked by the Golden Gate and San Francisco Bay bridges. *1937. H:34½ in (87.5 cm).*

NEW YORK WORLD'S FAIR Designed by Nembhard N. Culin, this is a colorful bird's-eye view of the futuristic Perisphere, Trylon, and Helicline buildings. *1937. H:29 in (73.5 cm).*

MID-CENTURY
MODERN
1940–1970

A NEW OPTIMISM

AS COUNTRIES RECOVERED FROM WORLD WAR II, DESIGNERS SEIZED ON FRESH OPTIMISM AND USED NEW MATERIALS TO CREATE A WORLD UNLIKE ANYTHING THAT HAD GONE BEFORE. THE NEW DESIGNS WERE EASY TO MASS-PRODUCE AND SOON BECAME MAINSTREAM.

FLOOR LAMP Designed by Gino Sarfatti, this *Triennale* three-arm lamp has enameled metal shades and handles on a polished brass frame. *1950s. H:62 in (157.5 cm).*

THE POSTWAR MOOD

The end of World War II in 1945 brought peace, but it did not immediately restore prewar levels of supply and demand for goods, let alone prosperity. The only nation to emerge richer from the war was the United States, for it alone had escaped invasion, occupation, or bombardment. Elsewhere, recovery took time, in some cases well into the 1950s.

However, as economies started to grow and people began to prosper again, the demand for consumer goods escalated as never before. It was met by a breed of designers excited by the possibilities of mass production and enthusiastic to work with the host of new materials being made available to them. And with the beginnings of youth culture, a new market for modern, fashionable goods—many the result of wartime inventions—was born.

CHARLES AND RAY EAMES

The war did bring one benefit, however, for many of the techniques pioneered for military purposes were now available for peacetime application. One of the most surprising benefits came from the technique of molding a piece of plywood in two directions, originally developed by Charles Eames for the US Navy in 1942 to make leg splints for injured servicemen. After the war, Charles and his wife, Ray, adapted this technique to produce some of the most striking and innovative furniture of the 20th century.

Charles Eames was an architect and draftsman, and Ray Eames an abstract expressionist painter: in their work, they perfectly expressed the modernist aim of combining industry and art for social good. Their mission was "getting the most of the best to the greatest number of people for the least amount of money," which is why they used mass-produced

materials such as aluminum, fiberglass, molded plywood, and plastic, all of them affordable, flexible, and fresh. They also used the latest production techniques, such as aluminum casting, new ways of bonding wood, and that dual-direction plywood molding. But they applied the techniques to a looser, more sculptural style of furniture, owing more to the sinuous curves of a Brancusi sculpture than to the rigorous straight lines of a Le Corbusier or Bauhaus chair.

SOFT MODERNISM

Charles and Ray Eames, however, were far ahead of most American designers, for the United States had mostly been slow to accept modernism, particularly modernist furniture design, in the

TWA TERMINAL The simple, sweeping, arching forms of the Trans World Airlines Terminal at John F. Kennedy International Airport in New York are typical of Eero Saarinen's designs. The building was completed in 1962.

VERNER PANTON CONE CHAIR The chair is upholstered with fabric-covered foam on a star-shaped chromed-metal base. It was designed in 1958. *H:33½ in (85 cm).*

THE HOMEWOOD Patrick Gwynne created a modern, clean-lined interior in his Surrey home. An Eames lounge chair and ottoman sit alongside other pieces from the era, including a biomorphic sculpture.

interwar years. Their work was also far ahead of anything being produced in Europe, but this changed in the late 1940s with the development of new designs in Scandinavia. During the 1930s Scandinavian designers, notably Alvar Aalto and Bruno Mathsson, had developed a style best described as soft modernism. Inspired by nature, the look was curving and organic. It took a gentler, more ergonomic approach that used wood, with which Scandinavia is abundantly endowed, rather than plastic or steel.

Alvar Aalto, a Finnish designer, had famously remarked that metal furniture was uncomfortable in the cold and was "unsatisfactory from a human point of view." He and others developed a design style that used natural materials and forms and emphasized craftsmanship and traditional rather than high-tech manufacturing techniques. This softer approach to modernism can also be seen in the work of the Danish designer Arne Jacobson, whose Ant and Egg chairs were sculptural in shape, combining soft lines with strict attention to detail.

NATIONAL DIFFERENCES

Soft modernism appealed to consumers looking for comfort and reassurance after the war, not just in Scandinavia but in Italy too. Here, Gio Ponti and

Carlo di Carli introduced a sensuousness into furniture design not seen since Art Nouveau. Elements of this new approach can also be seen in Australia, where the influence of Charles and Ray Eames was strong, in Japan, where a hybrid modernism used local styles, and in Germany.

In France, however, designers went in another direction, adding decorative effects to the basic modernist style in order to sell their individually made items at high prices to an affluent elite. In Britain, despite the best endeavors of the 1951 showcase Festival of Britain, consumers by and large rejected the modernist look—however soft or hard—as being too close to the Utility range of

furniture forced on them by rationing during the war.

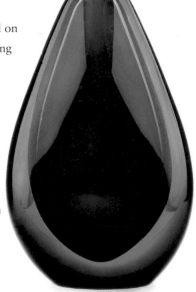

OVOID GLASS VASE
One of the big names in Murano glassmaking of the 1950s, this Seguso Vetri d'Arte vase was designed by Flavio Poli. *c.1960. H:12 in (30.5 cm).*

ELEMENTS OF STYLE

The multifarious strands of mid-century design make this a loose and mercurial era. The transition between 1950s formality and 1960s hedonism turned prevailing fashion on its head in a short span of time. A climate of scientific discovery informed many new developments in this period, while the shortage of materials after the war resulted in the need to design functional objects that were simple and easy to manufacture. This gave rise to the idea of "good design," a concept coined by Edgar Kaufman at the Museum of Modern Art in New York.

CASED MURRINE GLASS
REINTERPRETATION OF TECHNIQUES
In this age of innovation, even time-honored techniques were reinvented. Charles and Ray Eames revolutionized Thonet's 19th-century techniques for steam-bending wood, while in Italy the glassmakers of Murano updated traditional decorative methods to infuse glass with new color and variety.

GEORGE NAKASHIMA TABLE
WOOD
Early in this period, manufacturers working in wood dominated furniture design. Designers such as Finn Juhl and Hans Wegner sowed the seeds of the Scandinavian style with their simple and organic forms. In the United States, George Nakashima kept Japanese woodworking traditions at the fore of fashion.

MIDWINTER PLATE
DOMESTIC TASTE
A new domesticity saw the reinforcement of gender stereotypes after the disruption of war. Young homemakers were enticed by a huge array of labor-saving devices and bright new abstract patterns. The vogue for entertaining led to mass-produced tableware, oven-to-table crockery, and the hostess cart.

PSYCHEDELIC FABRIC
POP
The distinction between high and low art was eroded by a new generation of artists in the 1960s. Popular culture was taken more seriously, and in response it threw up outrageous and informal commodities in tune with the outlook of the newly empowered youth movement.

FAIENCE CHARGER
CRAFTSMANSHIP
Many artisans still practiced craft skills, often in tandem with more industrial work. The Studio movement pervaded the decorative arts, from ceramics and glass to furniture and metalware. Many of the styles and techniques developed by artist-craftsmen were adopted in time by industrial designers.

MURANO GLASS VASE
EXUBERANT COLOR
From the subtle naturalistic hues of Scandinavian glass to intense day-glo fluorescence, color was all-important. Designers used it in an unashamed bid to be noticed, discarding all rules regarding proper combinations. Drab colors were seen as old-fashioned and stuffy.

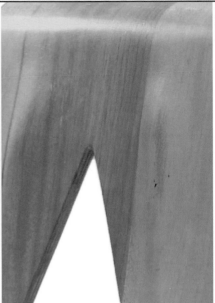

PLASTIC TELEPHONE
FORM AND FUNCTION
A culture of convenience encouraged the production of highly specialized goods that demonstrated fitness for purpose. Designers questioned traditional design in everything from the chair to the telephone. This telephone was designed to fulfill its purpose, curving to fit neatly from ear to mouth.

FLYING SAUCER FLOOR HEATER
FUTURISTIC DESIGN
The space race was one manifestation of the Cold War that grabbed the attention of the world. In the period leading up to the first Moon landing in 1969, globe shapes and representations of UFOs and satellites proliferated, from Sputnik lighting fixtures to the JVC Videosphere television.

BENT PLYWOOD TABLE
NEW MATERIALS
The war effort led to great advances in materials technology, which then brought new developments to the consumer market after the Allied victory. Inventive designers incorporated aluminum, stainless steel, improved plywoods, and even a spray-on plastic polymer into their work.

STACKING PLASTIC ASHTRAYS
FANTASTIC PLASTIC
Injection-molding technology gave designers new freedom. Manufacturers took to plastics enthusiastically, reveling in their potential to hold more or less any form or color. As more and more affordable and versatile synthetic materials hit the market, the range of consumer goods available exploded.

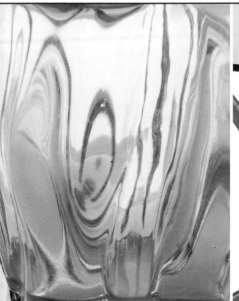

IITTALA VASE
NATURAL INSPIRATION
Designers drew freely from natural forms in this period, though rarely without adding a stylistic twist. Scandinavian glass and ceramic artists were drawn to the colors and textures of their local landscape, while Pop artists enjoyed the juxtaposition of depicting natural forms in unnaturally vivid colors.

VLADIMIR KAGAN TABLE
CLEAN LINES
The legacy of early modernism meant that the Cubist influence was still at work. As the 1960s progressed, this angular geometry waned, replaced by a more organic aesthetic. Many designers eschewed surface decoration, allowing these simple shapes and clean lines to take center stage.

HENNING KOPPEL BOWL
BIOMORPHIC FORMS
Biomorphic design—abstract forms fused with shapes found in nature—was first used in the 1930s by Surrealist artists to create ceramics and metalware. Natural forms were stretched and warped to achieve an effect both familiar and alien by adherents of the Scandinavian style, most notably by Henning Koppel.

ATOM BALL CLOCK
ATOMIC TECHNOLOGY
The dawn of the atomic age saw designers borrow microscopic natural forms such as atomic structures. Introduced at the Festival of Britain in 1951, this style was adopted enthusiastically in the United States. The Atomium, built in Brussels for the 1958 World Expo, represented the peak of atomic design.

FURNITURE

A TASTE FOR TRADITIONAL-LOOKING FURNITURE WITH A CLEAN,
MODERN EDGE IMMEDIATELY AFTER WORLD WAR II LATER GAVE
WAY TO A PERIOD OF FRIVOLOUS EXPERIMENTATION.

ROSEWOOD SIDEBOARD Designed by Børge
Mogensen, this rosewood-veneered sideboard is characteristic of contemporary
Danish design in its clean lines and tapering legs. The sliding doors have
book-matched veneers and indents for handles. *1958. L:93¼ in (238 cm).*

SCANDINAVIAN TRENDS

During the 1950s, Scandinavian designers became more prominent than ever before. They impressed the world with a pared-down vision of modernity that paradoxically relied on traditional materials and working practices. The industrialized killing of the war years had exposed a shocked public to the barbarous face of modernism; they no doubt found the cozy familiarity of carefully worked teak furniture reassuring.

The Danish designer and architect Finn Juhl grew up wanting to be an art historian, and although he was dissuaded from this career by his father, it was reflected in his respect for tradition. In collaboration with the cabinet-maker Niels Vodder, Juhl created highly sculptural pieces of furniture inspired both by the free-form expression of abstract art and by organic, natural forms. He won five gold medals for his exhibits at Milan Triennale shows during the 1950s, and his success helped to whet an international appetite for Scandinavian design, paving the way for other talented individuals to make a similar break.

Børge Mogensen, a close contemporary of Juhl and a fellow Dane, was influenced in his early career by Kaare Klint, an architect and designer who combined interests in Classical historicism and ergonomics. During the 1940s, Mogensen headed the Danish Cooperative Wholesale Society, a position that put him at the heart of trends in Danish manufacturing and retail. Armed with a detailed knowledge of Danish consumerism, Mogensen set about producing tailored furniture such as his 1954 Boligens Byggeskabe cabinet system. He was trained in the Danish craftsman tradition and worked primarily in wood, crafting his work with smooth, clean lines. This helped him reach a wide audience, even among those who were wary of modern design.

NEW IDEAS FROM THE OLD WORLD

During the 1930s, the United States benefited from a huge influx of fresh talent, as modernist designers fled the growing instability of Europe and forged new lives for themselves across the Atlantic. One reason why they found their adopted homeland to be so receptive to their ideas was the groundwork that had already been laid on their behalf by George Nelson. A two-year tenure at the American Academy in Rome offered Nelson the chance to travel around Europe interviewing the stars of

HANS WEGNER

Another of the high-caliber Scandinavian designers to find success in this period was Hans Wegner, who produced one of the most acclaimed chairs in the modern canon, model JH501. Known simply as The Chair to its many fans, it was born of what Wegner referred to as the "continuous process of purification" that is the kernel of all good modern design. Its status was enhanced further when CBS purchased 12 of them for use in the famous 1960 televised debates between Kennedy and Nixon. Although there is nothing revolutionary in the teak frame and woven seat construction, the design itself has a timeless elegance.

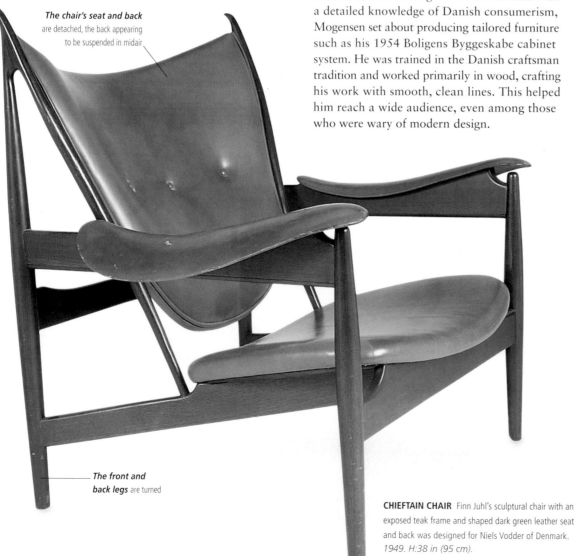

The chair's seat and back are detached, the back appearing to be suspended in midair

The front and back legs are turned

CHIEFTAIN CHAIR Finn Juhl's sculptural chair with an exposed teak frame and shaped dark green leather seat and back was designed for Niels Vodder of Denmark. *1949. H:38 in (95 cm).*

THE CHAIR In Wegner's model JH501 the back rail seamlessly becomes the armrests, raised on four tapering, dowel legs. It has been dubbed the ultimate blend of form and function. *1949. H:30 in (76 cm).*

GEORGE NELSON CABINET The white porcelain pulls and tapering, brushed-metal legs of this Herman Miller rosewood-veneered cabinet by George Nelson are typical of his *Thin Edge* series. *1950s. W:55¾ in (141.5 cm).*

HOME OFFICE DESK George Nelson's all-in-one walnut desk on a tubular brushed-metal frame is a clever combination of a leather-covered writing surface, a range of storage cabinets, and a mesh file basket. It was designed for Herman Miller. *1948. W:54¾ in (138 cm).*

avant-garde architecture and design. He published these interviews upon his return home, thus introducing the American public to figures such as Walter Gropius, Ludwig Mies van der Rohe, and Gio Ponti.

George Nelson's own career as a furniture designer was launched when D. J. DePree, the president of the Herman Miller manufacturing company, saw his Storagewall modular system featured in the pages of *Life* magazine. DePree immediately offered Nelson the design directorship at Herman Miller, and the company then quickly rose to a position of prominence, rivaled only by Knoll in its dominance of the American modern furniture industry.

INNOVATIVE DESIGNS

As large American companies such as Knoll and Herman Miller became more established, they were less willing to take the kind of creative risks that had made their names in the first place. Budding designers such as Wendell Castle and Vladimir Kagan were compelled to work with smaller outfits or produce their own furniture. Kagan's sculptural, organic furniture forms, with trademark splayed legs and sinuous frames, look like direct descendants of Finn Juhl's earlier wooden chairs.

However, companies such as Dunbar made the work of the American designer Edward Wormley more widely available. The Italian designer Gio Ponti proved that extraordinary new things could be achieved even with traditional methods and materials when he unveiled his *Superleggera* (Super-light) chair in 1952. Weighing in at just 3¾ lb (1.7 kg), it was the lightest mass-produced chair of its time.

The simplicity of Ponti's design was echoed by that of former employee, Franco Albini, and fellow Italians Gino Colombini and Marco Zanuso, as well as Frenchman Jean Prouvé. Ponti's richly embellished collaborations with Piero Fornasetti were the antithesis of modernist minimalism.

***SUPERLEGGERA* CHAIR** This dining chair with two horizontal back slats and a woven seat was Gio Ponti's version of a simple, rustic-looking chair, designed for Cassina of Italy. *1957. H:32 in (81 cm).*

CONTOUR CHAIR Armchairs with matching ottomans were a popular contemporary form. This example, designed by Vladimir Kagan, has a sculpted walnut frame and retains its original dark brown Kagan swirl chenille upholstery. *H:36 in (90 cm).*

AMERICAN STUDIO

Modernist design quickly became the status quo in the United States, where prosperous and fashion-conscious consumers were enjoying the boom years in the aftermath of World War II. Unwilling or unable to fit into this prescribed vision of corporate modernity, a number of solitary designer-craftsmen doggedly pursued their own unique visions.

The pioneer of this reclusive approach was Wharton Esherick, known as the "Dean of American Craftsmen," who first took to carpentry in 1924 when it became clear that his career as a painter would never take off. Esherick pursued a solitary existence in the Pennsylvania hills, working against the grain by striving toward the perfection of his handicraft at a time when craftsmanship was considered to be a relic of the past. Despite this, he did not work in total isolation from the wider world, absorbing influences from emerging modern art movements into his work. The result was

MODERN TO CONTEMPORARY The timeless style of George Nakashima's furniture means it is perfectly at home in the garden room of a house in Osaka, designed by Chitoshi Kihara. *c.2000.*

sculpted, functional forms that blurred the boundaries between furniture and high art.

Esherick chose to settle near Rose Valley in Delaware County, previously the site of a utopian Arts and Crafts experiment. His early work echoes the heavy aspect of much Arts and Crafts furniture, and exhibits a pronounced vernacular streak—he produced a series of chairs for a local theater fashioned from ax handles, for example. In time he developed his own idiom, a kind of tactile, free-form furniture that was much imitated by his spiritual successors.

SLAB COFFEE TABLE The free form top of this cherrywood coffee table, complete with fissures, is typical of George Nakashima's work. *1956. W:61½ in (154 cm).*

GEORGE NAKASHIMA

Born in Spokane, Washington, George Nakashima took a circuitous route that brought him to the same locale as Esherick. An MIT (Massachusetts Institute of Technology) architecture graduate, Nakashima worked in Paris and Tokyo before undergoing a transcendental experience in an Indian ashram that informed his later work.

On returning to the United States, Nakashima found himself interred with other Japanese Americans after the bombing of Pearl Harbor in 1941. After his release he settled in New Hope, Pennsylvania, where he established a studio and devoted himself to working with wood. Nakashima

was given the Sanskrit name Sundarananda, meaning "one who delights on beauty" by his guru. His struggle to remove the demands and constraints of the designer's ego from his work led him to a deep appreciation of his chosen material, firmly within the Japanese tradition that was so admired by Frank Lloyd Wright.

Nakashima's dramatic designs rely entirely on the qualities inherent in the wood for their effect. He selected his wood carefully, preferring pieces that had remarkable burls, good color, and other notable features such as natural "uro," or recessed areas. Many of his pieces have an unworked free edge, with the intention of expressing the form of the wood as much as possible. Nakashima threw the ebullient natural beauty of his wood into sharp relief by combining it with man-made elements, including angular, geometric members and decorative joinery such as butterfly splays.

THREE-LEGGED STOOL The flared dowel legs of this stool have been mortised through the seat and are joined by graduated stretchers. Designed by Wharton Esherick, the stool is carved "WE 1966." *W:16½ in (42 cm).*

PAUL EVANS

Another denizen of the New Hope scene, Paul Evans initially trained as a silversmith before establishing his own studio and beginning to accept commissions for pieces of monumental furniture. During the 1960s he designed for Directional Furniture, a progressive company based in North Carolina, and headed their factory for a time before downsizing once more to work from his own studio in the late 1970s.

Paul Evans's Cityscape range has echoes of Paul Frankl's Skyscraper line (*see p.272*) in both name and look, although Evans's work is far more sculptural. His massive doors and room dividers in particular straddle the boundary between functional furniture and art installations. His sinuous, stalagmite-form table bases are, like much of his oeuvre, constructed from bronze and steel. Evans's early training as a metalworker instilled in him a fundamental understanding of these materials.

Custom commissions for wealthy clients allowed Evans to fund the opening of a New York showroom in 1979, thus bringing his work to an even wider audience.

BRONZE DINING TABLE
The sculpted base of this Paul Evans table is of serpentine stalagmite form. It supports a round-edged plate-glass top. *1960s. W:87½ in (222 cm).*

PHILLIP LLOYD POWELL

During the 1950s Evans shared a showroom in New Hope with Phillip Lloyd Powell, another exponent of studio furniture. Powell gained widespread recognition after his work was exhibited at America House, next to the Museum of Modern Art in New York, which had championed the modernist cause. His furniture incorporates diverse materials, from metal and wood to slate and marble, chosen for their tactile qualities and the ways in which they contrast with one another. Powell's work is highly sculptural and each piece is unique—even handles on individual items will seldom match because, in Powell's words, "they don't have to, like people don't match." One of his favored woods was walnut, as it is particularly soft and can be sculpted with specialist tools such as the spoke shave, a skill at which he was especially adept.

ROOM DIVIDER The front of this steel room divider comprises sculpted compartments, treated in reds, greens, and purples with gold-leaf accents. Signed "Paul Evans." *1967. W:96 in (244 cm).*

NEW HOPE CHAIR AND OTTOMAN In walnut and black leather, this is Lloyd Powell's most iconic design. *1956. H:32¼ in (82 cm).*

COFFEE TABLE This Phillip Lloyd Powell coffee table has a circular slate top and lower shelf, on three chip-carved plank legs with hammered-metal hardware and casters. *1960s. H:36¼ in (92 cm).*

ARABESCO **COFFEE TABLE** This beech-veneered plywood coffee table is typical of designer Carlo Mollino's idiosyncratic style. Originally produced by Apelli & Vareso in 1949, this example is a reissue produced by Zanotta of Italy. *2004. W:50¾ in (129 cm).*

The perforated plywood frame is bent to provide a magazine rack below the plate-glass table top

S-CHAIR Designed by Verner Panton for Thonet, this was the world's first single-piece cantilevered chair made from molded plywood. *1965. H:34 in (85 cm).*

The chair is shaped to fit the human frame, with swooping, organic curves

BENT PLY

As the modernist movement matured, desire for the shock of the new ebbed, and designers became comfortable revisiting established methods and materials, especially if they could find novel ways to use them. The century-old technology of laminated plywood construction provided the basis for a large proportion of the most iconic furniture of the time. The war had resulted in great advances in laminate technology, and one of the biggest draws of the material was that the same design could be finished with any number of different lacquer, paint, or veneer coatings, offering consumers choice—something they were beginning to demand more of.

The versatility of laminated plywood had been comprehensively explored in the mid-19th century. In the United States, John Belter had exploited its suitability for extreme shapes and pierced decoration, while Michael Thonet had pioneered the steam-bending process in Austria. Their influence can be seen in Carlo Mollino's elegant *Arabesco* coffee table, designed in 1949. The plywood frame represents a synthesis of the Art Nouveau stylings of Antonio Gaudí with the free-form surrealism of Salvador Dali. Mollino was an eccentric designer, obsessed with the occult, and much of his work came from private commissions; the most vociferous exponents of plywood furniture were industrial designers who were interested in large-scale production.

THE SEARCH FOR A PERFECT FORM

The reductionist obsession shared by many mid-20th-century designers prompted them to eliminate every extraneous feature from their furniture; many imagined the perfect form to be one constructed from a single piece of material, without joins or breaks. Charles and Ray Eames struggled with this concept in the 1940s.

While working as an assistant for Arne Jacobsen during the early 1950s, the young Verner Panton contributed to the design of the celebrated 3100 model, better known as the Ant chair. Originally conceived for use in a canteen, this chair was designed with easy stacking in mind and became the most successful mass-produced chair of the 1950s. The seat and back are molded from a single piece of plywood, and the tubular plastic (later metal) legs are attached to the seat with a single bolt.

PUSHING THE LIMITS OF PLYWOOD

In 1956 Panton took this reductionism to its logical conclusion with his S chair. The first cantilevered design in plywood, the S chair was manufactured by Thonet, the spiritual home of bentwood furniture. Its distinctive curves have been borrowed and copied dozens of times since its first production.

Others also chose to explore the sculptural possibilities of plywood. George Nelson's Pretzel chair, for example, was named for the manner in which the top rail and arms twist and bend. A company named Plycraft manufactured dozens of furniture designs on behalf of individuals, including company president Paul Goldman, who were interested in pushing plywood to its artistic limits. The Cherner chair, thought to have been

The seat and back are made from a single sheet of bent laminated wood

CHERNER CHAIR This walnut-veneered, bent-laminated-wood chair with armrests was designed by Paul Goldman in 1957 but attributed to Norman Cherner at the time. It is based on George Nelson's Pretzel chair. *1957. H:31 in (78 cm).*

Plywood with curves that emulate the female form

The chair stands on simple, tubular-steel legs

TEAK-VENEERED CHAIR This teak-veneered plywood chair was designed by Robin Day for London's Royal Festival Hall in celebration of the 1951 Festival of Britain. Produced by Hille International Co., this example was made in 1956. *H:31 in (77.5 cm).*

NOTORIOUS CHAIR

This iconic and much-parodied image of Christine Keeler straddling what looks like an Arne Jacobsen chair was taken by photographer Lewis Morley at the height of the Profumo scandal in Britain in 1963. The aperture beneath Keeler's elbows shows that this is not in fact a genuine Series 7 chair but one of the many imitations that found their way onto the market. Nevertheless, the use of the chair for this powerful image demonstrates that Jacobsen's designs were still regarded as being bold and sexy a decade after they first appeared.

SERIES 7 CHAIR The seat and back of this chair are made from a single sheet of shaped and molded plywood. It has a tubular-steel base with rubber-capped feet. *1955. H:30 in (76 cm).*

designed by Paul Goldman but attributed to the architect and designer Norman Cherner in order to give it more credibility, is remarkable for the precariously slim transition between the one-piece molded seat and back. Combined with slender applied arms and legs, this chair manages to convey both the great strength and fluid grace of plywood.

The revival of British industry, celebrated at the 1951 Festival of Britain, depended on designers to supply economic, interesting products for mass production. Ernest Race provided the event with one of its most talked-about designs: the cast-aluminium BA chair. Robin Day, winner of the Museum of Modern Art's Low Cost Furniture competition, became design director of British manufacturer Hille in 1950 and fulfilled exactly that brief. Day's molded plywood 661 chair, designed for the Royal Festival Hall, was followed by the immensely successful Hillestak model.

THE EASTERN AESTHETIC

With a venerable tradition of woodworking behind them, Japanese designers took to plywood construction with aplomb, achieving international recognition. More accustomed to sitting on mats than on chairs, they took the Western idea of the seat—one that is alien to their culture—and infused it with a peculiarly Eastern aesthetic. Reiko Tanabe's geometric Murai stool, for example, makes use of a patchwork construction technique known as *yatoizanetsugi*. It is part of the permanent collection at New York's Museum of Modern Art.

Sori Yanagi accompanied French designer Charlotte Perriand on her tour of Japan when she visited the country in 1940. The cultural exchange between the two may have been the inspiration behind Yanagi's foray into chair design. In accordance with his maxim "True beauty is not made; it is born naturally," Yanagi's Butterfly stool takes its form from the natural world. It is constructed from two bent and shaped plywood forms bolted together with a brass stretcher—suitable for mass production and yet sacrificing none of its elegance to the machine-making process. The perfect symmetry of its form, in

particular the upswept seat, is reminiscent of the gateway to a Shinto temple. Both the Murai and the Butterfly stools rely upon the grain of their wooden veneer in lieu of any other surface decoration.

MURAI STOOL Reiko Tanabe designed a laminated, molded beech stool with teak veneer for Tendo Mokko in 1961. The example shown here is a reissue. *H:14¼ in (36 cm).*

BUTTERFLY STOOL Designed by Sori Yanagi, this rosewood-veneered stool is made from two sheets of laminated and molded beechwood, joined together by a single stretcher. *1956. W:16½ in (42 cm).*

The minimal, geometric design is achieved by bending each piece in three directions

CHARLES AND RAY EAMES

CHARLES AND RAY EAMES DEFINED MID-CENTURY AMERICAN MODERNISM. THEIR WORK WITH THE US GOVERNMENT, THE SMITHSONIAN INSTITUTION, AND BLUE-CHIP COMPANIES SUCH AS IBM PLACED THEM AT THE HEART OF 20TH-CENTURY AMERICAN IDENTITY.

ESU-400 STORAGE UNIT A multipurpose storage unit with four sliding doors and five drawers designed for Herman Miller, the ESU-400 is supported on a slender steel frame with polychrome side and back panels. *1950. H:48¼ in (122 cm).*

RAR CHAIR The iconic Rocking Armchair Rod chair, shown here in salmon, has wooden rockers, a metal-rod frame, and a fiberglass-reinforced molded-plastic seat. It was designed for Herman Miller. *1948–50. W:24½ in (62 cm).*

EERO SAARINEN

The collaboration between Eero Saarinen and Charles Eames for the Organic Design in Home Furnishings competition left an indelible mark on Saarinen's personal aesthetic. Like Eames, he developed an interest in office furniture systems, and his career followed a similar trajectory as he explored new materials. Among Saarinen's most distinctive contributions to furniture design are the spreading columnar bases of his Pedestal group, which he hoped would "clear up the slum of legs" that restricted movement and comfort in the dining room.

TULIP TABLE The elliptical laminated top of the Tulip dining table is supported on a pedestal base. Saarinen designed it for Knoll Associates. *1957. W:96 in (244 cm).*

Charles and Ray Eames were mentored by Eliel Saarinen, father of Eero, at the Cranbrook Academy of Art in Michigan. Charles initially trained as an architect, while Ray came from the avant-garde New York art scene, where she had experimented with molded and pressed plywood sculpture. Together, their goal was to create furniture that could be mass-produced at an affordable price.

One of their first products was a molded plywood chair developed from a concept Charles had worked on with Eero Saarinen for the Organic Design in Home Furnishings competition in 1940. During World War II, Eames had worked on commissions for the US navy, producing splints, stretchers, and airplane nosecones in plywood. Their extensive research into the plastic properties of plywood produced some true classics such as the 1945 LCW (lounge chair wood) and L cm (lounge chair metal), both of which had molded plywood components.

The Eames' commitment to providing their customers with choice can be seen in the range of materials in which these chairs were offered, from paint to leather and even animal hide. Their influence increased the options offered to consumers, as their contemporaries drew on their experiments to produce a wealth of plywood chairs in many designs.

NEW MATERIALS

The development of fiberglass-reinforced plastic made it possible to construct a chair seat and back from a single piece of material, representing the culmination of the Eames' earlier trials with plywood. The Plastic Shell Group was the first series of unlined plastic chairs to be mass-produced, the result of work for the International Competition for Low-Cost Furniture Design.

Unveiled in 1950, the line initially included the RAR (rocking armchair rod) and DAR (dining armchair rod) models and was expanded in later years. The "rod" component of these names refers to the metal rod bases that supported the fiberglass shell seats. *La Chaise*, another fiberglass design conceived for the same competition, proved too expensive to put into production at the time.

CTW TABLE This CTW (coffee table wood) table has a molded ash-plywood circular tray-top on bent plywood legs. It was designed for Herman Miller. *1946. H:34 in (86.5 cm).*

Charles and Ray Eames continued to design chairs throughout the 1950s and 1960s, most of them made and distributed by Herman Miller. The long relationship between the Eames and this venerable company was first forged when they designed the Herman Miller showrooms in Los Angeles.

The 670 lounge chair and 671 ottoman, with their luxury rosewood veneers, represented the Eames' first foray into the high end of the market and were an immediate success. Their willingness to embrace new materials also saw them using steel rods, aluminum, and Naugahyde upholstery.

Later in their careers, the Eames shifted the focus of their work from furniture to film, photography, and exhibition design.

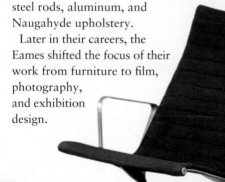

SWIVEL CHAIR This American Herman Miller Aluminum Group Model No. EA117 swivel chair has the original purple upholstery over an aluminum frame and star-shaped base. *1958. H:34 in (86.5 cm).*

DKW-2 CHAIR The Dining Bikini Wood (DKW) chair has a welded and bent-steel-rod seat and frame and is raised on wooden legs. It was designed for Herman Miller. *1951. H:33 in (84 cm).*

LA CHAISE The molded fiberglass seat and back are raised on five polished-steel rods, which rise from an oak star-shaped base. The lack of upholstery emphasizes the sculptural shape. Designed in 1948, this version is a 1990s edition from Vitra AG of Germany. *W:53 in (134.5 cm).*

MODERN MATERIALS

While Scandinavian designers first found fame with their innovative use of wood, many of them turned to more modern materials in the later 1950s. Sheet metal proved more versatile even than plywood, and its relatively cold and unwelcoming surface could be softened with fabric upholstery.

Some of the earliest steps toward this new vision were taken by Eero Saarinen. The son of a Finnish architect but a naturalized citizen of the United States, Saarinen represented the fusion of Scandinavian modernism with American corporate aesthetic. Having already collaborated with Charles Eames to win a competition run by the Museum of Modern Art entitled Organic Design in Home Furnishings, Saarinen unveiled his Model 70 chair in 1947. Constructed from molded fiberglass with foam cushions and fabric upholstery, it was soon dubbed the Womb chair in recognition of the invitation to curl up that was offered by its soft contours. Saarinen himself described the chair as being "biological." Its influence was far-reaching, inspiring a number of designs with a similar organic abstraction.

This strain of mid-century modernism was eminently suited to ambitious commissions that aimed to create harmonious environments in which even the smallest details contributed to an overall ambience. The undisputed master of this kind of obsessive total design was Arne Jacobsen. The Royal Hotel in Copenhagen, the world's first designer hotel, is one of his architectural masterpieces. Jacobsen produced the Swan and Egg chairs, two of the most recognizable furniture designs in the modern canon, for the hotel lobby. Their soft, enveloping forms and bright upholstery helped to create an interior aesthetic that contrasted with the angular uniformity of the exterior of the building.

THE CONE CHAIR

A hotel commission also lay behind one of Verner Panton's biggest successes—the Cone chair. Developed for the restaurant his parents owned within the Komigen guesthouse in a provincial Danish town, this chair caused a global sensation. After it was spotted by a local entrepreneur, Panton agreed to put it into production. The racy photo shoot he devised for a magazine article promoting his design featured naked models—quite enough to court controversy in the stuffy 1950s. When the chair made its New York debut, the police demanded it be removed from the shop window

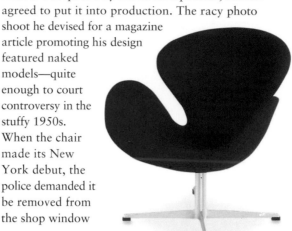

The organic form of the Egg and Swan chair is characteristic of Jacobsen's style

EGG CHAIR Made of foam upholstered in wool and supported on an aluminum star-shaped base, the high-backed Egg chair was designed by Arne Jacobsen for Fritz Hansen of Denmark. *1957–58. H:42 in (106.5 cm).*

SWAN CHAIR Arne Jacobsen's chair is made of fabric-covered foam on a molded fiberglass seat, with a swivelling cast-aluminum base. It was designed for Fritz Hansen of Denmark. *1957–58. H:29¾ in (74 cm).*

The heart-shaped back of the chair is constructed from bent sheet metal for stability

The chair takes its name from the womblike design of the seat

WOMB CHAIR Eero Saarinen's chair and ottoman, designed for Knoll Associates, are made from fiberglass upholstered in foam-filled fabric over a bent tubular-steel frame. *1948–50. H:40 in (102.5 cm).*

HEART CHAIR Verner Panton's sculptural chair takes inspiration from the work of Arne Jacobsen. The metal frame and foam construction is fully upholstered in a bright red fabric. *1958. H:40 in (101.5 cm).*

BUTTERFLY CHAIR This early model of the chair designed by Antonio Bonet, Jorge Ferrari Hardoy, and Juan Kurchan has a leather seat. *1950s. H:34¼ in (87 cm).*

DIAMOND CHAIR, MODEL 421LU This sculptural chair has a vinyl-coated, bent and welded steel-rod body and frame, and was designed by Harry Bertoia for Knoll Associates. It would have had a thin, upholstered cushion. *1950–52. W:33¼ in (84.5 cm).*

SOUND SCULPTURES

The royalties paid by Knoll Associates to Harry Bertoia for his immensely successful furniture line allowed him to concentrate on sculpture for the rest of his career. His oeuvre is instantly recognizable, consisting of serried rows of metal rods. Bertoia experimented with different types of metal, favoring strong, lightweight alloys such as beryllium copper, and with various shapes of rod, some capped with cylinders or disks to accentuate their kinetic qualities. The result was a series of sonorous sculptures that played a kind of music when touched by the wind or a hand. Bertoia even released a soundtrack, entitled *Sonambient,* of the sounds produced by these works of art.

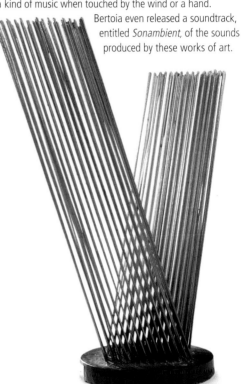

V SCULPTURE In this sculpture by Harry Bertoia, two opposing groups of gilded bronze rods are mounted on a circular bronze base. *1960s. H:8 in (20 cm).*

after crowds stopping to look at it blocked the street. Like the Heart, its sister chair, the Cone was based on a very simple geometric form. In designing it, Panton had deliberately steered away from his preconceived ideas of what a chair should look like.

ORGANIC SHAPES IN METAL

Emboldened by the phenomenal success of these radical designs, other designers looked back to the tubular-metal furniture of the prewar European avant-garde and breathed new life into it, bringing it in line with the organic shapes of mid-century modernism. Tubular metal frames and legs were already staples of the genre, featuring heavily in the work of Charles and Ray Eames, among others.

The Argentinian design collective Grupo Astral, comprising architects Antonio Bonet, Juan Kurchan, and Jorge Ferrari Hardoy, designed the Butterfly chair (Sling chair or A chair) in 1938. A modernization of Joseph Beverly Fenby's 1877 Tripolina chair, the Grupo Astral model was simply an angular bent and welded iron-rod frame slung with shaped leather upholstery. Later models were made with canvas seats rather than leather. The chair was extremely popular and is still produced today.

More remarkable was the Bertoia Collection, designed by Harry Bertoia for Knoll in the early 1950s. The wire construction he used was revolutionary and surprisingly delicate—as Bertoia said, his chairs were "made mainly of air."

Warren Platner took the idea further, drawing on the benefit of his five years' experience under Eero Saarinen. Aiming to produce furniture with the grace of Louis XV pieces, he relied on the beauty of his nickel-plated steel rods for decorative effect. The Platner Collection, issued by Knoll, included his 1725 table and stools, compared in the catalog to sheaves of wheat. The hundreds of metal rods that make up these pieces all had to be welded by hand.

The glass table top seems to float above the elegant, spindle-shaped base

DINING SET With a nickel-plated steel-rod construction, the four stools are upholstered with foam and the table has a glass top. It was designed by Warren Platner for Knoll Associates. *1966. Table: H:28 in (71 cm).*

PYRAMID CONE CHAIR Designed by Verner Panton for Plus Linje of Copenhagen, this chair is of sheet metal construction with foam and cotton upholstery. *c.1960. H:37½ in (95 cm).*

BALL CHAIR The near-spherical shell of this Eero Aarnio chair is lined with blue fabric-covered foam and is mounted on a painted aluminum base. It was designed for Asko Oy of Finland. *1963–65. H:78 in (198 cm).*

The chair swivels on its own axis over the base

COOL PAD An early 1970s bedroom is furnished with sculpted plastic chairs by Eero Aarnio. The look is completed by cool white walls, a gold shag carpet, and a Roy Lichtenstein print.

PASTIL CHAIR Designed by Eero Aarnio for Asko Oy of Finland, the fibreglass-reinforced polyester Pastil chair is molded to fit the shape of the sitter. It can be rocked from side to side. *1967–68. W:36 in (92 cm).*

PLASTIC FURNITURE

Good value, durable, colorful, and very versatile, plastic made an impact on the furniture industry during the 1950s and 1960s that was nothing short of sensational. Plastic, and plastic-reinforced fiberglass, allowed designers to realize at a stroke the ambitious forms they had been working toward through their exploratory use of plywood and sheet metal. The advent of injection-molding technology removed all barriers, making it possible to mass-produce almost any shape quickly and cheaply.

Continuing along the trail-blazing trajectory that had taken him into new territory when most of his contemporaries were busy rediscovering their Scandinavian heritage, Verner Panton conceived his single-piece, cantilevered plastic chair in 1959. Production was delayed for years and the Panton chair finally debuted in 1967. By this time, the radical design was in complete harmony with the Pop Art furniture that was then at the height of fashion, exemplified by iconic pieces such as Eero Aarnio's Ball chair.

THE INFLUENCE OF AARNIO

Like his later Pastil (or Pastilli) chair, Aarnio's Ball was constructed from fiberglass-reinforced plastic. Particularly hardy as well as waterproof, this versatile material allowed consumers to use these products indoors or outdoors—the Pastil could even be floated on water. Consumers were also offered a choice of colors, the Ball originally being produced in black, white, red, and orange.

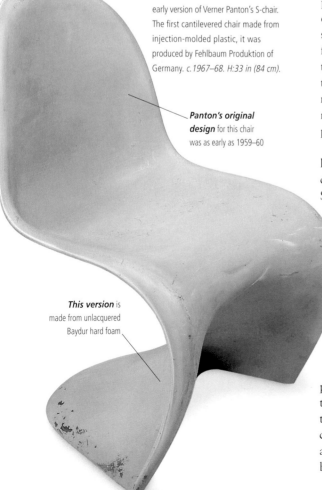

STACKING SIDE CHAIR This is an early version of Verner Panton's S-chair. The first cantilevered chair made from injection-molded plastic, it was produced by Fehlbaum Produktion of Germany. *c.1967–68. H:33 in (84 cm).*

Panton's original design for this chair was as early as 1959–60

This version is made from unlacquered Baydur hard foam

The premise of the Ball chair could not be more simple; it consisted of a hollowed, sliced sphere raised on a circular swivel base. The scope it presented for customization ensured its longevity—a cocoon insulated from the outside world, the chair was converted by some users into a listening station by the addition of speakers. Others used it as a base from which to make telephone calls.

The shape of the Pastil rocking chair is extrapolated from a lozenge, or a piece of candy—the very epitome of the Pop movement. As Aarnio's most celebrated furniture designs, these two chairs share more than an aesthetic connection. The form of the Pastil is based on the void space of the Ball, and together they form a perfect, solid sphere, although this was not the original intention.

Peter Ghyczy's Garden Egg chair is influenced by Aarnio's Pastil and is again suitable for indoor or outdoor use. In this cult chair, the foam upholstery was protected from the elements by the backrest, which folded down to create a watertight seal. The space-age pod design roots this chair firmly in the 1960s. Ghyczy built upon the success of the Garden Egg by founding his own studio and producing exclusive furniture for the top end of the market.

LUIGI COLANI

Maverick designer Luigi Colani has built his career on plastics and created some extraordinary furniture in the process. His 1971 *Zocker* (Gambler)

ZOCKER Made from seamless yellow polyurethane, this Top System *Zocker* designed by Luigi Colani is both a seat and a desk. *1971–72. H:24½ in (62 cm).*

chair, or *Sitzgerät* (Sitting Apparatus), evolved from a smaller model originally conceived as a piece of child's furniture. Colani is a firm believer in the importance of the ergonomics of good design, and the *Zocker* chair was designed to fit the contours of the human body. As well as functioning as a standard chair, it can be straddled, the backrest forming an integral table.

THE LURE OF PLASTICS

The Italian designer Joe Colombo was also fascinated by plastics and, like Colani, he was interested in multifunctional designs. His 1969 Tube lounger, composed of four hollow cylinders that can be attached together in any configuration, is a typical example of his functional, versatile design. He beat Verner Panton to the finish line in 1967 with his Universale 4860 chair, making it the first full-size injection-molded chair on the market; the detachable and interchangeable legs made his chair more versatile but sacrificed some purity of design. While Joe Colombo is well known for his chairs, lamps, and other household designs, he was also obsessed with storage units and carts. His greatest achievement in this particular field was the Boby

storage cart, a wheeled unit with rotating drawers that has been a bestseller ever since its inception in 1970.

The first designer to successfully draft a single-piece molded chair of traditional four-legged design was Vico Magistretti. His Selene chair used S-shaped legs, which gave it the required structural strength.

The lure of plastics was to prove irresistible even to the leading lights of the studio furniture movement. Wendell Castle's Molar Group furniture products, dating from the late 1960s, saw the designer apply his vision to the material that defined the age. One of the biggest attractions for Castle was the possibility of coloring plastic in any shade. "One day it just dawned on me that everything I had been making was brown," he said.

STORAGE CART Designed by Joe Colombo, this cart has hinged drawers and compartments stacked one above the other. It is made from injection-molded ABS plastic and was produced by Bieffeplast of Germany. *1970. H:21 in (53 cm).*

GARDEN EGG CHAIR The fiberglass-reinforced polyester shell of this chair is hinged at the back and lifts up to reveal an upholstered interior. When closed, it has a flattened ovoid form. It was designed by Peter Ghyczy for Reuter Produkts of Germany. *1968. L:32¼ in (82 cm).*

MOLAR GROUP COFFEE TABLE As the name suggests, the range was inspired by the shape of molar teeth. This is one of the few designs in plastic by Wendell Castle. *1969. H:23 in (58.5 cm).*

The shape of the table top is mirrored in the base

The table has a swivel action at the point where it is narrowest

FURNITURE GALLERY

Postwar modernist furniture explored new, often sculptural forms. This development was aided by the birth of new materials such as laminate and plastic that allowed for greater flexibility in design. Bright primary colors were fashionable and often covered the entire structure, making a bold statement. Wooden furniture remained popular, with the simple, elegant designs produced in Scandinavia influencing designers worldwide.

KEY

1. Coffee table by Isamu Noguchi. 1944. H:14½ in (37 cm). ③ 2. Double school bench designed by Jean Prouvé, for Ateliers Prouvé-V.S.A. c.1948. W:47¼ in (120 cm). ③ 3. Greta Magnusson Grossman coffee table with three circular tops laminated in primary colors. c.1965. W:58 in (145 cm). ⑤ 4. Austrian coffee table, the red synthetic top with swiveling, detachable gray-plastic tray. 1960s. D:24½ in (62 cm). ① 5. Ebonized chest-on-stand by Tommi Parzinger, the drawer with silver-leaf front. c.1952. H:36 in (90 cm). ③ 6. Pair of low bronze tables by Philip LaVerne, decorated with an Asian motif. 1960s. H:17 in (43 cm). ③ 7. Jean Prouvé wall-hanging cabinet with a single sliding door and enameled metal compartments. 1950s. H:116½ in (296 cm). ⑤ 8. Sideboard by Finn Juhl. c.1950. L:82 in (208 cm). ③ 9. Coffee table by Roger Capron, its top with geometrically shaped tiles. 1960s.

1 Isamu Noguchi coffee table

2 Jean Prouvé school bench

3 Greta Magnusson Grossman coffee table

4 Austrian coffee table

5 Tommi Parzinger chest-on-stand

6 Philip LaVerne tables

7 Jean Prouvé cabinet

8 Finn Juhl sideboard

10 Paul McCobb credenza

9 Roger Capron coffee table

11 Tommi Parzinger sideboard

W:47¾ in (121.5 cm). ③ **10.** Paul McCobb credenza with sliding cloth doors and two adjustable shelves. c.1950. W:60 in (152.5 cm). ③ **11.** Custom-designed sideboard with orange-lacquered finish by Tommi Parzinger. 1950s. W:84 in (213.5 cm). ⑤ **12.** Malitte seat system by Roberto Matta, consisting of five foam elements. 1966. H:62 in (157.5 cm). ⑤ **13.** Oskar Hodosi Fleur seat, made of polyurethane and foam-rubber padding with purple fabric. 1969. H:33 in (84 cm). ③ **14.** Mezzadro stool by Achille and Pier Giacomo Castiglioni. 1957. H:20 in (51 cm). ① **15.** Pair of George Nelson Coconut chairs. 1955. L:39¾ in (101 cm). ④ **16.** Pelican chair by Finn Juhl. 1940. H:28 in (71 cm). **17.** Sessel Karuselli armchair designed by Yrjö Kukkapuro, with fiberglass and leather seat and chrome base. 1965. H:35½ in (90 cm). ③ **18.** Allunaggio outdoor stool, with steel legs and an aluminum alloy seat, by Achille and Pier Giacomo Castiglioni. 1965. H:29 in (74 cm). ③ **19.** Fibreglass Group armchair by Erwine and Estelle Laverne. H:29¼ in (75 cm). ②

12 *Malitte seat system*

14 *Mezzadro stool*

13 *Oskar Hodosi Fleur seat*

15 *George Nelson Coconut chair*

16 *Finn Juhl Pelican chair*

17 *Sessel Karuselli chair, designed by Yrjö Kukkapuro*

18 *Allunaggio outdoor stool*

19 *Fibreglass Group armchair*

CERAMICS

MID-CENTURY CERAMICS ENCOMPASSED BOTH MASS-PRODUCED
WARES AND THE STUDIO POTTERY MOVEMENT, WHICH CONTINUED
TO BLUR THE BOUNDARIES BETWEEN CERAMIC CRAFT AND FINE ART.

LARGE BOWL This is an early and unique example of Bjørn Winblad's studio work. It is handpainted in a design typical of his themes of folklore and fairy tales. *1956. D:18½ in (47 cm).*

Organic, asymmetrical designs, like this one, are typical of the 1950s

REPTIL VASE Designed by Stig Lindberg for Gustavsberg of Sweden, this yellow-glaze vase has a textured surface reminiscent of the reptile skin after which it is named. *1950s. H:7¼ in (18.5 cm).*

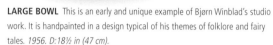

TEAPOTS These matte-glazed porcelain teapots, designed by Ulla Procopé for Arabia of Finland, betray Asian influences in the rounded shape of the pots, the flattened lids, and the cane handles. *c.1957. H:6 in (15 cm).*

SCANDINAVIAN CERAMICS

Mid-century Scandinavian ceramics occupied a curious middle ground between factory production and art pottery. Some of the larger companies opened public galleries at their premises, both enhancing their image within the community and subtly encouraging competition among their designers. In 1932 the Finnish company Arabia established a studio in which artists could work free from the pressures of the factory environment and production quotas, which proved to be an extremely fruitful venture in terms of generating new design ideas.

During the late 1940s, Arabia designer Kaj Franck responded to the austerities of war by producing the aesthetically and financially lean Kilta service. This economy of style became a hallmark of Scandinavian ceramic design, and was instrumental in the success achieved by Finnish factories at a series of Milan Triennale shows throughout the 1950s. Franck gathered a talented team around him at Arabia that included Ulla Procopé, whose well-proportioned table- and ovenware had a sculptural quality that belied its functional role.

Swedish potters enjoyed success on the same scale as their Finnish neighbors. The 1930 *Stockholmsutsällningen* (Stockholm Exhibition), directed by architect Gunnar Asplund, highlighted the extent to which Swedish ceramicists had embraced the modernist ideals of the Bauhaus, and marked the beginning of a golden age that peaked in the 1950s.

The Gustavsberg pottery followed the lead established by Arabia and founded an experimental studio in 1942. Many of the designs that successfully made the migration from the drawing board to the production floor were devised by Stig Lindberg, the dominant figure of Swedish pottery in this period, who took over artistic directorship of Gustavsberg in 1949. His work for the company included a series of hand-painted faience bowls in the 1940s and 1950s, and the Reptil range of textured vases and bowls in various matte and, less frequently, gloss glazes during the 1950s. His work is mostly associated with his plates, dishes, and bowls that mimic natural, organic forms.

INSPIRATION FROM NATURE
This kind of biomorphic style also prevailed at Rörstrand, another Swedish factory. Both Carl-Harry Stålhane and Gunnar Nylund had a background in sculpture before turning their attentions to ceramic design, and this is evident in their pieces. Both worked primarily with stoneware, producing vessels with decorative schemes steeped in the French abstract traditions of the Cubists and other modern art movements.

RÖRSTRAND BOWL Biomorphic forms and motifs were not uncommon in Scandinavian design, as in this oblong bowl with a spiral relief pattern designed by Carl-Harry Stålhane for Rörstrand of Sweden. *L:8 in (20 cm).*

MARSELIS VASE The geometric Marselis pattern is seen in a striking green glaze on this Royal Copenhagen Alumina faience vase by Nils Thorsson. *1950s–60s. H:4¼ in (11 cm).*

The most enduring of the products issued by the Rörstrand factory in the mid-20th century was Louise Adelborg's Grace porcelain dinner service. The repeated relief pattern depicting ears of wheat is typically Scandinavian in its homage to the sustaining bounty of nature.

This love of the Scandinavian countryside can also be seen in the work of Danish polymath Bjørn Winblad. His early slip-decorated ceramic forms, first exhibited in 1944, draw on the woodland and water spirits of Nordic folklore. Winblad used archaic Scandinavian potter's tools such as a cow horn and goose quill to manipulate his slip (clay and water mix), giving it a naive, even crude aspect that makes his subject matter all the more unsettling.

ROYAL COPENHAGEN
In Denmark, potter Gertrud Vasegaard successfully lobbied first Bing & Grøndahl and then Royal Copenhagen to tailor their materials and production methods in order to realize her own artistic vision. This extraordinary flexibility demonstrates both the high esteem in which Vasegaard's stoneware vessels

were held and the willingness of Scandinavian industry to accommodate its best designers. This certainly paid dividends for Royal Copenhagen, which found huge sales with Grethe Meyer's simple dinner services and a porcelain service of organic design by Henning Koppel in the early 1960s.

The output of the Alumina factory that produced earthenware ranges for Royal Copenhagen was dominated by designs by Nils Thorsson. His Marselis range of affordable, functional wares was decorated sparingly with ribs and geometric patterns picked out on solid glazes in natural tones.

STIG LINDBERG
Frederick Sigurd (Stig) Lindberg wanted to forge a career as a painter until he was taken under the wing of Wilhelm Kåge at Gustavsberg in 1937 at the age of 21. His tenure at the firm went on to span almost 50 years, lasting right up until his death in 1982. Lindberg's output was extremely diverse, ranging from wall plaques with applied figural decoration through folk-inspired wares, and his celebrated leaf-decorated dishes to the starkly geometric and monochrome Dominio series of platters. Lindberg remains one of Sweden's favorite cultural figures and his legacy continues to exert an enormous influence on contemporary Scandinavian ceramic design.

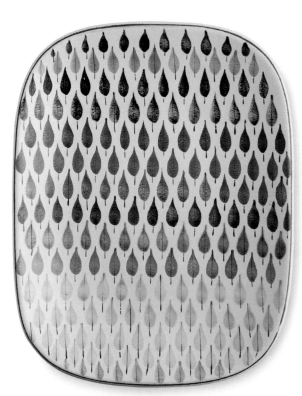

SWEDISH FAIENCE PLATTER One of Stig Lindberg's popular leaf-decorated ceramics, this platter was designed for Gustavsberg of Sweden. *c.1948. L:12½ in (31.5 cm).*

LAMP BASE Designed by Carl-Harry Stålhane for Rörstrand of Sweden, this porcelain lamp base is square in form and has an abstract design repeated in reverse on alternate sides. *c.1970. H:9¾ in (24.5 cm).*

SALAD BOWL In Lindberg's earthenware salad bowl designed for Gustavsberg, the shape is accentuated with simple stripes that radiate from a "stalk" at one end of the bowl. *c.1950. H:9½ in (24 cm).*

THE MASS MARKET

The mid-century notion of the happy home ruled by a dedicated housewife was a powerful driving force behind the rampant consumerism of the age. One of its most enduring legacies is the matching dinner service. While fine porcelain tableware had been the preserve of the wealthy, cheaper ceramic services were more democratic and their use permeated every strata of society.

One of the most remarkably successful lines of mass-produced tableware started life outside a factory. When Russell Wright began to draft the first designs for his American Modern dinner service in 1937, the manufacturers he approached were unwilling to invest in it. He eventually persuaded the Steubenville Pottery of Ohio—a previously bankrupt firm—to resume operations and take up the challenge. The organic style of this new service was informed by Surrealist art; the hard ceramic appears soft and mutable, bringing to mind Dali's melting clocks. Wright was perhaps also paying tribute to his Quaker background by exercising great restraint and keeping the shapes simple and free of extraneous ornament. The progressive color scheme he developed included a pale pink shade called Coral and a green, named Seafoam.

The Steubenville Pottery's gamble paid off. Wright accompanied the 1940 launch of American Modern tableware with a marketing campaign advertising the service as a starter set, appealing to the home-making instincts of young couples. It flew off the shelves, earning Wright a million dollars in royalties and becoming the biggest-selling dinner service ever.

STEUBENVILLE TEAPOT
Russell Wright designed his American Modern range in the late 1930s and Steubenville produced it from 1940 to 1961. The Bean Brown seen here was an early color. *L:10 in (25.5 cm).*

Similar organic forms and unusual colors can be seen in the Town and Country service designed by Eva Zeisel for the Red Wing Pottery in the 1940s. The handles of her dishes resemble fish tails and her pitchers have handles and spouts that look as if they have been peeled back from the mouth of the vessel.

CERAMICS IN THE UK

Imitation of Wright's phenomenally successful dinner service was widespread, and not limited to the United States. Roy Midwinter, sales director of the Midwinter pottery in Staffordshire, was advised by an American buyer to travel to the west coast of the United States to learn from Wright's

PRIMAVERA PLATE The Stylecraft shape of this plate is characteristic of Midwinter's embracement of American designs. *Primavera* was designed by Jessie Tait. *c.1954. D:9½ in (24.5 cm).*

FIESTA WARE

Frederick Hurten Rhead, artistic director of the Laughlin China Company in East Virginia, introduced Fiesta ware in 1936. His use of primary colors, geometric forms, and industrial production resulted in a range of ceramics for everyday use that the Bauhaus would have been proud of. The forms consist of little more than plain, circular and globular shapes, decorated simply with concentric circles in relief. Bright glazes in tones of yellow, red, blue, and white complete the minimalist modern aesthetic. Unusual design features include the "cut-out" section of the pitcher with a thin strip of ceramic forming the handle, following the circular outline of the body. Loop handles on the teapot and cups continue this single-minded devotion to the circle. Fiesta ware was particularly popular in the postwar period. It was undoubtedly an important influence on Russell Wright and, through him, on British potteries such as Midwinter.

FIESTA WARE CRUET SET Strong, bold colors were, and still are, a hallmark of the Fiesta ware range, as seen here in this pair of cobalt-blue salt and pepper shakers. *1930s–50s. H:2½ in (6.5 cm).*

FIESTA WARE PITCHER
Frederick Hurten Rhead's pitcher, here in yellow, exemplifies the Art Deco styling of the range, with its aerodynamic, near-spherical form and concentric-circle decoration. *1930s–50s. H:7 in (18 cm).*

TUREEN WITH LID
The geometric decoration emphasizes the tureen's tapered form. It was designed by Marianne Westmann for Rörstrand in 1956, with production continuing until 1969. *H:8¾ in (22 cm).*

BOHUS BERSA BOWL This high-fired earthenware bowl, transfer-decorated with a geometric leaf pattern, was designed by Stig Lindberg for Gustavsberg in 1960 and stayed in production until 1974. *D:6¼ in (16 cm).*

production if he wanted to make the most of the American export market. He did just that, and once British postwar austerity measures were lifted, he had his modelers design an entirely new line of shapes called the Stylecraft range.

After the Stylecraft wares were launched in 1953, the enthusiastic reception they received was due in no small part to the decorative schemes devised by Jessie Tait. Her 1954 Primavera pattern, comprising cartouches of diverse shapes containing a mix of stylized floriform and geometric motifs, was an early success. Another favorite was the Zambesi pattern, made up of handpainted zebra stripes with rims and handles painted in red. Terence Conran also contributed patterns to the Stylecraft line, including Plant Life, Chequers, and Melody, the names evoking the mix of floral, geometric, and symbolic decoration that the range encompassed.

The Homemaker pattern, designed by Enid Seeney for Ridgway in 1956 and sold by Woolworths in Britain, is a quintessentially mid-century design. Among other motifs, the repeating pattern includes a Robin Day armchair and a Sigvard Bernadotte sofa. Ridgway also produced the Barbecue pattern in a similar style, depicting kebabs ready for grilling.

POOLE AND PORTMEIRION

Mass-produced Scandinavian ceramics such as those made by Rörstrand were a rich mine of inspiration for Alfred Read, head of design at Poole Pottery from 1952 to 1957. The works had been largely rebuilt following the war, and Read reinvigorated the pottery's output, introducing a range of contemporary shapes such as the Peanut vase, available in various sizes. These new forms were decorated with either a solid color glaze or Read's own banded patterns that incorporated stylized ferns and other natural forms as well as more abstract geometric designs.

HOMEMAKER TRIO SET The transfer-printed design by Enid Seeney for Ridgways features domestic motifs on a striated ground. *c.1957. Cup: H:2¾ in (7 cm); Saucer: D:5½ in (14 cm); Plate: D:7 in (18 cm).*

The textile designer Susan Williams-Ellis started production at the Portmeirion Pottery using blanks she obtained from Gray's Pottery. The different diameters and lengths suggested to her a cylindrical coffee set, which is exactly what she produced. The enforced simplicity of her shapes proved an instant hit, encouraging her to experiment with surface decoration. In 1963 Williams-Ellis unveiled her Totem pattern, consisting of embossed geometric shapes and available in blue, amber, and olive.

PEANUT VASE This Poole Pottery Peanut vase is decorated with the geometric PKT pattern in alternating strips of blue and red with white. It was designed by Alfred Read and painted by Gwen Haskins in around 1953, and remained in production into the 1960s. *H:13½ in (34 cm).*

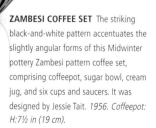

ZAMBESI COFFEE SET The striking black-and-white pattern accentuates the slightly angular forms of this Midwinter pottery Zambesi pattern coffee set, comprising coffeepot, sugar bowl, cream jug, and six cups and saucers. It was designed by Jessie Tait. *1956. Coffeepot: H:7½ in (19 cm).*

STUDIO POTTERY

The fledgling studio pottery movement went from strength to strength during the mid-20th century, as the seeds of creativity planted by Bernard Leach and Shoji Hamada began to flourish. The new generation at the Leach Pottery in St. Ives included David Leach, son of founder Bernard, and Janet, who became Bernard Leach's third wife in the early 1950s. While David Leach's work is mainly functional, with interior glazes and plain outer surfaces, Janet Leach developed a more eclectic idiom, building complex bottles, flasks, and vases from multiple thrown forms accompanied by coiled constructions.

The volcanic glaze gives a heavily textured surface, which is characteristic of Beatrice Wood's work

VESSEL AND VASE In these two fine sculptural forms by Beatrice Wood, the vessel has a blue-green mottled volcanic glaze and the tapered vase a uranium-red volcanic glaze. Both are signed "Beato." Vessel: H:6 in (15 cm); Vase: H:15½ in (39 cm).

The near-spherical vessel has a short neck and very small opening

The most prolific of Bernard Leach's early pupils was Michael Cardew, who revived a defunct pottery in Gloucestershire and, together with a local potter, rediscovered historical slip-decoration techniques. Then, in 1942, Cardew performed a complete volte-face and swapped the production of traditional English red earthenware with slip-trailed designs for teaching at an art college in the Gold Coast (now Ghana) in West Africa. Opting to stay in the area, he later opened the Volta Pottery and lived in Britain and Africa until 1965. His studies of traditional Nigerian pottery and his own experiments led to his publication of *Pioneer Pottery*, still valued by contemporary potters for its extensive technical notes.

Shoji Hamada's influence was most evident in the work of William Staite Murray, who was involved with Wyndham Lewis and the Vorticist movement in the early 20th century. Already a potter, after meeting Hamada in the 1920s, Murray became interested in Asian high-fire glazes. He constructed his own kiln at Rotherhithe in London, where he attempted to recreate classical Chinese effects such as the dark temmoko glaze.

AMERICAN STUDIO POTTERY

Many of the boldest advances in studio pottery at this time were made in the United States by individuals with a background in the fine arts. Beatrice Wood, the daughter of San Francisco socialites, attended the prestigious Académie Julian in Paris before settling in New York and falling in with a group of actors and Dadaists. Her relationship with Marcel Duchamp and Henri-Pierre Roché is supposed to have inspired the novel

The bowl is covered with a typical ash-green glaze

STONEWARE BOWL Designed by Katherine Pleydell-Bouverie, this elegant bowl of simple form bears an impressed seal mark and is incised "280." 1940s–60s. D:5¾ in (14.5 cm).

POTTERY JUG This simple, baluster-shaped, brown-glazed pottery jug with incised decoration is by Michael Cardew. 1940s–60s. H:9½ in (24 cm).

and subsequent film, *Jules et Jim*. Wood did not become interested in ceramics until she was in her forties, by which time she had become an adherent of the Theosophical Society. This occasioned her move in 1948 to Ojai, California, to be close to Jiddu Krishnamurti.

Wood's pottery is primarily sculptural; many of her vessels have tiny apertures that make them unsuitable for any practical use. During this period she developed a range of volcanic glazes in bright colors and earth tones characterized by myriad tiny pits on the surface of her vessels. Other characteristic features of her varied output include the use of applied decoration inspired by India.

MAIJA GROTELL

A generation of teacher-practitioners in the United States propagated the concept of modern studio pottery and its place in ceramic tradition. One of

OTTO AND GERTRUD NATZLER

Husband-and-wife team Otto and Gertrud Natzler were born in Vienna. After winning a silver medal at the 1937 World's Exposition in Paris, they settled in southern California. They divided their work between them, according to their own specialties: Gertrud worked the wheel while Otto formulated the glazes and fired the pots. They quickly won respect in their small community of California ceramicists by insisting on using the local clay at a time when many of their contemporaries preferred to import it from elsewhere. Gertrud initially concentrated on fashioning bowls because they were more likely to sell, but, as her fame spread, she began to produce other vessels including gourds and bottles as well as reproductions of natural forms including seed pods and shells. Otto's porous glazes, at first considered defective by many commentators, included Crater, Pompei and Lava. His experiments with kiln conditions included the introduction of drafts at various stages of the firing and the use of many different reduction agents.

BOWL AND VASE The large, hemispheric bowl is covered in a gunmetal and deep-purple crystalline glaze, with oxblood flashes to the exterior, while the monumental bulbous vase is covered in a blue-green striated volcanic glaze. *1960s. Bowl: H:7¾ in (119.5 cm); Vase: H:17½ in (44.5 cm).*

FOOTED BOWL This fine Maija Grotell stoneware footed bowl has a sheer, flowing, umber luster glaze to the exterior and a white, crackled interior. The bowl is incised "MG." *1940s–60s. D:9 in (23 cm).*

the most dedicated was Maija Grotell, who had studied under Alfred William Finch in her native Finland before settling in the United States in 1927. Her most long-lived teaching post was at the Cranbrook Academy of Art between 1938 and 1966, which brought her into contact with leading exponents of American mid-century modernism, including Charles Eames. It was thanks to Grotell's research into glazes that Eero Saarinen was able to include glazed bricks in his design for the General Motors Technical Center. Among her many innovations were a number of bright turquoise hues made using copper oxides.

Grotell's skill at the wheel was such that she could throw perfect pots of immense weight. She would often repeat the same design, improving it by increments until she finally reproduced exactly the form she had in mind before moving on to her next project.

Among the many pupils that she inspired was Toshiko Takaezu, born in Hawaii. Takaezu was enthused by Grotell's Scandinavian interest in landscape,

combining it with her own Zen Buddhist beliefs. As her career progressed, Takaezu became entranced by Abstract Expressionism, making her wares progressively less functional. This eventually culminated in a series of ceramics built together from numerous component thrown vessels.

SLAB VASE Janet Leach's stoneware slab vase is decorated at the front with brushstrokes of brown on a speckled blue, white, and buff ground. The vase bears the impressed mark "JL." *1940s–60s. H:11 in (27.5 cm).*

Celadon glaze is a traditional Chinese glaze

LOWERDOWN POTTERY FOOTED VASE David Leach's vase has curved and fluted decoration and a celadon glaze. It is impressed with the "DL" seal. *1960s. H:5½ in (13.5 cm).*

The design is inspired by Japanese pots

FIGURES AND FORMS

During this mid-century period, a growing number of studio ceramicists started to use pottery as a canvas for figural forms and other ideas that had previously been the preserve of fine art. Many of these ceramicists were classically trained artists who had either switched from a career behind the easel or were eager to expand their repertoire in a different medium.

Trained as an artist at Stanford University and in London and Paris, Henry Varnum Poor felt that ceramic art was the only medium to offer him complete control of his work. His oeuvre, mainly dishes and vases with painted and sgraffito figural decoration, was motivated by a mistrust of the march toward conformity and perfection that characterized corporate modernism in the United States. His priority, he said, was to gain intimate knowledge of his medium: "Clays are like wines—part of the flavor comes from knowing the hillsides and vineyards that grew the grapes."

FOLK ART TRADITIONS

Edwin and Mary Scheier learned the art of pottery while watching over kilns on behalf of colleagues at the Federal Art project in Tennessee during the late 1930s. Finding that they were increasingly drawn to the medium, the couple embarked on a tour of the southern states, discovering the folk art traditions of the region. They set up a studio in Glade Spring, Virginia, after spotting untapped deposits of red clay there. Their work soon

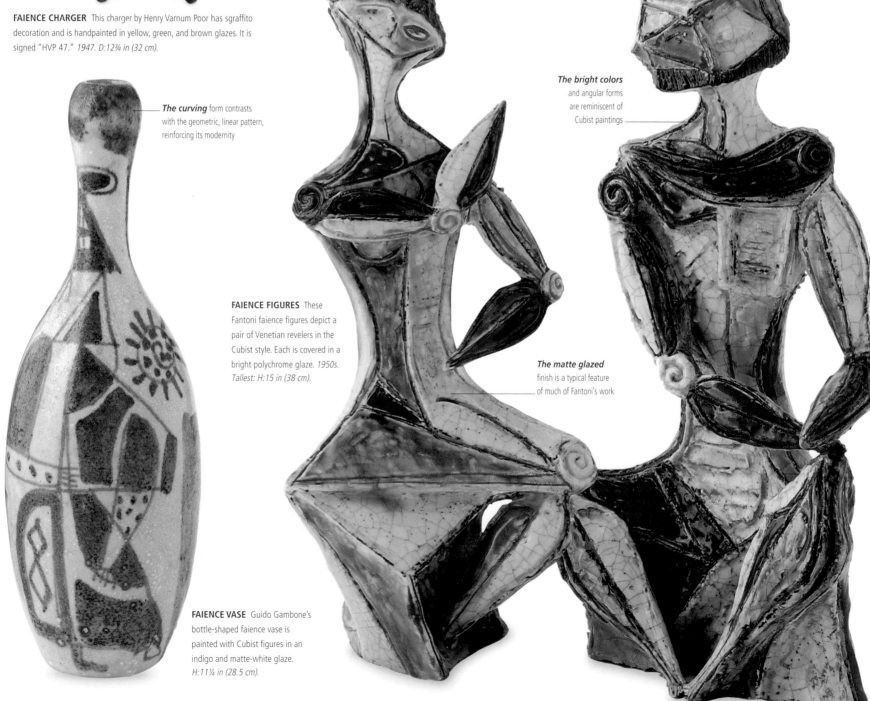

FAIENCE CHARGER This charger by Henry Varnum Poor has sgraffito decoration and is handpainted in yellow, green, and brown glazes. It is signed "HVP 47." *1947. D:12¾ in (32 cm).*

The curving form contrasts with the geometric, linear pattern, reinforcing its modernity

FAIENCE FIGURES These Fantoni faience figures depict a pair of Venetian revelers in the Cubist style. Each is covered in a bright polychrome glaze. *1950s. Tallest: H:15 in (38 cm).*

FAIENCE VASE Guido Gambone's bottle-shaped faience vase is painted with Cubist figures in an indigo and matte-white glaze. *H:11¼ in (28.5 cm).*

The bright colors and angular forms are reminiscent of Cubist paintings

The matte glazed finish is a typical feature of much of Fantoni's work

garnered national acclaim, and they were invited to teach at the University of New Hampshire.

In 1946 the Scheiers took a sabbatical to train workers for Puerto Rico's ceramics industry, developing an appreciation of that country's art and its African influence. They believed that ceramic vessels could convey "some aspect of the human spirit" and dealt with basic human themes such as birth and protection. Edwin's simple line drawings, done by combining sgraffito and relief decoration, give their work a naivety reminiscent of tribal art.

ANCIENT EUROPEAN FORMS

The figural tendency in mid-century Italian studio pottery was expressed most eloquently by two Florentine potters—Guido Gambone and Marcello

Fantoni. Gambone's exaggerated stoneware and earthenware vessels often have simple, painted decoration and thick lava glazes. Despite his modern techniques, his work frequently harks back to ancient Etruscan pottery in its simplicity.

Fantoni was a far more prolific practitioner who gathered around him a vast pool of talented students. Like Gambone's work, Fantoni's ceramic sculptures and vessels reference Etruscan forms. His sympathies for modern art and his Italian heritage combined to create something new and unique.

Frenchman Georges Jouve also looked back to ancient European forms, even as he explored modern techniques. He did much to develop the art of ceramic glazing, his use of selenium leading to some extraordinarily vivid colors.

FRENCH AND SPANISH FORMS

Some of the most individualistic ceramic works of the period were wrought by the titans of modern art. Pablo Picasso worked with potters Georges and Suzanne Ramie at the Madoura pottery in Vallauris, France, from 1947. He would manipulate clay bottles the Ramies had

MAINS AU POISSON Picasso's ceramic plate, designed for Madoura, is molded with two black hands and a fish in terra-cotta, green, and cobalt. This is 37 from an edition of 250, stamped "*Empreinte Originale de Picasso/ Madoura Plein Feu.*" *c.1954. D:12 in (30.5 cm).*

left to dry into figural and animal shapes, working against traditional ceramic form.

His own designs are decorated with stylized depictions of the body, similar to those in his drawn and painted work.

Joan Miró was equally comfortable with clay and canvas. He worked alongside Spanish ceramicist Josep Llorens Artigas during World War II, painting the potter's vases and plaques. Miró eventually started to mold his own forms based on objects he found around Artigas's farm, indulging his Surrealist's impulse to elevate the accidental to high art.

At the height of his fame in the late 1950s, Jean Cocteau found refuge from public expectation in the workshop of Philippe Madeline in Villefranche-sur-Mer. He developed a method of "drawing" directly onto terra-cotta, and became so enthused with this new medium that he found it hard to bear the frustration of waiting for his chargers and vessels to cool after the firing process.

EARLY SCHEIER FOOTED FLOOR VASE Decorated with typical tribal imagery, the vase is covered in a volcanic bronze glaze against a graduated matte-turquoise glaze. *1966. H:22½ in (56 cm).*

FOOTED VASE An example of Georges Jouve's work, this ceramic vase has an applied high-relief sun with rays and face, with incised compass directions above and below. *c.1948. H:12 in (30.5 cm).*

CERAMICS GALLERY

Mid-century modernism saw a dichotomy in the production of ceramics. The simple shapes that were fashionable could be produced cheaply in factories, yet studio ceramics also enjoyed a renaissance. Scandinavian design was highly influential, especially the bold patterns that were handpainted onto studio pieces and transfer-printed onto mass-produced wares.

KEY

1. Villeroy & Boch Acapulco pattern tray, with printed marks. 1960s. L:12 in (30 cm). ①
2. Troika pottery wheel vase, modeled in relief with a face design, painted marks. 1970s. H:7¾ in (19.5 cm). ① **3**. Midwinter pottery Plant Life pattern plate designed by Terence Conran. 1956. W:11¾ in (30 cm). ① **4**. Denby Arabesque pattern handpainted coffeepot designed by Gill Pemberton. 1964–70s. H:12¼ in (31 cm). ① **5**. Swedish Gustavsberg wall plaque by Lisa Larson, with a stylized bird design. 1960s. W:11 in (28 cm). ① **6**. Tête-à-Tête porcelain tea set by Trude Petri for KPM Berlin. c.1950. Saucer: D:5 in (13 cm). ② **7**. Portmeirion Tivoli pattern Seraph coffee set designed by Susan Williams-Ellis. c.1964. H:12¼ in (31 cm). ① **8**. Midwinter pottery Cannes pattern celery vase designed by Terence Conran. 1960. H:6¾ in (17 cm). ① **9**. Antonio Prieto ovoid vase,

3 *Terence Conran plate*

2 *Troika pottery wheel vase*

5 *Gustavsberg wall plaque*

1 *Villeroy & Boch tray*

4 *Denby Arabesque coffeepot*

6 *Trude Petri tea set*

7 *Portmeirion coffee set*

decorated in sgraffito. 1950s. H:10¼ in (26 cm). ③ **10**. Danish Royal Copenhagen Tenera vase by Bert Jessen, with a stylized flower design. 1970s. H:7½ in (19 cm). ① **11**. Ebb Tide large conch basket by A. Hull, with a stylized fish handle. c.1960. H:10 in (25.5 cm). ① **12**. H. J. Wood Piazza ware vase. c.1957. H:9½ in (24 cm). ① **13**. Richard Batterham cut-sided bowl, with a green-gray glaze. 1960s. H:5¾ in (14.5 cm). ① **14**. Norwegian Stavangerflint bowl, with handpainted decoration. 1950s. H:4½ in (11.5 cm). ① **15**. Danish Palshus Torpedo vase by Per Linnermann-Schmidt, in a blue haresfur glaze. 1950s. H:8¾ in (22 cm). ① **16**. Italian Bistosi Rimini Blu vase decorated with impressed symbols and a blue glaze. c.1960. H:8¼ in (21 cm). ① **17**. Royal Haeger shell vase with molded marks. 1950s. H:7 in (18 cm). ① **18**. Troika St. Ives Pottery chimney vase, with a green-blue glazed ground and geometric embossed panels. c.1970. H:8 in (20 cm). ②

10 *Bert Jessen vase*

9 *Antonio Prieto vase*

8 *Terence Conran vase*

11 *Ebb Tide conch basket*

12 *Piazza ware vase*

13 *Richard Batterham bowl*

16 *Bistosi vase*

14 *Stavangerflint bowl*

15 *Torpedo vase*

17 *Royal Haeger shell vase*

18 *Troika St. Ives chimney vase*

GLASS

MID-CENTURY GLASS DESIGN WAS LED BY SCANDINAVIAN FACTORIES

AND BY MASTER GLASSMAKERS IN MURANO WHO SUCCESSFULLY

REVIVED THE ANCIENT CRAFT OF THEIR ISLAND.

APPLE VASE Ingeborg Lundin's Apple vase, designed for Orrefors of Sweden, has extremely fragile-looking thinly blown walls and a short neck to suggest the stalk of the fruit. *1957. H:14½ in (37 cm).*

COLORED GLASS

The flawless surfaces and soft natural hues of vessels produced by the Orrefors factory in Sweden exemplify Scandinavian glass design of this period. Nils Landberg's delicate *Tulpanglas* was an early, iconic Orrefors shape, manufactured in various permutations of proportion and color. Its slender, attenuated trumpet stem balances the long, flutelike bowl. He also devised a pitcher with a distinctive ice-catching lip that remains in production.

Landberg's abstractionist treatment of the tulip found a mirror in Ingeborg Lundin's Apple vase, which has a globular body and a diminutive neck that is reminiscent of an apple's stalk. Both Landberg and Lundin used color and form in a way that aimed to incorporate the Scandinavian landscape into their work. These references to the natural world are often subtle or oblique, as if seen through mist and rain beneath a darkening sky.

The cool colors and organic forms seen on glass manufactured by the Danish firms Holmegaard and Kastrup represent a veritable celebration of the chromatic possibilities of glass. Both firms are known for the clarity of their glass. Per Lutken succeeded Jacob Bang as staff designer at Holmegaard in 1942 and used splashes and streaks of color to enliven his clear and opaque white glass forms. The colored opaline feet of his *Vintergaek* (Snowdrop) range are echoed in the opaline patches that mottle their otherwise clear glass bowls.

Lutken employed similar techniques in his sculptural work. His free-blown forms dating from the 1970s are made from semi-opaque white glass with streaky brown, red, and blue inclusions.

TULPANGLAS A hallmark of Swedish design, this is an elegant form with a tulip-shaped bowl on a tall, slender stem. It was designed by Nils Landberg for Orrefors. *1957. H:21 in (51.5 cm).*

Lutken's Carnaby glass vases paved the way for the bold plastic forms and colors of Michael Bang's later Palet range. Bang joined Holmegaard in 1968 and helped bring the company into the Pop era. His Palet tableware used a layer of opaque white glass cased with a brighter color, a combination that made his pieces resemble the plastics that were so crucial in other decorative art of the period. It was the first Holmegaard range to use bright red and yellow cased glass.

RIIHIMÄEN LASI OY GLASSWARE

A trio of female designers—Helena Tynell, Nanny Still, and Tamara Aladin—was largely responsible for the mid-century success of Riihimäen Lasi Oy. Tynell joined the firm in 1946 and is best remembered for her textured forms such as the Emma vase. This geometric mold-blown vase with patterning is also known for its jewel-like colors, which include a brilliant ruby red. Tynell's even more complex Pironki vase was manufactured in pale translucent shades, the edges appearing darker and so giving the form more definition.

KAJ FRANCK

Also in Finland, the multi-talented Kaj Franck turned his attention to glassware on behalf of Nuutajärvi Notsjo. Many of his designs were produced in a range of strong colors in recognition of a public appetite for colorful glassware that grew ever more voracious from the 1950s onward. Some of Franck's earliest experiments in this direction resulted in his 1952 *Saippuakupla* (Soap Bubble) line of simple and elegant oviform colored glass vessels.

As Franck became more ambitious, he began to set himself new challenges. Among these was his self-imposed quest to devise a carafe that didn't

KASTRUP VASE This vase is typical of Jacob Bang's work with its clean lines, austerity, and lack of surface decoration. It concentrates instead on form and color. *1950s. H:8¼ in (21 cm).*

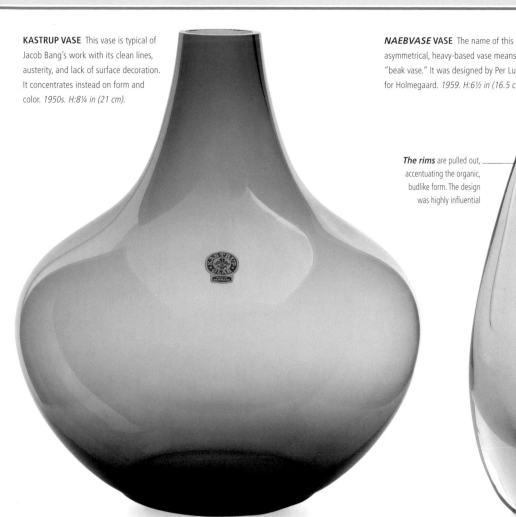

NAEBVASE VASE The name of this asymmetrical, heavy-based vase means "beak vase." It was designed by Per Lutken for Holmegaard. *1959. H:6½ in (16.5 cm).*

The rims are pulled out, accentuating the organic, budlike form. The design was highly influential

BLUE VASE Kaj Franck produced a number of minimal designs for Nuutajärvi Notsjo. Here, a tall, blue-case vase stands on a thick, clear-glass base. *1960s. H:12 in (30 cm).*

require a handle and so could be made more quickly and cheaply. His solutions included a waisted design from 1954 that the user could grip around the middle. This was made available in a rainbow of bright translucent colors, accompanied by matching tapering tumblers. He later came up with a decanter form with a handhold neck and an idiosyncratic stopper in the form of a speckled pink, red, and blue rooster.

Franck's Luna range of functional pressed glass tableware was prompted by Nuutajärvi Notsjo's acquisition of new glass-pressing machinery in the early 1960s. The advent of simpler and more efficient low-cost production meant that these wares could be offered inexpensively in a choice of shades. They were launched in 1968 in clear, amber, and green glass, later to be followed by more colors as sales picked up.

EMMA VASE Designed by Helena Tynell for Riihimäen Lasi Oy, this is a mold-blown and cased vase. *c.1976. H:8¼ in (21 cm).*

PIRONKI VASE This mold-blown cased vase of shaped form was designed by Helena Tynell for Riihimäen Lasi Oy. *c.1974. H:8¼ in (21 cm).*

THE GRAAL TECHNIQUE

The arresting Graal technique was invented at Orrefors around 1916 and was extremely popular in the 1950s and 1960s. The process involves engraving the desired motif onto a colored glass vessel before reheating it and casing it within an outer shell of clear glass, which is then blown into the final form. The internal reflections of the clear glass refract and multiply the original design, producing an interesting optical effect.

Edvin Öhrström, Vicke Lindstrand, and glass master Gustav Bergkvist developed Ariel glass during the late 1930s, naming it after the character in Shakespeare's *Tempest*. It is similar to Graal glass with the addition of trapped air between the cased layers.

FISH VASE Designed by Edvard Hald, this is an exceptional example of a Graal vase, with the various layers clearly visible. The fish design is one of several produced by Hald for Orrefors. *1937. H:7¼ in (18.5 cm).*

TEXTURED GLASS

The superlative skills of Scandinavian glassmakers were by no means limited to colored glass. They also excelled in the field of textured and engraved glass, none more so than Timo Sarpaneva and Tapio Wirkkala, who designed for the Finnish firm Iittala. Their careers followed a similar path—both had a background in sculpture and worked with metal, plastic, and wood as well as with glass. Both were also invited to contribute designs to Murano glassmakers. They began their careers at Iittala within a few years of each other, Wirkkala in 1946, and Sarpaneva in 1950.

GLASS AS SCULPTURAL ART

Sarpaneva in particular played a crucial role in the elevation of Scandinavian glass from functional household necessity to sculptural art. He achieved this through an involvement with Iittala that was prolonged and intense. Even if his Lansetti I and Orkidea designs were, strictly speaking, vessels on account of the inclusion of void space in their interiors, they were completely impractical for use as vases. These decorative cased glass sculptures formed part of Sarpaneva's prize-winning exhibit at the 1954 Milan Triennale.

Sarpaneva's Arkipelago range combines controlled bubble inclusions with a wavy, ridged surface—the small shot glasses juxtapose cast stems decorated in this manner with clear, unblemished blown bowls. However, one of Sarpaneva's most successful designs was his 1967 Festivo candlestick, cast in a charred wood mold in a similar fashion to his signature Finlandia line of 1964.

Tapio Wirkkala used a series of fine cuts, comparable to the Inciso technique used by Murano factories, to produce his *Kantarelli* (Chanterelle) bowl, in which the unpolished vertical lines echo the flutes of the chanterelle mushroom. His Tuonen Virta vase, issued in a limited numbered edition,

LANSETTI II Timo Sarpaneva's sculptural vase for Iittala is made from colorless glass surrounding a white opaque-glass hollow core. *1952. H:11 in (27 cm).*

*The **sculptural shape** of the vase is reminiscent of a lancet and typical of Sarpaneva's style. It has perfect balance of form*

uses the same technique to depict a scene from the *Kalevala*, the Finnish national epic poem.

Wirkkala was preoccupied with the degree to which clear glass was visually akin to ice, and his mold-blown *Jäävuori* (Iceberg) glasses are perhaps the most literal manifestation of this in his work. Textural and chunky, they share a similar aesthetic with his *Kanto* (Tree Stump) range. Wirkkala's *Paaderin Jää* sculptures were also designed to resemble cracked and melting ice.

VICKE LINDSTRAND

The most prominent figure in mid-century Swedish cut glass was Vicke Lindstrand. His cased glass designs for Kosta Boda in the early 1950s use textural ribbed effects and spiraling stripes. Lindstrand's various talents also stretched to book illustration, and this can be seen in the designs he drafted for Kosta Boda's talented engravers, who used cutting, engraving, and acid-etching techniques. Some of the

KANTO The gently rippled form of Tapio Wirkkala's squat, thick-walled vase suggests a tree stump and ice. It was designed for Iittala. *1947. H:4½ in (11.5 cm).*

THE BATH A bathing nude is engraved on this vase designed by Vicke Lindstrand for Kosta Boda. *1950s. H:8¼ in (21 cm).*

most accomplished specimens use a combination of engraving methods. Lindstrand's Bath vase, for example, features a milky delineation of a figure stepping into water represented by sharp, clean-cut concentric circles.

COPPER-WHEEL ENGRAVING

Lindstrand also produced textural designs for Orrefors, this work being characterized by thick-walled vessels with copper-wheel engraving. The Orrefors stable included a number of talented engravers, the most celebrated of whom was Sven Palmqvist. After studying sculpture at the Académie Ranson in Paris, Palmqvist completed his training at Orrefors's in-house glass-engraving school. He was especially adept at figural representation and also had an interest, like so many of his contemporaries, in natural forms.

Other notable contributors to this rich seam of Scandinavian glass design include Gunnel Nyman, who was among the first to give expression to the region's developing organic style through her work with Nuutajärvi Notsjo in Finland. Much of her best work, including her combinations of heavy crystal glass with trapped bubbles or opaque white glass strands, was done in the late 1940s before her career was cut short by her untimely death in 1948.

In Sweden, self-taught glass worker Gerda Strömberg and her husband, Edward, took over the Eda glassworks in 1933. They renamed their new venture Strömbergshyttan and produced chunky decanters, bowls, candlesticks, and other forms with thick walls and austere engraved decoration.

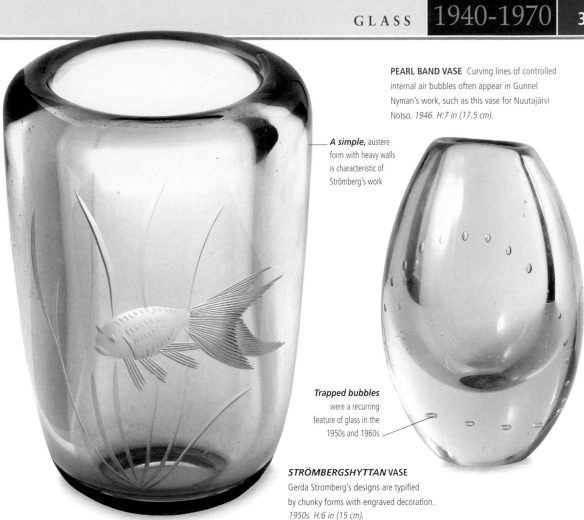

PEARL BAND VASE Curving lines of controlled internal air bubbles often appear in Gunnel Nyman's work, such as this vase for Nuutajärvi Notso. *1946. H:7 in (17.5 cm).*

A simple, austere form with heavy walls is characteristic of Strömberg's work

Trapped bubbles were a recurring feature of glass in the 1950s and 1960s

STRÖMBERGSHYTTAN VASE
Gerda Stromberg's designs are typified by chunky forms with engraved decoration. *1950s. H:6 in (15 cm).*

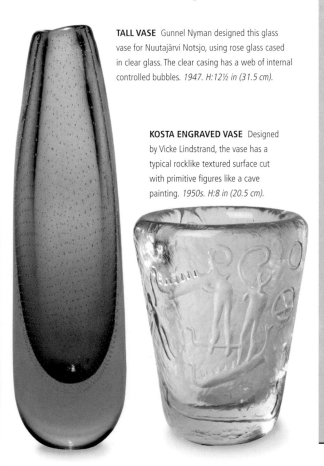

TALL VASE Gunnel Nyman designed this glass vase for Nuutajärvi Notsjo, using rose glass cased in clear glass. The clear casing has a web of internal controlled bubbles. *1947. H:12½ in (31.5 cm).*

KOSTA ENGRAVED VASE Designed by Vicke Lindstrand, the vase has a typical rocklike textured surface cut with primitive figures like a cave painting. *1950s. H:8 in (20.5 cm).*

THE INFLUENCE OF LANDSCAPE

Showing the typical Scandinavian identification with landscape, glass designers drew extensively on their surroundings for inspiration. The prevalence of wood and ice in the local terrain, and their domination of everyday life in the frozen north, held a particular fascination for Timo Sarpaneva and Tapio Wirkkala.

In 1961 Wirkkala built a traditional wooden house in Lapland as a refuge where he could observe the landscape and translate it into his work. His Turned Leaf vase for littala is scored with dozens of thin line cuts—a stylized representation of the infinitesimal veins that are found on real leaves.

Timo Sarpaneva's Finlandia range of textured glass, which was first made in 1963, was cast in carved and fired alderwood molds. Each piece is unique, as the molten glass charred and reshaped the molds each time they were used. The resultant effect has been compared to both tree bark and cracked ice, the two most characteristic features of the Scandinavian winter landscape.

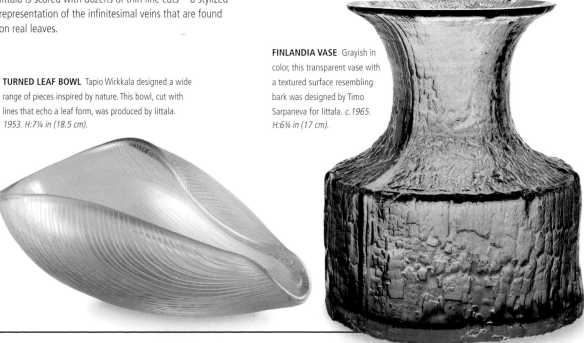

FINLANDIA VASE Grayish in color, this transparent vase with a textured surface resembling bark was designed by Timo Sarpaneva for littala. *c.1965. H:6¾ in (17 cm).*

TURNED LEAF BOWL Tapio Wirkkala designed a wide range of pieces inspired by nature. This bowl, cut with lines that echo a leaf form, was produced by littala. *1953. H:7¼ in (18.5 cm).*

ORIENTE VASE Combed multicolored bands and silver foil inclusions decorate this rare Barovier & Toso *Oriente* vase of baluster form, designed by Ercole Barovier. *c.1940. H:7 in (18 cm).*

FRATELLI TOSO *STELLATO* VASE Designed by Pollio Perelda, the vase has star-patterned murrines laid onto a clear glass body. The bright colors are typical of the period. *1953. H:11 in (28.5 cm).*

TIMELESS MURANO

A combination of new blood and old glassmaking dynasties taking a renewed pride in their work revived the glass industry of the Venetian island of Murano during the 20th century. Since the Middle Ages, this region had specialized primarily in hot decorating techniques such as blowing and lampwork, and it was these areas that were reinvigorated by key figures such as Dino Martens, Ercole Barovier, and members of the Toso family.

The Aureliano Toso glassworks, established in 1938, enjoyed enormous critical and commercial success from the mid-1940s, producing vessels designed by Dino Martens. His background in painting prompted him to reinterpret traditional Muranese decorating techniques, often to startling effect. His *Oriente* range combined pinwheel murrines, bright enamel coloring, and inclusions of aventurine metal oxides and powders within the same piece to produce tapestry-like glass vessels with powerful visual impact.

THE *ZANFIRICO* TECHNIQUE

In tandem with Anzolo Fuga, Martens reworked the traditional Venetian *zanfirico* technique for the AVEM factory. Named after the 19th-century Venetian art dealer Antonio Sanquirico, who revived this ancient process, the *zanfirico* technique consists of heating multicolored glass rods, twisting them together, and encasing them within a clear glass shell, resulting in an intricate filigree effect. It is just one manifestation of *filigrana* glass, meaning any type of glass that relies on colored

rods or threads for decorative effect. Murano factories had been practicing variations on this basic theme since the island's 15th-century heyday and now they began to infuse it with a new exuberance in the form of bright, bold colors.

INTARSIO GLASS

Ercole Barovier gave up his medical training to join the family glass factory in 1919. Like Dino Martens, he was influenced by abstract painters—his *Oriente* range for Barovier & Toso (not to be confused with the Aureliano Toso product of the same name) uses shining foil inclusions and swirling bands of color to produce an effect not seen before in glassware. Barovier was wholeheartedly

TEARDROP JUG This Aureliano Toso *Oriente* jug is of teardrop form, with a handle and various inclusions, among them zanfirico rods and plates and a large star-shaped murrine. It was designed by Dino Martens. *c.1954. H:13 in (32.5 cm).*

The glass is designed to look like a stained-glass window

The base is in the form of a floral pinwheel

INTARSIO VASE This Barovier & Toso *intarsio* vase has a clear glass body overlaid with an irregular mosaic of diamond-shaped tiles and a stylized floral motif at the base. *1961. H:12¼ in (30.5 cm).*

ATHENS CATHEDRAL VASE A rare Barovier & Toso Classically-inspired vase designed by Ercole Barovier, this piece is composed of clear glass overlaid with opal-white, blue, and green Athens murrines. *1967. H:13 in (33 cm).*

MURRINES

The use of murrines was by no means a novelty in the 20th century, but Ermanno Toso elevated the technique to a previously unattained status. Murrines are made by slicing thin sections from long canes of clear and colored glass with designs running through them. Flowers, spirals, and abstract designs have featured heavily in 20th-century murrines. Once the cut sections have been laid out in the required formation, molten glass is rolled over them, incorporating them onto the body of the vessel. Certain types of murrine are associated with particular makers or factories. Shown below is a Fratelli Toso factory sample board with various murrines dating from the 1950s to the 1970s.

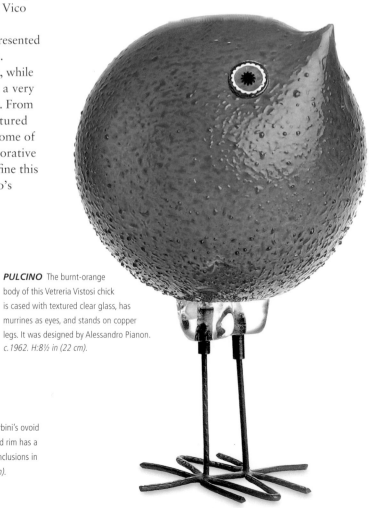

KIKU MURRINE VASE The clear glass body of this Ermanno Toso vase is densely covered with blue, orange, black, and white murrines, some with yellow centers. *1950–58. H:10¼ in (26 cm).*

engaged in the modernization and reinterpretation of antiquated Muranese techniques, and during the 1960s he used the *intarsio* method to create a series of patterned vases. These were made by laying out mosaic patterns of thin glass patches that were then encased in clear glass. When the gather—the mass of molten glass collected on the end of the glassmaker's pipe—was blown, the *intarsio* sections would morph and distend at different rates, depending on their position on the vessel. The resultant patterns are a fusion of geometric order and organic mayhem.

PERIPATETIC DESIGNERS

Many key figures working on Murano during this period migrated from factory to factory, often on a freelance basis. Alfredo Barbini, who eventually founded his own company, was no exception. His mid-century work is characterized by a Scandinavian restraint, with a palette limited to one or two colors and very simple forms. His use of the *inciso* technique developed by Venini, where the surface of the glass is scored with intricate series of horizontal bands, is typical of his work. Cold working techniques such as this were unusual in Murano at this time.

The peripatetic way of working that was shared by Barbini and some of his peers was a boon to the glass factories, which could benefit from the diverse skills of many

different designers. The Vistosi factory, founded in 1945, reaped the rewards of associations with many of Europe's most outstanding draftsmen, including Fulvio Bianconi, Etorre Sottsass, Vico Magistretti, and Peter Pelzel.

Some of the glass produced at Vistosi represented the whimsical side of mid-century Murano. Alessandro Pianon's charming stylized birds, while undoubtedly amusing, nevertheless exhibit a very high degree of skill on the part of the maker. From the murrine eyes to the textured finish, they showcase some of the sophisticated decorative techniques that define this period in Murano's long history.

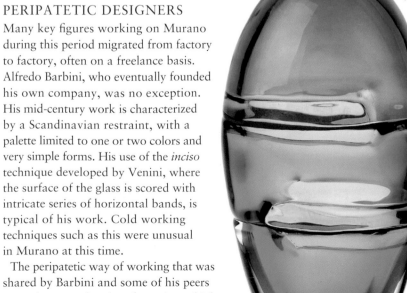

OVOID VASE Alfredo Barbini's ovoid vase with a narrow inverted rim has a double horizontal band of inclusions in ocher. *1968. H:9¼ in (24 cm).*

PULCINO The burnt-orange body of this Vetreria Vistosi chick is cased with textured clear glass, has murrines as eyes, and stands on copper legs. It was designed by Alessandro Pianon. *c.1962. H:8½ in (22 cm).*

MODERN ITALIAN GLASS

The 20th-century renaissance of Murano glassmaking was not wholly reliant on updated versions of old techniques. The prevailing climate of creativity threw up many original forms and decorative treatments that peripatetic workers and designers helped to disseminate between competing factories. One of the key ingredients was color, and vivid hues predominated, most frequently used in crystal-clear transparent glass to catch the light better.

SOMMERSO GLASS

One of the most prevalent of the new techniques developed in the Murano factories was *sommerso* cased glass, which was perfected by Carlo Scarpa for Venini during the 1930s. The name *sommerso* (which translates as "submerged") is a fair evocation of the decorative effect produced by *sommerso* vessels, which can look remarkably like blocks of glass suspended in a colored liquid. S*ommerso* glass production is extremely demanding, as it requires the maker to manipulate

globs of molten glass evenly without the glass falling out of its line or developing bubbles.

The Cenedese factory produced a wide range of *sommerso* vases designed by Antonio de Ros, which have a clear outer layer sheathing one or two bands of colored glass, usually at one side of the vessel. However, Flavio Poli, working for Seguso Vetri d'Arte, became the foremost producer of this type of glass during the mid-20th century. His elliptical *Valva* vases in particular allow the cased color combinations to come to the fore, untrammeled by decorative embellishments. In his *Siderale* range, the more technically remarkable vessels are made up of concentric circles of cased glass in alternating colors.

VALVA **VASE** A *sommerso* ovoid vase with purple and red glass cased in solid clear glass, designed by Flavio Poli for Seguso Vetri d'Arte. *c.1952. H:9½ in (23.5 cm).*

VENINI

In his capacity as artistic director at Venini between 1934 and 1947, Carlo Scarpa was responsible for many other innovations that helped cement the reputation of Paolo Venini's fledgling company. Among these are an opaque milky white glass known as *Lattimo* and a matte glass with a

OCCHI **VASE** Tobia Scarpa's tall, square-section vase, designed for Venini in 1959, has overlaid red murrines with colorless centers. *c.1960. H:13 in (32 cm).*

D-SHAPED VASE Cobalt blue is cased in solid clear glass in this *sommerso* vase designed by Antonio da Ros for Vetreria Gino Cendese. *c.1962. H:10½ in (26.5 cm).*

PULEGOSO VASE Archimede Seguso's elegant vase has a translucent green layer of randomly bubbled *pulegoso* glass, above which are orange swirls and a clear top casing. *c.1948. H:12½ in (32 cm).*

CANNE VASE Designed by Gio Ponti for Venini, this vase has the bright colors that are characteristic of much contemporary Italian glass design. The stripes are produced by overlaid colored canes. *1955. H:11½ in (28.5 cm).*

TESSUTO VASE The design of this vase is such that one half has green and black stripes and the other green and white. It was designed by Carlo Scarpa for Venini in 1940 and produced in a limited edition of 100. *1980. H:13½ in (34 cm).*

FAZZOLETTO BOWL Designed by Fulvio Bianconi and Paolo Venini for Venini, this handkerchief-shaped bowl was widely copied throughout Europe. Stripes were a more common decoration than the spots seen here. *1949. H:6¼ in (15.5 cm).*

FULVIO BIANCONI

The extraordinary partnership between graphic designer Fulvio Bianconi and Milanese lawyer-turned-glass-designer Paolo Venini was a driving force behind some of the greatest successes of mid-century Murano glass. As befits a designer who said, "Mistakes are what I like best," Bianconi was a consummate risk-taker who constantly explored and tested the properties and limitations of glass. His trademark flair for caricature informed his series of glass figures based on stock characters from the Italian folk tradition of the *Commedia dell'Arte*. Other figures, dressed in regional costumes, poked fun at the tourist tat hawked by the more derivative Murano factories.

Bianconi's patchwork *Pezzato* vases, created from fused glass panels of different colors, found immediate popularity when they were first introduced in 1950.

VENINI PEZZATO VASE The clear glass body of Fulvio Bianconi's vase is overlaid with tesserae (squares of colored glass) in the Paris colorway. *1950s. H:8¼ in (20.5 cm).*

faint iridescent sheen called *corroso*. Scarpa also developed his own variations of traditional Venetian filigrana decoration, including the spiraling *mezza filigrana* and the complex *tessuto* technique, which resembles woven textile threads. By the time Paolo Venini died in 1959, his factory was regarded as one of the most proficient and sophisticated in Murano.

Carlo Scarpa's son, Tobia, joined the firm that same year and continued in the trailblazing vein that had been established by his father. One of his most distinctive creations are the *Occhi* vases, which have clear glass murrines, or "eyes," set within a colored body.

ARCHIMEDE SEGUSO

Master glassblower Archimede Seguso brought the Seguso Vetri d'Arte factory to international prominence from the 1940s. His use of the bubbly *pulegoso* glass, first devised for Venini by Napoleone Martinuzzi, was a notable success. He was also responsible for realizing Flavio Poli's designs for a range of miniature glass animal sculptures. Seguso's twisted *Polveri* vases combined organic forms with gold powder inclusions and are quite unlike anything else produced by Murano factories during the 1950s.

THE *FAZZOLETTO* VASE

As Murano factories attracted greater esteem, the market for their wares expanded commensurately. Smaller factories determined to profit from this boom quickly appropriated the most commercially attractive designs.

One of the most widely copied mid-century Muranese forms is the *Fazzoletto* (handkerchief) vase, developed by Paolo Venini in collaboration with Fulvio Bianconi in 1948–49. This eccentric design has become a fixture of the Murano canon, appropriated by innumerable competitors.

The distinctive shape of the *Fazzoletto*, which resembles an inverted draped handkerchief, has been produced in innumerable patterns, shapes, and sizes. Many of the variations continue the handkerchief theme with patterns of spots or stripes. From around 1950 it became a feature on sideboards and coffee tables throughout Italy and farther afield.

BLENKO BOTTLE Wayne Husted's Persian blue tapering bottle with stopper is made from crackle-effect glass. This color was produced in 1959 only, but it was available in other colors until 1964. *1959. H:28¾ in (73 cm).*

The elaborate stopper is almost half the height of the finished piece

STUDIO GLASS

The range of art glass produced by specialist manufacturers during the mid-20th century was extremely diverse. Consumers were in a position to choose between molded, blown, and cut forms in an enormous array of colors and decorative styles.

The old London firm of Whitefriars—by now relocated to suburban Wealdstone on the outskirts of London—received a shot in the arm in 1951 in the form of an invitation to exhibit at the Festival of Britain. The company built on the momentum this opportunity generated by appointing top Royal College of Art graduate Geoffrey Baxter to the design team in 1954. His early soda glass forms have the uncluttered clarity of the colored Scandinavian glassware produced by Orrefors or Holmegaard.

TEXTURED GLASS

The Knobbly vases created by chief designer William Wilson in 1964 signaled a change in direction at Whitefriars, but it was Geoffrey Baxter who made the most wholehearted foray into textured glass with his Textured range in 1967. Baxter created molds for his glass from natural phenomena such as pieces of tree bark but also used a curious assortment of detritus, including copper wire, nail heads, and bricks to produce his deep relief effects.

The Bark, Drunken Bricklayer, and Banjo vases, all dating from the 1960s, were blown in cast-iron molds copied from Baxter's prototypes constructed from these bits of flotsam and jetsam. Their appeal was enhanced by the fresh range of Pop colors, including tangerine, kingfisher blue, and meadow green, and a gray tone called pewter.

BLENKO GLASS

In the United States, Blenko was one of the most innovative glass producers. After World War II, William

DRUNKEN BRICKLAYER VASE This kingfisher blue vase designed by Geoffrey Baxter for Whitefriars resembles three bricks stacked awkwardly one on top of the other. *1969. H:13 in (33 cm).*

BANJO VASE The bright color and geometric form of this tangerine Banjo vase, designed by Geoffrey Baxter for Whitefriars, reflect the influence of Pop culture during the 1960s. *1967. H:12½ in (32 cm).*

WHITEFRIARS VASE This small, bulbous amethyst vase was part of the Blown Soda range designed by Geoffrey Baxter in 1962. *H:4 in (10 cm).*

SHERINGHAM CANDLE HOLDERS Five King's Lynn candleholders of varying heights and colors follow a design by Ronald Stennett-Wilson. Each has a series of disks forming its stem. Wedgwood continued this design after 1969. *1967. Tallest: H:14 in (36 cm).*

H. Blenko Jr. became the third generation to join the family firm and his arrival coincided with that of Winslow Anderson, the first in-house designer employed by the Blenkos. Trained as a ceramicist, Anderson had no experience with glass but was nevertheless given carte blanche to design the new range of vases and tableware produced between 1948 and 1953. His most famous creations include the sculptural Horn vase and the 948 decanter, its bent neck the result of a happy accident on the blowing floor.

When Anderson left Blenko, he was replaced by Wayne Husted, who produced oversize designs with large, sculptural stoppers. These playful, decorative vessels were caricatures of traditional functional forms. The Blenko glass of this period was produced in vibrant colors, a legacy of the firm's origins in the stained-glass industry. Some have famous associations: Rose, for example, was much loved by Jackie Kennedy.

NEW AND TRADITIONAL CLASSICS

Smaller independent factories also found success. British glass designer Ronald Stennett-Wilson established the King's Lynn glassworks in 1967, employing Swedish makers to assist him. The firm's Sheringham candlesticks with multi-disk stems are a design classic, while the Brancaster glasses and candlesticks have hollow, attenuated stems that are reminiscent of Nils Landberg's *Tulpanglas*.

King's Lynn Glass was acquired by the Wedgwood Group in 1969.

Foremost among mid-20th-century studio practitioners were the British designer Sam Herman, who produced free-form shapes with decorative effects including trapped air and iridescence, and the American Dominick Labino, whose delicate Emergence series uses multiple casings.

Following World War II, the Czech glass industry was nationalized under the Communist regime and dozens of rival factories were brought into a single government-owned enterprise. However, individual glassmakers continued to flourish and to demonstrate the advanced engraving and cutting skills that have been a feature of Bohemian glass for generations. Many factories also produced pressed and cut glass.

TREE OF LIFE Designed by Jacob Landau and Donald Pollard for Steuben, this unique sculptural piece is both human and treelike in form. The surface is engraved with human figures. *1959. H:14½ in (37 cm).*

FREE-FORM VASE Multicolored swirling streaks with iridescent areas decorate this hand-blown studio glass vase by Sam Herman. *c.1972. H:10½ in (27 cm).*

CUT GLASS

Central European cut glass flourished during this period, despite the oppressive political climate. Work by masters such as Jiri Harcuba show great skill and sophisticated, often abstract, decorative expression. Vessels in Harcuba's oeuvre sometimes have concave lens panels set into one side to magnify the hand-cut decoration. Stylized and abstracted depictions of trees, birds, and animals, often incorporating geometric patterns, feature heavily in the cut glass of this period. Although clear glass predominates, some examples use layers of color to accentuate the cut designs.

WATERFORD VASE This clear and cased blue glass vase is of simple symmetrical form and has been engraved with a stylized swordfish motif. *c.1960. H:8¾ in (22 cm).*

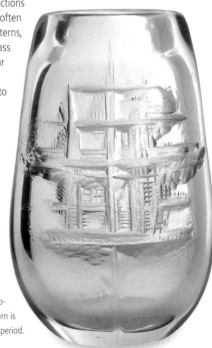

JIRI HARCUBA VASE This deep-cut, cross-hatched abstract pattern is typical of Harcuba's work of the period. *1965. H:8¼ in (21 cm).*

GLASS GALLERY

Mid-century glassware saw an explosion of modern forms and bright colors. Designers experimented with textures and patterns, and the revolutionary studio glass movement began during this period, with beautiful handcrafted and original pieces created. In Scandinavia, designers drew their inspiration from nature to make sculptural glassware, while on the island of Murano, ancient techniques were reinvigorated and used in new ways.

1 Orrefors vase

2 Boda Sun Catcher

4 Stuart barrel vase

3 Fluted Fiesta ware plate

5 Higgins rectangular dish

6 Ravenhead tumbler

7 Viking purple decanter

8 Pilgrim decanter

9 Isle of Wight bottle

10 Fenton crimped bowl

Wight studio glass bottle. 1974–79. H:15 in (38 cm). ① **10**. Fenton Coin Dot double crimped bowl. c.1950s. D:10½ in (27 cm). ① **11**. Caithness Glass lamp base by Domhnall O'Brion. 1960s. H:3½ in (9 cm). ① **12**. Dartington vase by Frank Thrower, with molded, textured Greek key design. H:3½ in (9 cm). ① **13**. Mold-blown glass vase designed by Pavel Hlava. 1959. H:14 in (36 cm). ① **14**. Mdina double-cased fish vase by Michael Harris. 1969. H:11½ in (29 cm). ① **15**. Murano triple-cased sommerso cut glass ashtray. 1960s. H:4 in (10 cm). ① **16**. Finnish Riihimäen Lasi Oy mold-blown vase by Tamara Aladin. c.1970. H:9¾ in (25 cm). ① **17**. A canne cased vase designed by Anzolo Fuga. c.1960. H:9¾ in (25 cm). ③ **18**. Blown and cut crystal glass vase by Monica Morales Schildt for Kosta Boda. 1957. H:9 in (23 cm). ①

11 *Caithness glass lamp base*

12 *Dartington Glass Greek key vase*

13 *Pavel Hlava vase*

14 *Mdina fish vase*

15 *Murano ashtray*

16 *Tamara Aladin vase*

17 *Anzolo Fuga vase*

18 *Crystal glass vase*

LIGHTING

FROM LIQUID PLASTIC POLYMERS AND POLISHED CHROME TO
ARTICHOKES AND GIANT PILLS, MID-CENTURY LIGHTING DESIGNERS
REVELED IN USING MODERN MATERIALS AND SCULPTURAL FORMS.

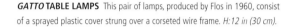

SCULPTURAL LIGHTING

The same advances in materials technology that gave rise to Pop furniture design also transformed lighting, which was even more experimental and bold. Versatile plastics were the key to this, since the globes, curves, and colors of Pop lighting would have been far more expensive to reproduce in any other medium.

Joe Colombo explored the multifaceted applications of plastic in a table lamp which he designed for Kartell in the 1960s. The opaque plastic shade diffused the light evenly, while the silvered plastic base mimicked the more expensive chromed finish that had been a prominent fixture of earlier modernist light fittings. Each segment was molded in an organic shape in much the same way as Gae Aulenti's *Pipistrello* (Bat) lamp for Martinelli Luce, which took its name from its folded, organic plastic shade.

The telescopic shaft meant that it could be used as either a table lamp or a floor lamp, according to the owner's wishes.

The longstanding partnership between Achille Castiglioni and Flos—two of the heavyweights of mid-century Italian lighting design—produced

***GATTO* TABLE LAMPS** This pair of lamps, produced by Flos in 1960, consist of a sprayed plastic cover strung over a corseted wire frame. *H:12 in (30 cm).*

some of the most remarkable lamps of the period. Founded in 1960 by Dino Gavina and Cesare Cassina, Flos quickly became a market leader through its associations with a host of leading designers. The company's first products were a series of lamps made from liquid polymer sprayed over a wire frame. Designed by Castiglioni, the Viscontia and *Gatto* lamps were very similar to the Bubble lamp range that was made in the United States by Howard Miller to designs by George Nelson. Nelson had first seen this space-age cocooning material used in New York Harbor to protect shipping in 1947 and was immediately inspired to put it to a more decorative use. Many variations of these lamps were made, from globes to more complicated shapes.

BULBOUS LAMP This table lamp with a bulbous, opaque plastic shade on a silvered spreading plastic base was designed by Joe Colombo for Kartell of Italy. *1960s. H:16 in (41 cm).*

***PIPISTRELLO* LAMP** Designed by Gae Aulenti for Martinelli Luce, the *Pipistrello* table lamp has a black-enameled metal base and white, hard plastic shade. The stainless steel shaft is telescopic. *1967. H:36 in (91.5 cm).*

DALU TABLE LAMPS Vico Magistretti's Dalu lamps, influenced by astronaut's helmets, were molded from hard red plastic in a single piece. They were produced by Artemide. *1969. H:10½ in (27 cm).*

BUBBLE LAMP This George Nelson lamp, designed for wall mounting, has a walnut panel with an adjustable-height tubular-aluminum arm. It was produced by Howard Miller. *1955. H:20 in (51 cm).*

COMMERCE VERSUS ART

Flos's rivals within the Italian market also took advantage of the versatility of plastic in order to create sculptural Pop designs. Vico Magistretti, who designed many of Artemide's best-selling

ISAMU NOGUCHI

The concept of light as sculpture was explored in depth by Isamu Noguchi. Born in Los Angeles, Noguchi grew up in Japan but trained as a sculptor in the United States, where he then spent most of his life.

His Akari design, named after the Japanese word for light, debuted in 1951. Produced in Gifu, Japan, using traditional materials such as paper made from mulberry bark, Noguchi's lamps fuse the Eastern paper lamp aesthetic with Western design concepts, making use of both man-made and natural materials. Noguchi was especially drawn to the ephemeral qualities of the paper lantern form, remarking of his own lamps that "they seem to float, casting their light as in passing."

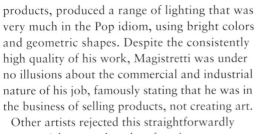

AKARI 31P A tubular, black-enameled metal structure covered with Japanese paper, Isamu Noguchi's standard lamp pays homage to the monumental *Infinite Column* sculpture by Brancusi that stands at Tirgu-Jiu in Romania. *c.1960. H:75 in (190 cm).*

products, produced a range of lighting that was very much in the Pop idiom, using bright colors and geometric shapes. Despite the consistently high quality of his work, Magistretti was under no illusions about the commercial and industrial nature of his job, famously stating that he was in the business of selling products, not creating art.

Other artists rejected this straightforwardly commercial approach and preferred to concentrate on the sculptural quality of their work. Serge Manzon, for example, said of his own creations, "My objects cannot be marketed industrially. They are living aesthetic sculptures." In the 1970s Manzon created a series of "perfect" simple furniture forms. These prototypes for ideal design have ideological and aesthetic roots in the Bauhaus experiment (*see p.248*).

Some of the most iconic work of this period occupies a space between functional lighting and artistic sculpture. The *Pillola* lamps by Cesare Casati and Emanuele Ponzio for Ponteur are a prime example of this. The design is fun, funky, and fresh, and the chosen form is quintessentially Pop—just as Warhol found art in a Campbell's soup can, so Casati and Ponzio found it in a pill. There is also an implicit acknowledgment of the growing culture of drug-taking, among both youth movements and tranquilizer-using adults.

DISTORTIONS OF SCALE

The close scrutiny of everyday objects encouraged by enlarging them to ridiculous proportions is another hallmark of the Pop Art movement and the increased interest in product design that it helped to bring about. Gaetano Pesce's 1970 Moloch floor lamp is a particularly witty manifestation of this trend—a giant version of the best-selling Luxo or Anglepoise desk lamp first popularized by the Jac Jacobsen company. Every detail is correct, down to the giant springs, but this room-filling design would never fit on a desk. In what was surely a

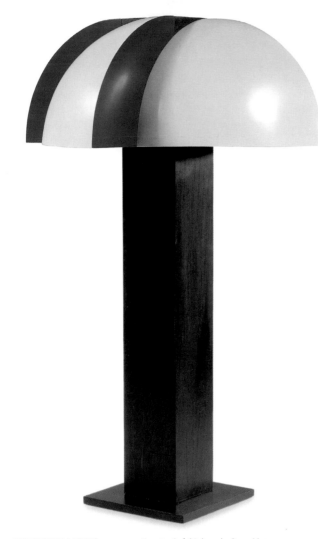

SCULPTURAL LAMP The square-section stand of this lamp by Serge Manzon is covered with purplewood veneer, while the shade is composed of ivory- and red-lacquered metal semicircles. *c.1975. H:39¾ in (98 cm).*

mischievously facetious remark, designed to poke fun at corporate modernism, Pesce said, "Moloch was conceived for a practical need: to illuminate large American skyscraper lobbies."

PILLOLA **LIGHTS** In Cesare Casati and Emanuele Ponzio's design for Ponteur, a collection of lights made from ABS hard plastic in the form of oversize pills are set on plastic ring stands. The lamps can be angled into different positions on the floor. *1968. H:22 in (55.5 cm).*

RODS AND RAYS

The importance of electric lighting in creating harmonious and coherent interiors had been a continuous theme since the end of the 19th century. However, where their predecessors, particularly in the Arts and Crafts movement, had sought to create unobtrusive lighting that blended into the overall scheme, mid-century modern designers produced fixtures that were features in their own right.

The Danish firm Louis Poulsen laid the ground by means of its collaborations with many of the boldest designers of the day, including Verner Panton. His Moon Visor ceiling lamp, produced by Poulsen from 1960, was composed of concentric plastic bands that could be manipulated around a central metal rod to produce different levels of illumination. This could range from muted to bright light, giving the same effect as a waxing and waning moon. The Flower Pot hanging fixture, designed later in 1968, was available with single or multiple plastic fittings in deep blue and orange colors, some with psychedelic swirling patterns.

Like Panton's, the lamps of sometime Poulsen collaborator Arne Jacobsen are firmly rooted in the 1960s by their globular forms.

THE PH ARTICHOKE

Perhaps the most iconic mid-century lamp produced by Poulsen was the PH Artichoke. Designed by Paul Henningson, this complex piece was handcrafted from 72 individual steel leaves mounted on a cage of struts. Arranged in staggered rows to resemble the leaves of an artichoke, they diffuse the light evenly. It was originally commissioned for the Langelinie Pavilion Restaurant in Copenhagen Harbor, but Henningson's design proved so popular that Poulsen put it into production and, despite a high price tag, it was a bestseller.

ITALIAN DESIGN

A more restrained, often linear, attitude to lighting design was expressed by the trio of companies that dominated post-war Italian lighting design. Arredoluce, Flos, and Arteluce benefited from the regeneration of Italian industry that peaked in the mid-1960s, at the height of the Pop Art craze.

Arredolucc was formed in the 1950s, originally producing chandeliers. Acclaimed designers such as Gino Sarfatti—who went on to found Arteluce—helped cement Arredoluce's reputation for innovation and high style.

The company was responsible for the Milan Triennale, which remains an archetype of the stylish fixtures produced by Italian firms during this

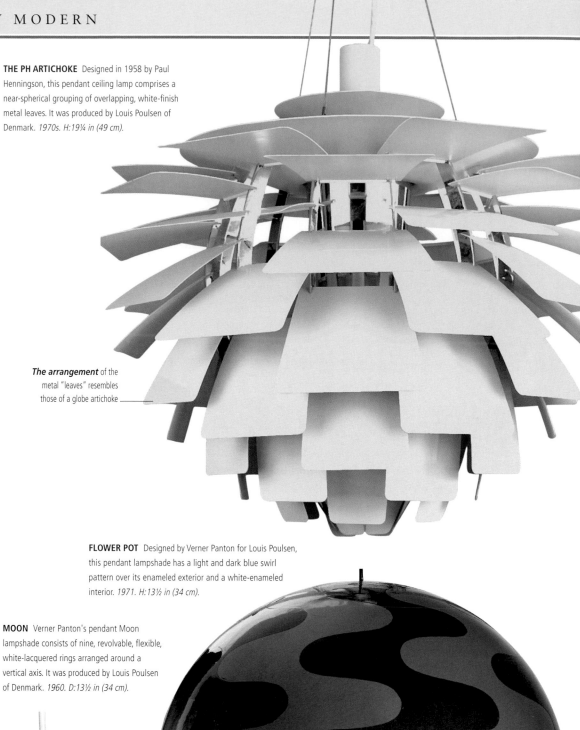

THE PH ARTICHOKE Designed in 1958 by Paul Henningson, this pendant ceiling lamp comprises a near-spherical grouping of overlapping, white-finish metal leaves. It was produced by Louis Poulsen of Denmark. *1970s. H:19¼ in (49 cm).*

The arrangement of the metal "leaves" resembles those of a globe artichoke

FLOWER POT Designed by Verner Panton for Louis Poulsen, this pendant lampshade has a light and dark blue swirl pattern over its enameled exterior and a white-enameled interior. *1971. H:13½ in (34 cm).*

MOON Verner Panton's pendant Moon lampshade consists of nine, revolvable, flexible, white-lacquered rings arranged around a vertical axis. It was produced by Louis Poulsen of Denmark. *1960. D:13½ in (34 cm).*

PENDANT LAMP Arne Jacobsen's elegant aluminum pendant lamp shade has a white-lacquered interior. It was possibly made by Ateljé Lyktan of Sweden. *H:12 in (30.5 cm).*

TRIENNALE FLOOR LAMP Produced by Arteluce, this lamp has three arms in a brass finish with brown leather-covered handles, three enameled shades, and a circular white-marble base. It is marked "Made in Italy." *H:60 in (152.5 cm).*

Each of the enameled shades is a different color: white, teal, and black

material to a supporting role being typical of Achille Castiglioni's irreverent approach to design. The more radical Toio lamp makes features of industrial components—an example of Italian "anti-design."

In the United States, radical mid-century lighting in the Atomic style included the avant-garde T-3-C lamp by James Harvey Crate. Nominally resembling a spacecraft, the cork feet and finials also bring to mind electrons orbiting a nucleus.

period. Versions with colored shades proved especially popular and could be found in fashionable interiors across Europe. The more abstract strain of Arredoluce's output is exemplified by the Eye (or Cobra) lamp with its Cyclopic magnetic fixture in the center of a slender chrome shaft.

Arteluce was formed in 1939 in Milan. Gino Sarfatti drafted the majority of his firm's early designs himself and, as it grew in stature, the company attracted the talents of leading designers such as Marco Zanuso and Franco Albino.

CASTIGLIONI DESIGN

In 1974, Arteluce was taken over by Flos, which achieved dominance thanks to the superlative design skills of the Castiglioni brothers. Their contributions to the Flos catalog of 1962 included the Arco and Taccia models. They quickly became fixtures of modish interiors and have since achieved classic status within the genre.

The monumental Arco floor lamp in particular is synonymous with mid-century lighting design. The long, bowed steel arm and aluminum reflector are held in place by a block of Carrara marble acting as a counterweight, the relegation of this noble

The shaft is made of polished chrome

EYE LAMP This piece has a black-enameled metal base and an adjustable fixture on a magnetic socket. Produced by Arredoluce of Italy, the design is attributed to Angelo Lelli in 1964. *H:24½ in (62 cm).*

T-3-C TABLE LAMP This rare Heifetz lamp by James Harvey Crate has a spring-mounted reflector over black-enameled metal and spun aluminum components. The ball finials and feet are cork. *1951. H:24¼ in (61.5 cm).*

TOIO FLOOR LAMP Designed by Achille Castiglioni for Flos, this floor lamp has unusual components such as a transformer and a car headlight. *1962. H:78¾ in (200 cm).*

SERGE MOUILLE

Metalworker and sculptor Serge Mouille began to create lighting fixtures in the early 1950s after an approach from Jacques Adnet of La Compagnie des Arts Français. His most famous designs include the *Oeil, Flammes,* and Saturn lamps. He viewed the dominant Italian designs as "too complicated," preferring a simpler aesthetic. The "teated" shape of his aluminum shades was designed to disperse light over as wide an area as possible. The development of neon strip lighting prompted Mouille to experiment with lamps that combined both fluorescent and incandescent light sources. He won commissions to design lighting for many large institutions, including universities and cathedrals.

DOUBLE-ARMED LAMP This Serge Mouille lamp has two aluminum shades, each with black exteriors and white interiors, and black-painted rods and ball joints. *c.1955. H:70 in (180 cm).*

LIGHTING GALLERY

Mid-century modern lighting was heavily influenced by the space age, the real possibility of space exploration being a source of contemporary excitement as well as a springboard for the imagination. Many lamps of this period echo the form of flying saucers or satellites. The forms are futuristic, and mix smooth shapes with angular lines. Another trend was the move toward sculptural forms (many influenced by the Surrealists and by artist and sculptor Jean Arp) as well as minimal, linear designs.

KEY

1. Red-lacquered metal book light. 1950s. H:15¾ in (40 cm). ① **2**. Serge Manzon metal lamp inspired by flying saucers. H:19¾ in (50 cm). ⑤ **3**. Verner Panton VP-Globe lamp, a plexiglass sphere containing aluminum disks. 1970. D:19¾ in (50 cm). ③ **4**. Brass desk lamp by Pierre Paulin for Philips. c.1955. W:17 in (41 cm). ① **5**. Chrome-plated Stilnovo Mini Topo desk lamp by Joe Colombo. 1968. H:14 in (35.5 cm). ① **6**. Painted and textured plaster table lamp with original parchment shade. 1950s. H:32½ in (83 cm). ① **7**. Fontana Arte desk lamp in brass and enameled metal. c.1960. H:18¼ in (46 cm). ② **8**. Heifetz Company floor lamp with magnetic ball-and socket pivoting

1 Metal book light

2 Serge Manzon metal lamp

3 Verner Panton VP-Globe lamp

4 Pierre Paulin desk lamp

5 Mini Topo desk lamp

6 Table lamp with parchment shade

7 Fontana Arte desk lamp

8 Heifetz Company floor lamp

9 Kaiser & Co. table lamp

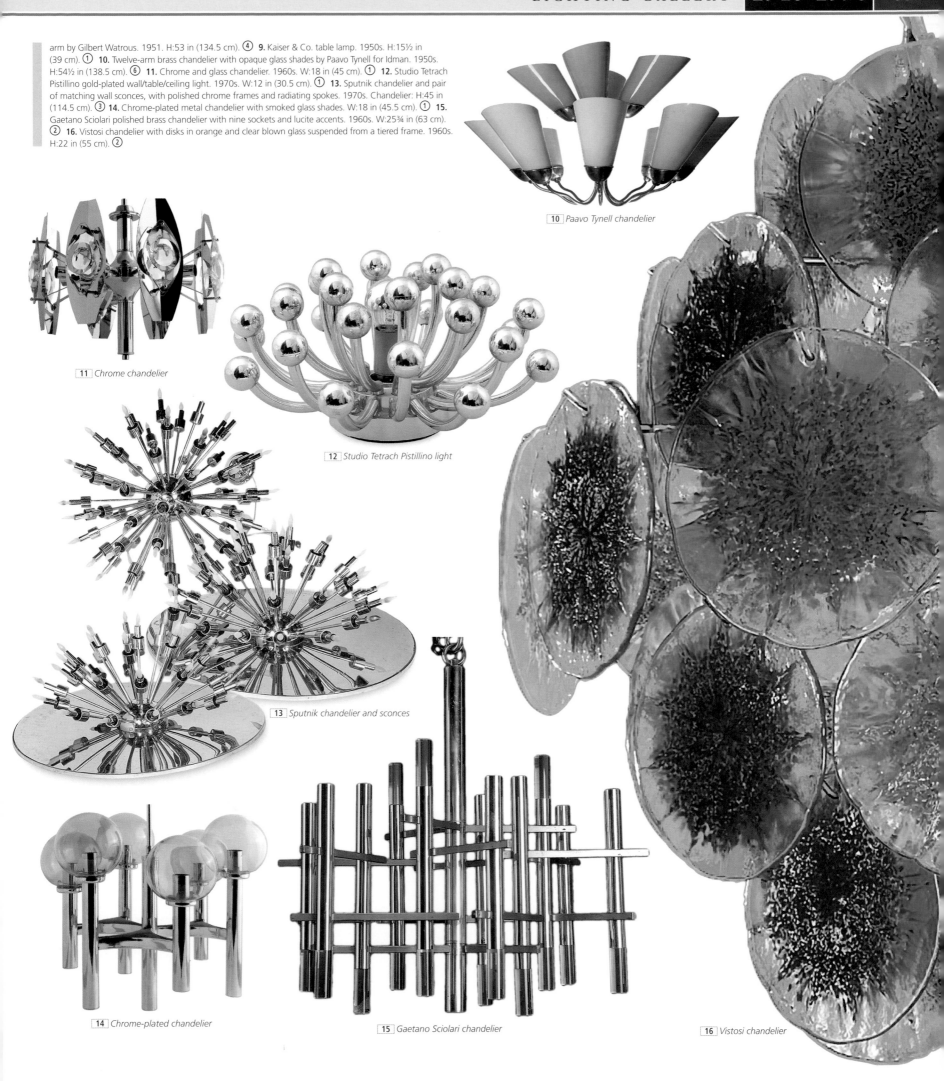

arm by Gilbert Watrous. 1951. H:53 in (134.5 cm). ④ **9.** Kaiser & Co. table lamp. 1950s. H:15½ in (39 cm). ① **10.** Twelve-arm brass chandelier with opaque glass shades by Paavo Tynell for Idman. 1950s. H:54½ in (138.5 cm). ⑥ **11.** Chrome and glass chandelier. 1960s. W:18 in (45 cm). ① **12.** Studio Tetrach Pistillino gold-plated wall/table/ceiling light. 1970s. W:12 in (30.5 cm). ① **13.** Sputnik chandelier and pair of matching wall sconces, with polished chrome frames and radiating spokes. 1970s. Chandelier: H:45 in (114.5 cm). ③ **14.** Chrome-plated metal chandelier with smoked glass shades. W:18 in (45.5 cm). ① **15.** Gaetano Sciolari polished brass chandelier with nine sockets and lucite accents. 1960s. W:25¾ in (63 cm). ② **16.** Vistosi chandelier with disks in orange and clear blown glass suspended from a tiered frame. 1960s. H:22 in (55 cm). ②

10 Paavo Tynell chandelier

11 Chrome chandelier

12 Studio Tetrach Pistillino light

13 Sputnik chandelier and sconces

14 Chrome-plated chandelier

15 Gaetano Sciolari chandelier

16 Vistosi chandelier

METALWARE

AFTER THE WAR, ALUMINUM AND STAINLESS STEEL ALLOYS
PROVIDED A NEW AND CHEAPER ALTERNATIVE TO THE USE
OF SILVER AND GOLD IN DECORATIVE METALWARE.

FLUID LINES

During World War II, huge advances were made
in the industrial application of aluminum and
stainless steel alloys. After the war, these materials
became increasingly available and popular within
the decorative arts.

Nevertheless, precious metals such as gold and
silver did not lose their appeal. One Scandinavian
silverware firm remained peerless during this
period: Georg Jensen, for whom Henning Koppel
in particular created outstanding functional forms.
Characterized by fluid lines and sinuous curves,
Koppel's work is a blend of the biomorphic and
the sculptural. Tapio Wirkkala produced similarly
modest and elegant silverware, often based on his
stylized perceptions of natural forms.

AUSTERITY AND FUNCTIONALITY

In addition to this organic modernism, many
designers at Georg Jensen invigorated the
company's output with other reinterpretations of
modernism. For example, Sigvard Bernadotte's
designs are typified by classic geometric shapes

WATER PITCHER
Henning Koppel designed this stunning,
sculptural silver water pitcher of organic
form for Georg Jensen of Denmark.
1950s. H:12 in (30 cm).

Koppel is renowned for the
biomorphic forms he created

The satiny surface
of the piece was created
using a technique
developed by Jensen

The hammered surface
is typical of Devlin's work

*The texture of the
body* of the jug is
repeated on the handle

WATER JUG Stuart Devlin's silver water
jug has a flared form with hammered
effect and an abstract gilt handle. It bears
an impressed "SD" seal and hallmarks for
London. *1973. H:11¼ in (28.5 cm).*

with a strong element of streamlining, while Jørgen Jensen became known for his sleek, mannered interpretation of modernism.

Austere and functional, Arne Jacobsen's designs also contributed enormously to the dominance of Scandinavian style during this period. They are typified by his AJ range of cutlery, designed in 1957, which featured in Stanley Kubrick's film *2001: A Space Odyssey*, and by the Cylinda line of tableware, designed around 1968. Both retain a futuristic aura.

The Royal College of Art played a crucial role in the drive to revitalize British industry after the war. Professor Robert Goodden was tutor to, among others, the metalworkers Robert Welch and David Mellor. After graduation, Mellor returned to Sheffield, the center of Britain's steel industry, where he worked on behalf of various

manufacturers. His strong belief in mass production saw him collaborate with many of the biggest names in British industry, including Elkington. He also produced a pared-down cutlery set called Thrift for the government's Ministry of Works, designed specifically for use in institutions such as hospitals and prisons, as well as in train stations.

Similarly, Robert Welch combined a devotion to industrial design with a latent sympathy for the modernist ideal. He subscribed to the Scandinavian philosophy of designing simple, everyday objects that were functional, beautiful, and affordable for most people. His stainless-steel Connaught tea service and Bistro cutlery set became staples in cafés and restaurants across Britain.

In the United States, Russel Wright, famous primarily for his ceramics, also produced metal tableware in a new, streamlined form, and often in aluminum. In Italy, Lino Sabbattini—the great Italian master of silver design during this period—produced objects for daily use that combined grand elegance with the modernist aesthetic.

A TASTE FOR EMBELLISHMENT

Gerald Benney, who had trained in an Arts and Crafts workshop, studied under Goodden at London's Royal College of Art and traveled extensively in Scandinavia. All these diverse influences appear in his modernist work. Benney developed a textured finish for silver in the late 1950s, which he later used on pewter. This was extensively copied by other designers.

The Australian designer Stuart Devlin, another graduate of the Royal College of Art, produced simple forms with rich, decorative embellishment. In order to find a market for his work, Devlin had to temper the prohibitive cost of his

intricate hand-tooled finishes. The result was striking textured finishes that were far removed from the clean surfaces preferred by adherents of the more austere Scandinavian style.

In the United States, the metalware designs of polymath designer Tommi Parzinger were equally distinctive. Reluctant to subscribe to any particular school, Parzinger fitted his furniture with his own handcrafted metalware, and designed a range of brass accessories for the American manufacturer Dorlyn. Among the designs that became iconic are his classical geometric shapes adorned with banding and accentuated loops.

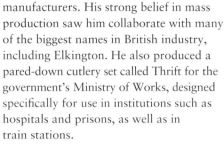

MEXICAN MARTINI PITCHER Designed by William Spratling in sterling silver, this pitcher has a distinctly modernist shape with no surface decoration. *1961–67. W:5½ in (14 cm).*

SAUCE LADLE Lino Sabbattini's elegant silver-plated sauce ladle with a wooden handle was designed for Christofle & Cie of France. *c.1950. H:10¼ in (26 cm).*

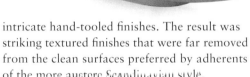

SILVER VASE This silver elongated vase was designed by Tapio Wirkkala for Kultakeskus of Finland. *1955. H:7½ in (19 cm).*

COFFEEPOT Designed by Tommi Parzinger for Dorlyn Silversmiths, this tall brass and stainless-steel coffeepot has horizontal bands adorning a tapering body. *c.1950. H:16½ in (42 cm).*

PRIDE TEAPOT David Mellor designed this silver-plated teapot for Elkington as part of a range of silverware that included cutlery. *1957. L:9 in (23 cm).*

METALWARE GALLERY

Mid-century modern metalware is characterized by simplicity and elegance. The style is of modern, clean lines where the form itself is the decoration, and there is very little added ornamentation. As this streamlined effect could be achieved by using inexpensive materials, most commonly stainless steel, silversmiths saw a decline in trade. However, they were able to edge back into the market and display their talent by creating handcrafted pieces with interesting textures that appealed to the sensibilities of the time.

KEY

1. Old Hall stainless steel Alveston tea set designed by Robert Welch. c.1962. Teapot: W:9½ in (24 cm). ① **2**. Stelton Cylinda line coffeepot designed by Arne Jacobsen. c.1970. H:8 in (20 cm). ① **3**. Deakin & Francis silver ashtray with textured rim and gold wash. Birmingham hallmarks for 1971. D:4 in (10 cm). ① **4**. Black wire and raffia wine pourer by Desmond Sawyer. c.1950. H:7 in (18 cm). ① **5**. Set of four Danish Krenitware enameled metal bowls designed by Hebert Krerchel in 1954. Largest: D:6¼ in (16 cm). ① **6**. Stelton Cylinda line cocktail shaker in stainless steel designed by Arne Jacobson. c.1970. H:9 in (23 cm). ① **7**. Georg Jensen bowl designed by Henning Koppel, design no. 980. 1950s. D:15 in (38 cm). ⑥ **8**. Pair of silver vases by Hans Bunde for Carl M. Cohr. 1963.

1 Old Hall tea set

2 Cylinda line coffeepot

3 Silver ashtray

4 Wine pourer

5 Krenitware bowls

6 Cylinda line cocktail shaker

7 Georg Jensen bowl

8 Pair of silver vases

H:7 in (18 cm). ② **9.** Silver cruet set by Gordon Hodgson with ivory and black stained hardwood inserts, hallmarked for London 1969. H:2½ in (6.5 cm). ② **10.** Pair of Danish Meka sterling salt and pepper shakers in the form of fish with enamel decoration. H:2¼ in (5.5 cm). ① **11.** Viner's stainless steel candleholder with textured gold-plated stem, designed by Stuart Devlin. H:6 in (15.25 cm). ① **12.** Candleholder sculpture by Nagel, composed of individual sections that can be assembled into any combination. 1960s. H:11 in (28 cm). ① **13.** Viner's stainless steel flower holder or bud vase by Stuart Devlin with gold-plated domed top. c.1969. H:3 in (8 cm). ① **14.** Condiment set by Frantz Hingelberg for Aarhus in silver and black bakelite. 1950s. Sugar sifter: H:5¼ in (13.5 cm). ② **15.** Viner's stainless steel wine goblet with textured gold-plated stem by Stuart Devlin. c.1970. H:5½ in (13.5 cm). ① **16.** Pair of Old Hall stainless- steel triple candlesticks designed by Robert Welch. H:9 in (23 cm). ① **17.** Set of six silver goblets with textured lower sections, a hollow base, and bowl interiors with gold wash. 1974. H:6¼ in (16 cm). ②

9 *Silver cruet set*

10 *Meka salt and pepper shakers*

11 *Viner's candleholder*

12 *Nagel candleholder sculpture*

13 *Flower holder*

14 *Condiment set*

15 *Viner's goblet*

16 *Old Hall candlesticks*

17 *Silver goblet*

PRODUCT DESIGN

THE AMERICAN DREAM WAS FULFILLED POST-WAR THROUGH THE CONSTANT
ACQUISITION OF NEW GOODS, WHILE IN BRITAIN HAROLD MACMILLAN TOLD
HIS ELECTORATE THAT THEY HAD "NEVER HAD IT SO GOOD."

THE CONSUMER DREAM

During the 1950s it was hard to escape the idealized image of the nuclear family living in their perfect suburban home that was propounded by advertising in print and on television. This branded vision of happiness relied upon consumerism to perpetuate itself. Hand-in-hand with the smiling family and the suburban house, came the car in its garage, the fashionable furnishings, the labor-saving appliances, and the state-of-the-art communications equipment. Manufacturers were eager to encourage this insatiable demand for novel products and even designed obsolescence into their goods, thereby conditioning the buying public to covet the latest thing and throw away the old. This fetishizing of consumer goods was driven in part by the designers who made them so attractive in the first place.

KOMET ENTERTAINMENT SYSTEM The angled high-varnished case houses a 21-in (53-cm) television set, radio, Telefunken tape deck, Imperial record player, and speakers. It was produced by Kuba of Germany. *1957–62. H:85 in (216 cm).*

Families had begun to gather around the wireless in the 1920s, but since that time its design had changed beyond recognition, new plastics such as bakelite being used to produce stylish, streamlined designs. However, during the 1950s, radio began to face increasing competition from television, which soon became the dominant mass-media source. The television sets of the 1950s and early 1960s were often designed to be the centerpiece of the living room, representing the high esteem in which this revolutionary new technology was held.

Surely the most ostentatious entertainment center ever made, the Komet Super Luxus Automatic was an enormous walnut and wenge-wood housing for a television, cassette tape deck, and

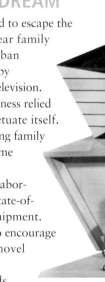

BOOMERANG This Philco Model 49-501 Transitone brown bakelite radio was named Boomerang on account of its angular design. *1949. W:11½ in (29 cm).*

JVC VIDEOSPHERE The design of this television set, based on an astronaut's helmet, was influenced by the American Moon landing of 1969. *1969–70. H:13 in (33 cm).*

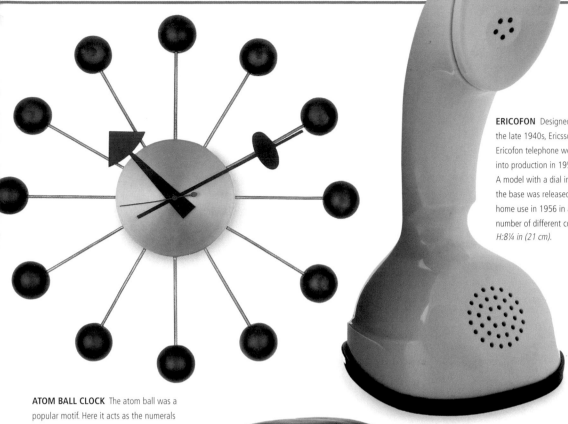

ATOM BALL CLOCK The atom ball was a popular motif. Here it acts as the numerals of a wall clock, designed by George Nelson for the American Howard Miller Clock Company. *1947. D:13 in (33 cm).*

ERICOFON Designed in the late 1940s, Ericsson's Ericofon telephone went into production in 1954. A model with a dial in the base was released for home use in 1956 in a number of different colors. *H:8¼ in (21 cm).*

"JUST WHAT IS IT...?" The poster for a retrospective exhibition of the work of Richard Hamilton in 1976 has as its main image a 1956 collage designed by Hamilton. *1976. H:30 in (75 cm).*

RADIO NURSE Designed by Isamu Noguchi for America's Zenith Radio Corporation, this bakelite radio has a typical late 1930s and 1940s streamlined look. *1937. H:8¼ in (21 cm).*

TRIMPHONE An iconic British design from this era, the plastic Trimphone (TRIM for Tone Ringer Illuminated Model) was available in three two-tone colors: blue, green, and ivory. *1964. L:7¾ in (19.5 cm).*

turntable. The angular, sculptural top section conceals eight speakers as well as the relatively small screen—the technology for larger screens had not yet come into existence. Later in the 1960s, less obtrusive but equally distinctive designs began to proliferate. The Videosphere by JVC, based on an astronaut's helmet, made its debut in 1969, the year of the first Moon landing.

CATCHING THE CONSUMER'S EYE

Eye-catching design was so vital for attracting consumers that many manufacturers hired famous names to help them. Isamu Noguchi's Radionurse, designed to transmit sounds from a baby's crib to its parents elsewhere in the house, looks like a cross between a robotic nanny and a samurai's kabuto helmet.

Marketing its 1963 turntable cabinet as "a stereo set for individualists," the German manufacturer Wega loudly trumpeted Verner Panton's input. A product of the more understated approach to design that began to take hold in the 1960s, it is sleek, simple, and geometric, the buttons and dials arranged in tidy rows on the top.

Pioneering companies willing to take risks with product design often found the rewards were great. Ericsson's Ericofon telephone handset, first produced in 1954, was a functional but unusual one-piece design with the dial in the base. Available in 18 colors, it was a bestseller and even broke into the notoriously difficult American market. The market leader in Britain was the Trimphone, designed by Martyn Rolands and produced on behalf of the General Post Office, which operated the national telephone exchange at the time. Thousands of people rented these handsets from the GPO, the more daring among them paying extra for a two-tone model.

Richard Hamilton satirized the ubiquity of such products in his 1956 collage *Just What Is It That Makes Today's Home So Different, So Appealing?* Advertising is represented by the woman vacuuming the stairs, while a black arrow extols the virtues of the brand of appliance she is using.

3300 STEREO SYSTEM This 1960s German Wega model 3300 stereo system housed in a molded white plastic case was designed for the company by Verner Panton. *1963. H:17¼ in (43.5 cm).*

POP AND PLASTICS

JUST AS EARLY MODERNISTS WERE INSPIRED BY ABSTRACTIONIST ART MOVEMENTS SUCH AS CUBISM, MID-CENTURY DESIGNERS FOUND NEW STIMULATION IN THE POP ART MOVEMENT THAT BEGAN IN THE LATE 1950S.

Like Cubism, Pop Art was initially a reaction against the art establishment. Young artists like Richard Hamilton, David Hockney, and Peter Blake rejected abstract expressionism, which they considered to be too high-minded and cerebral, and turned instead to everyday objects. They aimed to reconnect art with the normal lives of ordinary people. Critic Lawrence Alloway first coined the term Pop Art in 1958 in recognition of the way the movement eliminated the distinction between high art and low art, or popular culture. It is characterized by bright colors, collage, pastiche, convenience, and innovation. Leading advocates of the style made their work available in a variety of media, releasing art from the constraints of the gallery. Peter Blake devised the cover art for the Beatles' album, *Sergeant Pepper's Lonely Hearts Club Band*, one of the most frequently reproduced images in the Pop canon.

THE SOUPER DRESS Influenced by Andy Warhol's images of Campbell's soup cans, this papery cellulose dress reflects the disposable nature of the Pop culture of the time. *1966–67. L:38 in (96.5 cm).*

FAMOUS FOR 15 MINUTES

The movement surfaced in the United States, where Andy Warhol became its most prolific exponent. His exaltation of the mundane was most famously expressed by his various sculptural and graphic treatments of Campbell's soup packaging. At his Factory studio in Manhattan, Warhol employed teams of workers to assist in the production of his silkscreen prints—in effect turning art into an industrial process. Warhol prophesied that "in the future, everyone will be world famous for 15 minutes," acknowledging the disposable culture that had come to dominate modern life.

This emphasis on transience and intensive production made plastic a natural ally of the Pop movement. Novel, cheap, disposable, and accessible, it had the added benefits that it could take on just about any form or color. Molded plastic forms were designed to save space and contribute to a clutter-free lifestyle. Helen

COATHANGER This elaborate American plastic coathanger is charged with classic 1960s images and design motifs: the mirrored pebble glasses, lurid colors, and psychedelic swirls. *H:13½ in (34 cm).*

PENTAGRAM ASHTRAYS A group of interlocking Pentagram stacking ashtrays, made from molded plastic, each in a different bold color. They are marked "DO Reg No. 954.589 *PENTAGRAM.*" *Each: H:1¾ in (4.5 cm).*

POP SHAPES The red-and-white cased glass vase by Holmegaard, named Carnaby, has an opacity, color and shape mimicking contemporary plastics such as the *La Bomba* plastic picnic set. *Vase: 1961. H:8¾ in (22 cm); Picnic set: c.1975. H:15½ in (39 cm).*

von Boch's *La Bomba* picnic set, for example, slots neatly together to form a portable capsule when not in use.

THE PREDOMINANCE OF PLASTICS

The deluge of witty, throwaway designs from this period ranges from the sublime to the ridiculous. Some, like the inflatable Blow armchair produced by Zanotta, remain in production today. Like Gruppo DAM's *Libro* chair, it is representative of the new style of furniture demanded by consumers used to more informal living.

Plastic played such a pivotal role that products made from other materials were sometimes designed to look like it. Per Lutken's Carnaby vases—the name itself an allusion to one of the focal points of Swinging London—are glass made to resemble plastic.

BLOW ARMCHAIR Designed by Gionatan de Pas for Zanotta of Italy, this armchair was made of radio-frequency welded PVC. It was the archetypal example of disposable Pop Art plastic furniture. *1967. H:33 in (47 cm).*

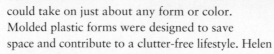

***LIBRO* CHAIR** Gruppo DAM's lounge chair is designed to resemble an open book. The aluminum frame has polyurethane foam "pages" upholstered in black and white vinyl. *W:31½ in (80 cm).*

FLOWERS Andy Warhol's *Flowers* is from a portfolio of ten screenprints. It is signed on verso, framed, and published by the American firm Aetna Silkscreen Products, Inc. *c.1970. H:36 in (91.5 cm).*

TEXTILES

REFLECTING EVERYDAY FASHION ON THE STREET AND IN THE HOME,
TEXTILE DESIGN IS A BAROMETER OF POPULAR TASTE. MID-CENTURY FABRICS
ENCOMPASSED THE RANGE FROM FLORAL TO GEOMETRIC PATTERNS.

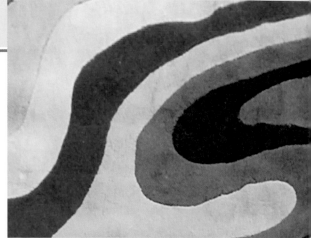

ABSTRACT DESIGNS

Lucienne Day, partner of British designer Robin Day, changed the face of British interiors with her designs for a huge range of textile products. Calyx, her most celebrated pattern, takes its name from the parts of a flower that protect the bud. The highly stylized floral design is made up of vertical stems and roughly delineated, semi-circular buds. Inspired by a trip to Scandinavia, where Lucienne and Robin had seen the subtle allusions to natural forms expressed by designers in that region, Calyx was commissioned for the Festival of Britain in 1951 and originally retailed through Heal & Son.

Day's next design for Heal & Son was Flotilla, which, like Calyx, was made with the screen-printing method. This had been used industrially since World War I, but it was not until the 1950s that more durable screen materials and advances in stencil technology made it viable for mass production. Day's association with Heal & Son continued until 1974 and resulted in dozens of acclaimed designs.

Other prominent British manufacturers of textiles included David Whitehead and the Edinburgh Weavers. Artists such as John Piper and Henry Moore contributed designs to these firms.

The resurgence in the crafts movement saw textile artists such as Richard Landis and Anni Albers hand-weaving colorful fabrics. Albers also designed colorful textiles, as did Alexander Girard, who worked for furniture manufacturer Herman Miller.

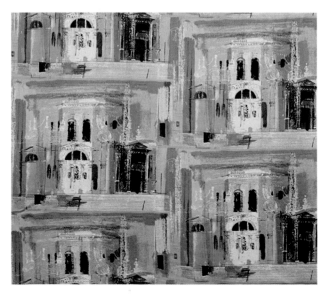

CHIESA DELLA SALUTE Produced by Sanderson, this pair of curtains has a screen-printed design by John Piper that features the Venetian church of the same name. The design was commissioned for Sanderson's centennial. *c. 1965. H:78¾ in (200 cm).*

CALYX FABRIC One of many fabrics designed by Lucienne Day for Heal & Son, Calyx was screen-printed. *1951.*

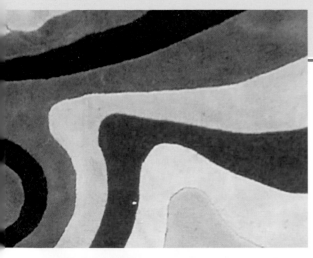

FANDANGO This length of patterned fabric was designed by Maija Isola for Marimekko of Finland, and is an elegant duotone repeating floral print. *1963. L:82½ in (210 cm).*

SWIRL-PATTERN RUG Produced by Edward Fields, this room-size rug has an overall random swirl pattern in black, white, red, and purple. *W:108 in (274 cm).*

SPECTRUM The bold, geometric shapes in strong colors on this velvet fabric are characteristic of much of Verner Panton's work with patterns. It was produced by Mira-X of Switzerland. *c.1975. W:47¼ in (120 cm).*

AREA RUGS

The more transitory lifestyle that many Americans led in the postwar years meant that they frequently moved home and abandoned their carpets. Edward Fields pioneered the concept of the "area rug" in the early 1950s as a solution to this. In partnership with the designer Raymond Loewy, Fields introduced a range of five patterned rugs for the living room. Names such as Infinite Star, Legend, and Stellar highlighted the futuristic nature of his designs. Fields's rugs became a huge success when they went on sale at Lord & Taylor's on Fifth Avenue.

Other interior designers followed suit, including icons of 1960s fashion such as Pierre Cardin. Aiming to create a homogeny between street fashion and interior furnishing, Cardin began to retail a line of rugs and other textiles that echoed the motifs he used in his clothing designs. His output was thus dominated by swirls, concentric circles, and ellipses in purples, reds, and blues. Much of Cardin's work and that of his contemporaries was indebted to key figures from the art world such as Andy Warhol; the optical effects of Bridget Riley's Op-Art were another key influence.

PANELS AND WALLHANGINGS

Verner Panton's Spectrum textile designs for Mira-X were indebted to Riley's oeuvre. His repeating swirls and geometric blocks were composed of graduated colors chosen to blend with other Panton-designed elements within an interior to create a unified environment. Mira-X produced fabric panels of Spectrum designed for use as wall hangings. This concept quickly became very popular, and throughout the 1970s many companies produced imitations. Finlayson of Finland, for example, retailed a pattern called Soundwaves, made up of bouncing waves of white, cream, brown, and black bands. The name as well as the design were calculated to tap into the consciousness of the youth movement.

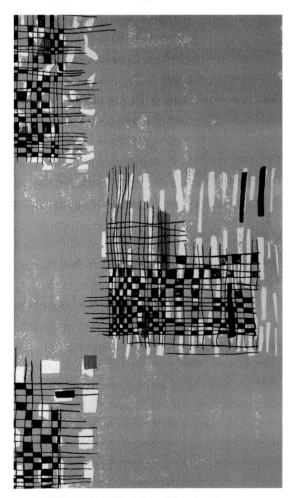

QUARTO FABRIC Typical of the designs which Lucienne Day produced for Heal & Son during the late 1950s, this framed panel of fabric has blocks of single color alternating with geometric patterns. *1960. H:35¾ in (91 cm).*

DEKOPLUS FABRIC This length of synthetic fabric was produced by Dekoplus and possibly designed by Pierre Cardin. The pattern comprises large, off-center circles in shades of blue. *c.1970. L:23¼ ft (7.24 m).*

POSTERS

THE COMMERCIAL ART OF THE MID-20TH CENTURY LIFTS THE LID
ON THE ASPIRATIONS, ANXIETIES, AND ABOVE ALL FASHIONS THAT
PREOCCUPIED PEOPLE DURING THESE TUMULTUOUS YEARS.

GRAPHIC DESIGN

The early experiments in modern
typography by the Constructivists and
the Bauhaus, and their overall avant-
garde design style, found their way to
the United States through the many
prominent artists who fled to the
United States in the years just prior to
World War II. Here they blossomed
into a new kind of graphic design.
Corporate America flocked to
designers such as Paul Rand to
commission logos that would embed
their name and identity firmly in the
public mind. This revolution in
information design was spearheaded by
Ladislav Sutner and by Charles and
Ray Eames, who released their first
educational film, *A Communications
Primer*, in 1953.

THE POWER OF PROMOTION
During World War II, the Royal
Society for the Prevention of
Accidents harnessed the power of
modernist graphic design to promote
worker safety—an impressive and
progressive campaign that stood
out markedly from the drab and
uninventive images normally associated
with the style. Many of these posters
were designed by Tom Eckersley, who
went on to create witty and dynamic

BOAC Tom Eckersley created this striking image for the airline BOAC. Coupled
with the slogan "It's A Small World By Speedbird," the poster shows the globe
being traversed by an abstract bird/plane image. *1947. H:39 in (99 cm).*

OLIVETTI TYPEWRITERS Frederic Henri Kay
Henrion's Post-Surrealist image of an eye above a
typewriter makes a symbolic link between the eye
and the machine, as manifested by the dotted line.
1950s. H:119½ in (299 cm).

PSYCHEDELIC POSTERS

Inspired by the sinuous whiplash curves of Art Nouveau
from an earlier era and by the hallucinogenic effects of LSD,
psychedelic poster design thrived as a means of advertising
the rock gigs, multimedia shows, and assorted happenings that
defined the acid wave that spread out from San Francisco in
the late 1960s. Promoters including Bill Graham and the Family
Dog commissioned this work by approaching underground
illustrators such as Chet Helms and Stanley Mouse, who were
invariably members of the scene. The style is characterized by
inflated lettering, day-glo colors, and surrealistic imagery. It was
later commercialized by artists such as Peter Max.

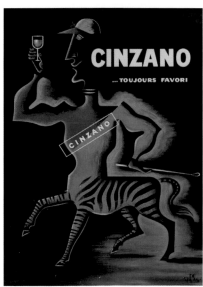

CINZANO A reworking of
the Cinzano emblem created
in 1910, this poster (*far left*)
was designed by Jean Carlu. It
makes use of the *ligne souple*
(supple line)—a green halo
on a dark background. *1950.
H:63 in (160 cm).*

4 GITANES CAPORAL The four
different kinds of Gitane cigarette
available are each accompanied
by an image of a Romany-type
woman in a headscarf. Designed
by Jean Colin of France. *1950s.
H:63 in (160 cm).*

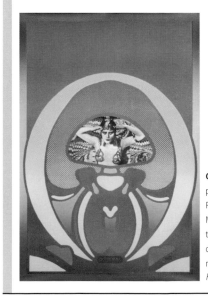

CLEOPATRA This
poster by American
Pop artist Peter
Max is typical of
the psychedelic art
of the age and was
much copied. *c.1967.
H:36 in (91 cm).*

images for a variety of clients including Shell and London Transport. His work is characterized by subtle flourishes such as the logo of the London Underground appearing in place of the pivot on a pair of scissors in his *Victoria Line* poster. In contrast to this practical approach, the advertising work of Frederic Henri Kay Henrion shows the influence of the Surrealists, his juxtaposition of a giant eye with an Olivetti typewriter being reminiscent of Man Ray's *Indestructible Object*.

MOVIE POSTERS

The mid-20th century was a golden period in cinema history, and the posters that advertised films such as *Rebel Without a Cause* and *Breathless* are suffused with the glamour and intrigue that kept people flocking to the theaters despite the advent of television. Artwork for movies such as *The Day the Earth Stood Still* highlights a preoccupation with space and science fiction, while the Bond franchise was sold on a steady stream of guns, girls, and gambling.

Barbarella, one of the seminal films of the 1960s, is the epitome of Pop. From the big hair to the kinky boots sported by Jane Fonda, the film and the artwork that went with it represent a distillation of the exploitative yet whimsical preoccupation with sex that pervaded the 1960s.

Behind the Iron Curtain, film posters took on a very different countenance. Rather than concentrate

THE DAY THE EARTH STOOD STILL An American poster for the sci-fi movie bears the hallmarks of contemporary fantasy and sci-fi design: a composite image featuring various scenes from the film and the use of bold, sans-serif type. *1951. H:41 in (104 cm).*

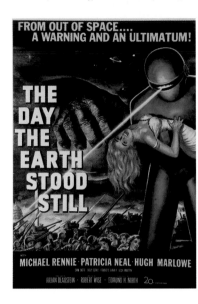

BARBARELLA In this rare Argentinian poster for the sci-fi/fantasy film starring Jane Fonda, the image is of Barbarella superimposed on a psychedelic pink and yellow background. *1968. H:43 in (109 cm).*

DR. NO The movie poster for the first-ever James Bond film, starring Sean Connery, shows Bond and the various "Bond" women, each in a different single color. The 007 logo, with gun, also features. *1962. H:41 in (104 cm).*

on images of the stars, they presented atmospheric and highly individual interpretations of the film's content. Wiktor Górka's artwork in Poland for *Cabaret*, starring Liza Minnelli, features a Nazi swastika composed of stocking-clad dancer's legs—an altogether darker and more intriguing representation than that used on Western posters.

Polish artists such as Lucjan Jagodzinski, Wiktor Górka, and Frantiszek Starowieyski worked on behalf of the state film distribution industry. They flourished from the mid-1950s when the government repealed restrictions on graphic representation, allowing more freedom of design, and their work is much sought-after today.

VERTIGO Featuring artwork by Saul Bass, this Argentinian poster bears the Spanish title for the French novel from which the film is adapted. *1958. H:43 in (109 cm).*

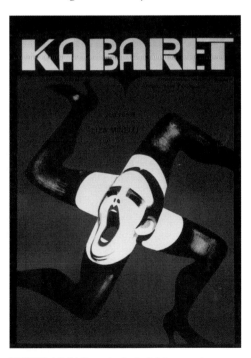

KABARET A Polish film poster for the Bob Fosse movie *Cabaret*. The striking image, with Liza Minelli's head at the center of a swastika made up of four performing legs, is by Wiktor Górka. *1973. H:33 in (84 cm).*

THE BIRDS The Czech poster for the Hitchcock movie with artwork by Josef Vyletal has an eerie image featuring a collage of Max Ernst's Surrealist painting *Attirement of the Bride. 1970. H:33 in (84 cm).*

POSTMODERN AND CONTEMPORARY
1970 ONWARDS

ECLECTIC DIVERSITY

AS A REACTION TO THE MODERNIST OBSESSION WITH FORM AND FUNCTION, DESIGNERS EXPERIMENTED WITH WITTY, IRREVERENT, COLORFUL WORK. THEIR INDIVIDUALISTIC APPROACH CONTINUES TO ENCOMPASS HIGH TECHNOLOGY AND TRADITIONAL CRAFTS.

IGNITED LUNAR LUNACY
Updating the ancient glassmaking technique of murrines, this sculptural vase crosses into the realms of art. *c.2003. H:40 in (101 cm).*

POSTMODERNISM BEGINS

The name itself sits uncomfortably, for we now appear to be living in a follow-on age rather than an age in itself, and there is always the suspicion that, in future years, postmodernism may acquire its own name in its own right, or perhaps be retitled as pre-something or other as yet undefined.

Postmodernism owes its birth to the ending of the modernist dream, that utopian belief that it was possible to create a better world using the power and potential of the machine and of industrial technology. That dream began before World War I, flourished in the interwar years, and managed to survive in a different form after World War II. It ended as the optimism of the 1960s gave way to the reality of a high-inflation and high-unemployment economy in the 1970s. As oil prices soared and gasoline was rationed, the previous optimism was replaced by a cynicism that infected all contemporary culture. The *Zeitgeist* of the 20th

century was further shaken by the failure of American technological superiority in Vietnam as well as the ephemeral qualities of Pop. Many people now saw that modernist culture had come to a dead end. When the world's economies began to grow again in the 1980s, the main motor was self-interest and personal enrichment at the expense of community. Without any all-embracing culture to make sense of this change, postmodernist thinkers suggested that the only appropriate response was to plunder the past for inspiration. Art, architecture, design, and fashion revived past styles at random, leading to such inspired creations as Philip Johnson's modernist AT&T skyscraper in New York with its Chippendale pediment.

THE MEMPHIS GROUP

The main feature of postmodernism is wit, the incongruity between what is expected and what something really is. One of the most ironic, and

most innovative, of postmodernist design outfits is the Memphis Group, formed in Milan, Italy, in 1980. "Memphis tries to separate the object from the idea of functionalism," said their leader, Ettore Sottsass. "It is an ironic approach to the modern notion of philosophical pureness. In other words, a table may need four legs to function, but no one can tell me that the four legs have to look the same."

Memphis designs are characterized by bold color and inventiveness. The designers were comfortable taking risks, mixing motifs from different eras and ethnic groups, and combining expensive and inexpensive materials. Each item can be viewed as furnishing, art, and fashion accessory and grabs attention in a way that fitted well into the conspicuous consumption of the 1980s.

A NEW REALISM

By the early 1990s this colorful mix of styles and ideas was losing favor, and designers reacted by looking for more subdued—although not necessarily less colorful—means of expression.

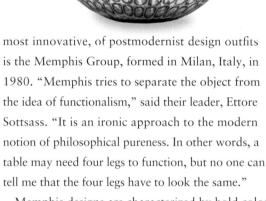

GUGGENHEIM, BILBAO Architect Frank Gehry designed this museum, opened in 1997, to look like a ship, in keeping with its setting in the Spanish Basque port. The reflective titanium panels look like fish scales, continuing the marine theme.

TAHITI TABLE LAMP
This design by Ettore Sottsass does away with the traditional lampshade. Instead, a halogen bulb is housed in an enameled metal structure that sits on a plastic laminate base. *1981. H:25½ in (65 cm).*

THE BIG WHITE HOUSE, SUSSEX The house includes work by postmodern and contemporary designers such as Sottsass, Mendini, and Arad. The interior is truly contemporary in its eclectic mixing of styles from the mid- to late 20th century.

The economic crash of 1987 was the beginning of the end for the culture of greed that had dominated the 1980s. This, combined with political uncertainty following the collapse of communism, a growing environmental awareness, and the threat of terrorism, made the 1990s and early 21st century a more subdued period. Design became simpler and more true to its materials, with wicker and clear acrylic in common use.

THE DIGITAL AGE

Of crucial importance to the recent development of postmodernist design has been the impact of the digital revolution, driven by the extraordinarily fast growth of the Internet, cell phones, and the computer industry. Designers now use computers as an essential tool in creating a product, largely doing away with the need to draw up detailed designs and make models. What results can be smooth and technical in appearance, a look that has long defined electronic consumer goods and now features in the decorative arts as well.

The ease of communication that enables designers to access and share ideas and images at speed also creates an international culture that changes fast and frequently. With materials sourced from all over the world and manufacturing increasingly relocating to low-wage countries, postmodernist design is now the first truly global style.

THE LANGUAGE OF MICHAEL GRAVES With a typically postmodern playful element, this exhibition poster uses the designer's name as the material for a typographical picture. *1983. W:18 in (45.5 cm).*

ELEMENTS OF STYLE

Postmodernism was an eclectic genre, absorbing a number of radical concepts and trends. Paramount was the rejection of the "form follows function" tenet of modernism: designers felt encouraged, even obliged, to challenge the preconceived ideas of good design. In doing so they were able to reexamine the natural properties of various media—especially glass, plastics, wood, metals, and ceramics—and reinterpret the styles of the past. The results are daring, unconventional, and often ironic.

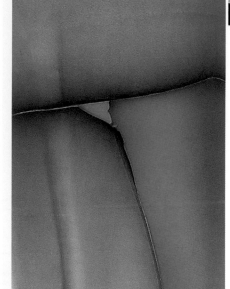

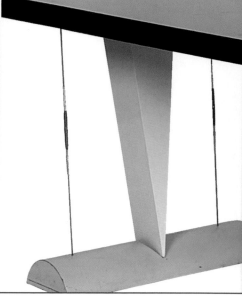

GAETANO PESCE *OSSO* TABLE LAMP

INDIVIDUAL DIVERSITY

The economic climate created a prosperous elite to fund custom creations. This provided a secure environment in which designers could produce the ultimate expressions of their own creativity. They did not confine themselves to one discipline, but chose instead to experiment across the decorative arts.

DANNY PERKINS MALIBU GLASS SCULPTURE

COLOR

Color was key for postmodern designers, sometimes elevated to a status equal to form or function in a piece. Designers often relied on their creative use of color to provide the visual impact of a piece—especially by combining bright or clashing colors and through the use of extraordinary patterns.

PETER SHIRE SINGLE-PEDESTAL DESK

ASYMMETRY

Perhaps the clearest expression of anti-modernism was asymmetry. Designers deliberately avoided symmetry, through color, structure, or materials. The results often challenged the accepted norms of conventional design, making pieces difficult to make sense of, even displeasing to the unaccustomed eye.

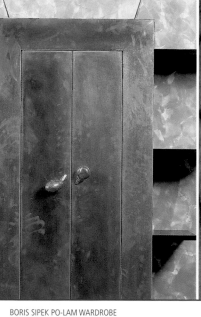

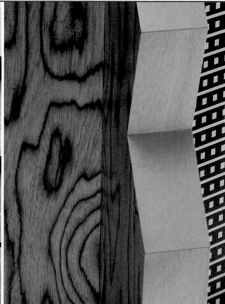

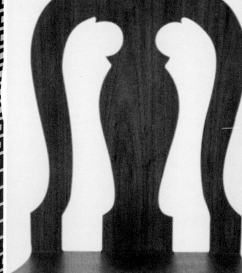

BORIS SIPEK PO-LAM WARDROBE

MIXING MATERIALS

The use of two or more utterly different materials was a common anti-modernist device. Costly materials such as heavy marble, semiprecious metals, and leather were teamed up with cheap and garish plastics or synthetic textiles. Designers also gave cheaper materials an expensive-looking finish, as here, where the marbling is simply a paint effect.

ETTORE SOTTSASS IVORY TABLE

SURFACE DECORATION

For many postmodern designers, the challenge of visual impact outweighed the importance of form or function. To this end, they experimented with a wide range of materials for surface decoration. Of particular significance was the popularity of plastic laminates imitating anything from wood grains to animal hides and exotic textiles.

ROBERT VENTURI QUEEN ANNE CHAIR

HISTORICAL APPROPRIATION

As in previous eras, postmodern designers looked to the past for inspiration. Borrowed motifs appeared variously across the decorative arts, sometimes combining several from different eras in one piece. The aim was to challenge the accepted symbolism of archaic forms by presenting them in an unexpected, irreverent way.

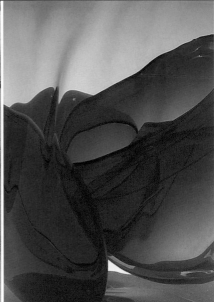

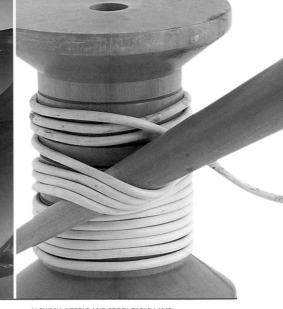

FRANTISEK VIZNER SPHERICAL VASE

SIMPLE FORMS

Early postmodern designers such as those associated with the Memphis group gave their work impact by using simple, conventional shapes in unconventional ways. As the movement waned and a new minimalism emerged, unornamented forms found favor in metalwork, ceramics, and sculpture.

MOI VOLKOV MARILYN SCULPTURE

POPULAR CULTURE

A theme across all disciplines was an obsession with popular culture and consumerism. Some designers incorporated instantly recognizable images such as cartoon characters, film idols, and punk motifs. Others recycled objects from contemporary living—a nod to anti-consumerist sentiments.

DALE CHIHULY HARRISON RED BASKET SET

UNIQUE CRAFTS

Tired of the precision manufacturing of the modern age, and of all the new plastics that had emerged since the 1950s, some designers returned to handcrafts as an alternative. They explored the natural properties of wood, glass, metals, and ceramics, producing a host of unique pieces.

ALCHIMIA NEEDLE AND SPOOL TABLE LAMP

HUMOR

In moving away from conventional forms, it was not uncommon for designers to incorporate unexpected, often witty, elements in their work. Examples of humor include objects with one function designed to resemble something with another, as here, or oversize versions of everyday objects.

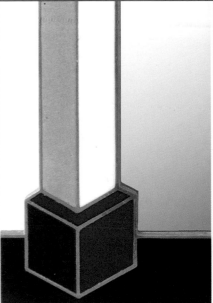

WENDELL CASTLE CALIGARI PIANO

REINTERPRETATION

Postmodern designers were adept at giving conventional forms a new and humorous lease on life. Here, a Steinway piano is painted in the abstract expressionist style. Other reinterpretations include Alessi's micro-architectural style of domestic appliances and the adoption of zoomorphic (animal-like) or anthropomorphic (human) forms.

MARC NEWSON FELT CHAIR

NEW MINIMALISM

By the end of the 1980s some designers rejected busy, symbolism-charged designs and turned to a new minimalism. Using materials with plain surfaces—glass, brushed metals, clear or single-color plastics, and untreated woods—designers began to make products where the simplicity of the medium accentuated the form of the work.

ADRIAN OLABUENAGA METAL PHOTOGRAPH FRAME

ARCHITECTURE

Architecture was one of the first disciplines to adopt the theories of postmodernism, and a number of architects also became involved in the decorative arts. The result was the appearance of architectural forms and motifs across all disciplines, but in particular in the designs of Michael Graves and Robert Venturi.

ALCHIMIA ATROPO TABLE

GEOMETRIC LINES

Geometric patterns were used to striking effect by postmodern designers, particularly in furniture design, textiles, and ceramics. Geometric lines—whether structural or decorative—might also be reinterpretations of popular stylistic genres such as Art Deco, or of designs specific to different cultures such as the Aztecs.

FURNITURE

DRAWING ON A DIVERSE RANGE OF SOURCES, AND PAYING LITTLE ATTENTION TO FUNCTION, POSTMODERN FURNITURE DESIGNERS REJECTED THE LESSONS OF MODERNISM IN FAVOR OF A MORE ECLECTIC APPROACH.

SEEDS OF POSTMODERNISM

In an essay entitled *The Return of Historicism*, written in 1961, the celebrated British architecture and design critic Nikolaus Pevsner referred to a new trend among architects and designers for borrowing from the past. Since the emergence of the modern era in the early 1920s, architects and designers had steadfastly refused to look back, focusing only on the future, so Pevsner described this new development as postmodern.

ARCHITECTURAL DESIGN

What Pevsner had spotted was the seeds of a movement in architecture and design that only fully began to flower during the latter half of the 1970s, reaching its zenith a decade later. The appropriation of the past (usually by adopting stylistic conceits from bygone eras) was an important ingredient in the postmodern style, as

Pevsner had pointed out early on, and so too were references to popular culture (such as movies and cartoons), the use of unusual materials, and a theatrical use of color. Low on the list of priorities of the postmodern designer was function, which had been so important to earlier generations.

AGAINST MODERNISM

The reasons for there being such a strong backlash against the rational, reductivist methods of modernism were numerous. Robert Venturi, the American architect, designer, and theorist was an early spokesman for postmodernism (particularly through writings in his highly influential books, *Complexity and Contradiction in Architecture*, first published in 1966,

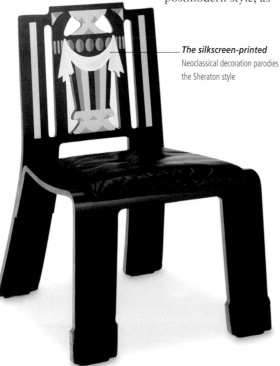

The silkscreen-printed Neoclassical decoration parodies the Sheraton style

KNOLL SHERATON 378 CHAIR Designed by Robert Venturi, this chair, of molded plywood with a black leather-upholstered seat pad, playfully recalls the Neoclassical furniture design epitomized by Thomas Sheraton. *1984. H:33¼ in (84.5 cm).*

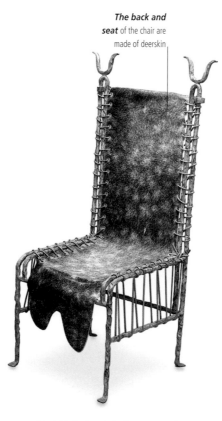

The back and *seat* of the chair are made of deerskin

BARBARE CHAIR Elizabeth Garouste and Mattia Bonetti based the design of this chair on an African tribal throne. It has a patinated bronze frame onto which a deerskin is laced. *1981. H:46½ in (118 cm).*

FRANKFURT F1 SKYSCRAPER CABINET Designed by Norbert Berghof, Michael Landes, and Wolfgang Rang, and made by Draenert GmbH, this cabinet is veneered in various exotic woods. The doors open to reveal a detailed interior including two secret compartments. *1985–86. H:92 in (230 cm).*

The Mickey Mouse ears compare with the two-part headrest on Toshiyuki Kita's earlier Wink armchair

AKABA S. A. GARRIRI CHAIR This black leather and metal-framed chair was designed by the Spanish artist, designer, and cartoon enthusiast Javier Mariscal. c.1988. H:38 in (96.5 cm).

LITTLE BEAVER ARMCHAIR AND OTTOMAN Designed by Frank Gehry for Vitra, these pieces form part of his Experimental Edges series, which exploited the expressive qualities of corrugated cardboard. The series evolved from Gehry's 1972 mass-produced Easy Edges cardboard furniture line. 1987. Armchair: H:32 in (81 cm).

Laminated cardboard gives the piece a startling, cutting-edge expressivity

PLAZA DRESSING TABLE Memphis, the Milan-based collective of young postmodern designers, dominated early 1980s design with innovative pieces such as this dressing table in laminate and briar-root wood by the architect Michael Graves. c.1981. H:89 in (226 cm).

The shape of the piece is architectural

ETHNIC INFLUENCES

Besides the many cursory references made to the past in postmodern furniture, there was also a proliferation of interest in ethnic design styles—most famously and explicitly in Elizabeth Garouste and Mattia Bonetti's controversial *Objets Barbares* and *Objets Primitifs* collections of 1981. By alluding to indigenous design languages, designers asserted their indifference to the drive toward an essential, international style that united designers of the modern era.

The fact that the complex and contradictory style of postmodernism (to paraphrase Robert Venturi) found its full voice during the late 1970s is no coincidence. This was a time of global economic uncertainty and the furniture industry, like many others, was at a low ebb. Without much commercial work to keep them busy, many designers began to pursue more individual, experimental projects and took the time to develop the convoluted design vocabularies common at this time. Even when money began to pour back into the furniture industry during the 1980s, this period of intense intellectual activity shone through—most remarkably in the intriguing work of the Memphis group (see p.390).

BAMBI CHAIR With its apparent structural instability and frail form, this brass, maple, organza fabric, and steel limited-edition chair designed by Borek Sipek embodies extravagance and whimsy. 1983. H:29½ in (75 cm).

FORREST MYERS ARMCHAIR This La Farge chair looks like a gravity-defying ball of yarn unraveling from a box. Made from tubular black metal and copper panels, it a variant of Myers's sculptural wire material drawings. (Unmarked). W:31½ in (79 cm).

CRAFTSMANSHIP

One of the most significant paradoxes of the postmodern movement (a movement that was riddled with them) was the fact that despite the fascination with so-called "low rent" popular culture, the furniture was almost invariably expensive. A chair made out of cardboard would be sold in an upmarket gallery to wealthy collectors, and a chair with Mickey Mouse ears—an image that you could see adorning many cheap, mass-produced products—was only available in limited numbers. Many of the furniture designs that were so indebted to the culture of quick turnover and disposability were lovingly produced by craftsmen in antiquated workshops. It was precisely these sorts of inconsistencies, however, that postmodernism embraced.

and *Learning from Las Vegas*, 1972). He described his fascination with the speed of contemporary culture and its obsession with surface. These, he argued, were just as interesting for architects and designers to explore as the pursuit of pure form and technical expertise. Venturi's furniture designs for Knoll (1978–84) made extensive use of plastic laminates and veneers (very postmodern materials), and played with entirely tongue-in-cheek references to past design styles, thereby commenting on—and indeed celebrating—what he saw as culture's largely superficial interest in history.

The sculpted metal seat forms an experimental, irregular structure

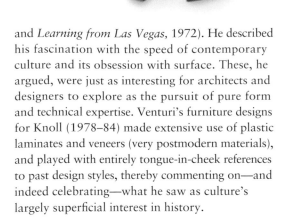

S-CHAIR Tom Dixon designed his steel-framed S-chair, inspired by Verner Panton, in 1988, and it was adapted by several manufacturers. This straw example by Cappellini is also available in woven cane, felt, and latex. c.1991. H:39½ in (100 cm).

Woven marsh straw lends the piece sinuous movement and expression

The bold structure rejects the excesses of earlier postmodern design

MONO SIDE TABLE One of a set of four, this table by SCP was designed by Konstantin Grcic. German-born Grcic took a democratic approach, advocating accessible and understandable furniture design. 1995. H:29½ in (75 cm).

KNOTTED CHAIR This chair by Cappellini was designed by Marcel Wanders. Made of carbon fiber and epoxy resin, it is a successor to Forrest Myers's sculptural and eccentric armchair, but has a regular, functional form. 1995.

CONTEMPORARY FURNITURE

The 1980s was a decade of excess in all areas of design. This was a reaction to the sobriety of modernism, which had been under attack since the 1960s. But by the end of the 1980s, as stock markets declined and belts were tightened, attitudes began to change. After almost 15 years of overt postmodernism and its rich, complex style, people felt the need for simpler, cleaner designs.

During the later years of the 1980s and into the 1990s, the clashing colors drained out of furniture. Clear glass and acrylic were more widely used, as were natural materials such as exposed wood and wicker. When color was employed, it was used on its own—pattern and surface decoration were considered little more than an unnecessary distraction. The obsession with laminates and mixing materials evaporated, too, as designers began to revive the modernist spirit of "truth to materials."

Many of the old modernist values seeped back into furniture design. A love of clean lines, pared-down forms, and an interest in utility were typical of designers in the 1990s. Despite this, however, many of the privileges won for designers by postmodernism lived on. Designers were aware, for instance, that function was not the be-all and end-all of furniture. They knew too that a certain amount of idiosyncrasy was welcome and that humor was an acceptable ingredient of design.

FREEDOM FROM CONSTRAINTS

Jasper Morrison, the British designer who led the move toward the more streamlined design style of the 1990s, stated in an interview that the most important designers for him were early modernists such as Eileen Gray and Marcel Breuer. Morrison also pointed out how important postmodernism was—particularly the Memphis group—by explaining: "It's not the most practical kind of design but it had the effect of freeing everything up, to show that we don't have to accept all these constraints and ridiculous rules about how one should design—design should be open to different ways of working."

BIRD ROCKING CHAIR Designed by Tom Dixon for the Italian firm Cappellini, this wooden-framed, multi-density foam rocking chair shows a contemporary emphasis on functionality. This piece is more suited to industrial production than many of Dixon's more intricate designs. c.1991. H:35 in (89 cm).

The clean lines and removable single-color cover made the Bird Chair relatively simple to manufacture

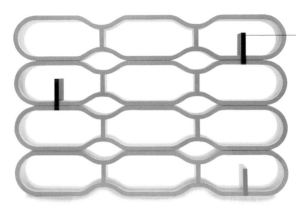

The shelves are held in place by plywood book ends

BRICK BOOKSHELVES This modular storage system consists of a number of honeycomb-shaped lacquered-plywood shelves stacked one on top of the other. Available in a range of colors, it was designed by Ronan and Erwan Bouroullec for Cappellini. *Each module: H:19¾ in (50 cm).*

DESIGN AND PERSONALITY

During the 1990s designers felt able to pursue their own personal styles, something that was made easier by advances in technology. The growing sophistication of computer programs and manufacturing techniques meant that mass-produced furniture became increasingly refined. Giving objects a personality, however, was not only about the designer expressing himself, but also something of a marketing ploy. In an increasingly crowded market, furniture needed to stand out from the crowd and appeal to consumers from not only a practical but also an emotional point of view. For this reason, soft, subtly curvaceous shapes were also popular during the 1990s, as was furniture whose forms resembled natural objects, such as birds and trees.

Italy had produced many of the most important designers of the 1950s, 1960s, 1970s, and 1980s, and this continued as the century drew to a close. As the world's most important country for furniture manufacture, Italy went from strength to strength. Companies such as Cappellini, B&B

Italia, and Edra produced some of the most interesting furniture of the decade. Many of the firms employed foreign designers. In fact, this era is notable for a global cross-pollination of ideas.

CHANGING INFLUENCES

Jasper Morrison, Tom Dixon, Ron Arad, Marc Newson, Konstantin Grcic, and many others all spent formative years in the United Kingdom, most of them attending the highly influential Royal College of Art in London. France, on the other hand, gave the design world Philippe Starck, whose sleek, witty designs dominated the latter years of the 1980s and early years of the 1990s (*see p.392*) and the Bouroullec brothers.

At the beginning of the 21st century, Ronan and Erwan Bouroullec were undoubtedly the designers in greatest demand, as companies appreciated the subtle sophistication of their furniture designs. Dutch design at the end of the 20th century was important mainly because of Droog, a loose collective of designers including Richard Hutten, Marcel Wanders, and Hella Jongerius, which reintroduced a political and conceptual element into their designs that had not been seen since the late 1970s.

At the turn of the century, after a roller-coaster ride through the extremes of modernism and postmodernism, design had arrived at a point where the lessons of both had been learned and designers were equipped to follow their own paths and develop their own ideologies.

GAETANO PESCE

Few designers in history have followed their own instincts with as much conviction as Gaetano Pesce, a designer born in Italy in 1939. Paying little heed to custom, convention, or prevailing design trends, Pesce has said that his only commitment is to "communicating feelings of surprise, discovery, optimism, stimulation, sensuality, generosity, joy, and femininity." A veteran of numerous Italian avant-garde design and architecture movements of the 1960s and 1970s, Pesce moved to New York in 1980 and established a series of companies dedicated to producing his own designs. Taking great pleasure in making what he calls "poorly made" products, his designs at the end of the 20th century were often made from resin in a rainbow of colors, and were idiosyncratic in the extreme.

NOBODY'S CHAIR Designer Gaetano Pesce continues to experiment with new forms and materials. This Zero Disegno for Etro limited-edition chair comprises panels of colored polyurethane-based elastic resin inlaid with silk fragments. *2004. H:34¾ in (88 cm).*

BERNINI BROADWAY 6 CHAIR This limited-edition chair designed by Gaetano Pesce was available in blue, red, or black, with the color of the thermochromatic plastic seat changing slightly with the heat of the sitter. The nine sprung feet give a pleasant rocking feeling. *2001. H.29½ in (75 cm).*

ETRUSCAN CHAIR This glass and stainless steel chair was designed by leading glass sculptor Danny Lane. It shows off Lane's particular skill in glass cutting and embraces the salvage look branch of postmodern style. *1986. H:34¾ in (88 cm).*

The seat and back are made of high-strength 1-in (25-mm) glass

The single yellow feather is subtle yet makes a dramatic impact

FEATHER STOOL Shiro Kuramata's design for Ishimaru & Co. features a translucent acrylic block base with internally cased feathers and an aluminum backrest. It looks more like a piece of sculpture than a chair. *1990. H:21¼ in (54 cm).*

WENDELL CASTLE

INVENTIVE AND ADVENTUROUS, WENDELL CASTLE IS A ONE-OFF
WHO HAS FREQUENTLY ENTERED TERRITORY TRADITIONALLY
OCCUPIED BY SCULPTURE. WITH HIS RICH, ECLECTIC STYLE,
CASTLE QUICKLY BECAME THE DARLING OF AFFLUENT
AMERICAN ART AND DESIGN COLLECTORS.

LOUNGE CHAIRS This rare and early pair of stacked
oak laminate chairs illustrates Castle's 1960s style of
curvy wooden furniture. Once other designers latched
on to it, Castle's work changed direction. *1967.
H:33 in (82.5 cm).*

The open-minded approach taken by
Wendell Castle to art, design, craft, and
industry has allowed the American-born
designer and artist to operate across the
borders of all four fields since he started
his career in Kansas in the early 1960s.
During this decade,
Castle became well
known for his
organically shaped,

CALIGARI PIANO Combining
the jazzy angularity of abstract
expressionism with tradition and
fine craftsmanship, Wendell Castle
teamed up with Steinway & Sons
to create this striking indigo and
white piano and bench. *1990.
W:69¾ in (177.5 cm).*

sculptural furniture carved from stacked,
laminated wood. His fame reached greater heights
in the 1980s, when he became known as a leading
exponent of the Studio Craft movement.

Castle's move away from the curvaceous wooden
furniture he made in the 1960s to his more eclectic
output of the 1980s was a gradual process. By the
1970s, the stacked, laminated wood process that
he had developed had been adopted by numerous
other American designers, and Castle felt a desire
to move on.

FINE FURNITURE

Around the 1960s and 1970s, Castle was also
impressed by the work of John Makepeace, a
designer based in England who used a team of
highly skilled craftsmen to create extravagant,
unique pieces of furniture in a diverse range of
exotic materials. On Makepeace's advice, Castle
employed an English craftsman named Stephen
Proctor, putting him in charge of his New York
studio. During this time Castle also took on Silas
Kopf and Donald Sottile, two other highly
competent technicians. Although Castle had never
previously placed much importance on technical
virtuosity (believing it distracted both the maker
and the user/viewer from the overall impression of
the piece), he saw that it would prove essential in
realizing his ideas for what he called his range of
"fine" furniture.

At the end of the 1970s Castle was invited by
the Memorial Art Gallery in Rochester, New York,
to curate an exhibition of historical furniture
borrowed from the Metropolitan Museum
of Art. This curatorship inspired him
to start a new so-called

"fine" style of his own. His first piece of this period
was the Lady's Desk with Two Chairs (1981),
made of English sycamore and decorated with
ebony and plastic dots. The piece, according to
Castle, "picked up where Émile-Jacques Ruhlmann,
the last of the great *ébénistes*, left off." Castle's
plundering of the past, as seen with the Lady's
Desk, has often been described as a postmodern
trait, but Castle himself denies it, referring to his
work of the early 1980s as historical classicist.
Indeed, Castle does seem to treat past styles with a
degree of reverence and attention that was hardly
conjured up by the more cynical, magpielike
designers of postmodernism.

ENERGETIC AND SYMBOLIC

Castle's work from the mid-1980s to the 1990s
can really only be described as postmodern. Paying
only a passing interest to function, his furniture of
this era occupies itself far more with form, color,
and conceptual content. Having seen the work of
the Italian Memphis group (*see p.390*), Castle
(a designer who always knew a hot trend when
he saw one) allowed his work to become far more
expressive, energetic, and rich in symbols. Surface
pattern became increasingly important too as he
began to paint, stain, and lacquer the wood that
he used. One of Castle's most successful series of
furniture of this type was the 1986 Dr. Cagliari
collection. Inspired by the tense, awkward
atmosphere created by the
film sets in the classic 1920s
horror film, *The Cabinet of
Dr. Cagliari*, Castle's furniture
is purposefully angular and
patterned with brushstrokes to
make it appear almost camouflaged.
Another decorative device that Castle
often used at this time was forms
resembling pots or plants, adding a
touch of the absurd to his furniture.

URN CABINET This
typically postmodern piece
combines a bold, abstract
polychrome composition on
the single door, concealing
two drawers and two shelves,
with a Classical form—the
urn—employed as supports.
1991. H:70½ in (179 cm).

ANGEL CHAIR The labor-intensive Angel Chair series is
considered by many to be Castle's finest achievement. This
memorable piece, entitled Night Voyages, is made of wood
and patinated bronze. *1991. W:63 in (157.5 cm).*

Wendell Castle 1990

ANGEL CHAIR DESIGN This signed and dated pencil and gouache painting by Wendell Castle shows the geometrical Bolstered Egos Angel Chair and illustrates a postmodern "form over function" aesthetic. The seat of the real chair is made of mahogany. *1990.*

FURNITURE GALLERY

Furniture designers took the freedom of expression granted to their mid-century predecessors and used it to push design as far as they could. An element of historical and cultural reference often leads to playful pieces that defy preconceptions of what a chair or table should be. The result is exuberant extremes.

KEY

1. Metal-framed mirror and lamp by Nanda Vigo. 1986. ④ **2.** Geoffrey Harcourt/Artifort Cleopatra sofa of upholstered foam and tubular steel. 1973. W:74¼ in (185.5 cm). ② **3.** Armchair by Toshiyuki Kita, 1984, reissued by Tendo Mokko, 2004. H:26½ in (67.5 cm). ① **4.** License to Build sofa/children's game made from high-resilience foam by Matali Crasset of France. 2000. ③ **5.** Bird personal desk made of burr elm, wych elm, and Lebanon cedar by John Makepeace. H:39¾ in (101 cm). ⑦ **6.** McCain recycled plastic chair by Beata Bär, Gerhard Bär, and Christof Knell. 1994. W:18½ in (47 cm). ① **7.** Stainless steel armchair with a leather seat cushion by Jonathan Singleton. H:41 in (104 cm). ④ **8.** Eighteen chest-of-drawers by John Makepeace. H:53 in (135 cm). ⑧ **9.** High-Heel chair with

2 | *Geoffrey Harcourt sofa*

3 | *Toshiyuki Kita armchair*

4 | *Matali Crasset sofa*

6 | *Recycled chair*

1 | *Nanda Vigo mirror*

5 | *Bird desk*

7 | *Stainless steel armchair*

8 | *John Makepeace chest of drawers*

9 | *High-Heel chair*

10 | *Mats Theselius armchair*

leopard-print upholstery, attributed to David Bury. c.1980. W:19¼ in (49 cm). ① **10.** Armchair with an elkskin seat by Mats Theselius for Källemo AB of Sweden. 1991. ④ **11.** Magis Tam Tam rotational molded polyethylene stool by Matteo Thun. 2002. H:14 in (35 cm). ① **12.** Side table made from panels of red and clear rubbery plastic by Gaetano Pesce. 2002. H:19¼ in (49 cm). ① **13.** Pierre Sala notebook table. H:28¼ in (72 cm). ② **14.** Gary Knox Bennett Table #8, in patinated bronze with an arrow-shaped top and three tapered legs. H:19 in (48 cm). ③ **15.** Kick Table by Toshiyuki Kita for Cassina. 1983. H:20½ in (52 cm). ② **16.** Fish Bench by Judy McKie. **17.** Tavolo table, made of cast bronze with a glass top by Sandro Chia. 1989. H:31½ in (80 cm). ⑤ **18.** Table Table, a center table with an inset leather surface on printed MDF by Clementine Hope. H:30 in (76 cm). ① **19.** Sgaboo foam rubber and plastic stool by Markus Benesch for Post Design. 2005. H:17½ in (44 cm). ①

⑫ *Gaetano Pesce side table*

⑪ *Matteo Thun stool*

⑬ *Notebook table*

⑭ *Gary Knox Bennett table*

⑮ *Kick table*

⑯ *Fish bench*

⑰ *Tavolo table*

⑱ *Center table with leather inset*

⑲ *Sgaboo stool*

PRODUCT DESIGN

MANY DESIGNERS WORKED ACROSS A RANGE OF DISCIPLINES, FROM FURNITURE TO CERAMICS AND FROM GLASS TO KITCHEN GADGETS. THE POSTMODERN STYLE BEGAN WITH ALCHIMIA.

ALCHIMIA

Throughout the 1960s and early 1970s, a number of Italian designers had begun to chip away at the prevailing idea that form must follow function, a concept that was core to the values of modernism. However, it was not until the birth of Studio Alchimia in 1976 that this idea, and all that it entailed, was finally and unceremoniously consigned to the trash can.

Studio Alchimia was formed when designers Alessandro and Adriana Guerriero invited a number of their friends to design some new work—not for the purposes of putting it into production but to include in an exhibition in a Milan gallery. Free from commercial constraints, the designers—including Alessandro Mendini, Paola Navone, and Michele De Lucchi—didn't hold back and produced a collection of experimental work.

It was the work's eclecticism, however (what Mendini called its "kaleidoscopic beauty"), that came to define the Alchimia style. In 1979, in a clear statement that the rigid rules of modernism—summed up by the architect Mies van der Rohe as "Less is more"—were being purposefully flouted, Alchimia produced a collection of bastardized Bauhaus furniture. Marcel Breuer's concise Wassily chair of 1925, in the hands of Alchimia, became a steel frame smothered in flaps of exuberantly patterned fabric. Echoing the sentiments of fellow rebel Robert Venturi, who retorted "Less is a bore," Alchimia's leader Alessandro Mendini stated: "The act of making signs is what counts today."

KANDISSA MIRROR This lacquered-wood framed mirror designed by Alessandro Mendini unites a traditional design with modern influences such as Kandinsky's paintings. Fewer than ten examples of this mirror exist. *1978. H:39 in (100 cm).*

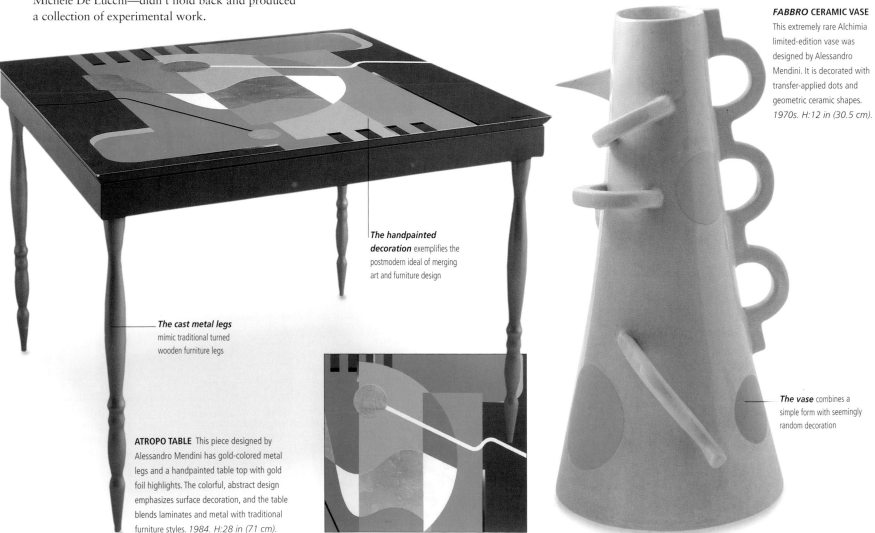

The handpainted decoration exemplifies the postmodern ideal of merging art and furniture design

The cast metal legs mimic traditional turned wooden furniture legs

ATROPO TABLE This piece designed by Alessandro Mendini has gold-colored metal legs and a handpainted table top with gold foil highlights. The colorful, abstract design emphasizes surface decoration, and the table blends laminates and metal with traditional furniture styles. *1984. H:28 in (71 cm).*

***FABBRO* CERAMIC VASE** This extremely rare Alchimia limited-edition vase was designed by Alessandro Mendini. It is decorated with transfer-applied dots and geometric ceramic shapes. *1970s. H:12 in (30.5 cm).*

The vase combines a simple form with seemingly random decoration

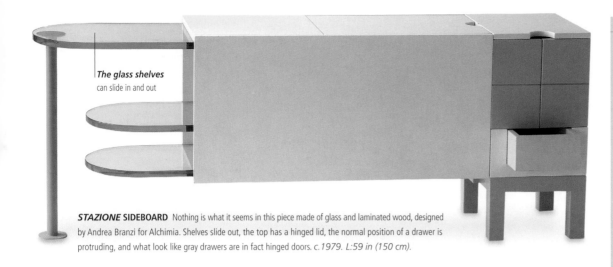

The glass shelves can slide in and out

STAZIONE SIDEBOARD Nothing is what it seems in this piece made of glass and laminated wood, designed by Andrea Branzi for Alchimia. Shelves slide out, the top has a hinged lid, the normal position of a drawer is protruding, and what look like gray drawers are in fact hinged doors. *c.1979. L:59 in (150 cm).*

REDISCOVERING SOUL

The members of Alchimia believed that the success of the production line had sterilized the field of design. The early modernist's dreams of marrying art and industry had, by the 1970s, become all too true and the search for "practical efficiency," as Mendini put it, had meant that design had lost touch with "the object's soul." In an attempt to recover some of the romance of design, the work produced under the Alchimia banner reveled in a riot of clashing color, pattern, and purposefully awkward forms.

One of the most radical ploys pursued by Alchimia's designers was to produce objects that employed a wide variety of materials. Mendini talked of a "confusion of craft and industry," as "low" materials such as painted metal and plastic laminate were combined with "high" materials such as crystal glass or polished briarwood. The ever-eloquent Mendini described Alchimia's look as "full and violent."

Alchimia's sphere of activity during the late 1970s and throughout the 1980s encompassed not only furniture design but also graphic design, stage sets, and fashion. No design discipline, it seemed, remained unaffected by the Alchimia crusade. In his role as contributor to numerous design publications (some of which he also edited during one time or another), Mendini ceaselessly promoted Alchimia and its message of Banal Design. An intentional echo of Bel Design—a phrase much used during the post-war era to describe design of good taste and honest practicality—Banal Design followed the idea that the discordant, complex nature of life at the end of the 20th century made it pointless to pursue the pure forms with which designers had previously been so obsessed. Embracing contemporary culture, in forms both high and low, became Alchimia's concerted aim.

FINAL YEARS

The aggression, energy, and strong voice of the Alchimia group meant that their influence spread far and wide. Their essentially anarchic approach to design struck a strong chord with young designers across the globe. Commercially, however, Alchimia was never much of a success. When the Museo Alchimia (a shop dedicated to selling the group's products) opened in Milan in 1988, it was little surprise that it folded shortly afterward. The fact that the group championed style over substance also condemned them to a limited life-span. By the end of the 1980s, most of the designers who had worked under the Alchimia banner had moved onto other things. The short life of Alchimia, however, remains one of the most thrilling episodes in recent design history.

Without the input of Alessandro Mendini, the tireless Italian designer and theorist, it would be fair to say that the design world at the end of the 20th century would have been a far duller place. Born in Milan in 1931, Mendini's early career as a partner in the firm Nizzoli Associati was unremarkable but at the beginning of the 1970s he began to find his voice.

As the most prominent member of the radical Alchimia group, he established himself as a designer of great invention and intellect. His clear ability to create products that made people sit up and take notice soon attracted the interest of a number of manufacturing companies, including Swatch (the Swiss watch manufacturer) and Alessi (the homeware manufacturer). As Art Director of Swatch in the late 1980s, he helped make them one of the most popular and prominent brands of the time, and his work for Alessi has similarly done much to establish the identity of the Italian company.

VENINI MURANO VASE
Alessandro Mendini designed several series for Venini in the 1980s. This large glass vase is of elongated globular form and is clear cased with vertical lines in turquoise, red, and blue. *c.1980. H:15½ in (39.5 cm).*

NEEDLE AND SPOOL LAMP This table lamp designed by Lapo Binazzi consists of a turned wood thread spool and needle, with the cord acting as the thread. *1982. Needle: L:21 in (54 cm).*

PROUST ARMCHAIR
Designed by Alessandro Mendini, this armchair was inspired by Louis XV *bergères*. The finely carved wooden frame is painted in the style of the French pointillist painter Paul Signac and upholstered in matching pointillist fabric.

ETTORE SOTSASS

Although Ettore Sottsass is best known for his founding of (and subsequent work with) the Memphis design group of the 1980s (*see p.390*), he can still be considered one of the most important designers of every decade that he has worked in from the 1950s to the 2000s. Despite working prolifically across design disciplines, Sottsass's energy and talent always ensure high standards.

ARCHITECTURAL BACKGROUND

Born in 1917 on the border of Italy and Austria, Sottsass studied architecture in Turin, graduating in 1939. His father, also called Ettore, was an influential Italian architect. Having studied under the protomodernist architect Otto Wagner in Vienna, Sottsass's father became a key member of the Italian Rationalists, an avant-garde group that took up the cause of modernism at a time when the Fascist regime favored less radical, more Neoclassical tendencies in design.

Despite (or perhaps because of) his father's adherence to the functionalist creed of modernism, Ettore Sottsass has always espoused a freer, more sensual style. There was an early indication of these leanings when in 1956 he chose to travel to New York to work for the celebrated American designer George Nelson. During the postwar period, American designers had loosened the straitjacket of European modernism by experimenting with organic forms and expressive colors, which attracted the young Sottsass.

WOLF HOUSE, RIDGEWAY, COLORADO Designed by Ettore Sottsass and built with project architect Johanna Grawunder from 1987 to 1989, this was the first architectural project to embody themes employed by the Memphis group: the importance of painted color, choice of materials, and surface finishes, and providing just as much attention to the exterior and garden as to the interior.

THE OLIVETTI YEARS

On his return to Italy in 1957, Sottsass began working for Olivetti, the office equipment firm that was then at the forefront of a technological revolution. Entirely new products such as computers and electronic calculators were being developed, and Sottsass soon became the primary

IVORY TABLE Designed by Sottsass in his Memphis period, the table of polychrome laminate is made in three parts: one straight, one jagged, and one wavy. It has a circular glass top. *1985. H:40 in (100 cm).*

BIEDERMEIER SOFA Designed by Ettore Sottsass, this sofa is made from colored plastic-laminated plywood with foam rubber padding. *1983. H:54 in (137 cm).*

The sofa legs are an irreverent pastiche of Classical columns

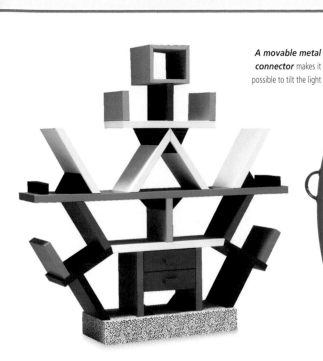

A movable metal connector makes it possible to tilt the light

TREETOPS STANDARD LAMP
This brightly colored, lacquered metal lamp was designed by Sottsass for the Memphis group. c.1981. H:71½ in (180.5 cm).

SOL FRUIT BOWL Sottsass reworked the traditional tazza form to create this quirky glass fruit bowl for the Memphis group. 1982. H:10½ in (26 cm).

CARLTON BOOKCASE Sottsass designed this hallmark geometric set of shelves with diagonal bookends for Memphis. The surfaces are made of brightly colored, laminated wood. 1981. W:74¾ in (190 cm).

ASTEROIDE TABLE LAMP Designed by Sottsass for Poltronova, this fluorescent lamp is reminiscent of neon lighting seen in Las Vegas. 1968. H:28½ in (72 cm).

designer responsible for deciding what form these objects took. It was at Olivetti that Sottsass learned how important it was for a product to communicate with its user, a skill that became apparent in all his subsequent work. His early designs for portable typewriters, computers, and electronic calculators (which many buyers would never have handled before) used simple color coding schemes and tactile forms to ensure that they did not appear too forbidding.

THE FLAMBOYANT 1960S
Throughout the 1960s, Sottsass continued to develop many technical products for Olivetti, as well as working on increasingly flamboyant furniture and lighting designs for the Italian firm Poltronova. During this decade he also began to experiment with glassware and ceramics, something that became a lifelong obsession.

Following travels to Asia and the United States, references to the two diverse cultures of these countries began to crop up in his work, most notably in his Shiva range of ceramics (1964) and his Pop Art–inspired Asteroide light (1968).

CHANGING CLIMATE
The 1970s were not the most productive years for Sottsass (as was the case for many designers), because the harsh financial climate meant that money for manufacturing new designs was scarce. Despite this, Sottsass remained at the cutting edge by involving himself with the numerous radical design groups that were springing up in Italy, many of whom were more interested in ideologies than actually making products.

In 1973 Sottsass helped to establish Global Tools, a short-lived group dedicated to making

design democratic by teaching people simple systems of design that used everyday objects.

During the late 1970s Sottsass briefly became part of Alessandro Mendini's Studio Alchimia (see p.386). Sottsass, however, has always been an essentially open-minded designer. "For me, design is a way to discuss life, social relationships, politics, food, and design itself," he once wrote. Mendini's dogmatic and, at the time, destructive approach to design meant that they did not work together for long. Despite this, Mendini's meticulous deconstruction of the values of modernism—primarily achieved by creating products that flew in the face of functionalism—paved the way for the acceptance of the Memphis group that was founded by Sottsass in the 1980s (see p.390).

The Memphis group (formed in Sottsass's Milan apartment in December, 1980) did not have any specific agenda, unlike many of the design groups that existed during the 1970s. The dilettante nature of Memphis designers was summed up by the name Sottsass chose for the group—as his partner, Barbara Radice, wrote at the time, Memphis meant: "The blues, Tennessee, rock 'n' roll, American suburbs, and then Egypt, the Pharaoh's capital, the holy city of Ptah." Sottsass's refusal for his designs to be pinned down was still apparent.

THE LATER YEARS
Following the phenomenal success of Memphis, Sottsass (who was 71 by the time the group dissolved in 1988) became one of the most revered figures in design. Far from resting on his laurels, however, Sottsass worked harder than ever throughout the 1990s—sometimes on his own independent projects and sometimes through his guiding of Sottsass Associati, the company that he

had set up in 1981. Working on everything from the design of complete houses to ceramics and minor details such as door handles, Sottsass continued to outshine designers far younger than he was.

The piece is a postmodern play on the tribal totem

BITOSI TOTEM This handpainted ceramic sculpture has 11 components bolted together through the middle with an iron rod. 1964–96. H:21 in (53.5 cm).

THE MEMPHIS GROUP

Formed in 1980 and disbanded eight years later, the work of Memphis, a group of primarily Italian designers, has come to symbolize 1980s design. Characterized by loud, brash color, a playful approach to function and form, and a willingness to employ a broad palette of materials, Memphis's output was wildly ambitious and willfully idiosyncratic. Crossing a wide range of disciplines (furniture, lighting, ceramics, and even clothing and jewelry), Memphis was also a great commercial success.

Despite its basis in the technology-obsessed and materialistic 1980s, the ideology behind Memphis was quite different in many ways. First, Memphis was a collective—a very 1960s concept—and a seemingly successful one at that.

EARLY INFLUENCES

Memphis's most influential member, Ettore Sottsass, was a veteran of numerous short-lived design collectives that existed during the 1960s and 1970s. He continued to believe in the idea of a collective consciousness. Indeed, many Memphis designs were produced in the immediate aftermath of long, often wine-fueled, gatherings at Sottsass's Milan apartment. Second, technology was of limited interest to Memphis designers. While they did use some up-to-the-minute materials and manufacturing methods, they relied primarily on Milanese craftsmen to produce their pieces.

Despite these paradoxes, there were many aspects of Memphis that were entirely of their time. Most obviously, there was the international flavor of Memphis designs, reflecting the increasing ease of global travel and communication (the fax machine was a much-employed tool of the Memphis designers). Memphis designers also enjoyed a freedom that was unknown in other design groups of the 1970s. Besides the input of the main Italian members of Memphis (Sottsass, Michele De Lucchi, Marco Zanini, Aldo Cibic, and Barbara Radice), there

KRISTALL TABLE This geometric table was designed by Michele De Lucchi for the Memphis group. It is made from patterned, laminated wood and plastic-covered steel. *1981. H:19¾ in (50 cm).*

FIRST CHAIR Made from plastic-coated tubular metal and laminated wood, this "first" chair was designed by Michele De Lucchi for the Memphis group. *1983. H:33 in (84 cm).*

The yellow box head and black and white striped neck are shaped in an abstract animal form

OCEANIC TABLE LAMP Made from polychrome enameled metal, this table lamp was designed by Michele De Lucchi for the Memphis group. *1981. H:39 in (99 cm).*

were also contributions from France (Martine Bedin and Nathalie du Pasquier), Spain (Javier Mariscal), England (George Sowden and Gerard Taylor), Austria (Matteo Thun), Japan (Arata Isozaki and Shiro Kuramata), and the United States (Michael Graves and Peter Shire).

The preference by Memphis group designers for surface pattern rather than form was in keeping with the mood of the times. Many of their products were covered with colorful plastic laminates, giving them a smooth, shallow surface that was entirely different in character from that of metal, wood, or any other natural materials. This use of patterned laminate made Memphis products look two-dimensional, as if they were cut out from the pages of a magazine or comic strip.

MARKETING FOR SUCCESS

Memphis was one of the first design groups that counted among its key members a non-designer. Barbara Radice (who was Sottsass's partner in their personal as well as professional life) held the title of Art Director, but her skills essentially lay in her ability to write eloquently and effusively about

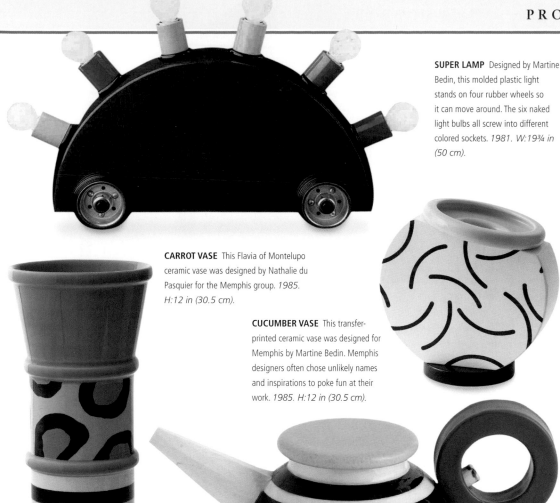

SUPER LAMP Designed by Martine Bedin, this molded plastic light stands on four rubber wheels so it can move around. The six naked light bulbs all screw into different colored sockets. *1981. W:19¾ in (50 cm).*

CARROT VASE This Flavia of Montelupo ceramic vase was designed by Nathalie du Pasquier for the Memphis group. *1985. H:12 in (30.5 cm).*

CUCUMBER VASE This transfer-printed ceramic vase was designed for Memphis by Martine Bedin. Memphis designers often chose unlikely names and inspirations to poke fun at their work. *1985. H:12 in (30.5 cm).*

STUDIO TEAPOT Designed by Peter Shire, this ceramic teapot with a funnel-shaped spout parodies traditional forms and is handpainted. *1996. W:9 in (23 cm).*

GIOTTO

Named after the 14th-century Florentine artist who set the Italian Renaissance in motion, the Giotto range of products was intended to have a similar revolutionary effect on the homeware market. Giotto gathered together a number of ex-members of the recently disbanded Memphis group including Ettore Sottsass, Nathalie du Pasquier, and Marco Zanuso Jr., as well as number of younger designers including Johanna Grawunder. The Giotto range of vases, fruit bowls, and other objects was as bold and audacious as much of the Memphis output. Unfortunately, poor publicity and manufacturing problems in China hastened the demise of Giotto. Instead of flooding the market as intended, the products eventually ended up as collector's items in expensive European art galleries.

GIOTTO JG4 VASE This blue ceramic vase designed by Johanna Grawunder sits in a sprung steel holder. *1992. H:9 in (23 cm).*

Memphis and in promoting the group's work to the international media and design cognoscenti. With Radice's help, Memphis became an almost overnight sensation, with pictures of their products reproduced across the world. The first Memphis exhibition in 1981 (at the Arc 74 Gallery in Milan) was an instant hit and by the end of the year a coffee-table book had already been produced about the group, their work, and their history. Such accelerated success was unprecedented.

The fact that the Memphis style was so readily accepted was largely thanks to the ground being prepared during the late 1970s by Alchimia, the radical design studio led by Alessandro Mendini (for which Sottsass and De Lucchi had also, briefly, worked). A riotous affront to the purist ideals of modernism, Alchimia successfully eroded the prevailing idea that design was essentially a practical pursuit. Like Memphis's output, Alchimia products often contained a broad sweep of cultural references. But whereas Alchimia tended to present them in an provocative and cacophonous manner, the Memphis designers preferred to blend them into a more seamless, unified whole.

The black-lacquered top forms an asymmetrical shape

BRAZIL SINGLE-PEDESTAL DESK Peter Shire designed this futuristic desk. It has a trapezoidal black-lacquered top on a pastel enameled steel base. *1981. W:81½ in (207 cm).*

A Memphis product, then, may have patterns that faintly echo African tribal designs—or their forms might bear some resemblance to American skyscrapers—but these references always take second place to the overall composition of the piece. In this way, Memphis was not as cerebral or as dogmatic as Alchimia, and this is perhaps why Mendini, a tireless theorist, never worked with the more instinctive, emotionally driven designers of the Memphis group.

REVOLUTIONS IN DESIGN

Toward the end of the 1980s, the backlash against modernism was beginning to subside. Designers were even beginning to show nostalgia for the more simplistic, sensual forms of the 1950s. While they found themselves returning to the pared-down shapes of modernism, however, they chose to ignore the ideals of rational reform that the earlier era promoted. Indeed, many designs that followed in the footsteps of postmodernism pursued form for its own sake, rather than being overtly concerned with function.

Philippe Starck, Ron Arad, and Marc Newson are in many ways typical of designers of this era. They display no allegiances to a particular movement or style, but appear to follow their own interests and ideas. A curiosity about materials allows them to explore different possibilities without committing themselves to one particular look. All three, however, seem to prefer the sinuous to the straight line, perhaps a reaction to the jagged or geometric look of much 1970s and 1980s furniture.

All three designers were influenced by living in several different countries, and their design style communicates itself across cultural borders. Appealing to both the head and heart, it creates a strong visual impact.

ÉTRANGETÉ 66 This teardrop-shaped glass object can be either a vase or a display piece. A typical Philippe Starck form, it was produced as a limited edition of 75 by the French company Daum. c. 1988. L:22 in (56 cm).

ALEPH SIDE CHAIR Starck designed this three-legged chair for the Royalton Hotel in New York. H:34 in (86 cm).

PHILIPPE STARCK

During the late 1980s and 1990s there was no bigger name in the design world than that of Philippe Starck. There appeared to be no household item that the designer had not turned his hand to: door handles, toothbrushes, sofas, telephones, and much more. His designs often involved stripping an archetypal object down to its bones in an essentially modernist manner, then adding a layer of postmodern whimsicality such as giving a chair legs made from different materials, or a lamp a shade shaped like a bull's horn. This formula proved incredibly successful and brought Starck a degree of international fame that was unprecedented for a designer.

Born in Paris in 1949, Starck claims he rarely attended classes at the furniture-design course in Paris where he enrolled, and is essentially self-taught. Possessing immense energy and ambition, Starck became the Artistic Director at Pierre Cardin at the age of 20. By the mid-1970s he was designing nightclubs, notably Les Bains-Douches in Paris, but his big break came when he was asked to design Café Costes near the Centre Pompidou. Completed in 1984, the interior was, like much of Starck's subsequent work, simple and coherent with a wealth of mischievous details. An oversize clock loomed over the space and the chairs only had three legs (one less for waiters to trip over).

After his work at Café Costes was published in magazines and newspapers around the world,

Starck was soon being courted by a number of (mostly Italian) manufacturers. His exuberant interiors for the Royalton Hotel (1988) and Paramount Hotel in New York (1990) confirmed his status as the world's most in-demand designer, and the 1990s was a prolific decade for Starck.

Although Starck primarily used wood and metal early in his career, his work during the 1990s was mainly made from plastic. This gave him greater flexibility of form and, crucially, made his furniture more affordable. Starck's furniture was usually slender and curvaceous and frequently had elements of zoomorphism—suggestions of wings, horns, and legs were common—giving it a cuteness that broadened its appeal.

By the mid-1990s Starck was working with companies around the world. Styling himself as the world's first truly international designer, and a superstar in the mold of a Hollywood actor, his profile in the 21st century is now lower. However, he continues to produce many critically acclaimed products and furniture.

VITRA WW STOOL Originally designed by Philippe Starck for Wim Wenders, the film director, this biomorphic-shaped stool is made of sand-cast aluminum with a pale green enamel finish. 1990. H:38 in (98.5 cm).

STARK MODERNISM Textured aluminum walls, floor-to-ceiling windows, atmospheric lighting, and bar stools with his trademark curvaceous legs are features of Philippe Starck's 1994 design for the Felix Restaurant in Hong Kong's Peninsula Hotel.

RON ARAD

Never afraid of making bold statements with his furniture and interiors, Ron Arad has been stamping his mark on international design since the beginning of the 1980s. Born in Tel Aviv in 1951, Arad moved to London in 1974 to study at the Architectural Association and has been in the city ever since, becoming a British citizen in 1994.

Arad studied under Peter Cook and Bernard Tschumi, two radical architects who emphasized that ideas and aesthetics were just as important as practicality when it came to architecture and design. Following these sentiments, Arad set up his own studio, called One-Off, in 1981 and began to produce a series of unique, experimental furniture designs. Arad's Rover chairs (1981), which used salvaged car seats welded to a steel base, were the most successful of a number of early designs that incorporated found objects. In the tradition of the *objets trouvés* beloved of surrealist and conceptual artists such as Marcel Duchamp, the pieces not only had a political, anticonsumerist element, but they also formed comments on the environmental concerns of the age.

Throughout the 1980s Arad continued to produce thought-provoking pieces, often using raw, industrial materials such as concrete and steel. By the end of the decade, however, he had wound down his One-Off studio and formed Ron Arad Associates, which was more commercially driven.

During the 1990s Arad designed numerous pieces of furniture for mass production, often using plastics. Although these pieces were still strident in their design, they had developed from his earlier "found objects" style. By the beginning of the 21st century Arad had proved himself as both a designer who appealed to more artistically minded buyers (indeed, unique Arad pieces in steel were achieving staggering prices at auction of over $50,000) as well as the mass market. His plastic Bookworm bookshelf for Kartell has been a bestseller since its introduction in the mid-1990s.

WELL-TEMPERED CHAIR The back, arms, and seat of this salvage movement chair are made from temper-rolled stainless steel, which is bolted into place with wing nuts. *1987. H:38¾ in (98.5 cm).*

ROVER CHAIR Arad's ready-made design for One-Off Ltd exemplifies the 1980s preoccupation with recycling. It is made of a salvaged Rover car seat mounted on a tubular-steel frame. *1981. H:37¾ in (96 cm).*

EMPTY CHAIR Made by Driade, this Arad chair consists of a bent, laminated plywood seating section on tubular-aluminum legs. *1993. H:39 in (99 cm).*

MARC NEWSON

The Australian Marc Newson is one of the most international and prolific designers of the Southern Hemisphere. "Coming from Australia, my design has been self-taught and instinctive," he says.

Born in 1962, Newson studied jewelry design at the Sydney College of the Arts in the early 1980s, but spent much time in the sculpture department. Largely cut off from the latest developments of the postmodern style that were spreading across Europe, Newson acquired an appreciation for Italian furniture of the 1960s and early 1970s. Furniture by designers like Achille Castiglione and Joe Colombo was relatively common in Australia, and Newson responded to the optimism and forward-thinking they displayed.

A love of the futuristic designs of the past has played an important role in the creation of Newson's style, as demonstrated by his Lockheed Lounge (1985), the piece of furniture that launched his career. First shown in a Sydney gallery, the sculptural lounger was made from fiberglass and riveted aluminum and bore many similarities to the 1950s aircraft from which it took its name. Following the global exposure of this audacious piece of furniture, Newson was invited to Tokyo to work with a new company called Idée. Given few financial or aesthetic constraints, he spent the period from 1987 to 1991 producing some of his most remarkable furniture and establishing his style.

Updating the organic forms of furniture that were so popular among American designers of the 1950s, Newson created a look that was both retro yet entirely of its time in its use of advanced materials and manufacturing techniques.

At the beginning of the 1990s Newson moved to Europe, where he worked for different furniture-makers in London and Paris. References to the beach culture of Australia continued to crop up in his work, however, in his use of bold shapes inspired by surfboards and eye-catching colors.

This chair was also manufactured with felt and leather upholstery

FELT CHAIR A characteristically sculptural design by Marc Newson for Cappellini, this armchair is made from a reinforced fiberglass body supported on a polished aluminum leg. *1994. H:34 in (86 cm).*

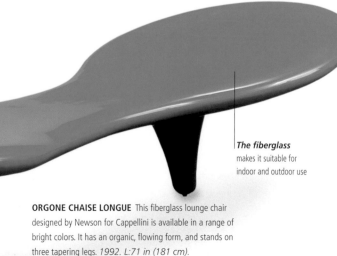

The fiberglass makes it suitable for indoor and outdoor use

ORGONE CHAISE LONGUE This fiberglass lounge chair designed by Newson for Cappellini is available in a range of bright colors. It has an organic, flowing form, and stands on three tapering legs. *1992. L:71 in (181 cm).*

NEW TECHNOLOGY

As consumers began to enjoy the benefits of increased leisure time, they placed greater importance than ever on the home as a place for rest, relaxation, and entertainment. In order to beautify this environment, designers turned their attention to the minutiae of daily life. The kitchen, reinstated as a hub of family life, became the focus of particular attention.

ALESSI DESIGN

The Italian design company Alessi has scored some of its most notable successes with appliances and gadgets for the kitchen. Philippe Starck's Juicy Salif citrus squeezer has become an icon of Alessi's achievement in this field. Despite its alleged impracticality, the Juicy Salif has sold well since its introduction in 1990. It is loved as a sculptural object first and a functional household item second. Other Alessi products have married functionality to eccentric design with greater success. Since first working for Alessi on the Tea and Coffee Piazza range, Michael Graves has contributed a steady trickle of designs to the company's catalog. His Kettle With Bird, first made in 1985, plays on the traditional notion of a whistling kettle by

attributing the noise to a plastic bird attached to the spout. Although most electric kettles automatically switch off once the water boils, Graves revived this time-honored warning signal as a witty postmodern embellishment.

The kettle is fashioned from molded stainless steel and the rivets around its base are designed in the same vein—as a reminder of and a throwback to archaic industrial techniques. The success of Graves's kettle design spawned a companion range of complementary products, all with the tubular blue plastic grip flanked by red spheres and the rivet detailing featured on the original.

Alessandro Mendini created a corkscrew called Anna G. for Alessi in 1994. By literally giving a face to Alessi's accessible, companionable design, Mendini created a phenomenon. From the original corkscrew the range has extended to include a cheese grater, a timer, a lighter, and a host of other products.

This personification of the product has been a constant feature of postmodern product design. The reference might be to a fictional character, as is the case with a pepper mill designed for Swid Powell by Robert and Trix Haussmann, which has large circular ears reminiscent of Mickey Mouse. Other products hint at this personification in a more abstract fashion,

HARLEQUIN VASE This figural piece by Alessandro Mendini is typical of his decorative and anthropomorphic designs. It is from a numbered limited edition of 99, plus nine artist's proofs. *2004. H:43¼ in (110 cm).*

The handle is shaped like a wing nut and resembles Mickey Mouse's ears

PEPPER GRINDER This piece was designed by the Swiss architects Robert and Trix Haussmann for the American company Swid Powell. *1986. H:5 in (13.5 cm).*

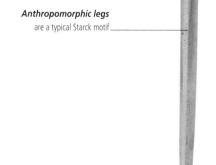

The juice runs down the body to be collected in a container placed beneath it

Anthropomorphic legs are a typical Starck motif

JUICY SALIF JUICER Philippe Starck designed this long-legged juicer, made of cast aluminum with polyamide feet, for Alessi. A gold-plated limited edition of this popular design was manufactured in 2000. *1990.*

Yum.

Think different.

AMERICAN iMAC POSTER The iMac was launched in 1998 and was touted as the most original new personal computer since the first Apple Mac in 1984. The design team, led by Jonathan Ive, introduced a new case design with translucent "Bondi Blue" plastic. The "Yum—Think Different, Apple Computers (Imac)" poster advertised the introduction of a new iMac model available in five new colors: Blueberry, Strawberry, Lime, Tangerine, and Grape. *1999. H:36 in (91 cm).*

SWINGING MARILYN TEAPOT Matheo Thun's unusual teapot, designed for Alessi, is made of copper, base metal, and black plastic. The curves are formed from circle and tube segments. *1985. H:9 in (22.5 cm).*

ANNA G. CORKSCREW This corkscrew in plastic and chrome-plated Zamak metal was designed by Alessandro Mendini. It became an Alessi best-seller and spawned a range of objects featuring the Anna icon, such as peppermills, graters, and cigarette lighters. *1994.*

OLA T1000GD TELEPHONE This blue plastic telephone is organic in shape and was designed by Philippe Starck for Thomson. *1993. L:11 in (28 cm).*

Transparent casing and brightly colored motor parts emphasize how the machine works

DYSON VACUUM CLEANER This limited-edition Dyson DC02 De Stijl vacuum cleaner was named after the Dutch avant-garde design group's exploration of the relationship between color, form, and function. *1996. H:19¾ in (50 cm).*

or in name only, such as Mattheo Thun's Swinging Marilyn teapot.

APPLE SUCCESS
More recently, large corporations have become more design conscious to win sales in an increasingly competitive marketplace. Through a series of prominent advertising campaigns, Apple Computers has built a brand around creativity and has sought to separate itself from its competition using innovative product design ever since the launch of the Apple II, designed by Jerry Manock in 1977. Apple headhunted British designer Jonathon Ive to lead its design team in 1992. The iMac line, launched in 1998, represented a watershed in computer design. It was one of the first home computers to integrate the monitor and

the CPU within a single case. The iMac also had its own quirky circular mouse. The candy colors and transparent case of the iMac have made it an object to display and have been imitated by many other industrial products.

DYSON
The phenomenal success of James Dyson's 1983 vacuum cleaner must also owe much to its appealing design. It proclaims its "reinvention" with its appearance as much as through its advanced technology. This is another household appliance that consumers are happy to leave out on display rather than hide away in a closet.

CERAMICS

POSTMODERN POTTERY CAME TO OCCUPY A CURIOUS MIDDLE GROUND BETWEEN FUNCTIONAL OBJECT AND SCULPTURE. CERAMICISTS CREATED EXPRESSIVE AND FIGURAL SCULPTURE ALONGSIDE PRACTICAL PIECES.

PAUL SOLDNER CHARGER This charger is carved and handcrafted from white clay with glazes over a fossilized image of a fish. Soldner experimented with reduction chambers, used at the end of firing, to try to recreate traditional Japanese raku effects. *D:19¾ in (50 cm).*

ABSTRACT EXPRESSIONISM

In 1952 the influential critic Harold Rosenberg, responding to the abstract expressionism of key figures such as Jackson Pollock, famously redefined art as a process rather than a product. Peter Voulkos was the first of a generation of potters to transfer this same idea to the medium of clay. He began to develop the distinctive sculptural idiom that encompassed his stoneware stack, plate, and ice bucket forms in 1954.

REVOLUTION IN CLAY

Voulkos was at the forefront of the so-called Revolution in Clay that overturned accepted notions of what made good ceramic art. Whereas pottery and porcelain production had previously been linked with a relentless quest for perfection, Voulkos celebrated the raw qualities inherent in unworked clay. Although nominally based on, and named after, functional forms, Voulkos's sculptures are comprehensively torn, twisted, and gouged, and deliberately useless. The violence implicit in Voulkos's work is reminiscent of both Pollock's aggressive brand of Action Painting and the volatile geology of California, the clay of which he uses to create his vessels. Voulkos established the ceramic departments at the Otis Art Institute in Los Angeles and, later, at the University of California at Berkeley. His tenure at Berkeley lasted for more than 25 years from 1959 onward and gave Voulkos the chance to disseminate his radical ideas on ceramics among many of the most promising young potters of the day.

Paul Soldner was Voulkos's first pupil at the Otis Art Institute. Arriving from the University of Colorado at Boulder, Soldner found that Voulkos's new ceramics department was little more than an empty room, and he set about helping his new teacher to organize the new department. Soldner even devised his own modifications to the pottery wheel they had installed. His interest in the technical side of pottery was so strong that he was compelled to establish a firm to sell his own clay mixers.

EXPERIMENTING WITH GLAZES

Soldner was unusual among Voulkos's students in that he worked with traditional vessels rather than the abstract and sculptural forms favored by his mentor. His great legacy is the innovative work he did taking Japanese raku ware as his starting point. Although fascinated by the element of chance involved in the raku glazing process, Soldner felt no natural affinity with the traditional tea wares usually associated with the style. Instead he applied

STONEWARE CHARGER The tears, incisions, and random pattern in the iron oxide and brown glazes of this large platter by Maria Woo show the influence of Voulkos. *H:19¼ in (49 cm).*

TOTEMIC VESSEL Made by Peter Voulkos, this tall brown stoneware piece incorporates tears, gouges, and incised lines. *H:27 in (68 cm).*

EARTHENWARE VASE This sensual vase by Ken Ferguson has three large lobes, a handle in the shape of a mermaid, and a twisted spout. It is covered in a verdigris and gray dead-matte volcanic glaze. *H:7½ in (19 cm).*

PETER VOULKOS CHARGER This large stoneware plate in dark brown glazed clay is typical of Voulkos's work. It is freely formed and features expressive tears and roughly applied pieces. *1995. D:20¾ in (53 cm).*

raku glazes to modern forms and plunged them into water while the glaze was still molten, cooling them quickly and accelerating the already speedy process of raku glazing. Soldner also developed a low-fire salt fuming technique. Both of these new processes produce a range of unpredictable effects depending on the exact conditions in the kiln.

Ken Ferguson, a former student of Voulkos, also experimented with salt glazes on his high-fired stoneware. Ferguson proved to be an inspirational teacher and many of his charges have since become influential contemporary potters in their own right.

HOMEWARE AS ART

A band of female potters inculcated the British ceramics scene with a host of new ideas in the 1970s. Carol McNicholl made functional homeware using the slip-casting technique that has long been used to manufacture mass-produced homeware. Her individual pieces are, however, made entirely by hand and are gently subversive of traditional domestic forms. Her aim in this was to reestablish the home as a suitable venue for art.

Alison Britton trained under Hans Coper at London's Royal College of Art. Like Voulkos, Britton creates work that lies between utility and sculpture. She uses a slab-building technique to make vessels from sheets of clay, taking inspiration from sources as varied as ancient Asian works of art to modern art.

The most prominent American woman working in a similar style is Betty Woodman. Among her most celebrated works are a series of pillow-shaped pitchers with mottled majolica glazes that resemble both Tang dynasty Chinese sancai ware and the poured-paint technique of Jackson Pollock. The elongated necks and gracefully curved handles on these vessels are inspired by Greek and Etruscan forms that Woodman had seen when visiting the Mediterranean.

DRYSPACE POT This tall, boxlike piece was made by the British potter Alison Britton. It was built from slabs of clay rather than thrown on a wheel. *2003. H:18 in (47 cm).*

Striped decoration creates a dramatic effect

PATTERNED VESSEL Entitled New World Order, this piece by Carol McNicholl juxtaposes the expressive and unique nature of handbuilt clay with the repetitive qualities of the printed pattern. *H:9 in (22.5 cm).*

Woodman's glazes and exuberant use of color are painterly

PILLOW PITCHER Just one of the many forms that Betty Woodman employs, this piece, of white clay with an applied handle, is covered in green, magnesium, yellow, and gunmetal majolica glazes. *W:20 in (51 cm).*

THE FUNK MOVEMENT

Ceramics in this period moved on from its craft status. Encouraged by the freewheeling spirit of the 1970s, ceramicists made the most of the expressive and sculptural possibilities of their medium and produced a more varied body of work than ever before. Centered around the San Francisco Bay area, the Funk movement borrowed elements from Dadaism and Pop Art and used them to create a new ceramic idiom with a political and social agenda. The work of key figures such as Hui Ka Kwong, who made boldly decorated, symmetrical sculptural forms, is highly individual and characterized by a desire to communicate an emotional response to the world in the tradition of expressionist art.

This individualistic expressionism found a monumental exponent in Viola Frey. Her enormous columns and figures—often more than 10 ft (3 m) high—are so large that she was forced to chop them into sections to fire them. Frey would then paint the individual sections by hand before reassembling them to form the finished sculpture. The process of creation was an intuitive one for her—it was only after figures were complete that she would "discover if they are intelligent or not, if they are good or bad, or if they have any sense of humor." In time she would abandon even this limited self-interrogation and work almost compulsively.

Akio Takamori, a Japanese potter who settled in the United States, had a more personal relationship with his

art. He first realized it was possible to create expressionist ceramics when a traveling exhibition of Western works passed through the town where he was apprenticed to a master folk potter. The anti-authoritarian nature of these works was a revelation to Takamori and he traveled to Kansas to embark on a degree in Fine Art. Takamori's

CRUCIFIXION This Akio Takamori faience sculpture depicts two naked men flanking a crowd of people watching a crucifixion. It has an outline of a bloodied cross on the reverse. *H:21 in (53 cm)*.

The four-armed piece resembles a circus figure

FUNK POTTERY LAMP Hui Ka Kwong's piece has five sockets and two rows of arms on a flared base. The colorful trumpetlike form emphasizes the fun in the Funk aesthetic. *H:38 in (96.5 cm)*.

The figures are covered with a cadmium-yellow volcanic glaze

RED CLAY SCULPTURE This piece by Beatrice Wood is composed of three wall-like panels with five door-shaped openings. Within them are figures of single women and embracing couples, all mounted on a pine board. *W:60 in (152.5 cm)*.

RAZZ-MA-TAZZ This large vessel by Rudy Autio is characteristic of his style. In his pieces, which are often American West in theme, Autio blends curved, bulbous clay forms with painted figures. *1998. H:31 in (80 cm).*

DAVID GILHOOLY

Since enrolling in his first pottery class in pursuit of an elusive girl, David Gilhooly has become a leading exponent of the Funk ceramic movement. His work ranges from representations of animals named after old acquaintances to enormous pieces of junk food, replicated in clay in an effort to resolve his eating problems. Gilhooly's extensive FrogWorld series—a trawl through human history with frogs taking the roles of the main protagonists—threatened to take over his work, and he tried repeatedly to kill them off before finally consigning them to space. Gilhooly subsequently developed a distaste for clay, renouncing it forever in 1996. This might be considered something of a handicap for a ceramicist, but Gilhooly has continued his inimitable work in plexiglass.

FROGS IN BEANS This sculpture, one of the FrogWorld series, depicts three frogs frolicking in a cast-iron pot full of black-eyed beans. *c.1970. W:5 in (14.5 cm).*

The grotesque faces, covered in polychrome oxide glazes, capture the Bosch spirit

BOSCH TEAPOT Noi Volkov's earthenware teapot alludes to the instantly recognizable work of the Dutch Renaissance painter Hieronymus Bosch. The piece is about form and decoration and pays little attention to function. *2005. L:12 in (30.5 cm).*

BASKETFUL FOR JOHN This painted and transfer-printed piece is by the Funk ceramicist Richard Shaw, who is well known for his trompe l'oeil ceramics. It features items of his everyday life such as a deck of cards, a pack of cigarettes and matches, poker chips, paint, and a small cruise ship in a woven basket. *1992. W:15 in (38.5 cm).*

early work was conspicuous for its sexual content, while his later figures draw on memories of his childhood in Japan and depict entire communities in clay. The common theme uniting these strands in his work is his exploration of the relationship between the physical and the emotional.

ART INSPIRATION

A number of potters who have enjoyed long and varied careers have produced works that fit within the Funk agenda. Beatrice Wood, who died at the age of 105 after attributing her longevity to "chocolate and young men," created a number of obliquely evocative works during her later career.

Rudy Autio trained alongside Peter Voulkos at Montana State University in the late 1940s, aided by financial provisions made by the GI Bill of Rights—legislation to ease servicemen returning from the war back into civilian life. Like many 20th-century studio potters, Autio was influenced by prominent visual artists in his formative years. The impact on Autio of paintings by Henri Matisse and prints by Shiko Munakata is particularly evident in his flowing painted decoration. Autio's handbuilt vessels have a freedom of line and form that echo the sweeping contours of the figures he depicts in his work.

More recently, Noi Volkov has reached farther back into art history in his search for inspiration. His postmodern juxtaposition of the contemporary and the historical comes in the form of bizarre, faux-functional forms decorated with startlingly accurate re-creations of paintings by famous artists, from Hieronymus Bosch to Vincent Van Gogh. Volkov was a citizen of the Ukraine under Soviet rule and his attempts to use his extensive artistic training as a means for self expression attracted the attention of the KGB, who closed down his kiln. In 1989 Voulkov moved to the United States, where he has pursued his individual vision with vigor. Many of his unorthodox ceramic works incorporate everyday objects he has found, such as faucets and even a pair of jeans.

The Funk ceramicist Richard Shaw also uses everyday objects as a basis for his work, but he recreates them in clay. His pieces include ceramic representations of objects as diverse as dominoes, cruise liners, cigar boxes, and playing cards.

The folded shapes are all random and unique

VESSELS OF IDEAS

The postmodern reinterpretation of ceramic art did not revolve solely around expressive and figural sculpture. Numerous potters, including many who also explored sculptural representation, chose to work within the constraints imposed by traditional vessel forms.

Potters such as Takeshi Yasuda pursued a new minimalism that was a world apart from the outlandish models being made by Gilhooly and the other Funk ceramicists (see p.398). Yasuda embraced accident and chance, and his intense interest in the process of modeling his pots was rooted firmly in the tradition of Peter Voulkos, even if the

eventual results were far more refined. His celebrated Unfolding Vases were the result of a throwing error at the wheel. In attempting to create tall, tapering vessels with very thin walls, Yasuda overreached himself, and some of the pots collapsed. When he hung the ruined vessels upside down they stretched back into buckled versions of their original shapes.

He created his companion Folding series by allowing plates propped up on stands to collapse in on themselves within the kiln. Both of these concepts highlight the plasticity of clay—a quality that is usually evident only while it is being worked.

WALTER KEELER

English ceramicist Walter Keeler has been called Britain's leading maker of individual domestic wares. He plays with functional forms, for instance, by applying ceramic arms

THREE UNFOLDING VASES These warped porcelain vases by Takeshi Yasuda were made by collapsing the pieces on the wheel, then hanging them upside down. H:17 in (45 cm).

STONEWARE LIDDED JAR This jar by Walter Keeler is typical of his angular, often humorous tilting forms and attractive salt-glaze decoration. H:9 in (22.5 cm).

PORCELAIN SCULPTURE This piece by Karl Scheid consists of a series of slab-built vessels that are reminiscent of open books set back to back and side to side. c.2000. H:23½ in (60 cm).

The clean shapes are inspired by many forms, including 18th-century Staffordshire ceramics and oil cans

Speckled salt glaze

STONEWARE BOTTLE Jim Malone used the Korean hakeme technique—applying a white slip glaze in swirls with a stiff brush. c.2000. H:12¾ in (32.5 cm).

TAKAEZU STONEWARE VESSEL This spherical vessel by Toshiko Takaezu is simply decorated with random, leaflike brushstrokes in earthy colors, reflecting her interest in the natural world. Takaezu has made many vessels like this in a wide range of sizes. H:6 in (17 cm).

OCEAN I AND OCEAN 11 These two jugs by
Emmanuel Cooper are Western in shape and design, their
elegant and simple forms highlighted with his brightly
colored hallmark glazes. *Larger pot: H:8 in (20 cm).*

The rich blue glaze recalls Egyptian faience

The color has been randomly applied by brush and slip trailers

POPPY TEAPOT Janice Tchalenko's popular poppy design, along with designs
such as Peacock and Tornado, for Dartington Pottery update traditional forms
with free, handpainted decoration. They helped to revive primary colors in
mainstream ceramics. *1980s. H:8¾ in (22 cm).*

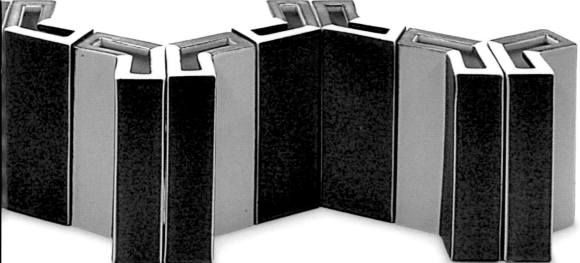

GRAYSON PERRY

An artist who works in many media but is best known for
his ceramics, Grayson Perry enjoys the conflict between
the colorful, naively decorative aspect of his pots and the
brutally frank way in which they deal with often disturbing
themes. His work mixes the autobiographical, dealing with
issues drawn from his own life and that of his alter ego,
Claire, with the political. He also uses ceramics to satirize
the work of other artists, poking fun at Alexander Calder's
mobiles and Jackson Pollock's pouring technique, among
other things. Unlike most studio potters who have tried
to elevate the status of pottery, Perry revels in its position
as a subordinate medium to painting or sculpture. Perry
accepted the 2003 Turner Prize with the words: "It's about
time a transvestite potter won the Turner."

PRECIOUS BOYS
Although traditional
in shape, this vase is
circled with figures at
the top and has a mottled
glaze overlaid with outlines of
fighter jets below them. *2004.
H:21 in (53 cm).*

resembling severed tree limbs to his vessels,
thus creating "extraordinary objects to do a
commonplace job." By forcing the user to negotiate
a network of thorny branches in order to brew a
pot of tea, Keeler interrupts an everyday action
and transforms it into something novel. As his
career has progressed, he has experimented with
stoneware and earthenware, raku, and reduction
firing, adapting his work to new processes and
techniques. His work can be seen as part of a
move to restore art to the home.

COLOR AND PATTERN

Other studio potters have worked toward the same
goal through their work with color and pattern.
Elizabeth Fritsch has produced coil-built stoneware
vases since training under Hans Coper in the early
1970s. She decorates her vessels with smooth layers
of slip in complex geometric patterns. Her palette
has ranged from pale colors early on, through bold
greens, reds, and blues to monochrome. Julian
Stair, on the other hand, has restricted color to
the natural tones of black basalt, white porcelain,
and red stoneware. His sparsely decorated work
includes functional pieces such as funerary urns,
teapots, and caddies as well as more abstract forms.

From the 1970s the British studio pottery
movement gradually grew away from its roots in the
Asian tradition. Emmanuel Cooper experimented
with glazes and produced a range of effects including
tactile volcanic surfaces. Janice Tchalenko opened
her studio in London in 1971, initially working
within the boundaries defined by Bernard Leach
before becoming enamored of the English style
rendered by his pupil Michael Cardew. As she
traveled to exotic locations, she learned from
diverse folk traditions. She fused her admiration
for the Renaissance French ceramicist Bernard
Palissy with Russian and Iranian decorative
styles, opening the floodgates for influences
other than the Oriental.

Tchalenko's work consists mainly of
unpretentious, functional forms that use repeat
patterns, stenciled motifs, and trailed glazes for
decorative impact. She brought her work to a wide
audience through an association with Dart Pottery
from 1984. Tchalenko has also produced unique
commissions including a range of pieces
representing the seven deadly sins. These pieces
were designed in collaboration with the team
behind the TV program *Spitting Image* for the
Victoria & Albert Museum in London.

FACTORY CERAMICS

Although the truly mass-produced ceramics of the late 20th century can be inferior in terms of both quality and appearance when compared with mid-century classics such as Russel Wright's American Modern, a middle tier of manufacturers, spanning the gap between the studio potteries and the cheap and cheerful factories, catered to a growing demand for well-designed homeware.

SWID POWELL

Nan Swid and Addie Powell, a pair of New York designers, exploited this new market with admirable aplomb. In Nan's own words, "I knew that very few people would ever live in houses designed by Richard Meier or Robert Venturi, but I thought they would like to experience that aesthetic level." Swid and Powell gathered a coterie of their talented friends around a table at the Four Seasons Restaurant and unveiled their business plan. They would commission these eminent architects and designers—Robert Venturi and Michael Graves among them—to create tableware and other useful objects for mass production. As leading proponents of the postmodern style in their architectural work, these individuals brought the same ideas to the designs they drafted for Swid Powell.

With his Grandmother mug, for example, Robert Venturi starts with a traditional motif—namely, a transfer-printed design of flowers—and gives it a contemporary 1980s twist by adding short pairs of parallel black lines. Venturi also used this underlying chintz motif on his chairs—in both instances the idea, as suggested by the name, is

to poke fun at the notion of taking tea with grandmother, the table spread with a 1930s floral tablecloth. Venturi's Notebook service, also designed for Swid Powell, juxtaposes standard dinner plates and serving dishes with a truly unexpected design based on the covers of school notebooks.

Michael Graves's Big Dripper teapot and Little Dripper creamer and sugar bowl make oblique external references to their intended function. The red cruciform bases symbolize the heat used to warm the vessels, bringing to mind a traditional stovetop kettle, while the blue wavy lines signify the liquid contained inside them.

GRANDMOTHER MUG AND PLATE
This Swid Powell ceramic mug and plate, designed by Robert Venturi, are decorated with transfer-printed pastel flowers and pairs of black lines. *1984. H:3¾ in (9.5 cm).*

LITTLE DRIPPER TEA SET Designed by Michael Graves for Swid Powell, this tea set consists of a transfer-printed tea- or coffeepot, a milk jug, a sugar bowl with a spoon, and a coffee filter holder. With typically postmodern appropriation from history, however recent, the set appears to be influenced by Art Deco and even Christopher Dresser. *1987. Teapot: W:9 in (23.5 cm).*

The blue waves obliquely hint at the object's function

FLASH CHEESE DISH This angular cheese dish decorated with blocks of geometric patterns was designed by Dorothy Hafner for the Rosenthal Studio Linie. *1985. W:7½ in (19 cm).*

ROSENTHAL POLLO STUDIO LINIE PORCELAIN VASE Tapio Wirkkala designed the Pollo range in three sizes, black or white. They were made in molds using a slipcast process. *H:4¾ in (12 cm).*

FLOWERS PLATE This plate, designed by Robert Venturi for Swid Powell, is decorated with stylized flowers—a traditional floral chintz updated for the postmodern generation.

OTHER FACTORY CERAMICISTS

Alessi, that other great democratizer of architectural design, achieved a feat similar to Swid Powell's in the field of ceramics and metalware. During the late 1990s Alessi issued a series of mugs and other vessels designed by Andrea Branzi. His Genetic Tales motif has adorned a number of products and also formed the subject of a book by the architect. The playful design features cartoon-like heads and symbols taken from mathematical equations to create a dialogue about similarities and differences, both between individuals and between cultures. Branzi has also produced other ceramics, notably the *Tatzine e Tatzone* (a wordplay on the Italian for "little cups" and "big cups"). This collection of objects, made by Tendentze, part of Alessi since 1989, has willfully perverse yet resolutely functional forms.

Through her work for Rosenthal, Dorothy Hafner has done much to popularize the postmodern aesthetic. Her angular Flash and Spirit shapes have been particularly successful, but it is her patterns that are most distinctive. Hafner's palette is diverse—extending to turquoise, orange, purple, and red—and always bright and bold. She plays with contrasts not just between colors but also between patterns, so checkered and striped areas mingle on the same piece with blocks of solid color. As well as work for Rosenthal's designer-led range Studio Linie, Hafner also creates individual platters and tureens in a similar style.

The Studio Linie range also includes pieces designed by Tapio Wirkkala, better known for his organic glass forms. He brings a similar aesthetic to his tableware for Rosenthal. The variation between the work done by Hafner and Wirkkala for the same brand of ceramics reflects Rosenthal's commissioning policy, and that of Swid Powell and Alessi: to offer the public a smorgasbord of contemporary design, as disparate as it is daring.

TENDENTZE *TATZINE* TEACUP AND SAUCER Designed by Andrea Branzi, the conical cup has a stylized face transfer on the handle. The cup can rest only on its saucer, a flat oval plate joined to a short cylinder that holds the bottom of the cone. *1986. H:3½ in (8.5 cm).*

MANITOBA CRUET SET This set of four pieces with a transfer-applied pattern was designed to sit in the corners of a tray by Matteo Thun for the Memphis group. *1982. Tallest: H:4 in (10 cm).*

VENTURI'S VILLAGE

With the Village tea set, Robert Venturi took Swid Powell's idea of bringing architecture to the table literally. The set is molded and decorated in the forms of miniature buildings.

The coffeepot, for example, references a Tuscan tower, while the teapot is based on a temple from the ancient world. Other pieces resemble more prosaic buildings, including one that looks like a child's drawing of a house. Other whimsical touches include the inscription "Amo Amas Amat" along the pediment of the temple-shaped teapot—this conjugation of the Latin verb "to love" is another nod to the ancient history of Italy.

VILLAGE TEA SET Robert Venturi designed this eclectic tea set for Swid Powell. The design recalls Venturi's 1977 Eclectic House series. The set, in form and decoration, plays on the traditional country cottage connotations of taking tea. *1986. Teapot: H:9 in (23 cm).*

The motifs are taken from different architectural and ceramic periods

CERAMICS GALLERY

By their very nature, postmodern ceramics are diverse and confound attempts to draw too many parallels between them. It is, however, possible to see common themes, including cultural commentary, inspiration from historical themes, and ironic humor. Some ceramicists defied function and made art pots which were purely decorative; others embraced mass production and designed tablewares which sold in their thousands.

KEY

1. Square platter by Vivika and Otto Heino, painted and incised with leafy branches. W:18 in (45.5 cm). ① **2.** Peter Max covered pot shaped as a man wearing a hat. H:8¼ in (21 cm). ① **3.** Ritzenhoff Dinner For Two set of transfer-printed oval dinner plates by Alessandro Guerriero. 1990. W:12¾ in (32 cm). ① **4.** Swid Powell Volumetric transfer-printed dinner plate by Steven Holl. 1986. D:12 in (30.5 cm). ① **5.** Swid Powell Beam transfer-printed dinner plate with gold highlights by Zaha Hadid. 1988. D:12 in (30.5 cm). ① **6.** Swid Powell Notebook transfer-printed dinner plate by Robert Venturi. 1984. D:12 in (30.5 cm). ① **7.** Rosenthal wall plate by Roy Lichtenstein. D:12 in (30.5 cm). ①

1 Square platter

2 Peter Max covered pot

3 Alessandro Guerriero dinner plates

4 Volumetric dinner plate

5 Zaha Hadid dinner plate

6 Robert Venturi dinner plate

7 Roy Lichtenstein wall plate

8 Robert and Trix Haussmann mug

9 Studio pottery abstract

10 Spirit of Art tea service

11 Marco Zanini cups on stand

8. Swid Powell Black Stripes pattern transfer-printed mug by Robert and Trix Haussmann. 1984. H:4 in (10 cm). ① **9.** Gordon Baldwin abstract piece. 1971. ① **10.** Spirit of Art tea service, after Keith Haring. 1992. Plates: D:13 in (33 cm). ③ **11.** Pair of cups on a stand by Marco Zanini. c.1990. ①
12. Covered pot by Ursula Scheid. **13.** Bitosso E-vasi double vase, the central urn-shaped vase sliding out of the main vase by P. Pallma and C. Vannicola. 1990. H:9¾ in (24.5 cm). ①
14. Wood-fired vase by Paul Soldner, with random painted and incised decoration. H:8½ in (21.5 cm). ② **15.** Win Ng squat vase, covered in volcanic glaze. 1960s. W:6½ in (16.5 cm). ① **16.** Pair of cornucopia vases on organic stands by Nancy Jurs. H:12½ in (32 cm). ① **17.** Ron Nagle bud vase with a four-sided structure attached to an angled one. W:6¾ in (17 cm). ④ **18.** Red clay wood-fired pot by Paul Chaleff. 1984. D:12 in (30.5 cm). ③ **19.** Sculptural vessel by Rudy Autio. H:20½ in (52 cm). ⑥

12 *Ursula Scheid pot*

13 *Double vase*

15 *Win Ng vase*

14 *Paul Soldner vase*

17 *Bud vase*

16 *Cornucopia vases*

18 *Paul Chaleff pot*

19 *Rudy Autio vessel*

GLASS

THE REVERBERATIONS OF THE "REVOLUTION IN CLAY" WERE FELT
THROUGHOUT THE ART WORLD, AS DESIGNERS IN OTHER FIELDS
WOKE UP TO A NEW WORLD OF POSSIBILITIES.

COLORFUL FORMS

The birth of the American studio glass movement can be traced back to a glassblowing workshop held at the Toledo Museum of Art in 1962. It was here that ceramicist Harvey K. Littleton and research scientist Dominick Labino perfected a miniature furnace and glass formula that finally made it possible for solitary artists to manipulate hot glass. Their collaboration led to the establishment of the first Fine Art program in glassworking, at the University of Wisconsin.

One of the first and most prolific students of this program has been Marvin Lipofsky. His relationship with glass has fluctuated—in his early California Loop Series he sought to bury the glass beneath flocking and paint. He also used mirroring and electroplating to coat his glass before finally coming to an acceptance of the inherent beauty of his chosen material, emphasizing its extraordinary propensity for color in particular.

Early in his career, Richard Marquis deliberately manipulated glass to make it resemble clay—he rarely produced clear pieces and frequently chose forms traditionally associated with pottery, such as teapots. Many of his techniques are drawn directly from the Viennese glassmaking tradition: a legacy of the time he spent in Murano. Marquis's enthusiastic use of murrines has even extended to the presentation of sample boards of these slices of transparent or opaque glass as complete pieces in

their own right. His Marquiscarpa vessels, decorated with murrines and based on ancient forms, take their name from a combination of Marquis and Scarpa in honor of Venetian architect Carlo Scarpa. The complicated construction of these pieces is made up of blown, fused, slumped, and carved elements.

Other studio artists such as Pauline Solven resisted this temptation to produce convoluted pieces and instead focused on simple blown forms.

It is testament to the willfully perverse attitude of many postmodern designers that Dan Dailey developed a passion for working with Vitrolite plate glass at a time when it was out of fashion. The opaque plate glass had been a popular structural material during the 1930s but was no longer manufactured when Dailey began working,

making it necessary for him to scavenge for it wherever he could. His Vitrolite, *pâte-de-verre*, and bronze decorative additions provide, in his own words, an "element of deluxe" to his colorful blown forms.

COLLABORATIONS IN PRODUCTION

A recent trend in the studio glass community has led to solitary craftsmen surrounding themselves with assistants and dividing the process of manufacture between them, each specializing in a specific skill. Dailey's glass forms can be the product of up to a dozen individuals working on his original vision. As the artist explains, "I couldn't do what I do alone physically. My skills are not at the level of all my friends."

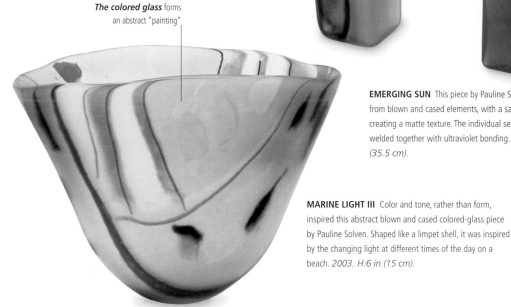

The colored glass forms an abstract "painting"

EMERGING SUN This piece by Pauline Solven is made from blown and cased elements, with a sandblasted finish creating a matte texture. The individual segments were welded together with ultraviolet bonding. *2000. H:14 in (35.5 cm).*

MARINE LIGHT III Color and tone, rather than form, inspired this abstract blown and cased colored-glass piece by Pauline Solven. Shaped like a limpet shell, it was inspired by the changing light at different times of the day on a beach. *2003. H:6 in (15 cm).*

The murrines have different designs such as hearts and stars

CRAZY QUILT TEAPOT This colorful and humorous piece by Richard Marquis is made of free-blown colorless glass overlaid with multicolored murrines. *1988. H:7 in (18 cm).*

THREAD VASE Mary Ann (Toots) Zynsky's richly colored vase was made by layering many fine, colored glass threads, then fusing them together in a kiln using a mold. *c.1990. H:7 in (19.5 cm).*

The colors resemble the plumage of an exotic bird

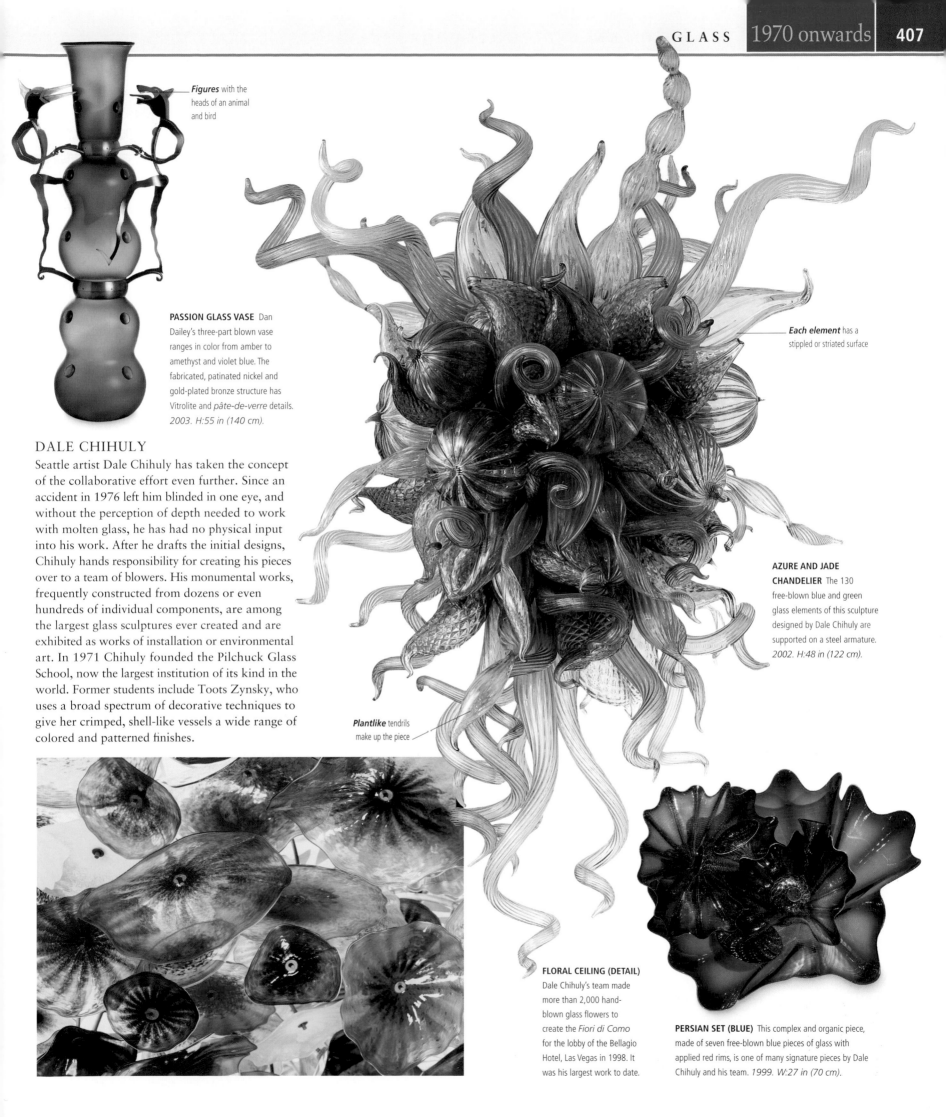

Figures with the heads of an animal and bird

PASSION GLASS VASE Dan Dailey's three-part blown vase ranges in color from amber to amethyst and violet blue. The fabricated, patinated nickel and gold-plated bronze structure has Vitrolite and *pâte-de-verre* details. *2003. H:55 in (140 cm).*

DALE CHIHULY

Seattle artist Dale Chihuly has taken the concept of the collaborative effort even further. Since an accident in 1976 left him blinded in one eye, and without the perception of depth needed to work with molten glass, he has had no physical input into his work. After he drafts the initial designs, Chihuly hands responsibility for creating his pieces over to a team of blowers. His monumental works, frequently constructed from dozens or even hundreds of individual components, are among the largest glass sculptures ever created and are exhibited as works of installation or environmental art. In 1971 Chihuly founded the Pilchuck Glass School, now the largest institution of its kind in the world. Former students include Toots Zynsky, who uses a broad spectrum of decorative techniques to give her crimped, shell-like vessels a wide range of colored and patterned finishes.

Each element has a stippled or striated surface

AZURE AND JADE CHANDELIER The 130 free-blown blue and green glass elements of this sculpture designed by Dale Chihuly are supported on a steel armature. *2002. H:48 in (122 cm).*

Plantlike tendrils make up the piece

FLORAL CEILING (DETAIL) Dale Chihuly's team made more than 2,000 hand-blown glass flowers to create the *Fiori di Como* for the lobby of the Bellagio Hotel, Las Vegas in 1998. It was his largest work to date.

PERSIAN SET (BLUE) This complex and organic piece, made of seven free-blown blue pieces of glass with applied red rims, is one of many signature pieces by Dale Chihuly and his team. *1999. W:27 in (70 cm).*

CLEARLY OPTICAL

Optical glass, first available on a large scale from the 1940s, is a flawless glass used in the manufacture of lenses and prisms. Its fundamental quality is that it allows as much light as possible to pass into and through it. This has made it attractive to glass artists wanting to explore the intrinsic clarity of glass, or its reflective and refractive properties. Other makers have found alternative, but equally novel, ways in which to explore the properties of their medium.

Sidney Hutter has investigated the vase form more thoroughly than most contemporary glassmakers and studies his works from a decorative rather than a functional perspective. His compositions are built up of dozens of thin, transparent glass plates, cut and stacked to resemble a vase in silhouette

but in fact they are completely solid. To extend the boundaries of his chosen form, Hutter often removes sections from groups of plates in order to create impossibly top-heavy loads. Although the glass from which Hutter constructs these pieces is perfectly clear, he often uses pigmented glues. When viewed on a plane parallel with the surfaces of the plates, light passes directly through the clear glass without picking up any color. When viewed from any other direction, however, the dyed glues flood the vases with color, yielding a wide range of unexpected optical effects.

Hutter's choice of the vase shape represents a postmodern acknowledgment of the importance this form has assumed in the history of glassmaking. At the same time, however, he asserts its irrelevance in contemporary creative developments by making it completely nonfunctional.

TECHNICAL CHALLENGES

Many artists working with high-performance glass seem to revel in the technical challenges it presents. Colin Reid combines casting, cutting, and polishing to mimic natural forms such as rock, wood, and sand. His monumental Cipher Stone, cast to resemble Cotswold stone, has a magnifying lens set into one of its facets through which the viewer can make out chunks of text inscribed in English, Morse code, and binary. This stone is a reference to the Rosetta stone, updated for the digital age. Tom Patti's work, meanwhile, straddles a

The lens emphasizes the optical effects of the glass

R999 GLASS PIECE In this sculpture by Colin Reid, optical glass was cast into a mold where it picked up copper powder. The piece was then removed and the flat surfaces ground and polished on a machine. *2003.*

VASIFORM SCULPTURE This piece by Sidney Hutter is entitled *90 Degrees of 4 Colorwheel: Jerry Vision Vase #195.* It is made of clear glass plates stuck together with brightly colored glues. *2003. H:16 in (42 cm).*

The cut-out plate sections draw attention to the unusual construction of the piece

BLUE GLASS SCULPTURE This three-layered piece by Tom Patti entitled *Compacted Solarized Blue with Dual Ring* has an unusual convex base as a stand. *W:6 in (15 cm).*

boundary between art and engineering. He has developed a number of unique laminating and fusing techniques, transferring breakthroughs made in his architectural work to his glassmaking. Other innovations build on ancient techniques. Ronald Pennell, for example, uses a copper wheel to draw freehand sketches directly onto the surface of his glass vessels.

CZECH TRADITION
Glassmakers in the Czech Republic and Hungary have continued to build on their Bohemian heritage. Husband and wife team Stanislav Libensky and Jaraslava Brychtová first worked together in the 1950s. Their work is characterized by smooth surfaces and carefully modeled interior voids. As a professor at the Prague Academy

from 1963, Libensky influenced the cream of Czech glass artists. Frantsiek Vizner's solid blocks of colored glass, cast in subtly modified geometric shapes, clearly owe a debt to Libensky's work. Vizner's flawlessly smooth polished finishes stand in marked contrast to the textural edges of work by Hungarian sculptor Maria Lugossy. Yan Zoritchak, another Czech glassmaker of this period, settled in France in 1970 after studying under Libensky. Since the 1980s Zoritchak has produced smooth, clean-lined forms with plain outer surfaces and complex internal decoration, as in his *Messager de l'Espace* (Messenger from Space) series.

Czech glass was exhibited at various International Exhibitions, including Osaka in 1970, where it influenced glassmakers from around the world. Studios such as Studio Lhotsky—which specializes in cast glass—are widely known today.

ENGRAVED GLASS

As precision tools have become more accurate, glass artists have been able to achieve a wider range of effects using engraving and cutting techniques. Czech engraver Jiri Harcuba is the foremost exponent of glass portraiture. His extensive work includes three-dimensional depictions of artists and writers in blocks of clear glass. The features of the subjects are cut into the back of the glass block so that, when they are viewed from the front, they cast shadows on the perfectly flat surface.

In Scotland, Alison Kinnaird engraves figures on glass panels and solid blocks. Her more complex pieces combine Celtic knotwork with human figures, through which she passes light with optical fibers. Her use of dichroic glass produces intense colors while eliminating glare.

SPHERICAL VESSEL This cut, sandblasted, and polished dark green glass piece by the Czech glass artist Frantisek Vizner demonstrates his love of simple, geometric shapes and rich opaque color. *1970s. D:5 in (14.5 cm).*

Natural elements within the glass create an imaginary landscape

MESSAGER DE L'ESPACE This piece by Yan Zoritchak demonstrates the artist's preoccupation with the transparent and distorting qualities of glass. *2003. H:18 in (46 cm).*

A man and his dog are confronted by three figures, one of whom is holding a sunburst

FRANZ KAFKA'S PORTRAIT Jiri Harcuba's uses techniques such as diamond, stone, and copper wheel cutting for his engraved glass portraits. *1991. W:8½ in (21.5 cm).*

GREEN GLASS SCULPTURE This piece by Maria Lugossy is typical of her cast glass, which is characterized by muted colors, layering, and lenses. *1988. H:9¾ in (25 cm).*

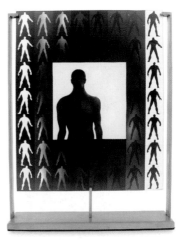

ECLIPSE Alison Kinnaird's engraved, sandblasted, and cased glass panel explores tone. It is adorned with figures and is mounted on a metal stand. *2001. Panel: H:11 in (29.5 cm).*

DOG DAYS A SUN FETISH Made by Karl Nordbruch and engraved by Ronald Pennell, this vessel is made from amethyst glass. Pennell's engravings are often concerned with past civilizations and cultures. *2003. H:8 in (20.5 cm).*

FIGURES AND MATERIALS

As the studio glass movement has matured, practitioners have begun to tackle more evocative themes. Human history, politics, and the relationship between people and their environment have all come under the scrutiny of glass artists with the confidence to explore such profound topics.

KILN FORMING AND CASTING

Describing himself as a "constructivist," Keith Cummings combines his cast and built glass forms with metals. Like many contemporary studio glassmakers attempting to reach beyond traditional vessel shapes, Cummings prefers to mold his forms in a kiln rather than blow them. His observational work draws on the landscape and ancient heritage of his native England. Alfred's Mirror, inspired by a 9th-century jewel owned by King Alfred, demonstrates how the intricate work required of the contemporary glassmaker compares with that of a jeweler. During his tenure at the University of Wolverhampton (previously Stourbridge College of Art), Cummings has helped nurture some of the finest talent on the contemporary glass scene.

David Reekie trained at Stourbridge during the late 1960s, where Cummings instilled in him the historical traditions of glass casting. Despite its status as a preeminent technique in the contemporary studio movement, glass casting was known in ancient Rome and has a longer history even than blowing. Reekie uses lost-wax casting—another Roman innovation—to produce his molds. The process of pouring, setting, and cooling the glass is both time-consuming and inherently risky; a single trapped air bubble can be enough to destroy hours of work.

The polished glass ovoid surmounting the opaque section resembles a winter sun

ALFRED'S MIRROR Keith Cummings's piece combines kiln-formed opaque glass, which looks almost like jade, with inlaid copper wire and bands. *2003. L:14 in (37 cm).*

The piece is inlaid with glass faux pearls

SEASON For this piece, Keith Cummings used cast kiln-formed opaque glass with metal additions, with cast and polished glass. *2003. W:5 in (13 cm).*

The new significance of glass as art has been explored by a number of artists. Dutch glassmaker Dick van Wijk combines geometric and figural forms in glass with more traditional sculptural materials such as marble, bronze, and steel. In France Georges and Monique Stahl work together, juxtaposing ethereal glass formations that represent figures, water, and air with hunks of metal, representing earth.

In the United States, William Morris uses glass to scrutinize the widening temporal rift that separates humanity from its pagan roots. Since working as the gaffer on Dale Chihuly's blowing team in the early 1980s, Morris has produced glass in eerily archaic forms, many of them based on ritual vessels such as the rhyton and shamanic rattles. His decorative techniques include acid-washing, etching, and the application of powdered glass and other minerals to give his work the semblance of great age. An important secondary theme in Morris's work is the repudiation of modern man's relationship with nature, and a desire to return to a more innocent age. To this end, Morris practices traditional bow-hunting skills in pursuit of a "pure" confrontation between man and beast.

These sentiments manifest

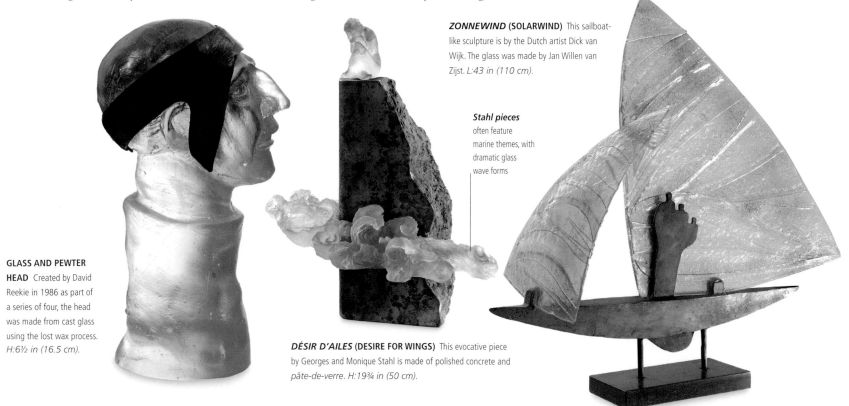

ZONNEWIND (SOLARWIND) This sailboat-like sculpture is by the Dutch artist Dick van Wijk. The glass was made by Jan Willen van Zijst. *L:43 in (110 cm).*

Stahl pieces often feature marine themes, with dramatic glass wave forms

GLASS AND PEWTER HEAD Created by David Reekie in 1986 as part of a series of four, the head was made from cast glass using the lost wax process. *H:6½ in (16.5 cm).*

DÉSIR D'AILES (DESIRE FOR WINGS) This evocative piece by Georges and Monique Stahl is made of polished concrete and pâte-de-verre. *H:19¾ in (50 cm).*

PAUL STANKARD ORB This unique paperweight from the Whitman Botanical series has an internal cased lampwork design of a honeycomb, two bees, moss, flowers, and lilies. *2004. D:4 in (11 cm).*

CROW VESSEL This William Morris urn consists of blown glass with glass powder coloring. Its amphora shape shows Classical inspiration, which is typical of Morris' work. *1999. H:20 in (51 cm).*

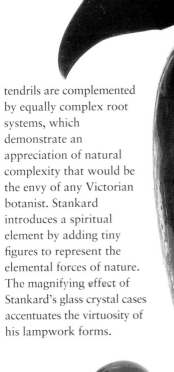

Thin canes of colored glass are melted and shaped by an oxyacetylene torch to produce a botanical picture

themselves in Morris's glass in the form of detailed depictions of birds and deer heads. The antediluvian aspect of Morris's work is made all the more jarring by his use of glass—an inherently fragile material that ancient cultures would have found impossible to manipulate into the forms that Morris achieves.

Fellow American artist Paul Stankard also relies on nature as his muse but, whereas Morris presents natural forms in the context of human interference, Stankard isolates them in clear glass cases and spheres, as if exhibiting natural beauty as an artwork in its own right. Stankard's expertise in the lampworking technique, where rods of colored glass are heated and engineered into precise shapes, is unsurpassed. His detailed flowers, leaves, and

tendrils are complemented by equally complex root systems, which demonstrate an appreciation of natural complexity that would be the envy of any Victorian botanist. Stankard introduces a spiritual element by adding tiny figures to represent the elemental forces of nature. The magnifying effect of Stankard's glass crystal cases accentuates the virtuosity of his lampwork forms.

GLASS COMBINATIONS

In the 1980s and 1990s glassmaking started to lose its status as a craft and was increasingly seen as an art form. Museums added contemporary glass to their collections and glassmakers began to experiment as they realized that, if something made from glass could be seen as a sculpture, there was no reason why glass could not be combined with other materials.

Designers such as Gernot Schlufer and Georges and Monique Stahl began combining concrete, petrified wood, metal, and marble with glass to create sculptures that sometimes do not appear to be made from glass at all. The new trend has been taken further by Jorg Zimmerman, who blows glass through netting to create inventive shapes.

The rough texture of the wood contrasts with the smooth glass

Prehistoric sources such as cave paintings inform Morris's work

LILAC-BREASTED ROLLER BIRD The work of Austrian Gernot Schlufer celebrates the unspoiled natural beauty and diverse animal and bird life of the Alps. *c.2000. H:8 in (21 cm).*

GLASS GALLERY

Postmodern glass is brightly colored, playful, and often witty. Studio art glass in particular displays freedom of form and technical experiment. As such pieces are purely decorative, they do not need to conform to any traditional functional shape. The United States and Italy lead the way in innovation.

KEY

1. Luigi Camozzo blown glass vase, with vertical canes. H:7 in (18 cm). ② **2.** Sculpture with hand-painted decoration by Ulrica Hydman-Vallien for Kosta Boda. 1999. H:15 in (37 cm). ② **3.** No. 8801 by Jörg Zimmerman of Germany. D:13½ in (34 cm). ③ **4.** Murrine cased vase by Vittorio Ferro at Fratelli Pagnin of Murano. 2004. H:9½ in (24 cm). ② **5.** Orange opaque half-globe and quarter-globe in clear glass by Milos Balgavy. D:9¾ in (25 cm). ⑤ **6.** Keith Brocklehurst pâte-de-verre bowl, legs cast with the piece. 1980s. D:7¾ in (19.5 cm). ③ **7.** Multicolored vase by Bertil Vallien for Kosta Boda. c.1985. H:8 in (20 cm). ③ **8.** Zip bowl by Kjell Engman. ① **9.** Bowl by Bertil Vallien for Kosta Boda. c.1980. H:4¾ in (12 cm). ① **10.** Vase by Philip Baldwin and Monica Guggisberg. H:18½ in (47 cm). ④

2 Handpainted sculpture

3 Jörg Zimmerman sculpture

4 Murrine vase

1 Luigi Camozzo vase

6 Keith Brocklehurst bowl

5 Globe sections

7 Bertil Vallien vase

8 Zipper bowl

9 Bertil Vallien bowl

10 Philip Baldwin and Monica Guggisberg vase

11 Dale Chihuly piece

12 Danny Perkins sculpture

11. A five-piece Harrison Red Basket Set by Dale Chihuly. 2003. H:11 in (28 cm). ⑥
12. Malibu, blown glass sculpture with painted decoration by Danny Perkins. 2005. H:47 in (119.5 cm). ⑤ **13.** Flaring bowl by Kjell Engman for Kosta Boda. W:10¼ in (25.5 cm). ① **14.** Vase by Alberto Donà, the clear glass encased with multicolored threads and strings. 2000. H:15 in (38.5 cm). ② **15.** Handmade vase by Licata. H:16 in (41 cm). ② **16.** Simon Moore jug with fins. 1986. H:13½ in (34 cm). ② **17.** One of Dante Marioni Green Trio of blown forms. 2001. H:29 in (73.5 cm). ⑥ **18.** Dinosaur by Lino Tagliapietra. 2003. H:15 in (38 cm). ⑦ **19.** Borek Sipek vase with ceramic bowl and glass stem. 1980s. H:24 in (60 cm). ② **20.** Vase by Gianni Versace for Venini. 1988. H:9¾ in (25 cm). ① **21.** Thick-walled three-sided vase with multicolored bands cased in clear glass by Fulvio Bianconi for Venini. 1992. H:10 in (25 cm). ⑤

13 *Kjell Engman bowl*

14 *Alberto Donà vase*

16 *Fin jug*

15 *Licata vase*

17 *Dante Marioni form*

18 *Dinosaur*

19 *Borek Sipek vase*

20 *Gianni Versace vase*

21 *Fulvio Bianconi vase*

LIGHTING

DURING THE LATTER HALF OF THE 20TH CENTURY, LIGHTING BECAME AN
INCREASINGLY IMPORTANT AND EXCITING FIELD OF DESIGN. IT STARTED AS
A VEHICLE FOR INNOVATION BUT BECAME A QUEST FOR QUALITY OF LIGHT.

85 LAMPS CHANDELIER
Designed by Rody Graumans for the
Dutch The Product Matters Company,
the chandelier is made of 85 15-watt
light bulbs. The individual parts of
this lamp are completely plain
but the combination makes an
opulent chandelier. *1993.
H:43½ in (110 cm).*

EXPERIMENTAL IDEAS

While tables, chairs, vases, and other objects
had been designed and made for centuries,
electric lights were still a relative novelty at
the beginning of the 20th century. The
fact that designers were free from the
weight of history in this respect
seems to have encouraged them
to express many of their most
creative ideas through the medium
of lighting design.

It was the designers of the 1960s who
really opened up the world of lighting design,
as the widespread use of plastic gave them a
wonderfully malleable material to work with.
Bright colors and bold shapes were used to
create designs where the actual light emitted
from the bulb was of secondary importance
to the object itself.

SOBRIETY AND INDUSTRY

The Middle East oil crisis of the early
1970s pushed the price of plastic up to
prohibitive levels, however, and
the levity that ran through
earlier lighting design soon
disappeared. A new, more
staid approach dominated
the early years of the 1970s as
designers returned to a more rigorous,
rational style of design (one that was eventually
to be labeled High-Tech). This reflected a new

Lamps with chips are touch-sensitive.
When lightly touched, they create a small
symphony of sounds

ALDA LAMP Of multicolored polyurethane resin,
this lamp was designed by Gaetano Pesce and
named after his mother. The brightly colored resin
lamp is made in large or small forms, with bells that
jingle to the touch or electronic chips. There is also a
wall sconce. *2004. H:24 in (71 cm).*

sobriety that had swept through Western society
following the fall in financial markets and the
uncertainty that surrounded the future of the
world's energy supplies.

By the late 1970s, however, this cautious and
considered approach to design—one that gave us
numerous lamps of geometric form produced in
muted colors—was submerged as a new generation
of designers developed a more abrasive and
energetic style. This attitude, particularly apparent
in Italy, was a clear sign of the frustration that was
felt by young people throughout the West whose
prospects, as the 1970s wore on, did not appear
to be improving.

Designers such as Gaetano Pesce, Alessandro
Mendini, and Michele De Lucchi produced lights
that defied convention by using a motley collection
of materials and loud, discordant color. Lamps no
longer looked like mathematicians' diagrams but
like artists' sketches. The Memphis group, led by
Ettore Sottsass, took this look into the 1980s,
although their work was a little more light-hearted
and less confrontational than the lighting designs
of a few years earlier.

As the 1980s developed, and consumer confidence
returned, lighting design became more playful once
again. However, in contrast to the straightforward,
fun-loving products of the Sixties, the lights of the
1980s were a little more cerebral in their design.
Many lights took on an anthropomorphic element
as sophisticated technologies made it possible to
create more complex forms.

Not all designers during the 1980s were
infatuated with new technologies, however. Indeed,
many made a conscious effort to avoid the cutting
edge and return to the virtues of craft. This
movement, variously known as the studio
movement, the craft revival, or (later on in the

INGO MAURER

When discussing lighting design of the later decades of the 20th century, one name stands out above all others—that of German designer Ingo Maurer. Having dedicated his career solely to lighting design since he set up Studio M in 1966, Maurer has created many of the most innovative and enduring designs of recent years.

As comfortable operating at the cutting edge of technology as producing sculptural pieces from primitive materials, Maurer is a designer of remarkable dexterity and invention. In reference to his monogamous relationship with lighting design, Maurer has said that "I have always been fascinated by the light bulb because it is the perfect meeting of industry and poetry."

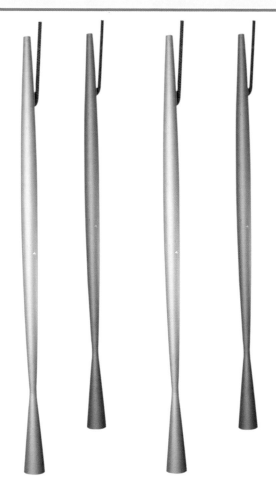

FIVE LIGHT FIXTURES These elongated brushed-steel forms, complete with purple nylon cords, were designed by Philippe Starck for the Paramount Hotel in New York. *H:47½ in (120.5 cm).*

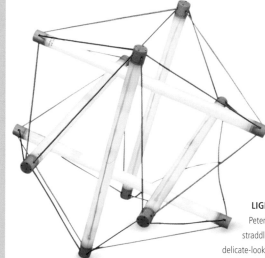

LIGHT STRUCTURE Ingo Maurer and Peter Hamburger's punning floor lamp design straddles modernism and postmodernism. The delicate-looking structure comprises tubular bulbs, acrylic, and electric cable. *1983. W:18 in (45.5 cm).*

BɪBɪBɪ TABLE LAMP Designed for Design M, this table lamp is constructed of porcelain, metal, and plastic. The styles of Ingo Maurer lamps are part art and part lighting. *1982. H:21¾ in (55 cm).*

decade) neo-brutalism or the salvage look, was a rebellion against the rampant consumerism that so defined the 1980s. Often using recycled objects or materials, designers pursuing this style worked independently and their output was on a very small scale. Lights that fall into this category often resemble sculptures that just happen to have a bulb or two attached.

MOOD LIGHTING

These whimsical and often wild designs were little seen during the 1990s, as lighting design became a subject that was approached with increasing gravity. Research began to show that lighting could seriously affect people's mood, productivity, and eyesight. The increased awareness of the psychological and physical impact of artificial lighting led designers to concentrate more on the quality of light from the lamps than on the objects themselves. A strand of wit pervaded the 1990s (notably in the inventive, amusing lighting of Droog, the Dutch design collective), but the fantastical designs that flourished in the 1970s and 1980s soon died out.

The reused materials are part of the salvage look

A NITE ON LINDQUIST RIDGE TABLE LAMP Designed by Gary Knox Bennett of California, the lamp is constructed with stovepipe housing with five flexible black and white shaft fixtures. It is inscribed with the title and the mark "In Oakland/GKB/ Anno 90." *H:22 in (56 cm).*

The metal frame has a lightly textured finish

NR 607 HALOGEN LAMP Designed by Gino Sarfatti for Arteluce, this pioneering table lamp is typical of the High-Tech movement and was the first to use halogen bulbs. *c.1971. H:12¼ in (31 cm).*

ITALIAN WIRELESS WL01C TABLE LAMP Designed by Andrea Branzi and distributed by Design Gallery Milan, the lamp is battery powered, creating a modern effect without the use of cords, cables, or wires. The main body is open, revealing the rice-paper shade. *1996. H:16¼ in (41 cm).*

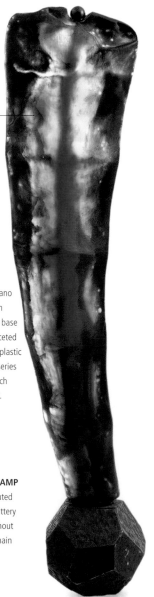

The shade is made of multicolored polyurethane plastic with unique coloring

***OSSO* TABLE LAMP** Gaetano Pesce designed this American limited production lamp. The base is of shaped and textured faceted cast metal and supports the plastic shade. The lamp is one of a series of ten different examples, each with random coloring. *1989. H:37½ in (95 cm).*

METALWARE

FROM SOLIDLY ARCHITECTURAL FORMS TO GOSSAMER WEBS, POSTMODERN
METALWARE TAKES ON DIVERSE FORMS. IT IS A BLEND OF HISTORICALLY
INFORMED DESIGN AND NEW IDEAS.

SCULPTURAL DESIGNS

What Peter Voulkos achieved for ceramic artists,
Albert Paley has done for the humble blacksmith.
In 1995 he became the first metal sculptor to
receive the Institute Honors Award, the highest
accolade awarded to non-architects by the
American Institute of Architects. Working
primarily in milled steel, Paley produces
monumental sculpture, architectural furniture
such as door handles, and smaller pieces like
paperweights and candlesticks. He has completed
many prestigious public commissions, including
the Portal Gates at the Renwick Gallery of the
Smithsonian Institution and Synergy, a ceremonial
archway in Philadelphia. Paley's work is not
mass-produced and tends to be site-specific,
incorporating decorative elements designed
to complement their immediate environment.

Designers with architectural backgrounds
have dominated postmodern and contemporary
metalware design, often working to commissions
from influential design houses such as Alessi and
Swid Powell.

SCALED-DOWN ARCHITECTURE

The prolific architect Robert Venturi, active in so
many spheres, produced a pair of candlesticks for
Swid Powell based on cutout silhouette designs
in a similar vein to his archly ironic series of
chairs for Knoll. Although based on conventional
columnar forms, Venturi's candlesticks confound
expectation by existing solely along two
perpendicular planes rather than as solid
tubes. In effect, Venturi turns the traditional
candlestick inside out.

Husband-and-wife team Robert and Trix
Haussmann designed several metal objects,
including an abstract aluminum chandelier for
the Swiss Pavilion at the Osaka International
Exhibition in 1970. The tiny candlesticks they
produced for Swid Powell during the 1980s
exhibit a stylized geometry that is reminiscent
of Art Deco. Steven Holl's 1986 candlesticks
for the same company have a verdigris-style finish
suggestive of age and wear. A cordlike strand of
metal snakes down from the sconce to
the base, giving the impression that
the candle is powered by electricity.

SILVER-PLATED CANDLESTICKS Robert
Venturi designed this pair of candlesticks
in two flat planes at right angles to one
another, blurring the distinction between
two and three dimensions. They were
produced by Swid Powell. *1986.*

SWID POWELL CANDLESTICKS Designed by
Robert and Trix Haussmann, these small silver-plated
candlesticks are stepped with a small base tapering
upward to a wider top. *1980s. H:2¾ in (7 cm).*

The brass insert is
shaped at the top and
flows down to the base

SUNRISE TALL CANDLESTICKS Designed by Albert Paley for the American
Ballet Theatre, the candlesticks are made of forged and fabricated steel with
brass inserts. *1993. H:20½ in (52 cm).*

The twisted strand of metal suggests the candle is powered by electricity

PAIR OF CANDLESTICKS Designed by Steven Holl and produced by Swid Powell, the candlesticks have a metal verdigris-style finish. The underside of the bases have a stamped facsimile signature. *1986. H:20¾ in (51 cm).*

CREVASSE VASES Designed by Zaha Hadid for Alessi, this pair of sculptural, undecorated vases is made of polished stainless steel. *2005.*

The design is influenced by Hadid's architectural training

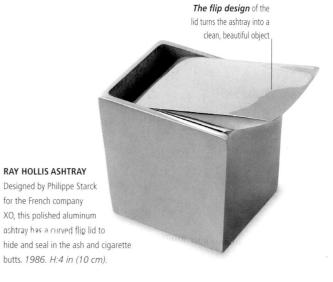

BLOW UP CITRUS BASKET Designed by Fernando and Humberto Campana for Alessi, this is part of a set of tableware. The lengths of stainless steel wires create a unique holder. *2004.*

The flip design of the lid turns the ashtray into a clean, beautiful object

RAY HOLLIS ASHTRAY Designed by Philippe Starck for the French company XO, this polished aluminum ashtray has a curved flip lid to hide and seal in the ash and cigarette butts. *1986. H:4 in (10 cm).*

The Italian design giant Alessi has been behind many of the most iconic pieces of mass-produced metalware of recent years. Through collaborations with the most innovative designers, the firm has developed a range of individualistic products. Iraqi-born architect Zaha Hadid, now settled in Britain, unveiled her Crevasse vase in 2005. Its sheer sides defer to the decorative properties of the stainless steel from which it is constructed. There is no concession to surface decoration—the involvement of the designer is evident only in the twisted, tapered form that resembles an awkward skyscraper.

The São Paolo–based Campana Brothers—lawyer Humberto and architect Fernando—designed the Blow Up series of products for Alessi in 2004. The range comprises a citrus bowl, trivet, basket, and centerpiece bowl that defy the concept of form. Constructed from a series of steel rods that appear to be suspended in space or bound by magnetism, the effect is every bit as striking as the exploded shed Cornelia Parker exhibited under the title *Cold Dark Matter* in 1991.

Many recent innovations in metalwork have come from improved materials and techniques. Others have been occasioned by changing social mores. The aluminum Ray Hollis ashtray, designed by Philippe Starck for XO, is a product of the increasing controversy surrounding smoky environments. A simple click of the lid seals any lit butts within the bowl, starving them of oxygen and so extinguishing them. It also prevents smoke and ash smells from escaping into the room. This is an

ashtray with non-smokers in mind—a design oxymoron. After working as an interior designer during the 1970s, Starck became interested in product design, founding Starck Product in 1979. His irreverently playful approach has won commissions from many of the biggest names in modern manufacturing.

ALESSI'S TEA & COFFEE PIAZZA SERVICES

Alessi became one of the first companies to produce architect-designed homeware when Alessandro Mendini commissioned the Tea and Coffee Piazza services in 1979. Robert Venturi contributed subtly engraved and gilded forms on a tray with a pattern based on Michelangelo's pavement at the Piazza Campidoglio in Rome. Japanese architect Kazumasa Yamashita came up with stark geometric forms with spindly spouts and knops in the shapes of letters representing the contents of each vessel. Charles Jencks, an American architect who has done much to clarify postmodern architecture through his

extensive writing on the subject, looked back to ancient Greek columns for his service. The four component pieces of Jencks's set, presented on a stepped tray, each exhibit subtly different fluting techniques. He also uses volutes and capitals based on the Greek Doric order. Despite these authentic touches, Jencks distorts his columnar forms by tapering, pinching, breaking, or otherwise manipulating them in an amiable parody. The Tea and Coffee Piazza services were exhibited in Milan in 1983 and a followup range called Tea and Coffee Towers, comprising 22 distinct services, was released in 2002.

The fluting recalls the shafts of Classical columns

TEA AND COFFEE PIAZZA SERVICE Designed by Charles Jencks, this set is an Alessi limited edition of 99 copies. It comprises coffeepot, teapot, milk jug, sugar bowl, and tray. *1983.*

USEFUL ADDRESSES

MUSEUMS AND GALLERIES

Australia
Powerhouse Museum
500 Harris Street Ultimo
PO Box: K346 Haymarket
Sydney NSW 1238
Tel: 011 61 2 92170111
www.phm.gov.au

Austria
Museen der Stadt Wien
Karlsplatz
A-1040 Vienna
Tel: 011 43 1 50587470
www.museum-vienna.at

Österreichisches Museum
für Angewandte Kunst
Stubenring 5
A-1010 Vienna
Tel: 011 43 1 711360
www.mak.at

Belgium
Musée Horta
Amerikaans Straate/rue Américaine
23–35, 1060 Brussels
Tel: 011 32 2 543 04 90
www.hortamuseum.be

Canada
Art Gallery of Greater Victoria
1040 Moss Street
Victoria
British Columbia V8V 4P1
Tel: (250) 384-4101
www.aggv.bc.ca

Glenbow Museum
130 9th Avenue SE
Calgary, Alberta T2G OP3
Tel: (403) 268-4100
www.glenbow.org

Ross Memorial Museum
188 Montague Street
St Andrews, New Brunswick E5B 1J2
Tel: (506) 529-5124

Royal Ontario Museum
100 Queen's Park
Toronto
Ontario
Tel: (416) 586-8000
www.rom.on.ca

Denmark
The National Museum of Denmark
Frederiksholms Kanal 12
1220 Copenhagen K
Tel: 011 45 3313 4411
www.natmus.dk

Egypt
Egyptian Museum
Tahrir Square, Cairo
Tel: 011 20 202 5782448
www.egyptianmuseum.gov.eg

Finland
Alvar Aalto Museum
Alvar Aallon katu 7, Jyväskylä
Tel: 011 358 14 624809
www.alvaraalto.fi/museum

Designmuseo
Korkeavuorenkatu 23, 00130 Helsinki
Tel: 011 358 9 6220540
www.designmuseum.fi

National Museum of Finland
Mannerheimintie 34, Helsinki
Tel: 011 358 09 40 501
www.nba.fi

France
Musée des Arts Décoratifs
Palais du Louvre
107 rue de Rivoli, 75001 Paris
Tel: 011 33 1 44 55 57 50
www.paris.org

Musée de L'École de Nancy
36–38 rue de Sergent Blandan
54000 Nancy
Tel: 011 33 3 83 40 14 8
www.nancy.fr

Musée du Louvre
Pyramide-Cour Napoléon, A.P. 34
36 quai du Louvre, 75058 Paris
Tel: 011 33 1 40 20 55 55
www.louvre.fr

Musée des Tissus
34 rue de la Charité, Lyon
Tel: 011 33 78 38 42 00
www.musee-des-tissus.com

Germany
Bauhaus
Gropiusallee 38, 06846 Dessau
Tel: 011 49 340 65 08 0
www.bauhaus-dessau.de

Germanisches Nationalmuseum
Kartäusergasse 1, D - 90402 Nürnberg
Tel: 011 49 911 13310
www.gnm.de

Staatliche Kunstsammlungen Dresden
Dresdner Residenzschloss
Taschenberg 2, 01067 Dresden
Tel: 011 49 3 51 49 14 20 00
www.skd-dresden.de

Vitra Design Museum
Charles-Eames-str. 1
D-79576 Weil-am-Rhein
Tel: 011 49 7621 702 3200
www.design-museum.de

Italy
Museo di Palazzo Davanzati
Via di Porta Rossa 13, 50122 Florence
Tel: 011 39 552 388 610
www.polomuseale.firenze.it/davanzati

Japan
Tokyo National Museum
13-9 Ueno Park, Taito-ku, Tokyo 110-8712
Tel: 011 81 3 3822 1111
www. tnm.jp

Netherlands
Rijksmuseum
Jan Luijkenstraat 1, Amsterdam
Tel: 011 31 20 6747000
www.rijksmuseum.nl

Norway
Kunstindustrimuseet
St Olavs gate 1, Oslo
Tel: 011 47 22 036540
www.nasjonalmuseet.no

Museet for samtidskunst
Bankplassen 4, Oslo
Tel: 011 47 22 862210
www.nasjonalmuseet.no

Russia
State Hermitage Museum
Palace Embankment
38 Dvortsovaya Naberezhnaya
St. Petersburg
Tel: 011 7 812 1109625
www.hermitagemuseum.org

South Africa
Stellenbosch Museum
Ryneveld Street, Stellenbosch, 7599
Tel: 011 27 21 887 2948
www.museums.org.za/stellmus

Spain
Museo Art Nouveau y Art Deco
Calle Gibralta 14, 37008 Salamanca
Tel: 011 34 92 3121425
www.museocasalis.org

Sweden
National Museum
Södra Blasieholmshamnen, Stockholm
Tel: 011 46 8 51954300
www.nationalmuseum.se

United Kingdom
American Museum
Claverton Manor, Bath BA2 7BD
Tel: 011 44 1225 460503
www.americanmuseum.org

Cheltenham Art Gallery and Museum
Clarence Street, Cheltenham GL50 3JT
Tel: 011 44 1242 237431
www.cheltenhammuseum.org.uk

Design Museum
Shad Thames, London SE1 2YD
Tel: 011 44 20 7940 8782
www.designmuseum.org

Geffrye Museum
Kingsland Road, London E2 8EA
Tel: 011 44 20 7739 9893
www.geffrye-museum.org.uk

Hunterian Museum and Art Gallery and Mackintosh House Gallery
82 Hillhead Street
University of Glasgow, Glasgow G12 8QQ
Tel: 011 44 141 330 4221
www.hunterian.gla.ac.uk

Victoria and Albert Museum
Cromwell Road, London SW7 2RL
Tel: 011 44 20 7942 2000
www.vam.ac.uk

The Wallace Collection
Hertford House, Manchester Square
London W1U 3BN
Tel: 011 44 20 7563 9500
www.wallacecollection.org

William Morris Gallery
Walter House, Lloyd Park, Forest Road
London E17 4PP
Tel: 011 44 20 8527 3782
www.walthamforest.gov.uk/wmg

United States
American Folk Art Museum
45 West 53rd Street
New York, NY 10019
Tel: (212) 265-1040
www.folkartmuseum.org

Delaware Art Museum
2301 Kentmere Parkway
Wilmington, DE 19806
Tel: (302) 571-9590
www.delart.org

The DeWitt Wallace Decorative Arts Museum
The Colonial Williamsburg Foundation,
P.O. Box 1776
Williamsburg, VA 23187
Tel: (757) 229-1000
www.colonialwilliamsburg.org

Elbert Hubbard Roycroft Museum
P.O. Box 472
363 Oakwood Avenue
East Aurora, NY 14052
Tel: (716) 652-4735
www.roycrofter.com/museum.htm

High Museum of Art
1280 Peachtree Street, N.E.
Atlanta, GA 30309
Tel: (404) 703-4444
www.high.org

Isabella Gardner Museum
280 The Fenway
Boston, MA 02115
Tel: (617) 566-1401
www.gardnermuseum.org

John Paul Getty Museum
Getty Center
Los Angeles, CA 90049-1687
Tel: (310) 440-7300
www.getty.edu

The Metropolitan Museum of Art
1000 Fifth Avenue
New York, NY 10028-0198
Tel: (212) 535-7710
www.metmuseum.org

The Museum of Modern Art
11 West 53rd Street
New York, NY 10019-5497
Tel: (212) 708-9400
www.moma.org

National Ceramic Museum
7327 Ceramic Road N. E.
Roseville, OH 43777
Tel: (740) 697-7021
www.ceramiccenter.org

Philadelphia Museum of Art
26th Street and the
Benjamin Franklin Parkway
Philadelphia, PA 19130
Tel: (215) 763-8100
www.philamuseum.org

Smithsonian Institution
Washington, DC 20013-7012
Tel: (202) 633 1000
www.si.edu

Stickley Museum
300 Orchard Street
Fayetteville, NY 13104
Tel: (315) 682-5500
www.stickleymuseum.org

Winterthur Museum
Winterthur, DE 19735
Tel: (302) 888-4907
www.winterthur.org

The Wolfsonian Museum of Modern Art
and Design
1001 Washington Avenue
Miami Beach, FL 33139
Tel: (305) 531-1001
www.wolfsonian.org

HISTORIC BUILDINGS

Austria
Schönbrunn Palace
Schönbrunner Schloßstraße 47, Vienna
011 43 1 81113 239
www.schoenbrunn.at

Belgium
Hôtel Solvay
224 avenue Louise, 1050 Brussels

Denmark
Rosenborg Castle
Øster Voldgade 4, 1350 Copenhagen K
Tel: 011 45 3315 3286
www.rosenborg-slot.dk

France
Château de Fontainebleau
77300 Fontainebleau
Tel: 011 33 1 60 71 50 70
www.musee-chateau-fontainebleau.fr

Château de Groussay
Rue de Versailles
78490 Montfort l'Amaury
Tel: 011 33 1 34 86 94 79

Château de Malmaison
Avenue du château
92 500 Rueil-Malmaison
Tel: 011 33 1 41 29 05 55
www.chateau-malmaison.fr

Château de Versailles
834-78008 Versailles
www.chateauversailles.fr

Hôtel de Soubise
60 Rue des Francs-Bourgeois
75003 Paris
Tel: 011 33 1 40 27 60 97

Germany
Neue Rezidenz, Bamberg
Domplatz 8, 96049 Bamberg
Tel: 011 49 89 179 080
www.schloesser.bayern.de

Charlottenhof
Sansoucci Park, Potsdam
Tel: 011 49 331 9694223

Schloß Charlottenburg
Spandauer Damm 20
Luisenplatz Berlin 14059
Tel: 011 49 331 9694202
www.schlosscharlottenburg.de

Schloß Neuschwanstein
Neuschwansteinstraße 20
87645 Schwangau
Tel: 011 49 8362 939 88-0
www.schloesser.bayern.de

Schloß Nymphenburg
Eingang 19
80638 München
Tel: 011 49 89 1 79 080
www.schloesser.bayern.de

Italy
Pitti Palace
Piazza Pitti 1
50125 Florence
Tel: 011 39 552 388 610
www.polomuseale.firenze.it

Reale Palace
Piazza Castello, Turin
Tel: 011 39 114 361 455
www.piemonte-emozioni.it/cultura/eng/
residenze_sabaude/pal_reale

Netherlands
Schröder House
Prins Hendriklaan 50
Utrecht
Tel: 011 31 030 2362 310

Portugal
Palacio Nacional de Queluz
Queluz, Lisbon
Tel: 011 351 214 343 860
www.ippar.pt/monumentos/palacio_queluz

Russia
Summer Palace
Letny Sad, 191186 St Petersburg
Tel: 011 7 812 314-0374
www.saint-petersburg.com

Pavlovsk Palace
Pavlovsk
St. Petersburg
Tel: 011 7 812 4702155
www.pavlovskart.spb.ru

Spain
Palacio Nacional Madrid
Calle Bailén, 28071 Madrid
Tel: 011 34 91 4548800
www.patrimonionacional.es

Sweden
Drottningholm Palace
178 02 Drottningholm
Tel: 011 46 8 4026280
www.royalcourt.se

Gripsholm Castle
647 31 Mariefred
Tel: 011 46 159 10194
www.royalcourt.se

The Royal Palace
Slottsbacken 1, Gamla Stan
Stockholm
Tel: 011 46 8 4026130
www.royalcourt.se

United Kingdom
Castle Howard
York, North Yorkshire Y060 7DA
Tel: 011 44 1653 648444
www.castlehoward.co.uk

Georgian House
7 Charlotte Square
Edinburgh EH2 4DR
Tel: 011 44 131 226 3318
www.nts.org.uk

Harewood House
Moor House
Harewood Estate, Harewood
Leeds LS17 9LQ
Tel: 011 44 113 218 1010
www.harewood.org

Hill House (The)
Upper Colquhoun Street
Helensburgh
Glasgow G84 9AJ
Tel: 011 44 1436 673900
www.nts.org.uk

Lotherton Hall
Lotherton Lane, Aberford
Leeds LS25 3EB
Tel: 011 44 113 2813259
www.leedsgov.co.uk

Osterley Park House
Isleworth
Middlesex TW7 4RB
Tel: 011 44 20 8232 5050
www.osterleypark.org.uk

The Red House
Red House Lane
Bexleyheath
DA6 8JF
Tel: 011 44 20 8304 9878
www.nationaltrust.org.uk

Rodmarton Manor
Cirencester
Gloucestershire
GL7 6PF
Tel: 011 44 1285 841253
www.rodmarton-manor.co.uk

The Royal Pavilion
Brighton BN1 1EE
Tel: 011 44 1273 292820
www.royalpavilion.org.uk

Standen
West Hoathly Road
East Grinstead
Sussex RH19 4NE
Tel: 011 44 1342 323029
www.nationaltrust.org.uk

Strawberry Hill
St. Mary's College
Waldegrave Road
Twickenham
TW1 4SX
Tel: 011 44 20 8240 4000

Temple Newsam House
Temple Newsam
Leeds LS15 0AD
Tel: 011 44 113 2645535
www.leedsgov.uk

United States
The Gamble House
4 Westmoreland Place
Pasadena, CA 91103
Tel: (626) 793-3334
www.gamblehouse.org

Marston House
3525 Seventh Avenue
San Diego, CA 92103
Tel: (619) 298-3142
www.sandiegohistory.org/mainpages/
locate3.htm

Nathaniel Russell House
51 Meeting Street
Charleston, SC 29402
Tel: (843) 723-1159
www.historiccharleston.org

Robie House
5757 S. Woodlawn Avenue
University of Chicago
Chicago, IL
Tel: (708) 848-1976
www.wrightplus.org/robiehouse

The Stickley Museum
at Craftsman Farms
2352 Rt. 10-West, #5
Morris Plains, NJ 07950
Tel: (973) 540 1165
www.stickleymuseum.org

FURTHER READING

Alessi, Alberto, *The Dream Factory: Alessi Since 1921* Electa/Alessi, Milan, 2001.

Andrews, John, *Arts and Crafts Furniture* Antique Collectors' Club Woodbridge, 2005.

Anscombe, Isabelle, *Arts & Crafts Style* Phaidon Press Ltd., London and New York, 1991.

Arwas, Victor, *Art Deco Sculpture* Academy Editions, London, 1995.

Arwas, Victor, *Art Deco* Academy Editions, London, 1992.

Aslin, Elizabeth, *19th Century English Furniture* Faber and Faber, London, 1962.

Baker, Fiona & Keith, *20th Century Furniture* Carlton Books, London, 2000.

Bangert, Albrecht and Karl Michael Armer, *80s Style* Thames & Hudson, London, 1990.

Battersby, Martin, *The Decorative Thirties* The Herbert Press, London, 1988.

Battersby, Martin, *The Decorative Twenties* The Herbert Press, London, 1988.

Benton, Charlotte, Tim Benton & Ghislaine Wood (eds.), *Art Deco 1910 to 1939* V&A Publications, London, 2003.

Casey, Andrew, *20th Century Ceramic Designers in Britain* Antique Collectors' Club, Woodbridge, 2001.

Duncan, Alastair (ed.), *Encyclopedia of Art Deco* Headline Books, London, 1988.

Duncan, Alastair, *Modernism* Norwest Corporation, Minneapolis, 1998.

Fahr-Becker, Gabriele, *Wiener Werkstatte* Benedikt Taschen Verlag, Köln, 1995.

Fiell, Charlotte and Peter, *1000 Chairs* Benedikt Taschen Verlag, Cologne, London, Paris etc., 1997.

Fiell, Charlotte and Peter, *Design of the 20th Century* Benedikt Taschen Verlag, Cologne, London, New York etc., 1999.

Fiell, Charlotte and Peter, *Modern Furniture Classics* Thames & Hudson, London, 1991 & 2001.

Fisher, Volker (ed.), *Design Now* Prestel Verlag, Munich, 1989.

Fleming, John and Hugh Honour, *Penguin Dictionary of Decorative Arts* Viking, London, 1989.

Forrest, Tim *The Marshall Guide to Antique China & Silver* Marshall Editions Ltd., London, 1998.

Frantz, Susanne K., *Contemporary Glass* Harry N. Abrams, Inc., Publishers, New York, 1989.

Gallagher, Fiona, Michael Jeffery & Nicolette White, *Christie's Art Deco* Watson-Guptill Publications, London, 2000

Giovanni et al., *Furniture by Wendell Castle* Founders Society, Detroit Institute of Arts, 1989.

Gleeson, Janet *The Arcanum* Warner Books, New York, 1998.

Greenhalgh, Paul (ed.), *Art Nouveau 1890–1914* V&A Publications, London, 2000.

Hamerton, Ian (ed.), *W.A.S. Benson* Antique Collectors' Club Woodbridge, 2005.

Hawkins Opie, Jennifer, *Scandinavia: Ceramics & Glass in the Twentieth Century* V&A Publications, London, 1989.

Jackson, Lesley, *20th Century Factory Glass* Mitchell Beazley, London, 2000.

Lesieutre, Alain, *The Spirit and the Splendour of Art Deco* Secaucus, New Jersey, 1978.

Levin, Elaine, *The History of American Ceramics 1607 to the Present* Harry N. Abrams, Inc., Publishers, New York, 1988.

Lewis, Philippa & Gillian Darley, *Dictionary of Ornament* Cameron & Hollis/David & Charles, 1990.

Livingstone, Karen, and Linda Parry (eds.), *International Arts and Crafts* V&A Publications, London, 2005.

Mendes, Valerie, *The Victoria & Albert Museum's Textiles Collection* V&A Publications, London, 1992.

Miller, Judith, *20th Century Glass* Dorling Kindersley, London, 2004.

Miller, Judith, *Art Deco* Dorling Kindersley, London, 2005.

Miller, Judith, *Art Nouveau* Dorling Kindersley, London, 2004.

Miller, Judith, *Arts & Crafts* Dorling Kindersley, London, 2005.

Miller, Judith, *Furniture* Dorling Kindersley, London, 2005.

Morrison, Jasper, *Everything but the walls* Lars Muller (Princeton Architectural Press), 2002.

Pile, John, *A History of Interior Design* Laurence King Publishing, London, 2005.

Radice, Barbara, *Memphis* Rizzoli, New York, 1985.

Raizman, David, *History of Modern Design* Laurence King Publishing, London, 2003.

Ramsey, L. L. G. (ed.), *The Complete Encyclopaedia of Antiques* The Connoisseur, London, 1962.

Ricke, Helmut, *Glass Art Düsseldorf*, Prestel, Munich, Berlin, London and New York, 2002.

Riley, Noël (ed.) *The Elements of Design* Mitchell Beazley, London, 2003.

Taylor, David A. and Jason W. Laskey, *Georg Jensen Holloware* The Silver Fund Plc, London and New York, 2003.

Thornton, Peter, *Authentic Décor: The Domestic Interior 1620-1920* Seven Dials, London, 1993.

Todd, Pamela, *The Arts & Crafts Companion* Thames & Hudson, London, 2004.

Venable, Charles L. et al., *China and Glass in America 1880-1980*, Dallas Museum of Art, 2000.

Venturi, Robert, Steven Izenour and Denise Scott Brown, *Learning from Las Vegas* MIT Press, Cambridge, MA, 1972.

Volpe, Tod M. and Beth Cathers, *Treasures of the American Arts and Crafts Movement* Thames & Hudson, London, 2003.

Whiteway, Michael (ed.), *Christopher Dresser* V&A Publications with Cooper-Hewitt, London, 2004.

Wilk, Christopher (ed.), *Modernism 1914-1939* V&A Publications, London, 2006.

Wood, Ghislaine, *Essential Art Deco*, V&A Publications, London, 2003.

Young, Robert, *Folk Art* Mitchell Beazley, London, 1999.

GLOSSARY

Acanthus leaf The fleshy, scalloped leaf of a Mediterranean plant that was a popular motif for furniture and metalwork.

Acid etching The technique of engraving a design into glass using hydrochloric acid. The longer the vessel is exposed to the acid, the deeper the relief.

Agate glass An opaque, marbled glass used to imitate vessels made from semiprecious stones such as agate, chalcedony, and jasper.

Albarello An Italian word for a waisted tin-glazed earthenware container made for pharmacies for drug storage from the 15th century in Italy, Spain, and the Netherlands.

Andirons (fire dogs) Two large iron rests placed in a hearth to hold logs, their fronts often made in reflective material, such as silver, brass, or polished steel.

Anthemion A fanlike decorative motif resembling the honeysuckle leaf and flower that was used as a repeat pattern on, among other items, Neoclassical friezes.

Appliqué A decorative technique in which pieces of one fabric are laid onto another fabric and stitched in place.

Apron The frieze rail of a table, the base of the framework of a piece of case furniture, or a shaped piece of wood beneath the seat rail of a chair.

Arabesque Stylized foliage arranged in a swirling, interlaced pattern and combining flowers and tendrils with spirals and zigzags.

Arita *See* Kakiemon.

Art pottery Handmade and/or hand-decorated ceramics dating from the late 19th century onward.

Bakelite A robust, nonflammable synthetic plastic invented by L. H. Baekeland in 1909.

Baluster A short bulbous post or pillar, such as a table leg, or one in a series supporting a rail and forming a balustrade.

Basalt ware (basaltes ware) A black, unglazed earthenware developed by Wedgwood in the 1760s.

Batik Method of producing patterned fabric by protecting parts of the cloth from dye with wax.

Beading A decorative Neoclassical border, often used on furniture, which has a single row of applied or embossed beads.

Bentwood A technique perfected in Austria by Michael Thonet in the mid-19th century that involves bending solid or laminated wood over steam to make curved sections for table and chair frames.

Bergère A French term for a large, informal, deep-seated chair. It usually has a caned or upholstered back and sides and a squab cushion.

Berlin wool work Embroidery worked in colored wools on a canvas background with published patterns and wools originally imported from Berlin.

Blackamoor A life-sized carved figure of a black slave in brightly colored clothes, originating in Venice, and used as a pedestal support for *torchères* from the 18th century.

Blanc-de-chine A type of translucent white Chinese porcelain that was widely copied in Europe. Wares include crisply modelled figures, cups, and bowls.

Bombé A French term used to describe a bulbous, curving form.

Bonheur-du-jour A French term for a small lady's writing desk that has a flat writing surface with tiered drawers and compartments at the back.

Bonnet An American term used to describe the domed or arched top found on clocks and highboys.

Boullework A technique named after the French cabinet-maker André-Charles Boulle, which involves the elaborate inlay of brass into tortoiseshell or ebony and vice versa. Other precious materials may also be used.

Bracket clock A spring-driven clock first made after the invention of the pendulum in the mid-17th century. The clock was designed to stand on a wall bracket.

Bright-cut engraving A form of engraving on metal, primarily used from 1770 to 1800, in which the metal was cut at an angle to create facets that reflected the light and glittered.

Brilliant cut The ideal form of cutting for diamonds, consisting of 58 facets.

Buffet A French term for a large, heavy display cupboard with open shelves, that was used for displaying silverware from the 16th century onwards.

Bureau A French term for a desk. A *bureau plat* is a flat-topped writing table. A *bureau à cylindre* is a roll-top desk. The sliding cover, made of slats of wood, hides the writing surface and pigeon holes. The most elaborate also contained candlesticks, clocks, and drawers.

Cabochon A French term for a smooth domed gem.

Cabriole leg A furniture leg with two curves forming an attenuated S-shape, like an animal leg. On chairs it often terminated in a claw-and-ball or stylized paw foot.

Cameo glass Glass made up of two or more separate layers of colored glass. The top layers are carved or acid-etched to produce a relief image and reveal the different-colored layers beneath.

Cantilever chair A chair with no back legs, in which the weight of the seat is supported by the front legs and base of the chair alone.

Carcass The shell of a piece of case furniture before the drawers, doors, shelves, or feet have been added.

Carriage clock A small spring-driven clock designed for traveling, developed in early-19th-century France. The case, usually plain or gilt brass, is rectangular with a carrying handle and often set with glass panels.

Cartel clock An ornate spring-driven wall clock made in France and Sweden in the 18th and 19th centuries, usually featuring a white enameled dial set in a carved and gilded wood or gilt-bronze frame.

Cartouche A panel or tablet in the form of a scroll with curled edges, sometimes bearing an inscription, monogram, or coat of arms, and used as a decorative feature.

Caryatid A full-length female figure of Greek origin that is used as a support for a piece of furniture.

Cased glass A type of glass that consists of two or more layers of different colors—the first, inner layer is blown and the second and any subsequent layers added on top. The layers fuse when reheated.

Cast iron Metal produced by casting iron with a high carbon content in molds of compressed sand. It is used for grilles, fireplace furnishings, furniture, and railings.

Caudle cup Two-handled silver or pottery cup with a lift-off cover to take caudle—a medicinal wine and gruel drink.

Celadon glaze A semi-opaque, distinctively colored olive green glaze that imitated jade, used in China, Japan, and South Korea.

Chaise longue A French term for an upholstered day bed that has a high support at one end.

Chalkware Ornaments made from plaster of Paris and decorated with bright colors, popular from the 18th to the mid-20th centuries in the United States and Britain.

Charger A large, often ornate, dish, principally for display but also for serving at the table.

Chasing A surface decoration on metals, especially silver, often used with embossing, made by hammering with a blunt ball-point chisel or punch to add fine details and texture to the metal's surface.

Chiffonier From the French term *chiffonière*, a small side cabinet with drawers. A *table en chiffonière* has longer legs and a shelf below the drawers.

Chinoiserie A decorative style in which fanciful, exotic motifs derived from Chinese originals were applied to European furniture, textiles, wallpaper, and ceramics.

Chrome A silvery metal usually plated on a base metal such as steel.

Chryselephantine A combination of ivory and metal, usually bronze.

Claw-and-ball foot A termination for furniture legs said to be based on Chinese examples of a dragon claw clasping a pearl.

Classical orders A column in Classical architecture, usually with a base, and always a shaft, capital (head), and entablature (upper part made up of an architrave, frieze, and cornice) decorated and proportioned as set out in Doric, Ionic, or Corinthian mode. The forms and motifs were borrowed extensively in the decorative arts from the Renaissance onward.

Cloisonné A method of enameling in which thin strips of metal are soldered onto the surface of an object to form decorative cells. These are filled with powdered enamel and then fired in a kiln.

Commode A French term for a chest of drawers; and also a small cupboard concealing a chamber pot.

Compote A dish with a long-stemmed base or foot, usually ceramic, used to hold fruit or sweetmeats.

Cornice An architectural term for a decorative, molded projection that crowns a piece of furniture, particularly tall cupboards or display cabinets.

Court cupboard A two- or three-tiered structure with open tiers to display plates.

Crackle glass (*craquelure*) A type of glass, also known as ice glass, that has a crackled surface produced by plunging hot molten glass into cold water.

Creamware A refined cream-colored earthenware developed in Staffordshire in around 1740 to rival imported porcelain.

Cristallo An Italian name for colorless soda glass, developed in Venice in the mid-15th century.

Crossbanding A decorative strip of veneer in contrasting wood that runs at right angles to the main veneer.

Crystalline glaze A glaze with crystals of zinc or calcium suspended in it, creating attractively patchy color, an effect produced by cooling the firing kiln extremely slowly.

C-scroll A carved or applied decoration in the shape of a C.

Cuerda seca A decorative technique used on pottery, in which the pattern outlines are drawn in wax or grease to prevent different colored enamels from running into each other.

Cut glass Glassware decorated with grooves and facets cut by hand or a wheel.

Damask A rich woven silk, linen, or cotton fabric with a satin weave.

Day bed *See* Chaise longue.

Decanter A decorative, usually handle-less, glass container with matching stopper, used for serving wine, sherry, and spirits that have been emptied (decanted) from the bottle.

Delft ware Tin-glazed earthenware inspired by Asian blue-and-white porcelain, which was made mainly in the town of Delft in Holland from the 16th century. Similar wares made in Britain are called delftware with a lower-case "d."

Demi-lune A French term for a half-moon shape.

Dovetail A joint in which two pieces of wood are joined together at right angles. Each piece of wood has a row of fan-shaped teeth, which interlock at the joint.

Dowel A small headless wooden pin used to join two pieces of wood.

Earthenware Pottery made from a porous clay body, which has to be waterproofed with a glaze.

Ébéniste The French term for a cabinet-maker, derived from the word for ebony. *Ébénistes* specialized in making veneered furniture.

Ebonized wood Wood stained black in imitation of ebony.

Electroplating A method of chemically depositing by electrolysis a layer of metal (usually gold or silver) onto any object (usually base metal) that will conduct electricity. It was used from around 1840.

Embossing The decoration of metals (or leather) using hammers to punch the material to produce a raised (relief) or impressed pattern. The details of the pattern are usually enhanced by chasing.

Enamel Colored glass fused by heating in a furnace to create a design or decorative finish on a metallic surface. Enamel can be produced in a broad spectrum of translucent or opaque colors.

Enamel colors A vitreous onglaze ceramic pigment that fuses when fired at a relatively low temperature, called *petit feu* (literally "little fire") in French. A full palette of colors was in use by the end of the 17th century.

Engraving A process for decorating glass and metal in which the design is cut with a sharp instrument such as a diamond point or wheel to create an image in small dots or intaglio or relief. Also a print made by cutting a picture into wood or metal, inking it, and pressing paper onto it.

Entrelac An interlaced tendril of Celtic origin, primarily used in jewelry-making.

Escutcheon A protective and usually ornamental keyhole plate, sometimes in the shape of a shield, on a piece of furniture.

Étui A pocket-sized case to hold small useful articles such as sewing accessories or writing sets, dating from the 18th to the 19th centuries and made of silver, gold, enamel, gilt metal, tortoiseshell, or lacquer.

Façon de Venise A type of gray-toned soda glass with elaborate *filigrana* or applied decoration, made in Europe from around 1550 to 1700, often by emigrant Venetian glassmakers.

Faience A French term for tin-glazed earthenware popular in Europe from the 16th and 17th centuries, corresponding to maiolica in Italy and Spain and Delft ware in Holland and England. Lightly baked and of a buff or pale red color, it was covered with white glaze to imitate porcelain.

Famille jaune, noire, rose, verte Terms used to classify Chinese porcelain by its color palette. In *famille verte*, green and iron-red predominate. *Famille jaune* used *famille verte* colors on a yellow ground and *famille noire* used a black ground. *Famille rose* used mainly pink or purple.

Fasces A decorative motif of a bound bundle of rods, often incorporating the head of an ax, the emblem of authority of the magistrates in ancient Rome.

Fauteuil A French term for a large, upholstered open armchair, first used at the Court of Louis XIV.

Fazzoletto An Italian word for a handkerchief vase—a vase that takes the form of a falling handkerchief.

Feather or herringbone banding A banding of veneer formed of two narrow strips laid together, with the grain of each running diagonally to produce a herringbone or feather effect.

Femme-fleur A sensual Art Nouveau motif, a hybrid of a female form and a flower.

Festoon A Classical decorative motif in the form of a garland of fruit and flowers tied with ribbons.

Fiberglass A strong, lightweight, and versatile material made from matted glass fibers bonded with a synthetic resin.

Filigrana A technique in which decorative threads of colored glass or rods are incorporated into a piece of glass.

Finial A decorative ornament on top of a household item, often in the form of an urn, an acorn, or a pinecone.

Flambé glaze A high-fired deep crimson glaze, which may flow in the kiln, creating flamelike streaks of purple or blue.

Flashed glass A thick layer of clear glass covered with a thinner layer of colored glass. This might be acid-etched, cut, or sandblasted to reveal the layer of clear glass underneath.

Flatware All flat table articles such as plates, spoons, and forks, but excluding those with a cutting edge (cutlery). It is also the collective name for all tableware, such as plates or salvers, as opposed to other wares, such as vases, which are termed hollow wares.

Flint glass An archaic term for English lead glass. It refers to glass made in the mid-17th century in which ground flint was the source of the silica.

Flute A tall drinking glass with an extremely narrow inverted conical bowl resting on a very short stem.

Fluting Parallel lines of shallow, concave molding (as opposed to reeding, which is convex) running from the top to the bottom of a column or column-shaped object such as a table leg.

Folk art Items such as painted furniture and treen, toleware, and pottery that are made by people with little or no formal training and reflect the traditional crafts and social values of their community.

Fraktur A form of folk art from Germanic Europe exported to colonial America with the settlers. Originally a style of broken lettering, it has come to describe a variety of illustrated texts including birth records, writing samplers, and rewards of merit.

Fretwork Originally Chinese, carved decoration consisting of intersecting lines with perforated spaces between them.

Frieze A Classical term used to describe the horizontal strip that supports a tabletop or the cornice on a piece of case furniture.

Fumed A term used to describe a technique in which a chemical was used to darken the natural color of a wood, usually oak, to make it look older.

Gadrooning A row of concave or convex flutes used along the edge of a surface.

Gesso A mixture of gypsum (plaster of Paris) and size, and sometimes linseed oil and glue. It was used as a base for carved and gilded decoration on furniture.

Gilding A decorative finish in which gold leaf or powdered gold is applied to wood, leather, silver, ceramics, or glass.

Giltwood Wood that has been gilded.

Glaze A layer of glass fused onto a ceramic body to make it watertight and stronger.

Goût grec A French term describing the renewed interest in ancient Greece and Rome that resulted in the Neoclassical style of the late 18th and early 19th centuries.

Grand feu See High temperature colors.

Greek key A decorative band of interlocking, geometric, hook-shaped forms.

Grisaille Decorative patterns painted on wood, glass, ceramics, plaster, or stone in a neutral palette of gray, black, or white to imitate marble or stone figure sculptures or relief ornament.

Grotesque A type of ornament in which real and mythical beasts, human figures, flowers, scrolls, and candelabra were linked, often in vertical panels.

Guéridon A French term for a small stand or table, first seen in the 17th century, that was usually ornately carved and embellished.

Guilloche A decorative motif that takes the form of a continuous band of strands twisted or braided together.

Highboy An American term for a chest-on-chest, often made with a matching lowboy—a low dressing table.

High-temperature colors The colors—green (copper oxide), blue (cobalt), purple (manganese), yellow (antimony), and orange (iron)—used to decorate tin-glazed earthenware until the 18th century, after which petit feu, or enamel colors, were more common. They are known in French as grand feu due to the high temperature used to unite them with the tin glaze.

Hyalith An opaque, jet-black or sealing-wax red glass made around 1819 in Bohemia.

Ice glass See Crackle glass.

Inciso The Italian term for incised glass. The technique creates many shallow, horizontal cuts across the surface of the glass.

Inlay A decorative technique in which different-colored woods, stones, or exotic materials are inserted into the solid wood surface or veneer of furniture.

Intarsia An Italian term for pictorial marquetry. It was often used for decorative paneling on furniture in Renaissance Italy and 16th-century Germany.

Intercalaire Cased glass where decoration can be applied on different layers.

Iridescence A lustrous, rainbowlike surface that changes color depending on how the light hits it.

Ironstone A hard white earthenware containing ironstone slag, patented by C.J. Mason in 1813.

Islamic wares Ceramics, glass, metalware, and furniture decorated with designs taken from Islamic art, especially flat, dense, repeating abstract patterns, pierced fretwork, interlacing, and calligraphic kufic script.

Istoriato Painted decoration found on Italian maiolica that depicts a story of historical, mythological, allegorical, genre, or Biblical origin.

Japanning A decorative technique in which furniture was coated with colored varnish to look like Chinese or Japanese lacquer.

Jardinière A French term for a large ornamental vessel, usually ceramic, for holding cut flowers or growing plants.

Jasper ware A fine-grained, unglazed, stoneware introduced by Josiah Wedgwood in 1775. It could be white or stained with metallic oxides, producing colored bodies, including the well-known blue, and was often decorated with white relief Classical-style figures.

Kakiemon A term for porcelain produced at Arita in Japan using a distinctive palette of red, yellow, blue, and turquoise. Well-balanced, the decoration is usually high quality, delicate, and asymmetric, sparsely applied to emphasize the white porcelain. The style was much copied in Europe.

Klismos chair A chair with a broad, curved top rail and concave saber legs that originated in ancient Greece.

Knop The decorative knob on lids and covers, or the cast finial at the end of a spoon handle. Also the decorative bulge halfway up the stem of a drinking glass, goblet, or candlestick.

Lacca povera An Italian term meaning "poor man's lacquer" that describes a form of decoration in which cut-out sheets of engravings were pasted onto furniture and varnished to look like lacquer.

Lacquer A resin produced from the sap of the Rhus tree that, once processed and dried, forms a hard, impermeable, smooth, and lustrous surface. Used from the 6th century, it was popular in Asia and particularly Japan where lacquered objects were highly prized. The lacquer is brushed onto a wood or composition base in very thin layers that are dried and polished.

Ladder-back chair A country chair with a back made up of horizontal rails, like the rungs of a ladder, between the uprights.

Lambrequin A decorative fringe, originally based on the scarf worn across a knight's helmet and its heraldic representation, found on drapery, furniture, silver, or ceramics.

Lamination The technique in which thin layers (laminates) of wood are sandwiched together with the grain at right angles for strength and glued.

Lampas A patterned textile similar to damask but heavier, and often referred to as damask.

Lampwork A delicate ornamental glass technique in which thin rods are shaped, bent, and heated to attach them to each other. The resulting designs are often embedded in paperweights and spheres.

Lattimo (milk glass) An Italian term for opaque white glass that resembles porcelain. Developed in Venice in the 15th century, in the 17th and 18th centuries it was made in France (called blanc-de-lait), Germany (milchglas), and Britain, and was often decorated with enameling and gilding.

Lava glass Iridescent gold art glass, known also as volcanic glass, developed and patented by Tiffany in the late 19th century, with an irregular form, and "dripping" decoration that resembles the flow of molten lava.

Lead crystal glass Glass with a high lead content, ideally suited to cut decoration. Perfected by George Ravenscroft in 1676, it is also popularly known as crystal or quartz crystal because of its brightness and light-reflecting quality.

Lead glaze A translucent glaze made from lead oxide and applied to pottery that has already been fired.

Leaded glass A technique of assembling pieces of cut glass (into windows, panels, or lamps) using small strips of lead known as "cames".

Lithography A printing process that was initially used on paper, but was also used for decorating ceramics from the late 1840s.

Lithyalin Opaque marbled glass designed to resemble hardstones. Invented by Friedrich Egermann and patented in 1828, it was used for beakers and scent bottles, often with cut and gilded decoration.

Longcase clock A tall narrow free-standing weight-driven clock, introduced around 1660. It is called a tallcase clock in the United States.

Luster glaze A shiny, iridescent glaze for ceramics, created by painting on a mixture of metallic oxides, such as gold, silver, and copper suspended in oil, before firing.

Lyre motif A decorative motif based on the ancient Greek musical instrument.

Maiolica In Italy, tin-glazed earthenware was known as maiolica because of the importance in the trading network of the island of Majorca, then called Maiolica. The term was first applied to Hispano-Moresque lusterwares from Spain, then to lusterwares made in Italy.

Majolica A corrupted form of the word "maiolica," this term was used in the 19th century for an elaborately modeled type of earthenware covered with thick colorful glazes in lead blue, purple-pink, turquoise, and yellow.

Mantel clock A type of clock designed to stand on a shelf or mantelpiece. The term is used to refer to bracket clocks, and also to describe some late 18th- and early 19th-century French clocks, often featuring gilt-bronze or marble cases embellished with figures, porcelain plaques, and a variety of Neoclassical motifs.

Marquetry A decorative veneer made from shaped pieces of wood in different colors placed together to form a pattern or picture.

Mauchlineware Wooden souvenir ware, including boxes and small household goods, that are usually made from sycamore and are decorated with printed transfers, frequently depicting a view.

Mica A shiny silica material that was combined with shellac by Arts and Crafts designers to create lampshades.

Micromosaic Miniature mosaics formed from elongated rather than square tesserae, popular in the 19th century.

Millefiori From the Italian for a thousand flowers, a glass technique often used in paperweights in which tile-like cross sections of brightly coloured canes are arranged in patterns and embedded in clear glass.

Mocha ware An inexpensive type of pottery derived from "mocha stone", a variety of moss agate with feathery markings. The decoration was achieved by dripping an acid colourant onto an aklaline ground: the chemical reaction formed treelike striations.

Mortise and tenon An early type of joint in which one piece of wood has a projecting piece (tenon), that fits into a hole (mortise) in the second piece of wood.

Mould blown A technique in which glass is blown into a mould to create a uniform shape, either by hand or as part of a mechanized process.

Mount A term for brass, ormolu, or bronze decorative details that were applied to furniture in the late 17th and 18th centuries.

Murrine A slice, usually patterned, of a coloured glass cane.

Nécessaire A small item of silver, leather-covered wood, porcelain, or enamel, which carries everything necessary to accomplish a task. A *nécessaire à coudre*, for example, contains the needles, bodkin, thread, thimble, and scissors necessary for sewing.

Needlepoint A form of lace created by embroidering stitches using a single thread and needle on paper that was cut away when the design was complete. Also embroidery on canvas using simple, even stitches over counted threads.

Objet de vertu A small accessory such as a snuff box, pomander, *étui*, or *nécessaire*, made of luxury materials, including porcelain, gold, silver, gemstones, or enamel, and valued more for beauty than function.

Opalescence A glass effect that is created when phosphates are added to the batch, it has a milky-blue appearance in reflected light and an amber tint in transmitted light.

Opaline glass A semi-opaque glass, developed in France in around 1825 by adding bone ash to the glass mix. This results in the "fire", whereby the colour of the glass changes when held to the light.

Ormolu Based on the French term *or moulu*, meaning "ground gold", a process of gilding bronze for decorative mounts.

Overglaze A technique in which enamels are painted onto fired and glazed porcelain, which is then fired again.

Palladian A restrained Classical style of architecture and decorative features that was derived from the works of the Italian architect, Andrea Palladio.

Palmette A Classical decorative motif based on the shape of a palm leaf.

Papier mâché A lightweight material made from paper and paste, which can be moulded into any shape. Pieces were often gilded, painted, japanned, and then varnished for decorative effect.

Parian ware A type of porcelain first made in England in the mid-19th century and named after the Greek island of Paros, which was famous for its white marble.

Parquetry A decorative veneer made up of a mosaic of small pieces of wood in contrasting colours pieced together to form a geometric pattern.

Pâte-de-verre From the French for "glass paste", ground glass is mixed with a liquid to form a paste, pressed into a mould and slowly heated to form the required shape.

Patera An oval or circular ornament on a flat surface, which is often decorated with a floral design, a rosette, or fluting.

Pâte-sur-pâte A ceramic term from the French for paste-on-paste, in which white slip is built up in layers to give a striking effect of depth on a dark background.

Patina A sheen on the surface of metal and furniture, the result of years of handling and a gradual build-up of dirt and polish.

Pearl ware A type of English creamware evolved by Wedgwood, in which the cream colour is counteracted by a blue-tinted glaze, and often printed or painted.

Pedestal The base that supports a column in Classical architecture. Since the Renaissance, decorative pedestals have been used as bases for vases, candelabra, lamps, and sculpture.

Pediment An architectural term for the triangular gable found above the portico of a Greek temple; a similar feature applied to the tops of large pieces of case furniture.

Pembroke table A small table, often with an elaborately inlaid top, with two frieze drawers, two drop leaves, and usually on legs with casters.

Pendulum A device controlling the timekeeping of a clock. A brass, steel, or wooden rod is made to swing in a regular arc by a flat or bulbous metal weight (bob) at the end.

Penwork A technique in which the en tire surface of a piece of furniture is japanned black before being worked with an intricate decorative pattern of white japanning.

Petit feu See Enamel colours.

Pilaster An architectural term for a flattened column attached to the surface of a building or piece of case furniture as a form of decoration, rather than for support.

Planishing A technique in which a sheet of metal is given a smooth or flat surface, either with rollers or, more usually, by supporting it on a stake then beating it with a planishing hammer, which has a broad, smooth, polished head.

Plique-à-jour **enamel** A technique by which a translucent enamel is held in an unbacked framework to produce an effect similar to that of a stained glass window when light is shone through it.

Plywood A flexible, composite wood made of several layers of laminated wood laid at right angles to each other.

Polyurethane foam A synthetic substance used to fill seat cushions and backs.

Porcelain A hard, dense, usually white ceramic first made in China in the late 6th century CE. It is translucent, watertight, and usually glazed. Soft-paste porcelain was developed in Europe in the 16th century as a substitute for the highly prized hard-paste porcelain being imported from China. It was made from a variety of ingredients, mainly white clay and ground glass, and was fired at low temperatures. A type of hard-paste porcelain was not made in Europe until 1709, when a formula was developed at Meissen. Made from kaolin and china stone, it was fired at higher temperatures.

Pratt ware A type of pottery made in Staffordshire, similar to pearl ware but characterized by a strong high-temperature palette of blue, green, and yellow.

Pressed glass Glass that has been shaped by being pressed in a mould.

Prunt A blob of molten glass applied to a piece of glass as decoration, particularly associated with drinking vessels.

Putto An Italian term for "cherub" or "boy", which denotes a motif used during the Renaissance and the 17th century.

Quatrefoil A Gothic decorative motif, often used in tracery, of four asymmetrical leaves resembling a four-leafed clover. Similar motifs with three leaves (trefoil) and five leaves (cinquefoil) are also common.

Raku **ware** A kind of lead-glazed Japanese earthenware, typically irregular in shape and used especially for the tea ceremony.

Red ware An American term used to describe stoneware and, generally, provincial pottery with a porous red body, typically decorated with coloured lead glaze and trailed slip or sgraffito work.

Repoussé A French term for the relief decoration on malleable metals that have been embossed and chased.

Reverse painting An image that has been painted in reverse on the inner surface of glass, especially lamps.

Rocaille A French term meaning "rockwork", which denotes the asymmetrical rock and shell forms characteristic of the Rococo style.

Rock crystal The commonest mineral in existence, composed of pure silica. Found worldwide, it has been used in the decorative arts for centuries.

Rosso antico The name used by Josiah Wedgwood for an unglazed red stoneware he developed in the 1770s. Decorations were based on ancient Greek and Roman designs – hence the term "antico".

Rummer A 19th-century English drinking glass in the form of a goblet with a short stem. It sometimes has a domed or a square foot.

Salt glaze A hard translucent glaze, produced by adding salt to the kiln during firing at high temperature.

Sampler Originally a record of stitches and patterns made as a reference tool by professional and amateur needleworkers. By the 17th century samplers were used to show the skill of the embroiderer – often a young girl – and alphabets, inscriptions, and pictorial elements became ubiquitous on 18th-century samplers.

Sancai ware Three-coloured wares from China decorated with green, amber, and cream lead glazes, and used for burial figures and boxes.

Sang-de-boeuf From the French for ox blood, a brilliant red or plum-coloured glaze originally used for Chinese monochrome wares from the Kangxi period.

Schwarzlot From the German for black lead, a type of monochrome handpainted decoration in black or brown enamels applied to glass and ceramics and especially popular on bowls and beakers from around 1650 to 1750.

Sconce A candleholder designed to be mounted on a wall.

Screenprinting A printing technique in which ink is forced over a stencil supported on a mesh or screen (originally made of silk). The image can be built up by applying a succession of different colours over a series of carefully aligned stencils.

Secretaire A French term for a large writing cabinet in two sections. The lower section has a fall front that drops down to provide a writing surface and reveals a number of pigeonholes and drawers. Above this there is a bookcase or glazed cabinet.

Serpentine Wavy or undulating. A commode with a serpentine front has a protruding central section flanked by concave ends. Serpentine stretchers are curved cross-stretchers.

Settle A wooden bench that has a high back and open arms.

Sgraffito From the Italian for little scratch, a form of decoration made by scratching through a surface to reveal a lower layer of a contrasting colour, typically done in plaster or stucco on walls, or in slip on ceramics before firing.

Shagreen Shark or ray skin, used by some furniture designers as an inlay. It is also known by the French term *galuchat*.

Slip A homogeneous mixture of clay and water, usually finer and richer than the clay body it covers. Slips are used for coating, to provide colour and a smooth surface.

Slipware Pottery with one or more coatings of more refined clay, which is then decorated with designs trailed on in different coloured slips. The name of the potter and the date may be added. The lead glaze finish gives a characteristic yellowish colouring.

Soda glass The earliest form of glass, made from soda and lime. The glass is light and often tinged with yellow or brown.

Sommerso From the Italian for submerged, a glass technique that involves casing one or more layers of transparent coloured glass within a layer of thick, colourless glass.

Spatter ware Cheaply decorated pottery, common in Staffordshire, in which the colour was applied with a sponge, creating a blurred effect.

Spelter A term for zinc or an alloy of zinc and lead or aluminium, used as a substitute for bronze for mass-produced cast items, such as candlesticks and figures.

Splat The flat, vertical, central part of a chair back.

S-scroll A decorative carved or applied ornament in the shape of an S, developed during the Rococo period.

Stained glass A term for coloured, stained, or enamelled glass, often used with lead strips in an abstract or figurative design, set in an iron framework and used in an architectural context, usually a window, or as a decorative panel.

Stoneware A type of ceramic that shares characteristics of earthenware and porcelain. The body is made of clay mixed with a fusible stone that makes it watertight, although salt glaze or lead glaze are also added for decorative effect.

Streamlining A term borrowed from engineering and used to describe American Art Deco furniture with smooth, clean-lined shapes in the 1920s and 1930s.

Stretcher A rod or bar extending between two legs of a chair or table.

Stringing Narrow lines of inlay on a piece of furniture, used to create a simple, decorative border around drawer fronts or table tops.

Studio pottery The work of independent artist potters working in individual studios or with other like-minded potters wishing to express their own artistry without commercial pressures.

Style rayonnant A style of painting on ceramics that resembles lacy embroidery. The patterns on plates and dishes radiate inwards from richly decorated borders. It was first used on blue-and-white faience in the late 17th century at Rouen in France.

Swag A Classical decorative motif of a hanging garland of fruit, husks, flowers, or laurel leaves.

Tall case clock *See* Longcase clock.

Tapestry A weaving technique in which coloured weft threads are woven into an undyed warp thread to form a decorative or pictorial design. The different coloured weft threads are wound on bobbins and woven as far as the warp thread that marks the edge of a particular area of colour. Thus each part of the design is built up independently. The term also applies to wall hangings and furnishings made by this method.

Temmoku glaze A Japanese term, used originally to describe Chinese stoneware cups with a streaky black/brown glaze, favoured by the Japanese as tea ceremony wares. Named after the Tianmu mountains in China, the term is now used to describe almost any pottery or stoneware with a thick black/brown glaze.

Tenon *See* Mortise and tenon.

Tesserae The small pieces of glass used to make mosaics.

Tessuto A design in glass that looks as if threads or strips of glass have been woven together over the body.

Tin glaze A glaze technique used to make the opaque white coating on maiolica, faience, and Delft ware. After a first firing, the pottery was dipped into a glaze of oxides of lead and tin, which produced a porous white surface. It was then decorated and fired again, possibly with the addition of a lead glaze.

Toleware A term for *tôle peinte*, the French name for painted tinware, used for lampshades and hollow wares.

Transfer printing A process for decorating ceramics in which an engraved copper plate is covered with ink, prepared with metallic oxides. The engraved design is then transferred to paper, which while wet with pigment is pressed onto the surface of the object. The design is then fixed by firing.

Treen A term for carved or turned wooden household items made in rural communities in Europe and North America.

Trefoil *See* Quatrefoil.

Tubular steel Lightweight and strong hollow steel tubes, which can be bent into any shape.

Tunbridgeware Small wooden domestic objects and also, rarely, work tables. The surfaces are decorated with patterns created from an intricate mosaic of coloured woods, often as souvenirs of the spa town of Tunbridge Wells in south-east England where it was made.

Tureen A deep ceramic or silver bowl with a lid, two handles, and oval or circular in shape. Large tureens were for soup; small for sauce. They were made in sets or pairs.

Underglaze Decoration painted onto a biscuit (unglazed) ceramic body. As the colours have to withstand the full heat of the kiln, the palette is restricted.

Vellum A fine-grained, unsplit animal skin that has been prepared for writing on, or for book-binding. Also used by Carlo Bugatti to decorate and cover furniture in the late 19th and early 20th centuries.

Veneer A thin layer of fine wood that is applied to the surface of a furniture carcase made of a coarser, cheaper wood, for decorative effect.

Verdure A tapestry featuring leafy plants and/or wooded landscapes, sometimes with birds and animals.

Vermeil A French term for silver gilt: silver that is covered with a thin film of gold.

Vernis Martin A generic name to describe an 18th-century French japanning method on wood, named after the Martin brothers. Although less durable than the Oriental lacquering that inspired it, the attractive brilliancy and depth of *vernis Martin* made it a fashionable varnish for indoor panelling, furniture, small boxes, and even carriages.

Vitrine A cupboard with large glazed panels, originally designed as a bookcase but later used to display ornaments. From the mid-19th century vitrines often had mirror backs, which made it possible to view both sides of the displayed objects.

Vitruvian scroll A wave-like series of scrolls used as a decorative motif – carved, painted, or gilded – on friezes.

Volute A Classical motif, consisting of a spiralling scroll, thought to resemble the horns of a ram.

Wucai Meaning five coloured, a type of decoration on Chinese porcelain with washes of underglaze blue and overglaze coloured enamel. Outlines are usually in red or black.

DEALER ADDRESSES

Many of the items shown in this book were photographed at dealers or auction houses
that are either selling or have sold the piece. Inclusion in this book does not constitute or
imply a contract or a binding offer on the part of any contributing dealer or auction house
to supply or sell the pieces illustrated, or similar items, at the price band, where stated.

BETH ADAMS
Unit GO43/4, Alfie's Antiques Market
13 Church Street, London NW8 8DT
Tel: 011 44 20 7723 5613

BEVERLEY ADAMS
30 Church Street, London NW8 8EP
Tel: 011 44 20 7262 1576

NORMAN ADAMS LTD
8–10 Hans Road, London SW3 1RX
Tel: 011 44 20 7589 5266
www.normanadams.com

ALESSI
www.alessi.com

ALL OUR YESTERDAYS
6 Park Road, Kelvin Bridge
Glasgow G4 9JG
Tel: 011 44 141 3347788
Email: antiques@allouryesterdays.fsnet.
co.uk

ALTERMANN GALLERIES
Santa Fe Galleries, 225 Canyon Road
Santa Fe, NM 87501
Tel: (505) 983-1590
www.altermann.com

ALBERT AMOR
37 Bury Street, London SW1Y 6AU
Tel: 011 44 20 7930 2444
Email: info@albertamor.co.uk

ANTIQUE TEXTILES AND LIGHTING
34 Belvedere, Landsdowne Road
Bath BA1 5HR
Tel: 011 44 1225 310795
www.antiquetextilesandlighting.co.uk

ARK ANTIQUES
PO Box 3133
New Haven, CT 06515
Tel: (203) 498-8572
www.ark-antiques.com

ART DECO ETC
73 Upper Gloucester Road
Brighton, East Sussex BN1 3LQ
Tel: 011 44 1273 329268
Email: johnclark@artdecoetc.co.uk

AT THE MOVIES
17 Fouberts Place, London W1F 7QD
Tel: 011 44 20 7439 6336
www.atthemovies.co.uk

AUX TROIS CLEFS
117 boulevard Stalingrad
69100 Villeurbanne, France
Tel: 011 33 4 72 44 22 02

BARRETT MARSDEN GALLERY
17–18 Great Sutton Street
London EC1V 0DN
Tel: 011 44 20 7336 6396
www.bmgallery.co.uk

BEAUSSANT LEFÈVRE
32 rue Drouot, 7500 9 Paris, France
Tel: 011 33 1 47 70 40 00
www.beaussant-lefevre.auction.fr

BELHORN AUCTION SERVICES
PO Box 20211
Columbus, OH 43220
Tel: (614) 921-9441
www.belhorn.com

PIERRE BERGÉ & ASSOCIÉS
12 rue Drouot, 7500 9 Paris, France
Tel: 011 33 1 49 49 90 00
www.pba-auctions.com

AUKTIONSHAUS BERGMANN
Möhrendorfestraße 4
91056 Erlangen, Germany
Tel: 011 49 9 131 450 666
www.auction-bergmann.de

THE BIG WHITE HOUSE
www.thebigwhitehouse.com

BLANCHARD
86/88 Pimlico Road, London SW1W 8PL
Tel: 011 44 20 7823 6310

BLANCHET ET ASSOCIÉS
3 rue Geoffroy Marie
75009 Paris, France
Tel: 011 33 1 53 34 14 44

BLOCK GLASS LTD.
60 Ridgeview Avenue
Trumbull, CT 06611
Tel: (203) 556-0905
www.blockglass.com

DELORME ET COLLIN DU BOCAGE
11 rue de Miromesnil
75008 Paris, France
Tel: 011 33 1 58 18 39 05

BONHAMS, BAYSWATER
10 Salem Road, London W2 4DL
Tel: 011 44 20 7313 2727
www.bonhams.com

BONHAMS, BOND STREET
101 New Bond Street, London W1S 1SR
Tel: 011 44 20 7629 6602

BONHAMS, EDINBURGH
65 George Street, Edinburgh EH2 2JL
Tel: 011 44 131 2252266

BONHAMS, KNOWLE
The Old House, Station Road
Knowle, Solihull B93 0HT
Tel: 011 44 1564 776151

ROGER BRADBURY
11 Church Street, Coltishall
Norwich, Norfolk NR12 7DJ
Tel: 011 44 1603 737444

T.C.S. BROOKE
The Grange, Wroxham
Norfolk NR12 8RX
Tel: 011 44 1603 782644

BROOKSIDE ANTIQUES
44 North Water Street
New Bedford, MA 02740
Tel: (508) 993-4944
www.brooksideartglass.com

BRUNK AUCTIONS
PO Box 2135, Ashville, NC 28802
Tel: (828) 254-6846
www.brunkauctions.com

JOE DE BUCK
43 Rue des Minimes
B-100 0 Brussels, Belgium
Tel: 011 32 2 512 5516
Email: jdb-tribalart@belgacom.net

BUCKS COUNTY ANTIQUE CENTER
Route 202, 8 Skyline Drive
Lahaska, PA 18914
Tel: (215) 794-9180

BUKOWSKIS
Arsenalsgatan 4, Box 1754
111 87 Stockholm, Sweden
www.bukowskis.se

JOHN BULL (ANTIQUES) LTD
JB Silverware, 139A New Bond Street
London W1S 2TN
Tel: 011 44 20 7629 1251
www.antique-silver.co.uk

BURSTOW & HEWETT
Lower Lake, Battle, East Sussex TN33 0AT
Tel: 011 44 1424 772374
www.burstowandhewett.co.uk

CALDERWOOD GALLERY
1622 Spruce Street
Philadelphia, PA 19103-6719
Tel: (215) 546-5357
www.calderwoodgallery.com

CAPPELLINI
Sede Legale via A., Massena 12/7
20145 Milan, Italy
Tel: 011 39 031 759224
www.cappellini.it

CASSINA SPA
Via Busnelli 1, Meda, MI 200 36, Italy
www.cassina.it

CATALIN RADIOS
5443 Schultz Drive
Sylvania, OH 43560
Tel: (419) 824-2469
www.catalinradio.com

LENNOX CATO
1 The Square, Church Street
Edenbridge, Kent TN8 5BD
Tel: 011 44 1732 865988
www.lennoxcato.com

CHEFFINS
Clifton House, 1 & 2 Clifton Road
Cambridge CB1 7EA
Tel: 011 44 1223 213343
www.cheffins.co.uk

CHENU SCRIVE BERARD
Hôtel des Ventes, Lyon
Presqu'île Groupe Ivoire
6 rue Marcel Rivière
69002 Lyon, France
Tel: 011 33 4 72 77 78 01
www.chenu-scrive.com

CHEZ BURNETTE
615 South 6th Street
Philadelphia, PA 19147-2128
Tel: (215) 592-0256

CHICAGO SILVER
www.chicagosilver.com

CHINA SEARCH
PO Box 1202, Kenilworth
Warwickshire CV8 2WW
Tel: 011 44 1926 512402
www.chinasearch.co.uk

CHISHOLM LARSSON
145 8th Avenue
New York, NY 10011
Tel: (212) 741-1703
www.chisholm-poster.com

CHISWICK AUCTIONS
1–5 Colville Road, London W3 8BL
Tel: 011 44 20 8992 4442
www.chiswickauctions.co.uk

CLEVEDON SALEROOMS
The Auction Centre, Kenn Road
Kenn, Clevedon
Bristol BS21 6TT
Tel: 011 44 1934 830111
www.clevedon-salerooms.com

THE COEUR D'ALENE ART AUCTION
PO Box 310, Hayden, ID 83835
Tel: (208) 772-9009
www.cdaartauction.com

CONTEMPORARY CERAMICS
William Blake House
7 Marshall Street, London W1V 1LP
Tel: 011 44 20 7437 7605

GRAHAM COOLEY
Email: graham.cooley@metalysis.com

COTTEES
The Market, East Street, Wareham
Dorset BH20 4NR
Tel: 011 44 1929 552826/554915
www.auctionsatcottees.co.uk

COWDY GALLERY
31 Culver Street, Newent, Glos GL18 1DB
Tel: 011 44 1531 821173
www.cowdygallery.co.uk

MATALI CRASSET PRODUCTIONS
26 rue du Buisson, Saint Louis
F-75010 Paris, France
Tel: 011 33 1 42 40 99 89
www.matalicrasset.com

CUVREAU EXPERTISES ENCHÈRES
6 boulevard Saint-Vincent-de-Paul
40990 Saint-Paul-Les-Dax, France
Tel: 011 33 558 35 42 49

DAVIES ANTIQUES
Tel: 011 44 20 8947 1902
www.antique-meissen.com

DECO ETC
122 West 25th Street
New York, NY 10001
Tel: (212) 675 3326
www.decoetc.net

DECODAME.COM
853 Vanderbilt Beach Road
PMB 8, Naples, FL 34108
Tel: (239) 514-6797
www.decodame.com

DELORENZO GALLERY
956 Madison Avenue, NY
Tel: (212) 249-7575

THE DESIGN GALLERY
5 The Green, Westerham, Kent TN16 1AS
Tel: 011 44 1959 561234
www.designgallery.co.uk

DESIGN20C
www.design20c.com

GEOFFREY DINER GALLERY
1730 21st Street NW
Washington, DC 20009
Tel: (202) 483-5005
www.dinergallery.com

GALERIE MARISKA DIRKX
Wilhelminasingel 67
NL-6041 CH Roermond
Netherlands
Tel: 011 31 475 317137
www.galeriemariskadirkx.nl

PALAIS DOROTHEUM
Dorotheergaße 17
A-1010 Vienna, Austria
www.dorotheum.com

DREWEATT NEATE
Donnington Priory Salerooms
Donnington, Newbury RG14 2JE
Tel: 011 44 1635 553 553
www.dnfa.com

DREWEATT NEATE
The Nottingham Salerooms
192 Mansfield Road, Notts NG1 3HU
Tel: 011 44 115 9624141
www.dnfa.com

DREWEATT NEATE
Auction Hall, The Pantiles
Tunbridge Wells, Kent TN2 5QL
Tel: 011 44 1892 544500
www.dnfa.com

DROOG DESIGN
Staalstraat 7a–7b
1011 JJ Amsterdam, Netherlands
Tel: 011 31 20 523 50 50
www.droogdesign.nl

DYSON
www.dyson.com

THE END OF HISTORY
548½ Hudson Street
New York, NY 10014
Tel: (212) 647-7598

ETIENNE & VAN DEN DOEL
Anna Pauwlonastraat 105a
2518 BD, Den Haag, Netherlands
Tel: 011 31 703646239
www.etiennevandendoel.com

JILL FENICHELL, INC.
Brooklyn, NY 11238
Tel: (718) 237-2490
Email: jfenichell@yahoo.com

FESTIVAL
136 South Ealing Road, London W5 4QJ
Tel: 011 44 20 8840 9333

THE FINE ART SOCIETY
148 New Bond Street, London W1S 2JT
Tel: 011 44 20 7629 5116
www.faslondon.com

FINESSE FINE ART
Empool Cottage, West Knighton
Dorset DT2 8PE
Tel: 011 44 1305 854286
www.finesse-fine-art.com

AUKTIONHAUS DR FISCHER
Trappensee-Schößchen
D-74074 Heilbronn, Germany
Tel: 011 49 71 31 15 55 70
www.auctions-fischer.de

GALLERY 532
142 Duane Street
New York, NY 10013
Tel: (212) 964-1282
www.gallery532.com/

GALERIE HÉLÈNE FOURNIER GUÉRIN
18 rue des Saints-Pères
75007 Paris, France
Tel: 011 33 1 42 60 21 81

FRAGILE DESIGN
14/15 The Custard Factory
Digbeth, Birmingham B9 4AA
Tel: 011 44 121 224 7378
www.fragiledesign.com

FREEMAN'S
1808 Chestnut Street
Philadelphia, PA 19103
Tel: (215) 563-9275
www.freemansauction.com

RICHARD GARDNER ANTIQUES
Swan House, Market Square
Petworth, West Sussex GU28 0AH
Tel: 011 44 1798 343411
www.richardgardenerantiques.co.uk

GALLERY YVES GASTOU
12 rue Bonaparte, 75006 Paris, France
Tel: 011 33 1 53 73 00 10

THOS. WM. GAZE & SON
Diss Auction Rooms
Roydon Road, Diss, Norfolk IP22 4LN
Tel: 011 44 1379 650306
www.twgaze.com

SIDNEY GECKER
226 West 21st Street
New York, NY 10011
Tel: (212) 929-8789

THE GLASS MERCHANT
Tel: 011 44 7775 683 961
Email: as@titan98.freeserve.co.uk

LEAH GORDON ANTIQUES
Gallery 18
Manhattan Art and Antiques Center
1050 Second Avenue
New York, NY 100 22
Tel: (212) 872-1422
www.the-maac.com/leahgordon

GORRINGES, BEXHILL
Terminus Road, Bexhill-on-Sea
East Sussex TN39 3LR
Tel: 011 44 1424 212994
www.gorringes.co.uk

GORRINGES, LEWES
15 North Street, Lewes
East Sussex BN7 2PD
Tel: 011 44 1273 472503
www.gorringes.co.uk

GARY GRANT
18 Arlington Way, London EC1R 1UY
Tel: 011 44 20 7713 1122

HALCYON DAYS
14 Brook Street, London W1S 1BD
Tel: 011 44 20 7629 8811
www.halcyondays.co.uk

HALL-BAKKER @ HERITAGE
Heritage, 6 Market Place
Woodstock, Oxon OX20 1TA
Tel: 011 44 1993 811332

JEANETTE HAYHURST FINE GLASS
32A Kensington Church Street
London W8 4HA
Tel: 011 44 20 7938 1539
www.antiqueglass-london.com

GALERIE MARIANNE HELLER
Friedrich-Ebert-Anlage 2
69117 Heidelberg, Germany
Tel: 011 49 6221 619090
www.galerie-heller.de

HERMANN HISTORICA OHG
Linprunstraße 16
80335 Munich, Germany
Tel: 011 49 895 237 296
www.hermann-historica.com

HERR AUCTIONS
W.G. Herr Art & Auction House
Friesenwall 35, 50672 Cologne, Germany
Tel: 011 49 221 25 45 48
www.herr-auktionen.de

HIGH STYLE DECO
224 West 18th Street
New York, NY 10011
Tel: (212) 647-0035
www.highstyledeco.com

HOLSTEN GALLERIES
Elm Street
Stockbridge, MA 01262
Tel: (413) 298-3044
www.holstengalleries.com

HOPE AND GLORY
131A Kensington Church Street
London W8 7LP
Tel: 011 44 20 7727 8424

JONATHAN HORNE
Sampson & Horne Antiques
120 Mount Street, London W1K 3NN
Tel: 011 44 20 7409 1799
www.jonathanhorne.co.uk

JOHN HOWARD @ HERITAGE
Heritage, 6 Market Place
Woodstock, Oxon OX20 1TA
www.antiquepottery.co.uk

RICK HUBBARD ART DECO
3 Tee Court, Bell Street, Romsey
Hampshire SO51 8GY
Tel: 011 44 7767 267 607
www.rickhubbard-artdeco.co.uk

IMPERIAL HALF BUSHEL
831 N. Howard Street
Baltimore, MD 21201
Tel: (410) 462-1192
www.imperialhalfbushel.com

INGRAM ANTIQUES
669 Mt. Pleasant Road
Toronto, Canada M4S 2N2
Tel: (416) 484-4601

IVEY SELKIRK AUCTIONEERS
7447 Forsyth Boulevard
St. Louis, MO 63105
Tel: (314) 726-5515
www.iveyselkirk.com

JACOBS AND HUNT FINE ART AUCTIONEERS LIMITED
26 Lavant Street, Petersfield
Hampshire GU32 3EF
Tel: 011 44 1730 233933
www.jacobsandhunt.co.uk

JAZZY
34 Church Street, London NW8 8EP
Tel: 011 44 20 7724 0837
www.jazzyartdeco.com

JOHN JESSE ANTIQUES
Tel: 011 44 7767 497 880
E-mail: jj@johnjesse.com

JAMES D. JULIA, INC.
PO Box 830, Fairfield, ME 04937
Tel: (207) 453-7125
www.juliaauctions.com

LEO KAPLAN MODERN
41 East 57th Street, 7th Floor
New York, NY 10021
Tel: (212) 872-1616
www.lkmodern.com

AUKTIONHAUS KAUPP
Schloss Sulzburg, Hauptstraße 62
79295 Sulzburg, Germany
Tel: 011 49 7634 5038 0
www.kaupp.de

KELLER & ROSS
PO Box 783, Melrose, MA 02716
Tel: (978) 988-2070
www.members.aol.com/kellerross

JOHN KING
74 Pimlico Road, London SW1W 8LS
Tel: 011 44 20 7730 0427
Email: kingj896@aol.com

ANTIQUES BY JOYCE KNUTSEN
Email: knutsenglass@aol.com

GALLERIE KOLLER
Hardturmstraße 102
Postfach 8031, Zürich
Switzerland
Tel: 011 41 1445 6363
www.galeriekoller.ch

AUCTION TEAM KÖLN
Postfach 50 11 19,
Bonner Str. 528-530
D-50971 Cologne, Germany
Tel: 011 49 221 38 70 49
www.breker.com

DANNY LANE
www.dannylane.co.uk

LAW FINE ART LTD.
Ash Cottage, Ashmore Green
Newbury, Berkshire RG18 9ER
Tel: 011 44 1635 860033
www.lawfineart.co.uk

LAWRENCES' AUCTIONEERS
The Linen Yard, South Street
Crewkerne, Somerset TA18 8AB
Tel: 011 44 1460 73041
www.lawrences.co.uk

LIBERTY
Regent Street, London W1
Tel: 011 44 20 7734 1234
www.liberty.co.uk

ANDREW LINEHAM FINE GLASS
Saturdays only or by appointment
101 Portobello Road, London W11 2QB
Tel: 011 44 1243 576 241
www.antiquecolouredglass.com

LOST CITY ARTS
18 Cooper Square
New York, NY 10003
Tel: (212) 375-0500
www.lostcityarts.com

LOTHERTON HALL
Lotherton Hall, Lotherton Lane
Aberford, Leeds LS25 3EB
Tel: 011 44 113 2813259
www.leeds.gov.uk/lothertonhall

DAVID LOVE
10 Royal Parade, Harrogate HG1 2SZ
Tel: 011 44 1423 565797

FREDERIC LOZADA EXPERTISES
10 rue de Pomereu, 75116 Paris, France
Tel: 011 33 1 53 70 23 70
www.fredericlozada.com

LUNA
23 George Street, Nottingham NG1 3BH
Tel: 011 44 115 9243267
www.luna-online.co.uk

LYON & TURNBULL
33 Broughton Place, Edinburgh EH1 3RR
Tel: 011 44 131 557 8844
www.lyonandturnbull.com

MACKLOWE GALLERY
667 Madison Avenue
New York, NY 10021
Tel: (212) 644-6400
www.macklowegallery.com

JOHN MAKEPEACE
Designers and Furniture-makers
Farrs Beaminster, Dorset DT8 3NB
Tel: 011 44 1308 862204
www.johnmakepeace.com

MALLETT
141 New Bond Street, London W1S 2BS
Tel: 011 44 20 7499 7411
www.mallett.co.uk

LILI MARLEEN
52 White Street
New York, NY 10013
Tel: (212) 219-0006
www.lilimarleen.net

FRANCESCA MARTIRE
F131–137 Alfie's Antiques Market
13 Church Street, London NW8 8DT
Tel: 011 44 20 7724 4802

GALERIE MAURER
Kurfurstenstraße 17,
D-80799 Munich, Germany
Tel: 011 49 89 271 13 45
www.galerie-objekte-maurer.de

INGO MAURER
Kaiserstraße 47
80801 Munich, Germany
Tel: 011 49 89 381 60 60
www.ingo-maurer.com

MEMPHIS AND POST
Via Olivetti 9
200 10 Pregnan Milanese, Italy
Tel: 011 39 293 290 663
www.memphis-milano.it

AUKTIONSHAUS METZ
Friedrich-Eber-Anlage 5
69117 Heidelberg, Germany
Tel: 011 49 6221 23571
www.Metz-Auktion.de

ARTHUR MILLNER
Tel: 011 44 7900 248 390
www.arthurmillner.com

MODERNE GALLERY
111 North 3rd Street
Philadelphia, PA 19106
Tel: (215) 923-8536
www.modernegallery.com

MODERNISM GALLERY
1622 Ponce de Leon Boulevard
Coral Gables, FL 33134
Tel: (305) 442-8743
www.modernism.com

MOOD INDIGO
181 Prince Street
New York, NY 10012
Tel: (212) 254-1176
www.moodindigonewyork.com

MOSTLY BOXES
93 High Street, Eton,
Berkshire SL4 6AF
Tel: 011 44 1753 858470

THE MULTICOLOURED TIME SLIP
Alfie's Antiques Market, Unit S00 2
13–25 Church Street
London NW8 8DT
Email: d_a_cameron@hotmail.com

MUM HAD THAT
www.mumhadthat.com

NAGEL
Neckarstraße 189-191
70190 Stuttgart, Germany
Tel: 011 49 711 649 690
www.auction.de

LILLIAN NASSAU LTD
220 East 57th Street
New York, NY 100 22
Tel: (212) 759-6062
www.lilliannassau.com

JOHN NICHOLSON
The Auction Rooms, Longfield
Midhurst Road,
Fernhurst, Haslemere
Surrey GU27 3HA
Tel: 011 44 1428 653727
www.johnnicholsons.com

GALLERY 1930 SUSIE COOPER
18 Church Street, London NW8 8EP
Tel: 011 44 20 7723 1555
www.susiecooperceramics.com

NO PINK CARPET
Tel: 011 44 1785 249 802
www.nopinkcarpet.com

NORTHEAST AUCTIONS
93 Pleasant Street
Portsmouth, NH 03801
Tel: (603) 433-8400
www.northeastauctions.com

GALERIE OLIVIA ET EMMANUEL
Village Suisse Galeries 24 et 58
78 avenue de Suffren
75015 Paris, France
Tel: 011 33 1 43 06 85 30
www.artface.com/olivia

R.A. O'NEIL ANTIQUES
100 Avenue Road
Toronto, Canada
Tel: (416) 968-2806

ONSLOWS
The Coach House, Manor Road
Stourpaine, Dorset DT11 8TQ
Tel: 011 44 1258 488838
www.onslows.co.uk

OTFORD ANTIQUES AND COLLECTORS CENTRE
26-28 High Street, Otford
Kent TN14 5PQ
Tel: 011 44 1959 522025
www.otfordantiques.co.uk

PARTRIDGE FINE ARTS PLC
144-146 New Bond Street
London W1S 2PF
Tel: 011 44 20 7629 0834
www.partridgeplc.com

GAETANO PESCE
543 Broadway
New York, NY 10012
Tel: (212) 334-7134
www.gaetanopesce.com

DAVID PICKUP
115 High St, Burford
Oxon OX18 4RG
Tel: 011 44 1993 822555

SALLE DES VENTES PILLET
1 rue de la Libération B.P. 23
27480 Lyons la Forêt, France
Tel: 011 33 2 32 49 60 64
www.pillet.auction.fr

POOK AND POOK
463 East Lancaster Avenue
Downingtown, PA 19335
Tel: (610) 269-4040
www.pookandpook.com

PORT ANTIQUES CENTER
289 Main Street
Port Washington, NY 11050
Tel: (516) 767-3313
E-mail: visualedge2@aol.com

POSTERITATI
239 Centre Street
New York, NY 10013
Tel: (212) 226-2207
www.posteritati.com

PRITAM & EAMES
29 Race Lane
East Hampton, NY 11937
Email: PritamEame@aol.com

PURITAN VALUES
The Dome, St Edmund's Road
Southwold, Suffolk IP18 6BZ
Tel: 011 44 1502 722211

QUITTENBAUM
Hohenstaufenstraße 1
D-80801 Munich, Germany
Tel: 011 49 859 33 00 75 6
E-mail: dialog@quittenbaum.de

DAVID RAGO AUCTIONS
333 North Main Street
Lambertville, NJ 08530
Tel: (609) 397-9374
www.ragoarts.com

**DAVID RAGO/NICHOLAS DAWES
LALIQUE AUCTIONS**
333 North Main Street
Lambertville, NJ 08530
Tel: (609) 397-9374
www.ragoarts.com

R. DUANE REED GALLERY
7th Floor, 529 West 20th Street
New York, NY 100 11
Tel: (212) 462-2600
www.rduanereedgallerynyc.com

**DEREK ROBERTS FINE ANTIQUE
CLOCKS & BAROMETERS**
25 Shipbourne Road
Tonbridge, Kent TN10 3DN
Tel: 011 44 1732 358986
www.qualityantiqueclocks.com

ROGERS DE RIN
76 Royal Hospital Road, Paradise Walk
London SW3 4HN
Tel: 011 44 20 7352 9007
www.rogersderin.co.uk

ROSEBERY
74–76 Knight's Hill, London SE27 0JD
Tel: 011 44 20 8761 2522
www.roseberys.co.uk

ROSSINI SA
7 rue Drouot 75009, Paris, France
Tel: 011 33 1 53 34 55 00
www.rossini.fr

RITCHES AUCTIONEERS & APPRAISERS
288 King Street East
Toronto, Ontario, Canada M5A 1KA
Tel: (416) 364-1864
www.ritchies.com

R20TH CENTURY
82 Franklin Street
New York, NY 10013
Tel: (212) 343-7979
www.r20thcentury.com

HUGO RUEF
Gabelsbergerstraße 28
80333 Munich, Germany
Tel: 011 49 89 52 40 84
www.ruef-auktionen.de

SCP LIMITED
135–139 Curtain Road
London EC2A 3BX
Tel: 011 44 20 7739 1869
www.scp.co.uk

SENIOR & CARMICHAEL
Church Street, Betchworth
Surrey RH3 7DN
Tel: 011 44 1737 844316
www.seniorandcarmichael.co.uk

THE SILVER FUND
1 Duke of York Street
London SW1Y 6JP
Tel: 011 44 20 7839 7664
www.thesilverfund.com

PAUL SIMONS
Admiral Vernon Antiques Center
141–149 Portobello Road, London W11
Tel: 011 44 7733 326 574

BOREK SIPEK
www.sipek.com

SKINNER
63 Park Plaza, Boston, MA 02116
Tel: (617) 350-5400
www.skinnerinc.com

SLOANS & KENYON
4605 Bradley Boulevard
Bethesda, MD 20815
Tel: (301) 634-2330
www.sloansandkenyon.com

SOLLO:RAGO MODERN AUCTIONS
333 North Main Street
Lambertville, NJ 08530
Tel: (609) 397-9374
www.ragoarts.com

HANSEN SØRENSEN
Vesterled 19
DK-6950 Ringkøbing, Denmark
Tel: 011 45 97 32 45 08
www.hansensorensen.com

STARCK NETWORK
18/20 rue du Faubourg du Temple
75011 Paris, France
Tel: 011 33 1 48 07 54 54

STOCKSPRING ANTIQUES
114 Kensington Church Street
London W8 4BH
Tel: 011 44 20 7727 7995
www.antique-porcelain.co.uk

STYLE GALLERY
10 Camden Passage, London N1 8ED
Tel: 011 44 20 7359 7867

SPENCER SWAFFER ANTIQUES
30 High Street, Arundel
West Sussex BN18 9AB
Tel: 011 44 1903 882132
www.spencerswaffer.com

SWANN GALLERIES
104 East 25th Street
New York, NY 10010
Tel: (212) 254-4710
www.swanngalleries.com

SWORDERS
14 Cambridge Road, Stansted
Mountfitchet, Essex CM24 8BZ
Tel: 011 44 1279 817778
www.sworder.co.uk

TAKE-A-BOO EMPORIUM
1927 Avenue Road, Toronto
Ontario M5M 4A2, Canada
Tel: (416) 785-4555
www.takeaboo.com

TECTA
D-37697 Lauenförde, Germany
Tel: 011 49 5273 378 90
www.tecta.de

TELKAMP
Galerie Telkamp, Maximilianstraße 6
80539 Munich, Germany
Tel: 011 49 89 226 283

TENDO MOKKO
1-3-10 Midaregawa
Tendo, Yamagata, Japan
Tel: 023 653 3121
www.tendo-mokko.co.jp

TITUS OMEGA
Cross Street, Islington, London N1
Tel: 011 44 20 7688 1295
www.titusomega.com

TRIO
L24 Grays Antique Market
58 Davies Mews
London W1K 5AB
Tel: 011 44 20 7493 2736
www.trio-london.fsnet.co.uk

TWENTIETH CENTURY MARKS
Whitegates, Rectory Road
Little Burstead
Essex CM12 9TR
Tel: 011 44 1268 411000
www.20thcenturymarks.co.uk/

VAN DEN BOSCH
Shop 1, Georgian Village
Camden Passage
London N1 8DU
Tel: 011 44 20 7226 4550
www.vandenbosch.co.uk

GALERIE VANDERMEERSCH
Voltaire Antiquités-Vandermeersch SA
21 quai Voltaire
7500 7 Paris, France
Tel: 011 33 1 42 61 23 10

ROBERT VENTURI
www.vsba.com

VETRO & ARTE GALLERY
Calle del Capeler 3212
Dorsoduro, 30123 Venice, Italy
Tel: 011 39 041 522 8525
www.venicewebgallery.com

JOHANNES VOGT AUKTIONEN
Antonienstraße 3
80802 Munich, Germany
Tel: 011 49 89 33079139
www.vogt-auctions.de

VON SPAETH
Willhelm-Diess-Weg 13
81927 Munich, Germany
Tel: 011 49 89 2809132
www.glasvonspaeth.com

VON ZEZSCHWITZ
Friedrichstraße 1a
80801 Munich, Germany
Tel: 011 49 89 38 98 930
www.von-zezschwitz.de

JONATHAN WADSWORTH
Wadsworth's, Marehill, Pulborough
West Sussex RH20 2DY
Tel: 011 44 1798 873555
www.wadsworthsrugs.com

RICHARD WALLIS ANTIKS
Tel: 011 44 20 8529 1749
www.richardwallisantiks.com

MIKE WEEDON
7 Camden Passage, London N1 8EA
Tel: 011 44 20 7226 5319
www.mikeweedonantiques.com

WILFRIED WEGIEL
Cité des Antiquaires
117 boulevard Stalingrad
69100 Lyon-Villeurbane, France
Email: wilfriedwegiel@aol.com

WIENER KUNST AUKTIONEN
Palais Kinsky
Freyung 4, 1010 Vienna, Austria
Tel: 011 43 15 32 42 00
www.palais-kinsky.com

**MARY WISE AND GROSVENOR
ANTIQUES**
58 Kensington Church Street
London W8 4DB
Tel: 011 44 20 7937 8649
www.wiseantiques.com

WOOLLEY & WALLIS
51-61 Castle Street, Salisbury SP1 3SU
Tel: 011 44 1722 424500
www.woolleyandwallis.co.uk

WRIGHT
1440 West Hubbard
Chicago, IL 60622
Tel: (312) 563-0020
www.wright20.com

JUNNAA & THOMI WROBLEWSKI
78 Marylebone High Street, Box 39
London W1U 5AP
Tel: 011 44 20 7499 7793
E-mail: junnaa@wroblewski.eu.com

ZANOTTA
Via Vittorio Veneto 57
200 54 Nova Milanese, Italy
Tel: 011 39 0362 4981
www.zanotta.it

INDEX

Page numbers in *italics* refer to
illustrations/captions

A

Aalto, Alvar 251, *251*, 259, *259*, 315
Aarnio, Eero 328, *328*
Abstract Impressionism 337, 366, 377,
   396
Acier, Michel-Victor 69
Action Painting 396
Adam, Robert *51*, 53, *53*, 57, *57*, 65,
   78–79, 82
   style 102, 103
Adams, John and Truda 283
Adelberg, Louise 333
Adnet, Jacques 295, 357
Aesthetic Movement 111, 125, 128,
   148–149
African influence 269, 271, 276, *276*, 279
agricultural revolution 50
Aitchison, George 168
Aladin, Tamara 342, *353*
albarelli 16, 32, 67, *67*, 107
Albers, Anni 263, 368
Albert Memorial, London 120
Albini, Franco 319, 357
Alchimia design 377, 386, 386–387,
   387, 389, 391
ALCOA 300
Alcock, Sir Rutherford 99
Alessi, Alberto 260
Alessi design 377, 387, 394, *394*, 403,
   416, 417, *417*
Alhambra, Granada 13, *13*
Alloway, Laurence 366
Alumina ceramics 333, *333*
aluminum, Art Deco 300
Amelung, Johann Friedrich 73
American art pottery 202–203
American folk art 86–87
American Indian series 159, *159*
American Modern range ceramics 334,
   334, 402
American Revolution 51
Amphora range ceramics *200*, 200–201,
   204
An Túr Gloine 171
Anderson, Winslow 351
andirons: 19th-century 124, *124*, 125
   Rococo 43, *43*
animal figures/motifs: Art Deco 269,
   280, *280*, 284, 290, *290*, 309, *309*
   folk art 86
   Neoclassical 60
   19th-century 109, *109*
   19th-century American 111, *111*
   19th-century French *138*, 138–139, *139*
   19th-century Viennese 139, *139*
   Rococo 22, *22*
animaliers 138–139
Annaberg ceramics 30
apothecary jars (see also *albarelli*) 107
Apple computers 395
Apsley Pellatt glass 119
Arab Hall 147, 168, *168*
Arabia ceramics 333, *333*, 334
Arad, Ron 381, 392, 393, *393*
Arequipa Pottery 161
Argenta range ceramics 279
Arkipelago range glass 344
Arnoux, Leon 107
Arredoluce lamps 356–357, *357*
Arteluce lamps 356, 357, *357*
Artemide lamps *354*, 355
Artificer's Guild *146*, 175, *180*, 181,
   221
Artigas, Josep Llorens 339
Arts and Crafts movement/style 102,

123, 144–157, 356
   American 144–145, 320
Ashbee, Charles 144, 151, 171, 172,
   174, *174*, 176, *180*, 221, 246
Ashstead Potters 283
ashtray: Art Deco 296
   Jensen 302
   mid-20th-century *317*, 353, 362, 366
   Ray Hollis 417, *417*
Asian influence (see also Chinese
   influence; Japanese influence) 22, 23,
   32, 33, 36, 40, 97, 99, 107, 109, 397
Asko Oy furniture 328
Asplund, Gunnar 333
Atelier Martine textiles 306
ATO clocks 303
Aubusson textiles 22, 46, *46*, 47, *47*,
   135, *135*, 307
Augustus the Strong, Elector of Saxony
   34
Aulenti, Gae 354, *354*
Ault Pottery 238, 242, *242*
Ausbach porcelain 37, *37*
Autio, Rudy 399, *399*, *405*
AVEM glass 346

B

Baccarat Glassworks 72, 116, *116*, 119
Bailey, Henrietta 202, 203
Bakalowits & Söhne lamps *258*
Bakelite 296, *296*
Baker, Josephine 267, 268, 276, *276*,
   310
Bakewell, Pears & Co. glass 73
Baldwin, Philip *412*
Ballets Russes 271, 306
Ballin, Mogens 222, 261
Banal Design 387
Bang, Jacob 342, *343*
Bang, Michael 342
Barbe, Jules 121
Barbecue ceramic design 335
Barberi, Michelangelo 132
Barberi, Alfredo 347, *347*
Barlow, Hannah 164, *164*
Barnsley, Ernest and Sidney *145*, 151,
   151
Barovier, Ercole 346, 346–347
Barovier & Toso glass 346, *346*, 347
barrel, 19th-century glass 121
Barye, Antoine-Louis 138, *138*
basin, Delft 33
baskets: Blow-Up *417*
   ceramic *341*
   silver 79, *96*
Bass, Saul 371
Batchelder ceramics 166
Batterham, Richard *341*
Baudisch, Gudrun *254*
Bauhaus 239, *239*, 242, *248*, 370
   ceramics 255
   furniture 248–249
   influence 272
   textiles 263, 307
Baxter, Geoffrey 350, *350*
Bayer, Herbert 239
B&B Italia furniture 381
beakers: Neoclassical 68, 75, 76, 77
   19th-century 117
   Rococo 22, 23, 38, 39
Beale, Lady Phipson *184*
Beardsley, Aubrey 189, 235, *235*
Beauties of America series ceramics
   109, *109*
Beauvais tapestries 47
Bedin, Martine 390, *391*
bedrooms: Aarnio 328
   Gropius 239
beds: Horta *195*
   lit en bateau 60
bedsteads, iron 125

Behrens, Peter 198, 234, 261
Bel Design 387
Bel Geddes, Norman 296, 300, *301*
Bell, Vanessa 263
Belleek ceramics, American 111
belt pin, Art Nouveau *220*
Belter, John Henry 101, *101*, 322
bench, Fish *385*
Benedictus, Édouard: *Relais* 128
Bennett, Gary Knox *385*, *415*
Bennett, John 111, *111*
Benney, Gerald 361
Benson, W.A.S. 172, 175, *175*, *180*,
   221
Bérain, Jean 28, 47, 66, *67*
Berghof, Norbert 378
Bergmann, Franz 139, *139*
Bergqvist, Gustave 343
Bergqvist, Knut 291
Berlage, H. P. 261
Berlin ceramics 69, *69*, 255, 281
Bernadotte, Sigvard 299, 334, 360–361
Bernhardt, Sarah 232
Berry, Mary Chase 163
Berthon, Paul 233, *233*
Bertoia, Harry 327, *327*
Bianchini-Férier textiles 306
Biancini, Angelo 279
Bianconi, Fulvio 347, 349, *349*, 413
Biedermeier style 50, *52*, 54, 61, 75, 77,
   79, 81, 103, 112
Big White House, Sussex 375
Billingsley, William 53, *53*, 69, *69*
Biloxi Art Pottery 160
Bimini Glass and Jewellery Workshop
   257
Binazzi, Lupo 387
Bing & Grondahl 200, *200*, 222, 279,
   333
Bing, Siegfried 193, 194, 212, 230
biomorphism 317, 333
bird figures 86, *107*, *139*, 164, 347, *347*,
   411
Birmingham Guild of Handicraft *174*,
   175, *181*
Bizarre range textiles 47, 88
Bizarre Ware 282
Blake, Peter 366
   Sergeant Pepper's ... album cover 366
Blenko glass 350–351
Blount, Godfrey 174
Blow-Up series products 417, *417*
Blue Room, Musée Carnavalet 25
Boch Frères ceramics 276, 279
Böck, Jos., porcelain 255
Bogler, Theodor 255
Böhm, August 120, *120*
Boizot, Louis-Simon 93
Bonaparte, Jérôme 61
bonbonnières: Art Nouveau 223, *224*
   Neoclassical 83
Bonet, Antonio 327, *327*
Bonetti, Mattia 378, 379
Bonheur, Isidore-Jules 139, *139*
Bony, Jean-François 89
bookcase: Art Deco *273*
   Arts and Crafts 151, *155*
   Carlton 389
bookend, Art Deco 303
bookmark, Arts and Crafts *180*
bookshelves: Bookworm 393
   Brick *381*
Bosch, Hieronymus 399, *399*
Boston & Sandwich Glass Co. 73, *73*,
   117, 119
Bothin, Henry E. 161
Böttger, Johann Friedrich 10, 30, 34, 67
bottle: Leach 256
   Marinot *259*
   mid-20th-century *352*
   Persian Blue *350*
   postmodern *400*

Rococo 39
Boucher, François 46–47, 88, 93
Boullework 44, *45*, 102, 130, *130*
Boulsover, Thomas 79
Boulton, Matthew 79, *79*
Bouroullec, Ronan and Erwan 381, *381*
Bouval, Maurice 231, *231*
Bow porcelain 37
bowl and pitcher, 19th-century *110*
bowls: Art Deco 293, 299
   Art Nouveau 204, 209, 211, 217
   Arts and Crafts 166, *175*, 177
   Daum 288
   early modernist 254
   Fazzoletto 349
   Gazelle 290, *290*
   Hamada 256
   Jazz 283, *283*
   Kalo Shop 179
   Knox 177
   Krenitware 362
   Leach 241
   mid-20th-century 362
   Neoclassical 72
   19th-century 107, *126*, 112
   pâte-de-verre 289
   postmodern glass *412*, 413
   punch 166
   Rie 257
   rose *180*
   Siren of the Sea 203
   Sol 389
   sugar (Dresser) 242
   Tiffany 300
   Zip *412*
boxes: Architex 302
   Art Deco 302
   Arts and Crafts *146*, *175*, *181*
   biscuit 126
   cigar *181*
   and cover 279
   folk art 86, *87*
   powder 302
   tartanware 132
Braden, Norah 257
Bradley, Will 235
Brandt, Edgar 288, 295, 299
Brandt, Marianne 259, *260*, 260–261
Brannam, C. H. 166, *167*
Branzi, Andrea 403, *403*, *415*
Brau, Casimir 299
Bredendieck, Hin 259
Breuer, Marcel *241*, 248, *248*, 249, 380,
   386
Brighton Pavilion, Sussex 61
Britten & Gibson, glass 170
Britton, Alison 397, *397*
Brocard, Philippe-Joseph 121
Brocklehurst, Keith *412*
Brongniart, Alexander 69
bronze: Art Nouveau 190, 191, *191*,
   218, 219, 231, 232
   Chinese 12
   cold-painted 139, *139*
   Egyptian 10
   gilded (ormolu) *124*, 125, *125*
   19th-century 124–125
   19th-century French *138*, 138–139, *139*
   19th-century Viennese 139, *139*
   Rococo clocks 45
Brouwer, Theophilus 161
Brown, Edith 203
Brychtová, Jaroslava 409
buffets, 19th-century 101, 103
Bugatti, Carlo 195, *195*
Bulow-Hube, Viviana Torun 223
Burden, Bessie 185
bureau cabinet, Rococo 27
bureau à cylindre 57
bureau plat, Rococo 25, *25*
Burne-Jones, Edward 121, 170, 184,
   231
Bursley Ware ceramics 204

Burt, Stanley 159
bust, Art Deco 284
   Neoclassical 92, *93*
Butler, Frank 164
Byrdcliffe Arts Colony 154, *154*
Byzantine art 12–13

C

cabinet system, Boligens Byggeskabe
   318
cabinets: Art Deco 271, 275
   Art Nouveau 191
   Arts and Crafts 148, *156*
   display 156, 275
   Frankfurt F1 Skyscraper 378
   inlaid 155
   Mackintosh 245
   mid-20th-century 319, 330
   music 156
   19th-century *104*
   19th-century Gothic 102
   Urn 382
cabochons, ceramic 165
cachepot, Art Nouveau 198
Café Costes, Paris 392
Cairo bazaar 134
Caldas de Reinha ceramics 107
Calder, Alexander 401
California Loop series glass 406
Camozza, Luigi *412*
Campana, Humberto and Fernando 417,
   417
candelabra: Art Nouveau 223, *224*
   Jensen 302
   Neoclassical 54, 79
   19th-century 112, *122*, *124*, *127*
candlesticks: Art Deco 299
   Art Nouveau 221, *224*
   Brancaster 351
   Empire 60
   Flèche 298
   Kalo Shop *179*, 302
   mid-20th-century 363
   Neoclassical 78, 79
   19th-century 107
   Olbrich 260
   postmodern 416, *416*, 417
   Rococo 43, *43*
   Sheringham *350*, 351
   Sunrise 416
   Tudric *180*
Canova, Antoine 92
Cantagalli ceramics 107
Capellini furniture *380*, 381, *381*
Capodimonte porcelain 36
Capron, Roger 330
Carabin, Rupert 231
Caranza glass 215
card tray, Art Nouveau 190, *224*
Carder, Frederick 210, 290
Cardew, Michael 257, 336, *336*, 401
   Pioneer Pottery 336
Cardin, Pierre 369, *369*
Carlin, Martin 56
Carlton Ware 276, 282
Carlu, Jean 370
carpets (see also rugs): Caucasian 135
   Chinese 135, *135*
   French 135, *135*
   Persian *134*, 134–135
   Swinging Woman 307
   Turkish 135
Carr, Alwyn C. *181*, 221
Carriès, Jean (Joseph-Marie) 198
Carter, Charles 283
Casati, Cesare 355, *355*
casket, Arts and Crafts 151
Cassandre (Adolf Mouron) 310, *310*
Cassina, Cesare 354
cast iron, 19th-century 102, 125, *125*
Castiglione, Achille 354, 357, *357*, 393
Castle, Wendell 319, 329, 377, 382, *382*

"cathedral" style 102
Catherine the Great 59, 78, 89
Catteau, Charles 279, *279*
Cawardine, George 295, *295*
Cazaux, Édouard 279
Cellini, Benvenuto 122, 138
Celtic influence/revival 99, 122, 123, 144, 146, 175, 176–177, 182, 221, 242
Cenedese glass 348
centerpieces: Art Deco *301*
   Art Nouveau 224
   19th-century *122*
Century Guild 170
Ceramic Art Co. 111
ceramics (*see also* porcelain)
   American art 163
   American Belleek 111, *111*
   American folk 87
   Art Deco British 282–283
   Art Deco French 278–279
   Art Deco gallery 284–285
   Art Deco Italian 279
   Art Deco Scandinavian 279
   Art Nouveau American 202–203
   Art Nouveau French 198–199
   Art Nouveau gallery 204–205
   Arts and Crafts gallery 164–165
   basalt ware 53, *53*, 55, 64–65, 74, 93
   Bauhaus 255
   bleus de Nevers 67
   blue-and-white 109, *109*
   chalkware 111, *111*
   Chelsea Keramic 161, *162*
   Constructivist 255
   creamware 64, *64*, 66, 67
   Delft ware/delftware 33, *33*, 66
   Doulton 148, 164, 183, 281, 283
   earthenware 31, 33, 66, 93
   faience fine 67
   faience, French 32, *32*, 66–67, 106, *316*, 333, *333*, 338
   faience, German ("fayence") 33, 67, 67, 107
   faiences parlantes 67
   Funk 398–399
   German stoneware 30, *30*
   Greek *10*, 11
   Grueby 159, 162
   Hispano-Moresque 32
   Islamic fritware 13
   Iznik 13, *13*, 97, 99
   jasper ware 53, 64, 65
   Lotusware 111, *111*
   maiolica 16, 17, 33, *33*, 66, 67, *67*, 106, 107
   majolica 107, *107*
   Mannerist 17
   Martin brothers 164
   mid-20th-century gallery 340–341
   mid-20th-century mass-produced 334–335
   mid-20th-century Scandinavian 332–333
   mocha ware 110
   Neoclassical British 53, 55, 64–65
   Neoclassical gallery 70–71
   19th-century American 110–111
   19th-century English 108–109
   19th-century folk revival 106–107
   19th-century French 106
   19th-century German 107
   Ohr 160–161
   pâte-sur-pâte 200
   pearl ware 53, 64, *64*
   postmodern 400–401
   postmodern American 396–397
   postmodern British 397, 400–401
   postmodern mass-produced 402–403
   Queensware 64
   red ware 65, *65*
   red ware, Pennsylvania 87, *87*, 110, *110*
   Rockingham ware 110
   Rookwood 158–159
   rosso antico 55, 65, 74
   Ruskin 165
   salt-glazed 31, *31*
   Satsuma earthenware *148*

slipware 31, *31*, 87
spatter ware 110, *110*
studio pottery 256–257, 316, 336–339, 401
tin-glazed 31, 106–107
toleware 87, *87*
Wiener Werkstätte 254–255
Ceramics for Shiva range 389
chairs: Akaba S. A. Garriri 379
   Aleph *392*
   American Classical *61*
   Angel *382*
   Ant (3100) 315, 322
   Argyle *244*, 245
   Art Deco 270, 271, 274
   Art Nouveau *193*
   Arts and Crafts 155, *157*
   Ball 328, *328*
   Bambi *379*
   Barbare *378*
   Barcelona 249
   Barrel 252, *252*
   Bergère 266
   Bernini *381*
   Bird *380*
   Blow 366, *366*
   Breuer 239, *241*, 248, *248*
   Bugatti *195*
   Butterfly 327, *327*
   Cabaret Fledermaus 247
   Cherner 322–323, *323*
   Chieftain *318*
   Coconut *331*
   Cone 315, 326–327
   DAR 324
   Diamond (421LU) *327*
   DKW2 324
   early modernist 240, 241, 247, 252
   Egg 315, 326, *326*
   Empire 60
   Empty *393*
   Etruscan *381*
   Federal *50*
   Felt 377, *393*
   First *390*
   Fleur *331*
   Garden Egg 328, *328*
   Group *331*
   Heart 326, 327
   High-Heel *J04*
   Hill House 245
   Hillestak 323
   JH501 ("The Chair") 318, *318*
   Jugendstil 196, *197*
   klismos 54, 60
   Knotted *380*
   La Chaise 324, *324*
   LC2 *Grand Confort* 250–251
   LC2 Love Seat *250*
   LCM 324
   LCW 324
   Libro 366, *366*
   Little Beaver *379*
   Lounge *382*
   Mackintosh *328*, 240, 244, 245, *245*
   mid-20th-century 319, *331*
   Model 70 ("Womb") 326, *326*
   Modernage *274*
   Morris 150, *150*, 154
   MR10 *249*
   MR20 *249*
   Neoclassical 57, 58, 59, 62
   New Hope *321*
   19th-century 100, *100*
   19th-century Gothic *98*
   19th-century revival 103, *103*, 105
   Nobody's *381*
   Nonconformist *251*
   Oak Hall *150*
   Old Point Comfort *273*
   Panton 328
   Pastil 328, *328*
   Pelican *331*
   Plastic Shell Group 324
   postmodern *376*, *379*, *384*
   Pretzel 322
   Proust *387*
   Pyramid Cone *327*

Queen Anne 23, 26, 27, *27*
RAR 324, *324*
reclining (Hoffmann) 246, 247
Red-Blue 238–239, *249*
rocking (Stickley) *153*
Rococo 20, 25, *25*, 26
Rover 393, *393*
S 322, *322*, 328, *380*
S33 249, *251*
Sandows 251, *251*
Selene *329*
Series 7 323, *323*
Sessel Karuselli *331*
Sheraton 378, *378*
661 323
670 324
Superleggera 319, *319*
Sussex 151, *151*
Swan 326, *326*
Tank 251, *251*
Transat 271
Tripolina *327*
umbrella-back 57
Universale 4860 329
Wassily 248, *248*, 386
Well-Tempered *393*
Zigzag *249*
Zocker 328–329, *329*
chaises longues: B306 *251*
   19th-century 103
   Orgone *393*
   Regency 61, *61*
Chaleff, Paul *405*
champagne buckets: Art Deco 298
   85 Lamps *414*
   mid-20th-century *359*
   Onondaga Shops 153
   Tiffany *173*
Chantilly porcelain 23, 36
Chaplet, Ernst 198
chargers: Arts and Crafts *166*, 175
   blue-dash 33
   Cliff 268, *286*
   Leach *256*
   mid-20th-century *316*, *338*, *339*
   19th-century *107*
   postmodern *396*
   Staffordshire *31*
Charles III of Spain 89
Charles X of France 112
   style *74*
Charlotte, Queen 64
Chartres Cathedral window 15, *15*
Chase Brass & Copper Co. 296, 300, *300*, 301
cheese dish, Flash *403*
Chelsea-Derby porcelain 68
Chelsea Keramic Art Works 161, 162
Chelsea porcelain 37, *37*, 83
chenets see andirons
Chequers ceramic design 335
Chéret, Jules 231, 232–233, *233*
Cherner, Norman 323, *323*
Cherry Valley Collection furniture 153
Chessa, Gigi 279
chests of drawers: Art Deco *274*
   Neoclassical 63
   postmodern *384*
chests-on-chests: Neoclassical 63
   Rococo 27
chests-on-stands: Art Deco *273*
   mid-20th-century *330*
Cheuret, Albert 305
chiffoniers: Arts and Crafts 154
   19th-century American *103*
   Regency 61
Chihuly, Dale 377, 407, *407*, 410, *412*
Chinese art 12
Chinese influence (*see also* Chinoiserie)
   Neoclassical 89
   postmodern 397
   Rococo 27, 32, 33, 40
Chinoiserie 23, 36, 40, 67, 83
Chiparus, Demètre 308, *308*
Chippendale, Thomas 25, 27, 57, 128
   The Gentleman and Cabinet-Maker's

Director 27
   style 102, 103
chocolate cup set, Neoclassical 68
chocolate pot, Rococo 42, 43
Christofle silverware 298, 299
chrome, Art Deco 296, *296*
chryselephantine 308
Chrysler Building, New York 266
Cibic, Aldo 390
cigarette case, Art Nouveau 225
Cityscape range furniture 321
Classical orders 11, 54, *54*, 80
Classical style/influence 10, 16
   Art Deco 269, 278, 279, 286, 288, 290
   Neoclassical 50, 52, 54, 60, 64–65, 69, 74–75, 80, 81, 89, 92, 93
   19th-century 97, 100–101, 103, 109, 112, 113
   Rococo 22, 25, 26
Clews, Ralph and James 108, *109*
Cliff, Clarice 268, 282, *282*
Clifton Art Pottery 163, *163*, 167
clock garnitures 130, *130*
clocks: Act of Parliament 81
   Aesthetic 183, *183*
   Art Deco 304–305
   Art Nouveau 226–227
   Arts and Crafts 182–183
   Atom Ball 317, *365*
   bracket 44, 45, 81
   cartel 44, 81
   desk *183*
   globe 131, *131*
   Lalique 304, *304*, 305
   longcase 80, 80–81, 81, 183, *183*
   Mackintosh *183*
   mantel 81, 96, 130, 177, 182, *183*, 226, 227, 305
   Meissen 96
   mystery 131
   Neoclassical 80–81
   19th-century 130–131
   19th-century American 130–131
   Passement astrological 44
   pendule religieuse 45, *45*
   regulator 45
   Rococo 22, 44–45
   Rohde/Miller 305, *305*
   shelf *130*
   Skyscraper 305
   striking 81, *81*
   table *304*, 305
   Tiffany *183*
   Tudric 177, *181*, 183, 226
   wall *182*
Cluthra range glass 242, 290
Coalbrookdale cast iron 125
Coalport porcelain 51, 52, 53, 70, 111
coaster holders, M. Brandt 260
coathanger, 1960s 366
cocktail set, Manhattan 300
cocktail shakers: Art Deco 296, 301, *301*, *303*
   Cylinda *362*
   Jensen 299, *303*
   Manhattan *301*
Cocteau, Jean 339, *339*
coffee can and saucer, Neoclassical 70
coffeepots: Cooper 283
   Cylinda *362*
   folk art 87
   Jutta Sika 255
   mid-20th-century *340*, *361*
   Neoclassical 69, *79*
   Rococo 37, 42
coffee sets (*see also* tea/coffee services)
   Art Deco copper *303*
   mid-20th-century 340
   19th-century *126*
   Zambesi 335
Colani, Luigi 328–329, *329*
Colbert, Jean-Baptiste 46, 47
Cold Dark Matter (Parker) 417
Colin, Paul 276, 310, 311
Collings, J. K.: *Art Foliage* 121
Colombini, Gino 319
Colombo, Joe 329, *329*, 354, *354*, 393
Colonial revival 103

Colonna, Edward 193, *193*, 212, 229
commodes: Art Deco 274
   Empire 60
   Neoclassical 63
   19th-century *101*, *104*
   Rococo 23, *24*, 25
compact, Art Deco *303*
Compiègne, Château de *60*
comports: Art Deco 298
   Art Nouveau 225
   Neoclassical 73
   19th-century *111*
condiment stand, 19th-century *126*
confiturier, Neoclassical 78
Conran, Terence 335, *340*, 341
Consolidated Lamp & Glass Co. 286, 291, *291*
Constructivism 240, 241, 255, 260, 370
Consulat period 59
conversation seat 101
Cook, Peter 393
Cooper, Emmanuel 401
Cooper, Nancy 140
Cooper, Susie 282, *283*
Copeland ceramics 113
Copeland & Garrett porcelain 93, *93*
Coper, Hans 257, *257*, 397, 401
copperware: Art Deco *303*
   Arts and Crafts 178, *178*
   19th-century *127*
corkscrew, Anna G 394, *395*
Cornille Frères textiles 307
Cotswold School 151, *151*, 181
Coty, François 286
couture, influence of 280
coverlet, Art Deco 307
Cowan Pottery 283, *283*
Cozzi porcelain 70
Craft Revival 414
The Craftsman 152, *152*, 153
Craftsman Workshops 178
craftsmen's marks 147, *147*
Crane, Walter 168, 170, 185, 227
Crate, James Harvey 357, *357*
Craver, Margaret 301
credenza, mid-20th-century *330*
   19th-century *104*
Crespin, Paul 28
Cressent, Charles 25
Circusscii ceramios 30
crewelwork 147, *184*
cruet sets: Manitoba *403*
   mid-20th-century *363*
Crystal Palace 118, 128
   Medieval Court 128
Cubism 241, 255, 268, 306, 317, 333
cuerda seca technique 203, *203*
Culin, Nembhard 311
Cummings, Keith 410, *410*
cups: Art Nouveau 188
   19th-century 120, *126*
   postmodern *404*
cups and saucers: Neoclassical 68, 69, *70*
   Rococo 36, 37
   Tatzine 403
cupboards: armoire 17, *104*
   court 100, *100*
   Jugendstil 196, *197*
cutlery (flatware): Acorn 299
   AJ 360
   Bistro *361*
   Jacobsen 361
   Jensen 222, 223, 299
   Mackintosh 260
   Pyramid 299
   Thrift *361*
Cuvilliés, François 25
Cuypers, Pierre 102
Cymric line silver 176, 176–177
   clocks 183
Czescheka, Carl Otto 238, 262

D
d'Aprey ceramics 32
Dadaism 398
Dailey, Dan 406, *407*

Daily Express Newspapers entrance hall, London 267
Dakon, Stefan 280, 281
Dali, Salvador 322, 334
Daly, Matthew A. 159
Dannecker, Johann Heinrich 92
darning samplers 91
Dart Pottery 401
Dartington Glass 353
das Gupta, Philip Kumar 310
Daum Frères glass 189, 191, 191, 208, 208–209, 288, 293, 295, 392
Dawson, Nelson and Edith 221
Day, Lucienne 368, 368, 369
Day, Robin 323, 368
De Coene Frères furniture 271, 271
de Feure, Georges 193, 229
de Jully, Lalive 78
de Lamerie, Paul 28, 28
de Lasalle, Philippe 88–89
De Lucchi, Michele 386, 390, 390, 391, 414
de Morgan, William 168, 168
de Pas, Gionatan 324
De Pree, D. J. 319, 305
de Ranieri, Aristide 226, 227
de Ros, Antonio 348, 348
De Stijl 240, 242, 249
de Vez glass 217
Dearle, John Henry 145, 185
decanters: Art Deco 292
    Art Nouveau 214
    mid-20th-century 352
    Neoclassical 73, 76
    948 351
    19th-century 118
Deck, Theodore 198, 200
Décorchemont, François-Émile 289, 289
Dedham ceramics 163, 163
Delaherche, Auguste 198, 198, 256
Delaunay, Sonia 306, 306
    Compositions, Couleurs, Idées 128
Dell, Christian 259, 259
Della Robbia ceramics 166
Derby porcelain 37, 53, 68, 69, 71
desk fan, Art Deco 296
desk stand, 19th-century 127
Deskey, Donald 273, 273, 295, 307
desks: Art Deco 273
    Bird 384
    Brazil 391
    Bugatti 195
    early modernist 247
    Gothic revival 155
    Lady's Desk with Two Chairs 382
    mid-20th-century 319
    postmodern 376
    Queen Anne 40
Desvres ceramics 106
deutsche Blumen decoration 67
Devlin, Stuart 360, 361, 363
di Carli, Carlo 315
Diderot, Denis 50, 83
Diederich, William Hunt 309
digital design 375
dining room, Art Nouveau 189
dining set, mid-20th-century 327
dining suite, F.L. Wright 252
dinner services: American Modern 334, 334
    Grace 333
    Kilta 332
    Neoclassical 66
    Rococo 43
    Town and Country 334
Directional Furniture 321
Directoire period/style 59, 89
dishes: Huguenot silver 28
    Iznik 13
    Mannerist 17
    mermaid 224
    mid-20th-century 352
    red ware 110
    Spode transfer-printed 65
    Staffordshire 31, 108
Dixon & Sons, James 242
Dixon, Tom 380, 381
Doat, Taxile 200
Doccia porcelain 36
Dominio series ceramics 333

Donà, Alberto 413
door hardware, Arts and Crafts 147, 147
doorway, Art Nouveau 188
Dorflinger, Christian, glass 119
Dorlyn Silversmiths 361, 361
Dorn, Marion 307
Doulton & Co./Royal Doulton 148, 164, 183, 281, 281, 283
Dr. Caligari collection 382
Dresden porcelain 115, 115
dress, Souper 366
Dresser, Christopher 121, 238, 240, 242, 242, 260
    The Art of Decorative Design 238
    ceramics 240, 255
    Principles of Decorative Design 242
    signature 241, 241
    silver and metalware 122, 125, 175, 221
dressing tables: Art Deco 272
    postmodern 379
    Queen Anne 27
Drewry, George 79
Droog design 381, 415
du Paquier porcelain 34, 35
du Pasquier, Nathalie 390, 391
Duchamp, Marcel 336, 393
Duesbury, William 68
Dufour wallpapers 89
Dufrêne, Maurice 218, 219, 269, 270, 299, 304–305
Dufy, Raoul 47, 278, 306
Dunand, Jean 276
Dunbar furniture 319
Dupas, Jean 278, 310
Durand, Victor 291, 291
Dwight, John 30
Dyson, James 395

E

Eames, Charles and Ray 314–315, 315, 316
    A Communications Primer (film) 370
    furniture 322, 324, 324, 327
Eastlake, Charles 103, 103, 150
    Hints on Household Taste 120
Eckersley, Tom 370, 370–371
Eda glassworks 345
Edinburgh Weavers 368
Edra furniture 381
Edwards, Emily 164
Egermann, Friedrich 74, 75, 77
Egyptian art 10–11
Egyptian style/influence: Art Deco 266, 268, 276, 276, 288, 305
    Neoclassical 10, 51, 53, 53, 60, 65, 69, 79
    19th-century 99
Eichwald Pottery 204
Eisenloeffel, Jan 261, 261
Elkington & Co. metalware 123, 242, 242, 361, 361
Ellis, Harvey 153, 153, 252
Elmslie, George 171
Elton ceramics 167
embroidery: Art Nouveau 229
    Berlin woolwork 91, 137
    crewelwork 147, 184
    mourning 137
    pictures 137, 137
    samplers 90–91
Emergence series glass 351
Empire style 10, 50, 59, 60, 69, 75, 81, 112
enameling: Arts and Crafts 146, 175
    on glass 23, 38–39, 75, 75
    overglaze (petit feu) 22, 22
    plique-à-jour 219, 219
Engman, Kjell 413
Enlightenment 20–21, 50
entertainment system, Komet 364, 364–365
entrelac work 221
Epstein furniture 273
Ericsson telephones 365
erotica 83, 83
Esherick, Wharton 320, 320

ethnic influence 379
Etling glass 286
Etruscan influence 339, 397
étuis, Neoclassical 83, 83
Evans, Paul 321, 321
ewers: Dresser 242
    Hanau 32
    Huguenot silver 28
    Neoclassical 66, 78
    19th-century 117
    Renaissance 17
exhibition arch, postmodern 387
exhibitions:
    Barcelona International Exhibition (1929) 249
    Brussels (1897) 189
    Der gedeckte Tisch (1906) 247
    Exposition Coloniale, Paris (1931) 276
    Exposition Internationale des Arts Décoratifs et Industriels Modernes, Paris (1925) 259, 267, 286, 291, 298, 300, 307
    Exposition Universelle, Paris (1878) 120, 121, 198, 206, 210; (1889) 159, 208, 229; (1900) 189, 193, 194, 200, 201, 211, 221, 229, 231, 232
    Great Exhibition, London (1851) 112, 114, 114, 120, 128, 128, 139, 144, 168
    International Exhibition, London (1862) 99, 120, 170
    Les Années "25" (1966) 266
    Louisiana Purchase Exhibition 1904) 155
    Munich Glaspalast (1897) 196
    New York (1853) 120
    Philadelphia Centennial (1876) 120
    Stockholm (1930) 333
    Vienna Secession (1900) 245, 247
    World Fair, New York (1939) 299
    World's Exposition, Paris (1937) 336
exoticism: Art Deco 267, 276
    Arts and Crafts 168
    Neoclassical 61, 82
    Rococo 25

F

Falconet, Étienne-Maurice 92–93
Fallingwater, Bear Run, PA 252
Fantoni, Marcello 338, 339
Farny, Henry François 159
Farquharson, Clyne 290
fauteuils: Neoclassical 60
    19th-century 101, 101
    Rococo 25, 25
Federal style 50, 58, 58, 61, 81
Felix Restaurant, Hong Kong 392
female form: Art Deco 269, 296, 280–281
    Art Nouveau 190, 190, 201, 201, 220, 226, 230, 230, 231, 231
femme-fleur motif 191, 191, 220, 220, 221, 230
Fenby, Joseph Beverly 327
fender, Arts and Crafts 181
Fenton glass 352
Ferguson, Ken 397
Festival of Britain (1951) 317, 323
Feuillâtre, Eugène 188, 219, 219
Fields, Edward 369, 369
figures: Aigle, les Ailes Deployées 138
    Angela 281
    animal see animal figures
    Aphrodite 309
    Autumn 115
    bird see bird figures
    Chien Braque ... 139
    Corn Girl 284
    Counting Coup 140
    Dancer of Kapurthala 308
    Dijin—Cheval à la Barrière 138
    Duke of Wellington 93
    female 190, 200, 201, 201, 230, 231, 280–281, 284, 285, 308–309
    Gardener with a Basket 115
    Grecian with Torch 309

Harlequinade 281
Horse and Jockey 139
Hygeia 70
Janle 308
The Last Drop 140
Lion and Serpent 138
Madam Kitty 284
Marietta 281
Marquis de Méjanes 93
The Mask 281
The Medicine Man 140
mid-20th-century 338
Minerva 93
    Neoclassical 70, 92
    19th-century French bronze 138–139
    19th-century porcelain 113, 115, 115
    Parian ware 113, 113
    Rococo 34, 34, 37
Saving the Flag 140
Staffordshire 109, 109
Stag and Hound 309
Sunshine Girl 281
Suzanne 286
Taureau Beuglant 139
Un Taureau se Défendant 138
Tiger Devouring a Gavial 138
Una and the Lion 113
filigrana 39, 346, 349
Finch, Alfred William 337
Finlandia range glass 344, 345, 345
Finlayson textiles 369
Fiorentino, Rosso 17
Fiori di Como ceiling, Las Vegas 407
Fire Painting technique 161
fire polishing technique 209
firedogs see andirons
firescreen: Art Deco 303
    Art Nouveau 193
Fisher, Alexander 146, 221
Fjerdingstad, Carl Christian 299
Flash range ceramics 403, 403
flasks: maiolica 67
    19th-century 99
flatware see cutlery
Flaxman, John 93, 118
Flögl, Mathilde 262
floor heater, Flying Saucer 317
Flos lamps 354, 354, 356, 357, 357
flower bricks, delftware 33
flower holder, mid-20th-century 363
Foley Intarsio Ware 205, 227, 227
folk art, American 86–87
folk crafts 97, 99
Follot, Paul 218, 219, 266, 270, 299
Fontaine, Pierre-François-Léonard see Percier and Fontaine
Fontana Arte lamps 358
Fordham, Montague 175
Forms range glass 342
Fornasetti, Piero 319
Frainersdorf ceramics 205
Fraktur documents 87, 87
frame, picture/photo: Art Nouveau 221, 224
    Arts and Crafts 176
Franck, Kaj 332, 342–343, 343
François I of France 17
Frank, Jean-Michel 295
Frankenthal porcelain 36
Frankl, Paul 272, 295, 305, 305, 321
Frazer, Walter 164
Frederick II, "the Great," of Prussia 20, 82
Frederick William I of Prussia 20
Frederick William II of Prussia 59
French Revolution 51, 69
Frey, Viola 398
Fritsch, Elizabeth 401
Frost, Edward Sands 137
Fry, Laura 159
Fry, Roger 263
Fuga, Anzolo 346, 353
Fuller, Loïe 201, 232, 231
Fulper Pottery Co. 163, 163
Funk movement 398–399, 400
furniture: Adam 57
    American Federal 58
    American studio 320–321, 329
    American workshops 154–155

Art Deco American 272–273
Art Deco British 273
Art Deco French 270–271
Art Deco gallery 274–275
Art Nouveau Austrian 197
Art Nouveau French 192–193, 231
Art Nouveau German 196–197
Art Nouveau Italian 195
Arts and Crafts gallery 156–157
    contemporary 380–381
    contemporary Italian 381
    craftsmen's guilds 151
    Empire 60–61
    Glasgow School 244–245
    late-20th-century gallery 384–385
    mid-20th-century American 318–321, 324
    mid-20th-century gallery 330–331
    mid-20th-century Italian 319
    mid-20th-century metal 327
    mid-20th-century plastic 328–329
    mid-20th-century plywood 317, 322–323, 324
    mid-20th-century Scandinavian 318, 324, 326
    Morris & Co. 150–151
    Neoclassical European 58–59
    Neoclassical French 56, 57
    Neoclassical gallery 62–63
    19th-century Colonial revival 103
    19th-century gallery 104–105
    19th-century Neoclassical revival 102–103
    19th-century Renaissance revival 100–101
    19th-century Rococo revival 101
    postmodern 379
    postmodern American 382
    Rococo American 26, 27
    Rococo English and Low Countries 26–27
    Rococo French 24–25, 56
    Stickley 152–153
Fürstenburg porcelain 36
Futura range ceramics 283, 283, 285
Futurism 241, 255

G

Gaillard, Eugène 193, 193, 218, 219, 219
Gallé, Émile 190, 190, 191, 192, 206, 206
Gamble House, Pasadena 173
Gambone, Guido 338, 339
garden seats 107
Gardner ceramics 113
Garouste, Elisabeth 378, 379
Gaskin, Arthur 176
Gate, Simon 291, 291
gate, wrought-iron 299
Gates, William 163
Gaudí, Antonio 322
Gauguin, Paul 198, 218, 229
Gavina, Dino 354
Gaw, Eleanor D'Arcy 178
Gehry, Frank 374, 379
Genetic Tales motif 403
Genu, Joseph-Gabriel 78
geometric style 268, 288, 298, 307
George I style 26, 40
George II style 26, 27
George III style 62, 82
George Prince of Wales (George IV) 60–61
German Workshops 197
Ghyczy, Peter 328, 329
Gilhooly, David 399, 399, 400
Gillander, J., & Sons, glass 119
Gimson, Ernest 151, 151
Giotto range products 391, 391
Girard, Alexander 368
Glasgow School 197, 234, 240
    furniture 244–245
    influence 258, 260
    metalware 175
    textiles 262
Glasgow School of Art 151, 175, 244
glass: acid-etched 118, 191, 206, 206,

208, 209, *209*, 288, *217*
agate 74–75
Amberina 117
American studio 406–407
Ariel 343
Art Deco American 290, 291
Art Deco British 290
Art Deco French 288–289
Art Deco gallery 292–293
Art Nouveau Austrian 210–211
Art Nouveau gallery 216–217
Aurene *190*, 210, *210*
Beinglas 74
Bohemian 39, *39*, 74–75, *75*, 116, 117, 120, 133, 291, *291*, 351
brilliant cut 119, *119*
Burmese 117
cameo 116, *116*, 121, *168*, 190, *190*, 206, *206*, 208, *208*, 209, *209*, *217*, 288
cased 75, 116, 344, 348
colored 39, 52, 74–75, 342–343
copper-wheel engraved 345
Cranberry 116, 117, *118*, 119
cristallo 38, 39
Crown Milano 117
cut 53, *53*, 72, *72*, 118, *118*, 119, 289, *289*, 290, *290*, 351
Cypriote 173
Czech 409
Daum Frères *189*, 191, *191*, 208, 208–209, 288, *293*, 295
Depression 291
early modernist 258–259
enameled 23, *38*, 38–39, *75*, *75*, 191, 208, *208*
engraved *73*, 75, 118, *290*, 291, *291*, 409, *409*
Favrile 173, 212
flashed 75, 170
flint 73
frosted 215
Gallé *190*, *190*, 191, 192, 206, *206*
Glasgow 176
Goldrubinglas 39
gorge de pigeon 83
Hyalith 54, 74, *74*, 116
ice (crackle) *118*–119
intarsio 347
intercalaire *209*
iridescent 191, *191*, 210, 210–211, 211, 212
Lalique 276, 286, *286*
lampwork 411, *411*
lattimo 39, 348
Lava 212, 216
lead crystal 39, 72
leaded/stained *121*, 147, *147*, 170, 170–171, *171*, 190, 191, 215
Lithyalin 74, 116
marbled 54, 74
marquetry 206, 209
martelé 209
medieval stained 14–15, *15*
mid-20th-century American 350–351
mid-20th-century British 350, 351
mid-20th-century Italian 346–349
mid-20th-century Scandinavian 317, 342–345
Milchglas 38, 39, 74
Mildner 75
mottled 288, *288*
molded 286, 291, 305
Murano 16–17, *120*, 120, 290–291, *315*, 316, 344, 346–349
murrine *315*, 316, 347, *347*, 412
Neoclassical 52, 72–75
Neoclassical American 73, *73*
Neoclassical gallery 76–77
Neoclassical Irish 72
19th-century American 117
19th-century British 116, 117, *118*–119
19th-century French 116–117
"Old German" 120
opalescent 171
opaline 74, 116, *116*
optical 408
Orrefors 290, 291, *291*, 295

pâte-de-verre 210, 289, *289*, 406
Peachblow 117, 117, *118*
potash 39
pressed 73, *73*, *269*, 291, 343
Pulegoso 349, *349*
reverse-painted 173, *214*, 214–215
ribbed 215, 344
Rococo 38–39
rock crystal 119, *119*
Roman 11, *11*, 74–75, 117, 210, 211, *211*
Rubinglas 39
Sandwich 73, *73*
Schwartzlot 23, *38*, 39
sculpture *see* glass sculpture
soda 38, 39, 350
sommerso 348, *348*
stained *see* leaded/stained
studio 350–351
Swedish 38
textured 344–345, 350
Tiffany 210, 212, *212*
uranium 116
Vaseline 117
Venetian *see* Murano
verre de fougère 39
Le Verre Français *209*, 288, 289, *293*
verre de soie 210
verres parlants 206
Vitrolite plate 406
Waldglas 39
Whitefriars 176
Zwischengoldglas 39, 75
glass sculpture, postmodern 412
Alfred's Mirror *410*, 410
Cipher Stone 408
Compacted Solarized Blue ... 408
Désir d'Ailes 410
Emerging Sun 406
Malibu 376
Marine Light III 406
Messager de l'Éspace 409, *409*
90 Degrees ... 408
Persian Set 407
portraiture 409, *409*
R999 408
Season 410
Zonnewind 410
glasses, drinking: Brancaster 351
Jällvuori 344
Neoclassical 73, 76, 77
Pokal 120
Rococo 39, *39*
rummers 72, *73*, 77
spa 133, *133*
Tulpenglas 342, *342*, 351
glazes: Art Nouveau 190, 198, 199, 200
Arts and Crafts 147, 161, 163
crackle 279
crystalline 200
eosin 199
flambé 165, 198
flint enamel 110
Grueby 147, 162
Iris *159*, 159
Jewel Porcelain 159, *159*
lava 339
lead 31
luster 13, *168*, 198, 199
Matte 159, *159*
Ohr *147*
porous 336
raku 396
Rookwood 147, 158, 159
Rouge Dalpayrat 198
salt 31, 397
Sea Green 159, *159*
Standard 158, 159
temmoko 336
tin 31, 106
Vellum 159, *159*
volcanic 336
Wilson 257
Glenny, Alice Russell 235, *235*
Global Tools 389
Gobelins tapestries 46–47
goblets: Art Deco 291
Arts and Crafts *180*
Jensen 223

mid-20th-century 363
Neoclassical 75, 77
19th-century *117*, *118*, *121*, 123
Rococo 21, 39
Godwin, E. W. 148
Goebel und Hutschenreuther ceramics 281, *281*
Goldman, Paul 322, *323*
Goldscheider ceramics 226, 227, *269*, 280, 280–281, 309
Goodden, Robert 361
Gorham Silver Co. 221, *221*
Górka, Wiktor 371, *371*
Goss, Baron 138
Gothic style/revival 14–15, 27
Art Nouveau 195
Arts and Crafts 144, 146, 148, 155, 175
19th-century 96, 98, 102–103, 121, 122, 144
Gouda Ceramic 201
Goupy, Marcel 278, 289, 292, *293*
Goût grec 56, 78, 79, *83*
Graal technique 343, *343*
grand feu decoration 32
Grand Tour 50, 54, 132
Grant, Duncan 263
graphic design 370
Grasset, Eugène 233, *233*, 235
Graumans, Rudy *414*
Graves, Michael *375*, 377, 379, 390, 394, 402, *402*
Grawunder, Johanna *388*, 391, *391*
Gray & Co., A. E., ceramics 282
Gray, Eileen 251, *251*, 263, *263*, 276, 307, 380
Greek art/influence 11, 397
Greene Brothers 173
Grenfell, Wilfred 137
Gropius, Walter 239, *239*, 248, 255, 319
Grossman, Greta Magnusson *330*
Grotell, Maija 337, *337*
grottoesque style 16, 17, 164
Groussay, Château de 97
Grueby Faience/Pottery 159, 162
Grupo Astral furniture 327
Gruppo DAM *366*, *366*
Guerbe, Raymond 294
Guerriero, Alessandro and Adriana 386, *404*
Guggenheim Museum, Bilbao 374
Guggisberg, Monica 412
Guild of Handicraft 144, 171, 174–175, *180*, *181*, 221, 246
Guimard, Hector 193–194, *194*, 200, 218, *218*
Gurschner, Gustave 231, *231*
Gustav III of Sweden 59
Gustavian style 50, 59, *59*, 62, 63
Gustavsberg ceramics 279, *322*, 333, *333*, *334*, 340
Gwynne, Patrick 315

H

Hadid, Zaha *404*, 417, *417*
Hadley, James 148
Hafner, Dorothy 403, *403*
Hagenauer Werkstätte 309
Hagia Sophia, Istanbul *12*, 13
Hald, Edvard 291
Haley, Reuben 291
hallstands: Art Nouveau 197
Arts and Crafts 156
19th-century Gothic 102
Hamada, Shoji 256, *256*, 336
Hamburg American Clock Co. 182, *182*
Hamburger, Peter *415*
Hamilton, Richard 366
Just What Is It That Makes Today's Homes... 365, *365*
Hampshire Pottery *163*
Hanau ceramics 32
Hancock & Sons ceramics *167*
Handel Co. lamps 216, 217, *217*
handcrafts 99, 146

postmodern 377, 379
Hanke, R., ceramics *255*
Harcourt, Geoffrey 384
Harcuba, Jiri 351, *351*, 409, *409*
Hardoy, Jorge Ferrari 327, *327*
Hardy, Charles 275
Harradine, Leslie 281, *281*
Harrison, John 243
Hartmann, Ferdinand Aloysius 79
Harvey, Agnes Bankier 175
Haseler, W. H., metalware 176
Haslemere Peasant Industries 174
Hassall, John 234, 235
Haupt, Georg 59
Haussmann, Robert and Trix 394, *394*, 416, *416*
Haviland ceramics 278
Hawkes, Thomas 290
Hawkes, Thomas G., & Co., glass 119
Heal, Ambrose/Heal & Son 145, 273, 368, *368*
Heifetz Co. lamps *358*
Heiligenstein, Auguste 289
Heintz Art Metal Shop 178, *179*, 180
Heintz, Otto 178–179
Helms, Chet 370
Henderson, Marion 175
Henningson, Paul 356, *356*
Henri II style 101
Henrion, Frederic, Henri Kay 370, 371
Hepplewhite, George 57, 58, *58*, 128
The Cabinet-Maker and Upholsterer's Guide 58
style 102
Herbst, René 251, *251*
Herculaneum 10, 54
Herczeg, Klara 280
Herman, Samuel 351, *351*
Heywood-Wakefield furniture 272
highboy, Rococo 27, *27*
Hille furniture 273, 323
Hillier, Bevis: *Art Deco of the 20s and 30s* 266
Hirschfeld, N. J. 159
Hisui, Sugiura 311
Hlava, Pavel 353
Hobbs, Brockunier & Co. glass 117
Höchst porcelain 36
Hocking Glass 291
Hockney, David 366
Hodosi, Oskar 331
Hoffmann, Josef 211, 238, 240, 245
furniture 246, 246–247
glass 258, *258*
metalware 260
textiles 262, *262*
Hogarth, William 83
Industry and Idleness 28
Holkham Hall, Norfolk 26
Holl, Steven 416, *417*
Holmgaard glass 118, 342, *343*
The Homewood, Surrey 315
Honesdale glass *209*, 209
hood ornaments 286, 296, 299
Horta, Victor 189, 194–195, *195*, 226–227, *227*, 229
Horti, Paul 159
Hôtel de Soubise, Paris *21*
Houdin, Robert 131
Houdon, Jean-Antoine 92, 93, *93*
Houses of Parliament, London 102, *103*
Hubbard, Elbert Green 145, 154–155, 173, 178
Huber, Patriz 197
Huet, Jean-Baptiste 89
Huguenots 28, 43
Hukin & Heath silverware 221
Hunter, David 172
Husted, Wayne 350, 351
Hutten, Richard 381
Hutter, Sidney 408, *408*
Hutton & Sons, William, silverware 221, *221*
Hylinge, Sweden 59

I

ice bucket, Tudric 176
ice pail, Neoclassical 71

Idée design 393
Iittala glassworks *317*, *344*, 345, *345*
Île de France, SS 286
iMac computers 395
Image, Selwyn 170
Imberton, I. J. 121
Imperial Porcelain Manufactury 112, 113
inciso technique 344, 347
Indian Sporting series ceramics 108
Indiana Glass 291
indianische Blumen decoration 67
Industrial Revolution 50–51, 108
inkstand, Neoclassical 73
19th-century 107
inkwells: Arts and Crafts *180*
folk art 87
Tiffany 179
inlay: Arts and Crafts 147, *147*
19th-century 102
International Silver Co. 300
Irvine, Sadie 202, 203
Islamic art 13
Islamic influence 17, 121, 147
Isokon 249, 273
Isozaki, Arata 390
istoriato style 67, 107
Ive, Jonathan 395, *395*
ivory 231–232

J

Jacob-Desmalter furniture 60
Jacob, Georges 59
Jacobsen, Arne: furniture 315, 322, 323, 326, 326
lamps 356, 356
metalware 361, 362
Jacobsen, Jac, lamps 355
Jacobson, A. Drexler 283
Jacquemart & Bénard wallpapers 89
jade, Chinese 12
Jagodzinski, Lucjan 371
Jallot, Léon 193, *269*, 270–271, *271*
Japanese Influence: Art Deco 278, 283
Art Nouveau 195, 219, 221, 233
Arts and Crafts 148, 168, 183
early modernist 241, 242, 252, 257
19th-century 99, 111, 117, 119, 121, 122, 128
postmodern 396
Rococo 33, 36
Japanese Palace 34, *34*
japanning 23, 40
Jardin des Plantes, Paris 138, *139*
jardinières, 19th-century 107, *121*
jars: Egyptian-style 276
owl 164
postmodern 400
Jarves, Deming 73
Jarvie, Robert 301
Jarvie Shop silverware *179*
Jazz Age style 268, 283, 299
Jean, Auguste 216
Jeanette Glass 291
Jencks, Charles 417, *417*
Jensen, Georg/Georg Jensen Silver 222, 222–223, *223*, 261, *261*, 299, *299*, 360, 360–361, 362
Jensen, Jørgen 361
Jerome, Chauncey 131
Jesser, Hilda 254, *254*
Jewell, Alvin A., metalware 125
jewelry: Cartier 276
Jensen 222, 223, *223*
Lalique 220, 286
Joel, Betty 273, *273*
Johnson house (F. L. Wright) 252
Johnson, Philip 374
Johnson, Dr Samuel 84
Jones, Owen: *The Grammar of Ornament* 99, *99*, 121, 128, *128*, 168, 212, 221, 242, *242*
Jongerius, Hella 381
Joor, Harriet 203
Jouve, Georges 339, *339*
Jucker, Carl 259
jugs: Art Deco 284
Art Nouveau 218

Arts and Crafts 166
bellarmine 30, *30*
claret 76, *225*
Cooper *283*
harvest *110*
Jensen *261*
mid-20th-century *360*
Neoclassical *64, 72*
19th-century ceramic *107, 114*
19th-century glass *119, 120, 121*
Ocean *401*
Oriente 346
Orrefors *291*
postmodern glass *413*
red ware *110*
Rococo 31, *34*
Jugend 234
Jugendstil 195–196, 234
Juhl, Finn 316, 318, *318, 330*
juicer, Juicy Salif 394, *394*

K

Kagan, Vladimir 317, 319, *319*
Kåge, Wilhelm 279, *279,* 333
Kaiser & Co. lamps *358*
Kalhammer, Gustav *263*
Kalo Shop 179, *179,* 301
Kammerer, Marcel 197, *197*
Kandem lighting 259, *259*
Kändler, Johann Joachim 34, 114, *115*
Karhula-Iittala glass 259
Kartell products 354, *354,* 393
Kastrup glass 342, *343*
Kauffer, Edward McKnight *310,* 311
Kaufman, Edgar 316
Kayserzinn silverware *244*
Keeler, Christine 323, *323*
Keeler, Walter *400,* 400–401
Kelmscott Press 154
Kendrick, George Prentiss 162
Kent, William 26, *26*
Kenzan VI, Ogata 256
Kerr, William B. 221
Keswick clocks 182–183
kettles: Behrens *261*
Kettle with Bird 394
King, Jessie M. 176, 262, *263*
King's Lynn glassworks 351
Kinnaird, Alison 409, *409*
Kip, Karl 178
Kirk, S., & Son, silverware 123, *123*
Kirschner, Marie 211
Kiss, Paul 295, 299
Kita, Toshiyuki *384*
kitchen equipment, late-20th-century 394–395
Klee, Paul 263
Klimt, Gustav 245
Klint, Kaare 318
Knoll furniture 319, 327, 379, 416
Knowles, Taylor & Knowles ceramics 111, *111*
Knox, Archibald 146, *176,* 176–177, *177,* 221, 226, 229
Ancient Crosses on the Isle of Man 176
Kohn, J&J, furniture 197, 246, 247, *247*
Kopf, Silas 382
Koppel, Henning 222, 333, 360, *360*
Körting & Mathiesen lighting 259, *259*
Kosta Boda glass 344, *344*
Kothgasser, Anton 75, *75, 77*
Krehan, Max 255
krug, fayence 67
Küchler, Rudolf 230
Kühn, Heinrich Gottlieb 114
Kunckel, Johann 39
Kuramata, Shiro *381,* 390
Kurchan, Juan 327, *327*
Kwong, Hui Ka 398, *398*

L

La Farge, John 171
La Jaoul, Paris (Le Corbusier) *250*
Labino, Dominick 351, 406
lacquer 40
imitation 23, 25

ladles: Japanese *126*
mid-20th-century *361*
Lagenbeck, Karl 159, 162
Lalique, René 190, 219, *286*
clocks 304, *304,* 305
glass 276, 286, *286*
jewelry 220, *220, 286*
lamps 295
lamp bases, mid-20th-century *333, 353*
lamps: Akari 31P *355*
Alda *414*
Anglepoise 295, *295,* 355
Arco *357*
Art Deco 294–295
Art Nouveau 191, *206,* 209, 211, 216–217, 231, *231*
Artichoke 356, *356*
Arts and Crafts *162,* 172–173
Asteroide 389, *389*
Bauhaus *239,* 258
BiBiBi *415*
Bubble 354, *355*
Dalu 354
Daum Frères 209, *209,* 294
early modernist *259*
Eye (Cobra) *357, 357*
Face 302
figurative 294, *294*
Flammes 357
floor 295, *295*
Flower Pot 356, *356*
Funk *398*
Gallé 206
Gatto 354, 354
Handel 216, 217, *217*
Lalique 295
Light Structure *415*
Luxo 355
mid-20th-century 354–357
mid-20th-century gallery 358–359
Mini Topo *358*
Moloch 355
Moon 356, *356*
MT8 *259*
Needle and Spool 377, *387*
newel post 173, *173*
A Nite on Lindquist Ridge *415*
NR607 *415*
Oceanic 390
Oeil 357
Osso 376, 415
Peacock 211
Pillola 355, 355
Pipistrello 354, 354
postmodern 414–415
Puffy 215, *215*
Saturn *357*
Super *391*
T-3-C *357, 357*
Taccia 357
Tahiti 374
La Tentation 295
Tiffany *173, 173, 191,* 212, *212*
Toio 357, 357
torchère 295, *295*
Treetops 389
Triennale 314, 356–357, 357
van Erp 172, *172*
V-P Globe *358*
WL01C 415
Landau, Jacob 311
Landberg, Nils 342, *342*
Landes, Michael 378
Landis, Richard 368
Lane, Danny 381
Lanel, Luc *298,* 299
lap desk, Neoclassical *83*
Larche, Raoul 219, 230, *230,* 231
Latona Tree ceramic design *282*
Laub- und Bandelwerk decoration 67
Laugier, Jean-Baptiste 66
Laughlin China Co. 334
Laurencin, Marie 271
LaVerne, Philip 330
Lawson Time Inc. 304
Le Bourgeois, Gaston 309
Le Brun, Charles 46
Le Corbusier *250,* 250–251, *251, 298*

L'Art Décoratif d'aujourd'hui 250
Pavillon de l'Esprit Nouveau 238
Vers une architecture 251
Le Coultre clocks 304
Le Verrier, Max 308, 309
Leach, Bernard *241,* 256, 256–257, *336,* 401
A Potter's Book 256
Leach, David 336, *337*
Leach, Janet 336, *337*
Leaping Deer design *283, 303*
Lebus, Harris 156
Lechevallier-Chevignard, Georges 278
Leger, Fernand *306,* 307
Legrain, Pierre 271, *276*
Legras, Auguste 209, *209, 289*
Leighton, Frederic *148, 168*
Leleu, Jules 271
Leman, James 28
Lenci figurines 281
Léonard, Agathon 200
Leuteritz, Ernst August 114, 115
Lewis, Wyndham 336
Libensky, Stanislav 409
Liberty & Co. 145, 165, 168
clocks 183, 226
metalware 176–177
textiles 185, 229
Lichtenstein, Roy 404
Liehm, J. K., ceramics *255*
light fixtures, Starck *415*
lighting *see* lamps; lights
lights, Mackintosh 258
lightshade, Art Nouveau *217*
Limbert, Charles 154, 155
Lindberg, Stig *332,* 333, *334*
Lindig, Otto 255
Lindstrand, Vicke 291, 343, *344,* 344–345, *345*
Linthorpe Pottery 242
Lipofsky, Marvin 406
liqueur set, Art Deco *300*
liquor set, Art Nouveau *255*
Lissitzky, El 255
lithography 233
Little Hermitage, St Petersburg *50*
Littleton, Harvey K. 406
Liverpool porcelain 37, *37*
Llewellyn, John 177
Lobmeyr, J. & L., glass *117, 117, 121, 121*
Lock, Matthias and Henry Copland:
New Book of Ornaments 128
Loetz glass *210,* 211, *211,* 258, 259, *259*
Loewy, Raymond 369
Löffler, Bertold 262
logos 370
Longton Hall porcelain 37, *37*
Longwy ceramics 279, *279*
Loos, Adolf: *Ornament and Crime* 250
Lorelei range ceramics 203
Lorenzl, Josef 281, 309, *309*
Loughlin, Homer, China Co. 283
loungers: Lockheed *393*
Tube 329
Lovet-Lorski, Boris 311
Lovet-Lorski, Jean 289
Lowestoft porcelain 37
Luce, Jean 289
Ludwig II of Bavaria 96
Ludwigsburg porcelain 36
Lugossy, Maria 409, *409*
Lundin, Ingeborg 342, *342*
Lutken, Per 342, *343,* 366
Luxval glass 286

M

McArthur, Warren 272, *273*
McCall, James 154
McCobb, Paul 330
Macdonald, Frances and Margaret 244, 245, 262
Machine Age style 269, 296
Mackintosh, Charles Rennie: clock *183*
furniture *238, 238,* 240, 244, 244–245, *245*
influence 153, 154
lights *258*
metalware 260, *260*
Mackmurdo, Arthur 170, 190
Macintyre ceramics 205
MacNair, James Herbert 244
McNicholl, Carol 397, *397*
Madeline, Philippe 339
Madoura Pottery 339
magazine stand, Arts and Crafts 156
Maggiolini, Giuseppe 59
Magistretti, Vico 329, 347, 354, *354–355*
mahogany 60, 80
Makepeace, John 382, *384*
La Maison de l'Art Nouveau 193, 212
La Maison Desny lamps 295
La Maison Moderne 219
Majorelle, Louis *191,* 192–193, *193,* 209, 288, *288*
Malevich, Kasimir 255, *255*
Maling ceramics 284
Malone, Jim *400*
Mannerism 17
Manning-Bowman clocks 304
Manock, John 395
Manzon, serge 355, *355,* 358
map samplers 91, *91*
Mappin & Webb silverware 299, *303*
marble 92
Marblehead ceramics 163, *163*
Marcks, Gerhard 255
Marcolini, Count Camillo 93
Margotin, Pierre 45
Marinot, Maurice 259, *259,* 271
Marioni, Dante 413
Mariscal, Javier 379, 390
Marot, Daniel 28
marquetry: Art Nouveau 191, *191,* 193, *193*
Neoclassical 52, 56, 59, 80, *80*
Rococo 25
Marquis, Richard 406, *406*
Marquiscarpa range glass 406
Marselis range ceramics 333, *333*
Martelé range silverware 221
Martens, Dino 346
Martin brothers 164, *164*
Martinelli Luce lamps 354, *354*
martini shaker, Art Deco *303*
Martinuzzi, Napoleone 291, *293,* 349
Massier ceramics 198, 199, *199*
Mathsson, Bruno 315
Matisse, Henri 47, *399*
Mauchlineware 133, *133*
Maurer, Inge 415, *415*
Mautner-Markhof apartment, Vienna 246
Max, Peter 370, *370,* 404
Maxim's, Paris 212
May, Sybille 284
Mayodon, Jean 269, 278, *278*
Mdina glass 353
medieval art 14–15
medieval influence 144, 170, 184
Meier-Graefe, Julius 219
Meissen porcelain 10, 21, *22,* 34, *34,* 67, 68, *68,* 70, 93, 96, 101, *114,* 114–115, *115,* 200, 281, *281*
imitations 115
mark *114,* 115
Mellor, David 361, *361*
Melody ceramic design 335
Memphis Group 374, 377, *379, 379,* 380, 382, 388, 389, 390, 390–391, *391,* 414

Mendini, Alessandro 386, *386–387, 387,* 389, 391, *394, 394,* 395, 414
Mêne, Pierre-Jules *138,* 139, *139*
Messager de l'Espace series glass 409, *409*
metalware (*see also* copperware; pewter; silverware)
Art Deco 298–299
Art Deco American 300–301
Art Deco gallery 302–302
Art Nouveau 220–221
Art Nouveau gallery 224–225
Arts and Crafts *147,* 180–181
Arts and Crafts American 178–179
Arts and Crafts British 174–175
early modernist 260–261
mid-20th-century 360–361
mid-20th-century gallery 362–363
Neoclassical American 79
Neoclassical mass-produced 79
19th-century 124–125
19th-century gallery 127
postmodern 416–417
Sheffield plate 79, *79*
Metro entrances, Paris 194
Meyer, Grethe 333
Meyr, Adolf 120
Meyrowitz clocks 305
micromosaic 99, *132,* 132–133
Middle Eastern influence 99, 168, 195
Middle Lane Pottery 161
Midwinter ceramics 316, *334,* 334–335, *335*
Mies van der Rohe, Ludwig 249, *249,* 319, 386
Mildner, Johann Joseph 75
Miller, Herman: clocks 305, *305*
furniture 272, 319, *319,* 324, *324,* 368
Miller, Howard, lamps 354, *355*
Minton ceramics 108, 112, 113, *113,* 148, *166*
majolica 107, *107*
Mira-X textiles 369, *369*
Miró, Joan 339
mirrors: Art Deco *274*
Art Nouveau *194*
Kandissa 386
postmodern *384*
Rococo 20, 23, 25
Miss Cranston's Tea Rooms 245
Mission-style furniture 152, 153, 178
modernism 267, 374, 386, 388, 392
early 238–329
mid-20th-century 314–315
Scandinavian 314–315
soft 314–315
modular system, Storagewall 319
Mogensen, Bjørn 318, *318*
Moholy-Nagy, Lázló 260
Molar Group furniture 329, *329*
Mollino, Carlo 322, *322*
Monart range glass 290
Moncrieff Glassworks 290
Mondrian, Piet *238, 240,* 249
money box, 19th-century *133*
Monroe, C. F., glass 121
Moorcroft ceramics 205
Moore, Bernard 166
Moore, Edward C. 212
Moore, Henry 368
Moore and Lindley: *The Ferns of Great Britain and Ireland* 121
Morris, May 184
Morris, William 144, 145, *145,* 146, 147, 174, 176, 194, 212
furniture *150,* 150–151
influence 152, 154, 228
stained glass *121, 170, 170*
textiles 184, *184,* 185, *185*
Morris, William (glass artist) 410–411, *411*
Morrison, Jasper 380, 381
Moser, Koloman 211, 238, 246
furniture 247, *247*
glass 259, *259*
metalware 260, *260*
textiles 262

Moser & Sons, L., glass 117
Mouille, Serge 357, *357*
Mount Washington Glass Co. 117, *117*, 121, *121*
mounts: Art Nouveau metal 191, *191*
porcelain 101
Rococo metal 23, 25, 43, *43*, 44
Mouse, Stanley 370
Moustiers ceramics 66, *66*, 106
Mucha, Alphonse 188, 229, 232, *232*
muffin dish, Arts and Crafts *180*
mugs: Black Stripes *404*
Grandmother 402, *402*
Staffordshire *30*
Muir, James Nathan 140, *140*
Müller, Albin 182, 254–255, *255*
Müller Frères glass 209, 295
Müller-Munk, Peter 296, 301
Munakata, Shiko 399
Munich Secession 196
Munthe, Gerhard 229
Murray, Keith *240*, 257, *257*, 290, 299
Murray, William Staite 257, 336
Musée Horta, Brussels *195*
Mussolini, Benito 279
Myott ceramics 282

N
Nabis group 229
Nagel silverware *363*
Nakashima, George 316, *316*, 320, *320*
Nancy School 191, 192–193, 208
Nantgarw porcelain 53, *53*, 69
Napoleon III 102
Napoleon Bonaparte 51, 53, 54, 60, 69
Napper, Harry 229
Nash, Arthur J. 210
Nash, John 61
Nasir al-din Shah of Persia 134
National Arts Club Studio 301
nature, influence of: Art Deco 268, 286
Art Nouveau 192, 200, 202, 208, 212, 215, 219
Arts and Crafts 146, 162
Neoclassical 53
19th-century 99, 107, 121, 123
Rococo 22
Scandinavian glass 345
Nauler, Otto and Gertrud *337*, *337*
Navarre, Henri 259
Navone, Paola 386
necessaires, Neoclassical 83, *83*
needlework *see* embroidery; textiles
Nelson, George 318–319, *319*, 322, 354, *355*, 388
Neo-Brutalism 414
Neoclassical style/influence 50–53
Art Deco 270, 277, 279, 300
19th-century 102–103, 112, 113, 114, 118, 121, 122, 123
Neuschwanstein Castle, Germany 96
Nevers ceramics 67, 106, *106*
New Bremen Glass factory 73
New England Glass Co. 73, 117
Newbery, Francis 244, 245
Newbery, Jessie 262
and Margaret Swanson: *Educational Needlework* 262
Newby Hall, North Yorkshire 57
Newcomb Pottery 202, *202*–203
Newlyn metalware *175*, *180*, 182
Newson, Marc 377, 381, 392, 393, *393*
Ng, Win *405*
Nicholas I, Czar 112
Nickerbocker Bar, *Empress of Britain* 296
Niderviller ceramics 67
Nielsen, Harald 223, 299
nightlight, Rococo *31*
Niloak Mission Ware ceramics *167*
Nippon ceramics *205*
Noguchi, Isamu *330*, 355, *355*, 365, *365*
Nordbruch, Karl *409*
Normandie SS 278, 286, 295, 298, 299
Northwood, John 118, 121
Norton & Fenton ceramics 110

Nuutajärvi Notsjo glass 342, *343*, 345, *345*
Nylund, Gunnar 333
Nyman, Gunnel 345, *345*
Nymphenburg porcelain 36, *71*

O
Oberkampf, Christophe-Philippe 89
Objets Barbares 379
Objets Primitifs 379
objets trouvés 393
objets de vertu, Neoclassical 82–83
Obrist, Hermann 190, 196, 229
Oeben, Jean-François 57
Ohr, George *147*, 160, 160–161, *161*, 256
Öhrström, Edvin 291, 343
Olabuenaga, Adrian *377*
Olbrich, Josef 247
Old Mission Kopper Kraft 178
Olerys, Joseph 66
Olivetti office equipment 388–389
poster *370*, 371
Omega clocks 304
Omega Workshops 263
One-Off studio 393, *393*
Onken, Oscar 155
Onondaga Shops 153, *153*
Op Art 369
Oppenard, Gilles-Marie 24
Oriente range glass *346*, 346–347
ormolu 125
Orrefors glass 290, 291, *291*, *294*, 342, *342*, 343, *343*, 344
Osler, F. & C., glass 118
Osterley Park, Middlesex *51*
Ott & Brewer ceramics 111, *111*
ottoman, Barcelona *249*
New Hope *321*
671 324
Overbeck ceramics *167*
overglaze 22, *22*, 31

P
Paestum 54
Pairpoint Corporation lamps 217, *217*
Palais Royal, Paris 24
Palais Stoclet, Brussels 247
Paley, Albert *416*, *416*
Palissy, Bernard 17, *17*, 107, 401
Palladian style 26, *26*, 56, 78
Palladio, Andrea 16, *16*, 26
Quattro Libri dell'Architettura 16, 128
Pallme-König glass 217
Palmqvist, Sven 345
pancake and corn set, Art Deco 300
panels, textile: Art Deco *306*, 307
mid-20th-century *369*, 369
La Veillée des Anges 229
Pankok, Bernhard 196
Panton, Verner 365
furniture 322, *322*, 326, 326–327, 328, *328*, 329
lamps 356, *356*, *358*
textiles *369*, 369
paperweight, Stankard *411*
papier mâché 82, 97, 98, 102
Papillon range glass 211
Paramount Hotel, New York 392
Paris ceramics 50, *70*
Park Lane Hotel foyer, London *307*
Parker, Cornelia 417
parquetry 52, 56, 80, 133
Parzinger, Tommi *330*, 361, *361*
pastille burner, Neoclassical *71*
pattern books 99, *99*, 102, 121, 128, *128*
Patti, Tom *408*, *408*
Paul, Bruno 197, *197*
Paul Revere Pottery 203, *203*
Paulin, Pierre 358
Pavely, Ruth 283
Peacock Room *148*
Pearson, John 174
Peche, Dagobert 254, *254*, 259, 262, *262*

Pelzel, Peter 347
Penfield, Edward 235
Pennell, Ronald 409, *409*
Pentagram design 324
penwork 98, *98*
pepper mill, postmodern 394, *394*
Percier, Charles and Pierre-François-Léonard Fontaine 59, 60, 69
Palais, Maisons et Autres Édifices Modernes ... 128
Recueil des Décorations Intérieurs 59
Perdrizet, Paul 206
Perelda, Pollio 346
perfume bottles: Art Deco 266, 286, *286*, 291, 292
Neoclassical *74*, *83*
perfume fountain, Rococo *43*
Perkins, Danny 376, *412*
Perriand, Charlotte 250–251, 323
Perry, Grayson 401, *401*
Perry, Son & Co. metalware 125
Perzel, Jean 295
Pesce, Gaetano 355, 376, 381, *381*, 385, 414, *414*, 415
Peter the Great 93
Petri, trude 340
Pevsner, Nikolaus: *The Return of Historicism* 378
Pewabic Pottery *163*
pewter 226
mid-20th-century 361
Tudric 176, *177*, *177*, 226, 231
Phänomen range glass 211
Philippe, duc d'Orléans 24
Phoenix Glass Co. 118, 291
Phyfe, Duncan 61, *61*
piano, Caligari 377, *377*, 382, *382*
Pianon, Alessandro 347, *347*
Piazza ware ceramics 341
Picasso, Pablo 339, *339*
picnic set, La Bamba 366
pie dishes, 19th-century *107*, 107
Pifetti, Pietro 25
piggins, Neoclassical 72, 76
pill box, Jensen 299
pillow, Arts and Crafts *184*
Piper, John 368, *368*
Piranesi, Giovanni Battista 54, 57, 72
pitchers: Fiesta ware 334
mid-20th-century 360, 361
19th-century *109*, 111, 118, 119, 120
Normandie 301
Pillow 397, *397*
Rookwood 158
Plant Life ceramic design 335
plant stand, Liberty 168
planters: Art Nouveau 231
Arts and Crafts 181
plaques: Art Deco 285
Art Nouveau 204
maiolica *33*
mid-20th-century *340*
Neoclassical 56
Rococo *32*
Wedgwood 103
plastic: Art Deco 267, 296
fiberglass-reinforced 324, 328
mid-20th-century 317, 328–329, 364, 366
plate of flowers, 19th-century *115*
Platel, Pierre 28
plates: Art Nouveau 203, *204*
Arts and Crafts *166*, *181*
Chinese *40*
Constructivist *255*
Delft *33*
early modernist *241*
Flowers *403*
folk art *87*
Grandmother *402*
Mains au Poisson 339
mid-20th-century *316*, 334, *340*, 352
Neoclassical 64, *65*, 66, 71
19th-century 107, *109*
19th-century Russian *113*
postmodern *404*
Rococo 22, *32*, 37, 43

Platner, Warren 327, *327*
platters, mid-20th-century 333, *333*
postmodern *404*
Pleydell-Bouverie, Katharine 257, *336*
Plycraft furniture 322
plywood 317, *317*, 322, 322–323, *323*, 324
Poiret, Paul 306
Polaroid Corporation lamps 295
Poli, Flavio 348, *348*, 349
Pollard, Donald *351*
Pollock, Jackson 396, 397, 401
Poltranova lamps 389, *389*
Pompadour, Madame de 68
Pompeii 10, *11*, 53, 54, 89
Pompon, François 278, 309
Ponteur lamps 355, *355*
Ponti, Gio 279, *298*, 299, 315, *319*, 319, 349
Ponzio, Emanuele 355, *355*
Poole Pottery 283, *283*, 335, *335*
Poor, Henry Varnum 338, *338*
Pop art/design 316, 342, 354, 355, 356, 366, 371, 389, 398
porcelain: Art Nouveau 200–201
biscuit 93, *93*
Chinese 12, *12*, 33, 36, 37, 40
Empire 112
famille rose 33, 37, 40
famille verte 33, 36, 40
hard-paste 10, 21, 34, 35, 67, 68, 93, 112
Imari 33, 40
Japanese 33, 36, 37, 40
Kakiemon 33, 36, 37, 40, 148
Neoclassical 68–69
19th-century German 114–115
19th-century Russian 112, 113
Parian ware 113, *113*
pâte-sur-pâte 113
Rococo 34–37
Rococo revival 112-113
soft-paste 35–36, 69
wucai 40, *40*
Portal Gates, Smithsonian Institution 416
Porter, Rufus 86
portière, Aubusson 47
Portland Vase 121, 209
Portmeirion Pottery 335, *340*
posters: Art Deco 272, 310–311
Art Nouveau 188, 232–235
Bauhaus 239
early modernist *241*
iMac 395
Japanese 310, 311
mid-20th-century 370–371
movie 371, *371*
Nord Express 310
postmodern *375*
psychedelic 370, *370*
Rockefeller Center 272
transport 310–311
Postgate, Margaret 283
postmodernism 374–377
pots: Arts and Crafts 165
Dryspace *397*
19th-century covered *115*
Ohr *161*
posset *33*
postmodern *404*, *405*
Potsdam Glasshouse 39
Poulsen, Louis, lamps 356, *356*
Powell, Addie 402
Powell, James, & Sons, glass 121, 170, 176, 290
Powell, Philip Lloyd 321, *321*
Powolny, Michael 281
Prairie House style 252
Prairie School 171
Pratt, F. & R., ceramics 64, *64*
Pre-Raphaelite movement 121, 170, 171, 231
Preiss, Ferdinand 308–309, *309*
Primaticcio, Francesco 17
Primavera ceramic design *334*, 335
Prior, E. S. 170
Procopé, Ulla 332, *332*

Proctor, Stephen 382
product design: Art Deco 296
late-20th-century 386–395
mid-20th-century 364–365
Prost, Maurice 309
Prouvé, Jean 319, *330*
Prutscher, Otto 258, *258*
Puerto Rican influence 339
Pugin, Augustus 103, 121, 122, 144, 170, 175
Puiforcat, Jean 298
Purcell, William 171
Purkersdorf Sanatorium 246–247
Purser, Sarah 171

Q
Quaint Furniture 153
Queen Anne style 26, 27, *27*, 40
The Quest 175
Quezal Art Glass 173, *211*
quilts: appliqué 99, 136, *136*
patchwork 136, 136
Quimper ceramics 66, *66*–67, 106, *106*

R
Racinet, Augustus 128
radiator cover, Art Deco 303
Radice, Barbara 389, 390–391
Radio City Music Hall 273, 295, 307
Radionurse 365
radios: Art Deco 296
mid-20th-century 364, *364*
Ramie, Georges and Suzanne 339
Ramsden, Omar 175, *181*, 221
Rand, Paul 370
Rang, Wolfgang 378
Raphael 16
Ravenscroft, George 39, 72
Read, Alfred 335, *335*
Red-Ashay glass 286
Red House, Kent 144
Red Wing Pottery 334
Reekie, David 410, *410*
Reeves, Ruth 307, *307*
Régence period/style 22, 28, 47
Regency period/style 50, *54*, 60–61, *61*, 72, 79, 84
Reid, Colin 408, *408*
Reinicke, Peter 114
religious symbolism 87
Rembrandt Art Guild 290
Remington, Frederic 140
Renaissance art 16–17
Renaissance revival 99, 100–101, 107, 120, 122, 123
repoussé work 22, *22*, 123
Reptil range ceramics *332*, 333
Reveillon, Jean Baptiste 89
Revel, Jean 47, 88
Revere Copper & Brass Co. 296, 300
Revere, Paul 79
revivalist styles 96–99
Revolution in Clay 396
Rhead, Frederick Hurten 161, 334, *334*
Rhead, Louis John 234, *234*
Richardson, Benjamin 118
Richardson, Henry Hobson 145
Richardson's glass 119, 121
Ridgway ceramics *109*, 335, *335*
Rie, Lucie 257, *257*
Riemerschmid, Richard 183, 196, 196–197, 198
Riessner, Stellmacher & Kessel (RSK) 200
Rietveld, Gerrit 238, 238–239, 248, *248*, 249, *249*
Riihimäen Lasi Oy glass 342, *343*
Riley, Bridget 369
Ritchie, Alexander 175
Rix, Kitty and Felice 262
Robertson, Hugh 161, *161*, 163
Robie House (F. L. Wright) 252, *252*
Robineau, Adelaide 166, *167*
Robsjohn-Gibbings, T.H. 272
Roché, Henri-Pierre 336
Rococo style/influence 21, 22–23, 69, 78, 83, 97, 195, 218, 221

19th-century 98, 101, 112, 114, 115, 122, 123, 130
Rodin, Auguste 230
Rodmarton Manor 145
Roentgen, David 57, 58
Roettiers, Jacques-Nicolas 78
Rohde, Johan 223, 223, 261, 299
Rohde, Gilbert 272, 305, 305
Rohlfs, Charles 147, 155, 155
Rolands, Martyn 365
Rookwood Pottery 146, 158–159, 162
room divider, mid-20th-century 321
Rörstrand ceramics 333, 333, 334
Rosenberg, Harold 396
Rosenthal ceramics 255, 281, 403, 403
Roseville Pottery 202, 283, 283
Rossetti, Dante Gabriel 121, 170, 170, 231
Rouen ceramics 32, 106
Rowlandson, Thomas: cartoon 85
Royal Bonn ceramics 205
Royal Copenhagen porcelain 200, 279, 281, 333
Royal Dux porcelain 201, 281
Royal Flemish range glass 117, 121
Royal Haeger ceramics 341
Royal Palace, Berlin 21
Royalton Hotel, New York 392
Roycroft/Roycrofters 154–155, 155, 172, 172, 173
    Copper Shop 178, 178, 180
    silverware 221
Rozenburg ceramics 201, 201
Ruba Rombic range glass 291, 291
Ruchet, Berthe 229
rugs: area 369
    Art Deco 306
    Gray 263, 263
    Grenfell 137, 137
    hooked 316–137, 137
    mid-20th-century 369, 369
    19th-century Persian 99, 134
Ruhlmann, Émile-Jacques 278, 298
    furniture 270, 271, 276, 276
    lamps 295
    textiles 306–307
Ruppelwerk metalware 260, 261
Ruskin Art Pottery 165, 165
Ruskin, John 99, 118, 144, 148, 194
    Fors Clavigera 174
Russell, Charles M. 140, 140
Russell, Gordon 273, 273, 290

S

Saarinen, Eero 314, 324, 324, 326, 337
Saarinen, Eliel 300–301, 324
Sabattini, Lino 361, 361
Sabino glass 286
Saint-Cloud porcelain 36
St. Ives Pottery 256–257, 336, 341
Saint-Louis Glassworks 72, 116, 116
Saint-Simon, Comte de 66
Saippuakupla range glass 342
Sala, Jean 292
Salon d'Afrique 276
salon suite, Jugendstil 197
saltcellar, 19th-century 123
salt dish, Art Deco 302
salt and pepper shakers: Art Deco 302
    Fiesta ware 334
    mid-20th-century silver 363
salts, pair of, 19th-century 123
salvage 393, 415
salver, Rococo 43
Salviati & Co., glass 120, 120
Salvini ceramics 204
samplers 90, 90–91, 91
Samson et Cie ceramics 113
sander, Rococo 32
Sandoz, Édouard-Marcel 309
Sanquirico, Antonio 346
Sarfatti, Gino 356, 357
Sarfatti, Margherita 279
Sarpaneva, Timo 344, 344, 345, 345
Sarreguemines ceramics 204
Satomi, Munetsugu 310
Saturday Evening Girls' Club 203

sauceboats: Huguenot silver 28
    Rie 257
    Rococo 43
Savonnerie carpets 135
Scandinavian design: furniture 318, 324, 326
    glass 317, 342–345
    silverware 222–223, 261, 299, 360–361
scarab motif 219, 219, 268
Scarpa, Carlo 348–349, 349
Scarpa, Tobia 348, 349
Scavini, Helen König 281
Schaper, Johann 38
Scheid, Karl 400
Scheid, Ursula 405
Scheier, Edwin and Mary 338–339, 339
Schloss Charlottenhof 54
Schmidt, Carl 159
Schmieg & Kotzian furniture 273, 273
Schneeballen technique 115, 115
Schneider, Ernest and Charles, glass 209, 267, 295
Schoen, Eugene 272, 273, 273
Schönbrunn palace 21
Schönheit, Johann Carl 93
school bench, mid-20th-century 330
Schreckengost, Viktor 283, 283
Schreyvogel, Charles 140, 140
Schröder House, Utrecht 238
Schufer, Gernot 411, 411
science, influence of 98
Sciolari, Gaetano 359
scissors, 19th-century 98
sconces: Arts and Crafts 146, 175, 181
    19th-century 124
Scott, Baillie 153, 176
Scott Morton Co., textiles 185
Scottish School 175
    clock 182
    influence 153, 155
    metalware 180, 181
    textiles 185
screens: Art Deco 270, 275
    metallic curtain 251
    Morris 184
sculpture (see also figures):
    American "Wild West" 140
    Art Deco 280–281, 308–309
    Art Nouveau 198, 230–231
    Basketful for John 399
    Bitosi Totem 389
    Frogs in Beans 399
    Funk 398
    glass see glass sculpture
    Neoclassical 92–93
    19th-century bronze 138–139
    Paaderin Jää 344
    postmodern 377, 400, 404
    sound 327, 327
    Tree of Life 351
Seaman, Maria 162
seat system, mid-20th-century 331
secretaires: à abattant 56, 57
    Art Deco 269, 271
    Chinoiserie (detail) 40
    Neoclassical 59, 63
    Rococo 23, 24, 26
secretaire, Federal 58
Seeney, Enid 335, 335
Segusa Vetri d'Arte 348, 348, 349
Seguso, Archimede 349, 349
servers: Art Deco 274
    Onondaga Shops 153
settees: Arts and Crafts 157
    19th-century 104
settles: Arts and Crafts 157
    19th-century 100
Sèvres porcelain 21, 36, 36, 68, 68, 69, 70, 93, 112, 112–113, 114, 191, 200, 278
    imitations 112
sewing clamp, 19th-century 133
sgraffito technique 31, 87, 87, 164, 164, 338, 339
Shapland & Petter furniture 197
Shaw, Richard 399, 399
shawls, paisley 135, 135

Sheerer, Mary G. 202
Shelley Pottery 282
Sheraton, Thomas 57, 58, 128
    The Cabinet-Maker and Upholsterer's Drawing Book 58
    style 102, 103
Shire, Peter 376, 390, 391
Shiriyamadani, Kataro 158, 158, 159
Shop of the Crafters 155
Sicard, Jacques 199, 199
sideboards: Aesthetic 156
    Art Deco 274
    Arts and Crafts 152, 154
    early modernist 247
    mid-20th-century 318, 330
    Neoclassical 58, 58
    19th-century 101, 103
    Stazione 387
Siderale range glass 348
signatures: Dresser 241
    Margotin 45
silk: bizarre 88
    Huguenot 28, 28, 47
    Lampas 88, 89
    Lyons 88, 88–89
Silver, Arthur 176
Silver, Rex 176
Silver Studio 176, 185, 229, 229
silverware: Art Deco 298–299
    Art Deco American 300–301
    Art Deco gallery 302–303
    Art Nouveau American 221
    Art Nouveau British 221
    Art Nouveau French 218–219
    Art Nouveau German 220
    Arts and Crafts 175
    Cymric 176, 176–177
    Danish 222–223, 261, 299; see also Jensen, Georg
    electroplated 123, 123
    Huguenot 29, 29
    Kalo Shop 179, 179
    mid-20th-century 360–361
    Neoclassical 78–79
    19th-century 122–123
    19th-century gallery 126–127
    Rococo 21, 42–43
Simonet, Albert 295
Simpson, Anna Frances 203
Sipek, Boris 376, 379, 413
Les Six 188–189
skonvirke 222
skyscraper style: clocks 305
    furniture 272, 272, 274, 321
Sloane, W. & J. 307
Smith, W. & A., souvenirs 133
Snischek, Max 262
snuff 84
snuff boxes: Neoclassical 54, 82, 82–83, 83, 84, 84
    19th-century 99, 132
Society of Blue and White Needlework 185
sofas: American Empire 61
    Art Deco 273
    Biedermeier (postmodern) 388
    early modernist 241
    Egyptian revival 242
    19th-century 101
    postmodern 384
Soldner, Paul 396, 396–397, 405
Solon, Albert 161
Solon, Marc Louis 113
Solven Pauline 406, 406
Sottile, Donald 382
Sottsass, Ettore 347, 374, 374, 376, 388, 388–389, 389, 390, 391, 414
Soubrier furniture
souvenirs, 19th-century 132–133
    Scottish 133
Sowden, George 390
speakeasy, New York 301
spectacle case, 19th-century 133
Spencer, Edward 175
spill-holders, 19th-century 109
spirit burner, 19th-century 115
Spirit range ceramics 403
Spode ceramics 65, 93, 108, 108

spoon, medieval silver 14
spoon warmer, 19th-century 123
Spratling, William 361
Sprimont, Nicholas 28, 28
Stabler, Harold and Phoebe 283
Stadler-Stoltz, Gunta 263
Stahl, Georges and Monique 410, 410, 411
stainless steel 361, 417
    Old Hall 363
    Viner's 363
Stair, Julian 401
Stålhane, Carl-Henry 333, 333
Stam, Mart 249
Standen drawing room 150
Stankard, Paul 411, 411
Starck, Philippe 381, 392, 392, 394, 394, 395, 417, 417
Starowieyeski, Franziszek 371
Stavangerflint ceramics 341
Stein, Creussen 30
Steinlen, Théophile 233, 233
Stennett-Wilson, Ronald 350, 351
stereo set, mid-20th-century 365
Steuben Glass Works 173, 190, 210, 210, 216, 290, 290
Steubenville Pottery 334
Stevens & Williams, glass 118, 119, 121, 121, 290
Stickley brothers furniture 144, 145, 152, 152–153, 153, 154, 173, 173, 178
Still, Nanny 342
stirrup vessel, early modernist 238
Stobwasser, Johann Heinrich 82
stools: Allunaggio 331
    Butterfly 323, 323
    Feather 381
    Magis Tam Tam 385
    Mezzadro 331
    mid-20th-century 320
    Murai 323, 323
    Regency 54
    Sgaboo 385
    Vitra WW 392
storage cart, Boby 329, 329
storage unit, ESU-400 324
Storer, Maria 158, 159
Storrow, James J. 203
Stourbridge glass 117, 118, 118, 119, 121, 210
Strauss-Likarz, Maria 262
streamlining 267, 269, 272–273, 296, 299
Strobach, Elly 284
Stromberg, Gerda and Edward 345, 345
Strombergshytten glass 345, 345
Stuart glass 292, 352
Stuchly, A. 204
The Studio 228, 229, 234, 235
Studio Craft movement 382, 414
Studio Lhotsky 409
Studio Linie range ceramics 403, 403
Studio M design 415
Studio Tetrach lamps 359
style rayonnant 66–67
Stylecraft range ceramics 334, 335
Süe et Mare: clocks 304
    furniture 271, 271
sugar sifter, Cliff 282
sugar urn, Neoclassical 79
Summerhouse ceramic design 282
Summers, Gerald, furniture 273
sun catcher, mid-20th-century 352
Suprematism 255
Surrealism 317, 334, 339, 371
Sutherland, Graham 47
Sutner, Ladislav 370
Swansea ceramics 53
Swatch watches 387
sweet tray, 19th-century 127
Swid, Nan 402
Swid Powell products 394, 394, 402, 402, 403, 403, 416, 417
Synergy archway, Philadelphia 416

T

tables: Arabesco 322, 322
    architect's 57
    Art Deco 271, 274, 275, 296
    Art Nouveau 192, 193
    Arts and Crafts 151, 153, 156
    Arts and Crafts American 144
    Atropo 386
    bonheur-du-jour 57
    console 25, 26
    CTW 324
    early modernist 249
    1852 250
    Empire 60, 60
    Gallé 192
    guéridon 60, 60
    Kick 385
    Kristall 390
    Majorelle 193
    mid-20th-century 316, 317, 320, 321, 330
    Mono 380
    Neoclassical 56, 59, 62
    nest of 246
    19th-century 103, 103, 104, 132
    19th-century Renaissance revival 99, 100, 100
    19th-century Rococo revival 101
    Notebook 385
    occasional (Wright) 252
    papier maché 97
    Pembroke 58
    postmodern 376, 377, 388
    Rococo 23, 24, 25, 27, 27
    1725 327
    sofa 62, 248
    Table 385
    Tavolo 385
    Tulip 324
table top, 19th-century micromosaic 132
tableware: Cylinda 361, 362
    Luna 343
    mid-20th-century 316
    mid-20th-century Scandinavian 332
    Neoclassical 78
    19th-century 122
    Palet 342
    Streamline 283
tabouret, Arts and Crafts 155
Tait, Jessie 334, 335, 335
Takaezu, Toshiko 337, 400
Takamori, Akio 398–399
Talbert, Bruce 150, 155
Taliesin Fellowship 252
Tanabe, Reiko 323, 323
tankards: fayence 67
    Neoclassical 74
    19th-century German 107, 107
tapestries: Aubusson 22, 46, 46, 47, 47
    Flemish 46, 47
    Gobelins 46–47
    Lady of the Unicorn 15, 15, 184
    Morris 145, 146
    Reeves 307
    Rococo 21, 22, 46–47
    verdure 46, 47, 47
tartanware 132, 133, 133
Tatlin, Vladimir 255
Tatzine e Tatzone line ceramics 403, 403
Taufschein documents 87
Taylor, E.A. 156
Taylor, Edward Richard 165
Taylor, Gerard 390
Taylor, William Howson 165
Taylor, William Watts 159
tazzas: Jensen 222
    maiolica 67
    WMF 224
Tchalenko, Janice 401, 401
tea 84
tea caddy 84, 84
tea canister, Neoclassical 71
tea cart, Aalto 251
tea/coffee services: Art Deco 284, 298, 303
    Art Nouveau 218, 225
    Connaught 361
    Diplomat 300

early modernist 261
Giaconda 298
mid-20th-century 340
Neoclassical 70
Spirit of Art 404
Tea and Coffee Piazza 394, 417, 417
tea kettle, 19th-century 123
tea sets: Little Dripper 402, 402
Village 403, 403
tea urns 79
Teague, W. D. 272, 290, 295, 301
teapots: Arts and Crafts 148, 174
Big Dripper 402, 402
Bosch 399
mid-20th-century 332, 334
MT4 260
Neoclassical 51, 65, 69
Ohr 160
Poppy 401
Pride 361
Rococo 31, 34, 42, 42
Studio 391
Swinging Marilyn 395, 395
TAC1 255
Teco ceramics 144, 163, 163
telephones 317, 365
Ericofon 365, 365
OLA T1000GD 395
Trimphone 365, 365
televisions 364
Videosphere 364, 365
Ten Broek, Willem 310, 310
Tendentze products 403, 403
Teren ceramics 205
Terry, Eli 131
Terry, Herbert, & Sons lamps 295
Tessuto technique 349, 349
Tétard, Jean 298, 298
textiles (see also carpets; quilts; rugs;
silk)
Art Deco 306–307
Art Nouveau 228–229
Arts and Crafts 147, 184–185
Calyx 368, 368
Chiesa della Salute 368
early modernist 262–263
Fandango 369
mid-20th-century 316, 368–369
Neoclassical 88–89
19th-century 134–135
Quarto 369
Rococo 46–47
Soundwaves 369
Spectrum 369, 369
Textured range glass 350
Theselius, Mats 384
Thieme House, Munich 197
Thonet, Michael 238, 241, 247, 322
Thorsson, Nils 333, 333
Thun, Matteo 385, 390, 395, 395
Tiffany & Co.: clocks 183, 183
glass 118
silverware 122, 299
Tiffany, Louis Comfort 171, 173, 178, 212
glass 210, 212, 212
lamps 212, 212, 215
Tiffany Studios 171, 173, 173, 178,
179, 212
tiles: Arts and Crafts 147, 162, 166
Iznik 168
medieval 14
Tinworth, George 164
toast rack, 19th-century 126
toiles de Jouy 89, 89
Toorop, Jan 234, 234
Tooth, Henry 242
Toso, Aureliano, glass 346, 346
Toso, Ermanno 347, 347
Totem ceramic design 335
Toulouse-Lautrec, Henri de 232, 233
Tournai porcelain 36–37, 37
Toussaint, Fernand 233, 233
transfer printing 65, 65, 109, 109
Traquair, Phoebe 175, 185
trays: Arts and Crafts 181
mid-20th-century 340
Trenchant, Jean 305
trio set, Homemaker 335

trophy cup, Arts and Crafts 180
Tschaschnik, Ilja 255
Tschumi, Bernard 393
Tudric line: clocks 177, 181, 183
vase 146
tumblers: mid-20th-century 352
spa 133, 133
Tunbridgeware 133, 133
tureens: mid-20th-century 334
19th-century 107, 109, 125
Rococo 37, 43
Tutankhamun 268, 276, 305
TWA Terminal, JFK Airport 314
Tynell, Helena 342, 343
Tynell, Paavo 359
Typenmöbel 197
typography 233, 240

U

UAM (Union des Artistes Modernes) 251
umbrella stands 107, 161
underglaze 31
Unger Brothers silverware 220, 220, 221
United Workshops for Art in Handicraft
196, 197
upholstery, 19th-century 99, 99
urns: Crow 411
19th-century 106, 125
Usonian model 252

V

Vacchetti, Sandro 281
vacuum cleaner, Dyson 395, 395
Val Saint-Lambert glass 286, 289, 289
Valentien, Albert 158
Valentin, Anne Marie 159
Vallien, Bertil 412
van Briggle, Artus 159, 191, 203, 203
van de Velde, Henry 227, 228
ceramics 198, 199, 200, 255
Déblaiement d'art 189, 194
furniture 194, 194
textiles 229
van Erp, Dirk 172, 172, 178, 178
van Gogh, Vincent 399
van Wijk, Dick 410, 410
vanity, Art Deco 274, 275
Varley, Fleetwood Charles 175
vases: Alexander 12
Amphora 200, 204
Apple 342, 342
Art Nouveau ceramic 191, 198, 199,
200, 201, 202, 203, 204, 205
Art Nouveau glass 189, 190, 209,
210, 211, 216, 217
Art Nouveau bronze 218, 231
Art Nouveau silver 219, 220, 221,
224, 225
Art Deco ceramic 276, 278, 283, 284,
285
Art Deco glass 267, 289, 290, 294,
295
Art Deco metalware 300, 301, 302, 303
Arts and Crafts ceramic 144, 158,
159, 161, 162, 163, 167
Arts and Crafts metalware 174, 180, 181
Athens Cathedral 347
Banjo 350, 350
Bark 350
Bath 344, 345
Bitoso E-vasi 405
Blown Soda 350
"burnt baby" 161
Canne 349
Carnaby 342, 366
Carrot 391
Chinese 40
Cliff 282
Crevasse 417, 417
Cucumber 391
cuerda seca 203
Daum Frères 208, 289
Drunken Bricklayer 350, 350
early modernist 240, 241, 242, 254,
255, 258
Emma 342, 343
Empire 50

Étrangeté 66 392
Fabbro 386
Fish 343
Futura 285
Gallé 190, 206
Giotto JG4 391
Handkerchief (Fazzoletto) 291, 349
Harlequin 394
Horn 351
Ignited Lunar Lunacy 374
Iznik 168
Japanese 40, 126, 148
Kanto 344
Kiku 347
King Tut 291
Knobbly 350
Lansetti 344, 344
Leach 241
Licata 413
Marselis 333
mid-20th-century ceramic 336, 338,
339, 340, 341
mid-20th-century glass 315, 343, 344,
347, 348, 351, 352, 353
mid-20th-century silver 361, 362
Naebvase 343
Neoclassical 52, 54, 69, 71, 72, 74
19th-century ceramic 98, 99, 106,
107, 107, 111, 112, 113, 115
19th-century glass 116, 117, 119, 121
La Nuit 199
Occhi 348, 349
Ohr 160, 161
Orkidea 344
Oriente 346
Passion 407
Peanut 335, 335
Pearl Band 345
Perruches 286
Pezzato 349, 349
Pironki 342, 342
Pollo 403
Polveri 349
postmodern 387, 396, 412, 143
Precious Boys 401
Propeller 242
Pyramid 285
Reptil 332
Rococo 36, 37
Rookwood 146, 158, 159
Ruba Rombic 291
Savoy 259, 259
Scarabées 219, 268
skyscraper 260, 260
Stellato 346
stoppered 199
Thread 406
Tiffany 212, 212
Tudric 146, 175
Tuonen Virta 344
Unfolding 400, 400
Valva 348
van Briggle 191, 203
Wedgwood 64, 65
Vasegaard, Gertrud 333
Vasekraft art pottery 162, 163
Velten-Verdamm ceramics 255
Venini, Paolo/Venini glass 290–291,
347, 348, 348–349, 349
Venturi, Robert 376, 377, 378, 378–
379, 386, 402, 402, 403, 416, 416,
417
Complexity and Contradiction in
Architecture 378
Learning from Las Vegas 379
Verneuil, M. P.: Étude de la Plante 128
Versace, Gianni 413
Versailles, palace of 20, 21
vessels: Dog Days … 409
New World Order 397
postmodern 400, 405, 409
Razz-Ma-Tazz 399
Totemic 396
Vibert, Alexandre 219

Victoria and Albert Museum, London
128
Victoria, Queen 113, 133, 134, 164
Vienna ceramics 69
Vienna (Austrian) Secession 233, 234,
245, 246
influence 155
Vigo, Nanda 384
Villa Cornaro, Italy 16
Villa of the Mysteries, Pompeii 11
Villeroy & Boch ceramics 225, 340
Villon, Jacques 271
vinaigrettes, Neoclassical 83
Vincennes porcelain 21, 36, 36
Vineland Flint Glasswork 291
Vintergaek range glass 342
Viollet-le-Duc, Emmanuel 194
Vistosi glass 347, 347
vitrines: Art Nouveau 192
19th-century 101
Vitruvius: De Architectura 16, 128
Vizner, Frantisek 377, 409, 409
Vodder, Niels 318, 318
Volkov, Noi 377, 399, 399
Volta Pottery 336
Voltaire 50
von Boch, Helen 366
von Buquoy, Count 54, 74, 120
von Eiff, Wilhelm 292
von Harrach glass 120, 216
von Klenze, Leo 55
von Nessen, Walter 300, 301
von Spaun, Max Ritter 211
von Schwartz, Johann 204, 205
von Tschirnhaus, Ehrenfried Walther 34
Vorticism 241, 336
Voulkos, Peter 396, 396, 397, 399, 400,
416
Voysey, Charles 150, 151, 176, 185,
185, 228, 228
Vyletal, Josef 371

W

Wagenfeld, Wilhelm 239, 259
Wagner, Otto 388
Wahliss, Ernst 201
wall hangings, mid-20th-century 369
wall masks 281, 281, 284
Walley, W. J. 166
wallpapers, Neoclassical 50, 51, 89, 89
Wanders, Marcel 380, 381
Walsh, John Walsh 290, 290, 293
Walter, Victor Amalric 289
Wardle, Thomas 176, 184, 185
wardrobe, postmodern 376
Warhol, Andy 366, 369
Flowers 366
Warren Telechron clocks 305
Wartha, Vince 199
Waterford Glass 118, 351
Waugh, Sidney 290, 290
Wave Crest range glass 121
weather vanes 125, 125, 127
Webb, Philip 150, 150, 151
Webb, Thomas, glass 117, 119, 121,
168, 168, 209, 209, 291
Weber, Kem 274
Wedgwood ceramics 53, 53, 64, 64–65,
65, 93, 109
Wedgwood, Josiah 53, 55, 64–65
Wega products 365
Wegner, Hans 316, 318, 318
Weisweiler, Adam 56, 57
Welch, Robert 361
Welden, William Archibald 296
Weller Pottery 190, 199, 199, 202, 205
Welles, Clara Barck 179, 301
West Bend Aluminum 300
Westmann, Marianne 334
Whall, Christopher 170
Wheeler, Candace 184
Whieldon, Thomas 64
whiplash motif 190, 195, 229, 229
Whistler, James McNeill 148, 148
White Bedroom (Mackintosh) 244
Whitefriars glass (see also Powell, James,
& Son) 121, 350, 350

Whitehead, David, textiles 368
Whitehead, Ralph Radcliffe 154
whatnot, 19th-century 104
Widdicomb, John 274
Wiener Werkstätte 246–247, 258
ceramics 254–255, 281
metalware 260
textiles 262–263, 306
Wieselthier, Vally 281
Wild Rose range glass 117
"Wild West" art 140
William and Mary style 27
Williams-Ellis, Susan 335
Wilson, Norman 257
Wilson, William 350
Wilton Royal Carpet Factory 185
Winblad, Bjørn 332, 333
Winchester Cathedral Gothic arches 14
Windbells ceramic design 282
wine coolers: Neoclassical 76
19th-century 106
wine pot, Japanese 128
wine pourer, mid-20th-century 362
Wirkkala, Tapio 344, 344, 345, 345,
360, 361, 403, 403
Wistaburgh Glassworks 39
Wistar, Caspar 39
Witzel, Josef Rudolf 234
WMF: clocks 226
metalware 190, 220, 220, 224, 225
Wolf House, Colorado 388
Wolfers Frères silverware 298
Wolfson, Helena 115
wood: carved 23, 25, 191, 191
exotic 23, 25, 26
laminated 100
mid-20th-century 316
19th-century 100, 102
Wood, Beatrice 336, 336–337, 399, 399
Woodall, George 121, 168
Woodman, Betty 397, 397
Woodroffe, Paul 171
Woodward, Ellsworth 202, 203
Worcester porcelain 37, 37, 68, 68, 71,
114, 148
Wormley, Edward 319
Wright, Frank Lloyd 153, 173, 240,
241, 250, 252, 252, 320
Wright, Russel 274, 295, 300, 334, 334,
402
writing box, 19th-century 133
writing tables: Mackintosh 245
Neoclassical 57, 58
Rococo 25
wrought iron, Art Deco 299, 299
Wyatt, James 79
Wyld, Evelyn 263
Wylie & Lochhead furniture 151, 197

Y

Yamashita, Kazumasa 417
Yanagi, Sori 323, 323
Yasuda, Takeshi 400, 400
Young, Grace 159, 159
Ypsilanti Reed Furniture Co. 273

Z

Zach, Bruno 309
Zambesi ceramic design 335, 335
zanfirico technique 346, 346
Zanini, Marco 390
Zanotta furniture 366, 366
Zanuso, Marco 319, 357
Zanuso Jr., Marco 391
Zecchin, Vittorio 293
Zeisel, Eva 334
Zimmermann, Jörg 411, 412
Zimmermann, Marie 301, 301
Zimpel, Julius 262
Zoritchak, Yan 409, 409
Zsolnay, Vilmos 199, 199
Zuber wallpapers 89
Zwollo, Frans 261
Zynsky, Toots 406, 407

ACKNOWLEDGMENTS

AUTHOR'S ACKNOWLEDGMENTS

The authors would like to thank the following people for their substantial contributions to the production of this book:

Photographer Graham Rae for his patience, humor, and wonderful photography, as well as John McKenzie, Andy Johnson, Byron Slater, Ellen MacDermott, and Adam Gault for additional photography.

All of the dealers, auction houses, and private collectors for kindly allowing us to photograph their collections, and for taking the time to provide a wealth of information about the pieces.

The team at DK, especially Angela Wilkes and Mandy Earey for all their skill and dedication to the project, and Anna Fischel for her invaluable support.

We would also like to thank the following for their help in the execution of this book: Anthony Barnes, Rago Arts and Auction Center, Lambertville; Pierre Bergé et Associés, Paris; Maison de Ventes Chenu Scrive Bérard, Lyon; Martina Franke; Julie Killam, James D. Julia, Inc., Fairfield; John Mackie, Lyon and Turnbull, Edinburgh; Ron and Debra Pook, Pook and Pook, Inc., Lancaster, PA; Paul Roberts, Lyon and Turnbull, Edinburgh; Rossini, Paris; Bernadette Rubbo, Sollo: Rago Modern Auctions, Lambertville; Nicolas Tricaud de Montonnière; Lee Young, Samuel T. Freeman and Co., Philadelphia.

PUBLISHER'S ACKNOWLEDGMENTS

Dorling Kindersley would like to thank Anna Amari-Parker and Janet Mohun for their editorial help, Sarah Rock, Katie Eke, Adam Walker, Lucy Claxton, and Romaine Werblow for their help with design, Caroline Hunt for proofreading, and Pamela Ellis for compiling the index.

PICTURE CREDITS

The publisher would like to thank the following for their kind permission to reproduce their photographs:

(Key: A-above; B-below/bottom; C-center; L-left; R-right; T-top)

akg-images 308 BL. Alamy Images AAD Worldwide Travel Images 374 BL; Bildarchiv Monheim GmBh 16 BL, 238 BL, 248 TR; Michael Jenner 144 L. Alan Moss 307 BR. Albert Amor 11 BR, 37 CC, BL, BC & BR, 211 TR. Alessi 394 BL, 395 TC, 417 TC, TR, BR. All Our Yesterdays 118 TC. Altermann Galleries 140 BC. Andrew Lineham 48 C, 74 TR & BL, 83 BC, 114 BC & BR, 117 BC, 119 TC, 120 BC, 133 BR, 121 TC, 216 no.2 & 3. Antique Textiles and Lighting 47 BL, 135 BC & CR. Antiques by Joyce Knutsen 119 BR. Ark Antiques 179 TL. The Art Archive Musee de l'Ecole de Nancy / Dagli Orti 189 T; Musée Historique Lorraine Nancy / Dagli Orti 207. Art Deco Etc 283 BL.

Arthur Millner 273 BR. At The Movies 371 TR. Auction Team Koln 364 TR. Auktionhaus Bergmann 60 TC, 62 no.15, 69 BL, 70 no.6, 9, 16, 75 BL, 77 no.12, 79 TL, 93 BC, 112 BL, 115 CR, 299 CCR. Auktionhaus Dr Fischer 2 C, 9 CL, 21 BR, 38 TR, BL & BC, 39 TC, TR, BL, BC & BR, 67 TC, 74 BR, 75 TC, TR & BR, 76 no.9, 77 no.14, 117 BL, 120 CC & BR, 121 CR, 156 no.6, 8 & 9, 206 BR, 215 no.10, 291 CC, 316 BL, 346 TL & TC, 347 TL & TC, 349 BR, 353 no.17, 385 no.13, 409 CR. Auktionhaus Kaupp 20 TR, 34 BL, 45 BR, 69 TC, 70 no.8, 94 C, 107 CR, 114 BR, 115 CC & BC, 122 BR, 126 no.10, 127 no.12 & 18, 131 BL. Auktionhaus Metz 34 TR & BR, 37 TL, 114 BL. Aux Trois Clefs 292 no.13. Barrett Marsden Gallery 397 TR. Beaussant Lefevre 24 BR, 25 CR, 42 TR, BR, 42 BR, 50 BC, 62 no.4, 63 no.11, 70 no.4, 72 BR, 93 TC, 278 TR. Belhorn Auction Services 341 no.11. Beth Adams 284 no.8. Beverley Adams 285 no.11. Blanchard 242 BC. Blanchet et Associés 47 TL. Block Glass Ltd 411 BR. Bonhams, Edinburgh 249 BC, 323 CR. Bonhams, Bayswater 249 BR, 250 BR, 259 BC, 260 BL, 323 TC, 345 TR & BCR, 368 CR. Bonhams, Bond Street 104 no.1, 130 TR, 366 CR. Bonhams, Knowle 91 TL, CR, BL & BR. Borek Sipek 378 CL. Bridgeman Art Library: 17 BL, 17 TL, 85. Brookside Antiques 118 CR, 121 TR, 209 BR, 211 BC. Brunk Auctions 101 BR, 136 BR. Bucks County Antiques Center 86 TR, 127 no.15. Bukowskis 59 TL, 62 no.2, 63 no.14, 292 no.4, 318 BR, 342 CR & BL, 344 CC, 392 BL, 393 BC, 413 no.2. Burstow & Hewett 341 no.18. Calderwood Gallery 194 TR, 204 no.7, 224 no.5, 230 BC, 266 TR, 270 CL, 271 TL & CR. Cappellini 380 TR. Cassina SPA 252 TR. Catalin Radios 296 CL, 305 TL. Cheffins 67 TR, 70 no.5 & 7, 105 no.12, 107 CL, 164 TL, 242 CC. Chenu Scrive Berard 66 BR, 194 TC, 270 TR. Cheryl Grandfield Collection 220 BC. Chéz Burnette 305 TR, 364 BR. Chicago Silver 179 BL & BR, 300 TC, 302 no.2. China Search 285 no.10, 340 no.1, 341 no.14. Chisholm Larsson 239 BR, 370 BC & BR, 371 BR, 395 TL. Chiswick Auctions 106 TR, 281 CR, 284 no.3. Christie's Images Ltd.: 227 L. Claudia Capelletti, Cappellini Design SPA 387 BR. Clevedon Salerooms 14 TR. Contemporary Ceramics 397 CR, 400 TL, BC & BL, 401 TL. Corbis: Peter Aprahamian 51 B, 169, 267 T, 307 TR; Condé Nast Archive 328 TL; Dean Conger 15 BR; Owen Franken 213; Michael Freeman 320 TR; Robert Harding 20 BL; Thomas A. Heinz 252 TL, 253; Historical Picture Archive 162 BL, 185 TR; Angelo Hornak 312 B; Robert Levin 325; Museum of the City of New York 301 TL; Gregor M. Schmid 50 BL; Setboun 392 BR; Herbert Spichtinger/zefa 98 BL; Adam Woolfitt 12 BL. Corning Musum of Glass 73 TR & BR. Cottees 283 BC. Cowdy Gallery 406 TR & TC, 408 CC, 409 BC, BR, 410 TC & TR. Cuvreau Expertises Enchères 278 BR. Danny Lane 318 BL. David Love 54 TL, 62 no.3. David Pickup 157 no.14. David Rago Auctions 111 CR & BC, 142 C, 144 BR, TR, 146 CL, 150 TR, 153 CC & CR, 154 BL & BR, 155 CL, CC, CR & BR, 158 BL & BR, 159 TL, TC, B Row (all), 160, TR, BL & BR, 161 TR, CR, BL, BC & BR, 162 BC & BR, 166 no.1, 2, 3 & 9, 167 no.12, 15, 16, 18 & 19, 171 TL, 172 TR & BL, 173 TL & BR, 178 BR, 179 TC, 180 no.1 & 10, 184 TC, 202 CR, BL, BC & BR, 203 TL, TR, CC & BL, 204 no.1, 8 & 10, 205 no.11, 13, 14, 15, 16 & 17, 210 BL, 211 BR, 216 BL, 214 no.5 & 7, 215 no.14, 15 & 16, 263 TL, TC, TR, CL, BL, BC & BR, 283 CR & BR, 285 no.14 & 15, 286 CL & BL, 287 CC, 289 BCR, 291 BR, 293 no.20, 301 BC & BR, 323

BR, 324 TR, CR & BL, 330 no.1, 3, 5 & 11, 337 CL, 338 TL, 339 BL, 358 no.6 & 7, 359 no.13, 15 & 16, 361 TR & BC, 394 BC & BR, 398 CR, 399 TR & CR, 405 no.17, 413 no.13 & 21, 495 no.15. David Rago/Nicholas Dawes Lalique Auctions 286 CC. Davies Antiques 281 TL. Deco Etc 8 C, 295 TL & TCL, 302 no.7, 358 no.6. Decodame.com 267 BR, 278 BL, 289 BCL, 298 CR, 300 BL & BC, 302 no1, 4 & 6, 303 no.11, 12, 13, 17 & 20, 304 TR & BL. DeLorenzo Gallery 270 BR, 272 BR. Delorme et Collin du Bocage 106 BL, 355 BL, 365 BR. Derek Roberts Fine Antique Clocks & Barometers 81 BR, 153 BC & BR. Design20C 353 no.15, 354 BR, 359 no.12, 364 BL. DK Images: British Museum, London 10l, 10 R, 14 R; Musee Carnavalet 25 TR. Dreweatt Neate, Donnington 9 C, 20 CL, 32 BR, 40 TR, 62 no.9, 65 BR, 67 BR, 71 no.19 & 20, 72 TR, 73 TL, 76 no.2, 4 & 8, 77 no.15, 16, 17 & 18, 101 TR, 103 BL, 105 no.16, 108, 115 BR, TL & BC, 117 TL, BR, 123 BR, 128 BL, 132 BR, 137 BL, 167 no.17, 175 BR, 180 no.7 & 9, 181 no.12, 18 & 21, 200 BR, 201 BR, 205 no.18 & 20, 281 BR, 292 no.9, 305 BC, 345 BL, 351 TC. Dreweatt Neate, Not tingham 224 no.7. Dreweatt Neate, Tunbridge Wells 133 TL & CL, 221 CL, 224 no.8. Droog Design 414 TR. Dyson 395 BR. Etienne & van den Doel 3 R, 7 L, 407 BR, 409 CL, BL, 412 no.5 & 10. Festival 334 CR & CBR, 335 TC, 340 no.4. Finesse Fine Art 299 CCL. Fragile Design 333 BR, 343 TC, 359 no.11 & 14, 366 TR, 369 BR. Francesca Martire 413 no.15. Frederic Lozada Enterprises 311 TR. Freeman's 27 BR, 50 TR, 57 BC, 62 no.8, 63 no.20, 86 BL, 90 BL, 92 BC, 97 BR, 104 no.2, 112 BR, 122 BL, 124 CL, CC & BR, 125 BL, 126 no.2 & 7, 130 BR, 131 TL, 135 CC, CL & BL, 137 CL, 141 CC, 157 no.16, 171 TR, 250 BL, 261 TL, 291 BC, 310 no.6, 331 no.15, 353 no.18, 354 BC, 367 CC, 385 no.13, 389 TC. Gaetano Pesce 414 BL. Galerie Helene Fournier Guerin 32 CC, 66 BL, 71 no.13. Galerie Marianne Heller 400 CR, 405 no.12. Galerie Mariska Dirkx 410 BC & BR, 411 CR, 412 no.3. Galerie Maurer 376 BL, 381 TR, CR, 384 no.1, 385 no.12, 17 & 19, 386 TR, BL, 387 BC, 398 CR, BR, 390 TC, 391 CC, CR, 394 BC, 402 TR, BC, 403 CR, 404 no.3, 4, 5, 6 & 8, 405 no.13, 415 BL, BC, BR, 416 BL, 417 TL. Galerie Olivia et Emmanuel 78 BL, 123 BC, 126 no.1, 127 no.11 & 17, 298 TR, 302 no.10. Galerie Vandermeersch 32 BL, 36 TR, 37 TR. Galerie Yves Gastou 271 BL, 295 BL. Gallerie Koller 2 L, 25 BR, 42 BL, 44 TR & BC, 45 BL, 59 BR. Gallery 1930 Susie Cooper 283 TC. Gallery 532 152 TR, BL, 156 no.7, 172 BC, 173 BL, 178 TR. Gary Grant 333 BL, 335, CR & BL, 340 no.3 & 7, 341 no.8. Geoffrey Diner Gallery 153 BL, 155 BL, 156 no.5, 157 no.10, 162 BL, 173 BC, 176 BR, 178 BL, 180 no.5, 186 C. Georg Jensen AS, Denmark: 222 BL. Getty Images/Hugh Sitton 13 TR. Gilbert Collection: 28 TC. Gorringes, Bexhill 105 no.13 & 15. Gorringes, Lewes 83 BL, 84 CR, 105 no.14, 130 BL, 131 CC & BR, 166 no.4, 5 & 8, 167 no.20, 215 no.9, 309 CR. Graham Cooley 341 no.16, 343 TL, 350 CC & BR, 351 BL & BC, 352 no.6, 353 no.11 & 14. Halcyon Days 84 TR & CL. Hall-Bakker @ Heritage 179 TR, 217 no.11. Hansen Sorensen 331 no.16. Hermann Historica OHG 100 BL. Herr Auctions 189 BR, 294 BL, 329 CR, 331 no.17, 340 no.6, 352 no.1, 361 CR, 378 BC, 388 CL. High Style Deco 273 TR, 274 no.2, 275 no.15, 302 no.5, 303 no.15. Holsten Galleries 372 C, 374 TR, 407 TR, 409 BL, 411 CL, 412 no.11, 413 no.17 & 18. Hope and Glory 93 TR. Hugo Ruef 30 BR. Imperial Half Bushel 123 BL. Ingo Maurer 415 TR. Ingram Antiques 341 BL. The Interior Archive: Tim Beddow 315 TR; James Mortimer 150 BR, 250 CL; Fritz von der Schulenburg 55, 59 TR, 60 BL, 97 B, 195 TL, 239 TL, 244 BL; Ivey Selkirk Auctioneers 219 CR. Jacobs and Hunt Fine Art Auctioneers Limited 204 no.9. James D Julia Inc 118 BL, 121 BR,

183 TL, 208 BC, 209 TC, 210 BC & BR, 211 BR, 212 TR, 216 BR, 217 TL, TR & BR, 214 no.8. Jazzy 274 no.3 & 6. Jeanette Hayhurst Fine Glass 73 BL & BC, 76 no.1, 5 & 6, 119 TR, 268 BL, 290 CR & BR, 292 no.11, 293 no.18. 343 TR & BR, 344 BR, 351 BR, 352 no.4, 412 no.6, 413 no.16. Jill Fenichell 111 BL & BR. Joe De Buck 276 TR. Johannes Vogt Auktionen 30 CC, 32 TR. John Bull (Antiques) Ltd 78 TC, 79 BC, 96 BR, 123 TR, 126 no.5, 6, 8 & 9, 127 no.13. John Howard @ Heritage 64 BR, 109 CR & BR, 181 no.19. John Jesse Antoques 254 BL, 271 BR, 281 TC, 294 BC, 296 BL. John King 296 TL. John Makepeace 384 no.5 & 8. John Nicholson 165 TR, 209 BCR, 257 BR, 328 TR, 312, 404 no.7. Sollo:Rago Modern Auctions 3 C, 7 CR, 249 TR, 252 CR & BR, 255 CR & BR, 256 CL, 273 TC, 274 no.5 & 10, 275 no.16, 276 TL, 284 no.4, 295 BC, 299 CR, 305 CR, 306 TR, 308 BC, 309 BR, 314 TR, 318 BL, 319 TL, TR, BL & BR, 320 CR & BL, 321 TR, CR, BL & BR, 324 TL, 326 TC & BC, 327 CR, 330 no.9, 331 no.19, 336 CL, 337 TR, 338 BR, 339 TR & CR, 355 TR, 355 TL, 357 TL, CC & BR, 358 no.8, 359 no.10, 366 TL & BR, 368 TR, 369 TL, 374 BR, 378 BL, 379 TR & BR, 382 TR, CL, BL & BR, 383 C, 384 no.2 & 7, 385 no.14, 390 BC, 391 BR, 392 TR, 393 CR, 396 TR, CR, BL & BR, 397 BC, 398 BL & BR, 400 BR, 404 no.1 & 2, 405 no.14, 16, 18 & 19, 409 TL, 415 TL & CC, 416 BR. Jonathan Horne 31 TL, 33 BC. Jonathan Wadsworth 47 TR, 134 TR & BR. Junnaa & Thomi Wroblewski 228 BR, 229 CL, CR & BR, 262 TR, BL & BR, 263 TR, 307 CC & CR. Keller & Ross 334 BL & BC. Law Fine Art 32 CR, 54 TR, 64 TR, 68 CL & BL, 69 TL, 70 no.10, 71 no.11, 12, 14 & 15, 151 CR & BR, 156 no.3, 157 no.13. Lawrences Fine Art Auctioneers 113 CR. Leah Gordon Antiques 199 BR. Lennox Cato 105 no.10. Leo Kaplan Modern 407 TL. Liberty plc (liberty.co.uk) 157 no.15. Lili Marleen 259 TC, 271 CC, 274 no.11, 275 no.13. Lillian Nassau Ltd 259 BL, 290 BL, 291 CR, 293 no.14, 351 TR. Liz Moore (liz@lizm.eclipse.co.uk): 28 R. Lost City Arts 324 BR, 327 TL, 330 no 10, 313 TL. Luna 365 TC & CR, 395 TC. Lyon & Turnbull 27 TC, 42 TC & TR, 45 TC & TR, 46 BL, 54 BC, 62 no.5, 7, 63 no.12, 16 & 18, 93 BR, 98 BL, 101 CL & BL, 104 no.3, 4, 5 & 8, 105 no.11, 126 no.4, 145 BR, 151 BL, 157 no.11, 166 6 & 7, 175 BL, 176 BL, 180 no.4, 181 no.15 & 20, 182 BL, 184 BL & BC, 185 CC & BR, 195 BC, 197 BR, 204 no.2, 215 no.17, 226 TR & BR, 227 BR, 228 TR, 236 C, 238 BR, 242 TR, 248 BR, 251 TC & TR, 257 BR, 258 TR, 260 TR, 263 BR, 264 BC, 273 CC & BL, 282 BL, 284 no.5 & 7, 308 BR, 309 CC & BR, 329 BL, 354 BL, 368 BL, 385 no.18. Macklowe Gallery 1 C, 2 R, 7 CL, 171 BR, 177 BR, 188 BR, 192 TR & BL, 193 TL, TC BC & BR, 195 BR, 198 BL, 190 BL, 199 TR & BL, 200 TR & BL, 201 TR & BL, 201 TL & TC, 204 no.5, 208 BR, 212 BL & BC, 214 no.1, 215 no.12, 218 TR, BR & BL, 219 TR, CL & BR, 230 BR, 231 TL, BC & BR, 289 BR, 293 no.19. Mallett 40 BC, 61 BC. 62 no.10, 289 TC & TR. Manx National Heritage: 177 TR. Mary Evans Picture Library: 114 BL, 440. Mary Wise & Grosvenor Antiques 113 BL. Matali Crasset Productions 384 no.4. Meissen.de: 35. Memphis and Post 379 CL, 391 TL. MGM Mirage/Bellagio Hotel 407 BL. Mike Weedon 168 CR, 206 BL, 214 no.4, 217 no.13. Moderne Gallery 275 no.14, 279 BC & BR, 284 no.9. 285 no.13, 292 no.10, 295 TCR & TR, 300 TR, 301 TR, 303 no.14 & 18, 331 no.12, 341 no.9, 357 CR. Modernism Gallery 273 TL, 274 no.1 & 9, 275 no.12. Mood Indigo 296 TR, 303 no.19, 334 TR. Mostly Boxes 82 CR. Mum Had That 332 CR, 334 BR, 343 BL & BC, 344 BL, 352 no.2 & 3, 353 no.16, 353 no.16, 361 BR. Nagel 59 BL, 92 CC, 168 CL. National Portrait Gallery, London: Lewis Morley 323 CRA.